MAYOR
Erastus
CORNING
Albany Icon, Albany Enigma

D1073457

MAYOR
Erastus
CORNING

Albany Icon, Albany Enigma

Paul Grondahl

STATE UNIVERSITY OF NEW YORK PRESS

Published by
STATE UNIVERISTY OF NEW YORK PRESS
Albany

© 2007 Paul Grondahl
All rights reserved
Printed in the United States of America

For information, address
State University of New York Press, Albany, NY
www.sunypress.edu

Production, Laurie Searl
Marketing, Susan M. Petrie

Library of Congress Cataloging-in-Publication Data

Grondahl, Paul, 1959-
 [Mayor Erastus Corning]
 Mayor Corning : Albany icon, Albany enigma / Paul Grondahl.
   p. cm.
 Originally published: Mayor Erastus Corning. Albany, N.Y. : Washington Park Press, c1997.
 Includes bibliographical references and index.
 ISBN 978-0-7914-7294-1 (pbk. : alk. paper) 1. Corning, Erastus, 1909-1983. 2. Mayors—New
York (State)—Albany—Biography. 3. Albany (N.Y.)—Biography. 4. Albany (N.Y.)—Politics and
government—20th century. I. Title.

F129.A353C675 2007
974.7'4304392—dc22
[B]   2007002077

              10 9 8 7 6 5 4 3 2 1

For my parents, in loving gratitude

Contents

Preface

The seed for this book was planted in Betty Corning's garden in the fall of 1992, where I spent a morning interviewing the widow of Erastus Corning 2nd for a *Times Union* profile. The autumnal mood was a harbinger of endings, both for Betty's beloved flowers and plants, and for the gardener herself, who suffered from emphysema and was tethered to oxygen tanks. I had a sense that not only Betty Corning would soon be passing, but that her family's story, and the entire chapter of Albany history that her husband's historic tenure as mayor represented, would soon fade with it. Already, the mayor and several key figures in the narrative were dead and others were old and infirm. If the story was not told now, the opportunity would be lost forever. This sense of urgency set me to work in earnest in the spring of 1993. Some biographers choose their subjects; I had Mayor Corning thrust upon me.

An unexpected symmetry emerged. I had interviewed Mayor Corning a decade earlier, in 1982, shortly before he was hospitalized with emphysema and now, during our interview sessions, I was watching Betty Corning die the same way in the house on Corning Hill where she had lived since their marriage in 1932. And yet, despite their fifty years of marriage and Mayor Corning's five decades in elected public office, little was known of the private man. Albany natives grew up assuming Corning's first name was Mayor, since he rarely appeared in public out of his guise as the aristocratic presence who sat behind the gray metal desk in City Hall since 1941. My purpose in writing this biography was to paint a full portrait of Erastus Corning 2nd, revealing both shadow and light, in an attempt to replace the reverential, one-dimensional view of Mayor Corning with a truthful, three-dimensional picture of the man.

After more than 200 interviews and archival research that took me from Albany to Maine to Groton to Yale and beyond, the pattern of Mayor Corning's life took shape in my mind more as a matter of thematic development than of chronology. The trajectory of his forty-two years as mayor was a flat line, after all, a numbing sameness he seemed to enjoy, deepening the Corning enigma. In both public and private realms, Corning preferred the unexamined life and he compartmentalized his experience to cement the essential mystery of his existence. He separated the various aspects of his life like spokes on a wheel, himself as the hub, each spoke radiating out from him but never overlapping or interacting with each other. The secret to his durability as a politician, as well as the root of his enigmatic personality, could be found in those individual spokes. It also helped explain the sense of melancholy and sadness that pervaded his life.

I have structured this biography so that each chapter represents a major theme in the mayor's life – a spoke, if you will. There was the spoke of his family's legacy in politics and business; his early years at prep school and college; his tangled family life with his biological family and his adopted family, the Noonans; and his relationship to Dan O'Connell and the Democratic machine's ward heelers. There were other spokes that offered profound contradictions: his blue-collar World War II buddies versus his Fort Orange Club friends and deep connections to Albany's elite society; his rough-hewn hunting and fishing guides in Maine versus his friendships with judges and business leaders. Other dominant themes that ran throughout Corning's life included his record on the environment, his rivalry with Nelson Rockefeller and his relationship with the press.

I've written the book so that each chapter can stand on its own, and can be read separately as a kind of story-within-a-story. The chapters are arranged to develop a progression of themes of Mayor Corning's experience that create a revealing portrait of Erastus Corning 2nd's life and times, public and private, the whole wheel of his career told through the spokes he had kept separate and distinct for so long. Erastus Corning 2nd was an exceedingly complex man and there are many levels of truth about his life. I present one truth here, as fully and as honestly as I could discern it, through the mayor's own papers and through the memories of those who knew him best.

Paul Grondahl
Albany

Acknowledgements

Until now, my writing has been mostly a series of sprints, but this biography was a four-year marathon that presented many difficulties and challenges, demanding a level of stamina I had not imagined. I couldn't have stayed the course for the long haul and completed the race without the support and assistance of so many. I owe a deep gratitude to scores of sources I can't name here, those hundreds of people I interviewed late into the night, who poured out their stories that brought the past alive for me.

I would like first to thank the Corning family for their cooperation, given freely and without condition. The mayor's daughter, Bettina Corning Dudley, offered insight, memories, letters and photographs, as well as her generous hospitality in Maine and guided tours of the mayor's special places there. The mayor's son, Erastus III, loaned documents and correspondence and discussed his father and family over lunches at the Fort Orange Club. Interviews with the mayor's grandchildren and other relatives were helpful, in particular the invaluable reminiscences and family photo albums supplied by a Corning cousin, Wharton Sinkler III.

Perhaps the single most important archival source was the Erastus Corning 2nd collection among the Corning Papers, a roomful of family documents dating from the early 1800s and housed in the McKinney Library of the Albany Institute of History & Art. Several members of the Institute's staff provided assistance. In particular, I would like to thank Wesley Balla, curator of history, for lending perspective and guidance; and to former librarians Jean Liska and Pam Norris, for maneuvering all those Corning boxes and helping me decipher their contents. A special thank you to the Institute's inimitable director emeritus, Norman Rice, for his support and encyclopedic knowledge of Albany.

Several other archives and libraries, and specific staff members, were helpful: Jeannine Marhafer of the Albany Academy; Tom Clingan of the Albany County Hall of Records; Jim Hobin of the Albany Public Library; Douglas Brown of Groton School; Jim Corsaro and Paul Mercer of the New York State Library, who guided me through the collections during a research residency program.

Many individuals loaned useful material. In particular, I'd like to thank the family of C.R. "Tip" Roseberry, for sharing tapes and notes on Corning research Tip had made shortly before he died. Thanks also to Joanne and James Lenden, John Curley, Rev. Charles Sheerin, Ruben Gersowitz, Gary Cobb, Clifford Manchester and many others for supplying helpful items.

For their hospitality or companionship during research travels, I thank the following: R.W.B. Lewis and his wife, Nancy, an inspiring literary partnership, for imparting advice and wisdom and making me feel as welcome as a family member while I was a guest at their home during a research trip to Yale University; Keith Marder, a supportive and generous friend and the *Times Union*'s all-time class clown, who made me laugh when I needed it most during a road trip to Groton; Sam Grondahl, my son and a great six-year-old road buddy during a long drive to Maine.

My colleagues at the *Times Union* have been a second family to me through good times and bad. It is impossible to mention everyone who provided support and a boost during this project, but I'll offer a partial list. Editor Jeff Cohen, for arranging a six-week leave at a critical juncture in the writing process; Bill Dowd, for the photo permission and the administrative details; Joann Crupi, Jim Gray, Colleen Fitzpatrick and Karen Potter, my kind, caring and supportive editors in the features department; Harry Rosenfeld and Harry Haggerty, for teaching me about journalism and about being a good person; Rex Babin, for his astute political insights and his true friendship; Fred LeBrun, for his wise counsel and kindness; Tim Spofford, Amy Biancolli and Chris Ringwald, for commiserating about writing a book; Ken Crowe, for being there for the long haul; cool people and talented artists too numerous to mention in the graphic design and photography departments; Skip Dickstein, for the author's photo and his friendship; Mike Virtanen and Doug Blackburn, for the camaraderie of our morning coffee runs; Darryl Campagna, Fran Ingraham, Michael Lopez and Tim Cahill, for putting up with me in their work pod; Barbara Delaney, a gentle soul and compassionate colleague whose death left a void in our department; Kathleen Dooley, for her sensitivity and motherly goodness; Mike Huber, for being the glue that holds it all together; Rob Brill, Ken Thurman, Rick Karlin, Teresa Buckley, Monica Bartoszek, Winnie Yu, Cailin Brown, Jane Gottlieb and Carol DeMare, for encouragement and enduring friendships; Gary Hahn, Jim Hickey, Larry VanAlstyne and Harry Loucks, for applauding my progress whenever we met; and many others I apologize for failing to mention. Also, for the great ones who got away to answer other callings: Vinod Chhabra, Cliff Lee, Joe Mahoney, Bob Whitaker, Joe Layden.

Outside the newspaper, many friends offered encouragement that lightened the load. I thank Chris Mercogliano, Walter Holmes, Jim Greenfield, Jeff Crane, Wendy and Scot Asher and the rest of the Morris Street gang, Jeanne Kobuszewski and the Saint Rose crew. Family members offered wonderful support throughout the duration of the project, especially when the going got tough. I thank my parents, Bonnie and Ken Grondahl, to whom I dedicate this book, and my brothers, Gary and Dave; my wife's parents, Jack and Charlotte O'Donnell, and my wife's brothers and sisters, Tim, John, Sheila and Ann.

I'm grateful to my publishers, Susanne Dumbleton and Anne Older of Washington Park Press, for believing in this project, for encouraging me to undertake it and for being so good to work with throughout the process. Serendipity and symmetry have played a big part in this book. Three of the first people I met in Albany when I came here in the fall of 1981 for graduate school at the State University of New York at Albany, outstanding literary men all, are deserving of thanks these many years later: Gene Garber, for encouragement and interest and writing a grant application letter on my behalf; Bill Kennedy, the best mentor a young writer could ever hope to find, who has always been supportive and generous to me, and whose peerless reconstitution of Albany in fact and fiction has been a source of profound inspiration; Bill Dumbleton, one of my favorite teachers, and now my editor, who took what had become the unbearable weight of the manuscript off my hands at a crucial moment and gave me hope and praise, even while his keen editorial skills helped shape and polish it into a much improved book.

None of this would have been possible, or meaningful, without the love and support of my wife, Mary, during each step of this marathon. She put up with my late nights in the attic, hammering away at the computer endlessly, and all those lost weekends when it was Corning time, enduring the disruptions to family life with understanding and encouragement. She was an early and enthusiastic reader of the manuscript. She believed in me and told me I could finish it even when I faltered. Along with her help and support, she kept me grounded and striving to strike a balance between work and play. Through it all, I have been blessed by the joy and happiness of two wonderful children, Sam and Caroline, whose laughter and kisses sustained me.

Introduction by William Kennedy
Pulitzer Prize-winning author of "Ironweed"
and the Albany cycle of novels

We used to think we knew Erastus Corning, those of us who grew up and old in the shadow of his very, very long career – 42 years in office, 1941 to 1983, longest-running Mayor in American history. We thought we knew his intellectual talent, his personal suavity, his ambition that never reached much beyond the city limits, his political wizardry at getting elected and extracting himself, and his party, from trouble, and his prestidigitational genius at manipulating public money. We even thought we knew about his private life, which provided the town with juicy gossip for four and a half decades.

But what we knew of Erastus was as true as love and just as false; for all that most of us ever saw was what the public Erastus let us see: his veneer. We guessed that what lay beneath that bright and shining surface was, alas, a figure of wasted talent and intelligence, and neglected ambition: a half-willing victim of a corrupt political cabal. We long ago decided he could be summed up in the phrase William V. Shannon used to sum up James Curley, the jovial rascal who became Mayor of Boston and Governor of Massachusetts: ". . . a self-crippled giant on a provincial stage." But however true that was of Erastus, it was also patronizing and unreflective of his complex motives for living and working as he did.

Paul Grondahl, in the biography that follows, gives us the Erastus Corning we didn't know. It is a candid and surprising book that humanizes an icon, revealing a loyal, thoughtful, and likable man who had to cope with lifelong psychic wounds inflicted by parents, by marital life, by subservience to Dan O'Connell – the brilliant political boss who became a surrogate father to him – and, not least, by his own obsession with power which, though subservient to Dan's steamroller obsession, was considerable.

This is an important book for Albany, for anyone interested in political power. It widens our vision (with a view from inside City Hall) of the O'Connell Democratic organization, which controlled Albany from 1921 until the Mayor died in 1983, making it the longest-running boss machine in American political history.

Erastus emerges from the book as a man doing something he loves: playing politics, governing, exercising power, and doing it all with a passion. But then, as happens with most passion, it aged into something unexpected. He was, willfully so, a superior machine politician who from the beginning loved the game. He remained so through his last six bittersweet years when, after Dan died, he finally became party boss; but in those years he was slowly dying of emphysema. He was the voice of upstate power that convinced Mario Cuomo to run for Governor. He was the Democrats' maestro of election mathematics, the great obfuscator when meeting the press, the vindictive executive who personally purged patronage lists of anybody tainted by links to a functioning Republican or maverick Democrat.

We encounter him excited by the election struggle, joyous in victory. But we see, too, his victory was won not only – as the party liked to boast – by his popularity, but also by multiple voting, buying votes, manipulating tallies, voting the dead, intimidating voters, and making the voting machine "dance" with multiple ballots cast by one man – by all this, and much more of the scallywaggery that goes with machine politics anywhere, but especially in a one-party town like Albany used to be, and, in a sense, still is.

The book anatomizes a fascinating and conflicted man, driven to live two family lives – a sterile one with his wife and children, a robust and vital one with the family of Peter and Polly Noonan, with whom he seemed truly at home for much of his life. We are treated to the traditional Erastus, urbanely at ease among the polite affluency of Fort Orange Club bankers, but who walks out of that club into the Maine woods and turns into a raunchy, ragged, besotted, bewhiskered and legendary snoring woodsman who drinks vodka for breakfast and fishes till he drops – his respite from City Hall's oppressive monotony.

The book assiduously follows him from Albany Academy to prep school at Groton, where he was a withdrawn, inarticulate scholar; on to Yale where, amid rollicking drinking and carousing, he became a history and English major and Phi Beta Kappa in his junior year. These are significant years: the young Erastus dominated by his father, Edwin, even though the father was largely absent from his life, busy with his steel mill and the new Democratic organization he'd founded with Dan O'Connell. Parental distance was a pattern Erastus would follow with his own children, often away from home, busy with politics.

His rituals on hunting and fishing trips, his loyalty to his fellow hunters, his lifelong friendships with the pals he made during his World War II Army hitch, these traits define a strength and loftiness of character that is at odds with the persona of the suave, double-talking con man who never gave us a straight answer about where the city's money went. But he jumps off these pages at us as a man after all: no longer that charmingly cool and dignified figure in the gray suit; here a flesh and blood creature who worked himself numb in the job, but also found ways to keep his soul throbbing with life. Paul Grondahl is a stellar reporter for the Albany *Times Union* and a fine writer, and his book is a substantial contribution to the annals of Albany politics, about which not much of lasting substance has been written in this century. But Mayoral partisans will not be entirely thankful for Grondahl's scholarship and humanizing efforts on Erastus's behalf, for his conclusions on the man, on Dan, and on their minions, are harsh.

He finds Erastus a tokenist on race, who used his most favored black man to spy on other blacks hostile to the machine; and he squashed black political opposition by arrest and intimidation. Macy's and Sears, who wanted to build department stores Downtown, met "so much interference from Corning and the machine that they opted instead to open in Colonie Center." Erastus also applauded construction of highway 787, which cut Albany off from the river, barricading all future waterfront development, and Grondahl deduces a citizen reaction to this: Shame on you, Erastus.

"Mayor Corning helped create, and presided over, a city in decline," Grondahl writes. "On [his] watch the city lost population; nearly 30,000 . . . Downtown suffered a steady hemorrhage of commerce . . . Albany's infrastructure [streets, sidewalks, city buildings, parks], from years of deferred maintenance, were . . . decrepit at the time of Corning's death."

"No theme emerges from his long reign except for stability, a numb sameness . . . that ultimately amounted to stagnation," Grondahl writes elsewhere. "Holding onto power was [the Democrats'] obsession; improving the city became secondary . . ."

We who came of age during the sixty-two-year rule of the invincible Democratic organization learned to live with stagnation, also with the much heralded graft. It was ubiquitous and, unlike the infrastructure, was given very serious attention by the organization's behavior, which flourished mightily while the town developed Alzheimer's. But even if we didn't accept the organization's behavior, we still liked Dan (some loved him), and we liked Erastus (he was harder to love, though a number of ladies managed it), and we loved the town, even when we could hardly recognize it as the swinging town that used to be. It'll bounce back, we said.

Erastus used to say that, too.

In a book I published some years ago, I referred to Albany as a city populated by political wizards and underrated scoundrels. Erastus was one of the wizards, also one of the scoundrels; but after Grondahl's book he will no longer be underrated.

Family Tree of Erastus Corning 2nd

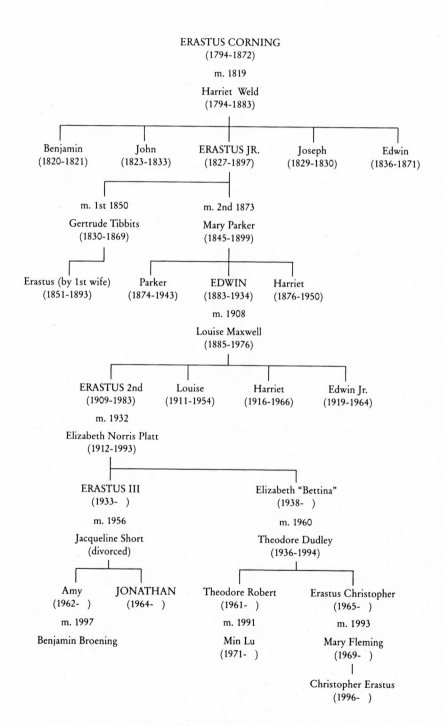

ERASTUS CORNING
(1794-1872)

m. 1819

Harriet Weld
(1794-1883)

| Benjamin (1820-1821) | John (1823-1833) | ERASTUS JR. (1827-1897) | Joseph (1829-1830) | Edwin (1836-1871) |

m. 1st 1850
Gertrude Tibbits
(1830-1869)

m. 2nd 1873
Mary Parker
(1845-1899)

Erastus (by 1st wife)
(1851-1893)

Parker
(1874-1943)

EDWIN
(1883-1934)

Harriet
(1876-1950)

m. 1908

Louise Maxwell
(1885-1976)

ERASTUS 2nd
(1909-1983)

Louise
(1911-1954)

Harriet
(1916-1966)

Edwin Jr.
(1919-1964)

m. 1932

Elizabeth Norris Platt
(1912-1993)

ERASTUS III
(1933-)

Elizabeth "Bettina"
(1938-)

m. 1956

m. 1960

Jacqueline Short
(divorced)

Theodore Dudley
(1936-1994)

Amy
(1962-)

JONATHAN
(1964-)

Theodore Robert
(1961-)

Erastus Christopher
(1965-)

m. 1997

m. 1991

m. 1993

Benjamin Broening

Min Lu
(1971-)

Mary Fleming
(1969-)

Christopher Erastus
(1996-)

(This genealogy represents only those Corning family members directly descended
from the original Erastus who figure prominently in the text.)

Chronology: Erastus Corning 2nd

1909:   Erastus Corning 2nd born on October 7, firstborn of Louise and Edwin Corning. They live at 156 Chestnut Street, Albany.

1914:   The Cornings move to Washington Avenue, across from the Fort Orange Club.

1916:   The mansion Edwin Corning built on the Upper Farm on the family estate at Corning Hill in Glenmont destroyed by fire just before the Cornings were to move in.

1917:   The mansion rebuilt and the Cornings move in. Erastus enters Albany Academy.

1921:   The Albany Democratic machine, formed by Edwin and Parker Corning and the O'Connell brothers, rises to power and takes City Hall with their candidate, Mayor William Stormont Hackett.

1922:   Erastus transfers to Groton School.

1928:   Erastus graduates from Groton, tied for top of his form with Joseph Alsop. That summer, Erastus tours Europe with his drama teacher, John Hoysradt. In the fall, Erastus enters Yale. His father, New York Lt. Gov. Edwin Corning, suffers a stroke and heart attack that ends his political career and leaves him an invalid.

1932:   Corning graduates from Yale. Erastus and Elizabeth "Betty" Norris Platt marry on June 23 in Philadelphia. Edwin Corning sets up his son in the insurance business. Erastus and Betty move into the gardener's house on the Upper Farm at Corning Hill.

1933:   Erastus and Betty Corning's son, Erastus III, born on June 20.

1976:   Mayor Corning's mother, Louise Maxwell Corning, dies on May 24 at 91.

1977:   After defeating Sen. Howard Nolan in the first and only Democratic primary of his career, Corning re-elected to a tenth term as mayor. Dan O'Connell dies on February 28 at 91. Mayor Corning fends off political rivals and becomes the first person in the machine's history to be both mayor and chairman of the Democratic organization.

1981:   Corning re-elected to eleventh term as mayor and claims the title: longest-tenured mayor of any city in America.

1982:   Corning admitted to Albany Medical Center Hospital for lung complications due to emphysema; later transferred to Boston University Hospital. He spends nearly one year hospitalized, mostly in intensive care, breathing with the aid of a respirator.

1983:   Corning prevails once more in his rivalry with Rockefeller as the region's tallest building, the 42-story South Mall tower, is officially named the Erastus Corning 2nd Tower on March 15. Corning is too ill to attend the bill signing ceremony. Mayor Erastus Corning 2nd dies in office on May 28 in Boston University Hospital at 73 after 42 years as mayor.

1984:   Mayor Corning's family and the Noonans fight in court over the mayor's lucrative book of business insurance accounts. The Noonans win.

1993:   Betty Corning dies on September 22 at 81.

1994:   The estate of Erastus and Betty Corning, including their personal and household belongings, sold at public auction on New Year's Day.

Chapter 1:

Mayor for Life: He Left His Heart in City Hall

"Once politics is in the blood, the only way they can take it out is embalming fluid."

*Malcolm Wilson, who spent 14 years as
Nelson Rockefeller's lieutenant governor and only
14 months as governor.*

It was a bitter cold day in late January, 1983, when Angelo "Joe" Amore – tailor to Mayor Erastus Corning 2nd of Albany for more than thirty years at his shop just around the corner from City Hall on State Street – was summoned to Boston University Hospital. It was an unusual request, but Corning was his best customer, so Amore didn't hesitate to make the long-distance service trip. Corning's loyal aide, Bill Keefe, had told Amore on short notice that there was room in the mayor's official car, the Buick with the "A" license plate. Matilda Cuomo, wife of Gov. Mario Cuomo, had canceled her intended visit to Corning in Boston at the last minute, and Amore joined Keefe, driver Dusty Miller and Judge John E. Holt-Harris Jr., one of Corning's closest personal and political friends, for the three-hour drive.

"The mayor had written to me, saying he had lost a little weight and wanted me to take in some of his suits," Amore said. It was typical understatement from the mayor, whose once robust 230-pound physique was gaunt, almost skeletal, and had deteriorated to perhaps 140 pounds of emaciated flesh draped haggardly over his six-foot two-inch frame. Corning had been hospitalized for the past seven months, spending much of that time in the intensive care unit, breathing with the aid of a respirator because of complications from emphysema and chronic lung ailments, as well as intestinal and coronary disease. Three months earlier, in October of 1982, the mayor had been transferred from Albany Medical Center

Hospital to Boston, where an experimental respiratory rehabilitation program – the only one of its kind in the country – had achieved some success
in weaning emphysema patients off the respirator.

Over the objections of friends and family in Albany who wanted him
to remain close to home, Corning had decided to try the Boston experiment. The mayor refused to relinquish the absolute control he wielded at
City Hall for forty-two years – the longest tenure of any mayor in the
country – and was determined to come back, against all odds and the
cumulative effect of several operations that had begun to seem like medical
acts of desperation. Those closest to him could see that he was dying, but
Albany's mayor for life refused to go gently into that good night.

One of the last things Corning was able to write was a statement of
goals shortly after being transferred to Boston. In labored penmanship,
Corning wrote this never-before published summation, a sort of treatise on
his purpose for fighting for life, from his hospital bed in Boston on
October 27, 1982:

> At seventy-three, I have had far more than my share of the good
> things in life, and I continue to truly enjoy it. I believe I have
> been productive and my basic goal is to continue to be so,
> accomplish things and not be a burden on others. My immediate
> goal is to get strong, and live easily with my present and any fur-
> ther handicaps, and to get back to the Mayor's office for a min-
> imum of eight to twelve hours a week to be able to handle
> essential matters on a regular and orderly basis. Looking at the
> future it is hard for me to look at goals more than five years
> ahead. My family is secure with interesting careers separate from
> mine. As to myself, I have agreed and just started on two oral
> histories. These should not be time consuming and completed in
> three to six months, perhaps as much as nine. In September of
> 1984 my term as chairman, Albany Democratic Committee,
> expires. I have to determine if I want to work to be elected for
> another two year term. My term as mayor expires December 31,
> 1985 and in April 1985 I must determine if I want to try for four
> more. If I were to answer today the answer would almost cer-
> tainly be no. I have simple changes to make in my insurance
> agency which I own 100%. I have a number of changes to make
> in transfer of real and personal properties, not time consuming

but interesting. Mrs. Corning and I plan to make a substantial memorial gift to our Church. I have plans to recognize as best I can some of those who have done so much to help me, to give real boosts along the road and just friends, too. There is a possibility I might want to stay on as Democratic County chairman till Sept. 1986 to have greater influence in picking my successor as Mayor. County Chairman is not a time consuming job. My negative goal at all times is: Don't be a burden. My positive goals should be reached generally in two to four years, with the future after that, reading history & nature and energy study, mild hunting and fishing and nature study. I would like to be a senior advisor with no ax to grind, but enjoying to the full the ability to help through long experience.

Throughout his life, Erastus Corning 2nd had been a masterful juggler. He was silky smooth and unflappable and made it look easy as he kept several balls in the air at once. He was a one-man City Hall, personally controlling the minute details of municipal affairs. He played many roles simultaneously: mayor and political boss, insurance company owner and astute bank director, blue-collar fishing buddy and blueblood club member, aristocrat and everyman, paternalistic provider and cunning political strategist.

Corning had been so many things to so many people, he may have gotten lost amid the personas. In the narrative of his life, Mayor Corning tried to mirror the mythic veneer overlaid upon him by a city and citizenry hungry for civic heroes. Despite four generations of outstanding accomplishment in the realms of politics and industry, the Corning family's sterling resume masks a family that, like all ordinary families, knew its share of pain and personal tragedy. Although many Albanians held him in blind reverence, Mayor Corning was far more human than his assuredly aristocratic bearing suggested. An accurate portrait of the mayor contains as much shadow as light, portions of darkness to balance the qualities of brightness and goodness the public most often wanted to find in him. The legacy of Mayor Corning is a life told through stories. Everyone in Albany seemed to have a story about the mayor. He possessed both a common touch and a larger-than-life cult of personality. A Corning encounter usually made a deep impression, a memory that lasted. He had a special ability to make people feel at ease, no matter what their station in life. His greatest quality was being able to meet people on their own terms, from the poorest to the richest, youngest to oldest, across any spectrum one cares to define. His door at City Hall was always open. His accessibility was as legendary as his approachability. He liked people.

And yet, he kept most people, even longtime friends, at arm's length. He practiced a smiling aloofness. Very few, if any, were granted entry into the intimacies of his interior life. What his closest friends and associates saw was a single branch, whichever branch Corning chose to reveal to them, and not the whole trunk and roots of the entire man. Robert Roche, Corning's family attorney, chose a different analogy to describe the compartmentalized nature of Erastus Corning's personality: "Erastus Corning was like a great novel with twelve amazing sub-plots. Nobody ever really figured him out. The story never really ended. He just died."

State Assemblyman John McEneny, a Corning protégé who dreamed of succeeding his political idol as mayor, viewed Corning in terms of a wheel metaphor: "Corning was the hub of a wheel and all the spokes plugged into the mayor, but none of the spokes touched each other or had any interaction. One spoke was for his judge friends, one spoke for his Maine buddies, another spoke for the Noonans and Rutniks, one for his World War II pals, a spoke for his local political allies, a spoke for state and national Democratic politicians, one spoke for his own family, another spoke for his Fort Orange and society friends, et cetera." McEneny believed that the strict separation of the facets of Corning's life served his intensely private and aloof personality and also strengthened the structure of the wheel itself. "The separate spokes might have contained people who didn't like each other and were even bitter enemies," McEneny said. "But the mayor kept them separate and distinct and each spoke worked for Corning and strengthened the overall wheel that only Corning controlled."

Control was an overriding theme of Corning's life. Growing up, Erastus had almost no control, living under the thumb of his father's subjugation, succumbing to Edwin Corning's obsession to mold a son who reflected his own political ambitions. Later, as Mayor Corning, he relinquished control out of deference to political boss Dan O'Connell, a substitute father figure. In his personal life, the mayor's continuation of an arid society marriage and cultivation of domestic respectability could be seen, once more, as dutiful son proffering control to a grieving mother and widow who lost a husband and three children in their prime in part because of the ravages of alleged alcoholism. Finally, with the death of his mother and Dan O'Connell less than one year apart, Corning had the opportunity, for the final six years of his life, to run the show himself and he galvanized power and control absolutely, with a micro-manager's possessiveness. After a lifelong quest for control, Corning was not about to relinquish it easily, even as he lay dying.

Back in Boston, for a time, the new year, 1983, had opened with promise for the ailing Albany mayor. Through sheer force of his personality, Mayor Corning, whose condition had indeed been improving slightly, convinced all around him that he would return to his office, Room 102 of City Hall, the only place he felt fully alive and in control: Mayor for life. Preparations were being made for Corning's return, as aides and ward heelers scurried about with the eagerness of serfs welcoming back their king from battle. The mayor's friend, developer Lew Swyer, and contractor Frank Letko had drawn up plans to install ramps and rails at his home at Corning Hill to make the house accessible to the wheelchair-bound Corning. A concrete pad was poured outside the house to hold oxygen tanks and Corning purchased a specially equipped van with wheelchair lift and special controls in January and had it parked outside the hospital in Boston so the mayor could drive himself home, home to City Hall.

"I went to see him in January and he had just bought the van," recalled Judge John E. Holt-Harris Jr., city traffic recorder judge and a close political and personal friend of the mayor's. "He and I talked about going out to the Alcove Reservoir in the van. Erastus was going to put special stops in the back of the van so the wheelchair didn't roll out when he was casting. He made a joke about it and said, 'That would be a hell of a thing if they found me in a wheelchair at the bottom of the Alcove Reservoir.'"

It was on that trip, too, that Corning's spirits were so high that he pantomimed out his hospital room window for a television crew outside. The mayor held aloft a bedpan, swinging it back and forth, pretending to pour it on the reporter's head and laughing with the glee of a Groton first former pulling a prank, Holt-Harris recalled. This was the same January trip on which Amore brought four custom made suits for Corning, made of a gray wool that the mayor himself selected in England. One of the suits Amore carried was forest green, the mayor's favorite color, which matched the green socks Corning wore to City Hall each day without fail – considered an eccentricity by most, but the habit was, in fact, due to Corning's color blindness.

Amore had made more than fifty custom suits and sports jackets for Mayor Corning over the years, some costing as much as $800, with a label inside the breast pocket of each: "Erastus Corning II." Amore knew the mayor's suit size by heart – forty-six long, forty waist, thirty-one inseam. "He had relatively short legs and a long torso for his height," the tailor said. "He'd come into the store and order three or four suits a year, always gray and blue pinstripes. He was very conservative in his dress. Nothing wild for the mayor."

Erastus Corning 2nd did not like surprises. Since childhood, reared in the military regimentation of Albany Academy and the Protestant Episcopalian sternness of Groton, his life was laid out for him with patrician perspicacity. Erastus had no say in being born into a gray wool pinstripe suit, a WASP Ascendancy uniform that he donned dutifully yet regretfully. There hadn't been many days since adolescence when Corning hadn't been expected to dress formally. Although such rigid style did not suit his other side, his earthy and profane side, Corning, at least in public, rarely shed the uniform of his aristocratic breeding. As a young boy at Albany Academy in the early 1920s, knickers, tie and jacket were required, except when replaced by a military uniform. At Groton, the suit was blue serge, with stiff Eton collars and black patent leather pumps at dinner. The suit at Yale was generally brown tweed. Corning's gray and blue pinstripes became a second skin during a half-century spent in politics. Going casual for the mayor, such as at the annual Democratic Party picnic, meant khakis, a blue blazer and buttoned-down Oxford shirt, sans tie. Corning once joked that when a new acquaintance asked him to go fishing, the man expressed surprise when the mayor showed up without jacket and tie.

Clothes make the man, it has been said, and the aphorism is especially apt in Mayor Corning's case. Clothing style is more than a metaphor for the mayor, who embodied the internal conflict of nature versus nurture. As a boy, left to his own devices, young Erastus was as carefree and free-spirited as his butterfly collector grandfather, Erastus Corning Jr., with the youngster spending his days on long naturalist rambles through the woodlands of Corning Hill, studying birds and plants, collecting specimens from the forest and reading voraciously books pertaining to natural history. That was the nature side of the mayor's personality. The nurture aspect was imposed upon the boy primarily by his overbearing father, Edwin Corning, who uprooted Erastus from his cheerful and unstructured life in Albany and replanted him in the lonely and competitive prep school groves of Groton's uncompromising academe. Moreover, despite Erastus' innate sensibilities and profound interest in natural history, the father forced the son into a narrowly defined path of politics and business that would continue the Corning family legacy. In one dramatic gesture, then, the destiny of Erastus and the city of Albany was determined by a father intent on making certain his firstborn lived up to that preordained image. As a result, since boyhood, Erastus Corning 2nd felt obliged to wear the uniform his father had tailored for him, and he spent a lifetime struggling to honor the suit of his father's memory and, at the same time, trying to shed its confining shape.

None of the dozens of fitting sessions Amore had conducted with Corning over the years prepared the tailor for the condition in which he found his most loyal customer at the Boston hospital. "He hardly looked like Mayor Corning," Amore recalled. "He had lost so much weight that he was just skin and bones. He'd had that tracheotomy and couldn't talk. He struggled to stand up so I could pin the suits to where they needed to be taken in, but he was so weak. We finally got a couple of nurses and they helped him stand while I took the measurements. He was so far gone, but he insisted he wanted to do this."

Corning's forty-inch waist had shrunken more than eight inches and the pants had to be taken in drastically, as did the jackets. Amore went about his work quickly and silently, marking the alterations with pins. Amore remembered feeling stunned and saddened, unable to find the right words to thank Corning for the many kindnesses the mayor had shown him since Amore emigrated from Calabria in southern Italy in 1960. Amore had worked at first for John Cerasoli at Albany's old Ten Eyck Hotel, before it was demolished, where Corning bought his suits, and later took over the business in 1965 with the mayor's encouragement. "I was afraid my English wasn't good enough to open my own store, but the mayor said I could do it and that he would help me," Amore recalled. "The mayor sent his friends to me and the business prospered. The mayor was as good as his word."

As Amore packed up his supplies, Corning slipped the tailor a note: "Joe, I'll be coming home in two weeks. I'll have Dusty pick up my suits then." Corning never made it home. The mayor was buried in the gray pinstripe suit that Amore had altered. The other three suits are preserved in garment bags in Amore's third-floor storage room of his shop at 123 State

Street. "I called Betty Corning [the mayor's wife] after the mayor died and she told me to keep them because she had no use for them," Amore recalled. "I've kept them all these years. I think I'll keep them always. I loved that man."

The altered suits, the custom van, the oxygen tanks and the special wheelchair ramps planned for Mayor Corning's triumphant return to City Hall – envisioned as something in the annals of Albany politics every bit as spectacular as Corning's homecoming as the combat-decorated G.I. Mayor in World War II – were left to gather dust. The hopefulness of January was quickly replaced by hopelessness and despair after Corning developed pneumonia and was placed back in intensive care, where he also developed arrhythmia, an irregular heartbeat. Still, in mid-February, 1983, Corning battled against a failing mind and loss of muscle control and scrawled out these notes from his hospital bed in the Boston intensive care unit: "Coughing up secretions is the easy way out but for the super plugs and thick secretions and copious quantities. Try at least four experiments by myself each day with suctioning with and without saline. Sit on stool in tub. Use hand held shower head. Much simpler, does the job. I will get a hospital supply co. representative. There will be twenty different things he will keep me supplied with." It was the last thing Erastus Corning 2nd ever wrote.

During his long decline in the hospital, the mayor had been robbed of all the legendary vitality that had made his return to City Hall seem possible. One by one, his faculties faltered. After he lost his voice and the use of his hands to write notes to visitors, his awareness of reality slipped away in a fog of pain and medication. He breathed with the aid of a respirator and was fed intravenously. The reminders such deterioration triggered in his memory during his own slow and torturous wasting-away must have been frightful, for he had watched his invalid father slide downhill like this and the image was seared into his consciousness: don't be a burden . . . don't be a burden . . . don't be a burden. It had become Mayor Corning's mantra in the hospital, a phrase he wrote over and over again, and now, after his fierce struggle, he no longer had the energy to fight the inevitable.

On February 22, Corning underwent surgery for removal of a tumor on his large intestine and to stop intestinal bleeding. Half of his intestine was removed. Several days later, he suffered a mild heart attack. Still, loyal aide Keefe continued to come to Boston with papers and reports, carrying in his briefcase the essential business of City Hall, which Corning, on his deathbed, refused to relinquish. "I made more than sixty-five trips to

Boston," Keefe recalled. "The toll collectors on the Mass Pike got to know me. They'd send me on my way with a get-well wish for Mayor Corning's speedy recovery."

On March 12, Corning was operated on to treat bleeding ulcers at the base of the esophagus, where it meets the stomach. Doctors termed his condition "life threatening" because of his age and other medical problems. At this time, Betty Corning asked Holt-Harris and the mayor's Albany physician, Dr. Richard Beebe of Albany Medical College, to meet with her in Boston. "The mayor was semi-comatose and hugely bloated and it was an extremely painful thing to see," Holt-Harris recalled. "We tried to elicit a reaction, but the mayor was not functioning. That wasn't Erastus Corning anymore. It was an enormous lump of flesh in bed with a face as big as a pumpkin. It was not my beloved friend."

Holt-Harris and Beebe conferred and knew what they had to do. "The doctors had been planning to do another operation and Betty wanted us to come and make them stop," Holt-Harris said. "She didn't have the energy anymore to fight them. Doctor Beebe sat the Boston medical team down and said they would not invade that poor man's body again. And that was the end of the discussion." A few weeks before, Corning had scrawled on a note to Holt-Harris: "I'm not going to make it. I shouldn't have come here." Holt-Harris discussed the mayor's sentiment with Beebe and they turned to Betty Corning and said, "I think the humane thing to do is to let him die now." "It was tragic at the end," Beebe said. "They try to keep someone alive and go overboard. He was courageous to the end. He didn't give up. He was a good patient and a very brave man. I never heard him complain." After two months of tenuously clinging to life, on May 28, 1983, the mayor died.

The moments when Mayor Corning – a man who seemed emotionally closed off to all, even his family – opened up were rare. One such example could be found in a Christmas letter Corning wrote on December 23, 1982, to his daughter from the Boston hospital, thanking her for the letter she sent the day before and trying to clarify, in shaky cursive and a mind medicated against pain, his life philosophy: "Number one, sentiment is good stuff. Number two, just a small piece of crisp bacon will make an entire sodium free breakfast much more enjoyable. Number three, we are not perfect by a damn sight and in politics that's very clear. Politics is the art of compromise, and politics and life in general are much the same." Corning then recalled his days at Groton School, raised under the stern religious certitude of its founder, Rev. Endicott Peabody, an educator "who never saw a bit of gray any place. It was right or it was wrong. That's all." But a long career in politics had taught Corning that life could not be so neatly divided into black and white. He wrote, "In politics, a modest amount of corruption is helpful in getting along. The word is not corruption in day by day existence, but it means pretty much the same."

Then the father's letter to his daughter drifted and rambled across a number of cloudy attempts to make meaning of the world and humankind's place in it, discussing the Big Bang theory versus creationism, before he gave up from fatigue. "Maybe some day I'll get smarter and explain," he concluded. His daughter never heard that explanation. Her father's condition continued to decline after Christmas and his ability to speak or write was soon gone.

The few instances when someone broke through Corning's tightly held reserve were remembered as special glimpses into the soul he worked hard to shield from view. As the mayor lay dying, his daughter read him "The Gift of the Magi" as he had done for her as a child. "We both cried and cried and it was a beautiful moment," Bettina recalled. During one of her visits to Boston, she brought her father wintergreen mints, the kind he loved to buy during the summers of her girlhood at the homemade candy and ice cream shop in Bar Harbor, Maine, but he was too sick at that point to eat them, to allow the memory of taste to transport him back to a moment when they were a young and happy and loving family for a time.

There was no apparent closure, however, when it came to the conflicting relationships of Mayor Corning with his wife, Betty Corning, and his longtime confidante, Polly Noonan. Even in the truth-telling moments expected of life's final chapter, the dying Corning managed to juggle his two lives, the public and the private, never resolving the secrets he had carried and buried for so long. Noonan, a frequent visitor to Boston, made sure to check the schedule with Keefe to determine the days when Betty Corning would not be at the hospital. The dual relationships continued until the end.

When it came to his estranged son, Erastus III, there were no moments of shared reconciliation in the hospital for a lifetime of regret and sadness between father and son. "There was no reconciliation, because a reconciliation implies there was damage that needed repairing and I wouldn't characterize it that way," the son said. "It wasn't good or bad. It was just nothing. I visited him in the hospital a few times, the last time a few days before he died, and nothing had changed. We simply had no relationship. He was focused on coming back to Albany to continue as mayor. He had convinced others of that, too. Everyone had lost all reason given his condition in my view."

Corning, the obsessive controller of all details, had used his wit and charm to win over even his doctors. He wanted to be back at his gray metal desk in City Hall, running his kingdom. When David Bray told Corning he intended to retire as superintendent of the Albany School District in 1982 at the age of seventy after a forty-eight year career in education, the mayor couldn't understand Bray's decision.

"Are you serious?" Corning asked.

"Yes, I think forty-eight years is enough," Bray replied.

"Not me. I'm never going to retire," the mayor had said. "They'll have to carry me out."

His words rang prophetic. Mayor Corning never made it back alive to his beloved City Hall. The closest he got was being wheeled over to the window in his Boston hospital room, where he could look out and, on a clear day, catch a glimpse of an Albany Street a few blocks away. Erastus Corning 2nd, America's most durable mayor, died in Boston, just off Albany Street, at 12:20 p.m. on May 28, 1983 at the age of seventy-three. Cause of death was cardiac arrest due to a pulmonary embolism, a blood clot that settled in the lungs.

Back in Albany on the day of the mayor's death, the city was cloaked in gray, overcast weather that felt like a shroud of doom. It was a Saturday. Downtown, word spread person to person in Albany's small-town way. "Is the mayor really dead?" a woman asked, brushing back tears, outside Saint Mary's Church, where, by 3 p.m., less than three hours after Corning's death, hundreds had gathered in the shadow of City Hall for a memorial mass. Even after his long, slow decline, the city seemed stunned. The pace of city life slowed perceptibly for the next couple of days in a stupor of disbelief. The mayor for life. Dead. Could Albany even go on? Citizens seemed unable to comprehend their city A.C., After Corning.

On Tuesday, Mayor Corning's body lay in state, casket closed, out of regard for his skeletal state, in the Episcopal Cathedral of All Saints. More than 8,000 mourners filed past, despite a heavy downpour that did not let up all day. At nine o'clock that night, Betty Corning left the cathedral with her two children, Bettina and Rasty, and they walked down South Swan Street, crossed Washington Avenue and entered the Fort Orange Club for a late dinner in the bastion of privilege and elite society the mayor's forebears had built to preserve what they perceived as the noblest qualities of Albany.

The next morning, the sun broke through the clouds, clear and bright, for the first time in several days as they buried Erastus Corning 2nd. The funeral cortege bearing the body of Mayor Corning stopped in front of City Hall – a pause heavy with symbolism – where a huge crowd numbering thousands lined the streets ten deep encircling the landmark building the mayor's grandfather had commissioned. The carillon in the City Hall bell tower played "God Bless America" and the throngs of Albany's citizens, many of whom had known no other mayor in their lifetime, wept openly and sang along through muffled sobs. At precisely 12:14 p.m., police motorcycles roared and the cortege quickly started up, gained speed and, within a moment, the mayor for life was gone from his city. Crowds estimated at more than 10,000 people lined Washington Avenue between City Hall and All Saint's Cathedral. The *Times Union* published a photograph of the hearse bearing Mayor Corning, stopped in front of City Hall for the last time, with the headline, "The End of An Era."

At the funeral service, Gov. Mario Cuomo read from the Epistle of St. Paul to the Corinthians: "Then cometh the end, when he shall have delivered up the kingdom to God, even the Father; when he shall have put down all rule and all authority and power. For he must reign, till he hath put all enemies under his feet. The last enemy that shall be destroyed is death." After the reading, the choir sang this anthem: "Thou knowest, Lord, the secrets of our hearts, shut not thy merciful ears unto our prayer; but spare us, Lord most holy, O God most mighty, O holy and most merciful Saviour, thou most worthy Judge eternal, suffer us not, at our last hour, for any pains of death, to fall from thee. Amen."

Everyone had a story about Mayor Corning and each one who had known him tried to eulogize the man, to sum up his legend.

"He was just the greatest," said his loyal aide, Bill Keefe, his voice choked with emotion.

"Albany has lost a great leader," said the new mayor, Thomas M. Whalen III.

"The Empire State mourns the loss of one of her grandest sons, Erastus Corning, the mayor," Cuomo said.

"His door was always open to those who sought him, even when he was advised to close it because of ill health," said the Republican State

Senate Majority Leader, Warren M. Anderson, a friend from the Fort Orange Club.

"Legends are hard to replace," said Albany Assemblyman Richard Conners, a machine Democrat who served on the Albany City Council under Corning for thirty-five years.

No one person can fully sum up the life and times of Erastus Corning 2nd. He did not reveal himself completely to anyone, not even family members. He was many different people, many different faces, a separate guise for each of the compartments of his life. In piecing together those various parts of his personality we begin to emerge with a more complete portrait of Erastus Corning 2nd.

Chapter 2:

Of Iron and Politics: The Corning Family's Roots

"Albany needed a club composed of gentlemen who represented that which was best in Albany, the men of distinction, of culture, of good manners, of high character, of attainments, of social quality, the men who were born on the top, as well as those who possessed the qualities which make good men and had risen to the top."

From the history of Albany's Fort Orange Club, founded in 1880 by Erastus Corning Jr. and others.

The Corning family burial plot at Albany Rural Cemetery commands the high ground, offering a sweeping view of the Hudson River Valley far beyond. The Corning plot is located in Section 31, in one of the oldest parts of the cemetery, founded in 1841 on the outskirts of Albany. The Corning site is a circular mound bordered on all sides by a gravel drive and shaded by a dozen trees – pine, maple, cherry, dogwood. The most striking feature is its isolation. The Corning plot is an island, self-contained and set apart. It is a very private orb, this grassy knoll the Cornings occupy in perpetuity. The plot is laid out like a wheel, with the railroad baron progenitor, the original Erastus, as the central hub from which the spokes of each successive generation radiate. On a map, the Corning family's final resting place mirrors the stern formality of military regiments, resembling troops encircled in rigid formation to repel an attack. And yet, despite the geographic isolation, even in death, the Cornings rub shoulders with their class, their kind. Neighboring monuments belong to John Boyd Thacher, Dean Sage, Maj. Gen. Philip Schuyler and assorted Pruyns and Lansings. It amounts to a roll call of Albany's former ruling class. Very WASP. Very Dutch. This cluster of monuments range from markers to mausoleums, and while some, like Mayor Thacher's, are extravagant edifices, they generally bear the restraint and discretion of old money.

If anyone took the time to visit the Corning plot on Memorial Day, 1995, it passed unnoticed. Nobody left flowers, or flags, or any trace of having paid their respects. It appeared as if nobody had been there in months. A long-decayed arrangement of autumn flowers moldered between the grave markers of Mayor Erastus Corning 2nd and his wife, Elizabeth. Otherwise, the site was barren of offerings of love or remembrance. Weeds and tufts of long grass sprouted between the gravestones. It was quiet and peaceful and the sense of being forgotten by time was absolute. The only sound on this afternoon – with a gathering sky filling with dark, ominous clouds amid warnings of severe thunderstorms – was the wind whispering through the leaves and pine needles on trees protecting the Corning glade, this fortification that holds its familial mysteries as surely as any rampart.

A visitor to the historic Albany Rural Cemetery, home to the grave of President Chester Arthur and other luminaries, would not be drawn to the Corning circle. The expansive plot contains four modest monuments and fourteen simple head stones on a site with room for fifty-six graves. There is nothing in the design or the epitaphs that would give a visitor any indication of the prominence and influence of the Cornings on the business and political life of Albany for more than 150 years. The dominant monument is reserved for the first Erastus, titan among merchants, maker of iron and railroads, creator of the family fortune in Albany, an empire builder who put his indelible stamp on the capital city on the Hudson in countless ways. It is from this Erastus that all wealth and prominence for the family flowed in Albany. He was the wellspring of greatness, the familial font, and his monument symbolizes such. Set on an imposing black granite slab measuring twelve feet by six feet, the top is a solid copper sculpture in the shape of a cathedral, with a roof in a cross pattern and a decorative border of carved plants beneath the eaves. One side is reserved for his wife, Harriet Weld Corning, born July 31, 1793 and died May 26, 1883. "I have waited for thy salvation, O Lord," reads her epitaph. Erastus Corning's reads, "My hope is ever in thee," next to his dates: Born December 11, 1794 and died April 8, 1872. Erastus and Harriet had five children: two died before their second birthdays, another lived only until the age of nine and two survived into adulthood.

For the most part, the Cornings were not expressive when it came to memorials. They list only the name of the deceased and the dates of their birth and death. Nothing is revealed, neither the agonies nor the ecstasies, the triumphs nor the failures, the joys nor the pains. Albany Rural Cemetery is the final resting place for a family that spans eleven generations of American life. The roots run deep in this country for the Corning name, which, according to lore, is believed to be derived from the French name *de Cornu*, "horn of a hunter," which then became Cornus and, finally, Corning in the English translation. The ancient Corning arms are said to have depicted the horn of a hunter and the motto, "*Crede Cornu.*"

The American tale for the Cornings began when Samuel Corning, a Puritan, born in England in 1616, left his homeland at the age of nineteen for reasons of religious persecution. One of ten children raised in the Belstone parish of Devonshire, England, Samuel Corning sailed to the colony of America, landing apparently at the popular port of Salem, Massachusetts, just up the coast from Boston, and eventually settled with his wife, Elizabeth, in Beverly, Massachusetts across the harbor from Salem. After eking out an existence for his first six years in the new world, it was in Beverly that Samuel Corning gained prominence after starting as a farmer in 1641 with one acre of land, on which he grew hemp. Corning quickly gained respect among his fellow settlers and they rewarded him with positions of responsibility, including his selection in 1665 to Beverly's first board of selectmen, which incorporated the town three years later. Samuel Corning established the family's deep and lasting interest in politics and, like successive generations of Cornings, was a proven vote-getter: Corning was elected five terms as a selectman. Moreover, trust in him ran so high he was named Beverly's collector of taxes in 1676. A few years later, the citizens turned to Corning again, this time to negotiate a settlement in a boundary dispute with neighboring Wenham, Corning's former hometown. Corning's other civic duties included acting as an early land planner when he served on several committees formed to lay out a blueprint for growth and development in the town. Beverly records also show Corning secured twenty trees for a windbreak and soil conservation, perhaps foreshadowing a tradition of land stewardship that reached down many generations and took hold in Mayor Erastus Corning 2nd. Samuel Corning and his wife, Elizabeth, had three children, a son, Samuel Jr., a daughter, Elizabeth, and a second girl named Remembrance. Samuel Corning Sr. amassed a large farm and substantial land holdings, the extent of which is unclear. His estate was divided at the time of his death in 1694, at the age of seventy-eight, between Elizabeth, his widow, and their three children.

Corning's only son, Samuel Jr., married Hannah Batchelder and the couple settled in Beverly on the family farm. They had four children, all boys: Samuel 3rd, John, Joseph and Daniel. Samuel Jr. died in 1714 at the age of seventy-three. His wife, Hannah, died in 1718 at seventy-two, ending the second generation of Cornings in America and extending the family legacy as proven leaders and prominent land owners.

The third generation of Cornings on American soil confirmed a family habit descendants find amusing, but historians find annoying – the repetition of certain names. Trying to tease apart the various Erastuses, for instance, can prove unnerving, for there were no fewer than eight Erastus Cornings in the family tree by 1995 and several had no middle name or distinguishing feature to differentiate them from each other. A ninth Erastus was born in 1996, the mayor's great-grandson. It was no wonder, then, that the third Samuel – although the family did not use junior or senior or numerals, Roman or otherwise – should be given the same name as his father and grandfather. The third Samuel and his wife, Rebeckah Woodbury, had five children: Hannah, Joseph, Josiah, Martha and Nehemiah. The son, Joseph, moved his family from Beverly to Norwich, Connecticut, before dying at the age of thirty-nine in 1718. His widow was left to raise their five children, who ranged in age from one year to sixteen years. After his father's death, the middle son, Josiah, married a Norwich girl, Jane Andrews, in 1733 at the age of twenty-four and they moved to Preston, Connecticut just west of Norwich in southeastern Connecticut near Long Island Sound and the Rhode Island border. This generation of Cornings, with their eleven children, had now earned the moniker of Connecticut Yankees.

The Cornings, at this point the fifth generation of Americans, now become a blur of Biblical names and a bushy family tree with a thick network of branches upon which hang a few leaves of historical interest. Josiah's son, Ezra, born in Preston in 1737, was the first of the Corning clan to forsake the familiarity of the country lifestyle for an early urban experience in Hartford, Connecticut, where Josiah worked as a shoemaker and ran a grocery store. He married a captain's daughter, Mary Hopkins, who died young, and then Josiah remarried twice more, fathering ten children in all. A cousin to Josiah, Joseph Corning, born in 1746 and a Whig, was taken prisoner by the British in the Revolutionary War, put aboard a prison-ship in New York and never heard from again. Another cousin to Josiah, Benjamin Corning, born in 1748, moved his family out of the Corning conclave at Preston to Voluntown, Connecticut, about ten miles to the north, on the edge of Pachaug State Forest. While Benjamin's uncle and other relatives had moved to Hartford and sought a living in the mercantile trade, Benjamin established himself as a farmer. This return to the family's agrarian foundation set the stage for the upbringing of the sixth American generation and the rearing in rural Columbia County in New York state of the first Erastus Corning, founder of the New York Central Railroad and great-grandfather of Mayor Erastus Corning 2nd, who so proudly bore his great-grandfather's name.

It is here that references to Corning family history blossom, for the original Erastus was the wellspring from which subsequent Corning achievement flowed. Erastus Corning set an unsurpassed benchmark for family accomplishment, a remarkable record of entrepreneurship forged by dogged determination. He possessed an uncanny sense for predicting business trends far ahead of the curve and then marshaling the forces of politics and commerce to bring his vision of the future into sharp focus. Although his was not a rags-to-riches story, the rapid rise and high level of wealth and prominence – both political and social – that Erastus achieved could not have been dreamed of by the five previous generations of Cornings working the soil in southeastern Connecticut.

Erastus Corning was the only family member, after all, who, up to this point, achieved the immortality of a life preserved in print. The fine biography, *Erastus Corning: Merchant and Financier, 1794-1872* by Irene Neu of Cornell University, published by that university's press in 1960, is a detailed chronicle of his entrepreneurship. Relying heavily upon business records and related legal documents, Neu delineates how Erastus came from a modest background to found the New York Central Railroad, earning wide acclaim as one of the richest and most powerful men in New York state, with a nationwide reputation as industrialist, land speculator and financier. As her book's title indicates, Neu focuses on Corning's business career and does not explore her subject's private life and does not offer a critical evaluation of the public impact of Corning's financial deals, which often were assisted by his political machinations.

Its strengths as a text on economics aside, Neu doesn't fully evaluate that nexus of politics and business, yet it is precisely that potent combination that Erastus Corning managed to exploit in such an early and innovative way that, I believe, largely accounts for his success. Leveraging business opportunities through political connections became a family legacy that Erastus Corning passed on to future generations.

Erastus Corning was born in Norwich, Connecticut on December 14, 1794, the sixth generation of Cornings in America, the grandson of Nehemiah Corning and the son of Bliss Corning, who married Lucinda Smith. Erastus' father served in the Revolutionary War and fought against the British alongside the family of his wife, Lucinda, who came from a long-established American family. Accounts of Erastus' father have called him unstable financially, even shiftless, and often on the brink of leaving his family destitute. Nonetheless, his boy Erastus grew into a bright and gifted child and, in 1802, at the age of eight, was chosen to attend a select school for outstanding students run by Pelatiah Perit, a recent graduate of Yale. Erastus was later taught by Rev. Daniel Haskell, also a Yale man. A Yale education would become in later generations of Corning men an unspoken rule. But Perit's school was costly and Bliss Corning did not have the money for Erastus to attend. In stepped the boy's uncle, Benjamin Smith, Erastus' mother's bachelor brother, who had no children of his own upon whom to shower his largess. Benjamin Smith recognized Erastus' unusually high aptitude and wanted to foster the boy's ability as his benefactor.

What makes the achievements of Erastus Corning all the more remarkable is that he accomplished them despite physical disabilities in an era that was not as enlightened as our own when it came to handicaps. Erastus Corning had fallen from his crib at the age of two and injured his hip to such an extent that for much of his life he could walk only with the aid of crutches. His sheer intellectual power and financial wizardry overshadowed the physical disabilities, though. In fact, accounts of Erastus Corning in newspapers of the day never mentioned his crippled condition or that he was hunched over and could walk only haltingly, supported by crutches.

In 1805, after more than a century and a half of Corning settlement in Connecticut, Bliss Corning decided – as was common after the Revolution – that it was time for his family to strike out for New York State. The Cornings followed the lead of other Connecticut neighbors and sought out new opportunity amidst the rich farmland of Chatham, Columbia County. Erastus Corning's uncle and benefactor, Benjamin Smith, now lived nearby in Troy. Smith was an early settler there in the late eighteenth century and was a prominent citizen of Troy, where he became co-owner of a hardware and iron store, Heartt and Smith. In 1807, when

Erastus was thirteen, he was given permission by his parents to leave the family home in Chatham (with eleven children, the boy's departure meant one less mouth to feed) to go to Troy to work in his uncle's store. It was there that Erastus, already well schooled in arithmetic, spelling and the classics, would learn the art of the deal. There were other lessons awaiting, particularly political ones. His uncle Benjamin was an ardent Jeffersonian who strongly influenced the young Erastus in that direction, which establishes the Corning family's zealous support of the Democratic Party despite the more familiar Republicanism of their later status as members of the wealthy class.

His uncle's store was a crossroads for buying and selling materials carried from New York up the Hudson River by sloop, items then re-sold to merchants who carried wares into the western interior by wagon or river portage. Erastus underwent a typical apprenticeship. He was in charge of cleaning up the store, sweeping the floors and straightening the inventory. His handicap apparently did not seem to deter him, nor did it stifle his progress. Within two years, when he was fifteen, his uncle encouraged the boy to begin a small side operation of buying and selling goods ranging from tobacco to sugar to lemons. His uncle helped him out with cash advances to purchase more goods and Erastus always immediately repaid his debts; even as a youngster, he understood the value of good credit.

Erastus wasn't afraid of a hard day's labor. He hobbled down to the Hudson wharf early in the morning for his boxes of goods, worked into the evening at his uncle's store, and to earn extra money did bookkeeping at night for other merchants. He'd occasionally hire a horse and buggy for a visit with his family in Chatham, where he lent money to his struggling father – although Erastus kept accounts of these loans to his dad in his ledger book. He was determined not to end up in the dire financial straits of his father. By early 1814, at the age of nineteen, Erastus was worth $500, a sizable sum considering the value of a dollar then and that he had scraped it together without assistance, by profits on his small side selling venture and by hustling freelance accounting jobs at night.

When young Erastus moved to Troy at thirteen, he became financially independent and lived in William Pierce's lodging house across from the hardware store. One of the other boarders was William L. Marcy, who later became governor of New York and for whom the state's highest peak, Mount Marcy in the Adirondack Mountains, is named. After six years in Troy, at nineteen, Erastus was ready to move on. The Troy years taught him much. He learned the mercantile trade and became interested in politics. With the blessing of his uncle, whose apprenticeship had run its course, Erastus took his $500 stake and went to work across the river in Albany for John Spencer and Company. It was a March day in 1814 and Albany would never be quite the same again.

What Albany offered Erastus Corning – aside from a more cosmopolitan air as the state's capital and the state's second most prominent city behind New York – was a deep connection, an intense intermingling, of the Dutch ruling class heritage and the corridors of political power. Erastus Corning found his niche on the periphery of Capitol Hill, on what is now South Broadway, known in the nineteenth century as "Hardware Row." Corning's promotion to clerk in the Albany operation was once again assisted by a benefactor, Joseph Weld, a Troy hardware merchant. Weld had recommended Corning to Spencer for the opening. Although Spencer was initially reluctant to hire a handicapped person, Corning won him over in an interview and his disability proved no impediment to his success. He also subsequently won over Weld's daughter, Harriet, whom he married on March 10, 1819.

Corning's rise in the Albany hardware trade was swift and decisive. Two years after joining John Spencer and Company, when Corning was twenty-one, he bought into the firm as a partner. In 1824, when Spencer died, Corning at twenty-nine became sole owner by purchasing the Spencer share from his deceased partner's heirs. One of the main goods traded by the hardware company – later named Corning and Norton after he took on John T. Norton as a partner – was iron imported from Sweden, England and Russia, and steel from Germany. Corning hired an agent in New York City to get him the best deals on imported iron and steel, which were then sailed up the Hudson by sloop and later by steamboat. The metal goods and other supplies were then either sold in Albany or shipped west by wagon to merchants along the young nation's sparsely populated interior.

Corning's learning curve as a young entrepreneur was a sharp one and he made rapid headway in the competitive arena of business by being a risk-taker. Corning was among the visionaries who early on foresaw the vast potential for an east-west link of trade and ignored the naysayers who criticized the Erie Canal as "Clinton's ditch." Only thirty years old, as thanks for his support, Corning was invited to help plan and participate in Albany ceremonies celebrating the opening of the 363-mile Erie Canal linking

Lake Erie with New York City via the Hudson River. Corning had a hand in importing material to build the eighty-three locks and was a backer of Gov. DeWitt Clinton, catalyst for the fifteen-year long engineering feat and masterwork of political maneuvering.

Corning's idealism and belief in forward-looking projects such as the Erie Canal, however, were balanced with a fierce pragmatism. Corning learned early on, for instance, how to deal with merchants who fell behind on paying up their accounts. Bankruptcy was common in the boom-or-bust western lands. Corning generally tried to negotiate terms with a failing merchant, to cut his losses and take a percentage of what he was owed. A lawsuit was a last resort that generally won nothing. Often, in a negotiated debt settlement, Corning wound up with some sort of collateral, particularly parcels of land – in Ohio or Michigan or Wisconsin – the foundation for his later interest in western land speculation.

Corning's partner, Norton, was not a risk-taker and ended their partnership after four years and sold back his share in 1828. Norton felt that Corning was too much of a speculator who allowed the firm to become over-extended with too many outstanding loans and not enough capital and cash flow – despite an average day's receipts of $2,000 in 1828. "Norton was doubtless right," Neu wrote, "since a tendency to overextend was a characteristic of Corning at almost any period of his career. It might be argued (as it was by Norton) that this was an entrepreneurial weakness, but from the long view it probably was not, for Corning's temerity in operating on slim reserves permitted him to go ahead when a more timid man might have faltered."

Perhaps his boldness in business was, in part, a response to his disabilities. In letters to friends, Corning sometimes complained about his lameness, particularly as a young man, when he expressed shame and loathing about his condition in respect to courting young women. Corning had no trouble, apparently, in his courtship of Harriet Weld. Their marriage was a union of similars. She, too, was from an old New England family, centered in Roxbury, Massachusetts, hers being the eighth generation of Welds in America. The Cornings had five children, all boys, although only two of their sons survived to adulthood. The family plot in Albany Rural Cemetery commemorates these lost innocents, with the three markers for their deceased children grouped in front of the couple's notable monument. Erastus Corning honored his mentors in the naming of his children. Benjamin Smith, named for his uncle and benefactor, died on September

18, 1821 at the age of one year, eight months and eighteen days. John Spencer, named after his Albany hardware partner, died on February 25, 1833 at the age of nine years, three months and twelve days. The third, Joseph Weld, died on August 14, 1830 at the age of seventeen months and six days. Erastus Jr. and Edwin were the surviving boys.

Corning's own life was marked by health concerns. At one point, he traveled south to recuperate from an unspecified illness. It was most likely a respiratory-related ailment, since lung trouble ran in the family. Erastus Corning 2nd, the mayor, was sent south on more than one occasion during Albany winters as a young boy suffering from asthma. The first Erastus Corning's strength and drive overcame the misfortunes of his life as he established himself, while still in his early thirties, as a prominent business and civic leader. He became known among merchants from Albany to New York City, Philadelphia to Boston, and along the western frontier. Naturally, this ambitious and entrepreneurial merchant moved into politics. In 1828, he was elected an alderman in Albany. That same year, he moved from a rental apartment on Beaver Street into a substantial rowhouse at 102 State Street in the heart of the residences owned by the city's ruling elite. Corning bought the house in the fashionable district for $18,000, using a bequest from his uncle Benjamin Smith, who had died two years earlier. Most importantly, through perseverance and grueling physical therapy, Corning was able to discard his crutches and walk with a single cane. He would need such determination for his next Albany incarnation.

After years as a middleman, buying and selling imported iron and steel, Corning had gained the expertise and had accumulated the capital needed to move from merchant to manufacturer and to control a product from beginning to end in addition to the middle – the entire cycle of production and sale. In 1826, Corning bought an iron mill on Wynants Kill, a creek just south of Troy, and named it the Albany Iron Works. The plant produced 825 tons of rolled iron each year from bar iron imported from Russia and Sweden. The rolled iron was cut primarily into nails and also band iron, nail plates, hoops and rods. Corning also recognized the benefit of diversifying, and invested in the early 1820s in banks and insurance companies. A visionary who understood that money was power, politics was power and new ventures were power, Erastus Corning seized power in all three realms. As early as 1831, Corning invested in railroads, still in their infancy at that time, most notably Mohawk and Hudson, a fourteen-mile road between Albany and Schenectady that was the state's first. He was elected to positions of leadership in both the Mohawk and Hudson and the Utica and Schenectady lines, the latter selecting him as president in 1833.

Corning's influence in the sphere of politics was growing just as rapidly. In 1834, as a prominent member of the powerful Albany Regency – the Democratic organization whose members included Martin Van Buren, a group some historians consider the country's original political machine – Corning was elected mayor of Albany by a divided vote of twelve to eight among the aldermen. The *Microscope*, a Whig paper, sought to discredit Corning by calling him "the wealthy nabob of State Street." The name calling didn't hurt Corning, who was re-elected to three more one-year terms as mayor (1835-1837). He was later elected a New York State senator (1842-1845) and a member of Congress (1857-1859 and 1861-1863). While Corning, by all accounts, performed competently in these positions, he seemed less motivated by a commitment to a life of public service than by the potent use of elected office as a means of gaining connections and political influence that would further enhance his business deals.

Corning's career was marked by an extraordinary ability to foresee connections and opportunities and shrewdly position himself to exploit those openings ahead of the competition. Corning perfected the corporate strategy of double-dipping – and even triple-dipping. For example, spikes from the Albany Iron Works were used in the building of the Utica and Schenectady Railroad, of which Erastus Corning happened to be president. Consider this typical convoluted chain of Corning command: His agents bought bar iron from Russia, the iron was rolled into nails at Corning's iron works, then sold from Corning's hardware store to Corning's railroad. Corning later invested in the source itself, the mining operations. Corning earned profit each step of the way – as beginning, middle and end man. Corning's business derring-do was a *tour de force* that attracted the attention and sometimes the wrath of competitors. Henry Burden, who owned the prosperous Burden Iron Works in Troy, battled Corning and his Albany Iron Works through the courts in scores of patent right infringement cases spanning three decades. Burden fought Corning not only over patent disputes, but over the flow of the Wynants Kill, which Burden claimed Corning unfairly diverted, resulting in unfair competition.

Corning's reign as Albany's iron king was not trouble-free. Fires destroyed the factory in 1849 and again in 1852, a combined loss of nearly $100,000 above what insurance policies reimbursed. Nonetheless, Corning rebuilt. Corning played hardball when it came to labor negotiations, too.

His factory's wages were never considered munificent to begin with, yet when production costs rose, company policy was to slash salaries. As a result, Corning's Albany Iron Works was rocked by labor disturbances and strikes several times. Corning's solution? Lock out the workers and let the factory sit idle until employees accepted Corning's provisos.

Corning never let such local concerns cloud his broader vision. He was an early investor in the Mount Savage Ironworks in Allegheny County, Maryland. It was there, in 1844, that the first heavy iron rails in the United States were made. Corning got in on the ground floor of an industry critical to the advancement of railroads in America. The former crippled boy that shop owners once shunned from hiring was now sitting at the throttles of one of the most powerful engines poised to drive America's Industrial Age.

In 1850, Corning was jubilant when the Mount Savage Ironworks churned out 1,000 tons of rails for his own Utica and Schenectady Railroad (doubling Corning's profits). Sometimes, his own multiple layers of profiteering got him into trouble. For instance, Corning wavered on his position toward import tariffs, a double-edged sword to a businessman who was both a domestic iron maker and a railroad president who needed cheap imported iron. He was a capitalist divided. Corning's ethics derived from the bottom line. At one point, he served as president of the Ironmasters Association of New York to work toward raising the tariff on foreign iron competitors. A few years later, he hired a lobbyist in Washington to argue against raising the tariff because he had two large rail mills in operation. Erastus Corning's malleable ethics were most in evidence during the Civil War, the early years of which he was an elected member of Congress. By supplying the Union Army with iron products, Corning secured a substantial profit for himself while the death toll climbed from the bloody conflict. A Democrat, Corning at first spoke out strongly against the Civil War and later criticized the Lincoln administration. Privately, he was sending his agents to Washington where, with the help of his Congressional connections, Corning's Albany Iron Works nailed down lucrative war contracts that amounted to production of eight tons a day to supply the war effort, mostly cannons and rail hardware. There was profit in war and Corning was not a squeamish capitalist.

Corning gained recognition as a fierce political enemy of Abraham Lincoln and worked actively against his election. Erastus Corning 2nd, the mayor, was fascinated by this historical footnote and often recounted the rivalry in correspondence he received from history buffs. In a November 8, 1951 letter to Joan Stroud of Spartanburg, South Carolina, the mayor wrote, "Thanks for the information about the correspondence between Lincoln and my great grandfather. I did know of it as my great grandfather was a rabid Democrat in those days and fought with Lincoln frequently. As a matter of fact, when my great grandfather was president of the New York Central Railroad, he tried to hire Lincoln as a general counsel to get him out of politics. Another interesting Civil War item, I think, is that it was my great grandfather's steel mill up in Troy that made the armored plate for the *Monitor*."

Corning's baiting of Lincoln – through a group of northern Democrats, known as the Copperheads, who opposed the war and sympathized with the South – drew a sharp written rebuke from the president himself in what some historians consider one of Abraham Lincoln's most remarkable political letters. Addressed to Corning "and others," Lincoln wrote a stinging defense of his war policy and a pointed criticism of the Corning-led Albany naysayers. An excerpt from Lincoln's handwritten draft dated June 12, 1863 from the Executive Mansion in Washington reads:

> . . . Prior to my installation here it had been inculcated that any State had a lawful right to secede from the national Union; and that it would be expedient to exercise the right, whenever the devotees of the doctrine should fail to elect a President to their liking; and accordingly, so far as it was legally possible, they had taken seven states out of the Union, had seized many of the United States Forts, and had fired upon the United States' Flag, all before I was inaugurated; and, of course, before I had done any official act whatever. The rebellion, thus began, soon ran into the present civil war; and, in certain respects, it began on very unequal terms between the parties. The insurgents had been preparing for it more than thirty years while the government had taken no steps to resist them. The former had carefully considered all the means which could be turned to their account. It undoubtedly was a well pondered reliance with them that in their own unrestricted effort to destroy Union, constitution and law, all together, the government would, in great degree, be restrained by the same constitution and law, from arresting their progress. Their sympathizers pervaded all departments of the government

and nearly all communities of the people. From this material, under cover of 'Liberty of speech' 'Liberty of the press' and 'Habeas corpus' they hoped to keep on foot amongst us a most efficient corps of spies, informers, supplyers, and aiders and abettors of their cause in a thousand ways.

Lincoln's letter goes on for several more pages. Historian James G. Randall deemed it "one of those dignified, carefully worded statements addressed to a person or occasion, but intended as a kind of state paper." The letter was widely published in newspapers and magazines of the day. Corning pooh-poohed the soaring oratory and deeply felt sentiments, calling Lincoln's missive "misty and clouded" and "a monstrous heresy" and "a plea for absolute power."

Even while Corning was criticizing the Lincoln administration and doing his utmost to prevent implementation of the president's policies, the iron baron of Albany was maneuvering to profit from the young nation's horrific conflict. In 1861, even though he was a member of Congress and barred by federal regulations from entering into a business contract with the government, Corning's Albany Iron Works secured the contract to make the iron plates for the famous ironclad warship, *Monitor*. The *Monitor* gunboat, with its inventive revolving turret, defeated the Confederate *Merrimac* on March 8, 1862, a turning point in naval superiority in the Civil War. Corning got around the sticky business of conflict of interest on the *Monitor* deal – which netted Corning personal profits of as much as $20,000 – by having his agents at the Albany Iron Works conduct the negotiations. "But they kept him [Corning] informed of the negotiations with Washington and later of the progress of the ironclad," Neu wrote. Corning played his Congressional colleagues with mastery. Just six days after the *Monitor* defeat of *Merrimac*, having sidestepped even the slightest hint of wrongdoing, Corning's ironworks closed a deal to supply iron plates for six additional gunboats slightly larger than the *Monitor* for $400,000 each – more than $100,000 of which was expected to be profit. It can be said that Erastus Corning made a killing in the Civil War.

After the Civil War, as he continued his visionary ways and explored a new steelmaking method developed in England, the Bessemer process, Corning once again became embroiled in a patent infringement lawsuit. Corning and his ironmasters were clearly violating an earlier American patent, according to Neu, but Corning prevailed by overpowering or buying out his challengers. By 1875, the Troy Bessemer plant owned by Corning and others was cranking out more than 270 tons of ingots a day, producing what was considered one of the best grades of steel to be found anywhere in the United States. The numbers were staggering. In 1872, the year Corning died, the Albany Iron Works was producing a remarkable 15,000 tons annually of cut nails, spikes, rivets, band, bar, rod, scroll iron, railroad car axles and other hardware for the railroads.

Corning's success lay in his innovative, organic approach to business in which he saw the whole of an industry, as well as its parts, well in advance of his competitors. Neu wrote, "Not a little of his early interest in railroads may be explained by his recognition of the new transportation medium as a first-rate market for iron." And, further, Neu commented, "No one who has worked with the Corning Papers can doubt the close tie-up between Corning the railroad president and Corning the iron manufacturer and dealer." In addition, Corning's political connections were used to buoy his considerable power and finances. ". . . He was not without political influence when it seemed desirable to exercise it," Neu wrote. "His association with the Albany Regency assured him of favors from his own party, and his friendship with Thurlow Weed [Albany newspaper publisher, a Whig, and political power broker], whom he had early taken pains to cultivate, gave him a strong ally among the opposition."

The power of the Albany Regency and the state's railroad tycoons was legendary, as indicated by a piece of legislation in 1858 that nearly ground state government to a halt. Corning and eighty-six prominent New York State capitalists lobbied hard for a bill that called for dropping the executive and legislative branches and turning power over to the directors of the New York Central Railroad. The bill was called "a burlesque memorial . . . intended as a joke" by the *New York Herald*, but it passed both the Senate and Assembly. The editorial writers of the *New York Times* were not amused in a March 3, 1858 editorial: "Of course it is intended as a joke, but it conveys a bitter satire – a satire which is deserved and just. Substantially, the Central Railroad has made and violated laws as suited their interests or their caprices. When the Democrats are in power, it is Corning, Richmond & Co. that direct and control. When the Republicans are in the ascendancy it is . . . guided by the same firm of Corning, Richmond & Co." The bill that would have created a railroad-controlled oligarchy was defeated in a general referendum on November 2, 1858. Remarkably, the statewide vote was close, 141,526 against and 135,166 in favor. This epitome of voter apathy and anger meant that just 6,360 votes stood between a democracy in New York state and a railroad-run State of Corning!

Corning's cornering of the political game at the local, state and federal levels was only the beginning. Corning shrewdly covered every angle. Through his directorship in Albany banks, including presidency of the Albany City Bank, and extensive banking connections, competing railroads were indebted to Corning for iron and occasionally had to ask for an extension of credit. Corning also served on the board of directors of the Michigan Central Railroad and made annual visits to inspect the line in which he was a major stockholder. More importantly, this railroad line served as a critical link between Corning's railroad in the east and his land speculation in the west. Furthermore, Corning was president of the Mutual Insurance Company of the city and county of Albany. He was a kind of one-man treasury, seemingly making profit everywhere he turned, as if he had a license to print money. The insurance business foreshadowed a source of personal wealth for his great-grandson, the mayor, owner of the insurance firm Albany Associates, which benefited from Corning's forty-two years as mayor.

Erastus Corning managed to deflect his failures with a dry wit that would become a Corning family trademark. When the Albany and Northern (Vermont) Railroad failed in the late-1850s, Corning, a director, not only suffered substantial losses, but so did friends whose investments he had solicited. There was a public outcry that "certain men should be hung," namely Corning. Corning replied dryly, "If at any future day this threat should be carried out I should like to have good company."

By the time he was in his early forties, the late-1830s, Erastus Corning, already a millionaire, stood astride Albany like a colossus, disability and all, and had become the city's most prominent citizen – risen from the stockroom of the hardware store on Broadway. His world was insular, comprising a triangle of commerce and residence from lower State Street to Broadway, but the House of Corning was built upon a substantial foundation of iron. From that solid base, he branched out into railroads and land development and banking and, ultimately, politics, which became the engine that drove his commercial possibilities. Corning's political clout stemmed from his involvement with the Albany Regency, the Democratic political machine of New York that controlled the state Legislature. The Albany Regency's chief architect and leader was Martin Van Buren, governor of New York, who used the state capital as his stepping stone to the presidency.

Corning's assistance to Van Buren's political career was rewarded when Van Buren got to Washington and championed lenient banking laws that allowed a bank to extend loans to its officers. Erastus Corning was an officer of more than one bank in Albany, ensuring him a steady source of working capital needed to fuel his ambitions for an expanding business empire, which gave Corning the bank president an inside edge over his competitors seeking loans from Corning's banks. During the Van Buren administration, Albany City Bank, of which Corning was president, was designated a bank of deposit for public funds. Corning's early political investment in Van Buren began to pay handsome dividends.

Corning also managed to combine pleasure with business. In the spring of 1840, Corning imported the first documented herd of Herefords in the United States. In the fall of that same year, he took his wife on a trans-Atlantic sailing journey, complete with a grand tour of Europe. Besides sightseeing excursions, Corning met with his British iron trading partners and tried to peddle some of Albany City Bank's stocks and bonds it held from New York State that had plummeted in value. Corning remained president of what later became The State Bank of Albany, until his death in 1872. He went daily to his office at the bank at 47 State Street and "was something of a trial to the cashier and clerks" because of his over-bearing demeanor; the bank staff breathed easier when Corning made his annual summer retreat to Newport, according to Neu.

Corning was not confined to his comfortable domain of State Street and Broadway, though. As an early and central backer of the Erie Canal, opened in 1825, Corning was among the progressive thinkers who saw exceptional business opportunities in westward expansion. Banking on a fledgling network of canals and, later, an integrated system of railroads to open up western lands as profitable trading partners, Corning became a major land speculator in the western New York communities of Corning, Irving and Auburn. He later branched out to Iowa, Wisconsin and Michigan, where he was a leading developer of the Sault Ste. Marie Canal that linked Lake Huron with Lake Superior. At each site, Corning and his investment associates controlled the fate of hundreds, even thousands, of acres of prime real estate.

The ownership of the renowned Corning Glass Works has long been mistakenly attributed to the Corning family. The town of Corning in the western part of New York, in Steuben County, situated along the Chemung River, was originally named Painted Post. The name was

changed to Corning by citizens grateful to the Albany financier for bringing the canal and railroad to the town along with substantial investment
and the development of hundreds of building lots. The Corning Glass
Works took its name from its location, not from any ownership by the
Corning family. The town fell short of Corning's vision for it as a major
inland shipping port and cosmopolitan city. Still, there is a monument to
Erastus Corning on the town green and today Corning is known internationally as the home of Corning Glass Works, which the citizens of
Corning enticed there in 1868 by putting up $50,000 in incentive money.

Corning's land speculation elsewhere was less prosperous. Despite
exerting leverage in the state Legislature and the U.S. Congress, federal
money for the townsite of Irving along the Cattaraugus Creek in
Chautauqua – which Corning hoped would become a booming railroad
terminus – never materialized and dreams of hitting the jackpot withered.
Not that Corning ever got severely burned in his land grabs. He was generally able to buy the acreage dirt cheap and recouped his investment even
in the worst market. And if his hunches were correct about future growth,
Corning's profits were enormous – selling for as much as ten times what
he had paid.

Occasionally, Corning's manipulation of the banking system, coupled
with favors from political friends in high places, drew criticism from the
press. For instance, Corning was a major shareholder in The American
Land Company, which purchased hundreds of thousands of acres of property during the 1830s in a dozen states, including massive tracts in Ohio,
Michigan, Arkansas, Mississippi, Tennessee and Florida. A scandal erupted
in the newspapers when investigation into the multi-million dollar land
speculation firm revealed that among those who had a financial stake were
President Martin Van Buren, Attorney General Benjamin F. Butler, Senator
Silas Wright and presidential advisor Amos Kendall – Corning associates
all, linked from their Albany Regency days. But the controversy died
quickly and the company paid handsome dividends to its shareholders
throughout the 1840s and 1850s, before the Civil War crippled the company because of its heavy position in the wartorn South.

Corning's image as a leading citizen and upstanding businessman was
further tarnished, albeit briefly, from his speculation in the so-called Half-
Breed Tract in Iowa. The 119,000-acre region in the southeastern corner of
the state originally was set aside in the early 1830s by the U.S. government
as an entitlement for the children of Native American women and white

men during what were common frontier-era unions. Congress passed a law allowing the half-breeds to sub-divide and sell off their land if they so chose. Corning and a handful of other shrewd speculators who formed the New York Land Company were waiting for just such congressional action (perhaps even playing a role in the legislation) and pounced on the property. The Half-Breed Tract affair ended up embroiled in controversy and in the courts, with accusations of bribing of judges and swindling the rightful owners out of their land – another passing storm of bad publicity that Corning seemed to weather with little ill effect.

It is difficult, of course, to hit a moving target and Corning the financier never stood still. He kept his investments moving forward at a dizzying pace, always looking ahead for the next big opportunity and simultaneously juggling numerous capital ventures. Corning amassed tens of thousands, even hundreds of thousands, of acres of land in Wisconsin and Michigan in a second phase of speculation, in the 1850s, and parlayed those holdings with investments in the creation of shipping-canal systems through those states – most notably the Green Bay and Mississippi Canal Company and the Saint Mary's Falls Ship Canal Company. Corning was a director, and briefly president, of both concerns. These few examples only hint at the extent of Corning's intricate land holdings in a dozen states. The Albany capitalist ruled this domain expertly, selling off parcels piece-meal, buying others, corresponding with agents and prospective buyers. Corning seemed to derive satisfaction from playing his own real-life Monopoly game, because he handled all land transactions himself after retiring from running his railroads.

If Corning's financial plate seemed full with his myriad business and political dealings, it was just a prelude for the enormous organizational and negotiating effort required of his greatest accomplishment, the creation of the New York Central Railroad. Consider Corning's coup: chartered in 1853, Corning raised $23 million in capital for the New York Central Railroad, making it the largest corporation in America at the time. In an era of intense infighting and turf battles among competing rail lines, Corning managed to merge a sprinkling of ten minor railroads – between Albany and Troy, Buffalo and Niagara Falls, Rochester and Syracuse – into a major and historic rail network. Once again, Corning played his Albany Regency trump card by gaining unanimous approval from the state Legislature for consolidation of the lines. Corning was elected the New York Central's founding president and held that position, despite considerable pressures from rivals, for a dozen years. He was at the height of his powers, the architect of a 300-mile interconnected railroad system stretching from Albany to Buffalo. Russell Sage, of Troy, a major capitalist himself with a reputation as a ruthless businessman, begrudgingly congratulated the New York Central's founder, and Sage's sometime rival, as "one of the greatest railroad men in the country" in a December 20, 1853 letter to Corning. Corning's sweetest deal, his financial *tour de force*, was complete. Corning enjoyed his usual pattern of profiting twice, even thrice, by owning the companies that made the iron and shipped the hardware that expanded the New York Central. The *New York Times*, the leading voice of criticism against Corning's *modus operandi*, pointed out that Corning was profiting to the tune of $250,000 a year by supplying iron to the railroad of which he was president. The negative press never picked up steam, though, and Corning ruled the Central with an iron fist, dismissing board members who questioned his practices, including former business associate Russell Sage. Neu wrote, "Corning, as usual, paid little attention to the tirades in the papers. Rather he concentrated his energies on the obtaining of proxies."

Corning's biggest test of leadership came with a challenge to his presidency in 1863, a decade after he formed the New York Central. Corning and his coalition, including strong support from Commodore Cornelius Vanderbilt, trounced the opposition. Vanderbilt was rewarded by Corning with board membership. Call it a Trojan Horse strategy by Vanderbilt, who shrewdly concealed his long-range motives to wrest control of the New York Central for himself. Even as Corning scored his impressive victory, there were other considerations. He was about to turn seventy, was in faltering health, and he had endured more rebukes about his iron company's profiteering. A bitter strike at the railroad's West Albany shops was directed at Corning and required troops of police to restore order. On April 28, 1864, at a meeting of the New York Central directors, Corning resigned as president.

Corning had not anticipated Vanderbilt's power play. Corning's Achilles heel, despite his progressive transportation vision, was a stubborn reliance on shipping cargo via the Hudson River. Corning had banked on the river for trade between Albany and New York City since his boyhood days as a clerk in the hardware store. Corning's prejudice for moving freight cheaply on the waterway (Corning held a financial interest in Hudson River steamboats) opened the door for Vanderbilt, who had amassed a fortune in ocean shipping. The Commodore built up the two rail lines, The Hudson River Railroad and the New York and Harlem, that eclipsed Hudson River steamboat freight service. Vanderbilt controlled the vital missing north-south railroad link in New York State and thus possessed the power to bring Corning and the New York Central to its knees. Vanderbilt used his leverage to toss out Corning and his board at the December 11, 1867 annual shareholders' meeting in the Albany offices of the New York Central. After fourteen years running the great railroad, often touted as "the road of the century," Corning was relegated to a spectator while Vanderbilt and associates seized control. The two towering capitalists never quarreled publicly, however, and apparently remained on good terms personally after the dust of the takeover settled. The far-flung financial empire of Erastus Corning – a traveler could ride coast to coast on railroads in which he held a financial interest – paid substantial dividends. When he died in 1872, Corning's estimated net worth was $12 million, an extraordinary sum in that day, making Corning Albany's wealthiest resident and one of the two or three richest men in New York – a state loaded with successful capitalists.

Although historians focus on his role as railroad tycoon, financier and empire builder, Corning's home life deserves some attention. Corning and his wife, Harriet, who encouraged her husband's shift from a Presbyterian upbringing to membership in the Episcopal church, opened their luxurious State Street mansion (on the site of today's Omni Hotel) to many guests. In addition to their five children, the Cornings raised four nieces – repaying, in a way, the debt he felt as recipient of his uncle's largess. The Cornings maintained a lavish lifestyle and threw large parties. One of their closest friends was John V.L. Pruyn, Corning's able assistant in railroad and other business affairs, and a neighbor just around the corner on Elk Street. Harriet and the youngsters spent summers at a family farm in Canaan, New York. The Cornings also owned summer homes in Sachem's Head, Connecticut and Newport, Rhode Island, where they were active in the social scene. The Cornings and their extended family also were a fixture at Saratoga Springs during the spa's busy summer social season.

But the Corning family's heart and soul, the place where it established a sense of permanency for successive generations, was at the 700-acre parcel in Bethlehem on the outskirts of Albany along the Normanskill gorge that became known as simply "The Farm." Erastus Corning purchased the wooded property and farmhouse in the 1830s in a district known as

Kenwood as a simple retreat for his family to escape summer's heat in Albany. Future generations would turn it into a sort of upstate Shangri-la.

In civic matters, Erastus Corning was a leader in Albany's major municipal projects during a boom era for public works. Working from the recommendations of architect Philip Hooker, Corning engineered the grading of State Street, leveling off the precipitous incline. In the early 1840s, Corning also leveled Madison Avenue, directing the work of 250 laborers and dozens of teams of horses which shaved down the sharp incline and filled in the fetid, unsanitary Ruttenkill stream. They used the loads of Madison Avenue soil also to fill in other dangerously steep ravines to render several side streets passable to horse and buggy for the first time.

In 1850, Corning also headed Albany's first water commission, which purchased for $150,000 all sources of drinking water that converged into Patroon's Creek; formed a forty-acre, 200-million gallon reservoir on the western edge of the city now known as Six-Mile Waterworks along Fuller Road in the Pine Bush; replaced wooden pipes with iron ones that were carried in brick-lined culverts beneath what is now Washington Avenue four miles downtown to the thirty-million gallon Bleecker Reservoir in the heart of the city. They also added two new auxiliary reservoirs in Albany known as upper and lower Tivoli lakes. Erastus Corning created the clean drinking water supply that the Democratic machine in his grandson and great-grandson's era would take credit for and ride to electoral success.

Not all Corning innovations were embraced. Over the opposition of many citizens who thought it would hamper navigation and bury river ferry companies, Corning built the first railroad bridge over the Hudson River at Albany. Corning's finesse closed the missing link that had hampered Albany's growth as a railroad terminal. Work began in 1856 and the bridge opened just before Corning's death in 1872. The half-mile span cost $500,000 and was built twenty-five feet above the river to let boats pass under. No dissent was heard when Corning bought 250 acres of the Van Rensselaer estate and used his influence to locate the vast repair shops for the New York Central Railroad in West Albany in 1853, creating hundreds of stable, well-paying jobs. They named Corning Street in his honor in West Albany, a memorial well deserved, according to Codman Hislop, who published a history of Albany in 1936. "Railroads brought prosperity to Albany and an end to the charge that the city was 'more Dutch than decent,'" Hislop wrote in his book, *Albany: Dutch, English and American*.

One of the enduring works of civic leadership for which Erastus Corning will be remembered is the All Saints Cathedral of the Episcopal Diocese of Albany. He was the catalyst for devising a strategic plan for the cathedral in 1871. Corning died a year later at the age of seventy-eight. The actual construction of the great cathedral, as well as other unfinished business, would be left to his son, Erastus Corning Jr. He is the only one among the five children who survived into his later years; three siblings died in childhood and his brother Edwin died in 1871 at age thirty-four.

When measured against his father's sparkling accomplishments, Junior, as he was known, was an unrepentant underachiever. It has been said that greatness in a family line seems to skip a generation, a kind of cyclical pause for mediocrity, and Junior confirmed that sociological generalization. The father's personality resembled the iron upon which he built his fortune, while the son was a dreamy idealist who let money flow through his fingers like spring runoff. He liked to spend it much faster than he made it and, eventually, the seemingly bottomless well of the Corning fortune ran dry. But what a fine time Junior had in reaching bottom. Almost immediately, Junior "began to scatter the millions bequeathed him," according to a newspaperman of the day familiar with Junior's ability to run through a $12 million inheritance. He lacked his father's business acumen, especially when it came to responding to volatile market conditions such as the free fall in steel prices in the late 1800s that caused Corning's fortune to drop $3 million, on paper at least, in a single day.

Born on June 16, 1827, Erastus Jr., the middle child and first to live beyond childhood, grew up as a spectacularly spoiled boy. His education was at private schools, including Union College in Schenectady, followed by a special business apprenticeship arranged by his father. As his father grew old and infirm, he handed over the reins of his various enterprises to Junior. This outsized silver spoon seemed to fit easily in the mouth of his son. Passed from father to son were the various presidencies and directorships: Albany Iron Works, Albany City National Bank, Albany City Savings Institution, the New York Central and Hudson River Railroad and the All Saints Cathedral, to name just a few.

Erastus Corning Jr. was not cut from the same entrepreneurial cloth as his father and the progenitor realized it. "Corning had little respect for the business acumen of either of his sons," Neu wrote. Albany businessman John Bigelow wrote this withering assessment to William B. Beach on May 29, 1876 about Erastus Corning Jr. "Corning of Albany," Bigelow said, "is a man of pleasure, who inherited a large fortune and a name associated with the triumphs of a political dynasty in this state in the last generation, of considerable influence. The heir, however, never had the ability to acquire these patrimonies, neither has he the ability to preserve them; and he has already squandered so much of them that he is only the shadow of a name."

Erastus Jr. was not the least bit interested in politics. He accepted the nominal appointment of city alderman, but once remarked that he was "reluctant to abandon his business for the uncertain and often unsatisfactory honors of the political arena." Historians said Corning could have had the Democratic nomination for governor in 1881, which went instead to Grover Cleveland after Corning declined the offer. Corning substituted his father's passion for politics and business with leisure activities, ranging from horticulture to animal husbandry to civic volunteerism. He became known around the world for his cultivation of flowers, particularly orchids. Erastus Jr. possessed, as Cuyler Reynolds noted, "ample means to gratify his fine taste."

Erastus Corning Jr. inherited the family farmstead, named it *Ta-wass-a-gun-shee*, an Indian variation of Tawasentha, meaning mouth of the Normanskill, and transformed it into an exotic paradise for flora and fauna. Corning continued to nurture the nation's first herd of Herefords established by his father. He also raised prize-winning Jersey cows, Southdown sheep and thoroughbred racing horses, sparing no cost in constructing numerous stables, training tracks and a mile-long oval horse racing track where he held stakes races and printed programs for spectators. The finesse of his breeding would pay off for his son, Parker, one of whose horses would win the prestigious Travers Stakes at Saratoga Racetrack.

Junior also erected a network of conservatories where he raised his world-renowned orchids and other flower varieties, employing master gardeners brought over from England, including William Gray, Frederick Goldring and Harry C. Eyres. Gray developed a new variety of orchids for Corning named the *Vanda Corningii*. Corning published a "Catalogue of Orchids" that ran nine pages and included more than 1,000 species and varieties of orchids he propagated. Corning was considered to have the "the finest orchid collection in the Western Hemisphere," according to Milan Fiske, of Burnt Hills, an officer of the Northeastern New York Orchid Society and an orchid scholar, who wrote in the March, 1986 issue of the society's newsletter, *Orchidoings*: "Greenhouses, a staff of orchid growers and thousands of the choicest varieties made Albany something of a mecca for the orchid fancier of a century ago. Warm houses, cool houses, houses given just to odontoglossums . . ." Corning gained recognition for developing new orchid varieties, among them one for Mrs. Erastus Corning, *Cattleya Corningiae*, and the *Phalaenopsis Harriettiae* (named for his daughter Harriet).

Orchids were only one aspect of Erastus Corning Jr.'s passion for growing plants. "The choicest floral productions of the world were to be found in his conservatories," according to Cuyler Reynolds. The Corning Farm became Junior's living experiment in horticulture. He imported tropical flowers from the Himalayas in India, from the Pacific island of Borneo, from the highlands of Mexico, Peru, Venezuela, Brazil and Madagascar. From foreign lands came ginkgo and tulip trees and other unusual species. He planted lemon and orange trees, cultivated grape arbors and banana groves. Corning also donated exotic floral specimens that were planted in newly created Washington Park, including Egyptian lotus and other rare water plants that were fashioned into a lush aquatic garden ringing the edge of the park – giving Lake Avenue its name.

Corning's desire for surrounding himself with all creatures great and small, all things bright and beautiful, didn't end there. He collected moths and butterflies. But this was no simple boyhood fascination. Over the course of his lifetime, the dedicated lepidopterist amassed one of the country's finest private collections, containing more than 10,000 specimens of moths and butterflies. Corning's extraordinary array today is in the permanent collection of the New York State Museum in Albany.

When he wasn't on The Farm, Corning was very much a man about town. Known as an easygoing fellow, a congenial sort who wasn't tight with his money, Corning got the reputation as something of an easy touch, freely offering handouts and loans, often to ill-conceived and short-lived business ventures. Corning was a founder and first president of the Fort Orange Club, incorporated in 1880, a bastion of WASP ascendancy and power. An oil portrait of Corning hangs in the foyer of the club, which occupies a luxurious Federal-style brick mansion built in 1810, located at 110 Washington Avenue near the Alfred E. Smith State Office Building. Its founding filled a gap as the only private club for men of means in the city. It replaced the defunct Albany Club at Lodge and Steuben Streets, which died of disinterest and an apparent lapse in elitism. Corning, the leading benefactor among the 182 charter members, intended the Fort Orange

Club as a private gathering place for the men of distinction in Albany. Corning was joined on the organizing committee by Grange Sand, Charles Emory Smith, John F. Rathbone, Frederick Townsend, Edward Bowditch, Samuel B. Ward, Robert H. Pruyn, Robert Lenox Banks, Abraham Lansing, Dudley Olcott, S.W. Rosendale and Charles P. Easton. How blue was their blood, how discriminating the articles of their constitution and how green their dues.

The Fort Orange Club blossomed quickly and thrived. The Bender property on Washington Avenue was purchased for $30,000. An initiation fee of $100 was set. The greenhouse, considered to be a frivolous use of cash (despite Corning's preoccupation with flowers and his donation of flowers to decorate the club for special events) was turned into a bowling alley – ladies were permitted to bowl until 2 p.m. daily. But the sport was not popular and the lanes were quickly scrapped. A bigger hit was the billiards tables and the lavish furnishings, including china and crystal place settings, for which the founders allotted $6,500. But such indulgences were not meant to pollute the supposedly puritanical ideals upon which the club was founded. "An organization of such men for social purposes could not be other than an advantage to a city, not only for what it might do, but for what it might suppress and frown upon," founder Grange Sand wrote in a 1903 club history. "No gambling has ever been permitted in the clubhouse, and public sentiment has sustained the strict enforcement of the rules against excessive drinking. The continued enforcement of these rules, and a discriminating care in the selection of members, are necessary if this club is to maintain its high position." These rules were swiftly passed by the membership and, according to early accounts, just as quickly broken as liquor flowed and bets were placed.

Erastus Corning Jr. was the heart and soul of the Fort Orange Club and had one of the longest tenures as president (1880-1892) in its century-long history. Subsequent presidents served one- or two-year terms, including the founder's son, Edwin Corning (1918-1920) and grandson, Erastus Corning 2nd (1967-1969). The Cornings were standard bearers for the proud elitism of the club, whose members began admitting women – after much foot dragging and being shamed into it by public opinion – in the mid-1980s. Still, the Fort Orange Club's motto remains: "Its history is a proud one; its standards have been high, its purposes beneficent, its membership honorable."

Frivolous as some of his pursuits might have seemed, Erastus Corning Jr.'s horticultural and collecting indulgences should not overshadow his stewardship of major civic projects. When the old City Hall was destroyed by fire in 1880, Erastus Corning Jr. was tapped to head the commission to build a new one. Most of the valuable records and documents were saved in the mysterious blaze, but the forty-eight-year-old structure was burned to the ground. Corning envisioned a larger, more imposing edifice. The grand Romanesque design by H.H. Richardson was built of Long Meadow brown stone, four stories tall, with a tower that reached 202 feet high on the same site as the razed building. Construction took two years (1881-1883) and cost $325,000, raised mostly by a bond issue, with the cost split between the city and county. This City Hall would truly become a House of Corning, home for forty-two years to the building catalyst's grandson, Erastus Corning 2nd, the longest-tenured mayor of any city in the history of the United States.

Erastus Corning Jr.'s pursuit of the good life and the pleasures of beautiful living things was marred by the disappointments and setbacks in his family. Corning married Gertrude Tibbits in 1850 and they began a family immediately. Their son, Erastus, born on May 26, 1851, endured a life marked by sickness and frustration. "A serious illness in youth left him with an impaired constitution, which was a handicap, effectively preventing his engaging actively in the great Corning enterprises," Cuyler Reynolds wrote. The unnamed disability, perhaps mental illness, caused young Erastus to drop out of St. Paul's, the prestigious prep school in Concord, New Hamsphire, and the boy was sent to Europe to study under a private tutor – "the gentler, quiet pursuits of life . . . the world of art and nature," according to Reynolds. His mother died in 1869, when her son was seventeen, and Erastus Corning remarried in 1873; his second wife, Mary Parker, was a member of the same Albany social circle and daughter of the State Supreme Court Judge Amasa J. Parker.

As he began a new family with his second wife, Erastus Corning Jr. set up his son from Gertrude Tibbits with a job at the Corning Iron Works, but his namesake suffered an unexplained "breakdown and was ever after an invalid" who traveled abroad in search of therapeutic cures, Reynolds wrote. In a manner reminiscent of his grandfather (the first Erastus), the third Erastus managed somewhat to overcome his disabilities with a coterie of friends and a life of the mind that focused on books, paintings, flowers and nature. His apparent psychological problems did not sour him and he was, instead, "a most lovable man," wrote Reynolds. A Brooklyn minister's daughter found him so. On January 13, 1879, Grace Fitz-Randolph Schenck, daughter of the Rev. Noah Schenck, married Corning. They had two children, including a son, named the fourth Erastus, who grew into manhood, and a daughter, Gertrude Tibbits, who died at the age of ten, in 1897, the same year her grandfather, Erastus Jr., passed away. Of Junior's son, the third Erastus, Reynolds summed up: "He was eminently qualified to take rank with the best of Albany's captains of industry and keenly felt the lack of physical equipment that held him to a life of inactivity, but he fought life's battle manfully, and left behind a cherished memory."

For reason of disinterest and illness, then, for two generations the Corning family wealth lacked a prudent fiscal guardian. What was built upon a foundation of iron and seemed so permanent and monolithic, one of the great fortunes in New York State, dissipated like a vapor. When Erastus Corning Jr. died in 1897 at the age of seventy – succumbing to a heart attack while driving a fast trotting horse, the man-child chasing his bliss still – he was survived by his second wife, Mary Parker, and four children. On probate, when the accounting was done, Erastus Corning Jr.'s estate, which started the ledger with an inheritance in excess of $12 million, was in the red. Junior had had quite a run, it seemed, depleting all his assets. The bottom line was this: He died in debt, owing $125,000 to his creditors.

But Erastus Corning Jr., despite his legendary spendthrift ways, would leave a memorial to the more serious side of his nature. The Cathedral of All Saints, like City Hall, was the house that Junior built. "As a founder of the Cathedral of All Saints, he [Corning] ranks second only to the bishop," wrote George DeMille, an Episcopal priest who worked at All Saints and wrote its history, *Pioneer Cathedral*. The cathedral was to become the headquarters of the Episcopal diocese in Albany and an inspiring structure of soaring spires and lofty ideals for the faithful in the region. It would have to be a marvelous building, indeed, to rival St. Peter's Church, the ornate Episcopal house of worship on State Street where the city's wealthy ruling elite were christened, married and buried. The Cathedral of All Saints grew out of an incorporation formed in 1881, named The Corning Foundation for Christian Work in the Diocese of Albany. Episcopal Bishop William Croswell Doane was a close friend of the Corning family and he had found sites for a cathedral on the prominent corner of Lark and State streets, and on Washington Avenue, but both parcels were determined to be too costly. Instead, Erastus Jr. took matters into his own hands. He donated land that had once been used by his father for an iron foundry on the east side of Swan Street between Elk and Lafayette. Corning bought the surrounding lots and presented the parcel to Doane as the site for the new cathedral. It was 1882 and Doane and Corning were in a hurry. Their haste was unfortunate.

"Right here, of course, the bishop and leaders made their greatest mistake, a mistake that has affected the whole future of the cathedral," DeMille wrote. DeMille argued that cathedral catalysts should have waited until they had the resources to buy the entire block, which then contained only small houses, so that the cathedral could have been placed magnificently in the middle. "The result would have been superb," DeMille wrote. Instead, the cathedral is so tucked away that a visitor easily misses the grand edifice on a tour of downtown Albany. It is hardly visible from the main thoroughfare, Washington Avenue, and is overshadowed by the State Education Building, an Albany jewel on a prominent site that could have been the cathedral's location. As it is, All Saints is a neglected gem, practically hidden from the rest of downtown Albany. DeMille wrote, "Despite Mr. Corning's generosity, they were pressed by an impatient bishop. There was very little money available, comparatively, and the bishop, a young man in a hurry, wanted, as soon as possible, a usable building of cathedral size." Whenever funds faltered, the bishop could count on the deep pockets of Erastus Corning Jr., whom DeMille described as "a devout churchman" – with a devotion to attending services that did not extend to his grandson, Mayor Erastus Corning 2nd, who was about as common a sight in the pews of All Saints as a Republican in City Hall.

All Saints was designed by the architect R.W. Gibson, who designed three of the five cathedrals of the Episcopal Church in New York State – Christ Church in Rochester and St. Paul's Church in Buffalo, in addition to All Saints. The Albany cathedral's foundations were laid June 1, 1884. Construction costs topped $320,000 (minus the undetermined value of the land), which was considered a very tight budget. Another challenge for Gibson was Doane's impatience. Since the diocese had no cathedral at this point, Doane – who hobnobbed with Albany's millionaires in town and at Northeast Harbor in Maine where the Cornings had an estate – was in a rush to cut the ribbon on this religious and social status symbol. Gibson's architectural notes indicate he felt hurried, spurred by Doane, and that the difficult deadlines caused him to devise in a rushed manner innovative engineering techniques to meet the load requirements

of the lofty, airy interior. Gibson chose distinctive red Potsdam sand-
stone for the exterior, which announced itself strongly and, in a small
way, attempted to overcome the overlooked nature of its location. In his
1961 book, *American Architecture and Other Writings*, Montgomery
Schuyler, the eminent architectural historian, called All Saints Cathedral
"about the most important church erected since Trinity (in Boston) . . . a
design in a free and somewhat Hispanicized English Gothic, which in
much of the detail, however, shows a reversion to Romanesque."

Architecturally, in terms of Albany as a whole, All Saints Cathedral
extended the Gothic tradition seen in the Roman Catholic Diocese's
Cathedral of the Immaculate Conception across town. Despite the lack of
a centerpiece location, and the fact that limited funds forced Gibson to
drop a few of his visual flourishes, All Saints Cathedral stands as an indisputable stroke of genuine architectural artistry. It is the greatest accomplishment, in terms of lasting value and religious and cultural permanence,
of Erastus Corning Jr. And it is the house of worship where subsequent
generations of Cornings were celebrated, mourned and blessed before
being sent to their final resting place at Albany Rural Cemetery. DeMille
summed it up this way: "And so it stands, a monument to the vision and
drive of William Croswell Doane, the architectural genius of Robert W.
Gibson, and the generosity of Erastus Corning and his son."

Despite the flamboyant lifestyle of Erastus Corning Jr., who spent the
family fortune and died in debt, the butterfly-collecting dreamer possessed
the pragmatism to marry into the Parker's long-established wealth in his
second marriage. His widow, Mary Parker Corning, a descendant of judges
and capitalists, could provide the old money comfort for her three children
by tapping into her family's font of means. At the time of their father's
death in 1897, the three Corning children from that second marriage –
Parker, twenty-three, Harriet, twenty-one, and Edwin, fourteen – continued to require the financial support that came from their mother's side of
the family. That notion of sociological and psychological traits skipping a
generation in the Corning family held true for this group, too. The sons of
the free-spirited, free-spending plant and animal lover abruptly severed any
connection to their father's benignly wastrel ways and reverted to the hard-
nosed capitalism of their grandfather, the first Erastus, family fountainhead
and empire builder. While their father showed virtually no interest in politics and precious little command of business, the sons early on learned to
harness and exploit that nexus between industrialism and political connec-

tions that established the Corning family fortune in the first place. Although their father had depleted vast cash reserves and bank accounts, he hadn't totally run the far-flung Corning industries into the ground. It was a family dynasty built upon iron, after all, and that solid manufacturing base proved difficult for even a head-in-the-clouds idealist like Erastus Corning Jr. to destroy. His sons, therefore, did not enter manhood without means or victims of bankruptcy. They inherited the bank directorships, which gave them access to capital, and the iron foundries – potential engines of wealth with the right president at the controls. Parker Corning, recently graduated from Yale at the time of his father's death, would prove just such a skilled and iron-willed entrepreneur in steel and felt manufacturing who could overturn his father's business incompetence. Parker grew up before his time and became the man of the house while still in his twenties, relied upon by his mother as the breadwinner. Parker also took his sister and little brother, Edwin, a Groton student, under his wing and became their guardian and tutor during the family's long and arduous climb back to prominence in business and politics after their father's precipitous fall from the pinnacle their grandfather had established. Those years, the rebound era, were marked by grueling work and incremental change.

Meanwhile, there were intriguing offshoots along the maternal branches of the Corning family tree. Despite his indifference to attending church services and keeping at arm's length the Episcopal faith in which he was raised, Mayor Erastus Corning 2nd expressed pride in it and in connections to the ministry in his background. His maternal grandmother, Ellen Blackmar [Maxwell], was born in West Springfield, Pennsylvania on July 6, 1852. Her parents, Protestant missionaries, soon moved Ellen and her older brother, F.M. Blackmar, to northern India. There, they not only performed church work, but were recruited as taskmasters by the ruling British at the height of the Raj. The mayor proudly offered stories of their adventures in India and discussed family photos of his grandmother riding elephants as a young girl and being raised by Hindu nurses. Ellen married the Rev. Allan James Maxwell in September, 1879 in Lucknow in northern India near the southern border of Nepal. Their daughter, Louise Maxwell, was born in Cawnpore, just south of Lucknow along the sacred Ganges River, on January 13, 1885. Rev. Maxwell died of cholera in Lucknow on October 7, 1890, leaving Ellen a widow and a single mother of five-year-old Louise. She supported herself and her daughter with her writing, publishing several novels, beginning with *The Bishop's Conversion* in 1892, which drew on her experiences in a missionary family in India. She wrote fast and for cash. Maxwell's popular Victorian novels, largely autobiographical, were turned out at a rate of one per year in a purely mercenary spirit. Other titles included *Lieutenant Loring's Chance, The Way of Fire, Three Maids In Hawaii* and *A Millstone About His Neck* in 1897. In the early 1890s, the widow Maxwell moved her family from northern India to Hawaii. It was on that Pacific island that Maxwell, forty-two, met and married her second husband, fifty-five-year-old bachelor Admiral Albert S. Barker, on October 26, 1894.

The rear admiral was an Annapolis graduate and a career Navy man who ended up with a forty-five year record in the service, having reached the highest echelons of the Navy, commanding the entire North Atlantic Fleet. That position took Barker on lengthy naval missions that required that his wife and stepdaughter stay behind in New York City. Barker wrote an autobiography based on diaries kept during his decades at sea, *Everyday Life in the Navy*, a 422-page volume published by his family. Barker mentioned his wife just twice, and then only briefly. The Navy was his life and his life was the Navy. He traced his military heritage to a cousin, Commodore William Barker Cushing, a Civil War hero noted for destroying the ship *Albermarle* in battle. The foreword to Barker's book said of him: "This background of naval service, together with his Puritan and Pilgrim ancestry tracing to the Mayflower in four distinct lines, gave to the Admiral a high purpose, a true simplicity, with strong impulse for accomplishment, so typical of the old Navy, and so clearly mirrored by his pen." Barker turned over control of the Atlantic fleet and retired in 1905. He died in 1916, and his wife outlived him by a decade.

Ellen Maxwell's daughter, Louise, born in India and raised in Hawaii, eventually came to New York City when she was in her early twenties. In the summer of 1908, when Louise was twenty-three, she was vacationing in the Adirondacks when she was reunited with Edwin Corning, Erastus Corning Jr.'s youngest child, two years out of Yale and the secretary and treasurer of The Ludlum Steel & Spring Co. of Watervliet – the firm in which his father had held a major financial stake. Louise and Edwin had met in New York City a few years earlier, brought together by mutual friends and Groton alumni, Warren Low and his wife. Corning found love when he least expected it.

"I've lived very quietly at the Farm with my brother," Edwin Corning wrote to his mentor, the headmaster of Groton, Rev. Endicott Peabody, on October 2, 1908. Corning was uncharacteristically candid and revealing of his heart and motivations. "I found out very quickly that to work ten hours I need a lot of sleep, so going out at all has been out of the question." It was a fluke that Edwin and Louise got back together in the Adirondacks, at all, Corning told Peabody. "This year, when I expected no vacation (vacations being against Mr. Ludlum's idea of a company officer), I had the good fortune to hurt a knee quite badly while spending a Sunday at camp, with the result of a ten days' rest there and the opportunity to realize shortly afterward, the hope which I had been having for a year or more." In his handwritten letter, Corning crossed out the term "carry out" and replaced it with "realize," indicating he had set his cap for Louise Maxwell some time before. "I hope to be married in December – to Louise Maxwell, the stepdaughter of Admiral Barker of Washington," Corning wrote. "She is the daughter of a missionary to India, and seems to have inherited his perceivable fondness for church and church work. You will approve, I know, when you have seen her. In one sense she is rather old fashioned, in as much as I expect to do the smoking and drinking for the family."

At the time of his marriage, Ed, as his friends called him, voted "Nerviest" in his class of 1906 at Yale, was an outgoing, confident young fellow of twenty-five who already was beginning to become active in Albany County Democratic politics. At Yale, he was known as a fearless football player who made up in determination what he lacked in size and physical ability. And it seemed to be so in courtship also, although Louise, as would later be seen in the rearing of her son the mayor, was not deficient herself when it came to possessing a strong will. Theirs was an intense and brief courting period. Following a few short months of dating, at the end of the summer, on September 8, 1908, they became engaged. They were married on the twenty-fifth of November that same year. Their first child was born on October 7, 1909 and, bound by tradition, they named him Erastus – the fifth Corning to be so christened. By Corning standards, the young family lived in modest accommodations at 156 Chestnut Street, along Brides Row. This grouping of pleasant, nicely appointed brick townhouses in Albany's Center Square neighborhood was home to newlyweds of a certain social standing who were getting on their feet financially until they moved up into a mansion. The Cornings followed this typical course.

When Edwin and Louise Corning and their son, Erastus, moved to the Upper Farm on Corning Hill in Glenmont – equally divided in acreage in comparison to Parker's Lower Farm – they lived in luxury, with a magnificent estate and many servants. In a few short years, Edwin and Parker rode the steel and felt operations they had inherited to a level of substantial wealth, with no ceiling to their rising fortunes in sight. Parker later became renowned for conspicuous shows of consumption and extravagances his younger brother tried to emulate. In his own right, Edwin was known for breeding champion Irish wolfhounds and for quirky habits, such as carrying a suit coat pocket full of uncut emeralds, diamonds, rubies, sapphires and other rough gems. He'd frequently remove his glittery companions, observe their sparkle in his palm, and shake them like so many pairs of dice, before returning them to his pocket – some sort of strange Corning mojo. Edwin had something of a jewelry obsession. He had Tiffany's send up the latest styles of rings, necklaces, earrings and bracelets and then illegally had an Albany craftsman copy the Tiffany patterns and fashion replicas for his wife out of glass and other cheap materials. A Corning cousin, Wharton Sinkler III, passed down those family anecdotes, but was uncertain whether they signaled Edwin Corning as a cheapskate, a thief, or an eccentric. Among the certainties was Edwin's prodigious appetite for expensive single-malt Scotch and fancy black cigarettes known as Egyptian Deities. Edwin Corning's genteel lifestyle paled, however, in comparison to the extravagance of his older brother, Parker. There was a fierce competition between the brothers in matters of business and politics. Their mother, Mary, and sister, Harriet, seemed powerless to temper the rivalry as they occupied the uneasy middle ground between the brothers. Edwin was the baby of the family, after all, and Parker was nine years older and much larger physically. Parker was outsized, starting with his booming personality that seemed suited to his large brooding eyes and rough-cut, pronounced features that upstaged Edwin's soft, almost feminine, face and narrow eyes. Their political roles were reversed. Parker was considered "less in the limelight than his younger brother Edwin" when it came to the Albany Democratic machine and its "position of affluence and power," according to the *Albany Evening News* of May 24, 1943. That assessment came long after Edwin Corning failed in early bids for political control within the Democratic ranks, but he was able to shrug off rejection and continue to build his power base.

Edwin wrote once more to Peabody at Groton in 1908: "My fondness for politics has not died out. I can't afford time or money to go in very deeply, but I'm still an ardent Democrat. We made our attempt to throw out our local leader – one "Packy" McCabe – but Murphy and Cowens threw us out in the Convention. I don't blame them much, for though I believe we won, the regulars had all the reports. So we're behind McCabe till after the election, and then we will go for him again." Finally, after several tries, the coalition necessary to wrest control from McCabe and his cronies and to defeat the dynasty of the Republican Barnes machine was formed: Edwin and Parker Corning together with the Albany O'Connell brothers, Dan and Ed and Solly. This team represented a new political union that reached across traditional political chasms. The O'Connell-Corning organization joined for the first time in Albany a coalition of immigrants, particularly Irish who had helped dig the Erie Canal, and the working-class from the South End and the city's downtown ethnic wards with the uptown affluent sections and defectors from a traditionally Republican patrician class, who switched allegiance to the Democrats as followers of the Cornings. The class-merging strategy was brilliant. The Democratic O'Connell-Corning organization was victorious in 1921 and Albany politics was transformed for generations to come. "I'm in politics for the fun I get out of it," Edwin Corning told a newspaper reporter. The following year, in the 1922 election, Parker Corning brought the reach of the Albany Democratic machine all the way to Washington by defeating Charles M. Winchester Sr. by a wide margin in a race for Albany's Congressional seat.

In substantial ways, because his own father was largely absent and unavailable to him, Erastus Corning 2nd's uncle, Parker, loomed large as an influence in the development of the personality of his nephew, Albany's eventual mayor for life. Parker Corning was born in New York City on January 22, 1874. Like his younger brother Edwin and future generations of Cornings, Parker was sent first to Albany Academy, but then transferred to St. Paul's Prep School in Concord, New Hampshire, rather than Groton, where scores of Cornings did their college preparatory work. Parker followed Corning tradition, however, by going on to attend Yale, from which he graduated in 1895. At Yale, Parker Corning, a rugged six-foot two-inch tall athlete, was on the crew and cricket teams and competed in other sports on an intramural basis. He was active in the Psi Upsilon fraternity and the secret society, Wolf's Head, and was a big man on campus, invited to all the important parties and doings. His classmates sometimes poked fun at his pretensions to being a member of the English gentry and gave him the nicknames Prince, Albany Hasty and Prince Chocolate. Upon graduation, Parker's father set him up with a company and installed the twenty-one-year-old as vice-president of Albany Felt Company, which, today, as Albany International, is the world's largest producer of products for forming, pressing and drying paper in the global paper industry. "Not only did Erastus Corning Jr. have abundant capital, but he also had a son, Parker, who was about to graduate from Yale with no definite plans for the future. With his father's full moral and financial support, Parker Corning decided to stake his future with Duncan Fuller," Lorna Skaaren wrote in a corporate history published in 1995 for Albany Felt's centennial. Fuller and Corning formed the company in 1895 with a small felt mill in Kenwood, on the outskirts of Albany within present-day Glenmont, on a corner of the property that comprised the 700-acre Corning Farm where Parker Corning, and two previous generations of Cornings, had lived. The Corning family's prize-winning herd of Southdown sheep were willingly fleeced and gave up top grades of wool for felt production. In five years' time, the company's stock increased from the initial $40,000 to $150,000 behind Parker Corning's relentless drive. "Parker's father died in debt, so Parker considered it his duty to recoup the family fortune," said his grand-daughter, Anita Corning Iglehart Swatkovsky. "He had to work very hard for many years to keep the family going and he felt he couldn't have a wife and a family and maintain them in the accustomed luxury of the Cornings, so he married late."

There is no family account of how Parker Corning met his eventual wife, Anne Cassin McClure, but it was an attraction between opposite ends of the social spectrum. The Corning family was dubious. She was poor and divorced and, the whispers went, was after the Corning money. Besides, she was Catholic and he Episcopalian. Parker, at thirty-six, was nearly ten years older than she was; she had a son from her previous marriage. She was practically from the peasantry, compared to the Cornings' slowly replenishing wealth.

Anne Cassin was born in Rensselaer in 1883, the daughter of John J. and Ellen (Walsh) Cassin. She grew up in a working-class Irish household, strictly Catholic, and attended parochial schools in Rensselaer and Albany. Her mother died when she was a young girl and her father struggled to provide for her. She was raised partly by relatives and had few possessions.

Her first marriage, to Archibald McClure, a pub keeper in Rensselaer, ended in divorce at a time when divorces were not common or socially acceptable, neither in the Corning's social circles or in Anne's Catholic background. Swatkovsky characterized McClure as a drunk and womanizer and Cassin was granted one of the early divorces in the state's history because of his infidelity. Family pressure swirled around Parker Corning to call off the marriage, most strongly from his younger sister, Harriet, but he was undeterred. McClure, both of whose parents were deceased, was a single mother raising a son, Barclay Jermain McClure, when she married into the prominent Corning family on October 31, 1910.

The new Mrs. Corning set herself the task of throwing open the windows on the family's musty, rigid ways. She dumped the heavy, ornate Victorian furnishings in the Corning mansion on the Lower Farm when she moved in and replaced them with a rustic Adirondack Great Camp style, rough-hewn and woodsy. "I remember there were lots of animal heads on the walls," Swatkovsky said. Parker and Anne Corning had acres of lawn and tennis courts and two swimming pools and a large network of horse and cattle stables. "It was an extremely lavish lifestyle," Swatkovsky said. "My grandmother loved to spend money. She had incredible jewelry (the real thing, as opposed to Edwin's knockoffs). She loved owning and breeding thoroughbred race horses. My grandfather just couldn't say no to her." The couple had one child together, a daughter, Mary Parker Corning, born in 1912, who was roundly spoiled. "I remember her telling me how she had her own stable of horses when she was eighteen and servants in every home they owned," Swatkovsky said. The Cornings had additional homes in Washington, D.C.; Old Westbury, Long Island; New York City; Saratoga Springs; and their beloved estate in Bar Harbor, Maine, known as Sea Urchin.

As their respective fortunes grew, relations between the brothers, Parker and Edwin, were lukewarm at best. It was partly a wives' spat, Swatkovsky said, because the brothers seemed to work well together in their overlapping business ventures of steel and felt. "They had two separate worlds. We never went from Parker's Lower Farm to Edwin's Upper Farm on Corning Hill," Swatkovsky said. "And I don't remember hearing about the two families visiting in Maine between Parker's estate in Bar Harbor and Edwin's in Northeast Harbor."

Martha "Patty" Becker, born in 1914, a lifelong Corning family friend and sister of William Thompson Jr., a classmate of Mayor Corning's at

Groton and Yale, recalled the rivalry between the two brothers. "Edwin couldn't keep up with Parker's lavish lifestyle," Becker said. "Edwin tried to buy the fastest Chris-Craft yacht, the biggest Dusenberg car, the best of everything. But he couldn't keep up with Parker." The middle sibling, Harriet, also drove a wedge between the two brothers. "Harriet never spoke to Parker again after he married that divorced woman," Becker said. "Poor Edwin sat in the middle and tried to reconcile them, but she wouldn't budge. They had very strong wills, all of them, and Harriet and Parker never mended the split."

But Parker and Anne Corning were madly in love and on the move: socially, politically, economically. He continued to gain renown for his horse and cattle breeding and his wife moved into thoroughbred horse training. Best known among the horses that carried the Corning colors was the colt, Attention, which in 1941 beat the Triple Crown winner and famed superhorse Whirlaway by a length and a half to win the Arlington Classic. In addition, Mrs. Corning and trainer Mary Hirsch, an unusual female owner-trainer duo for that day, teamed up to win the prestigious Travers Stakes at Saratoga in 1938 with their thoroughbred Thanksgiving.

Parker Cornings' five houses kept him and his wife in the glare of high society – a craving for celebrity that never seemed to grip Edwin. In the Albany area, Parker Corning was a member of the Fort Orange Club and Albany Country Club, Saratoga Golf, Schuyler Meadows and the North Woods – golf being one of the couple's favorite pastimes. The Cornings entertained often at their various residences, traveling between them in a burgundy Rolls-Royce with chauffeurs in matching burgundy livery. They were well suited for the extravagances of the Roaring '20s. The many parties exacerbated Parker's mounting drinking problem. That was one aspect, at least, that Parker shared with his brother. "Edwin was a hard drinker and had to have a leg amputated in part because of the booze," Becker said. "When they took him off the liquor after the operation, the staff would catch him doctoring up his afternoon tea with booze." Heavy drinking was part of the Corning family legacy. Both Edwin's daughters, Louise and Harriet, were alleged alcoholics and both died before the age of fifty largely due to liver complications attributable to reported alcoholism, according to Harriet's son, Wharton Sinkler III, a Groton graduate who trained as both a physician and Episcopal minister. The affliction to differing degrees affected Edwin's two sons, Eddie, who allegedly once had a drinking problem and who died at age forty-four from injuries and a lengthy coma sustained in a car accident, and Erastus 2nd, the mayor, a heavy drinker who engaged in drunken binges to the point of blackouts.

Parker Corning moved easily from the worlds of agriculture to society to business to politics. A Democrat, he was elected to Congress in 1922 as a member of the House of Representatives from the 28th District of New York, one of the Democratic machine's early successes. Among Corning's notable Congressional accomplishments were legislation that created the Port of Albany and helped to bring about the construction of a new federal building. Corning was assigned to the prestigious Interstate and Foreign Commerce committees in Congress. As chairman of the subcommittee on bridges, he leveraged federal support of the Parker Dunn Memorial and Troy-Menands bridges that now span the Hudson River – nearly a century after his grandfather, Erastus Corning, had built the first railroad bridge across the Hudson at Albany amid much controversy. One of his last pieces of legislation in 1936 before retirement was the minting of the fifty-cent coin for the 250th Dongan Charter celebration in Albany, where his nephew, Erastus Corning 2nd, five years hence would be installed as mayor. These are two examples of the many ways, cutting across business and politics, in which the Corning legacy resembles the family burial plot at Albany Rural Cemetery, an unbroken circle that closes around itself in insularity and protective posture.

Parker Corning was "attracted by the social as well as the political elements of his role as a congressman," according to the *Albany Evening News* of May 24, 1943 and kept company with political heavyweights including former Gov. Alfred E. Smith, Vice-President John Nance Garner, Speakers Longworth and Gillette, Representatives James W. Wadsworth and Rhode Island's Sen. Peter G. Gerry. Corning nurtured those important connections and also accepted the advice and orders issued by the Albany Democratic machine forged among himself, his brother Edwin and the O'Connell brothers. It was an unbeatable combination, those power bases in both Albany and Washington. Parker Corning was elected to seven terms in Congress as representative from the 28th New York District, which comprises Albany County and part of the city of Troy. He retired on July 16, 1936 at the age of sixty-two.

Corning retired partly out of a mounting anger against President Franklin Delano Roosevelt and his New Deal policies. "A close personal friend of Alfred E. Smith, Mr. Corning has been openly identified with the

Liberty League and has taken issue at times with some of the New Deal policies," the paper reported on July 17, 1936. The Democratic Congressman's opposition was due in part to Dan O'Connell, the Albany political boss, who viewed Roosevelt's social welfare programs as a threat to the machine's effective use of patronage to win votes and ensure loyalty from working-class citizens who needed the machine's jobs for survival – effectively an O'Connell-Corning welfare state. Parker Corning was known to bristle publicly at mention of Roosevelt's "brain trusters" and voted against FDR on several issues, including attempts to continue the National Relief Agency and other social welfare programs, as well as the Guffey coal control act. Corning, a director of three Albany banks, also differed with FDR on the administration's banking policies. As president of the Albany Felt Company and director of the Ludlum Steel Company (his brother Edwin's business), Corning criticized FDR's tariff proposals and, despite being a Democrat, said he could not follow the Roosevelt program on tariff reductions because it threatened domestic felt companies like his by permitting foreign materials to compete successfully against home industry.

Parker Corning's retirement was taken in stride by leaders of the powerful Albany Democratic machine, which could practically guarantee election of the next machine-backed candidate. There was a notion to keep the seat in the family. Parker's nephew, Erastus Corning 2nd, twenty-seven and a state Assemblyman, who "gained some prominence at the last legislative session," according to the *Albany Evening News*, was on the short list of Parker's successors but was not tapped by O'Connell. Uncle Dan had a more politically important assignment in Albany in mind for Erastus, whom he had begun grooming, that would bring the Corning family full-circle once more from the original Erastus. Parker Corning's vacant Congressional seat remained in Democratic control and eventually was won, with the machine's backing, of course, by Leo W. O'Brien, newspaper reporter, member of the Albany Port Commission and machine loyalist.

The end of Parker Corning's political career began his own slow decline. His wife was nearing the end of a prolonged battle with cancer and died on April 3, 1943 at her home in Kenwood at sixty. She was buried in Albany Rural Cemetery. Financially, Parker had managed to avoid the heavy losses suffered by his younger brother, Edwin, in the stock market crash of 1929 by selling off his margins before the bottom fell out. Still, like his father before him, Parker couldn't make it as fast as he spent it and began borrowing against his holdings in Albany Felt's stock. His heavy debts often left the company in a weakened financial condition. Even after his large sell-offs of stock, Parker Corning retained 22,730 shares, or fifty-eight percent interest in Albany Felt, worth hundreds of thousands of dollars. But his heirs were forced to liquidate the stock to pay off the creditors of Parker Corning's estate, according to Skaaren, author of the company history. Parker Corning, once a millionaire many times over, died essentially broke at the age of sixty-nine on May 24, 1943, seven weeks after the passing of his wife. He also had cancer and had been seriously ill and hospitalized for about three weeks before he died in the Albany Medical Hospital. Her death was "the beginning of the end for Parker Corning," according to a friend quoted in *The Knickerbocker Press* on May 24, 1943. Many family members and relatives remarked on Corning's singular devotion to his wife and how his vigor left him when his wife took ill. "Parker told my mother he was tired of life without his beloved Anne," his granddaughter said.

According to his obituary in *The Knickerbocker Press*, Parker Corning "had a good clear business head" and a talent for "diagnosing the future," which helped Albany Felt stock to rise from $40,000 a hundred fold, to $5 million, during his tenure. His death left a void in the company's leadership, leaving control up for grabs in a power play between the remaining principals. "Corning was the only individual who had been with Albany Felt since the beginning," Skaaren wrote. "His death marked the end of an era."

Tragedy struck the extended family of Albany Felt and the Cornings. Following Parker Corning's death, directorship of the company was passed to Lewis Parker, a cousin of Mayor Corning's and also a Yale graduate who started in an entry-level production job in 1928 at Albany Felt fresh out of college. Lewis Parker died in 1957 at fifty after choking to death while dining with his wife and some friends in New York City. The death marked the end of a Corning connection to Albany Felt, what is today Albany International, with its press fabric manufacturing plants scattered around the world with annual sales totaling hundreds of millions of dollars, although exact figures are not made public.

Meanwhile, although somewhat overshadowed by his older brother, Edwin Corning, the mayor's father, notched significant successes in business and politics in his own right. In 1906, the year he graduated from Yale, Edwin was set up in business by his father, as Parker had been. Edwin wrote in the notes for his third year Yale reunion, "After a summer's loaf, I went to work in the fall of 1906 for the Ludlum Steel & Spring Company, then building a plant at Watervliet." The Corning family had held a financial interest in Ludlum since 1854, when the first Erastus bankrolled James Horner in re-activating the old Pompton Furnace, which operated in Pompton Lakes, New Jersey for more than a century. Pompton produced metal during the Revolutionary War for American cannon balls and links for the giant chain stretched across the Hudson to block British warships, according to *33 Magazine*, a steel trade publication that carried an article on the history of Ludlum Steel, which Mayor Corning saved in his personal files at City Hall.

It was at Ludlum Steel where Edwin Corning, soon to become company president, would rise to the position of captain of Albany area industry. Edwin Corning related his quick climb up the corporate ladder at Ludlum in an October 2, 1908 letter to his mentor, Groton headmaster Rev. Endicott Peabody:

> This company in which I have a small interest gave me a job when I graduated. I started as time keeper, and gradually absorbed the work of pay master and sort of general superintendent of the new plant we were building here. We started to manufacture just before the panic, but have pulled through without losing much money, and with our force of men intact and thankful for the work which we made or got for them. This summer about twenty of our men worked on the Farm. At this year's stockholder's meeting, I was elected a director and later made secretary and treasurer to save a raise in pay, I fear. Most of my time I try to spend in the mill. I am more or less of a poor blacksmith, but take pride in my ability as a tool dresser. I like the work and the men I am with and believe the company will do very well financially in good times. I believe the Prince or Pauper idea holds in the steel business. I know the Pauper end of it does.

Corning was being modest. William E. Ludlum, president and general manager when Corning joined the firm in 1906, quickly discovered Corning's business acuity and turned over to Corning the running of the Watervliet steel mill while Ludlum devoted most of his time to their plant in New Jersey. Corning's older brother, Parker, a vice-president at Ludlum (he returned the favor and made Edwin a vice-president at Albany Felt) let Edwin carry most of the weight. "My brother has taken advantage of the dullness of all business to wander 'round the country, shooting, sightseeing and enjoying himself. Consequently, a good bit of his work falls on me. However, the more the work the easier it is to do it and I like it," Edwin wrote to Peabody.

Edwin was responsible for the prestige and profitability of Ludlum, which became widely known for high-quality steel railroad car springs and for crucible cast steel. Corning first had to dig the company out of a financial hole, though. Three years before he started, in 1903, disaster struck the New Jersey operation when its power-supplying dam on the Pompton River gave way. The floods destroyed the mill, forges and furnace pits. Corning proved himself an innovator in the field and oversaw the building of modern facilities at Watervliet, including electrically operated furnaces, which allowed Ludlum to become a pioneer in the making of alloy steels. By 1914, Ludlum reportedly was the only firm in the world making its steels by the new electric-arc furnace process. As president of Ludlum Steel from 1910 to 1930, Corning was the catalyst for other historic firsts in the steel industry that were achieved at the Watervliet facility.

According to a trade industry magazine account in September, 1976, "It was estimated that over ninety-five percent of the exhaust valves on American World War II planes were made by the owners or licensees of Ludlum patents. The first commercial heat of stainless steel ever produced on this side of the Atlantic was poured from a Ludlum furnace in the summer of 1919." Once again, the Corning circle came around, from the first Erastus, whose iron was used in Civil War cannons, to his grandson Edwin's steel helping to build America's World War II bombers.

On another front, Corning's flagship patent was on Silicrome steel, an alloy of silicone and chromium, which was highly heat-resistant. Corning's plant turned out the beautiful architectural steel for the spire of the landmark Chrysler Building in New York City. At the Watervliet steel plant, Corning also forged a deep and abiding camaraderie among his workers. He was a boss who didn't mind rolling up his sleeves and getting grease under his fingernails; he could turn a wrench as well as the next assembly line worker. A few old-timers, who retired from the Watervliet plant, now Altech Specialty Steel, recalled stories passed down among workers about Edwin Corning running the operation in the late-1920s. They seemed to like Corning and Corning liked them, at least in second-hand anecdotes. One retiree, in his eighties, recounted for me in 1994 a story about how Mayor Erastus Corning, when he was a young boy, would run around the plant or have lunch with his father in the oak-paneled executive dining room while making a special visit.

Tragedy was never far from the core of Corning family narrative. In 1928, at the zenith of his political and business careers, Edwin Corning – just forty-five years old, but grossly overweight and a heavy smoker and drinker – suffered a heart attack and began a long health decline. He never again was a guiding force at Ludlum on a daily basis. Part of the stroke might be attributed to the stress of Corning's disastrous losses leading up to the stock market crash of 1929. Corning was a special agent in the New York Stock Exchange firm of Gurnett & Company from 1928 to 1932 and he had invested heavily in the stock market on the crest of Coolidge prosperity. In 1926, the net worth of Corning's estate was $1.7 million. Then came the crash. "I am rather pulling in my horns as far as the market is concerned," he wrote his stockbroker. In 1931, Corning said it was "utterly impossible" to duplicate his 1926 donation of $1,000 to the Yale Alumni Fund. "I had an attack of acute dilation of the heart two and one-half years ago, which has naturally cut my earning power very considerably," he wrote the Yale solicitors.

Before the financial ruin of 1928, though, Edwin Corning reached heady heights in the political realm, all the way to the office of lieutenant governor under Gov. Al Smith, and he was Smith's probable successor when the popular governor ran for president in 1928. Corning's successes with the O'Connells in controlling Albany County politics with their Democratic organization was well known – so well, in fact, that Corning was tapped to bring the same sort of winning political strategy statewide, beginning in 1926 when he was named chairman of the New York State Democratic Committee. Edwin Corning had risen from city to county to state politics and, at least in a peripheral way from his brother, Parker, the Congressman, and more directly from his connection to Al Smith, to the national political arena. His Yale classmates had detected this drive early on; "Nerviest in his class" summed up Edwin Corning. In essence, Smith made Corning his political point man not only in Albany, but across the entire state and beyond. Smith was repaying a favor, since it was Edwin Corning who acted as upstate campaign chairman for Smith's gubernatorial runs and Corning was a catalyst behind the drive to get Smith nominated for the presidency in 1928. When Corning was inaugurated as lieutenant governor in Albany on January 1, 1927, he was joined by friends locally and from Maine at the party. Corning was flooded with congratulations and telegrams, which he answered with variations of this January 3, 1927 reply to the Women's Democratic Club of New York City: "I certainly hope that I will be able to live up to the high expectations which you seem to place in me. So far I have had nothing to do, but tomorrow I start presiding over the Senate which is about the only thing the Lt. Gov. has to do under the reorganization plan," Corning wrote.

As Democratic Party chairman and lieutenant governor, Corning had to field a flood of requests for jobs and political favors. The bulk of Corning's correspondence in the posts came from the Democratic County Committee of the County of New York: Corning was very much in the pocket of Tammany Hall, which made no pretense of sending Corning his marching orders. Like father, like son: the situation differed only in venue between Edwin Corning and Tammany and Mayor Erastus Corning 2nd and Dan O'Connell. As lieutenant governor, Edwin Corning was rarely in Albany and traveled seemingly non-stop around the state, putting out political brush fires as Democratic chairman. It wasn't easy to solve the problems, though, since Corning reported that the state Democratic committee was in debt in November of 1927. Corning also mentioned in his letters in the late fall of 1927 that poor health was hampering his political and business activities, although he wasn't specific about the symptoms. Looking forward to forgetting his struggles during a summer respite, he wrote on June 23, 1927 to Sen. James Truman of Oswego: "I don't know what my plans are for August. If the Governor plans to be out of the State, I have got to be here. If he is in the State, I want to spend as much time as I can at Northeast Harbor, Maine."

Even as he dealt on a daily basis with power brokers ranging from state parks architect and Secretary of State Robert Moses and Tammany Hall boss Edward J. Flynn, Corning struggled to control his consumption of liquor during this strenuous phase in his career. Ironically, Corning liked to tell his son, Erastus, and his legislative colleagues that he was the first lieutenant governor since Prohibition came in who had not kept liquor in his office next to the Senate Chamber. "He was far from being a *dry* professionally, politically or personally," his son, the mayor, told a Capitol symposium in 1981. Heavy drinking was one of the contributors to Corning's downturn in health, he confided to his longtime friend and Yale classmate, William Godfrey of Philadelphia in December of 1927.

Meanwhile, when he wasn't pouring the Scotch, Corning carried water for Gov. Al Smith in more ways than one, particularly in battling the prejudices against Smith, a Catholic, in his bid for the presidency. Corning promoted religious tolerance in a February 20, 1928 letter to Lena Todd of Cuba, N.Y. "There are narrow minded bigots in every faith, and it is a comfort to know that the majority of us who are Protestants take a more liberal view of things," Corning wrote. "The very idea that a man should be barred from office on account of his religious belief is abhorrent. Many of our early ancestors came to this country to avoid just such religious intolerance."

In the summer of 1928, with the November election approaching and Al Smith pushing hard on the presidential campaign trail, the pressure for Corning to run for Smith's vacant seat as governor was mounting. Corning seemed willing to accept the fate of the powers that be when he wrote on July 5, 1928 to Tammany operative Judge George Olvany of New York City: "Last evening Governor Smith practically told me to discontinue [holding back Corning-for-governor supporters] and endeavor to make an upstate canvass," Corning wrote. "Under the circumstances I have written the men to whom I sent telegrams earlier in the day to discontinue their activities. I have not changed in any way my views on the subject but accept the decision of my superior."

The matter soon became moot due to Edwin Corning's heart attack and stroke on a train from New York City to Maine in early August, 1928. Corning wrote to George R. Van Namee of New York City, FDR's campaign manager, from the Corning's Maine estate, Stoney Point, in Northeast Harbor: "Shortly after I got up here from New York I was sent to bed by the doctor with instructions to stay there for two or three weeks, as I have had a recurrence of a strained muscle in the heart which affected me some years ago and which I am afraid will preclude the possibility of my doing anything active in the next two months. The Governor is being appraised of the situation by Dr. Elting. I will, of course, be governed by his wishes."

Corning had accepted his political fate by then, realizing that he had been stricken with a career-ending malady. He wrote a $5,000 check to the election committee of FDR for governor and Herbert H. Lehman for lieutenant governor on October 26, 1928. Despite his weakened condition, politics was a lifelong attraction from which Corning would never recover. Corning wrote on November 2, 1928 to Judge Charles Herrick of Albany: "The doctors told me it was O.K. to come down, and I got here Tuesday after a very comfortable trip, with no noticeable effect on my heart. However, I am going to continue to take things easy for a few weeks, but hope to see you before long. Everything in Albany County looks mighty good to me. I think the whole county ticket will be safely elected."

Corning couldn't divorce himself completely from the gubernatorial race, either, even though he wound up watching from the sidelines in the 1928 campaign. He kept up on FDR's statewide barnstorming by way of state Comptroller Morris Tremaine, a close friend, who briefed Corning on FDR's performance as a disabled candidate in an October 25, 1928 letter:

> We were all surprised on the trip about Roosevelt's ability to stand the trip. . . . He worked harder than anyone else and came up each morning feeling much better than any of us. In fact he wore us all out. His difficulty seems to be entirely with his knees, and as you know he wears braces that have to be locked when he stands up so that his knees cannot bend. While this looks awkward at times it apparently is nothing more than an inconvenience. He walks with a cane and usually takes someone's arm, besides. He motors in an open car and seems to love the whole thing. The enthusiasm for him is more than he expected, and it is always spontaneous. Tommy interjects that he heard your brother Parker make a speech the other night. He said it was short, concise and to the point – like all the Cornings, steadily improving, better and better every day.

Corning remained a loyal Democrat despite the disappointment of the end of his political career, offering his congratulations to his victorious successor, Lt. Gov. Herbert Lehman on November 28, 1928: "This is a very belated letter of congratulations on your nomination, due to the fact that I have been combating an illness for almost four months, and therefore must ask your forgiveness," Corning wrote to Lehman. Corning used the letter to discuss housekeeping chores regarding the lieutenant governor's job, such as hanging of the official photograph in the reception room, protocol for inauguration ceremonies, the budget of the lieutenant governor's office ($4,000 per year for a secretary and $5 per day for a stenographer and a messenger during session) and other perks. "These are personal appointments and no organization should ask that they go through the organization," Corning wrote. Corning also made his pitch for Lehman to retain the services of his own appointees, George Harder, a former newspaperman, lawyer and expert on Senate procedure as secretary; and a young lad named Anthony Tardio as messenger. Corning was trying to be helpful to

Lehman, a compatriot in the Democratic Party, but his letter was tinged with sadness over passing the torch. "Though I was naturally heart broken over Governor Smith's defeat and the loss of New York State at the same time, I was delighted to see Franklin, you and Morris Tremaine all come in winners," Corning wrote to Lehman.

In essence, Corning told Lehman that the lieutenant governor's position was largely ceremonial, a no-brainer. "I will be glad to go as fully as may be necessary into any details connected with the office of Lieutenant Governor, and for Heaven sake do not bother your head about the technicality of presiding," Corning wrote on November 28, 1928. "It may be a little awkward for a week or so, but you'll swing into the routine in no time. Perhaps once or twice during the Session some strange technicality may come up in which case the simplest and, in fact, the only thing to do, is to lean down and ask the Clerk what the proper ruling is." Corning got in one parting shot. While the job may be no sweat, the office was. "By the way the office is being cleaned, varnished and a new carpet put in," Corning concluded. "But nothing under Heaven will ever ventilate it in a half decent manner."

Lehman responded to Corning a week later, on December 5, 1928, and apologized for the delay. He blamed his tardiness on the fact that he had been meeting with Roosevelt at Warm Springs, Georgia, where FDR received water therapy for his polio. "I was very glad indeed to hear from you again and to learn that you are quite recovered from your recent illness," Lehman wrote from his Manhattan apartment. "I had kept more or less in touch with your progress with your brother. I know that it must have been a source of great disappointment to you to have been laid up during these recent exciting months."

Lehman said he already had negotiated with a secretary that worked with him on the campaign, but he'd save a spot for Corning's messenger. "I had a letter some time ago from your brother Parker about your messenger boy, Anthony Tardio, and I promptly advised him that I should be very glad to continue him in his present position," Lehman wrote. Lehman asked Corning to recommend a stenographer, too. As for the job itself, Lehman conceded some trepidation. "I am a little scared about it all, but I imagine that I will get used to it fairly promptly. At any rate, I am going to follow your advice and not bother my head much about the details, and lean for guidance just as heavily as may be necessary on the clerk."

Corning didn't let his illness – "a slight attack of heart trouble that confined me to the house for five or six months" is how he downplayed it in one letter – hold him back long from his twin loves, business and politics. "If my health ever permits I may get back in a mild way into politics, not from an office holder's point of view, but probably one of the people pulling the strings in the town of Bethlehem, County of Albany, and if you get back in I am quite sure we will be able to get together on most anything," Corning wrote to Judge Jeremiah Mahoney of New York City on January 4, 1929.

Corning told his longtime buddy Jacob Herzog, an officer with the National Commercial Bank & Trust Co., that he was back at the steel mill, too, after turning the reins for a time over to his brother, Parker. "I have been up to the Works for quite a time and I am now thoroughly in charge thereof," Corning wrote to Herzog on May 3, 1929. "My working and playing hours are gradually increasing and before long I hope to be back in full swing, at least as far as the Steel Works and play go."

Such hopefulness never came to fruition. Corning did not make a full recovery from his career-ending heart attack and stroke in 1928. He was essentially an invalid for the last six years of his life, unable to return to an active role in politics or to take hold of the helm of the steel mill once more. He turned over the presidency of Ludlum Steel to Hiland D. Batcheller. Corning spent many of his final, declining months at Stoney Point in Northeast Harbor, staring out to sea from a specially built sick room at the rising and falling of the tides.

Corning, whom his son, Erastus, recalled as "a heavy and sedentary man" in an interview with William Kennedy, was diagnosed with arteriosclerosis. He had a leg amputated by a surgeon friend in New Haven, Connecticut, where Corning maintained contacts from his Yale days, but the results of the operation were not good. Corning was admitted to the hospital for a second leg amputation in Bar Harbor, Maine on August 7, 1934, but died on the operating table, a fifty-year-old man. Heavy smoking and alleged alcoholism added to his health problems and cut short his life, as it would his children's, according to his descendants. Edwin Corning's last will and testament revealed that his real and personal property, left to his widow, Louise, amounted to less than $20,000. The millions that had once been the family fortune, partly regained during his generation, had sifted through the Corning fingers once again. The missionary's daughter, who had come from India to Hawaii to New York with a mother left a widow herself at a young age, would be on her own once more. Louise would need all the iron will she could mine from her mother's experience, since she was a forty-eight-year-old widow left with four children and a meager inheritance aside from the estate and farmland outside Albany and the summer compound in Maine.

As for Edwin Corning's son, what remained after the father's death was a twenty-five-year-old man uncertain of his father's legacy. The mayor was fond of polishing the family chestnut, the legend of his father's political paradise lost. Corning told and re-told the story over the years, but the essential narrative was this. Al Smith, while embarking on his 1928 presidential campaign, had tapped Edwin Corning to be his successor as governor of New York state. Corning initially demurred, but finally gave in to the wishes of Smith and the Democratic Party faithful. The track to the Executive Mansion was greased for Corning, but his heart attack and stroke on the eve of the foregone conclusion of the state Democratic convention left the incumbent party with no machine-backed candidate. They scrambled to draft a worthy replacement for Corning, the mayor's story went, and found a young state senator from Hyde Park by the name of Franklin Delano Roosevelt. And here is where the mayor would pause in his father's legend, fix his listener with a gleam in his eye, his thin lips turning slightly upward in a proud grin, wait just a few more beats for emphasis and intone, "And the course of history was changed forever."

But was Edwin Corning truly being groomed to become the governor of the Empire State? Had Smith and Tammany actually tapped him for the state's highest job? Or was the Corning family legend merely a psychological consolation prize for an invalid dying a slow death, one limb at a time, of hardening of the arteries? The lieutenant governor's son, the mayor, who had been mentioned as an attractive gubernatorial candidate himself several times, but who seemed to possess no ambition for the job, recounted the family myth so often he seemed to have bought into it. Or had he? The standard biographies of Smith and Roosevelt do not mention Edwin Corning as Smith's chosen successor, with Corning receiving little more than a footnote in scholarly books written by historians specializing in New York State politics of that era.

No less a source than Leo O'Brien, the late newspaperman, longtime confidante of Dan O'Connell, machine-backed Congressman and expert on local political history, seemed to contradict the Corning legend with this account in his January 14, 1961 column in Albany's *Knickerbocker*

News. O'Brien's piece was included in *A Loyal and Well Beloved Son of Albany*, a commemorative memorial chapbook dedicated to William Stormont Hackett, Albany's sixty-seventh mayor, who died on March 4, 1926 in a car accident in Havana, Cuba. The book was published with the assistance of the Board of Trustees of City Savings Bank of Albany, whose members included Parker Corning.

O'Brien wrote:

> I know you will recall the Democratic state convention at which Al Smith, nominated by the Democrats for President, was casting furiously about for a gubernatorial candidate who could carry New York for himself and for Smith. The late Peter G. Ten Eyck of Albany was considered, as were others, before the finger of fate pointed in the direction of FDR. And yet, if it were not for a bump in an obscure street in Havana, Roosevelt would not have been the candidate for Governor in 1928 and never would have run for President. Because William S. Hackett of Albany was Smith's choice, as early as 1925, as the Democratic candidate for Governor. Hackett himself had told me so before he departed for his ill-fated trip to Havana. So did another Albany resident, who was present when Smith told Hackett that he, Smith, expected to be nominated for President in 1928 and that he wanted Hackett to be nominated Governor.

William Kennedy said Hackett's untimely death left the door open for Corning. "Corning, in 1927, became lieutenant governor under Smith and the next heir apparent to the governorship. Smith did offer it to him in 1928, but Edwin declined," Kennedy wrote in *O Albany!* Mayor Corning apparently harbored some doubts about his father's story of missed gubernatorial opportunity and set out to conduct his own research into the matter. He received a reply from John Forner Jr., counsel to Lt. Gov. Malcolm Wilson, regarding the mayor's request for official papers from his father's two-year tenure as lieutenant governor between 1926 and 1928. "So far as anyone is able to determine, there are no official papers kept of the Lieutenant Governor," Forner wrote back to Corning on May 4, 1961.

Gov. Malcolm Wilson can be considered the tiebreaker in the Corning-groomed-as-governor story. Wilson spent a record thirty-six years in the state Legislature, fourteen of them as Rockefeller's dutiful lieutenant governor and less than one year as governor to fill Rockefeller's unexpired term. Wilson told me in an interview at Albany's Fort Orange Club how Mayor Corning's mother, Louise, invited Wilson to visit her at the Upper Farm of Corning Hill in 1959 when Wilson was first elected lieutenant governor. "I've never told this story to anyone," said Wilson, who thought Mrs. Corning's request rather odd. He was a conservative Republican and a disciple of Rockefeller, whom the Cornings, diehard Democrats, knew socially from Northeast Harbor in Maine but didn't countenance politically and considered a foe. Wilson recalled:

> I went to see her at her house on Corning Hill. She was very kind and we sat down and she started to tell me a story. She said very few people knew that in 1928, the state Democratic Party wanted to run her husband for governor. He didn't want that at all, she said. But they leaned on him and harassed him and passed resolutions that forced him to go along with their plans. One evening, he came home and told his wife he had to give in and he had accepted the gubernatorial nomination and that night he had a heart attack and stroke from which he never recovered. That was a few days before the state Democratic convention and they were desperate to find a replacement, so they looked around for someone else to run for governor. They got a senator from Hyde Park by the name of Franklin Delano Roosevelt and that changed the course of history.

After her tale had ended, and the tea she had poured for the lieutenant governor had grown cold, Louise Corning said she had a gift for Wilson. And the Democrat presented the Republican with the gavel her husband used during his term as lieutenant governor under Al Smith. Mrs. Corning said she wanted Wilson to have it. "I was immensely touched," Wilson recalled. "I used her husband's gavel the whole time and I still have it. It was a kind gesture on her part and a way for Edwin Corning somehow to live on in politics."

Chapter 3:

Thy Father's Will Be Done:
The Early Years of Erastus Corning 2nd

"O world, all bright and brave and young
With deeds unwrought and songs unsung,
For all the strength thy tasks will give
We greet thee, we about to live."

From Groton School Hymn, by Phillips Brooks

The sense of determinism from his family's legacy in politics was so strong, one could say Erastus Corning 2nd was on a collision course with Albany's City Hall since birth. Literally. One warm afternoon, in the summer of 1910, when baby Erastus was nine months old, his English governess, Miss Cook, went on a routine walk, pushing the firstborn of Edwin and Louise Corning in a baby carriage. Miss Cook met up with her friend, Annie Gwladys Evans Pritchard, a recent Welsh immigrant and a nanny, who worked for a neighbor of the Cornings, the Townsends, who lived on Lark Street, just around the corner from the Cornings at 156 Chestnut Street on Brides Row.

"The two nurses were walking their babies in carriages past the Capitol on Washington Avenue," recalled Grace (Pritchard) Holmes, whose mother, the Townsend's nurse, often recounted the incident. "Miss Cook was distracted somehow, looked away and temporarily let go of Erastus' baby carriage. Almost instantly, the carriage started gathering speed and momentum down the hill. It was heading straight for City Hall. My mother, who was twenty at the time and quite strong, rushed down the street and rescued the carriage, baby and all, and Erastus was safe and sound."

Grace Holmes added this post-script: "Many years later, my mother marched into City Hall, met with the mayor and told him the story. My mother used to tell all her friends she was the one who saved Erastus

Corning in his runaway carriage and he wouldn't be around to be the longest-tenured mayor in the country if it wasn't for her." Pritchard died in 1984 at the age of ninety-five.

Corning escaped the rogue stroller incident unscathed, unlike his namesake, the original Erastus, whose spill from a crib as a baby left him crippled. The disability didn't stop the first Erastus Corning from becoming Albany's richest and most prominent citizen, though, and a four-term mayor. He also graded the hills around City Hall, making them less steep, thus slowing his great-grandson's baby carriage enough, perhaps, to prevent disaster. Such are the labyrinths of Albany history.

After he outgrew the baby carriage and was perambulating on his own, the natural world became the favorite realm for young Erastus 2nd after his father moved his family out of the city and onto hallowed Corning ground at Corning Farm. Young Erastus indulged his passion for collecting flora and fauna on frequent rambles through his own private wooded wonderland. The playground in which Erastus could exercise his naturalist leanings must have seemed immensely vast to a small boy. The Corning Farm – split between the upper farm for Erastus' father and the lower farm for the boy's uncle – comprised some 700 acres. The Corning parcel stretched for more than a mile from the Hudson River all the way up the steep grade known as Corning Hill, to what is Route 9W today, and was a full half-mile wide. It would take a boy the better part of a day to walk from one end to the other. A densely wooded parcel, developed only at its eastern and western margins, the bulk of the land was wild and untamed, protected from the civilizing effects of construction by its deep and rugged ravines and the gorge cut by the Normanskill Creek on one end, bordered by Island Creek on the other.

It must have seemed a magical place to a boy and the Cornings christened the land with a name apropos of its legacy. *Ta-wass-a-gun-shee*, they called it, a Native American word also meaning "Lookout Hill." The easterly edge of the Corning farm lay at the mouth of the Normanskill, which the Indians had used as a burial hill and called Tawasentha, "The Place of the Departed Spirits." The land was owned by Joel Rathbone, who built a summer home in the early 1800s and named it Kenwood, for a village in Scotland. Rathbone's property was purchased by the Cornings in the early-nineteenth century. Today, the property is on the edge of the Town of Bethlehem near the border with Glenmont. But to the Cornings, for more than a century, it was always simply The Farm.

It was in these woods at The Farm that Erastus developed his lifelong love for nature and the environment. His tutelage in naturalist knowledge began early. As with many things a boy of his social class learned at that time, hired help taught Erastus about the outdoors. Miss Cook, the English governess, put her stamp on Erastus' interests early on. "Miss Cook knew everything there was to know about nature and she taught the Corning children about it," said Mary Arthur Doolittle, a playmate and close friend of Erastus' younger sister, Harriet, who had an older sister, Louise, and younger brother, Edwin Jr. (Eddie). Doolittle's father, Hiland Garfield Batcheller, worked as an executive for Edwin Corning at Ludlum Steel and took over the day-to-day operation of the prosperous Menands foundry after Edwin Corning suffered a heart attack and stroke in 1928. "All of the Corning kids were interested in the outdoors because of Miss Cook, but 'Rastus especially. Nature was the most important thing to him. 'Rastus would take long walks in the woods, gather wildflowers and other objects from nature."

This fascination with flora and fauna became deep and abiding. On June 15, 1976, three years shy of his seventieth birthday, when others might have retired to more sedentary retirement pursuits, Mayor Corning sent off for a supply of ants and catalogs from a mail-order company called Cord-Body McMurray Ant. The mayor enclosed fifty cents for sample ants and said he was interested in perhaps purchasing grasshoppers, inchworms and beetles stocked by the company. The mayor had not outgrown the boy who loved bugs.

Miss Cook oversaw these early nature lessons, often leading the four Corning children and their friends on long nature walks around the Corning farm. Erastus' parents were otherwise occupied. The mayor's mother spent most of her free time tending her sprawling formal English garden and Erastus picked up a lifelong love of gardening from her. But between gardening, frequent entertaining, and her charitable work, Mrs. Corning had limited time to spend with Erastus and his siblings. "Sometimes, I just wanted her to come down off her cross because she tried to do so much for her causes," said Norman Rice, director emeritus of the Albany Institute of History & Art and longtime family friend who spent several summers as a houseguest of Mrs. Corning at the Upper Farm. Meanwhile, Erastus' father was consumed with running his steel business and political life on the local, state, and national levels. Servants filled in the major gaps in child rearing left from the lack of parental involvement. Also, the Corning children learned to entertain themselves in solitary pleasures. For Erastus, that meant reading, nature walks, plant and animal collection and identification, bird watching, fishing in the pond near their house, and horseback riding. "All the Cornings rode, of course, because they had quite a stable and the kids each had their own pony," Doolittle recalled. "When they were very little, they rode in a pony cart. Miss Cook taught each of them to ride and she taught me, too. We'd ride all over the countryside and down to the Normanskill."

As with his grandfather's orchids, butterflies, moths and more, the young Erastus' passion became collecting. He collected stamps, trader tokens, coins, campaign buttons, old letters, prints of Albany, and natural history books. "I started collecting all these things when I was nine or ten and it seemed the natural thing to do," Corning told a *Times Union* reporter in 1970. Two of Corning's prized items were a $5 bill issued in 1863 by Albany City Bank, with the signature of his great-grandfather, and a $5 bill from 1890 issued by Albany National Bank signed by his grandfather, Erastus Corning II (also known as Jr.). Erastus Corning used the Arabic 2nd, to distinguish him from his grandfather in a family that didn't believe in middle names.

The best part of a day's visit to the Corning farm for Doolittle in the early 1920s was the magical kingdom known as The Playhouse, a little cabin far out in the woods of the Upper Farm, no adults allowed. The children played any games they wished inside their special space, under the direction of Miss Cook. Friends still recall the Corning Christmas play of 1924, written by Harriet, a precocious eight-year-old girl, with parts for her sister and two brothers, Louise, Erastus and Eddie, and cameos by the children's ponies, as well. Rehearsals were held in The Playhouse. In time, The Playhouse became their rotating nature exhibit, a kind of museum of natural history. "The Playhouse was a marvelous place that was full of wild stuff the Corning kids collected on their walks," Doolittle said. "I remember plants and birds' nests and stuffed owls and raccoons and foxes and anything interesting we had found in the woods. You could walk for miles on their property and you never knew what you were going to find."

Sometimes, they found trouble as a result of their mischief. Erastus had always been told by his nanny and mother not to play on the railroad bridge that crossed the Normanskill Gorge at the northern end of the Corning property. Getting stuck on the trestle by an oncoming train was terrifyingly high drama and grave danger for a boy, especially for the great-grandson of the founder of the New York Central Railroad, who read histories of the railroads and knew a thing or two about the power of locomotives. Erastus recalled his bridge adventure in a letter written to George Hecht on November 23, 1981. Hecht, a Cornell Cooperative Extension agent with Albany County had walked Corning's Glenmont Farm at the mayor's request, to assess its potential timber value (rather poor), when Hecht "almost got hit by a train on the bridge." Recounting an incident when he was eleven or twelve, Corning replied, "I had the same trouble with that railroad bridge something over sixty years ago and I certainly don't want to try it today."

But Erastus was not a troublemaker. In fact, he could be considered something of a mama's boy, raised by female servants and his very proper and strong-willed mother, since Erastus' father, Edwin, had a full life running Ludlum Steel, Albany machine politics, and laying the groundwork for his statewide political aspirations. While his father did not have much time for Erastus, he was known to enjoy children when possible and displayed at times a childlike spirit and sense of playfulness. "My younger sister was very quiet and Mr. Corning always called her Mouse and tried to draw her out," Doolittle recalled. "He was wonderful with kids and we liked going into his library. Even if he was busy, he'd welcome us in and show us something interesting."

Although each child had their own nanny and were encouraged to pursue solitary interests, as a young boy, Erastus' closest playmates were his two sisters, Louise, two years younger, and Harriet, seven years his junior. His little brother, Eddie, was a full decade younger and Erastus was already away at Groton by the time Eddie was four years old. The two brothers later developed a close friendship centered on fishing in Maine, but the pair didn't have much of a chance to bond until after World War II, when both were busy with families and careers. A close boyhood friend of Erastus was his cousin, John Ewart "Jack" McElroy, who was the same age as Erastus. The two attended Albany Academy together and were classmates and members of the same fraternity at Yale. McElroy grew up at 2 Elk Street, along the stretch designated Quality Row, amid the luxury of Albany's old money. The inter-connectedness within the Dutch city's WASP elite, which centered on the Fort Orange Club, St. Peter's Episcopal Church, First Dutch Reformed Church and the Episcopal Cathedral of All Saints, is difficult to tease apart. For instance, McElroy's wife was Cornelia Ransom, whose brother, Andrew Ransom, married

Corning's sister, Louise. Their brief and unhappy marriage was dissolved in Nevada, where Louise's mother brought her daughter for a quick divorce.

During Erastus' boyhood, his parents maintained a busy social schedule, which afforded the Cornings, father and son, even less time together. McElroy remembered that when Erastus wanted to learn something, his father hired someone to teach the boy, rather than try to carve out the time himself to work with Erastus. "I remember his father hired a man to teach Erastus about the outdoors and he showed Erastus how to set up a trapline for small animals down at Corning Farm," McElroy recalled. "Erastus was interested in all kinds of nature things and we liked fishing together. He was wonderful company and I enjoyed being with him."

Although he rarely discussed his childhood with friends, in his later years, Corning, after he had been mayor for more than three decades, began to confide in his secretary, Thelma Dooley. Corning sometimes told Dooley stories about his spending each summer amid the society set in Northeast Harbor, Maine as a young boy. "He said they were basically raised by a nanny and when they went out of the house they had to sign out in a book and sign in when they returned," Dooley recalled. "They were smart kids, though, and they started getting around this rule by forging each other's names, but the nanny eventually caught onto their trick." Roberta Miller, a secretary for the mayor, heard similar stories from Corning about absentee parents. "The mayor told me his mother's full-time job was running the house and servants and all the social obligations so he was basically raised by a nanny," Miller said. The mayor put it plainly once to Rice: "My mother was a true aristocrat." Erastus' sister Harriet's son, Wharton Sinkler III, retained a lasting image of the mayor's mother commanding the household as the center of her domestic universe from the upholstered comfort of an antique sofa, sipping an afternoon cocktail, rye whiskey and water on the rocks. "She had a habit of just rattling the ice in her glass when she finished, signaling the servant to bring her another," Sinkler recalled. "She had that regal quality where she didn't have to ask, didn't have to say a word. Just rattle the ice in the glass. But she always stopped after two drinks. She had that discipline and self-control, unlike her children who so sadly succumbed to alcoholism to varying degrees."

Another lifelong pal of Erastus' was William L. Thompson Jr., a classmate at Albany Academy and Groton School. The two parted ways in college – Thompson went to Harvard – but resumed their close friendship in

Albany after graduation. Thompson, the son of a wholesale drug business owner, was from a Republican family and lived in Troy. Despite the political differences, Thompson and Corning managed to remain close friends their entire lives (Thompson died in 1991). Their parents were in the same social circles and had become good friends. The Thompson and Corning families vacationed together in Maine and Erastus' younger sister, Harriet, was named for a Thompson aunt. "We grew up playing with the Corning kids all the time," recalled Thompson's sister, Martha Becker, known as Patty. She was six years younger than the mayor, and fell between the mayor's two sisters in age. "I remember the mayor and his two sisters were very close and they all seemed very bright. But Erastus was always somewhat quiet. I don't think he was a social type. He made just a few close friends, which is how I remember his father being."

Neither the life of the mind, nor his passion for the natural world, would replace in young Erastus the ache of the absent father. Family friends who knew Erastus his entire life suggest that the lack of fatherly closeness and constancy in Erastus' formative years accounts in part for his somewhat distant, aloof personality. It is a cycle of disengagement, of a lack of intimacy between father and son, that Erastus passed on to his own estranged son, Erastus III, an inheritance handed down to the mayor through at least two previous generations. When put in context of the mayor's time and social class, however, such a sense of emotional distance between father and son was commonplace.

"Erastus was sent away to boarding school when he was twelve, his father was working all the time, was heavily involved in politics and even when the Corning family spent the summer together in Maine, their father stayed behind in Albany mostly to work," Becker recalled. "Erastus really only came back to Albany full-time after graduating from Yale in 1932 and his father died in 1934. I can't see how that can be a very close relationship."

"There were a lot of unresolved father and son issues with the Cornings," Sinkler said. "I remember when Rasty (Erastus III, the mayor's son) was in college, he came down to our house in Philadelphia and talked with my mother and stepfather and said his parents simply did not understand him. My parents were genuinely concerned for him and worried about his deep unhappiness, but they seemed powerless to step in between father and son."

While there was a basic shyness in Erastus, it was by no means a crippling introversion. His was a temperament of quietude that caused him to choose the solitude of the woods over the boisterous chumminess of the playing fields and locker room. From earliest boyhood, Erastus took pleasure in solitary pursuits. At home, he was surrounded with a large, carefully selected library that was strong on classic English literature and the established canon. Early on, he became, and remained throughout his life, a voracious reader. In his youth, Erastus read the great English poets and novelists, the acclaimed histories and biographies, and devoured any book he came across pertaining to natural history and outdoor sports, particularly hunting and fishing – even if his mother frowned upon such topics as unworthy of her son's time. Although it wasn't his first choice, the boy couldn't avoid an interest in reading about politics, which engulfed him from all sides down through the generations as determinedly as his baby carriage lurched toward City Hall. The fate of Erastus Corning 2nd never seemed in doubt.

The Corning book collection of more than 1,000 volumes in the family home at the Upper Farm included many valuable first editions, such as collectible volumes of Charles Lamb, the nineteenth-century English essayist and Romanticist, and Lamb's letters and correspondence with his circle, including Coleridge, given to Edwin Corning by the writer P.G. Patmore, father of the English poet Coventry Patmore. There was also the complete works of Mark Twain, as well as full sets of Longfellow, Wilde, Cather and Hawthorne. Some of the mayor's favorites as a boy were the series of humorous novels about the rural Irish gentry by E.O. Somerville and her cousin, Violet Florence Martin, who wrote under the pen name of Martin Ross. But for sheer reading enjoyment, in Erastus' book, nothing could top the short stories of the American master, O. Henry. In later years, the mayor would read his son and daughter O. Henry stories and recite passages by memory. The library also contained several family Bibles, some of which contained Corning genealogical records. A love of literature ran deep in the family. The mayor's maternal grandmother, Ellen Maxwell, had been a novelist in the Victorian age. And, of course, Erastus received an unavoidable early tutorial in politics. His father had a copy of *The History of Tammany Hall* by Gustavus Myers, with the title page marked by his father's signature, Edwin Corning, 1917. There also was an autobiography of Martin Van Buren, published in 1918 by the American Historical Association, a gift book signed from Lewis Parker to his cousin, Edwin Corning. There was the three-volume *Political History of the State of New York* by D.S. Alexander, published in 1906. For a lesson in the bare-knuckle hurly-burly of Albany machine politics, which he'd later discover firsthand, Erastus received an early primer reading Frank R. Kent's 1928 book, *The Great Game of Politics*. If the young Erastus hadn't had his fill of politics yet, he could always crack his father's bound copy of *Al Smith's Campaign Addresses, 1928*, which the governor autographed to his lieutenant governor, Edwin Corning. The Corning family history made its way into more than one book. The library contained a copy of Frank Walker Stevens' 1926 volume, *Beginnings of New York Central Railroad: The Early Railroad Career of Erastus Corning*. So important were books to the Cornings that the first Erastus received full leather binding treatment by Joel Munsell for *Catalogue of the Library of Erastus Corning*, published in Albany in 1874.

Books were never far from the reach of Erastus as he moved between the city, the country, and the Maine woods. The mayor's parents, Edwin and Louise, were married in 1908. They were living in Albany's Center Square neighborhood when Erastus, their firstborn, arrived in 1909. The Corning couple's townhouse at 156 Chestnut Street, just off Lark Street, was part of Brides Row, a block of solid and respectable, if not opulent, brick residences for newlyweds of Albany's ruling class. Still just three years out of Yale, Edwin Corning, nonetheless, had big plans and he began dreaming about building a grand residence befitting the president of fast-growing Ludlum Steel. He had social appearances to think of, too, and family precedent for opulent domiciles. Edwin's grandfather and father lived across from each other on lower State Street, the son in a house built in 1790 by Mayor Philip Schuyler Van Rensselaer, brother of Albany's last patroon. Huybertie Pruyn Hamlin, related to the Cornings through marriage, recalled the Corning residence in the 1880s as "a beautiful house, with a garden at the rear, and there we played croquet in the summer, and in the winter coasted on a toboggan slide," Pruyn wrote in her memoirs, *An Albany Girlhood*, describing a lush backyard grotto with rock gardens, cascading water spouts and ponds with carp named for prominent Democratic politicians of the day – Samuel Tilden, Horatio Seymour *et al.* The grounds kept Mr. Gray, the Corning's Scottish gardener, quite busy. He filled the house with vases and china tubs of flowers. "Sometimes, when giving a dinner, they had the table arranged so that a sunken zinc tank was in the center holding water," Pruyn recalled. "Around the edge were Farleyens ferns and lovely orchids and small gold fish swam around tiny rocks and islands."

Edwin's father, Erastus Corning Jr., died in debt in 1897 when Edwin was just fourteen and the State Street mansion had to be sold, but there was always The Farm, vast acreage in the family since the early 1800s, and land was wealth. But first, there was one more brief stop in the city before the Cornings became country squires. When the mayor was five years old, his parents moved from Chestnut Street to a larger house on Washington Avenue next to the Thacher Home, almost directly across from the Fort Orange Club, an elite private club the mayor's grandfather helped establish. The newlyweds were biding their time as Edwin Corning built up a substantial cash flow at Ludlum Steel and the family could afford to construct its dream house. By the time Erastus was ready to enter Albany Academy at the age of eight, the Cornings had moved to The Farm on the southern outskirts of Albany and lived as gentleman farmers. At *Ta-wass-a-gun-shee*, in pre-World War I optimism, Edwin built his family The House of Corning, a sprawling center hall Colonial home, an imposing brick structure with tall gables and a half-dozen chimneys leading from its many fireplaces and eleven bathrooms. That's what family friends remember eight decades after it was built: eleven bathrooms. What luxury.

It was called "The Big House" and it is where Erastus grew up in richly appointed splendor, though modest compared to Edwin Corning's first and even more grandiose vision. "The Cornings had built a much larger mansion before The Big House," Doolittle said. "But it burned down just before they were supposed to move in. They lost a lot of money in the fire and were forced to scale back on some of the extravagances for The Big House." Details of the 1916 fire are sketchy, and insurance did not cover the heavy financial loss. Sinkler recalled: "Family legend had it that the mayor's father called the chief of the local fire department and said, 'This is Edwin. My house is burning down.' The fire chief was drunk and thought he was playing a trick and calling himself Ed Wynn, the comedian. As a result, the house burned down." Whatever the details, the fire's devastation was tempered somewhat by Edwin Corning's stroke of good fortune in winning a farmhouse kit at a home show at Albany's Washington Avenue Armory in 1920. The six-bedroom brick house he won and had assembled on the western edge of the farm served as the gardener's quarters until Erastus and Betty were married in 1932 and it became the newlyweds' home, although they maintained a residence on South Lake Avenue in Albany to fulfill the requirement that the mayor live within the city limits.

The Big House that Edwin Corning hastily had rebuilt after the fire – and eventually moved into on March 16, 1917 – could not rival in size or architectural indulgence the extraordinary mansion and estate his brother, Parker, owned just down Corning Hill on the Lower Farm. Still, Erastus came of age amid a dozen or more spacious rooms and servants galore, all of it surrounded by the tasteful elegance of old money. The livingroom housed a Steinway grand piano. Oriental rugs covered the oak floors. Antiques filled the rooms, alongside decorative and functional game tables; the Cornings were known for a sense of play and for entertaining regularly. "They worked hard, but never forgot how to play," it was often said of the Cornings. An elaborately carved eighteenth-century mahogany desk commanded attention in Edwin's library. The dining room table was surrounded by two dozen nineteenth-century Chippendale mahogany chairs. The mayor's parents liked paintings of Oriental landscapes, nature scenes and Maine coastal images. There were nineteenth-century prints, as well, of Antarctica and whale fishing. His parent's nineteenth-century mahogany double bed was a four-poster. His mother's dining room cabinets were filled with numerous silver tea services, Louis Philippe and Crown Derby china, commemorative Yale plates and Garden Club of America dishes by Wedgewood. A prized heirloom, now at the Albany Institute, was a one hundred-ounce sterling silver covered tureen and stand made in 1851 by Ball, Tompkins & Black of New York and given to the original Erastus by the Utica and Schenectady Railroad.

The Big House was only the centerpiece of the Upper Farm where Erastus grew up. The home also had seven outbuildings, a half-mile horse racetrack, barns and greenhouses where the world-renowned Corning orchids were raised. There were still herds of livestock left over from the mayor's grandfather's days as a renowned cattleman. There were extensive greenhouses that once contained grapes, lemons, oranges and bananas. But the magnet for relatives and friends of the Corning children was the swimming pool. Just after World War I, Edwin Corning installed a large, poured concrete in-ground swimming pool, believed to be the first in the Albany area. It was a big draw. "The swimming pool was a big, marvelous one and everyone thought it was wonderful. We had never seen anything like it," Doolittle recalled. "I remember it was a bother to keep clean and they had a lot of trouble with algae, but we loved it." The servants, of course, took care of such details.

Soon enough, however, Erastus' sylvan idyll at the Corning Farm would come to an end. His unstructured, joyous rambling through the woods, riding ponies around the property, romping with his sisters and their friends, collecting natural specimens and studying them at The Playhouse, fishing for hours and roaming purely for pleasure and not purpose – the delicious freedom of his charmed boyhood – were drawing to an abrupt close. In the fall of 1917, a month before his eighth birthday, family tradition reared its head in the form of Albany Academy. There was no question as to what school Erastus would attend. It was the school where his father, and assorted other Cornings, were first enrolled. "The Cornings were like that when it came to tradition, very strict on doing things the same way the family had always done them," Sinkler said. "Parents often model a secret life for their children. The path was laid out for Erastus from the time he was born."

Erastus spent five years at the old Albany Academy, which now houses the Albany Board of Education offices, located in Academy Park at Park and Elk streets, amid the city's most architecturally prominent triangle and bounded by the state Capitol, City Hall, the Court of Appeals and state Education Building. Some architectural historians consider it one of the most elegant historic corridors in the country. For Albany Academy, the estimable Phillip Hooker was chosen to design the Georgian building that is considered one of the finest creations of the famous Albany architect. The formidable facade was constructed of Nyack freestone, a brooding, dark red brownstone that suggested an air of somberness. The structure was imposing, with two wings, a cupola and spacious classrooms. The cornerstone was laid July 29, 1815. The structure cost $91,000, a fortune in that day.

Albany Academy had been founded by a group of influential citizens headed by Mayor Philip S. Van Rensselaer, who appealed to the Board of Regents in February, 1813, for permission to operate a school. Something of a junior version of The Fort Orange Club, the self-appointed educators established an institution that met their high standards and would teach their boys (girls were not considered worthy of such an educational investment at this juncture in Albany history) how to lead their city, their state, their country. Such was the WASP aristocracy's burden, its sense of *noblesse oblige*. The Regents granted their approval in March, 1813 and the first session of Albany Academy was held in a small wooden building at the southeast corner of State and Lodge streets owned by Albany's first patroon, Kiliaen Van Rensselaer. The magnificent Hooker building succeeded those temporary quarters. In the ensuing 180 years, Albany Academy developed a rich legacy. Joseph Henry, who later became Secretary of the Smithsonian Institution, demonstrated the theory of the magnetic telegraph for transmitting sound there in 1828. Renowned theologian and philosopher Henry James Sr., father of the celebrated novelist Henry James Jr., was a student at the Academy who was badly burned in 1824 when a hot-air balloon experiment failed and caught fire. The burns were so severe, James' leg eventually had to be amputated. Among the illustrious roster of Academy students was *Moby Dick* author Herman Melville and the eminent jurist Learned Hand, who spent fifty years on the bench, a federal district court judge who has been called "the greatest judge never to be appointed to the Supreme Court."

Hand, who was born at 224 State Street just around the corner from the Academy, began attending at age seven in 1879. Hand criticized the overly rigid education. "Hand's memories of his lower-school years were predominantly unpleasant – a sense of 'being scared,' perhaps an understandable reaction from a sheltered youngster finding himself amid two hundred or so other boys for the first time," wrote Hand's biographer, Gerald Gunther in *Learned Hand: The Man and the Judge*. Hand decried "the lack of intellectual excitement" and recalled that he encountered stimuli at the Academy only as "the competition for grades and the satisfaction of completing assigned tasks."

Erastus Corning's experience at Albany Academy was not unlike Hand's. Erastus, something of a loner, lost in his reading and his naturalist preoccupation, was immediately thrust into the world of Albany Academy's two hundred boys and he seemed to have been overshadowed by his more aggressive peers. In fact, Erastus apparently made almost no impression at all at Albany Academy when he entered the Class of 1928 on September 18, 1917.

"I always considered it curious, and something of a mystery, that I never knew Erastus Corning at Albany Academy," said Edwin Shultes III. Shultes, a few months younger than Erastus, entered Albany Academy in the fall of 1918 at the age of nine. Shultes later was a classmate of Corning's at Yale (both graduated Phi Beta Kappa, Class of '32). Shultes practiced law for a leading Albany law firm after graduation and, despite his being a Republican, remained a social friend of Erastus' over the years. "I knew everyone at the Academy, we all knew each other and the classes were tight-knit. Erastus and I were both Class of '28, and yet I didn't know Erastus there," said Shultes, who was editor-in-chief of the school newspaper, the *Fish and Pumpkin*. "All I can figure is that we were in different classrooms and Erastus was either not involved in school activities, or was very shy, so I never really got to know him."

Another classmate of Corning's at Albany Academy was Jacob Herzog, whose father, Lester Herzog, ran a coal company and became a Democratic ward leader for the O'Connell-Corning machine when it overthrew the Barnes GOP regime in 1921. Lester Herzog's reward from his friend, William Hackett, the newly elected Democratic mayor, was the position of public works commissioner. Despite the political connections and the fact that both Corning and Herzog counted William Thompson Jr. among their best friends, Herzog never felt close to Corning at Albany Academy.

"Bill was one of our best friends, Bill and Erastus went through Groton together and Bill always said Erastus never really joined the group," Herzog recalled. "Erastus just wasn't outgoing and he always held even Bill at arm's length. Bill thinks it was a basic shyness with Erastus. Bill and I talked about that a lot, about how Erastus never let anyone get really close to him, how he remained an enigma. I believe it began when he was a boy just starting school."

School files at Albany Academy fail to fill in gaps during Erastus' enigmatic career at Albany Academy. Records show Corning entered Albany Academy on September 18, 1917 into Preparatory Department C. Erastus, eight years old, was one of fourteen boys in the class. Upon entering the school, Erastus was fitted with a military uniform: eighteen large brass buttons festooned the front of the gray jacket, overwhelming the boy's scrawny chest, which he tried to puff out, his neck held rigid by a stiff collar as he posed for a school portrait in full military dress. The gray trousers, with black piping down the leg, were held up by a wide white belt and thick brass buckle. The uniform ensemble was completed with white gloves and a black patent leather military cap with more brass insignia and a cone headpiece. In addition, there were mock rifles made of wood and painted white for these miniature warriors. Military drills were a major extracurricular activity at Albany Academy and a place where a boy could excel as much as in the classroom.

Even the youngest boys were incorporated into Albany Academy's School Battalion, inaugurated in 1870, consisting of three companies with their commissioned officers all under the command of a major. Participation in the daily afternoon military drills was mandatory. "This military training develops an erect carriage, neatness in dress, the habit of prompt obedience, and the ability to command others. As an incentive to thoroughness certain medals are awarded annually to the best drilled members of the Battalion. This military organization forms an essential part of the school life, supplying a daily interest to the boys, culminating in the important military events of the Competitive and Guidon Drills. Instruction in cavalry drill was suspended during the War," according to the 1928 *Class Book*.

Despite the competition encouraged in the military drills, sports were not heavily emphasized and the focus was on intramural participation. Contests against other schools were almost non-existent. "In athletics the Academy aims not, primarily, to turn out a winning team but to develop the habit of taking systematic exercise," the class book said. "A regular instructor is employed to organize and supervise the games. All boys – but especially those who are disinclined to play – are encouraged to engage actively in the sports peculiar to each season." Growing up, Erastus was tall and skinny and suffered as a young boy with respiratory illnesses and other frequent sicknesses, and thus never developed into an exceptional athlete. He played baseball and boxed, his only team sports, with limited success. His preference was for solitary sports; the only ones he pursued in adulthood were fishing, hunting and golf.

The Albany Academy has always prided itself on a well-rounded college preparatory curriculum that was fast, focused and disciplined. "It aims to furnish the most thorough preparation at the earliest age, the average age of the graduating class being seventeen. This is accomplished by concentrating the work of the pupil on preparation for college, never allowing him to be sidetracked by anticipating college studies or to scatter his energies over a large number of subjects, interesting but comparatively useless. This makes a direct savings of two years in school life, with the additional advantage of an early entrance upon professional life," the class book stated. The walls of the chapel had portraits of benefactors Thomas W. Olcott, Gen. Stephen Van Rensselaer, Peter Gansevoort, Henry Pitt Warren and Dr. Philip Ten Eyck – Academy benefactors and the city's Dutch ruling class. Although Corning's heritage was English, he had the right pedigree to assume the WASP ascendancy that was the ultimate goal of prep schools. In order to achieve lofty intellectual goals, Erastus and the other boys were kept on a short tether. The scattershot, purely-for-pleasure reading Erastus had done as a youngster was finished. Everything at the Albany Academy was done with a clear purpose. No wasted thinking, no wasted time. Erastus entered during the waning days of one of the school's most revered headmasters, Henry Pitt Warren, who became headmaster in 1886 and held the job until his death in 1919. Warren's successor, Islay F. McCormick, contributed to the Academy's well-deserved reputation for academic excellence. The teachers were primarily women in the lower levels, the Preparatory Department (ages six through twelve), which Erastus attended – the last time he would be taught by nurturing women in his academic career. "These are permanent teachers of widely recognized ability in their several departments, possessing a force of character and a power of personality that is calculated to develop all that is best in a boy," the class book said.

Throughout a boy's career at Albany Academy, the course of studies was rigid and narrow: Reading, Language, Arithmetic, History, Geography, Drawing/Music. When Erastus entered Class C at the age of nine, his classes consisted of phonic analysis, sentence structure, spelling, penmanship, letter writing, dictation, multiplication, units of measure, history stories, sand table, and (his favorite class) use of maps and natural forms of land and water. Two years later, in Class A, he was reading *Kingsley's Greek Heroes* by John Tetlow and *Tales of Ancient Greece* by Rev. George W. Cox. Grammar lessons were supplemented with French conversation. History of the United States and geography of the western continent were the most appealing to Erastus. The school guideline called for two to three hours of study at home daily, divided between afternoon and evening sessions. "Few young boys can play all the afternoon, and study with profit in the evening," the class book advised. "Parents are urged not to allow their sons to make social engagements for any of the first four evenings of the week." Corning, a diligent student, rail thin as a boy, apparently did not linger long in The Buttery, the two cafeterias in the Academy where "wholesome, well-cooked food" was served for lunch. Discipline was drilled into young Erastus at every juncture in the school day; moral bearing and obedience was at the foundation of the institution: "A dishonest boy finds that he is despised by his classmates and either changes his habits or leaves the school. Besides, association with boys from good families encourages gentlemanly bearing and high standards of conduct."

By all accounts, Erastus toed the line at Albany Academy and quietly followed all the rigid rules and staunch regulations. He earned excellent grades. Not only was the Albany Academy tradition draped over him as starched and confining as his military uniform, but there was no escaping the sense of duty-bound service and excellence expected from his own family, who were large financial benefactors of the Academy. Erastus was a Corning, after all, and Corning achievement was expected of him. Despite being detached and emotionally remote from his son, Erastus' father engineered his son's educational and career track in the same way his had been relentlessly shaped, with the regularity and cold, hard logic of the family's steelmaking plant. There was a symmetry in the multi-generational Groton-Yale, Groton-Yale, Groton-Yale Corning tradition and the mold was not to be broken with Erastus. Edwin Corning began corresponding about his son's fate in 1921, when Erastus was twelve, with Rev. Endicott Peabody, the founder and headmaster of Groton School in Groton, Massachusetts, where his father joined a line of Cornings.

There was a twinge of parental protection about sending the shy and socially reticent Erastus off to boarding school at the tender age of twelve, but his father and grandfather and other assorted Cornings had undergone the same ritual. Duty called. Still, Edwin Corning wrote to Peabody on April 3, 1922, "I cannot say that I look forward very much to having him leave us, but it is a fine thing to know the school that he is going to."

The negotiations had begun and the correspondence between Edwin Corning and Peabody took on the tone of a business transaction. Edwin Corning wrote to Peabody on January 12, 1922, "I suppose you would probably want him to enter the first form. If he stays at the Albany Academy next year he will enter the third form which would make him enter college when he was just seventeen years old, which I consider too young." The father went on to tout his son's class standing – he ranked in the first quarter of thirty-five pupils in his class for the last couple of years – and wondered whether his son's limited Latin coursework at the Academy would hinder him at Groton. "If he has sufficient Latin probably he is far enough along in his studies to enter the first form. I would rather like to take him out of school now and turn him loose on the farm until he leaves for Groton. He has now completed the same work that I had at the Boys Academy before going to Groton, and you may not remember but during my first form year I headed the class every month due entirely I think to my preparation for Groton, as I never did any such thing after the first form year." Corning's father did not oversell his son's abilities in sports to the Groton headmaster. "While not a probable athletic star he manages to hold his own in football, hockey, baseball and is more or less of an expert swimmer and a fair horse back rider, besides being a pretty good trapper and a fairly good shot."

Peabody was suitably impressed with the boy. More importantly, the fervent desire that Erastus attend Groton coming from his father, a Groton man who had maintained a personal correspondence with his former headmaster over the years, insured Erastus' acceptance. But Islay F. McCormick, the headmaster of Albany Academy, realized the fine student he was losing in Erastus and didn't let his charge go after five years at the Academy without a struggle. McCormick, delaying in responding to requests for Erastus' transcripts from Albany Academy, engaged in a subtle tug-of-war with Peabody and Groton for enrollment of the boy: "Dr. McCormick doesn't take very kindly to boys leaving the Academy for boarding school, but I think I will succeed in getting his cooperation before long," Erastus' father wrote to Peabody on April 22, 1922. McCormick relented and surrendered the still-unformed piece of clay he had been shaping for the past five years at Albany Academy and shipped young Erastus off to his rival educator in Groton, writing Peabody: "He is a fine boy and I dislike to see him go, but I congratulate you on your acquisition." Against his own desires, the acquisition property was sent off that fall of 1922 – in his father's chauffeur-driven Dusenberg – to follow a Corning's predetermined pathway.

The soaring Gothic spires of St. John's Chapel that seem to pierce the clouds above Groton School must have looked impossibly high to Erastus Corning, a smallish, thin and often sickly twelve-year-old boy who arrived under the long shadow cast by their daunting ideals in the fall of 1922. The spires rivet one's attention upon entering the wrought-iron gates of Groton in the northeastern corner of Massachusetts, in an area of Yankee privilege marked by stately Colonial homes and gentlemen's estates. The spires are a kind of psychological signpost pointing to the great expectations burdening the boys granted access to those portals. The spires also stand as sentinels over the rigidly designed, tightly contained Groton campus, a half-dozen formidable brick structures impersonating English manors and forming a wall around a broad oval lawn and circular driveway – like wagons that have been circled against attack – a design of impregnability not unlike the Corning burial plot at Albany Rural Cemetery. "A great WASP Ascendancy fortress," was how Corning's classmate, Joseph Alsop, the eminent Washington political columnist, described Groton in his memoirs. This WASP Ascendancy, as embodied in the Groton students, Alsop wrote, "was substantially richer and enjoyed substantially more leverage than other Americans" and also "felt a right – even a duty – to set the tone for the rest of the country."

Theodore Roosevelt attended Groton. So, too, did Franklin Delano Roosevelt. FDR had passed through the same gate at Groton and viewed the same spires two decades before Corning, and so would boys who later became President of the United States, Secretary of State, Secretary of the Treasury, Attorney General, Ambassador, Foreign Minister, Congressman, state legislator, and mayor. W. Averell Harriman, Francis Biddle, Douglas Dillon, McGeorge Bundy, Dean Acheson – the *Who's Who* list could go on and on. There were children and grandchildren of the financier J.P. Morgan and a thick slice of the greatest wealth in the nation represented by Harrimans, Webbs, McCormicks, Vanderbilts, and Stillmans. These boys were considered the aristocracy of America and their fathers had membership in the most exclusive clubs, such as the Somerset, the Knickerbocker, the Philadelphia or the Baltimore clubs. Harriman's biographer, Rudy Abramson, wrote: "In an atmosphere of uncompromising regimentation, Dr. Peabody's charges absorbed reverence for the social order, confirmed their place in it, and came face-to-face with their responsibilities. Groton was where the Protestant establishment renewed itself – the school of Roosevelts, Whitneys, Vanderbilts, an academy for America's first families."

In 1922, as young Erastus entered this inner sanctum of WASP Ascendancy and its century-old status quo control on American politics, the Fascists were marching on Rome, Italy's King Victor Emanuel III invited Benito Mussolini to be Prime Minister and the Communist Revolution was codified with the establishment of the Union of Soviet Socialist Republics. But such cataclysmic world events caused nary a blade of grass to bend out of place on the verdant Groton campus, with its WASP Ascendancy certainties: "their faith unshaken, their principles immovable," was part of the school's Graduates' Prayer new boys entering Groton with Corning would be taught.

We have no record of young Erastus' first, indelible impression of Groton as he entered the gate – certainly in a suit, dark gray or navy blue, a brown suit being considered too informal for the school – and slammed headlong into the imposing edifices that amounted to a kind of symbolic arranged marriage that his father had engineered for him. For a boy who had known the freedom of roaming the backwoods of Corning Farm in Glenmont indulging his passion for unfettered naturalist ramblings, and who had attended the Albany Academy when it was housed in a single building on familiar downtown Albany turf, the utterly foreign world of Groton must have jarred Erastus.

When Corning arrived with twenty-two other boys entering "First Form," the lowest level, roughly equivalent to seventh grade, the future mayor received an instant primer on Grotonian hierarchy. The First Formers were required to hand over whatever money they brought with them, from which they were provided a weekly stipend of twenty-five cents, a nickel of which was expected to be dropped into the collection plate at Sunday chapel services. The Groton School headmaster, Rev. Endicott Peabody, the school's founder, icon and guiding light, addressed a gathering of Erastus' class in Saint John's Chapel shortly after their arrival. He didn't waste time setting the strict tone: Joseph Alsop wrote in his memoirs that this "awe-inspiring" man "did his level best to drill his boys in the gentleman's values of sport, religion, and learning. The result was a fiercely rarefied and homogeneous environment in which obedience and conformity were commended by one's teachers as well as by one's peers. Independence, in almost any form, was punished."

Peabody was born in 1857 in Salem, Massachusetts. His great-grandfather amassed wealth by trade with China and India. After attending a British prep school, Cheltenham, and Trinity College, Cambridge, Peabody became an Episcopal minister. He retained British manners, a taste for cricket, and the dry humor he picked up in England during his school days. In 1884, the twenty-seven-year-old Peabody established Groton, an American boarding school masquerading as Cheltenham. Very British, indeed. "Every endeavor will be made to cultivate manly, Christian character, having regard to moral and physical as well as intellectual development," Peabody wrote in a manifesto outlining his new school's philosophy. The Groton way was austere, almost monastic: supper dress was starched white shirts, stiff Eton collars, ties and spit-shined black leather pumps; morning chapel was mandatory after a cold shower at the crack of dawn; washing was with cold water only at long group sinks that functioned as communal troughs in the basement. The day began with chapel service and ended with evening prayer. Each boy was required to take a Sacred Studies course each term. Severe punishments were meted out by

Peabody for swearing, telling religious jokes, fooling around in chapel, or gambling. Groton alumnus George Biddle described Peabody as "some splendid eleventh- or twelfth-century crusader; the militant Christian, half warrior, half priest."

It was young Averell Harriman who once offered his father this assessment of Peabody: "You know, he would be an awful bully if he weren't such a terrible Christian" – meaning terrifying. Harriman's biographer, Abrahamson, wrote, "Under Peabody's stern guidance, boys scarcely out of their mother's laps began their academic preparation for Harvard or Yale and their moral and physical tempering for the leadership of the nation's vital institutions." Peabody considered all the Groton students "his boys" and he was a fiercely paternal presence, deciding what was right and best for "his family."

The writer and artist George Biddle, Class of 1904, wrote in his memoir: "The Groton code was snobbish rather than military, precise rather than regimented, socially conservative rather than actually hostile to scholarship. . . . My indictments against Groton are these. Its effect was to stifle the creative impulse. Its code could tolerate a feeling of shame for one's brother; and by and large, in many small ways, it was intellectually dishonest . . . During my years there, I was on the edge of a nervous breakdown."

It was evident early on at Groton that the willful Erastus, through whom an independent streak ran long and deep, was among those who found Peabody's control smothering. In response, Corning sought ways to open forbidden windows and to allow some fresh air into the rarefied atmosphere. "They really drilled the discipline into us and I think 'Rastus found that difficult," recalled classmate Alexander Forbes, a fellow member of the class of 1928. "They worked hard to make us conform, which I did, but I remember 'Rastus was a free-thinking guy with his own ideas and there was something of the rebel in him."

Before long, Erastus became familiar with "the cellar," a kind of purgatory, a dark and mythic place beneath the dormitories "where all punishments for being 'fresh' were decided on and sentence carried out," the 1928 class yearbook said. The cellar also would become Corning's crucible, a term, as the boy would know from his father's steel business, which defined the container where substances were heated to high temperatures. As First Formers, the runts of Groton, Erastus and his twenty-two fellow classmates who entered in 1922 – six years away from their graduation – were subject to all manner of hazing from upper classmen. The upper classmen were granted the power to police the First Formers and boys in the lower forms and to assign in the student's file "black marks" for alleged infractions.

It didn't take much – an errant glance, a perceived lack of deference, a wayward word – for a terrified First Former to receive that ominous command, "The Second Form wishes to see you downstairs," followed by the frightful march down the wooden stairs to the cellar. The ritual went like this: "Down with your pants." Then the belts "whistled," as one chronicler described it. "Some were stoic and bit their lip, some shrieked, and some were never licked at all," their class yearbook reported. The punishments meted out on the First Formers ranged from "a mild beating" to being "beaten purple and red," according to the yearbook. The First Formers had to rest content in the knowledge, even as they heard and felt the whistle of the belt on their backsides, that their day would come, that "the wheel of fortune swings round" and they'd have their turn "wielding the lash upon refractory new kids," in the words of the yearbook. Another punishment was known as "pumping." Biddle described this time-honored Groton practice in his memoir. "Over the lavatory faucet a fourth-former sat with a stop watch. A first offender was given only about ten seconds. The water came from the open spigot with tremendous force and the stream could be concentrated in violence by thumb and forefinger. Besides the culprit was winded and frightened and held upside down during the pumping. He was being forcibly drowned for eight or ten seconds. Then he was jerked to his feet, coughing, choking, retching. He was asked if he understood why he was being pumped. It wasn't hazing, remember, it was discipline."

Corning did not chronicle his pumpings or other frightening and humiliating episodes of hazing at the hands of upper classmen, but no first former escaped the punishment. Those were the worst aspects of Groton, but even in the best of times, the young Erastus seemed vaguely unhappy and filled with an unexpressed melancholy. It wasn't a matter of thriving at Groton; it was a matter of surviving. But his father had pushed the boy onto the Groton path and desired Erastus to be sculpted into the Peabody mold with such fervor that the youngster was afraid to disappoint. Erastus apparently learned not to express the sadness and disappointments he felt at Groton, so as not to unduly disturb his father who was so intensely immersed in business and politics back in Albany.

Peabody, called "The Rector" by the boys, tried to soften the stern environment of Groton with some semblance of a family feel. He'd pass out Necco mints for the boys to chew while he read them stories from P.G.

Wodehouse at night. He invited the boys to play parlor games at his house in the evening two nights a week. "The family atmosphere was lost at Groton, despite the Rector's attempts," said Rev. Charles W. Sheerin, an alumnus and former faculty member who lives in Albany and was a friend of Erastus and Betty Corning. "Instead, the boys learned WASP reticence and you can see that in the mayor by the way he compartmentalized his life. The influence of Peabody on those boys was overwhelming. I'm sure Erastus got into politics not only because of his father, but because of the sense of social service Peabody drilled into him at Groton."

Others in his class wrote down for posterity what Erastus Corning surely was feeling himself in his Groton melancholy. One was Corning's close friend, classmate Richard Bissell, who went on to become a top official in the Central Intelligence Agency. Bissell's recollections of Groton were published in 1996, *Memoirs of a Cold Warrior: From Yalta to the Bay of Pigs*. Bissell wrote, "In the first year or two at Groton especially, I suffered a great deal from homesickness. Instead of returning each day to a warm and friendly family setting, I went to a dormitory after evening school and had to live with boys my own age, most of whom I didn't like and most of whom didn't like me. I was shy, I wasn't a good athlete, and I was scared of them."

Bissell and Corning, both fundamentally shy, shared other personality traits, as well as a connection to Maine, where their families spent summers, and the two became good friends. Even if the young boys managed to avoid the hostilities and harassment of the upper classmen for a time, life at Groton was never easy or designed for comfort. Bissell wrote, "Life at Groton seemed to me austere; our time and space were rigorously structured." He described the dormitory's rows of cubicles, sparsely furnished, offering only partial privacy with seven-foot high partitions and curtains instead of doors. Within this austere setting, Corning seemed to take pride in a rebellious streak that flouted the school's rigidity. "I succeeded in getting three black marks today for kicking someone under the table," Erastus wrote to his mother in October of his First Form year. Five years later, he mentioned to his mother in a letter that three black marks caused him to be evicted from his large room with a bathroom in it to a tiny cubicle upstairs as punishment. He mocked his upperclassmen judge and jurors, though, by noting "the beds are much bigger and wider upstairs and we can stretch out in them."

Corning received his lashings like the rest down in the cellar that first year at Groton, but in his second year, the wheel of fortune, as the yearbook predicted, had indeed swung 'round. When Philip Boyer, a cocky kid and top baseball prospect, got into a scrap with Erastus, the son of the Albany steelmaker refused to back down. "I'll see you after supper downstairs" was the formal challenge Corning made to Boyer and down they went to that crucible below the dormitories. His classmates had gotten wind of Corning's fighting words and they pushed and crowded to claim ringside seats atop large boxes containing winter boots. A white, dusty stone floor was the canvas for Corning and Boyer as they punched it out in "the battle of the century which none of us will forget," according to the yearbook. No word on the outcome of the fight for the record, but 'Rastus, as his classmates called him, was remembered at Groton as a good boxer and he was a year older than Boyer. Erastus emerged from the cellar with a new toughness, tempered in the way steel is, confident of challenging the old order of Groton, at least a little, and buoyed by the admiration of his Second Formers.

"He wasn't very big at Groton and didn't sprout until Yale, but he wasn't afraid of anybody. He used to get in a fight about every other day. He could hold his own, though," recalled Charles Devens, the most popular student in the class, elected officer in top positions, star athlete and captain of the baseball team, who went on to pitch in the major leagues for the New York Yankees.

Although Erastus was away from home for the first time at Groton, making tentative forays into independence, he remained very much under his father's influence and the boy's interests, to a large extent, mirrored those of his father during his boarding school days. Erastus was the spitting image of his father physically, as well, comparing pictures from their early years at Groton. Erastus had his father's delicate face, Romanesque nose slightly upturned, high cheekbones, full lips and wide-set blue eyes with a deep intensity. In academics their interests merged, too. For instance, Erastus was very much interested in Latin when he entered Groton. Edwin Corning had won Groton's coveted Latin Prize as top Latin student in 1902, the same award Franklin Delano Roosevelt had received in 1900. The Latin Prize did not go to Erastus in 1928, but other scholastic prizes did, and academics became the currency with which Erastus purchased his sometimes difficult passage through Groton. His years of making his own fun around the Corning Farm, hours spent in solitary pleasure fishing in Maine, and a voracious reading habit, particularly about the outdoors, accounted for some of the aloofness classmates expressed about Erastus at Groton. There was something of the loner in Erastus, yet students were naturally drawn to him because of his impressive intellect.

"He was one of the smartest guys I ever met," said Dr. F. Sargent Cheever, Corning's classmate in the class of 1928 and retired dean of the Pittsburgh University Medical School. "Groton is very competitive and we were ranked and examined at the end of every month. Erastus was always at the top or very close to the top. In a very bright class, he was one of the brightest stars."

Despite his scholastic superiority, Corning was not at the center of his First Form universe at Groton, preferring to move in an orbit on the fringes. "I remember he was somewhat shy when he got to Groton and it took him awhile to get over that," Devens said. Devens recalled that Corning did not become fast friends with him, or the chosen few at the center of Groton social life, but, instead, sought his company in boys who were outsiders. In that regard, Corning found a kindred spirit in Joseph Alsop. Besides a formidable intellect rivaled only by Corning at Groton, Alsop had pedigree, too. Ancestors on his father's side included some of the wealthiest men in America. His maternal grandmother was the sister of Theodore Roosevelt and his mother was Eleanor Roosevelt's first cousin. Despite the fact that Alsop was a cousin to the Roosevelts, who were among Groton's patron saints, Alsop remained a tortured outcast at Groton. Alsop could boast guests at his family's house that included FDR (then governor of New York) and William Amory Gardner, one of the founders of Groton School, but this name dropping didn't relieve the merciless humiliations aimed at Alsop – who was fat, bookish, inept at sports and friendless. "A Groton winter term is grim under the best of circumstances," Alsop recalled in his memoirs. "A Groton winter term without human company was grim beyond imagining. So those few months were a desolate and lonely period; indeed, it was the only time I'd ever thought seriously of taking my own life."

Corning, refusing to join in the taunts of his classmates, instead befriended the ostracized Alsop. "Corning was someone who had weight in the class by virtue of his intellect and he wasn't someone who was teased or ridiculed for being close to Alsop," said classmate Alexander Forbes. Corning and Alsop were a formidable pair of intellects. Alsop and his brother, Stewart (Groton Class of '32), went on to become two of the most revered – and feared – journalists in Washington. The Alsops became close personal friends of John F. Kennedy and other presidents and became viewed almost as policy consultants. The pair wrote the syndicated political column, "Matter of Fact," and were the authors individually and collectively of several books.

At Groton, Joseph Alsop was the class eccentric, brainy and odd, always lugging a stack of books with his name labeled on each. Besides being pudgy and timid, Alsop had a soft, almost feminine face and he was the one cast for female parts in school plays – as was Corning. Despite his limited athletic ability, Corning could mix easily with any of his classmates and was not at all an oddball, but Erastus found in Alsop a kindred spirit. Both possessed brilliant minds and they matched each other academically stride for stride. "From the very beginning at Groton, I did well academically," Joseph Alsop wrote. "Term after term, the future mayor of Albany, Erastus Corning, and I would divide first place in our form."

Corning developed a close friendship with Alsop, who was later revealed as a homosexual. In his biography of the Alsop brothers, Robert W. Merry cited irrefutable evidence of Joseph Alsop's sexual preference. "Joe, whose life had been one of bachelorhood . . . harbored a dark personal secret. He was homosexual. Privately, some of his friends speculated about his sexuality, but no one ever asked him about it, and he discussed it with only his very closest friends or with those who knew because of their own connection with the homosexual community."

Homosexuality was a fact of life at Groton, according to Rev. Charles W. Sheerin, who speaks from deep knowledge about the school. Sheerin is an alumnus and former Groton faculty member who is an Episcopal minister and longtime friend of the Cornings who is semi-retired and assists at St. Peter's Episcopal Church in Albany. Sheerin, class of '44, taught the mayor's son, Erastus Corning III, during Sheerin's twelve-year career at Groton. A third-generation Episcopal minister, Sheerin's uncle, John Fays Williams, was chaplain at Groton beginning in 1929. He speaks with authority about Groton. "Homosexuality was certainly there, but there was very little to my knowledge despite the boarding school setting," Sheerin said. "It certainly went on. We all knew who the masters were and who the boys were who went in for that sort of thing. A boy's boarding school has inherent homosexual tendencies. The dorms are run by bachelors. It's a twenty-four-hour-a-day job, and undoubtedly some of the masters were homosexual."

While at Groton, Corning and Alsop planned to room together at Yale, which Alsop's father and grandfather had attended. But Joe Alsop broke tradition at the last minute and entered Harvard. Merry described in his biography the effeminate aspects of Alsop at Groton, including an "almost ladylike interest in people's clothes and things of that nature." The nature of the relationship between Alsop and Corning at Groton is unclear, but rumors swirled about them, according to classmates.

Bissell, Corning and Alsop, who were not much suited to success on the athletic fields where the stars of Groton shone brightest, looked to fit in elsewhere: the Dramatic Association, the Civics Club, and the board of the school literary journal the *Grotonian*. Alsop was literary editor and Bissell the press editor. Corning's father had been editor of this literary journal in 1902, but Erastus had to settle for the *Grotonian*'s business editor, which meant he had to sell the advertisements. While the job was not a plum assignment and previous business editors had run the *Grotonian* into financial difficulties, Corning kept the journal solvent. Erastus had the help of his father, who took out large ads in the *Grotonian* for Ludlum Steel, and his uncle, Parker, who bought ads for Albany Felt. Erastus got his mother to sell subscriptions, and the family connections produced ads from the City Savings Bank of Albany and the New York State National Bank of Albany. Corning's work didn't go unnoticed. "The business department had the finances so completely in hand that the *Grotonian* never had any financial trouble, nor was it necessary to reduce the size of any issue," the editors wrote. In the yearbook photograph of editors of the *Grotonian*, Corning, unlike his straight-legged peers, sat with his legs crossed in a pose of studied cool. Corning, ever exhibiting his individuality, also was the only one wearing knickers in the picture.

In his fifth form year, 1927, Corning joined ten other Groton classmates in completing one of the highlights of their prep school careers: researching, writing and publishing a book on China titled *That Untravell'd World: An Elementary Introduction to the Study of China*. It was the first time Groton students had ever undertaken such a major task. Corning wrote chapter seven, a recounting of the history and philosophy of the religions of China. In remarkably erudite fashion for a seventeen-year-old, Corning summed up in fifteen pages the meaning of Confucianism, Taoism and Buddhism. "At that time in my life, I was interested in comparative religion," Corning told a *Times Union* reporter in a

1973 feature article. "I read quite a lot about all religions. I wouldn't say it was extensive reading, but it wasn't superficial either."

The China book was 181 pages long; the students financed its printing themselves, each putting up $50. They sold out the print run of 200 copies and Corning recalled each student earned a profit of about $2.50 on the venture. Mostly, it was a learning experience that laid the groundwork for the later success of its participants. Some of those who joined Corning in publication of the book were classmates Bissell (top CIA official); Alsop (celebrated journalist and writer); F. Sargent Cheever (chancellor at University of Pittsburgh); Dwight W. Morrow Jr. (federal education official whose father was ambassador to England under Hoover and whose sister, Anne Morrow, married famous aviator Charles Lindbergh); and Howard Page Cross (prominent New York City architect).

Another school activity that brought Alsop, Corning and Bissell together was the Civics Club, a society formed in the early 1900s to foster an interest in current events among students. The three boys were among fourteen students involved. Each was given a topic for consideration, ranging from literature to archaeology to finance to sports. Alsop had art; Bissell had international politics; and Corning, in an odd bit of foreshadowing, had national politics. Discussion sessions were held weekly with a faculty member.

In sports, Corning made tentative attempts, but he never had the skill of close friend William L. Thompson Jr., of Troy, whose family knew the Cornings socially long before the boys were sent to Groton. Thompson, tall and strong, looked far more mature than Corning, and was one of the most popular boys in their form. He was chosen prefect, or student leader, of Hundred House – a dormitory so named because it housed one hundred students. Thompson played football, rowed crew, captained the wall scaling team, oversaw the Athletic Association and was a manager of the gym.

On the playing fields, Corning was not in the same league as Thompson or Devens. In the fall of their First Form year, Corning and his classmate Devens played a match of "fives," a rare variation on handball found in England and adopted at Groton. Devens beat Corning "very badly" in their fives match, Erastus wrote to his father in November of 1922, conceding that Devens was "a great player." Corning's competitiveness broke through. He kept practicing and seeking out matches in fives, playing almost every day, but he never improved enough to make the fives team at Groton, on which Devens was a top player. "Corning was a damn nice fellow and I got along well with him, but he wasn't much of an athlete," Devens said.

Corning managed to make the team only in baseball in his final year at Groton. He had been on the second squad, or junior varsity, in football as a sophomore, or Fourth Former, but gave up the sport after that. On the baseball team, Corning was a little-used substitute who played right field and had a weak bat. Nonetheless, his coach let Erastus play in a few games so that he could earn his sole athletic letter at Groton. In his senior year, 1928, in a game against arch-rival St. Mark's, Corning was put in as a pinch runner in the sixth inning for Boyer – the boy Corning beat up in the cellar fistfight. Corning was thrown out trying to steal second. Groton won anyway, 7-1, and Corning wasn't asked to forfeit his letter despite going hitless on the season.

Corning enjoyed some success in other sports. He had learned to ice skate on the frozen pond at Corning Farm and at Albany Academy, which had a hockey team. In his final winter at Groton, partly in order to counter the drudgery of the season at boarding school, Corning was an organizer of a hockey squad that played outdoors on a pond near campus. In the spring of 1928, Corning, an avid golfer, gathered students interested in the game and became president of the Golf Association. "Erastus played a lot of golf and I knocked the golf ball around with him a bit, but I wasn't a good golfer the way Erastus was," recalled Cheever. Still, his classmate could see the organizational and leadership qualities quietly, tentatively coming to the fore in the future mayor. That was further evident as a senior when Corning had the demanding job of manager of the Athletic Store, where school items were sold to family and friends visiting on weekends.

At the same time, Corning continued to shine academically. Besides being at the top of his form for overall academics, Corning was particularly outstanding in mathematics and won a class prize in math, which had been his favorite subject at Albany Academy.

It seems remarkable that he could continue to excel, particularly in math, given how much schoolwork Corning missed at Groton due to illness. He spent many days in the school infirmary with chronic colds and flus during the winter months and suffered sporadic coughs and sore throats in spring and fall, as well. At one point, the school nurse had Erastus write home for a cod liver oil prescription. Eventually, more serious action was required to fight the recurring colds. In January, 1925, Erastus was sent home to have his tonsils removed, causing him to miss several weeks at Groton. At the time, Corning's father wrote to Peabody: "Dr. Cox strongly urges that he be sent south some time next week for at least two weeks, preferably Aiken (South Carolina) or some point where it is not too warm but where he could be out of doors and exercising. I would like to know what your views on this subject are. I dislike to see him miss the work but he is attending conscientiously to his work here at home, and if worse comes to worse we could have him tutored if necessary next summer." Peabody wrote back: "Erastus should have no great difficulty in catching up with his class, for he is a boy of ability and conscience." A year later, Erastus was having another sick spell that required an extended stay at home. "Erastus arrived promptly and as far as I could see none the worse for his journey, though he certainly does look pretty well drawn out," his father wrote to Peabody on February 9, 1926. "The doctor looked him over last evening and is having his blood count taken today. It looks to me just like a case of a boy who has been growing too fast . . . I will keep you posted on how Erastus is coming, and will get him back to school as soon as I can." The boy missed another two weeks of school and was still home, prompting his father to write Peabody once more. "I had expected to get Erastus back to school before this but his temperature still remains considerably sub-normal. If he goes out for a walk, he starts to sneeze when he comes in and the doctor tells me that he is in a condition to catch any illness that he might be exposed to. I am very much in hopes that the arsenic and iron hypodermic injections that started today will build him up rapidly."

The boy's physician again suggested a period of recuperation down South for the sickly Erastus, but Corning's father wrote to Peabody that he'd prefer it if Erastus got back to Groton as soon as possible so as not to miss more schoolwork. The headstrong father decided to take matters of health, as he had most everything else when it came to Erastus, into his own hands. The boy would go back to Groton instead of South for a period of recovery "unless the doctor is very insistent in which case I will bow to his judgment." Besides, Edwin Corning had a family vacation planned in Boca Grande, Florida in March of 1926 with his brother, Parker, and their families. Edwin Corning had already planned to take Erastus out of Groton a day before the official start of the Easter break so they could rendezvous in Washington, D.C. where Parker was a Congressman.

Edwin Corning monitored each step of Erastus' academic career. Erastus' father asked Peabody to have a special report – above and beyond the frequent testing, ranking and report cards – written up on his son's study habits by his professors. Douglas Brown, the Groton archivist, suggested that such a request was out of the ordinary and quite rare. Such reports could only be solicited by a parent and were done without the student's knowledge. The file compiled in October of 1926 on Erastus Corning, reports of which were stored in his student record in the Groton Archives, contained these evaluations: "Corning is thoroughly able. His work in French is distinctly good, though slightly erratic" (French teacher William E. Mott); "This year I have come in contact with Corning only in history class, in which he has done reasonably well. He seems handicapped by an inability to express himself fluently. There is certainly a good brain underneath a quiet exterior. He seems this year to be less hot tempered and perhaps also less egotistic" (history teacher T.J. Edward Pulling); "Very able and does satisfactory work" (Latin teacher S. Warren Sturgis); "Does fairly good work. He does not work as hard as he might. On the other hand, I feel that his ability has been overestimated, and that we cannot expect him to make a brilliantly high record" (English teacher Louis C. Zahner); "Conduct in dormitory is good. It is common talk among his form mates that he does not do a stroke of work" (English teacher Henry E. Tuttle); "A good scholar. Hard worker and satisfactory. A trifle opinionated and somewhat unfortunate manner, but will make good" (Greek teacher William S. Cushing).

While he oversaw his son's career at Groton, there is no record that Edwin Corning ever visited his son at the school. Edwin Corning instead would send a chauffeur to pick up Erastus or, as a sort of consolation prize, the father would send Erastus' younger sister, Louise, to visit in his absence. "I remember his sister, Louise, coming up to see him, but never his father," his friend Cheever recalled. That absence apparently became a learned behavior handed down from father to son. "I can't recall his father ever coming to Groton to visit Rasty," said Sheerin, who taught the mayor's son, Erastus III, at Groton.

Letters from Edwin Corning to his son generally focused on emotionally detached topics such as the father's political career and business activities – the price of Ludlum Steel stock or the details of patent infringement lawsuits against competitors – that were hardly typical subjects for most teenage boys. Erastus tried to hold up his end of this manly correspondence, rarely lapsing into the personal or emotional concerns of boyhood or the homesickness and loneliness many boys felt at the boarding school, Erastus included. He had confided in his classmate, Alexander

Forbes, that he was unhappy at Groton and glad to get out upon graduation. In letters to his father, however, Erastus, the dutiful son, maintained a stoic facade to please him and changed the subject by soliciting information about his father's rising political career. After receiving the Democratic nomination as lieutenant governor as Al Smith's running mate, Edwin Corning wrote on October 1, 1926: "It has been a pretty busy week with the Convention at Syracuse and the usual aftermath to a nomination, letters, telegrams, etc. which all had to be answered. I am naturally delighted to be on the same ticket with Governor Smith and think I have a reasonably good chance of election. For the next four or five weeks, however, things are going to be pretty busy."

Corning congratulated his father and did his best to campaign for his dad while at Groton. He got his mother to send Smith-Corning campaign buttons and Erastus talked up the ticket. His Democratic loyalties, however, were in the minority in the conservative Republicanism at Groton. Still, Erastus swam against the current. "I remember how loyal he was to Al Smith during the presidential campaign of 1928," Cheever recalled. "He kept a framed photograph of Al Smith on his desk and he was somewhat abused by the faculty and headmaster, who were pretty staunchly Republican as you can imagine. But that didn't budge Erastus one bit from his loyalty and support of Al Smith."

Throughout his Groton career, his mother, Louise Corning, remained at best a spectral presence on the periphery of her son's consciousness. She was barely in the picture save for her role to nurse Erastus back to health during his recurring illnesses. Clearly, Erastus was Edwin's project and the boy would fit the father's mold in matters of politics and business and social status. Louise backed off and quietly supported her husband's engineering of their son's future. By his final year at Groton, however, 1928, when Edwin Corning suffered the heart attack and stroke that rendered him an invalid, the relationship between mother and son changed irrevocably. The catastrophic health setback for his father required Erastus at age eighteen to become an adult suddenly, before his time, and the man of the house for his mother. The son whose rearing she had passed off to a governess, or who spoiled and coddled Erastus periodically and extravagantly from afar, in an instant became a partner and ally. The vague, tentative relationship that existed between the two during his Groton years crystallized into a pair of peers who needed to work together to hold the family together in Edwin's long, slow decline. The most important attribute mother passed to son was a silent strength and fierce will that endured through all adversity. "I believe Erastus wanted to be mayor and have a career in politics as a way of honoring his mother," said longtime family friend Norman Rice. "And the mayor's mother had a mantra. 'My son, Erastus the mayor.' She said that over and over to whomever she met."

The burden of his father's impaired condition and the forging of a new relationship with his mother as *de facto* head of household coincided with Erastus' final semester at Groton. At this same time, out from under his father's thumb, having overcome his initial shyness and his propensity to withdraw and become something of a loner, Erastus achieved the final stage of his blossoming sense of self in the Dramatic Society by landing one of the lead roles in the school play, *Kathleen*, adapted from a novel by Christopher Morley. The play was directed by John M. Hoysradt, a new master at Groton who taught history and drawing and also filled in as coach of dramatics for a teacher away on sabbatical.

Kathleen, a comedy about a pair of Oxford dons, was a gentle nudge at self-parody among the Grotonians. Corning and Forbes played the two male leads, roommates at Trinity College, Oxford. Forbes was cast as Randall King and Corning as Johnny Blair, a Rhodes scholar from Milwaukee. Other boys had to assume the female parts; Alsop played the leading woman character, Mrs. Kent, in black lace evening gown, replete with full jewelry, makeup and high heels. "Alsop's interpretation of the part was positively matronly in line and inflection blended with gesture to build a personality eagerly listened to by audience and actors," a student reviewer wrote in the *Grotonian*.

Erastus was cast in a leading role by Hoysradt, despite the fact that he had almost no acting experience, having appeared on stage just once before in a bit part. The *Grotonian* critic praised Corning's portrayal, though: "A natural actor, he played his double part with fluency and ease…. He shares high honors with Alsop." But the reviewer hoped for something more from Corning: "While applauding the winning streak that followed (or guided) Blair through the comedy (we felt he would anyway), we waited wistfully for a certain abandon that never arrived, the sort of thing that activated Forbes." Forbes remembered Erastus as "a very effective character actor who took to drama naturally and really enjoyed it."

His newfound love of the theater was due to Hoysradt. Besides boosting his self-confidence and bringing him outside himself, Corning's participation in *Kathleen* marked a particularly close relationship with Hoysradt, the drama coach, causing whispers among his classmates. What made their intimacy noticeable was the fact that at Groton there was usually a purposeful division between faculty members – called "masters" – and students. Forbes watched the association between Erastus and Hoysradt grow and deepen.

"The other masters didn't even know much about it because it evolved privately between the two of them," Forbes said. Hoysradt, new to Groton in 1927, young and unmarried, had a bachelor of arts degree. He lived in Hundred House dormitory as a prefect. Corning and Hoysradt – dark and handsome with deep-set eyes and a full mustache, his fingers caressing a cigarette in the Dramatic Society yearbook photo – were seen together often in the dorm, walking around campus, preparing for the play, or talking after class. Not only Forbes recognized the unusual friendship between master and student. Cheever said, "Erastus had one close friend among the masters, Hoysradt, who was very sociable with Erastus and was something of a mentor to him." Forbes characterized the relationship as something more, too. "I couldn't presume how close it was, but it was very close," Forbes said. "It wasn't a relationship between student and teacher. It was unusual, not quite a normal friendship, and very personal. It's a delicate thing to discuss."

In one regard, Hoysradt can be seen as the first adult male who lavished attention and concern on Corning. The drama coach and his tender affections arrived at the moment Erastus may have felt most alone and distant from his own absent father, whose intense devotion to business and politics had driven him to early coronary disease. Perhaps Hoysradt's intimate mindfulness was what the shy, sensitive Erastus craved and never received from his own father.

Forbes stopped short of characterizing the relationship between Corning and Hoysradt explicitly as a homosexual affair. Although there was no direct confirmation, strong circumstantial evidence fueled talk to that effect among Corning's classmates. "It was something we never found out about, but there might have been something physical," Forbes said. "Whatever it was, it didn't go on long. It was brief. But the closeness was there for anybody to observe. It was an especially close friendship that was out of the ordinary for teacher and student." Sheerin was not fazed by the revelation: "Groton's position was that a master's business was his own and some were known to be homosexual," the former Groton master said.

"The Rector did not take action unless the master overstepped his boundaries and got a student involved in a harmful situation."

In 1929, the Rector hastened Hoysradt's departure. Corning's drama coach left Groton on less-than-favorable terms after two years on the faculty. Forbes, who went on to Harvard and acted in Hasty Pudding productions there, followed Hoysradt's career at Groton. "He wasn't a leading figure at Groton and the school dropped him pretty quick," Forbes said, although the reasons were a mystery to him. In a letter from Hoysradt to Peabody in May, 1930, Hoysradt wrote, "You say that I have influenced boys against the school." Peabody had made it clear that he did not want Hoysradt to visit Groton after his brief teaching stint was terminated. Hoysradt acquiesced and replied to Peabody that he would "respect your wishes" about staying away from the school. Sheerin said Hoysradt's ouster was still being discussed a decade later. "We heard about Hoysradt," Sheerin said. "He overstepped Peabody's boundary."

After Groton, Hoysradt lived from 1929 to 1953 in Bronxville, New York and pursued an acting career in the theater in New York City. In 1953, he relocated to Los Angeles and landed parts in more than two dozen movies. But Hoysradt was best known as the grandpa in the television sitcom, "Give Me A Break," starring Nell Carter. Hoysradt, who died on September 15, 1991 in Santa Cruz, California, was married for the last twenty-five years of his life to Dorothy Hoysradt. His widow recalled her late husband mentioned Erastus Corning occasionally: "Oh yes, he was a friend of Corning's and I know they saw each other over the years at Groton functions. John told me Corning was from a leading New York family and that he had gone on to Yale and done well. I know they corresponded and they were rather dedicated to each other. Whenever my husband got a letter from Corning, he would tell me stories."

Dorothy Hoysradt also said her late husband was an avowed homosexual who had many sexual relations with young men throughout his life, including during their quarter-century long marriage. "He was a dyed-in-the-wool homosexual who had all kinds of homosexual experiences his entire life," Hoysradt said. "John always had young boys, aged seventeen or eighteen. If they traveled together alone, I'm sure John had a relationship with Corning. He always preferred the young boys." Hoysradt said her late husband had been arrested in San Diego for "taking young boys on excursions and molesting them," but avoided serving prison time by getting expert testimony from psychologists who said he was not a public menace and would not harm children.

"John had a lot of homosexual pornography and pictures of boys he had fallen in love with," Dorothy Hoysradt said. "John wasn't nasty about it. Homosexuality was beautiful to him. He'd bring his boys home once in awhile and he had a loft for guests in our house. But mostly he went away with them. When he was living in Hollywood for the six years he worked on 'Give Me A Break,' he had a hotel there and three boys living with him. I didn't go near the place."

Dorothy Hoysradt, eighty-eight years old at the time of the interview, recalled her husband's alcoholism and his early theater days on the East Coast when he lived with Orson Welles. The two men traveled together and were in plays. Hoysradt had written a memoir about his time with Welles, but it was never published. "Orson was a wild man and John got some bad habits from him, but John also was a marvelous man and was beautiful to me and our son," Dorothy Hoysradt said. Their son, fifty-eight-years-old at the time, had suffered a stroke several years before, but her husband had set aside money to provide for his care.

While they were rehearsing for the 1928 performance of *Kathleen*, Hoysradt and Corning – who shared a love of history as well as an interest in dramatics – planned a European vacation together. A month after Corning's graduation from Groton, in July of 1928, Hoysradt led him on a tour through the architectural and artistic treasures of Europe, particularly in Italy. Corning's parents approved the trip, but did not accompany their son. Apparently, neither did anyone else. "As far as I know, they went to Europe on their own, just the two of them," Forbes said. "That special closeness and intimate association between master and student was very unusual for Groton."

One outgrowth of the relationship between Corning and Hoysradt was an almost giddy sense of confidence and exuberance Corning expressed during the final months of his six-year tenure at Groton – an emotion rarely seen previously. Cheever recalled a dramatic flair the otherwise reticent Corning displayed at the final examination in Latin required before graduation. Cheever recounted it this way: "It was the last test and after that we were through with Groton. Erastus said the schedule of the exam was causing a great deal of difficulty because he had an important family birthday party that night in Bar Harbor, Maine. He said he could make it, but he would be cutting it close. Erastus' idea was to have the family limousine waiting outside the study hall while he finished the examination. He said the only way he could get to Bar Harbor on schedule was to finish the Latin exam in half the time allotted. So, I remember Erastus went in and sat down and started writing and writing and writing. He filled page after page and when the school clock tower rang out, he looked up, picked up his papers and said, 'This is where I say goodbye.' And he walked out, got into the limousine and was off. Just like that. Now, that's a *tour de force*." Cheever offered this postscript: Corning ended up achieving the highest score on the exam, received top honors for Latin in his class – just like his father in 1902 – and tied for top of form with Alsop.

Groton had introduced Erastus Corning to regimentation and the rigid code of order expected of the future guardians of the WASP Ascendancy. Although he chafed initially at the constrictions, his keen perceptive powers and intellect, along with a touch of theatrical training, taught him to play a convincing role even if his heart wasn't in it. While his relationship with the drama coach was intense and brief and an aberration that was a product of circumstances, it may have signaled a deep need for intimacies from a father figure and an outgrowth of his close friendship with Alsop. There is no indication that Corning displayed homosexual tendencies before or after the Groton experience.

Yale was the next stop along the path his father had laid out for him. Tap Day is a tradition cast in stone at Yale, the granite of the imposing edifices of the secret senior societies, castles of elitism framed by Gothic towers, high brick walls and wrought-iron gates. The secret societies gather in extravagant, fortress-like mansions covered with ivy, cloaked in myth and pervaded by deep mystery. Tap Day is an ancient ritual at Yale, the foundation of the school's social order as the three secret societies replenish their membership, each selecting fifteen of the best and the brightest seniors-to-be. It is a defining moment that divides senior Yalies into movers and shakers and also-rans. As Yale juniors had done each Tap Day for more than a century before him, Erastus Corning and his classmates dutifully gathered beneath a gnarled, old oak tree in front of Battell Chapel to await their destiny on May 16, 1931.

Erastus Corning was a tall, thin, academically bright, but still somewhat shy young man as he entered Yale. His classmates dubbed him 'Rastus. Perched in the top five percent of his class, he won the high oration appointment as a junior, earning him election to Phi Beta Kappa – a rare academic achievement for a junior. Outside the classroom, however, on the all-important social scale of Yale, 'Rastus registered only modestly. His extracurricular star had not shone as brightly as that of his father, Edwin (Class of 1906), or his uncle, Parker (Class of 1895) in their years at Yale. Erastus carried heavy baggage in feeling he had a lot to live up to!

Parker, a member of the crew team and an all-around swell on campus, and Edwin, a member of the football squad and active in student government, had been chosen to Yale's most prestigious fraternity, Psi Upsilon. This Greek house deemed worthy of membership the most important, popular and wealthy students at Yale. W. Averell Harriman, for example, scion of a vast railroad fortune, New York state governor, presidential candidate and adviser to presidents, was a member of Psi Upsilon.

In his junior year during the fraternity pledge season, Erastus, who was not particularly athletic or outgoing, did not make the grade of Psi Upsilon. Instead, Erastus had been picked for a second-tier fraternity, Chi Psi. And so, as Tap Day rolled around near the end of junior year, the scorecard on 'Rastus was spotty. He had the status of his father's and uncle's exploits at Yale going for him, he had prepared at Groton, and he was a top-notch student. That was in the plus margin. On the negative side, his only participation in competitive athletics came as a freshman, when he was on the boxing squad and the golf team. He did not have any intercollegiate team competition on his resume and he hadn't done much in the extracurricular department, except for the University Club, a service group with dozens of members that lacked a cache of exclusivity. What 'Rastus Corning did possess, however, was a trump card that carried a lot of weight. Both his father and uncle had been members of the secret society Wolf's Head.

Among the three secret societies at Yale, the most exclusive was Skull and Bones, whose members include former President George Bush, and a formidable list of America's elite. The runner-up in clout was Scroll and Key, which laid claim to the intellectual high ground and selected the leading academic lights. In the pecking order of elitism, Wolf's Head ranked third among the secret societies, but it was hardly a consolation prize. In all, just forty-five juniors among Erastus Corning's Class of '32, which numbered 890 students, would be chosen for the three secret societies on Tap Day.

"As soon as you got to Yale, you found out that its structure was a social pyramid," according to Robert Caro in *The Power Broker*, his biography of Robert Moses (Yale Class of 1909). "Its base was the select sophomore societies, its next step the even more select junior fraternities, its apex the three senior societies – Skull and Bones, Scroll and Key and Wolf's Head. Sixty years later, surviving members of the class of 1909 could still remember watching classmates burst into tears on Tap Day when they realized that they were not to be selected for a senior society."

Tap Day arrived for Erastus Corning on May 16, 1931, with high drama. As they did each year for this Yale rite of passage, faculty members took up position in the late afternoon in front of the chapel, and underclassmen staked out prime viewing areas, from the windows of Durfee Hall, to the branches of trees, to the perimeter of the campus green where the event took place. Hundreds of juniors who harbored any hope of being selected to a senior secret society gathered on the lawn in front of Battell Chapel. When the clock on the chapel struck five o'clock, a representative from Skull and Bones, Scroll and Key and Wolf's Head would emerge from each society's respective mansion. Each society emissary wore a derby, a blue serge suit and gold society pin in his lapel. The society representative would give the junior accepted for membership a whack on the back and intone the command, "Go to your room."

Corning's roommate, Dr. Daniel Catlin, recalled the buildup to Tap Day. "We had all been talking about Tap Day for weeks and weeks and it was a very big thing," Catlin said. "You had to stand on the campus green, turn your back away from the chapel and close your eyes. I remember 'Rastus and I were out there with hundreds of our classmates. It was crowded and we all wanted to be in Skull and Bones, of course. It was the most prestigious, the in crowd was part of it and Bones would tap the captain of the football team, the most popular person, that sort of thing." Catlin was not tapped and the disappointment, pain and humiliation of that moment lingered the rest of his life. "I didn't make the cut and never got tapped, but I was working like hell and bogged down in my pre-med work anyway," said Catlin, who became a cancer surgeon at Sloan-Kettering in New York City. "It hurt to know you weren't considered exclusive enough to be chosen."

In fact, the senior societies came in for a good bit of criticism in 1932, Corning's senior year. The uproar was led by Dick Bissell, Corning's bookish friend and fellow Groton alum, who, like Corning, was in the rare company of being elected to Phi Beta Kappa as a junior. As a senior, Bissell was editor of *Harkness Hoot*, the Yale undergraduate review. Bissell, who was not tapped for a senior society and was something of a social outcast among Yale's smart set, helped write the lead article in the May, 1931 issue of the *Hoot*. The title: "Senior Societies Must Go!" The incendiary piece called for "the abolition of an outworn, unwanted social system." Bissell's protest picked up steam, but the staunch conservatism and social clout of the secret society members won out over the eccentric crew backing Bissell, president of the Liberal club.

In identical fashion to his father and uncle before him, the Wolf's Head representative walked up behind Erastus, slapped him on the back and said, "'Rastus Corning, go to your room." Corning opened his eyes, walked toward the Wolf's Head fortress and felt, perhaps for the first time at Yale, that he had arrived. In profound ways, Wolf's Head foreshadowed Erastus Corning's approach to his future political life as practiced in the Albany Democratic machine. The two commandments of Wolf's Head, as with the O'Connell-Corning political organization, were these: loyalty and secrecy.

Wolf's Head Hall, as it is called, is a sprawling Tudor structure made of stone and half-timbers. The society, formed in 1883, was a reaction to the "poppycock" of Bones and Key, according to a Wolf's Head brochure Corning kept in his files at City Hall. "The Strength of the Pack is the Wolf. The Strength of the Wolf is the Pack" is the society's motto; its stated objective is "to unite its members in lasting personal friendship and loyalty to Yale." The society's writings speak of "the Wolf's Head experience," which is characterized by "beauty, warmth and friendship" within the society's "sacred portals." Wolf's Head also aspired to classical models and the members engaged in ritualistic speech, such as their greeting, "The Gods of Egypt bid us hail." Besides the fierce bond of secrecy, taken to the degree of a sworn oath to keep the workings of the society forever private, Wolf's Head stressed loyalty. This, too, was a prelude to the same unquestioned loyalty that would serve Erastus Corning so well in his later political career, for it was inviolate loyalty that fueled the Albany Democratic machine. A Wolf's Head pamphlet continued:

> The loyalty of her sons is in no small measure due to the sense of loyalty and friendship gained through experiences such as we all had in Wolf's Head. . . . Yale is strong and very, very special because of these institutions from which she draws her strength and which enrich the entire Yale Community . . . Trust is the medium of the Wolf's Head life, and it is this trust which subdues the principle of all its chambers to its character. For at the heart

of trust is the spirit of privacy which pervades this Hall. The Hall exists to shelter the beauty and truth of traditional privacy in an era when, as never before, life in private has been neglected . . . Life can never be fulfilled without a fulfilling life in private.

In addition to swearing an oath to maintain the society's secrecy, Wolf's Head members agreed to support each other. "They made a pact for life," Catlin said. "If one of the members needed help financially or got into trouble, the other members would help you out, no matter what."

The spirit of Wolf's Head was a kind of dreamy, gauzy camaraderie. An unidentified Wolf's Head member from the Class of 1919 wrote this ode: "When the wind blows over New Haven bitter with snow,/And the stars in the blue-black sky are chilly and small,/May there be a fire in this hearth, with logs aglow,/And fellowship in this Hall." Thomas F. Steyer, Wolf's Head member from the Class of 1979, put it this way: "Wolf's Head has become a type of sanctuary for us all, a place outside the rush of mainstream Yale life where we can be sure of comfort and friendship."

For one of the rare times during his career at Yale, Corning forged intimate and lasting friendships with the other fourteen members of Wolf's Head during his senior year. There was Edwin Sumner Hunt Jr. from Waterbury, Connecticut, a member of the lacrosse and crew teams and a colleague of Corning's on the University Club; Harry Towne Jones Jr., a baseball player; Marshall Hay Jones, who came from a long line of Yalies and was an outstanding athlete who played football, baseball and water polo. His father, John Elsworth Jones, was president of Globe Iron Company in Jackson, Ohio, and Jones and Corning often discussed the pros and cons of joining their families' iron operations.

Corning's closest friend at Yale, though, was Catlin, a native of St. Louis whose father was a Harvard-educated lawyer; classmates nicknamed Catlin "Dapper" for his snazzy dress. "Of all the roommates I had, 'Rastus was my favorite," Catlin said. "He was well liked by the rest of the class. He had a lot of friends. He was neat and clean and dressed nicely. And he had money so we could afford to get the hell out of New Haven on weekends. Mostly, we'd go to New York City. I remember we'd go to dances looking for women in the city. That was the era of debutante dances for women and it was a great time" – Corning's society connections made him an acceptable suitor.

Another close pal of Corning's at Yale was his cousin, John Eward McElroy, "Jack," also a member of the Class of '32. The two had practically grown up together. McElroy, six months younger than Corning, was in the same class at Albany Academy with Erastus, and their parents were close friends. McElroy's father, Charles E. McElroy, was an investment banker and businessman; the family lived on Elk Street across from Academy Park and traveled in the same circle as the Cornings. In fact, the mayor's sister, Louise, married Andrew Ransom, the brother of McElroy's wife, Cornelia (nee Ransom). The Cornings and McElroys were even more deeply intertwined, because McElroy's mother, Harriet, and Corning's grandmother, Mary, were both members of Albany's prominent Parker clan. And, like Corning's father and uncle, McElroy's father was a graduate of Yale (Class of 1896). With such a shared history, it was natural that Corning and McElroy chummed around together. In addition, both were members of the same fraternity, Chi Psi. Nonetheless, McElroy, despite the fact that he helped run the *Yale Record* as a sophomore and was active in the dramatic association, wasn't tapped for Wolf's Head. McElroy and Corning formed the core of an Albany connection at Yale that included fellow Chi Psi brothers William Peltz and John Easton, who were two years ahead of them. All had attended Albany Academy before Corning transferred to Groton and McElroy to the Taft School.

Fraternities like Corning's Chi Psi were at the center of social interaction at Yale. "We didn't live there, but we got all our meals there and we became very close with our fraternity brothers that way," Mayor Corning told me during a lengthy interview in his City Hall office in May, 1982 about his college years. The mayor repeatedly excused himself for a deep, hacking cough that rendered him speechless and gasping for air. "Excuse me for this lousy laryngitis," he apologized to me, at that time a long-haired graduate student in faded jeans and ratty sweater to whom the eleven-term mayor was a most attentive and respectful interview subject. A month later, Corning was admitted to Albany Medical Center Hospital for treatment of emphysema and bronchitis. He was dead the following year. Corning recalled Chi Psi with fondness. "We had some fads at Yale, like goldfish swallowing and things like that," the mayor told me. "I think they're perfectly good and kind of amusing, even joyous. There were quite a few fraternity initiations, but I think they've gotten away from that because over the years a lot of people got hurt." Corning sidestepped questions about hazing directed at him or, as an upper classman, orchestrated by him.

The class book was less circumspect than Corning about what it called "all the voodooism of fraternity life." Fraternity hazing often got physical, according to a class book anecdote. "Hollon Farr, our Class Officer, made some of the hooded brothers feel pain when he expelled them forcibly from a room in Vanderbilt just as they were putting their paddles on a wet, shivering, and naked candidate."

Corning could be a master of obfuscation in an interview, as he was when I prodded him on his Yale recollections. Corning would say he majored in English and history. He said he never wore his Phi Beta Kappa pin and he claimed not to recall his academic honors. "I forget if it was *cum laude* or *magna cum laude*," Corning said. (It was *magna cum laude*.) And when the talk came around to his drinking days at Yale, Corning reminded me with a characteristic twinkle of his eye that we were, after all, ahem, ahem, speaking of the Prohibition era. "We had a lot of activities in the dormitory," he said with a poker face. "We would have a group of friends gather together every week or two to have a bash." Corning did not elaborate whether or not those were fermented bashes.

The route between Albany and New Haven for the Cornings was well-worn; the family Corning tradition at Yale ran deep. Although the mayor's grandfather, Erastus Corning Jr., went to Union College, the Corning family had been sending its sons to Yale since 1891, with the expectation that they would receive the Ivy League training that perforce would extend the family's record of achievement in business and politics. Nearly a dozen Cornings and Corning cousins have graduated from Yale since the late-nineteenth century, with the mayor's father, Edwin Corning, and his older brother, Parker Corning, cementing this family custom.

Parker Corning, Yale class of 1895, was a joker who wrote facetiously in his class notes: "The earliest ancestor of whom much is known was St. Paul, but he was too good for the family and so they shook him. The blood is English, French and sporting." Parker didn't fit the family mold in other ways. He went to St. Paul's School in Concord, New Hampshire, rather than to Groton like other Cornings. Parker's Yale classmates joked about his love of things English, particularly cricket, and they gave him the nicknames Prince, Prince Chocolate, Prynes, Prunes, Albany Hasty and Chocolate.

Parker's younger brother, Edwin, called Ed – the mayor's father – was a hard-nosed competitor, particularly on the football field, where he excelled despite his modest size of six-feet and 187 pounds. The way Ed threw himself into the fray of the much larger players earned him the honor of being voted "nerviest" among his classmates of the Class of 1906. Unlike his son, Edwin showed early interest and ambition in politics at Yale, getting elected president of the civics club and to the governing board of the University Club, a private social club and restaurant. He also became deeply immersed in student government and was secretary of the City Government Club, a post that earned him a reputation as "biggest bluffer" among classmates. When it came to making sure his son and firstborn, Erastus, would follow his footsteps from Albany Academy to Groton to Yale, however, there was no bluffing on the father's part. In Edwin Corning's third year class reunion book (1909), the mayor's father was explicit about the destiny he intended for the newborn Erastus: "I am in hopes that my young son will turn up in New Haven in the early thirties, and feel sure that with the various other offspring of 1906 who will reach Yale about that time – and there are quite a lot of them – they and the rest of us will have some extra special parties." And so it was, as it had been for Erastus at Albany Academy and then at Groton and now at Yale, that the father dictated his son's future. Edwin even pushed his naturally intro-verted son to get more involved socially at Yale. "His chief trouble seems to be that he is quiet and would rather go off and shoot and fish by him-self than to wear a two-story collar and go out with the boys," Edwin Corning wrote to a friend.

In other ways, though, Erastus Corning received more of an educa-tion at Yale than his father bargained for. This was during Prohibition, after all, so Yalies learned how to make bathtub gin. The Depression had hit hard, too, but the Yale men still managed to make frequent trips in the full hormonal flush of springtime to court the co-eds at Smith College in Northampton, Massachusetts and further afield in search of eligible women. While the rest of the nation reeled from the Depression's eco-nomic hard times, the Yale men spent freely and became avid moviegoers. All things considered, Corning's four years at Yale were a breeze, a kind of endless summer. Corning wrote to his father infrequently, usually to report that his bank account was close to being overdrawn and that he needed money.

Corning and the 890 members of the Class of 1932 constituted the largest class that ever entered Yale to that point and they prided themselves on their prodigious appetites. Their class book boasted:

Maybe you hadn't heard that 1932 was known to the higher-ups as the biggest and worst little aggregation that ever hit Yale. Maybe you didn't know that this dignified and self-respecting Class is called the hardest-drinking, hardest-studying crowd of Croesuses that ever swamped York-Library, Wright and Vanderbilt. The depression may have reduced us to four percent beer, applejack, et alky, but we wrapped our heads in towels and got oration appointments just the same, if anybody knows what they are.

Corning and his classmates began their Yale career on September 26, 1928 for the start of Freshman Week, "designed to make us feel at home in New Haven before those mighty scions of the upper classes arrived to force us out of the picture," wrote the author of the '32 class book. Freshman Week was meant, in part, to put the newcomers in their place and to wipe away any residual prep school cockiness. The orientation was capped by a convocation in Woolsey Hall under the stern decorum of President James Rowland Angell and Dean Percy T. Walden. "We sank lower in our seats as each successive speaker impressed upon us how far we had to go and how insignificant we were to start with," according to the class book. "And we had met our masters; we were at the bottom of the ladder."

The freshman's place on the lowest rung was reinforced by Yale policy, such as the infamous nude posture photos and exams in the gym. According to the class book, all the freshmen were lined up in the gym, made to strip naked, analyzed for posture and photographed in the buff as part of a widespread obsession with posture and remedial posture exercises, particularly among Ivy League schools of that era. Yale was all-male then, but some students found it odd that swimming in the pool during gym class was done completely naked, a policy abandoned in the late-1960s.

Traditions thrived at Yale. Each academic year was ushered in with a century-old ritual: torchlight parade, chapel service and convocation speeches. The next morning at eight o'clock in Sprague Hall, college regulations were intoned and class schedules, determined by Dean Walden during Corning's tenure, were handed out. The keeper of the class schedules, Professor Hollon A. Farr (Yale 1896), was the Class of '32 class officer – a kind of academic warden who dispensed all favors relating to curriculum logistics. After Farr gave each student his destiny, it was off to the Yale Co-op or Whitlock's to buy textbooks before the first day of class.

While a strict hierarchy at Yale left a freshman with all the authority of an indentured servant, even first-year Yalies enjoyed far more latitude than Corning had experienced beneath Groton's vaunted rigidity, particularly on the matter of mandatory chapel attendance that Corning complained about at Groton. At Yale, Corning simply stayed away. In place of chapel, Corning and his classmates seemed to make an almost spiritual connection to the movies, attending the silent films and later talkies with an almost religious fervor. "We usually managed two movies on the Sabbath. It was a relief from Commons anyway," the class book said. "As freshmen, we got the movie habit and never have lost it." Movies became the social currency, the glue that held Corning's class – with all its cliques and the prep school pack mentality that tended to divide Groties from St. Paulies and St. Markies from Choaties – at least partly together.

When they weren't ogling Mae West in *Diamond Lil* or Bebe Daniels in *Rio Rita*, 'Rastus and the boys found plenty else to amuse themselves with in town. Prohibition and their ages of eighteen and nineteen didn't prevent their frequenting speakeasies, where they'd listen to jazz – Louis Armstrong's "I Can't Give You Anything But Love" was a tune singled out in the class book – and partaking of other pleasures. At the old Hyperion Theater in New Haven, the freshmen received their "official and patriotic welcome to town" at the hands (and more) of "Red Hot" Norma Noel and her Girls of the U.S.A. Their act was referred to, not so discreetly, as "sex struggles on the stage" in Corning's class book. There were other gin-induced debaucheries among the Yalies, too. "It didn't matter that Prohibition was in effect. We still did quite a bit of drinking," recalled Catlin. "Erastus and I drank quite a bit together, but we didn't get into trouble with it. It never became a problem for us. Erastus was always a fellow who had tight control over his life, even when he'd drink too much."

The game of trying to hide a booze-making operation in the dormitories became one of the most popular extracurricular activities for Corning's class. "I remember we'd make bathtub gin, really terrible stuff," Catlin recalled. "We'd buy it in gallon glass containers of pure alcohol, sneak it up to the dorms and use the bathtub to mix it with water and other stuff. It was lousy, but we'd drink it for the effect. Neither 'Rastus nor I were what you'd call hell-raisers." Corning was familiar, however, with "beer showers" at meetings of the University Club, to which he belonged, and he attended parties of friends who sent out invitations that read: "Come And Drive A Nail Into Your Coffin."

Other popular pastimes for Yale men were gin picnics at Vassar, a widely accepted form of seduction at the Seven Sisters college in Pough-keepsie, New York. Sporting events also provided a convenient excuse to get drunk. "Our cheer leaders found a new and better use for their mega-phones when the relation of megaphone to cocktail shaker occurred to them in the daze of their customary pre-game party," the class book writer recalled. Their excessive drinking, in fact, and the way they flouted author-ity concerning Prohibition, came to define the Class of '32 in a way few other of their activities did. Illicit booze was their crowning achievement, it seemed, and these foot soldiers in the army of the elite thrilled in the way bootleg liquor came to symbolize their break with the conformity of their conservative social class. "It is an indisputable fact that our Class consumed the largest quantity of Bromo-Seltzer and tomato juice in the history of the business and almost lifted the depression off its hind feet through this one thing alone," D. Nelson Adams bragged during his delivery of the class his-tory at graduation ceremonies on Class Day, 1932.

The sort of bravado they displayed about their drinking prowess car-ried over among Corning and his classmates when it came to the way they sloughed off the stock market crash and the devastation wrought by the Depression. Within the *Class Book of 1932* narrative, which ran to more than one hundred pages chronicling their time at Yale season by season and year by year, only a few paragraphs mentioned the economic cataclysm that wiped out much of Corning's father's fortune and that of so many other investors. If they mentioned the Depression at all, they joked about the dire financial situation: "In the early fall of 1929, just previous to the Stock Market crash, collectively and as individuals, we were utterly and hope-lessly broke. That may give you some idea of how poor we are at present. What with ever increasing grill bills, loans, interest rates, tailors' accounts, the Yale Hope Mission, the Class Fund, and the tuition, it is a wonder that we have not jumped off a tall building in Wall Street. Out of all this misery we have one great claim to fame: we were the originators of this great social class that has recently come into existence, these respectable people, the *Nouveaux Pauvres*." Among these "newly poor," a bank failure in New Haven their senior year was cause for a quip rather than consternation. Such economic ruin and the shock waves felt throughout the financial world surprisingly hardly registered amid the sheltered bastion of privilege that was Yale. Corning and his classmates managed to purchase the regula-tion uniform of their era, a pair of gray flannel slacks, white shoes and an

Anglicized tweed jacket. Corning added a bit of self-effacing humor when recalling his dandyish days as a Yalie. "I remember my senior year at Yale. when a buddy asked me to go fishing," Corning told me in May, 1982. "I said, 'Sure, but I've got to go get my jacket and tie first.'"

Corning stood tall, grown to his full height of six-feet two-inches by the time he left Yale, carried on a solid 190-pound frame. From his years spent tramping throughout the Maine woods, Corning had developed the cut of a rugged outdoorsman and he wasn't afraid of hard physical labor. Corning joined the boxing squad, as he had done at Groton, during his freshman year at Yale. He was handy with his fists, but lacked the skill and determination to move up to the varsity level and dropped out after a season.

Corning and his classmates had plenty of disposable income to spend at the Yale Golf Course, where they placed wagers on each hole, and at a nearby lawn and tennis club, where they placed bets on the outcome of their squash and tennis matches. Corning, in particular, spent a lot of time on the links. He donned a pair of knickers and joined the freshman golf team. The competition was stiff. "Only one man from 1932 could shine because both the classes of 1931 and 1933 contained some of the finest golfers in intercollegiate circles," according to the class book. Still, Corning was good enough to make the cut and was named a member of the freshman squad. Corning improved his game by competing in match play against Yale's best golfer, Dan England, of Pittsfield, Massachusetts, a friend of Corning's from the University Club. Even after the cash spent on golf and other sports, there was plenty left to run up substantial bills for dinner and drinks at several private clubs – the University Club; and Mory's, the campus pub that served the hallowed "green cup," a gallon-sized chalice filled with champagne and *creme de menthe* passed and guzzled between toasts; and the Oyster Bar, a new venue at that time for students looking for a place to unwind and socialize.

Given so many opportunities for diversionary pleasures, it's a wonder that Erastus Corning – who eventually came to like to join the fun and be part of a group, mainly fraternity life or social functions with Wolf's Head – managed to excel academically at Yale. An English and history major, Corning was a voracious reader and remained so throughout his life. The novel that swept the Yale campus his sophomore year was Ernest Hemingway's *A Farewell to Arms*, which spawned many Hemingwayesque contributions to the *Yale Literary Review*. But Corning's reading diet did not tend toward novels. "I suppose my favorite form of entertainment is reading and has been since my days at Yale," Corning told me in our 1982 interview about his college years. "I read practically no fiction. I read environmental material, history, biography, natural history, a real catch-all of stuff. The mix is unbelievable." He not only read deeply and widely, but his uncanny recall and extraordinary memory for what he had read was a key to his powerful intellect. "I've never seen someone who could absorb and remember information so easily," said his roommate Catlin. "He was able to make it look so easy. He was just incredibly bright. I was bogged down, working like hell on my pre-med work, and Erastus just sailed along. Phi Beta Kappa his junior year was a remarkable achievement."

Erastus was a naturally inquisitive student in love with knowledge and reading, to whom the class book chronicler observed: "A few adventurous souls can be seen creeping back from the Co-op or Whitlock's under heavy loads of books. These fellows are obviously Phi Beta material and should be watched carefully." Erastus Corning was Phi Beta Kappa material alright, but the fact that he earned the prestigious academic honor in his junior year put him among an exclusive group that could be counted on one hand among the 890-member class. "I remember Erastus took every math course Yale had to offer. He was so bright in math, that his senior year he just met with the head of the math department for an hour to talk about mathematical theory," recalled McElroy. "He didn't even have to take a final exam in math like the rest of us. He was exceptionally bright."

Corning himself referred to his academic achievements at Yale with characteristic understatement. "I learned a good amount and studied fairly hard at Yale," Corning told me. "I studied a lot of Shakespeare in my literature courses. And I remember my most interesting history course came in my senior year. It was just six of us students who were history majors and we made an extensive, substantial study of World War I reparations. As far as the Phi Beta Kappa goes, I guess it was a matter of being good in math. I never thought about it much and I never wore the pin around."

Politics remained on the periphery of activities at Yale for Corning, but nonetheless it played a small part in his college life. At Yale, as it had been at Groton, Corning's fierce loyalty to the Democratic Party was a matter of some amusement to his overwhelmingly Republican classmates who made the GOP's Herbert Hoover a runaway winner for president in a student straw poll at Yale in 1932. "We used to kid Erastus about being a Democrat, because you couldn't be a proper person and a Democrat, of course," Catlin said. "The important thing is that Erastus wasn't in any way a snob, people liked him and he made it easy to be his friend. I don't think politics got much in the way of our talk at Yale." Some of his classmates decided to avoid the topic altogether. "We never talked politics," said McElroy, Corning's cousin and close friend since boyhood. "I'm an ardent Republican and he's an ardent Democrat. We knew we could never change each other's minds, so we talked about everything else but politics. When you're very fond of somebody, you're willing to do that." Corning became friendly at Yale with Robert Wagner Jr., who was a year behind him. Both men's fathers were in politics and both sons would later become mayor, Wagner of New York City and Corning of Albany. "I mean, if we could be friends with Corning the Democrat, what about Wagner?" Catlin asked. "Bob Wagner was a Democrat and a Catholic besides, which was a double second-class citizen, after all."

By the time he reached Yale, Erastus had already been given a political apprenticeship at home, of course, whether he wanted one or not. Corning avoided involvement in student government at Yale, unlike his father, who was secretary of Yale's city government club as a senior in 1906. "My father was more interested in student government at Yale than I ever was because he was interested in politics and that was a way for him to learn about it," Corning told me. "When I was growing up, as early as I remember, my father had always been politically active, so I didn't have any great interest in learning about politics through student government."

Corning's career at Yale was rigid, steady and tightly controlled throughout, a precursor to his long tenure as mayor, not marked by the emotional extremes of highs and lows of fellow classmates. Compared to his truly adventurous and risk-taking friends in New Haven, Corning seemed exceptionally stable, a plodder who ran a safe pace, more of a conservative in spirit than a progressive. Next to someone like classmate Drayton Cochran, Corning looked as dull as a gray flannel suit. In the summer after his junior year, Cochran built a schooner, *Mable T.*, and planned to cross the Atlantic in 1931 with four classmates. Cochran and crew ended up marooned on the Canary Islands and they missed the first few weeks of their senior year – but what thrilling yarns they could spin of their sea voyage. So, too, could assorted Yale miscreants brag about their exploits, such as the test cheaters who were suspended and the organizers of a garden party gone amok that degenerated into a full-fledged riot. Even Dick Bissell, the odd and bookish Groton classmate of Corning's, who, along with a couple of his intellectual literati clique, got drunk and scaled the roofs of

Yale's academic buildings with mountain-climbing gear. Corning could boast of none of these hijinks. He took the safe route, the road most traveled, and received a textbook, albeit uneventful, Yale education. The most brilliant, mercurial and ultimately tragic classmate of Corning's was Eugene O'Neill Jr., son of the famous playwright, who was with Corning in several literature classes. O'Neill developed into a promising classicist and won many academic honors at Yale, including orator of his class at commencement. He spoke five languages and returned from postgraduate studies in Germany to teach classics at Yale. Compared to Corning's solidity and convention, O'Neill's life spun faster and faster out of control. He quit his professorship and became a heavy drinker, married three times and was thrice divorced by the age of thirty-five. He ended up in Woodstock, New York, still plagued by his demons, and committed suicide in the classicist mode – filling a bathtub and slashing his left wrist and ankle with a straight razor and then settling in the tub in Roman and Greek fashion. He left a note next to an empty bottle of bourbon in the bathroom: "Never let it be said of O'Neill that he failed to empty a bottle. *Ave Atque Vale.*"

Despite such tragic characters as O'Neill in their class, as a whole the 1932 group was carefree and pursued amour as studiously as their degrees. The class book writer painted this scene of spring lust at Smith College: And so the 'Hamp Habit' was born, by Sex out of Spring. Mad dashes after the last Saturday class. Eighty miles north to Northampton and a new lease on life. Undelivered telegrams, momentary confusion at getting dates – success – gin picnics – small talk and laughter, then a moving, throbbing silence. Damn eleven o'clock rules [Smith curfew was 11 p.m.]. Then eighty more miles back to New Haven to cool off in, with a pause at Farmington for 'Tosta Bun and Coffee'" – 'Goodnight, John!' Bed and another week to battle through."

Corning, in fact, commuted often to Philadelphia for his romance with Elizabeth Norris Platt. His frequent trips received a ribbing in the class history speech by D. Nelson Adams at Class Day commencement exercises: "It is also a genuine pleasure on this occasion to welcome home Erastus Corning, whom graduation has torn out of the fond arms of Philadelphia and brought again into the light of our midst. It gladdens and warms our hearts, as when the first blush of spring appears after a hard winter, or as when the first tumbler of Tom Collins disappears after a hard training season, to see something of Erastus after all these months." Corning's relatives were in the audience, and given his basic shyness, he no doubt wished he could have melted into his seat. But the mayor-to-be was quickly developing a poker face and had learned at home the art of emotional detachment.

It was in 1932, Erastus' senior year at Yale, that his romance with Elizabeth Platt blossomed. She came from Philadelphia society and he from Albany society; the two had met at the intermingling of those social circles in Maine's Northeast Harbor the summer before. Betty and Erastus were an attraction not of opposites, but of similars. Everything about the union was safe and cemented the status quo. Both were quiet, almost shy. They were conservative and proper and revered their mothers. Their mothers were both strong, independent women who ran their respective households – Betty's mother as a widower, Erastus' mother as the caretaker of an invalid. Both Erastus and Betty were tall and thin, slightly awkward physically, and felt more comfortable on the sidelines than at center stage. They shared a love of wildlife, the outdoors and nature's beauty. They enjoyed culture, the arts, and architecture. They were both Episcopalians. They both played bridge. For the mathematician, their match all added up. But was there romantic love? Passion? Ecstasy? If there was, it was not spoken of, not recorded, not conveyed in love letters, not observed by friends. It was a thoroughly acceptable commingling, befitting both. Erastus pursued Betty with probity. "In his senior year at Yale, Erastus was quite busy with his schoolwork, but he was driving down to Philadelphia from New Haven to see me quite a lot," Betty Corning recalled. Erastus would take Betty out to dinner and a play, or they'd attend parties together. Their favorite pastime was joining friends in Philadelphia or Yale for a bridge game. It was a brief, intense courtship for the couple.

Erastus' strong-willed mother, Louise Corning, the arbiter of acceptability on the relationship, gave her blessing to Betty. As judge and jury on her daughter's future, Mrs. Platt, likewise, was a hurdle Erastus had to clear. "I remember when he came to meet my mother for the first time, he arrived in his new green Packard roadster convertible," Betty Corning recalled. "He had the top down in September and he had terrible hay fever. He was sneezing and miserable and tears were streaming down his face and yet he pulled it off. My mother thought he was quite marvelous. It was quite a triumph for Erastus. That says a lot for how charming his personality was."

With her mother's blessing, Betty Corning began to contemplate marriage. Erastus was the only one for her. "I had had boyfriends before, but nothing like I felt for him," Betty Corning said. Betty's mother had to sign off first, though. "I remember I had to have my mother's permission because I wasn't twenty-one-years-old yet," said Betty Corning, whose husband-to-be was twenty-two-years-old at the time. They were engaged early in 1932, while Corning was still a senior, and a June wedding was planned. The engagement earned a mention in the Yale class book. "It was not an arranged marriage like some society marriages seem to be," Betty Corning said. "We were particularly happy and everyone else seemed enthusiastic about it. Mrs. Corning liked me and she was devoted to her Erastus and the same was true of my mother. Both of them approved. There wasn't much for me to do the rest of 1932. I did some volunteer work, but mostly, I was getting engaged."

The wedding was set for a week after Erastus' graduation from Yale. On June 23, 1932, Erastus and Elizabeth were married in Philadelphia, at St. Paul's Episcopal Church in Chestnut Hill by Rev. Malcolm Peabody, of the family of Episcopal ministers that founded Groton and were part of the social scene in Northeast Harbor. Erastus' sisters, Louise and Harriet, were bridesmaids, with Erastus' fellow members of Wolf's Head as ushers. The usher's gift was an exquisite Tiffany silver bowl engraved with their names. In wedding photographs, Betty appeared serene and poised in a white silk and embroidered lace designer wedding gown accented by a cumulus cloud of lace veil and train. She held a large bouquet of simple lilies, their long stems reaching to her knees and the straight, narrow silhouette cut of the gown as graceful and slender as the flower stalks. She appeared thin, almost gaunt, with large, wide eyes that gave her a resemblance to a young Joan Crawford. There was a classical grace about her, a fresh beauty that needed no makeup. Next to her, Erastus looked apprehensive and boyish in gray pinstriped trousers, black tuxedo tails and waistcoat, butterfly collar and gray formal tie with white spats over polished black shoes. Erastus' only disappointment was that his father, whom he had wanted as his best man, was too sick to attend the wedding. He chose not to pick a replacement as best man for the ceremony.

"I was a little nervous, I suppose, as I walked down that aisle and my brother gave me away," recalled Betty Corning, whose father was dead. "It just felt so much like it was the right thing to do. It was somewhat symbolic that Rev. Peabody married us, because our lives came full circle," Betty Corning said. The wedding reception was held in the brick-walled private oasis of Mrs. Platt, a noted flower artist, leading light of the Philadelphia Garden Club and an officer of the Garden Club of America who instilled in her daughter a lifelong love of horticulture. Mrs. Platt's garden was an

award-winning showcase, a stunning, colorful backdrop for the reception –
for which she supplied the floral arrangements. "It was a beautiful, sunny
day and my mother's garden was perfect," Betty Corning recalled. She estimated they had about 250 guests, a merging of the Platt Philadelphia circle
and the Corning Albany contingent. The couple stood in a receiving line
and were showered with blessings and best wishes for a long and happy marriage from family and friends. Her girlfriends stopped to admire Betty's
wedding ring, which was set with diamonds Erastus had chosen from
Corning family heirlooms and had placed in a setting of his choosing.

Erastus and Betty headed off to the Corning family camp on Webb
Pond in Maine for their honeymoon. "We fished and watched birds and it
was so lovely and relaxing to be together and all alone," Betty Corning
recalled. Their honeymoon as nature retreat started a family tradition:
three generations of Cornings have spent their honeymoons at Webb
Pond. After their Webb Pond idyll, however, they returned to the reality of
Albany, with great social connections but little in the way of genuine
prospects. Erastus didn't have a job. The couple had no visible means of
support. The Depression continued into that fall of 1932 and new jobs
were scarce. Betty Corning also was pregnant.

In an attempt to maintain their independence, as a temporary arrangement the couple moved into a modest apartment at 397 State Street across
from Washington Park for a time after the honeymoon, but struggled
financially as Erastus looked for work. As always, the mayor's mother protected her firstborn and favorite child from hardship, and soon brought
him back to where she wanted him to be, close to her on Corning Hill.
Mrs. Corning gave Erastus and Betty the gardener's house next to her
mansion on the Upper Farm for their residence. "We were lucky to have
been given the gardener's house," Betty Corning said. "Erastus didn't have
a job at that point, but he quickly got into the insurance business. That was
my father's and brother's business, so I was able to help him a little bit."

Financially, Betty had an inheritance from her late father, but Erastus'
father, an invalid, saw his fortune largely wiped out during the stock market crash. Edwin Corning had turned over the operation and control of
Ludlum Steel when he was stricken in 1928 and could not offer that company for his son. Instead, with a modest cash investment from his father,
Erastus was set up in insurance. Although it required little start-up cash,
Erastus had no experience and even less passion for the trade. But it was all

he had and it was his father's plan, so the dutiful son once more complied – a gray career for the young man whose father told the son to play it safe.

Corning's father arranged for Erastus to work with the Schenectady insurance firm of Ter Bush & Powell. Corning drove to Schenectady for training each day and passed the test for his insurance broker license. Using his father's business and political connections, as well as his capital, Corning quickly formed his own insurance firm, Albany Associates, in 1932. Ter Bush & Powell initially owned a one-third interest in the company and Corning one-third. He had the position of secretary-treasurer; David Ter Bush was listed as president. Corning's hard work at the new business attracted family friends and political allies as clients. "I remember those early years as very busy ones with Erastus studying insurance late at night and working all the time," Betty Corning said. The workaholic pattern was one he would repeat in politics. Eventually, in 1935, Corning became president of Albany Associates, the same year he was first elected to public office, as State Assemblyman. He later bought out Ter Bush & Powell's interest in the company and became its sole owner and stockholder.

Erastus and Betty Corning's firstborn, a son, arrived on June 20, 1933 – three days shy of a year after their wedding. They kept tradition and named him Erastus III. Betty hired a nurse for her son; she also had a housekeeper and cook working for her, a substantial payroll for a fledgling insurance broker, but cash advances from their mothers always tided over the newlyweds. "Being able to afford good help made it much easier on us," Betty Corning said. "We also could always ask for help from Mrs. Corning. We did everything together in those early years and it was wonderful living right next door. I was very close to her. But we also led our own lives. She might have had the urge to protect and spoil her son, like any mother, but she was much too wise to do that after we were married." Betty was used to a forceful mother and generally chose the path of least resistance among these two resolute women, both of whom were left widows when young (Platt in her thirties, Corning at forty-nine). Neither remarried. Betty certainly had her skirmishes with Mrs. Corning early on, but the two seemed to adjust to the fulcrum of power that very clearly tilted toward the mayor's mother.

Mrs. Corning, the mayor's forceful matriarch, ruled life around the Upper Farm, even Betty's and Erastus'. Louise Maxwell Corning planned the dinners and parties. She organized the lists of guests. She set the schedule for the family's summer gatherings in Maine. Betty Corning also had a sister in York, Maine and they rented a house on the beach together so the children could play together for a few summers. Mostly, it was Corning time and when Mrs. Corning made a request, it was followed as surely as an order.

"I wanted to go back to school, but I didn't have a chance to go back full-time, although I took some non-credit courses in Spanish and Japanese and enjoyed that," said Betty Corning. Their second child, Elizabeth, who preferred to be called Bettina, was born five years after her brother, in 1938. "I was very active in the Garden Club of America and did some volunteer work, but otherwise I stayed busy with my children and my gardening. I've lived in the same house for sixty years, which seems amazing, but the time seemed to go in a flash," Betty said.

Subsumed in the culture of the Cornings, Betty Corning watched from the sidelines as her husband followed family tradition and grew deeply interested in politics in the early years of their marriage. "He started getting involved in politics early on, but I didn't have any ambition in that field," Betty Corning said. "He grew up with politics practically his whole life through his father and other family members. I wasn't going to change that." Gradually, the young couple drifted apart as he pursued politics and she immersed herself in gardening. They began to lead parallel lives that seemed to intersect less and less. But the basic attributes that attracted Betty to Erastus never dimmed in her mind. "He always had a sense of humor, a great love of people and a deep kindness," Betty Corning said. "He was kind to everyone. For myself, I kept busy keeping the house, with the garden club, and taking care of the children."

And then, before she knew it, sixty years had passed, and Betty Corning, twenty-year-old bride, was eighty and living in the same house on Corning Hill, a solitary widow all alone.

Chapter 4:

One Man, Two Families:
The Unusual Home Life of Mayor Corning

"If you would have a lovely garden, you must have a lovely life."

Betty Corning's favorite saying. From a Shaker proverb.

The fall of 1932 was a time of abrupt change for Erastus Corning 2nd. In a few short months, the once irresolute Yalie, given to the art of flouting Prohibition by concocting bathtub gin and experimenting with other forbidden pleasures during his collegiate career, went from indulgent frat life to the real world. It was a crash course in adulthood. Graduation. Wham. Wedding. Wham. Set up by father in the insurance business. Wham. A baby. Wham. Family life. Wham. And, inevitably, politics. Double Wham. The track of WASP respectability was groomed and laid out in front of him as far as he cared to look. Wham.

In September of 1932, a few months after their nuptials and a honeymoon spent at the Corning family camp at Webb Pond in Maine, the newlyweds, Erastus and Elizabeth, were settling into the quiet domesticity of the Upper Farm on Corning Hill. Their house, known as "the gardener's house," built in a loose center hall Colonial style, had been bought by the mayor's father after it won first prize at a home show in the Washington Avenue Armory in 1923. The second story was added later and the house was used to house the Cornings' gardeners. For his part, Erastus felt responsible for helping his mother next door and strove to help ease her burden of caring for her invalid husband and holding the family together. The couple took up residence in the gardener's house – appropriately enough for Betty Corning, a gardener obsessed – a house constructed of brick and weathered cedar shingles that lent it the folksy air of backwoods Maine or back-cove Cape Cod.

A decade after the mayor's death, approaching the front door, framed by two white columns, one's eye was instantly drawn to an oval-shaped nameplate with the word "Corning" in fancy script. The nameplate was coated with a patina of age and weather. "Everything stays the same around here," Betty Corning, eighty years old at the time, told me by way of greeting at the house on Corning Hill. It was September, 1992, sixty years on from when Betty first moved in and assumed the role of materfamilias behind the gilded Corning nameplate and all that implied. Betty, a shy and tentative twenty-year-old new bride, faced the additional pressure of conducting her newfound domestic responsibilities under the watchful, sometimes critical, gaze of her forceful mother-in-law who lived just beyond a ravine and orchard in a stately mansion known in the family as "the big house." Joanne Lenden, a gardening protege of Betty Corning's who became one of Betty's closest friends in her final years, remembered meeting the mayor's mother in the early 1970s at the Ten Broeck Mansion while decorating for a Fort Orange Garden Club Christmas party there. "It was a driving snowstorm and Mrs. Corning pulled up in her limousine with her driver and announced she had come because she always brought variegated holly for the party at the mansion," Lenden said. "Variegated holly as a colorful Christmas green was something Betty and her mother-in-law could agree upon. From what I saw, Betty and Mrs. Corning weren't great buddies. Mrs. Corning was strong and formal and had a very patrician manner. She and Betty didn't seem terribly close." Wharton Sinkler III, son of the mayor's sister, Harriet, recalled the relationship between Betty and Mrs. Corning as "polite and distant."

Contrasting with the lifestyle of the mayor's mother ensconced in the mansion and surrounded by the trappings of comfortable wealth, albeit beginning to fade, the humble "gardener's house," where Betty and Erastus lived, was marked by an almost rustic simplicity, with the feeling of an unfinished camp on the second floor. That unpretentiousness seemed fine with the newlyweds, mirroring their understated tastes. Neither Betty nor Erastus appeared interested in the old-money opulence in which both were raised.

In the fall of 1992, the house, where Betty had been living alone for nine years after the death of her husband, had a feel of permanence, the timeless quality of a museum or shrine to Betty's image of what their marriage had been. It appeared as if the furniture, even the bric-a-brac, had not been rearranged in decades. The furnishings, although not of a quality sought by serious collectors, were classic and solid, mostly understated examples in the Colonial, Federal and particularly Empire style – fitting for the scion of the Empire-building family.

As a longtime widow, Betty Corning, who shared the large house with two cats, Charlotte and Emily, named after the Bronte sisters, clung fiercely to rituals in her frail, emphysema-ridden solitude. Without the help of a housekeeper, who arrived later in the day, early each morning Betty set a place for breakfast at the head of a formal dining room table, carefully placing the blue Staffordshire china and a silver coffee service just so. The *New York Times* and that day's letters and correspondence were stacked carefully to one side, near a bowl of seedless California grapes. An uneaten plain doughnut was tossed outside to feed the birds. The scene was so precisely etched that one could imagine this exact routine each morning, with Betty often alone, even while her husband was alive, for more than six decades.

Fall, of course, is one of the best times for planting trees and shrubs and Betty Corning dove into that task in the fall of 1932 when the newly-weds moved onto Corning Hill. "The land around this house was all bare when I arrived, and I planted everything you see," she told me in 1992. "When the first bird sets up its nest in a tree, that's when I feel I've done something worthwhile." Betty Corning had inherited her mother's passion for flowers and plants and her first efforts in their new home were spent landscaping and planting. The property around the house was a wild tangle of forest and undergrowth when the bride, just twenty years old, never having attended college or lived on her own for any extended period, moved in and tried to turn the house into a home. Betty's get-it-done instincts were put to good use; she set about making order out of chaos. "As soon as I was married and we had our own piece of land to cultivate, my interest in horticulture became a real obsession," Betty Corning told the Russell Sage College Class of 1987 at the Troy school's convocation, when the mayor's widow received an honorary doctorate. "My husband and I spent many, many happy hours working on our property. How grateful I am that our first energies went into digging holes for trees and hauling the endless buckets of water so essential to get them off to a good start for their future well-being."

Betty planted a fern-leaf beech tree at the entrance to their property on the Upper Farm at the crest of Corning Hill Road. During the six decades Betty lived there – the only house she ever knew as Mrs. Corning (aside from winter months at 116 South Lake Avenue in Albany in the '40s and '50s to meet the city residency requirement for mayor) – the beech grew into a huge shade tree soaring more than sixty feet high with a majestic, muscular trunk and a vast constellation of branches. The tree grew to be so massive that the gravel driveway was forced to take a jog to the left inside the white gate posts. "I planted that tree too close to the drive, and it's still pushing outward," Betty Corning, then eighty years old, told me, shaking her head at the vigor of the tree after all those years. "But I always told Erastus, 'I'll move the drive, but I won't move that tree.'"

For one-half century, Betty Corning was the quietly aristocratic, immovable presence behind the man, the myth, the exalted ruler, the icon of Albany. At her heart, Betty Corning was a gardener. She knew everything about nurturing and loving and raising a tender shoot into a hardy plant. She surrounded herself with all manner of beautiful flowers, plants, trees and shrubs throughout her obsessively tended gardens. Perhaps she retreated deeper into her gardening, friends said, in order to forget, even to deny, the lifeless nature of her marriage.

Even as her marriage withered, how marvelously Betty Corning's garden flourished. She became internationally known for her work in horticulture, winning numerous awards and judging famous flower shows and becoming an officer, like her mother, and later president of the prestigious Garden Club of America. She traveled to many foreign countries in search of rare plants or to share her knowledge in the field. But she always traveled without her husband on those garden tours. She had her life in gardening. He had his in politics. Their two worlds rarely merged. Her gardening received many important recognitions. A rare species of clematis she had discovered was named for her, Clematis Betty Corning. The Garden Club of America gave her its highest achievement medal in 1971. British author Sheila Macqueen wrote, "Betty Corning has done more for the beautification of America than anyone else, specifically through promoting legislation to remove billboards from major highways and by moving the Garden Club of America to lobby toward this legislation."

Betty traveled widely across the United States and around the world lecturing, judging, collecting and propagating rare plants. She planted gardens all around Albany and was a guiding light in the Fort Orange Garden Club. She turned her own home, greenhouse and property into a lush oasis of greenery. When I visited Mrs. Corning in her garden in 1992, she offered her visitor a long and detailed narrative about every shrub, every tree, every flower on the property. About her two children and four grandchildren she said nothing. Betty Corning seemed to pour all of her love and devotion and caring into those plants. "It all began some twenty years ago, my first primrose dreams and desires," Betty Corning wrote in the September, 1954 issue of the *Garden Club of America Bulletin*. "My first love and initial attempt was the *polyantha*, and here I was fortunate, for a more charming and tractable member of the clan does not exist."

Betty Corning was in all things her mother's daughter. She was the youngest of three children born to Dorothy Falcon Platt, who died in 1971 at the age of ninety. The *Garden Club of America Bulletin* eulogized her this way: "For fifty-eight of her ninety years, Dorothy Falcon Platt loved and served The Garden Club of America with all her remarkable qualities of heart, head and hand. She created beauty in paint, in words, in flowers, and in her surroundings. She was gay and witty, modest and kind, with a surpassing gift for friendship with all ages." Platt was a founding member of The Garden Club of America in 1913, having helped to establish The Garden Club of Philadelphia. She was president of both groups and was awarded numerous prestigious medals for her leadership role with The Garden Club of America. Betty's mother's illustrations were included in the 1953 edition of *Wild Flowers of America* and her paintings, embroidery and needlepoint designs were exhibited widely, including at the Philadelphia Museum of Art.

Betty was raised by her mother after her father's untimely death. Charles Platt Sr., an insurance executive, died at thirty-eight in 1918, when Betty was just six. His widow never remarried. Betty's older brother, Charles Jr., and older sister, Dorothy, lived with their mother in a stately residence in Philadelphia's affluent Chestnut Hill section in a neighborhood known as Laverock. The Platt family inherited, through Betty's mother, a large tract of property atop Falcon Hill known as Allonby Farm, named for a tiny coastal town in the Lake District of northwest England, from which Betty's mother's forebears emigrated. The first family member to arrive in America was John Sims, who settled in Burlington County, New Jersey in the early 1790s. On her father's side, John Patterson arrived in 1796 from Belfast, Ireland.

In many ways, Betty Corning's upbringing mirrored that of her husband. Both were raised by strong-willed mothers after their fathers died young, before their children knew them well. Both were, in some ways, in search of a father figure. Both grew up indulged amid old money luxury, waited on by servants, with plenty of money and mansions attached to sprawling farmlands where they could roam as children and develop their love of nature and cultivation.

In her childhood, Betty Corning's salmon-colored stucco mansion in Philadelphia's Chestnut Hill was called "Allonby" or "The Pink House" by local kids. Betty was nicknamed "Me-mouse" for her shyness and love of the nursery rhyme, "Hickory, Dickory, Dock." Her mother had the help of two housekeepers as Mrs. Platt, from a distance, reared Betty as she had been raised. Mother attended Agnes Irwin School, a private Philadelphia finishing school, but didn't graduate, spending her final year in Paris studying art. Betty didn't complete her private Philadelphia finishing school, spending her final year in Florence studying art. Mother learned French; so did daughter. Mother was active in the work of St. Paul's Episcopal Church in Chestnut Hill and served on the board of All-Saints Hospital there. Daughter was active in the work of All Saint's Cathedral in Albany and served on the board of Child's Hospital there. During World War II, mother headed the Victory Gardens in Chestnut Hill and daughter headed the Victory Gardens in Albany.

Betty's mother passed on many things to her daughter, but central was a deep reserve and sense of privacy, and, of course, an obsession for gardening, right down to a botanical inheritance for Betty regarding mother's passion for clematis. In a *Garden Club of America Bulletin* feature article on her garden, Betty's mother was shown amid the foliage in a print dress, white pumps, a strand of pearls and a straw hat, looking as if she was preparing for an Easter service. But she was hoeing the soil in what apparently passed for basic gardening attire in Chestnut Hill. The article called Dorothy Platt's garden "very special . . . lovely . . . a horticulturist's garden designed in perfect taste. Cleverly enclosed and divided by walls, trees and hedges, each charming section is individual. Two of Mrs. Platt's specialties are roses and clematis. Mrs. Platt grows bamboo to make supports for beans and tomatoes."

Betty wrote of her mother: "I had a closely knit bond with my widowed mother, who was one of those rare spirits loved equally by young and old. She was a talented artist – charming, intellectual, a poetess and a great gardener, and everything she undertook was laced with her warm sense of humor. I soon learned the value of that indefinable quality. . . . With my mother as mentor it was only natural that my interests should veer in the direction of horticulture."

While Betty's interests were firmly rooted in the garden, her overarching passion for plants was not fully embraced by her husband, whose interests began to veer in other directions. Despite the fundamental similarities of their backgrounds, Betty and Erastus were also a study in contrasts. His humor was bawdy and earthy, which would make her blush, while her demeanor was marked by a demure quality in all things and an almost Victorian propriety. He liked the hurly-burly of politics, an arena that held absolutely no interest for her. He liked to cuss and swear and drink Scotch with beer chasers. She was a quiet sort who discussed horticulture over tea poured from a silver service into dainty china cups. "Betty's emotional repertoire ranged from distantly polite to frighteningly frigid," said Wharton Sinkler III. "She could be pleasant, but in an instant she could turn as icy as could be. You never knew where the switch was. I have no recollection of her joking or enjoying a good laugh." Of the mayor's fabled "pecker bone" collection, taken from the erect penis skeletal structure of various animals, his daughter Bettina said, "We never told mother about the pecker bones. Oh, my word, she would have been scandalized."

Erastus and Elizabeth's first child was born on June 20, 1933, a son, named Erastus, designated the third – Roman number III as opposed to his father's Arabic 2nd – with no middle name. The baby's father was consumed with building up his fledgling insurance business and being introduced into the Albany political machine, an organization in which his once dominant father, now an invalid, was a fading legend. Erastus clearly was not a hands-on father and saw little of his firstborn during early childhood development. As a mother, Betty was incapable, it seemed, of transferring that same kind of affectionate dotage she bestowed upon her plants to the rearing of Erastus III, known as Rasty. A nanny and servants were responsible for much of little Rasty's upbringing, while Betty remained consumed with horticulture.

"Hardly a day goes by even now that somebody doesn't stop me on the street of Albany to tell me a story about my father and how wonderful he was and what he did for them," Erastus Corning III recalled in 1996, more than a decade after his father's death. "I find that so strange. I didn't know him. He was a complete stranger to me. I can count on one hand the recollections I have of him as a boy. Maybe once or twice fishing. That's about it." Erastus 2nd, like Edwin, his father, had difficulty expressing emotions or showing affection, even to his son, according to several family friends. "He was not a hugger" was the way his daughter, Bettina, put it. Neither parent was emotionally available to their children in a physical, tactile, caressing way, a contributor to the strain in their familial relationships, Bettina said. To a large extent, Rasty, and, to a lesser degree, Bettina, were raised by nannies as surrogate parents.

In a rare moment of familial exploration, the usually guarded Rasty poured out his embittered feelings toward his father to Bruce Bouchard, a founder and former artistic director of Albany's Capital Repertory Company. The two traveled together during a theater exchange trip to Russia in which Corning, who had lived and worked in Russia for many years, acted as translator and tour guide. "He went on and on about how unhappy his childhood was and how he hated his father, absolutely hated him," Bouchard said. "He told me the story of how he got interested in Russia. He was seventeen years old and looked on a map and decided on going away to Russia because it was the furthest he could get away from his father."

"I'm not blaming my father," the son said over lunch at the Fort Orange Club in April, 1996. "He didn't know his own father. He got married right out of Yale and then they had me. What kind of training for fatherhood was that? Basically, my father didn't have time for me and then they sent me away to boarding school and college. I went to Russia and I never came back to Albany until he was in the hospital." "Rasty was treated so badly from the day he was born," said Martha (Thompson) Becker, a family friend. "They just didn't make him feel like a member of the family. He more or less was left to grow up on his own. Betty was so stunned by what was happening to her own marriage that she forgot about her little boy."

When the boy was four years old, in 1937, his father, a twenty-eight-year-old state senator, the youngest member of the upper house in the State Legislature, was a rising star in the Albany Democratic organization. Betty Corning suffered a miscarriage following the birth of Erastus III. Betty and Erastus' second child, Elizabeth, named for her mother, was born on June 17, 1938. Her rift with her mother could be seen symbolically perhaps in the fact that she never used her mother's name, but preferred her nickname, Bettina. When Bettina had a miscarriage herself in 1964, her father revealed for the first time the fact that Betty had suffered the same loss. Corning struggled to express his emotions in a letter to his daughter on May 12, 1964. "Dear Bettina: I was very sorry to hear of the trouble you have had, and it must have given you a really rough week. I hope that you come along well now, and that you will be home and feeling much better very, very soon. Mummie had a miscarriage between the time Rasty and you were born and it is, of course, a tremendously disturbing thing – more mentally than physically – and I know it must have been so to you." And then the father quickly changed the subject to safer topics like the weather, the blooming lilacs and dogwood tree in the yard and his first sighting of a Tennessee warbler.

At the time of Bettina's birth in 1938, Erastus Corning 2nd, still a year shy of his thirtieth birthday, was one of the youngest senators ever elected to the New York State Legislature. In addition, he continued to tend his insurance company and to build a power base in Albany County politics. Bettina's mother was immersed in the Garden Club of America and still deeply imbedded in her own mother's Philadelphia garden club social circle.

"There were difficulties and lots of unhappiness growing up," Bettina Corning said. "I sometimes wonder why my brother and I didn't grow up to be completely schizophrenic. Since I've moved to Maine, I've become serious about meditation and primal therapy and have done a lot of healing. I think my brother, who's on his third marriage, is still deeply wounded and unhappy."

Rasty had reason to be confused growing up. At Albany Academy, where he attended his early years of school, the name Erastus Corning was both a burden and a curse for the son – an appellation whose reputation preceded him no matter how much he tried to become his own person. "When I look through family photo albums, I'm struck that you'll never find my uncle [Erastus III] smiling after the age of six or so," said another namesake, Erastus Christopher Dudley, the mayor's grandson, who named his own baby boy, the mayor's great-grandson, Christopher Erastus. "I know my uncle is an unhappy person. I would guess there were a lot of causes for the mutual separation between father and son, from being sent off to boarding school to Polly Noonan. The evidence is clear. It's just difficult inferring cause and effect." "The psychological wound in the relationship between Rasty and his father was deep and completely unresolved," said another grandson, Robert Dudley. "I don't think there was a simple explanation for their conflict."

At the Fort Orange Club in the spring of 1996, Rasty was having lunch in the tap room, off to the right rear of the main dining room, a rustic and informal space with wide pine floors and a bar with an Adirondack mural. We sat at a table for two, an arm's length away from where his father had lunch at "the long table" almost every workday during his forty-two years as mayor. The long table that afternoon had a couple of Corning's friends and old lunch regulars, Jim Lenden and Norman Rice. This is a club where guests carry weighty titles, where the men are greeted with "Hello, Senator" and "Well, hello, Judge" or "Good to see you, Governor." But the one greeting that stopped everyone in mid-sentence for nearly one-half century was reserved for the most powerful man in Albany: "Hello, Mayor." Mayor Corning needed no further introduction. Some joked they thought his first name was Mayor. And there was the son in 1996, christened with the same name, but without its reward. Nobody stopped to greet this Erastus Corning: there was no special treatment, no honorific title. The portrait of the mayor's grandfather, Erastus Corning Jr., at the entrance to the club he helped establish seems yet another unfair weight, a burden of family legacy, to drop upon the shoulders of Erastus III.

Outwardly, at least, sterling achievements across four generations granted the Corning family iconic stature in Albany; the historic tenure of the mayor was among the family's most prized legends. But at what cost? Inwardly, the mayor's children spoke of a home life marked by a profound sadness, of deep regret and unresolved issues. They described a mother and father seemingly incapable of a form of parenting that was anything other than vaguely distant. "My father was around so little for us growing up and he kept his political life totally separate from his family life and my mother had nothing to do with politics. So, they more or less each went their own way," Bettina Corning Dudley said. "You're talking to me about a stranger, a total stranger," Erastus Corning III said. "I didn't know him at all. His job was a seven-day-a-week job and then I left for school and never came back. There was nothing between us. It was a void." As was the case with his own upbringing, the mayor passed on the paradigm of absentee father. Betty Corning, too, seemed incapable of expressing her feelings to her children and retreated into an obsession for order and decorum. "My mother was so rigid and uptight, I remember she could never relax," Bettina recalled. "If I finished a drink in the livingroom, the glass, on a coaster, of course, wasn't dry a second before she whisked it away and wiped the spot." Neither parent learned to touch and to nurture their children. "I don't remember being kissed by my father," Bettina said. "But I do remember feeling loved by him. We didn't have a lot of time with him. Looking back on my childhood, I think I was a lonely child, feeling very much alone out there in the country."

For a brief time, though, when the children were young, in the early 1940s, the Cornings enjoyed a fleeting sense of being a happy family without the later searing resentments and psychological wounds that would so injure them. At that time, the Cornings made an annual migration in fall from their home at Corning Hill to their official residence at Morris Street and South Lake Avenue, a few blocks from the southwest corner of Washington Park. The family moved truckloads of personal belongings so that the children – Rasty at Albany Academy, Bettina at Saint Agnes – could get to school more easily in winter weather. The annual moves, oddly enough, were happy times, Bettina recalled, even though their main purpose was to fulfill the requirement that the mayor be a resident of Albany. But as the family began drifting apart and whatever cohesiveness it once possessed began disintegrating, they stopped moving into the city each fall and winter as the children were shipped off to boarding school. Bettina Corning recalled that her father read her bedtime stories and sang her lullabies as a young girl in the house at 116 South Lake Avenue. She said she could still hear his voice, low and soft, more than fifty years later, singing "Long, Long Trail" and "You Are My Sunshine" and "Rockabye, Baby." And when he was home to tuck his children into bed and bid them goodnight, which wasn't often, he'd read to them at bedtime, usually O. Henry stories. His daughter remembered him reading over and over "The Ransom of Red Chief," and, around Christmas time, "The Gift of the Magi."

It was in those early years that Bettina recalled their house as a place that resounded with moments of domestic harmony. "I remember we'd sit in the kitchen and my mom would make salad and my father would make chestnut stuffing and cook a partridge he'd shot," Bettina recalled. Her father would help his wife do the dishes and often times the mayor, tired from his workday, would fall asleep on the couch in the livingroom. Bettina remembered from her girlhood another one of her father's rituals. On the afternoon of New Year's Eve, Corning would make sourdough bread. "It was always sourdough and my father would leave it on the radiator to start to rise," his daughter recalled. "Then he and my mom would go out for New Year's Eve and they'd be home at midnight and we'd have sourdough bread and champagne. It was my father's special ritual." It didn't have to be a holiday when her father, if he had enough energy after dinner, would fetch *Webster's* dictionary and read definitions of words that came up in conversation. It was a favorite form of entertainment for Corning, perhaps a pastime he picked up at Groton. "He'd get that gleam in his eye, head off to the dictionary and carry it back reading about this hilarious word that would make us laugh every time," Bettina remembered.

Based on fond memories of her father when she was young, Bettina wrote this poem about childhood recollections after her father's death. It's titled "In Albany."

> We picked wild strawberries
> along the Normanskill;
> your hands hulled
> the sun-full fruit. You made
> jam for a feast at Flat Rock,
> where we hunted for frogs.
> We would wander
> on cool fall days,
> looking for partridge and woodcock
> in fields by the lake.
>
> You made chestnut stuffing.
> I got to stay up late and dine.
> Giddy at dinner,
> you would read us
> *The Ransom of Red Chief,*
> definitions out of *Webster's,*
> and we would laugh
> until we cried.
>
> We always shopped
> late on Christmas Eve,
> buying sandalwood soap
> for my mom and, when you thought
> I wasn't looking,
> a gold charm for me.

But the good times were short-lived and soon gave way to a long, emotionally sterile relationship in which Erastus and Betty Corning seemed to lead parallel lives. Friends recalled early on in the union the jovial voice that would answer the phone, on the first or second ring, at Corning Hill: "Erastus here!" But over the years, Erastus was there less and less. "From what I saw, she went her way and he went his and their paths rarely overlapped," said longtime family friend Norman Rice, who spent several summers as a houseguest of the mayor's mother in the big house. "If you want to know the truth, the mayor wasn't home much," said Bela Kollarits Jr., son of the caretakers who grew up on the Corning Farm in the gate house. "It wasn't a happy home from what I saw. The mayor and his wife would work in the garden together some, but they weren't together much." Kollarits is the son of the Cornings' longtime caretakers, Bela Sr. and Olga Kollarits, who lived on the property and worked for the family from 1961 to 1994 after fleeing the Communists in Hungary. They lived rent-free; their utilities were paid by the Cornings, who also gave the couple a weekly salary of $40, which was eventually doubled to $80 per week. "I felt sad for the mayor's wife," said Olga Kollarits, whose son translated her Hungarian. "It was heartbreaking. I'd rather not say anymore. But Mrs. Corning was a very lonely lady, so alone all the time."

While gardening filled Betty Corning's days and nights, when her husband was off building and protecting his political career, she sought outlets to occupy idle time and to provide the social contact she lacked on Corning Hill. One antidote was the Knit & Nibble group that Betty started at her home in the late-1930s. It was patterned after a gathering of Chestnut Hill society ladies her mother had formed in Philadelphia a generation before. Knit & Nibble, which met Tuesday afternoons on Corning Hill, consisted of a half-dozen women, acquainted through their husbands' membership in the Fort Orange Club. Knit & Nibble members would select a book to read out loud. Each Tuesday afternoon, they'd arrive at Betty's house with their knitting, along with a snack or dessert, for the Knit & Nibble gathering. One person would begin reading the book out loud for the others, who sat around in the livingroom, munching the food and knitting. After ten minutes or so of reading, the book was passed to the next person. "It was ostensibly a gathering to read new books, but mostly we'd sip tea, knit and shoot the breeze," recalled Jean Beebe. "Knit & Nibble was great fun," recalled Mary Arthur Doolittle. "It was initially formed for younger women new to Albany to help solidify their social connections. We soon became just a group of good friends."

Knit & Nibble ran concurrently with another women's social group, the Junior Friday Morning Club, and the members of the two overlapped to a large extent. There was Corning, Doolittle, Beebe, Martha Thompson and her eventual sister-in-law, Elizabeth Becker, as well as assorted Parkers and McElroys – related to the Cornings by marriage. The Junior Friday Morning Club had been formed in 1897; Betty Corning joined in 1951.

The format for the Junior Friday Morning Club, despite the fact that its meetings had been reduced from weekly to monthly by the 1950s, nonetheless remained constant over the years: two women would team up to research and write a kind of term paper that they would then present as a report for the continuing education and general edification of the rest of the group. "We let it lapse into a social thing for awhile, but then we women decided we didn't want to be frivolous all the time and it turned into quite an academic gathering," Doolittle said.

Beebe recounted Betty Corning's papers in a tribute she wrote after the death of her friend. "Her subjects were as diversified as her partners," Beebe wrote. Among Betty's papers were these: "Brief Background of a Day at the Races" with Mrs. Porter; "Turkey" with Mrs. McNamee; "Dolls" with Mrs. Becker; "Analysis of Creative Writing" and "China as Glimpsed Through a Flying Horse" with others. "In later years, her papers on travels to Singapore, South Africa and Egypt were so colorful and imaginative, her curiosity and shy wit showing through," Beebe wrote. Beebe further praised Betty Cornings' "friendship, scholarship and generosity" as well as her "alert intelligence and diligent spirit that drove her to get things done" and an "innate curiosity and appreciation of all things" in relation to her long association with the Junior Friday Morning Club.

Consciously or not, Albany's upper class had institutions such as these as a manner of WASP self-preservation. The Beebes met the Cornings in the 1930s at such a gathering, whose ulterior motive was to preserve blue-blood efficacy among the social elite of the capital city. "Benjamin Arnold and his wife, who lived in a mansion on State Street near Washington Park, gave dinner parties to encourage young society couples to get to know each other and that's how we met the Cornings, Parkers, McElroys and other prominent Albany families," recalled Dr. Richard T. Beebe, of the Baltimore Beebes, a Harvard man and graduate of Johns Hopkins Medical School, who arrived with his wife, Jean, to take a job at Albany Medical College, sans local social connections, in 1932, the year Erastus and Betty Corning were married. In essence, these clubs and social opportunities had, as their desired effect, the same purpose as the Corning family's traditional schooling at Groton and Yale – namely, to equip with adequate elan the next generation who would be carrying the torch of WASP Ascendancy.

For all this effort at preserving class and tribe, Erastus Corning 2nd was a man who did not fully connect with the institutions of private social club or family. Each required a certain emotional risk, a divulging and an opening up that was not in the mayor's makeup. However, what was lacking in loving contact with his closest friends and his own children, Erastus partly provided when it came to his grandchildren. He apparently felt remorse at his remoteness and sought to rectify it, doting on his four grandchildren. Whenever he got the chance he left them a richer inheritance of happy childhood memories than he had provided his own children. His daughter's son, Erastus Christopher Dudley, nicknamed Topher, was probably the mayor's favorite grandchild. Dudley, who grew up in Maryland, has fond boyhood memories of grandpa Erastus from Christmases at Corning Hill and summer vacations at Webb Pond in Maine. They shared a passion for coin collecting, fishing, long walks in the woods, gadgets and hot fudge sundaes.

The mayor repeated the same Christmas ritual each year. "Grandfather always got a nice, big tree and decorations. Grandmother was in charge of the details," Dudley remembered. "We'd open our presents early on Christmas morning and my mom [Bettina] would make breakfast. During the day, my grandfather would take some turkeys and food to shelters and I'd go along." His grandfather gave him unusual Christmas gifts. Dudley remembered a pen-sized pocket telescope his grandfather gave him as a young teen, which he saved. "He'd give me coins and he got me started in coin collecting," Dudley said, noting the mayor was a member of the Albany Numismatic Association. "I remember he loved zinc pennies from 1943. I never knew why. But he had thousands of them stored in tins." (That was the year Gov. Thomas Dewey tried to bring down the Albany Democratic machine with his investigations.) His grandfather also gave Dudley gifts of fishing gear. "He took me out on Webb Pond and taught me how to fish," Dudley recalled. "Fishing was a very serious thing for him, but he was just having fun with us kids."

Dudley continued family tradition and went to Yale, where he received a Ph.D. in molecular biology and now researches immune system development for the National Institutes of Health. He said he never acquired an appetite for politics despite the time spent with his grandfather. Hot fudge sundaes, though, were another matter. "My grandfather got me started on hot fudge sundaes and he'd order me one wherever we stopped," Dudley recalled. "He never ate much of the sundae himself. He just liked watching me eat them, I guess. I couldn't go anywhere around Albany with him, though, without getting stopped by people who wanted to talk to him or ask a favor. Anywhere we stopped, everyone knew him and wanted to shake his hand and talk. It was phenomenal." All things considered, Dudley said he is proud to carry on the name of his grandfather, the sixth-generation Erastus in the Corning family. "Down South, Erastus was a slave name and I've never been able to find out how it made its way up North," Dudley said. "People are always telling me how unusual it is as a name. So's Topher, which wasn't my choice, either. On the whole, I think being named Erastus has been a blessing," Dudley said. "What I'm left with in the end is the heart wrenching image of seeing how many people cared enough to line up to see his funeral procession. To think that many people cared about my grandfather that deeply is remarkable."

Dudley's older brother, Robert Dudley, a professor of zoology at the University of Texas, said the strongest impression his grandfather made on him growing up was what he called a "polymath passion," an intense interest in many disciplines, especially natural science, the environment and Native American history. "My grandfather had the book *League of the Iroquois* practically memorized," Robert Dudley recalled. His grandfather also gave him a gift of an arrowhead Corning had found in the fields of the family farm as a boy. But his grandfather gave him an even greater gift, a zest for knowledge, particularly zoology, and the means to pursue higher education. Dudley said his grandfather paid for the majority of his college tuition at Duke University. "He was always interested in and supportive of my academic career," said Dudley, who received a postgraduate Marshall Scholarship to conduct research at Cambridge University in England on insect and bird flight. "My regret is that my grandfather died shortly after I got the Marshall Scholarship. I wanted to show him all he did to support me through college had paid off."

Dudley was impressed by his grandfather's formidable intellect and felt he could have achieved success in larger spheres than Albany had he so chosen. "The universe is where we find it and my grandfather found it in microcosm," Dudley said. "He had a visceral connection to Corning Hill. That was his family's land and he knew every inch of the flora and fauna on that real estate." Dudley said his grandfather's avocations and intellectual pursuits knew no bounds, particularly in the field he calls "crypto-biology." Said Dudley, "He was interested in all that Loch Ness stuff. He was very interested in underwater photographs a scientist had taken at Loch Ness that I got from his lab. We discussed his penis bone collection. He read a lot about UFO studies and spontaneous human combustion, that sort of thing. He also followed the controversial theories of Charles Fort and Immanuel Velikovsky." In essence, what his grandfather was, Dudley asserted, was a man out of time. "He really fit the nineteenth-century terminology of natural scientist in that line of Emerson and Thoreau," Dudley said. "He was a hungry naturalist, sufficiently open-minded to be curious about everything. He just collected information, whether it was on penis bones or Native Americans."

When it came to his grandparents' marriage, Dudley didn't consider Betty and Erastus a good fit, despite similar backgrounds. "Betty was a classic East Coast WASP and so was my grandfather, at least to outsiders, but to those who knew him he was far more complex," Dudley said. "They probably tolerated each other's interests, but they weren't explicitly interested in each other. They led different lives. I don't sense that their marriage was a deep, close collaboration."

Dudley said he understood and respected his grandfather's essential atheism. "Implicitly in his psyche, I believe he embraced the biologist's view that we emerged as primates and in one way or another we return to that, rather than to God, at death," Dudley said. "And that was a fundamental difference between him and Betty, who put her faith in the Church."

Erastus Corning III's children, Amy and Jonathan, knew their grandfather with considerably less clarity, given the estrangement between their father and grandfather. They simply weren't around Albany much, either. Their father's executive position with Pan American Airlines resulted in a childhood spent on the move with homes in Moscow, France, London, Hawaii and New York City. In addition, the Corning children were further unsettled by the breakup of their parents' marriage, their father's remarriage and second subsequent breakup and, eventually, a third marriage. Amy Corning said her father divorced his first wife, Jacqueline, when Amy was six years old; he split with his second wife, Roseanne, when Amy was in college. "Our time was split between parents, and living overseas made it very difficult to spend time with our grandparents," said Amy Corning, who nonetheless remembered childhood visits with her grandfather in Maine and at Corning Hill during family vacations back to the States.

"I think to say my father and grandfather were divided is too strong a word," she said. "They were both very independent personalities. It's weird how little I heard about my grandfather, but my father never said much about him. They were similar in that respect that both had reserved demeanors and didn't like discussing personal matters." When she did spend time with her grandfather, Amy Corning called him "Gramps" and he seemed larger than life. "He'd come into the kitchen in the morning and give us a big 'Hi-Ho!' He'd have breakfast and make jokes for us at the table, teaching us riddles and limericks, and we just loved being around him. But he always had to go so soon, off to work."

She recalled her grandparents visiting her once in Moscow while they were touring Russian cities. Her strongest memory about her grandfather was a rescue on Webb Pond in Maine. "It was really early in the morning, just at daybreak, and I was eight years old and thought it would be really neat to take out the canoe by myself," Amy said. "All of a sudden, a strong wind came up, I was blown out into the middle of the pond and getting really scared because I couldn't get back. Next thing I knew, my grandfather was right beside me in another canoe, pulled me into his and towed my canoe back to shore with him. He didn't yell and wasn't mad at me, just kind of fierce and stern about what I'd done."

The international flavor of their upbringing served the Corning children well in their careers. Jonathan Corning is a pilot working for an international agency providing humanitarian air drops into Mozambique, Africa. Amy Corning, his older sister, followed in her father's academic path by majoring in Soviet studies at Harvard University. After graduation, she spent five years as a research analyst and production assistant with Radio Free Europe. She left that job when she was in her early thirties to pursue a doctorate degree in sociology from the University of Michigan in Ann Arbor, Michigan.

One long-running family rumor among Albanians that Amy Corning categorically denied is that her father was a spy or informant for the Central Intelligence Agency during his years in Moscow with Pan Am in the late-1960s and early-1970s. "Absolutely not," Amy Corning said, chuckling at the notion of her father as a spy, which she claimed not to have heard before. "There's no way. I lived with him there. I would have known." Her father flatly denied the reputed CIA connection, as well, in interviews with the *Times Union*. Still, the rumors persisted. At lunch at the Fort Orange Club in the spring of 1996, the question was put to him once more. "I deny it, but it's hard to prove a negative," he said wryly. "No question in my mind that Rasty was a CIA spy," said Douglas Rutnik, former son-in-law to Polly Noonan, himself a close political adviser, a kind of surrogate Corning son, and a hunting partner of the mayor's. "Why else study Russian transportation? He was mapping every inch of Moscow for us. He has his father's iciness for that kind of work. A very odd guy."

Swirling around all this discussion of family life is the deep-seated Albany mythology about the mayor and the Noonan family, a mythology based upon innuendo and surmise, with no definitive conclusion, but a mythology so widespread and long-lived that it cannot be ignored.

The story begins in 1937, when Corning, a member of the minority party in the Senate, blocked by the Republican majority, scored his biggest legislative victory by creating the Scenic Hudson Commission and getting it signed into law. The nine-member Commission, headed by Corning, was charged with "surveying scenic, historic and commercial assets of Hudson Valley." It was a progressive exercise for that day, anticipating by fifty years the Hudson Valley Greenway preservation movement. Corning's Commission received an appropriation of $15,000, part of which was designated to hire a secretary. When the woman who had been secretary left to take a job in Washington, D.C., there was a vacancy. The recipient of the Democratic machine patronage was Dorothea "Polly" Noonan.

Noonan remembered the hiring this way: "Erastus had a clerk named Daley who asked me to do some typing and dictation to fill in while they looked for another secretary. I filled in a couple of times and Mary Marcy [Dan O'Connell's faithful lieutenant in the machine, charged with doling out some of the patronage jobs] met with me and told me she'd like me to take the job with Erastus. I said I didn't want to work full time. But Mary Marcy said she really wanted me to do the job and I was one of Mary's girls, so I did." Noonan said O'Connell also gave her a nudge into the position. "Dan had a lot to do with me getting hired because of his friendship with my Uncle Hughie in the South End. I can tell you Erastus had very little say in who his secretary was and he certainly never hired me."

Regardless of how Noonan and Corning were brought together, immediately a chemistry developed between the suave, twenty-eight-year-old senator and his vivacious secretary, just twenty-two years old. They had plenty of time to get acquainted. The Commission was extended three years beyond its initial one-year deadline, with additional appropriations each year. Noonan remembered she had piles of typing to do for the job and she often would have to stay into the evening to finish. Noonan, politically savvy and well-connected in the machine, was very different from Betty Corning. She retained the scrappy perseverance of her working-class background. Earthy, brash and tough-talking, she laced her conversation with expletives. Physically, she was a striking, full-figured woman. Kate (Walsh) Grober, whose husband, George Grober, became an office assistant for Mayor Corning, recalled working with Polly Noonan in the early 1940s at the Internal Revenue Service. "She was a stunning girl, absolutely beautiful," Kate Grober recalled. "A real knockout" and "a china doll" were some of the other descriptions used by old-timers to describe Polly Noonan in the 1930s and 1940s. Although Corning and Noonan both were married (Noonan was wed in 1936 to businessman Peter Noonan), the gossip started almost immediately linking the dashing young senator and his saucy, self-assured secretary who could hold her own with the cigar-chomping, foul-mouthed ward heelers who fueled Dan O'Connell's cult of personality. From the outset of their lifelong relationship, Corning and Noonan were seen together around the Capitol, at political meetings, campaign dinners, Elks Club dances and committeeman strategy sessions – applying the lubricant of machine politics Corning was starting to make his life's work.

Judge Martin Schenck – a political ally and personal friend of Corning's since his youth, son of a jurist who was an intimate of Dan O'Connell's, and himself a State Supreme Court Judge backed by the machine – remembered meeting Polly Noonan in 1941 before he knew who she was. Schenck was campaigning door-to-door for ward leader and knocked on Noonan's door. "She was a very good-looking woman and my partner introduced me as a committeeman who was a good friend of the mayor's," Schenck recalled. "Out of the clear blue, Polly said, 'I'm a good friend of Mayor Corning, too. A very good friend.'" After she said it, Schenck detected a wink from Noonan. Over the years, Schenck, who played golf with Corning at Schuyler Meadows Country Club, would see a lot of Noonan. "She was the only person who called me Marty," recalled Schenck, who remembered seeing the mayor and Noonan dance cheek-to-cheek at Schuyler Meadows functions. "His relationship with Polly was one of those things you don't understand because Betty was the absolute greatest. It was all very strange, but it was something you did not kid Erastus about."

Betty Corning clearly knew what everyone in Albany was whispering about from the very beginning, her friends agreed. "All of Betty's friends did the same thing as Betty did. Put it out of our heads," said Betty's close friend, Jean Beebe. "We all knew the rumors and so did Betty, and it devastated her. History repeats itself. All the politicians did that."

The mayor's longtime associate Jacob Herzog also saw the Erastus-Polly relationship in historical terms. "Betty Corning was a lot like Nelson Rockefeller's first wife [Mary Tod Hunter], that old line Philadelphia reserve," Herzog said. "Look how Rocky fooled around all the time. Rockefeller and Corning were brought up in the same rigid social class and Corning married right out of college before he had time to fool around. And along comes this rude, crude, sexy Noonan woman and Corning was attracted to her. It's a law of physics, isn't it, that opposites attract?" Herzog illustrated his point with an anecdote from a few years before the mayor's death in 1983. Corning was sitting for a portrait with Herzog's wife, the painter Betty Warren. Corning periodically would pose at Warren's studio at her home in Albany. Corning was never accompanied by his wife; his companion at those portrait sittings was Noonan. Recalled Herzog: "I was joking with Erastus during one sitting and told him that the subject always falls in love with the painter. Polly was nearby and blurted out, 'He better not or I'll cut it off!'" Tales of Polly Noonan's earthiness are common and bear a certain similarity to Corning's own profanity, suggesting one aspect of their attraction.

Herzog was mystified by Betty Corning's tolerance of the situation, especially in a small town like Albany where the Corning-Noonan relationship was common knowledge. "I can't explain how Betty accepted it," Herzog said. "I'm sure she just denied it and ignored it." Family friend Mary Arthur Doolittle said, "Betty rose above it is what she did, and threw herself into her gardening." "You just didn't talk to Erastus or Betty about it," said family friend and the mayor's longtime physician, Dr. Richard Beebe. "The rumors flew and were magnified over the years, but we all just tiptoed around it. It was never mentioned."

Still, the relationship was a matter of speculation, in private, for Corning's close friends. "Polly must have had some sort of irresistible attraction for Erastus," Martha Becker said, revealing some of her own class attitudes. "She wasn't what you'd call a lady. I guess there was some of Ireland in Erastus from all that time with Irish politicians, after all. The genes jump around among generations, you know." Judge Francis Bergan, a political associate of the mayor's father and Dan O'Connell since the 1920s said: "It was a strange, incongruous relationship. They were so different in all regards, socially, intellectually and culturally. It was a very interesting human attraction, to say the least, and a very strange taste for Erastus because she was so far outside his class." More politically noteworthy, Bergan stressed, was the fact that O'Connell let it go. "Despite the political risk, Dan decided to stick with Erastus," Bergan said. "I think he liked Erastus so much, almost like a son, that he accepted Erastus with all his weaknesses, including his attraction to Polly."

Meanwhile, while Erastus and Polly were tackling new adventures together in politics, Betty Corning was back at home on Corning Hill, alone. If she felt trapped, it was a prison at least partly of her own making. "I don't know how Betty could stay in that house," Martha Becker said. "Divorces were becoming more common, but I think Betty weighed the pros and cons and liked the power that came with her position as wife of the mayor. The fact that she was Mrs. Erastus Corning in Albany solved a lot of the problems they had."

Contrary to public perception, the Corning children while growing up were not aware of the Noonan family. "I did not hear her name until I came back to Albany when my father was in the hospital in 1982," Erastus III said. "I never heard her name growing up. My mother never mentioned her. I found out about the whole thing after I came back to Albany and realized that everyone in town had known so long, but neither my sister nor me knew that name. People assumed I wasn't close to my father because of Polly Noonan. That's not true. I couldn't be angry with him over something I didn't know about." Bettina Corning concurred. "It seems rather strange, but we never knew about Polly Noonan," she said. "My mother was very good at shielding us from things like that." Betty Corning's strategy of shielding her children had worked. Despite their protests, both children were sent away to boarding school in adolescence – the son to Groton, the daughter to Westover School in Middlebury, Connecticut – and both attended out-of-town colleges and established careers out of the state. Long distances not only served the mother's indifferent and awkward mothering, but it kept the children in the dark about their father's other life with the Noonans.

In sharp contrast to Polly, Betty was reserved, basically shy in demeanor. She was gaunt, almost anorexic-looking in photographs as a young woman (her daughter later wondered aloud if her mother had an eating disorder). Betty dressed in the garb of her Chestnut Hill upbringing, a kind of perpetual debutante: full-length floral dress, a double-strand of natural pearls, white gloves, matching white patent leather purse and pumps. She preferred to immerse herself in her seedlings and plants and shrubs and trees. In sexual matters, friends say Betty Corning was so demure as to be considered almost frigid. In their second-floor bedroom at Corning Hill, the couple slept in separate, single beds with a gap in between and the mayor requested the same when booking hotel rooms for rare vacation trips he took with his wife.

Lawyer, lobbyist and Democratic gadfly Charlie Torche never missed a national political convention and recalled flying on airplanes with Corning and Noonan, the mayor's regular convention companion. "Corning had something going on with her, that's for sure," Torche said. "I saw them together all the time at the hotel together during the conventions. Polly was always with him."

Joe Picchi, a *Times Union* reporter since 1959, recalled flying on an airplane with Corning and Noonan returning from the 1974 State Democratic convention in Niagara Falls. Picchi was traveling with *Times Union* political reporter Vic Ostrowidzki. The reporters took the only empty seats, directly across the aisle from Corning and Noonan. "The mayor seemed a little nervous about having us right next to them, but not Polly," Picchi recalled. "She started right in with crude stuff, how Erastus can't get it up anymore. Corning tried to smile, but he looked like he wanted to die. They brought coffee. Corning was really nervous and fumbled getting the top off his creamer and finally took out his pocketknife. It was really embarrassing for the mayor. Polly kept going on and on."

In many ways, the Noonan children were closer to the mayor than the children that bear his name. "We were the only family he had," said Peter Noonan, Polly's son. "There's no question I was like a substitute son for him," said Douglas Rutnik, Noonan's former son-in-law. "He was like a father to me," said Penny Rutnik, Noonan's daughter. "He taught me to hunt and fish and to love the outdoors. He was with our family all the time." Consider these realities: Erastus Corning 2nd was a distant, largely unavailable father during his children's early years. When they reached adolescence, both son and daughter were sent off to boarding school over their objections – the mother's insistence prevailed over the father's ambivalence – further damaging an already weak bond with their father. Both went away to college, married and relocated overseas or out-of-state in adulthood, had families and raised children – distant strangers, for the most part, to their father. In the meantime, the Noonan family was just up the road, all the while, or just down the hill in the insurance office or right next door in the case of Floods Pond in Maine, where the mayor urged the Noonans to build a camp. In simplest terms, the Noonan kids were always around;

the Corning kids were not. When the Corning children were grown, the mayor gave the Noonan children a patriarchal boost when they established Aurora Insurance, an entrepreneurial assist he never provided his own children. And after the mayor died – despite a desperate and publicly humiliating legal challenge mounted by his son and widow – his greatest financial asset, the insurance business begun in the 1930s and known as Albany Associates, went not to his own progeny but to the Noonan children. "Those of us who were his close friends just couldn't believe that," said Judge John Holt-Harris Jr. "That was absolutely devastating. We didn't understand how he could have done that."

Gerald Mineau, who had worked as a broker since 1979 for Corning's insurance firm, Albany Associates, recalled how shocked and outraged he felt, along with the rest of the company's fifteen-person staff, when they learned Mayor Corning had passed them over in giving the business to the Noonans. "None of us knew the mayor had made that agreement with the Noonans, not even Otto Fausel, who'd been running the business for the mayor since just after World War II," Mineau said. "It hit us as a major shock. It felt like a complete betrayal to us by the mayor after all the years of loyal service we gave him. We all felt the business should have gone to his widow and the Corning family, for whom we would have worked. The value of the business was the name of the mayor and his drawing power and suddenly we didn't have that. The mayor's action speaks for itself. We were angry. We felt we had been stabbed in the back."

After Mayor Corning died in 1983, the battle for the late mayor's lucrative insurance accounts, known as his "book of business," was at the heart of a bitter court dispute between the Noonans and the Cornings. The legal feud erupted in the Albany press in February of 1984. Corning's family contended the client list was the mayor's personal property – inherited by his widow as part of his estate – while the Noonans claimed that as the new owners of Albany Associates, they had the rights to the account list.

Robert Roche, a former Albany County attorney and the lawyer who handled Corning family legal matters, represented Betty Corning and Erastus III in their legal bid to wrest the insurance books away from the Noonans. "Our contention was that the decision was wrong on the facts and the law," Roche said. "The court's decision was that the book belonged to the Noonan company, Aurora, even though there was no consideration given for that. I couldn't prove it, but my feeling is that as things changed and shifted in the mayor's life, he did not intend for that original agreement with the Noonans to remain in place." In the end, the Cornings lost and the Noonans won. The insurance business and its "book of business" remained with the Noonans. Erastus Corning III, with the help of Otto Fausel and Gerald Mineau and others from the defunct Corning Associates, tried to take business away from the Noonans by establishing a rival agency, Corning Associates, in 1984. But the venture died quickly.

If that bequeathing of the insurance business to the Noonan children, rather than to his own family, is not symbolism enough of the duality, the competing sides of light and shadow, for even the most staunch Corning loyalist, consider the oral history. In extensive interviews for this book about the mayor's personal and family life, in terms of sheer volume of concrete anecdotes and reminiscences of time spent with the man, the best sources on the mayor were Noonans and not Cornings. The Noonans had grown up with the mayor, sharing his passions for politics, hunting, fishing and other outdoor pleasures. The Cornings knew their father mostly from afar or through the clouded and pained lens of their mother's experience.

As Polly Noonan tells it, the mayor pursued her. "When Erastus left the Legislature for City Hall in 1942 after being elected mayor for the first time, Erastus wanted me to go to work for him as his secretary and I said no," Noonan said. "People were already talking about us and I was tired of the rumors. Erastus insisted. So, I went out to see Dan. I said I didn't want to go and Dan said I could stay in the Legislature with [Sen.] Julian Erway and that was that."

Under the tutelage of Mary Marcy – Dan's loyal lieutenant since the machine took power in 1921 and the one who rode herd over the women's wing of the organization – Noonan became a high-profile protege as one of "Mary's girls." Through her job in the Legislature and her role as trusted adviser to Corning, Noonan began to wield considerable clout within the machine, particularly as gatekeeper to state patronage jobs.

As they began to attend political functions together and Noonan was linked with winks and sly asides as Corning's "confidante" in newspaper stories, what a dynamic duo Noonan and Corning became in the machine. Even though Noonan no longer worked directly for Corning after 1941, their lives remained inextricably linked through politics and personal devotion. From their early years together, through old age and the mayor's death, Polly Noonan embodied the juicy marrow of life the mayor craved. From the mayor's own melancholy days at Groton and his drifting through Yale, he was squeezed against his own free-spirited personality into the rigid course of politics and business his father had preordained him to fulfill. As a go-along, get-along guy, Erastus learned to play those roles as if he cared, and his formidable intellect gave him quick mastery of any new situation. He was just waiting to break out of the smothering world of his mother, his family legacy, his subservience to Dan O'Connell, the never-ending minutiae and numbing routine of his job as mayor. Like his father before him with his drinking and cockfighting and consorting with the O'Connells' street-level political machine, Erastus liked to indulge his earthy side and to dabble in the pleasures on the other side of the tracks – forming liaisons with folks outside his class. The one element that endeared Corning most to the citizenry was his common touch and his chameleonic ability to meld with the culture of his present circumstance, whether it be the Fort Orange Club or some South End saloon. And in Polly Noonan, for a man who found his universe in microcosm, he had discovered a woman who synthesized Erastus Corning's complex and seemingly conflicting appetites. In Albany, Corning possessed unbridled political power and in Noonan he had found a person unafraid to challenge the king and her gutsiness appealed to him, fired him in a way that the reticence of women in his social milieu never did. Friends and political associates related numerous stories that illustrated the fact that Polly Noonan was the only person with the chutzpah to put the mayor in his place. Anecdotes abound about her cowing Corning like some Groton first-former. In Polly Noonan, Corning the power broker and the machine's marquee star, had finally met his match. "My mother just wouldn't take his crap," Peter Noonan said. "That was a major difference. Betty put up with everything and my mother called him on his bullshit and wouldn't tolerate it."

The Noonans are not reluctant to discuss their long and intensely personal relationship with the mayor. In fact, they described Corning's presence at their house almost nightly – meaning, of course, a corollary absence from Corning Hill, Betty and his own family – as the most natural scenario imaginable. During the week, the pattern of life went something like this. Many nights, after putting in a long day at City Hall, the mayor would drive up the Washington Avenue hill, alone, in his modest Chevy, making certain not to abuse the privilege of the mayor's official car, to the Fort Orange Club for dinner. He'd either meet a judge or politician or other guest for a scheduled dinner or simply take potluck dinner partners by seating himself at the "long table" – a communal place for single diners without company. After dinner, he might shoot a little pool or play a few hands of poker, but generally, at least two or three nights a week, he had a public function or political event to attend. It would be a speech or political meeting or fund-raiser or civic dinner or some official function he felt obligated to attend as the ever-congenial, always-available, mayor for life. Since his wife resolutely refused to attend these events and was never seen at such functions, Corning often attended alone, or he was accompanied, at least to overtly political functions where their companionship would not raise eyebrows, by Polly Noonan. After these functions, whether Polly Noonan attended or not, Corning often made his way back later in the evening not to Corning Hill but to Noonan Lane.

Polly Noonan vividly described the mayor's ritual. The mayor would come over to Noonan's house, where he would join Polly's husband, Peter Noonan, in the family room, an airy, open floor plan with sliding glass doors looking out onto the Noonan's extensive grounds with ponds, in-ground swimming pool and circular drive. Noonan talked about the mayor's presence, twelve years after his death, as if he had been there just the night before. "That was Peter's recliner," Noonan said, pointing to a black naugahyde model, "and that was where Erastus sat," she added, pointing to a brown cloth recliner just opposite. "They'd sit there, right across from each other, and drink their Scotch and watch sports on TV or read books or magazines and maybe talk politics or history. And I'd be sitting at this table, sewing or reading, joining in the conversation occasionally. Erastus would get up to get them refills on the Scotch and Peter would always complain that Erastus ruined it with water because Peter drank his neat."

Throughout all the gossip and innuendo and thinly veiled references to their alleged intimacies in the newspapers, the sub-text was that Erastus and Polly somehow conducted their relationship in secret. That was never the case. Whatever transpired between the two of them, Polly's husband, Peter Noonan, knew about it because they were a threesome as much as a couple. There was no subterfuge on Polly Noonan's part. In numerous photographs she displayed around her house, Corning was a frequent subject, posing with herself and her husband, with just her husband, with her children.

Thelma Dooley, Corning's secretary, got her job in City Hall through Polly Noonan, a friend of Dooley's in the Legislature where both worked for many years. Dooley was astounded about the openness of the relationship between Corning and Noonan. "I would crochet with Polly occasionally over at the Noonan's house and Polly's husband, Peter, would be there and Erastus would be there, too," Dooley said. "They acted like it was natural and nothing strange at all, just three friends getting together. I saw the three of them together several times socially and they all got along well."

Polly married Peter Noonan Sr. in 1936, the year before she went to work for Corning as his secretary on the Senate's Scenic Hudson Commission. They were married for fifty-two years until Peter Noonan died in 1988 at the age of eighty. Similarly, Betty and Erastus Corning were married for fifty-one years until the mayor's death in 1983 at the age of seventy-three. The two men shared common ground. For starters, both were businessmen. Peter Noonan, one year older than Corning, grew up in Watervliet in a working-class family, was bright and nimble in business, and worked his way up at Albany Car Wheel Factory, an iron foundry in Menands. Corning's family, of course, had a distinguished history in the iron industry and that forged a strong bond between Corning and Noonan. Noonan eventually became vice president and a part-owner and later sold out his interest. In 1949, Noonan went to work for Atlantic Cement just down-river from Albany in Ravena, as manager of industrial relations. His job involved a busy travel schedule in which he spent years on the road crisscrossing the country purchasing rights to mining operations for Atlantic Cement. Mining was another connection between Noonan and Corning, whose father and grandfather had financial stakes in mining companies. Eventually, Noonan was promoted to supervising director of nine cement plants scattered across the East Coast. Noonan retired at the age of seventy.

Throughout her life, Polly Noonan has steadfastly denied rumors of an alleged sexual relationship between the mayor and herself. Noonan also denied all rumors of alleged illegitimacy. Polly Noonan said, "That was the one rumor that hurt me most. It wasn't true. What is true is that Erastus is Penny's godfather, which I made him at Erastus' own request. Thank God none of my children looked like him." Many people interviewed dispute that, and those rumors have persisted despite Noonan's denials. Peter Noonan Jr. also dismissed the rumors. "I know all the rumors and it's not worthy of my comment. The mayor would get pissed off at what people were saying. We all would. But we just put up with it because my mother stood up to it all." The Noonans have spent decades dismissing these rumors and the attendant civic gossip, but both persist to this day. Polly Noonan said the shame and embarrassment of hearing the whisper of rumor throughout her life in the incestuous confines of Albany politics almost drove her to retreat from public life and her work as a machine lieutenant. "When the talk first started, I wanted to leave my job," Noonan said. "I was only twenty-two years old at the time, remember, and married. I told Dan I wanted to quit. Dan said, 'If you quit tomorrow, the gossip won't stop anyway.' I discussed it with my husband and Peter said, 'Polly, you stand your ground and don't let them run you off the porch.'" And then Polly Noonan added, in her own inimitable vernacular, "I came to the conclusion it was like shit; the more you stir it, the more it stinks."

Noonan's cousin, Jack McLean, a Corning hunting buddy and life-long friend of the mayor's, who also lived at the Noonan's home for a time after his tour in Vietnam, was unconvinced that Polly Noonan and Erastus Corning ever consummated their relationship. "If they wanted to, they could have," McLean said. "But you could never prove it by me. I lived in that house. I saw the mayor when he let his guard down. And I never saw anything sexual between him and Polly."

In dozens of extensive interviews, those closest personally, professionally and politically to Corning and Noonan, the ones who knew them best, both friends and enemies, reached the same conclusion. They said it might have looked like an affair to the outside world, that they themselves might have suspected it was, but, despite countless times seeing Polly and the mayor together during a relationship that spanned nearly fifty years, they never once caught the two in a compromising position. Not that Polly didn't make references to the mayor in coarse sexual terms. But that was her manner with many besides the mayor. Those who observed Corning and Noonan over the years witnessed countless times they attended dinners together (often with Peter Noonan making it a trio) or traveled to conventions together (without their respective spouses), even danced together. Many witnessed them drinking together, laughing together, smiling at each other, a few light shoulder touches, that sort of thing, but that was something Corning did with numerous men and women among the machine's ranks anyway. There are reports, too, of Polly Noonan cursing and browbeating the mayor in a way that no one else dared do that some found both shocking and suggestive of some sort of deep-seated control Polly held over Corning. That is the gist of the gossip and rumors that buzzed so incessantly in the ears of both families, up and down the Albany grapevine, for so many years. And, to date, no matter how much everyone thought the Noonan-Corning relationship was a no-brainer, it has remained solely in the realm of Albany myth. File it under unfounded rumor and unconfirmed gossip. There is not one person offering evidence of the mayor and Polly *flagrante delicto*. Nothing after scores of reporters since the 1940s tried to crack the case of what some Albanians have dubbed "The Big Lie;" nobody has, myself included, despite trying to uncover a smoking gun. Polly and the mayor might have been exceptionally careful not to show affectionate intimacy in public, but it's hard to believe they wouldn't have slipped up during five decades if their union was an ongoing physical one. It must be noted that Corning was never viewed by friends – beginning with his prep school and college classmates and continuing through his World War II pals and political associates – as a sexually promiscuous personality. Rather, those closest to him, both men and women, describe a man who leaned more toward the asexual side of the libido spectrum. When women flirted with the mayor and made it known they were available, he tactfully ignored their advances, according to men who drank with him in bars and observed this sexual interplay. It might be said his sexual drive matched his political ambition; he didn't mind the same old routine and a flat line. It would appear that his wife was not a highly sexual person and Erastus seemed accepting of that. For the mayor, the political cliché held true: power was his aphrodisiac. Juggling a thousand pieces of a political and municipal and personal puzzle stimulated Corning and he loved the control and power he wielded in his circumscribed kingdom of Albany. With that undiluted elixir of human experience daily passing through his veins at City Hall, the mayor had found his substitute for a passionate marriage. Polly Noonan, however, was at the core of those secret places for the mayor and the populace entertains several possible speculations for their long and loyal linkage. Whatever the scenario, how had Betty Corning and Peter Noonan possibly put up with it? The only person alive who could solve that mystery would only say so much.

Polly Noonan refused to be lured into a discussion of her sexual attraction to Corning and defined her relationship with the mayor thus: "I think it was close to love between us, a very close friendship. He was a nice, good friend," Noonan said. "We worked well together. I was interested in, and knew politics, where Betty didn't. Dan would always say, 'She goes with the job, Erastus.' Because I was running things for the Democratic organization in the Legislature and I was necessary. We grew close because we thought almost the same on political matters. That was natural, because Dan was mentor to both of us. He learned from Dan. I learned from Dan."

Polly Noonan stated flatly that she was never unfaithful to her husband and that Corning never enticed her to be. "I had the most interesting, bright, loving husband. There was no need to look anywhere else. There was never any question who I was married to," she said. "I was always a broad who knew what she wanted. The first time I met Peter, I told my girlfriend I'm going to marry that man and I did. We were married fifty-two years until his death. Nobody ever interested me before him and nobody ever interested me after him."

Corning and Noonan's husband were similar in many regards. Both were tall (Noonan six-foot one-inch, Corning six-foot two-inches) with lean, strong builds. Both loved hunting and fishing. They went golfing together. They enjoyed talking sports and politics with each other. And they shared something deeper, perhaps a kinship of brothers both had lost, and certainly an abiding respect for the same woman. Polly Noonan suspected they found in each other a kind of brotherhood. Corning's younger brother, Eddie, whom the mayor had been helping with jobs and political favors since college and whom he fiercely protected with an older brother's devotion, died in 1964 at age forty-five after years of diminished mental abilities following a car crash and lengthy coma. Peter Noonan lost his two brothers unexpectedly at about the same time. After the deaths of their brothers, the two men found in each other that missing male bond. "It developed into the closeness of brothers," Polly Noonan said. "They were closer than Erastus and me. Erastus and I were very close politically, but he and Peter filled each other's void. I can still picture them in those two recliners, night after night, drinking Scotch, watching sports on TV. And then they'd both fall asleep. I'd wake them up, send Peter upstairs to bed and tell Erastus to go home."

Polly Noonan was adamant when she stated that Erastus always went home. "Peter knew everything that went on between Erastus and me," she said. "I loved my husband and I didn't fool around. Peter was very religious and I'm a strong Catholic and I follow the commandments, including the death do us part wedding vow."

There were several times, Noonan conceded, when Corning, uncharacteristically, removed the masks of his many personas and revealed emotional truths. "He started to tell me about the trouble in his marriage on different occasions and I stopped him," Noonan said. "I knew it was not a completely happy marriage, but I told him his married life was not my business and I refused to hear it. That was a rule I put on our friendship. I didn't want to know about his marriage, then I couldn't be accused of getting involved in it." Polly Noonan said Erastus never broached the topic of divorcing Betty to marry her. "I would have killed him if he even suggested it," she said. "And Erastus knew divorce would have meant the end of his political career. Dan would have made sure of that. Dan did not allow divorce in the organization."

Noonan said she had empathy for both Erastus and Betty in the barrenness of their marriage. "I imagine Betty suffered as much from the rumors as I did," Noonan said. "I won't pass judgment, because love is a two-way street, but Erastus and Betty had practically no life together as a couple. She despised politics and that was his whole life. Erastus had plenty of faults, too, and wasn't blameless. It can't be easy to be married to a politician."

In the end, Polly Noonan suggested Erastus really fell in love with her family and she was just part of a package deal. "When he started hanging around our house so much, he'd always say, 'Polly, your family is so close. I wish I had that,'" Polly Noonan recalled. "I think what he wanted more than anything was a real family. Mine was the only one he had."

Polly Noonan offered these revealing remarks to me in the fall of 1995 – twelve years after the mayor's death and two years after Betty Corning died – during extensive interviews in her house that continued late into the night. She didn't seem to want to stop talking and the interviews had the feel of confession. Polly is a master obfuscator who put off reporters for decades with her standard line, "I'm taking it to the grave with me." As time went on, however, and other politicos seized power in Albany, the reporters stopped calling and Polly Noonan seemed something of a relic and irrelevant. She was history. I got the feeling as the stories tumbled out of her that here was a woman whose time was running out and her chance to tell her side of the story, to reclaim her relevance, was slipping away. She was seventy-nine years old at the time and in declining health and spoke more openly to me than anyone previously about her relationship to Corning. Her political star had faded, been almost extinguished, and she had a public falling-out at about this time with the new Democratic boss, Leonard Weiss. If not now, when? Still, she spoke only on her terms and answered or didn't answer my questions in her own inimitable way. She certainly didn't disclose everything, but, despite detractors who question her veracity, she spoke her version of reality, through her prism of experience.

In the fall of 1992, during a long, reflective morning I spent with Betty Corning for a *Times Union* feature article, she moved haltingly, struggling for breath, tethered to an oxygen tube to combat the advancing symptoms of her emphysema – the same lung disease that killed her husband nine years earlier. As we sat in Betty's garden – her retreat, her Eden, her alpha and omega – for the first time in our nearly three-hour conversation, I asked her about her legendary husband, the mayor. She didn't answer right away, as if considering her words, then began to tell an anecdote in her feathery, labored speech:

> I was in the Grand Union the other day and a woman came up to me, looked me over and asked, 'Are you Mrs. Corning?'
>
> I said, 'Yes, I am.' And she threw her arms around me and said, 'Oh, I knew him.'

"That's very touching to me," Betty Corning said. "My husband was very much loved by so many and still is. I miss him just as much now as I ever did."

It was revealing, despite Betty Corning's attempt to hide her true feelings behind a veil of properness, that she never talked about her husband directly during the lengthy interview and spoke of him only in an indirect, third-person manner. It seemed that if others held such a high regard for Erastus Corning, that was enough and she would continue to mouth the old contentments about her husband.

Similarly, I found very few references to Betty Corning in scouring the mayor's archives that included thousands of letters pertaining to politics and private life, speeches, correspondence and other files among Mayor Corning's vast collection of personal papers at the Albany Institute of History and Art's McKinney Library. A few times, Betty was mentioned in passing in one of the mayor's letters, generally regarding gardening matters or details about vacation plans or invoking her name disingenuously as an excuse to send regrets to a function Corning had been invited to but didn't want to attend, a rarity in forty-two years as mayor. Betty Corning was never mentioned in a negative light; it's just that she wasn't mentioned at all. Neither was the mayor much on his wife's mind in many hours of interviews. He had his politics and the Noonans and his outdoor sports; she had her gardening and Garden Club of America coterie and her women friends who volunteered at the cathedral and the hospital and other pursuits. The sad truth seemed to be that, for the most apart, they remained husband and wife in name, but in spirit they traveled separate roads whose paths rarely intersected. They appeared to be content and fulfilled in their own worlds, each without the other.

In 1996, sixty-four years after the newly married Betty and Erastus moved into the gardener's house on Corning Hill, the children sold the house. The new owners expressed plans of turning it into a bed and breakfast. The sale of the house was one of the last pieces in settling the estate of Elizabeth Platt Corning after her death on September 22, 1993. A large piece of land surrounding the house on Corning Hill remains with the two Corning children and is up for sale, but its ravines make it undesirable for development. Betty inherited her husband's assets – aside from the disputed insurance book of business that the courts ruled he had signed over separately to the Noonans – under the six-paragraph will he signed on February 19, 1938. Erastus Corning 2nd's last will and testament bequeathed everything "to my beloved wife, Elizabeth Platt Corning, to be hers absolutely and forever."

Betty Corning's will left a gross estate valued at $3.2 million. Of that, Bettina received $842,293; Erastus III got $717,293; and each of her four grandchildren was given $50,000 each in a trust. The Corning Hill house and property was appraised at $480,000, the Webb Pond camp and acreage at $125,000. Betty bequeathed $25,000 to All Saint's Cathedral, $25,000 to Child's Hospital and $15,000 to the Albany Institute of History & Art. She stipulated the Webb Pond camp be given to Bettina but that she make it available to her brother and his children "at such time and in such manner as may be mutually convenient." Betty also left to her former daughter-in-law, Jacqueline Corning of New Haven, Connecticut $1,000 "as a token of my affection for her." All the rest of the estate was designated to Bettina and Erastus III "to share and share alike." Her two children were named joint executor and executrix of Betty Corning's estate, but they are estranged from each other. "I think he tore out my page in his address book," Bettina said. She did not know her brother had moved to Charleston, South Carolina abruptly at the end of the summer of 1996 to open a gift shop with his third wife, Megan, until I informed her. "I don't have much contact with her," said Erastus III. "They don't talk at all and I'm the intermediary through whom messages pass from one to the other," Holt-Harris said. "That's sad, but that's the reality of Erastus' legacy, too."

For Betty Corning, the garden was more than a metaphor. It was her life, to the exclusion, many said, of her children, husband and a sense of family life. It's difficult to say which came first, Erastus' abandonment into a consuming passion for politics and his other family, the Noonans; or, Betty's retreat into her private life of plants. Laying blame at the feet of either spouse serves no purpose. The only fact that endures is that, for much of the fifty-one years of their marriage, it was a distant relationship. And, because each spouse maintained full schedules with their individual and separate pursuits, the decades passed swiftly. The gravel drive leading to the Corning house ends at the massive base of an oak tree that towers eighty feet. "I planted that oak as a teeny little slip of a sapling, and now it's a giant," Betty Corning told me in the fall of 1992. "People think trees take forever, but the years pass quickly and they grow right along."

On June 23, 1982, Patty Becker threw a fiftieth wedding anniversary for Erastus and Betty Corning at her large Colonial home in Loudonville. The Corning's longtime social set was invited. Becker's brother, Bill Thompson, one of Erastus' best friends, was on hand. There was Dr. Beebe and his wife. And perhaps a half-dozen others, who knew the Cornings from dinner parties and membership at the Fort Orange Club and the Garden Club. The guest of honor's son, Erastus III, was in town and Becker invited him to come. He declined. "That was so sad. I think it hurt his father, but he never let it show," Becker recalled.

Becker said the gathering of good, old friends was a poignant affair. Corning seemed comfortable enough among friends he trusted deeply to open up, at least a little, and to reveal a hint of his conflicting emotions about his marriage. Speeches and tributes and toasts abounded. It came the mayor's turn to speak. He rose slowly, somewhat red-faced and embarrassed, Becker recalled, his emotions loosened by alcohol. "He made some very touching remarks, all rather heartbreaking, actually," Becker said. "He said perhaps it would have been better if he hadn't gone into politics. He said maybe then his family would have been happier and things would have been better for them all."

Becker said the room grew silent and the guests seemed somewhat stunned, wondering what to make of the first emotional, heartfelt confession they'd ever heard from the normally taciturn mayor. "All I could feel was terribly sad for the man. He seemed deeply unhappy," Becker said. One of the fiftieth anniversary gifts Becker presented to Erastus and Betty was a commemorative ceramic serving plate. It was pale blue with a delicate flower motif and it read, "Betty & 'Rastus. June 23, 1932–June 23, 1982." That plate was one of the few personal possessions of his parents that Erastus III, at the request of his sister, did not sell at the estate auction. Among the several garbage cans of personal correspondence and memorabilia from his parents the son threw out were a set of postcards Betty wrote to her husband from China during a Garden Club trip in September of 1978. Norman Rice salvaged the postcards for their sentiment, as much as for their stamps. There were a dozen postcards, one sent dutifully each day, and each one began: "Dearest Honey" and concluded, "All Love, B." Rice let that paradox sink in without comment. During a visit to her parent's empty house in 1995, Bettina Corning found a use for the fiftieth wedding anniversary gift. She poured water onto the plate in hopes of reviving a memory, of watering the past and making it bloom forth once more with meaning and insight, rather than seething anger and resentment. Betty Corning's beloved geraniums, nearly a dozen in terra cotta pots, dominated the bay window ledges in the home, ledges lined with copper and filled with white crushed marble as a kind of livingroom greenhouse. Bettina Corning was visiting her parent's house on September 8, 1995, nearly two years after her mother's death, which was how long it had been since anyone had last watered or cared for her mother's prized geraniums in the window. All of the geraniums were brown and brittle, long dead, completely lifeless, all, that is, except two tiny and stubborn green shoots that somehow miraculously survived the two years without water or care. The daughter put the fragile geranium clinging tenaciously to life on the watery anniversary plate and hoped.

"This geranium is so symbolic for me," Bettina said, choking slightly on her words and brushing back tears. "My mother had the most incredible fortitude and endurance and my father sure as hell did, too. Somehow, their marriage lived on through difficult years. I'm going to bring this geranium plant back to life and give cuttings to my kids for them to grow. That's the way I want to remember my parents, the geranium that survived despite everything."

Chapter 5:

The Never-Ending Story:
Dan and Erastus and Their Durable Machine

"For some reason it brought back an expression that Dan O'Connell had: All dogs are nicer than most people."

Undated note from Mayor Erastus Corning 2nd to wildlife artist Wayne Trimm, who was finishing a wolf painting for the mayor.

During the denouement of the dance of death that is cockfighting, the stronger cock, its claw fitted with a razor-sharp piece of metal known as a slasher, begins clawing and pecking and shredding the other animal into oblivion in a crazed whirl of feathers and blood and primal savagery. This eruption of heart-stopping violence is rewarded with lusty applause from the spectators. This is what they come to witness and to wager on, this ultimate act of aggression. It is considered very bad form for the rooster's owner or a spectator to be so gripped by a twinge of remorse that he would enter the ring to halt the carnage and the losing cock's certain annihilation. Cockfighting, after all, is a blood sport that is meant to be a fight to the death. Two roosters enter the ring. Only one leaves victorious, and in one piece. The match goes on until one of the birds is maimed or killed. The analogy between cockfighting and politics as practiced in its most ferocious, atavistic form is an obvious one. The Albany Democratic machine was formed by two families, the Cornings and the O'Connells, whose bond of politics was a link of blood, the blood of the cockfighting ring. Little did it matter that cockfighting was illegal in New York, as was gambling on the outcome. With newly won cash in their pockets and blood still on their lips – in some instances, quite literally, since maimed gamecocks might anoint those in the front row with their mortal wounds – the Cornings and the O'Connells would repair to O'Connell's saloon to drink ale and talk politics and cockfighting. A perennial Albany question has been this: how did the aristocratic Cornings and the working-class O'Connells ever get together and stay together? Pundits and political scientists wanted to find some metaphysical explanation. But the answer seems ridiculously simple. It came down to the inexorable mix of beer, the blood sport of fighting chickens and politics.

Theirs was an alliance more profane than sublime, but it was a winning combination. The Democratic political machine fashioned by the O'Connells and Cornings seized power in Albany in 1921 and – despite a substantial erosion of its sphere of influence and power amid a cluster of major Republican victories – continues to shape city and county politics in the waning years of the twentieth century with remnants of the old committeeman and ward leader hierarchy. That's more than three-quarters of a century of Democratic dominance. The machine lives on today in vestigial form, reverent of its patron saints, even though there have been no O'Connells or Cornings involved for more than a decade. The machine's eight-decade dynasty is unprecedented in modern American political history. The O'Connell-Corning organization has endured longer than any other fabled political machine and its boss: longer than Tweed in New York, Curley in Boston, Prendergast in Kansas City, Long in Louisiana, Buckley in San Francisco, Hague in Jersey City, Crump in Memphis, Dennison in Omaha or Aldridge in Rochester. John Gunther described Albany's form of government in a memorable phrase (resonant in definition as both sewer and the defecation and procreation cavity in birds and reptiles) in his 1947 book, *Inside U.S.A.* as "a kind of political *cloaca maxima*, beside which Kansas City seemed almost pure." In international terms, you might call it a draw regarding the duration of Communist rule in the Soviet Union and the O'Connell-Corning machine. Both the Bolsheviks and the O'Connells and Cornings seized power at roughly the same time, in the World War I era, and, seven decades later, each began to break apart in the early 1980s – with the death of Corning in 1983 in Albany and the emergence of Gorbachev's *glasnost* and *perestroika* reforms in Russia that led to the fall of the Berlin Wall in 1989. Although there were few remnants left of the disintegrated Soviet Union in the 1990s, in the Albany County Democratic Committee, a few cogs of the machine's dictatorial powers appear durable enough to survive into the twenty-first century.

"The Albany machine is a dinosaur, the Jurassic Park of American politics," said Jon Teaford, a professor of political science at Purdue University and author of books on urban politics and Boss Tweed. "Albany's political structure has changed only at a geological pace. It's remarkable how long it has survived. Albany is Bossland. You couldn't name a city in the world in this century that has had the same political organization in power as long as Albany."

Warren Moscow, the erstwhile *New York Times* reporter, marveled at the timelessness of the O'Connell-Corning machine in his definitive 1948 text, *Politics in the Empire State*. "The Albany machine is probably closest to the ideal of the practical political machine," Moscow wrote. "It more nearly resembles the old-type Tammany organization, of Murphy's day, than any other extant. It is a prototype of the Irish-Democratic organizations so familiar in the cities of the north, but is much better than most now in existence. It has the vices of entrenched paternalism and plenty of the practical virtues as well. But, good or bad, the people of Albany like it." Moscow listed the machine's vices, from pressuring Albany saloonkeepers to put the O'Connell family's ale and lager, Hedrick's, on tap to assessment tampering to giving municipal contracts to its no-bid friends to the detriment of the taxpayer. "The boss system made money for the boss and for the party organization," Moscow wrote, "but it also made life more bearable for a lot of little people who had not access otherwise to government, who knew of its operations only through their contacts with the machine."

The Albany machine "infested every facet of life, legal and otherwise," noted Samuel G. Freedman in his 1996 book, *The Inheritance: How Three Families And America Moved From Roosevelt To Reagan And Beyond*. "More than anything, if you wanted a job you mortgaged your vote. The O'Connell version of patronage was like public works without the work," Freedman wrote. The O'Connell-Corning machine is "America's most durable urban machine. Albany is, in many ways, the archetypal machine city," M. Craig Brown wrote in a chapter titled "Machine Politics" in the anthology, *Experiencing Albany*. Brown, a former sociology professor at the State University of New York at Albany, wrote a government-funded study quantifying the distribution of political machines across cities and over time in America. Nothing came close to Albany. "What is it about this city that lends itself to the inertia of dominance?" Brown asked. He concluded the answer remained a riddle. What is clear is that Albany's machine in the 1980s resembled political machines elsewhere in the U.S. from the 1890s: Dan and Erastus, a couple of old fossils, resurrecting a dinosaur.

It's one for the history books, to be sure, and its lineage can be traced to the blood sport of cockfighting and the drinking culture of the saloon. The O'Connell-Corning machine's extraordinary strength and durability is due to the forged early union between working-class immigrants and upper-class aristocrats. It was in this potent union that Erastus as mayor for life was to play a significant and ceaseless role. The initial and fertile common ground between these two classes was the cockfighting ring.

Daniel Peter O'Connell, the archetypal political boss, was born on November 13, 1885. It was Friday the 13th. His father, John "Black Jack" O'Connell ran a saloon at Fourth Avenue and South Pearl Street. His mother, Mary (Doyle) O'Connell, bore and raised four sons who went on to give birth to a political machine the likes of which this country likely never will witness again. The O'Connell boys possessed a winning combination of fearlessness, intelligence and ambition. They soon became a dominant force in Albany's South End, an ethnic melting pot for newly arrived immigrants, particularly Irish, Germans, Italians and Jews. Dan spent a large part of his formative years at the family saloon, having quit formal schooling after the fifth grade, but he possessed abundant street smarts and political intuition that couldn't be learned in a traditional setting. Unlike his brothers, Dan chose to pursue his education outside the classroom walls. At the bar, Dan learned to speak fluent German with the immigrant patrons, a connection he would later exploit for votes cast in favor of Dan's machine candidates. Dan moved out beyond his turf in the South End and gained influence across the city with an amateur football club team he managed, the Delphinians. Dan used the opportunity of traveling football games to solidify a blue-collar social network throughout Albany County that sowed the seeds of the future political machine far and wide. Although he was not a polished public speaker, Dan compensated for a raspy, squeaky high-pitched voice through a squat, barrel-chested physique that lent him the forcefulness of a fire plug and a rough-hewn charisma that burned brightly in brown eyes exaggerated behind thick bifocals. Dan eventually took over bartending duties from his father, who also schooled him in the finer points of gamecock breeding, raising and fighting. "Black Jack O'Connell had trained fighting cocks in Ireland and he passed on his skills to Dan," said John E. Holt-Harris Jr., a patrician Albany attorney and the city recorder court judge who had a lifelong association with the Cornings and O'Connells. "The patricians like Edwin Corning [the mayor's father] would come into O'Connell's saloon. The O'Connells got the Cornings interested in cockfighting. And that was the entree for the O'Connells into Albany's patrician world."

Down through the generations, the Cornings have liked their drink. And, despite their Episcopalian reserve, the descendants of the original Erastus needed no coaxing to take a walk on the wild side. Mixing with the O'Connell boys, who came to be considered the lords of the South End, represented a symbolic crossover to the other side of the tracks for the Cornings. At the turn-of-the-century, the world of the Cornings was the WASP conclave of wealth and privilege around Elk Street, a patrician neighborhood surrounded by the city's great architecture: old Albany Academy, City Hall and the Capitol. This was the domain of bankers and industrialists, physicians and lawyers, permeated by the culture of old money. The Cornings had all the comforts a millionaire could buy. But they didn't have the visceral, illicit pleasure of the cockfight.

Holt-Harris, born in 1917, is the son of a politically connected physician who was appointed city bacteriologist. One of the elder Holt-Harris' patients happened to be Mayor Corning's father. Holt-Harris's son, the judge, was familiar with cockfighting from the aristocratic vantage point since boyhood. "The patricians became addicted to cockfighting," Holt-Harris said. "They all owned fighting cocks, especially the Cornings. The Cornings had a big fighting cock operation." Wealth couldn't ensure success in the blood sport, though. Cockfighting was a great social equalizer. "Cockfighting brought together the lower and upper classes like few other things," Holt-Harris said. "It was a poor man's sport because anyone could afford to breed, raise, groom and spur a fighter. And it also became a passion for the gentry who enjoyed the challenge of breeding a line of champion fighting cocks as they had with dogs and thoroughbred horses."

Since the mid-nineteenth century, when Erastus Corning Jr., the mayor's grandfather, began to amass his world-class collections of orchids, butterflies and moths, cattle, horses *et al.*, the Cornings were drawn to the mysteries of early genetic engineering. Fighting cocks were no different. In the early years of the twentieth century, Edwin – the mayor's father – and his brother, Parker, young and rising industrialists, divided the vast acreage of the Corning estate in Glenmont on Corning Hill into the Upper Farm and Lower Farm. Still, there remained plenty of room for raising fighting cocks amid their sprawling array of barns, stables, greenhouses and fields for their assorted livestock. The mayor's father, Edwin Corning, raised Irish wolf hounds as a hobby and had two champions of the breed at his estate. He interested Dan O'Connell in the breed and many later visitors to the home of the political boss on Whitehall Road recalled being jumped up on, and nearly knocked over, by Dan's pair of Irish wolf hounds. The boss was an iron-fisted disciplinarian with ward heelers, it seemed, but a softie when it came to training his dogs. The Corning brothers, Parker and Edwin, also each employed a crew of farm hands to raise their animals and their fighting cocks to the highest standards. It was more than a matter of pride in animal husbandry.

Cockfighting could mean big money to those who raised the most vicious, murderous roosters. "There was some heavy wagering," said Holt-Harris, who spoke from experience. Dan O'Connell told William Kennedy in a 1974 interview recounted in *O Albany!* that he, Dan, "beat Gus Melick out of sixty-five thousand dollars in a night, up in Foley's, in Troy. I beat him, seven to three."

Wagering on cockfighting was a double criminal offense and the mains, as the matches were called, required an underground quality. The location of an upcoming main was revealed only to insiders, the secret society of cockfighters and bettors. Bringing a man into the ring of lawbreakers involved an unwritten oath of loyalty – a blood oath, as it were. This loyalty the Cornings and the O'Connells later utilized as the foundation of their political dynasty. Charlie Ryan, one of Dan's closest friends, told Kennedy: "Dan said he'd never trust a politician with anything, but would trust a chicken fighter with his life." At the main, there were lookouts, a bookmaker, and the ring judge. O'Connell hosted some of Albany's biggest and richest cockfights at his summer home on Beaver Dam Road in the Helderbergs just above Thacher Park. "I saw a couple of fights up at Dan's summer place," Holt-Harris said. "There were a lot of men. Some were like me, more curious than devotees of that kind of thing."

O'Connell flouted the law by hiring George Kenfield, an Albany police sergeant, to handle his fighting cocks. O'Connell estimates he had 500 fighting cocks at a time, "perhaps the best in the world," he told Kennedy. Holt-Harris said that was hardly hyperbole. "Dan's chickens had notoriety among aficionados as far away as the Philippines," Holt-Harris said. "They were called the Albany strain. They were very valuable and in demand as breeding stock." The cockfights were Dan's stage as much as the political arena. "Dan would narrate the chicken fights, a bunch of meaningless terms to me," said Judge Francis Bergan, who attended several of O'Connell's big mains. "The Cornings were major cockfighters and they were joined by a lot of wealthy Albany people. Without cockfighting, there would be no connection between the O'Connells and their friends and the Cornings and theirs."

Bergan, born in 1902, is a former Albany newspaperman whom O'Connell befriended and convinced to quit journalism for a law degree. Bergan was rewarded as a machine-backed judge whose career began in Albany police court in 1930 and ended in 1972 with his retirement after nine years on the New York State Court of Appeals, the state's highest court. Bergan enjoyed a lifelong association with the O'Connells, particularly Dan, and the Cornings, beginning with the mayor's father. "Their machine was as solid as any you'll find on the American political scene," Bergan said. "It was a wondrous thing to behold."

Many knew about Dan's cockfighting, but few knew Dan also raised fighting dogs. So said retired state Supreme Court Judge Edward Conway, born in 1917, whose father, John Conway, was a longtime friend of Dan's and his personal lawyer. Conway was also a Republican, but Dan made a rare exception and they remained friends, as well as client and attorney. The Conways lived in a big house in Cohoes. "We'd raise chicks for Dan at our house and then bring them to Ravena, where he had a fighting cock trainer," Edward Conway said. "We used to go to cockfights with Dan in Saratoga and if a cock was killed, Dan would give my brother the feathers to make trout flies. Dan helped us out any way he could. I remember when our dog was killed by the neighbor's German shepherd, Dan gave us a pit bull from among his fighting dogs. It was named Coolidge after the president. That pit bull tore up that guy's German shepherd, but it also killed about five other dogs in the neighborhood in three days and my dad had to bring the pit bull back to Dan. Dan was sorry we couldn't keep it and later gave us an Irish setter."

For a young boy like Erastus Corning 2nd, who realized only that shadowy politicos in fedoras showed up at the family's mansion with mysterious regularity, growing up with the machine must have seemed as commonplace as drawing breath. The mayor remembered his first meeting with Dan O'Connell at about age five, a hazy boyhood memory he shared with John Treffiletti, a personal friend of the mayor's and Dan's for fifty years. "He didn't remember a lot of details, but Erastus met Dan briefly when he was five, which would have been 1914," said Treffiletti, a wholesale grocer and owner of Star Supermarkets, who raked leaves for O'Connell as a kid and later bought a house on Whitehall Road, not far from Dan's. That 1914 introduction of Erastus to Dan O'Connell roughly coincides with the stirrings of the alliance between the two families.

In an undated reminiscence typewritten and saved in his personal papers, Corning wrote, "At the start of W.W.I, when I was a small boy, the family moved from Chestnut Street to a big brownstone on Washington Avenue next to the Thacher Home and almost across from the Fort Orange Club. One day my father told me he was going to have some Democrats come to the house that afternoon and he would like me to meet some. I waited around all day and while a lot of people came and went, I didn't see any Democrats, and asked him about it afterwards. He told me that all the people were the Democrats, which was a surprise to me, but in the years succeeding I found the statement to be true."

The Cornings had deep pockets and they helped finance the establishment of the countywide Democratic Party political organization that culminated in Dan's 1919 victory in the race for Albany assessor, the only elected public office he ever held. Just back from World War I, where he served in the U.S. Navy aboard the *USS Prairie* for a two-year tour of duty beginning in June, 1917, Dan appeared in gaudy campaign banners wearing his sailor's uniform and depicted as a patriotic veteran and Democrat who captured the attention of an apathetic electorate. O'Connell's unexpected win exposed a chink in the protective armor of Albany's long-entrenched Republican machine run by William F. "Billy" Barnes, grandson of influential newspaper publisher Thurlow Weed. Barnes, the Harvard-trained "Boy Leader" had become owner of two Albany newspapers and had seized control of city politics in the 1890s. With Dan's election, in cockfighting parlance, the O'Connells and Cornings smelled blood, strapped on a slasher and went in for the kill, capturing City Hall in 1921 with their first candidate for mayor, William Stormont Hackett, a banker friend of Edwin and Parker Corning's. Dan borrowed a page from Tammany Hall boss George Washington Plunkitt, whose political philosophy could be summed up in a sentence: "I seen my opportunities and I took 'em."

In Hackett, the Cornings and O'Connells shaped the WASP aristocratic mayoral mold continued for the next six decades by John Boyd Thacher and Erastus Corning 2nd. The strategy was to have Irish Catholics in the background operating the gears of the machine and a Protestant titular head out front handling public relations and official duties in City Hall – a ribbon-cutter *par excellence* with patrician breeding and excellent diction. It was respectability they were after and Hackett filled the bill, a man who invented himself as an aristocrat, despite the fact he was Baptist and a member of his mother's church, Emmanuel Baptist in Albany, who came from a Scottish and Irish lineage. Born in 1866, Hackett grew up on Ferry Street in Albany's South End – O'Connell turf. "The South End Against The World" was the neighborhood slogan, a fierce pride and loyalty of tribe engendered by the O'Connells. Hackett dropped out of Albany High School after two years, at age sixteen, but his intelligence and drive won him a job as a law clerk. Hackett eventually moved into banking, working his way up to assistant treasurer at Albany City Savings Institution – Corning's bank and the place the patricians piled their wealth.

Hackett served as a reservist in the Army from 1890 to 1899 as a sergeant with Company A. With the explosion on the battleship *Maine* in the harbor of Havana, Cuba and the outbreak of the Spanish-American War in February, 1898, the thirty-two-year-old Hackett was called to the front. The request to report to wartime duty came from the captain of Company A, Frank Rockwell Palmer, who was Albany city comptroller and Hackett's boss at the bank. A memorial booklet later published about Hackett by the Cornings and his banking cronies recounted how, on the evening of April 26, 1898, when called upon to fight in the war, Hackett rose, said, "I greatly regret that I cannot" and then broke down. On many occasions afterwards, Hackett expressed his great regret that, on the one occasion when he had the opportunity of serving his country as a soldier, he chose not to go and fight.

A strong lesson was learned from Hackett's experience. Wartime service became a benchmark of the machine. Dan O'Connell parlayed his World War I Navy career into elected office and Mayor Erastus Corning 2nd was re-elected by the largest landslide of his career upon his return from fighting in World War II as the G.I.-Mayor. Harvey Lifset, one of the first lawyers drafted in Albany, came to know this unwritten military service policy firsthand. Lifset became a major with the Army's 82nd Airborne and was awarded five combat medals for his bravery during World War II's Battle of the Bulge. Lifset returned to a prosperous law practice after the war and decided to enter politics in 1956. He met with O'Connell at Whitehall Road. Dan already had the scouting report on Lifset, who spoke little during the brief meeting. "Dan said the combination of being a lawyer with a good war record was an unbeatable combination for a candidate," Lifset said. "Dan gave me his blessing. When Dan said it was a go, it was a go." Lifset was elected to the State Assembly and served six terms.

Foreign war zones had a strangely powerful impact on the arc of Albany politics. Even though he always regretted he didn't fight in Havana, Cuba, Hackett made a trip there during peacetime in 1926. Hackett was at the height of his popularity and zenith of his political career. Some insiders believed Gov. Al Smith, positioning himself for a run for president in 1928, had tapped Hackett in 1926 as his replacement candidate for governor in the year when he campaigned for the White House. Hackett went to Havana on February 26, 1926 seeking the therapy of a tropical climate for unspecified health problems. The car Hackett was riding in hit a bumpy patch of road, lost control and Hackett was killed on March 4, 1926 in Havana.

Edwin and Parker Corning organized a tribute to Hackett, publishing the commemorative booklet, *A Loyal And Well Beloved Son Of Albany*, and they offered a memorial service on March 5, 1926 at a special meeting of the board of trustees of the City Savings Bank of Albany. The board membership reads like a *Who's Who* of Albany ruling families: Parker Corning, Jacob H. Herzog, Peter G. Ten Eyck, James W. Cox, George H. Thacher, Samuel Hessberg, Anthony Brady Farrell and Thomas Hun. The machines aristocratic wing had groomed one of its own to succeed Hackett after his death. The next mayor was John Boyd Thacher II, a Princeton man and an excellent orator who matched the WASP City Hall front-man prerequisite. Thacher had money and had managed well the purse strings as the machine's comptroller beginning in 1921 and later was promoted to president of the Common Council. Hackett's grandfather and great-grandfather had been Albany mayors, too, like Corning's great-grandfather.

From the beginning, the O'Connell-Corning machine was something of a secret society. These men understood how such seemingly inscrutable organizations worked. They knew it from the illegal cockfighting network. They knew it from secretive fraternal groups like the Knights of Columbus or the Masons, to which many of the machine operatives belonged. They knew it from secret societies at their Ivy League schools, such as the Corning allegiance to Wolf's Head. They knew it from members-only social venues ranging from the Fort Orange Club to the Elks. The rules of each of these clubs hinged on certain principles. The first rule was exclusivity; membership was open only to a chosen few. The second rule was loyalty; you were expected to stick together and help out a fellow member in need for richer or poorer, in sickness and in health, like a marriage of sorts. The third rule was unity; you pooled resources and energies to defeat all challengers to your dominance. The fourth rule was confidentiality; you told nobody about what went on inside the club and were expected to take its secrets with you to the grave.

Erastus Corning 2nd was born into this secret society mindset and he accepted the rules and conditions of membership as part of the natural order. So did the others. Political rewards through machine loyalty was a generational phenomenon, almost an inheritance passed down from father to son in Albany. That was the case with Mayor Corning and dozens of others. The names of the mayor's close political associates during his forty-two-year City Hall reign are, like Corning himself, the sons and grandsons of the early members of the Democratic organization: Holt-Harris, Herzog, Schenck, McArdle, Kinley, Koreman, Joyce, Conway, *et cetera, et cetera.* "Family. Family. Family. That's what the organization is all about and we kept it all in the family," Judge Harold E. Koreman said.

A brief Koreman biography is illustrative of the birthright quality of the machine. Koreman was born in 1916 and raised in the South End – O'Connell turf. He knew the O'Connells from the neighborhood growing up. Their families were friends. An uncle, Ed Koreman, was an O'Connell alderman in the South End. Harold showed ambition by becoming the first lawyer in the family. Uncle Dan marked him as a promising kid to watch. Koreman landed a job with the FBI and left town in 1941 for five years, but returned to Albany and reaped the first of his political rewards in 1947 when he was hired by the machine's district attorney, Julian Erway, a life-long friend and fishing buddy of Mayor Corning. Koreman worked as an assistant district attorney until Corning made him his corporation counsel in 1954. The machine had bigger rewards in store for the good agent, a comfortable bench. Koreman rose from Surrogate Court Judge to state Supreme Court to Court of Claims, where he retired as presiding judge in 1986. In retirement, he keeps pictures of his three patron saints on a wall in his home: Dan O'Connell, Judge Francis Bergan and Mayor Corning. "Albany's a small town when you get down to it," Koreman said. "We all grew up together. Our families had associations going way back. See what I mean by family? It was the accepted order of things."

The O'Connell-Corning machine was the third such urban political organization to control Albany in unbroken succession dating back to the mid-nineteenth century. D Cady Herrick, a Democratic boss, held power for nearly twenty years before being overturned by the Republican machine run by Barnes, who, in turn, was beaten by the O'Connell-Corning machine. Not only did those on the inside of the exclusive club that was the machine accept its paternalistic structure, but so, too, did the general citizenry of Albany. Political scientists have shaken their heads in disbelief that the O'Connell-Corning machine could stay in power for so long in Albany. But there were many dynamics, and even, dare we say, genetic predispositions among Albanians toward accepting the machine's oligarchic rule. The first is what William Rowley in his insightful history of Albany in the 1800s termed a "patroon psychology." Rowley, a former Albany newspaper reporter and State University of New York at Albany journalism professor, published *Albany: A Tale of Two Cities, 1820-1880* in 1967 as his Ph.D. thesis in American history at Harvard University. In his study, Rowley suggested that Albanians were trained over the course of generations to act as docile sheep beneath the firm, guiding hands of a succession of shepherds. With Albany's Dutch colonial settlers, the citizens shrunk under the powerful patroons and adopted an attitude of obeisance. This pattern continued with the three-decade dominance of the Barnes Republican machine. Without so much as a breather of independence, Barnes' rule was followed up by seventy-five years of control by the O'Connell-Corning machine. An added layer of what we might consider in psychological terms as a syndrome of servitude among Albanians is the reliance on state government work – likened to puppies suckling at their mother's teats. "The history of Albanians is like sheep," said Dick Patrick, who grew up in Oneonta and came to Albany for a state job after graduating from Syracuse University. Corning hired Patrick away from the state in 1966, and he's been city planner ever since. Although not a native, he spoke with authority as an embodiment of the syndrome. "Albanians seem to be bred to be sheared. They have an inbred sense of being scared. They always expect the worst, I've found. They're naturally pessimistic and it's easy to lead those kind of people."

Examples of patroon psychology abound. Apparently, it didn't matter to the people of Albany that political boss Dan O'Connell had served time in prison for running an illegal – and fixed, by all accounts – baseball pool in the 1920s renowned across the Northeast as "The Albany Pool." A federal government investigation of the machine revealed that the O'Connell brothers rigged their pool with the help of hundreds of hired hands in

Albany and raked in a cut worth an estimated $820,000 in 1927, an extravagant sum in that day, a portion of which allegedly was kicked back to Edwin Corning, the mayor's father, who had been so generous during the genesis of the machine. The O'Connells purportedly also extorted money from competing baseball pool operators and bribed Albany police officers not only to look the other way, but to escort runners personally for the O'Connells when they transferred large sums of cash. William Kennedy covered the baseball pool scandal in detail in *O Albany!* and chronicled how the Ryans, twin brothers Charlie and Jimmy, became Dan's trusted lieutenants in the machine. Their father, James Ryan Sr., used his clout to get Dan sprung from the Federal House of Detention in New York City, where he was incarcerated in 1930 for his role in the baseball pool. Each morning, Ryan would have O'Connell driven to the Ryan's comfortable home in the Riverdale section of New York City for the day and then driven back to prison in the evening. O'Connell was as good as his promise to help out the family after old man Ryan died that same year, 1930. The Ryans moved to Albany and were set up through the benevolence of Dan and the machine, of whom it was said their word was as good as a contract and impossible to trace.

The patroon psychology was only one factor in any attempt to deconstruct Albany's mythic political organization. Whatever slim thread of independence remained in the citizenry of Albany was co-opted by the machine. Dan O'Connell always said he wanted a thousand little jobs instead of a few big commissioner-level patronage positions. Everyone in Albany, it seemed, got a little slice of the patronage pie or was related to somebody who did. There were all the old fellas raking leaves in the park, the lift operators running automatic elevators in City Hall, the surfeit of janitors in the city's buildings, the plethora of laborers on county road crews, the scores of clerical workers tucked away in forgotten cubbyhole offices in city and county agencies. Freedman in his book *The Inheritance* recounts what has come to be seen as a classic symbol of machine payroll padding and patronage corruption: that Dan's Albany County courthouse required seventy-two janitors for six floors while the Empire State Building employed just sixty for its 102 floors. One estimate put the number of full- and part-time city and county jobs controlled by the machine at about 5,000 – perhaps as high as fifteen percent of the county's entire adult workforce – attesting to Dan's philosophy of spreading the patronage broadly. In William Kennedy's *Grand View*, a drama about Albany's Democratic

machine performed in the city in 1996, a character in the play asked political boss Patsy McCall (a thinly veiled Dan O'Connell) if he owned any
property. "Yes we do," Patsy replied. "We own the city and the county."
O'Connell's real-life patronage employees worked for penurious wages,
but the number of jobs controlled by the machine was so exorbitant that
many households were given more than one position and the combined
salaries offered a livable income. There were perks to holding a machine
post, too, chances to moonlight or opportunities to make extra money
freelancing that came your way. Putting Hedrick's beer on tap at your tavern and buying insurance coverage for your company from Mayor
Corning's Albany Associates were only the two most obvious examples of
implied reciprocity within Albany's machine politics. Those who weren't
given a permanent position might receive seasonal employment or the
proverbial turkey or bin of coal or a few sawbucks to tide one over during
lean times – slapped into the palm personally by Dan or Erastus. Money, it
has been said, is the mother's milk of politics; small denominations sans
receipt was the invisible lubrication that greased the cogs of Albany's
Democratic machine. All these rewards came with strings attached. This
condition didn't even need to be voiced; *quid pro quo* was an unspoken
proviso no matter how small the gift. Remember us come election time.
Vote Row A. Democrats all the way. If you didn't, a machine pox upon
your house. There was an element of voodoo in the machine's tactics, too,
for the sheep of Albany believed the machine knew how each person voted
in the voting booth. The voodoo rumors included these: there was a
slightly different pitch to the clicking sound the Democratic and
Republican candidate levers made; there were elaborate systems of mirrors
or special peepholes cut in the ceiling above the booth; hawk-eyed spies
looked over your shoulder. There were a score of other voting intimidation
legends attributed to the machine, yet never confirmed.

The machine definitely bought votes, however, according to several
reliable insiders. The machine's vaunted $5 vote was fact, rather than fic-
tion. "Yes, there were $5 votes. I saw my dad give out $5 bills on election
day," said Ray Joyce Jr., born in 1923, whose father, Ray Joyce Sr., was a
ward leader and crony of Dan's. "Back in the '30s and '40s when times were
tough, that $5 meant a lot. My dad said he was given a stack of $5 bills equal
to the number of votes they needed to buy to reach the ward leader's goal."
Rev. Joseph Romano, a Catholic priest who had known Dan O'Connell for
many years, remembered a pastoral visit to a shut-in, a machine hack and

former public safety commissioner. "This was just a couple of days before an election and his bed was covered with stacks and stacks of $5 bills," Romano said. "Piles of money. I'd say it was more than $10,000. Right before the election. And he acted like it wasn't there." Not only did the Democrats buy votes, but they employed the time-honored Tammany tactic of voting early and often. One machine stooge boasted of voting more than three dozen times in a single election. In 1936, Albany County's Republican chairman Charles G. Wing claimed to have found one man who voted four times: as a dead man, a convict, an out-of-state resident, and, apparently for good measure, as himself. To machine loyalists, those bound by the secret society code, such voting fraud became a kind of badge of honor. Slang that glamorized the corrupt practices grew up in North Albany: "making the machine dance." Dan's boys took pride in making the machine dance to the tune of a dozen or more rapid-fire repeated yanks of the voting booth lever for Democratic candidates. When it came to such fabled fraud, nobody made the machine dance better than Dan and Erastus and their famous organization.

In his 1973 book, *Albany's O'Connell Machine*, Frank Robinson documented in detail the specific abuses, corruptions and underhanded methods for controlling the voters employed by the machine. We need not repeat his labors here, but in an interview twenty years after the publication of his iconoclastic volume, Robinson said little had changed in Albany. "The average person living here wasn't shocked or outraged by what I uncovered, because the machine had their hooks into almost everybody some way or another," said Robinson, who lives in Albany's Pine Hills with his family and is an administrative law judge with the state Public Service Commission. Robinson was a Republican ward leader, ran campaigns and was a losing candidate himself for city court judge in the 1970s, but has been less active politically in recent years. Robinson said years of research for his book turned his interest in the machine from obsession to revulsion to acceptance. "The Albany machine never resorted to physical violence like Tammany, because they didn't have to," Robinson said. "They started out so strongly with Hackett and had a free ride for decades and never needed the severe methods of control. The machine isn't dead in the 1990s, it's just metamorphosed. People still believe in its power."

A remarkable analysis of the urban political machine, perhaps the best behind-the-scenes explanation of its structure ever published, is Frank R. Kent's 1923 book, *The Great Game of Politics*. Erastus Corning 2nd read the Kent primer as a student at Groton and absorbed its penetrating insights. Kent wrote:

> The political machine makes for waste, extravagance, and inefficiency in the public service. It adds terribly to the taxpayers' burden. Its primary purpose is to get jobs, and in the pursuit of this it enormously swells the public payrolls. It breeds up a class of professionals who cost the country dear, and there is a long train of evil and undesirable things in its wake. But there is another side to the picture. In every community its excesses are exactly equal to the tolerance of the people. They have always the power to smash the machine and clean house whenever they become sufficiently aroused to use it. They may have a good or a bad machine in exact proportion to the energy of their desire, but a machine they must have. It stands in all great cities as a buffer between ignorance and helplessness on the one side and the red tape of the government on the other hand. It helps the poor, guides the ignorant, rescues the unfortunate, lightens the penalty for the sinful, and straightens out the bewildered.

John J. McEneny – Corning protégé, State Assemblyman and Democratic mayoral candidate in 1997 – summarized the machine's extraordinary control thus: "Great political power is an empire of favors due . . . not called in. Once they're called in, they're no good." One of the machine's favorite tactics of that sort of mental manipulation was to jack up the tax assessment each time a person purchased a home or property in the city. The new homeowner would get a visit from the machine's committeeman, who said he could help you get the assessment lowered – if you voted Democratic out of gratitude. The machine seemed so omnipotent, the sheep of Albany believed this, went along with what they were told and gave the helpful committeeman their allegiance. "What people didn't understand is that you could go down to City Hall and get the assessment reduced by yourself," Robinson said. "When I bought a house in the early '70s, the committeeman came around and I said go away. I was a Republican ward leader and still got my assessment lowered on my own without any hassle. It was all an illusion. The people of Albany lived under an assumed fear."

Those were the head games that the machine perpetrated on the psyche of Albanians with its real and implied threats – carrot-and-stick property tax assessment manipulation for political purposes. They only had to work those strong-arm tactics a few times to lay the groundwork for mental intimidation simply by suggestion. But demographics gave the machine even more solid footing for its entrenched power. Rowley pointed out that 1885 was a pivotal year in Albany's ethnic history. The state census that year revealed that Albany had become almost one-half Irish Catholic, many recent immigrants who arrived and dug the Erie Canal in the early 1800s. "It had become, in fact, two cities, one Anglo-Saxon Protestant, the other Irish Catholic," Rowley wrote in his thesis. Rowley added this:

> The striking thing about the development of Albany into two cities is not that they were so different but that they were so alike. Both were aristocratic in their social structure, with a marked distinction between the aristocrats and the poor; both aristocracies were conservative in their determination to preserve the power structure as it had developed, and both were adept in winning the acquiescence of the laboring class and the poor. The two cities did not merely coexist. They accommodated. And in that accommodation, they laid the foundation for the modern oligarchic structure of Albany society. The Irish joined the Yankees in perpetuating the tradition of conservatism and aristocracy that had been started by the feudal Dutch.

The machine simply merged these two cities within Albany under one banner and the bond was as strong as any of the forged steel manufactured at Corning's plant. As Jon Teaford, the Purdue political scientist pointed out, there were other contributing factors at work for the Albany machine's longevity. First, the political culture of New York state, which had spawned Tammany Hall, was conducive to a machine. "Dan O'Connell would have been lost in California, for example, which didn't have powerful ward bosses like New York," Teaford said. Second, Albany's demographics were stagnant. Population hovered between 100,000 and 130,000 from 1920 to 1995. The percentage of blacks in the city's population rose gradually, from 2.5 percent in 1920 to about fifteen percent in 1980. "It would have been harder for the machine to maintain its power if the population was less stable or if there was an influx of minorities demanding change," Teaford said. "Dan O'Connell wasn't worried about the Latino vote." Third, Albany is a city of senior citizens, ranking seventh in the nation in 1960 with nearly twenty percent of its population over the age of sixty-five. "A lot of the people voting for Erastus Corning in 1981 were the same people who voted for him in 1941," Teaford said. And, finally, the cult of personality exuded by Dan and Erastus was an unbeatable force. "You couldn't script the movie any better," Teaford said. "Erastus was the front man who looked good, sounded good and came from a good background. Dan was happy to stay behind the scenes and run the show."

Dan and Erastus, the be-all and end-all of the machine, its alpha and omega. Their relationship holds the key to what made the organization work so effectively for so long. During a political association that spanned one-half century, built upon almost daily strategy sessions, Dan and Erastus became as close as hand and glove, or, opposite sides of the same coin. They've been caricatured by journalists who portrayed Dan as the rough-hewn, cigar-chomping ward boss and Erastus as his urbane alter-ego. Those who knew them both and watched the two men interact and operate their machine over the years said those popular notions were too simplistic. The alliance was much more complex than that.

O'Connell met Erastus when he was a young boy and Dan kept his eye on Erastus as he grew up – a bright lad with good breeding, Edwin's eldest child – the way he might watch a promising fighting cock with winning blood lines. Erastus was hardly in Albany at all between the ages of twelve and twenty-two, away at Groton and Yale with summers spent in Maine. Those were the years that the machine rose to power and solidified its block-by-block control of Albany. Even though he didn't actively participate in politics in his youth, Erastus couldn't help but absorb an education in that area. It seemed to be in his genes. His great-grandfather had been mayor of Albany, his grandfather had been an alderman and his father was State Democratic chairman and Lieutenant Governor under Al Smith. He couldn't escape it. "My father always loved politics, my father loved to talk politics, and I knew political people ever since I was a little kid," the mayor told reporter Carol DeMare in June of 1981 for an extensive *Times Union* profile that was one of Corning's last in-depth interviews. Nonetheless, Corning added he had never harbored "any longtime vision of going into politics."

In fact, Erastus seemed to have no longtime vision for himself of anything. Even in young adulthood, he was the wandering boy of his youth, roaming over numerous areas of interest without focusing on any single one in a fashion similar to that with which he meandered through the hundreds of acres of woods at Corning Hill. Erastus was a dabbler, collecting coins and stamps, cataloging objects from the natural world, studying history and art and literature, pursuing fishing and hunting and the outdoors – that last being perhaps his most passionate avocation. In demeanor and personality, Erastus more closely resembled his grandfather, Erastus Corning Jr., the free-spirited orchid grower and butterfly collector with the extravagant mutton-chop sideburns. The free-spirited young Erastus seemed the antithesis of his great-grandfather, the original Erastus, or his father, Edwin, both of whom were driven to attain achievements of the highest order in business and politics with a single-minded purposefulness. In the Corning family tree, broad personality traits seem to skip a generation before repeating themselves.

This intellectual drift and absence of concrete goals in Erastus clashed with the rigid career path his father had mapped out for his firstborn son. Erastus had no choice in Groton and Yale and neither did he have a say about the insurance business in which his father set him up in 1932 after graduation and marriage. It was a source of conflict within Erastus. "He confided in me he wanted to go to Italy to study art and he yearned to be an artist," Holt-Harris said. "But his father had decreed the direction and Erastus was a dutiful son. Groton was the beginning of the end of his freedom." Said Corning cousin, Wharton Sinkler III, "I think they had us all enrolled in Groton within days of our births."

Corning's father never saw the fruits of his labor in shaping Erastus' destiny. He had been an invalid following a heart attack and stroke in 1928, the year Erastus graduated from Groton, and died in 1934 at age fifty-one, after being incapacitated for the final years of his life. At the time of his father's death, Erastus was two years out of Yale, working at the insurance company, married and the father of a son – as his private life spun out of control. "He was real wild at that age," Holt-Harris recalled. "He was drinking heavily, his bank account was always overdrawn and he made some big mistakes when he was drunk." This is about the time that Holt-Harris, then a student at Cornell Law School, met Corning one fall day at the Austerlitz Fish and Game Club, a private preserve where Holt-Harris went bird hunting. "I saw this tall, rugged young man emerging out of the woods lugging a field-dressed deer and looking for all the world like Paul Bunyan," Holt-Harris recalled. It was the future mayor. The two young men struck up a lifelong friendship.

Meanwhile, Dan O'Connell had been keeping tabs on young Erastus and he didn't like what he saw in the destructive ways of the son of his late friend and political associate, Edwin Corning. O'Connell changed the course of Erastus' directionless life. The political boss asked him to take the seat of his deceased father as delegate to the 1934 State Democratic convention. Erastus was one of those men who have greatness thrust upon them. The political grooming had begun. The Dan-Erastus alliance was born.

Dan liked to give his political cronies nicknames based on characters in the novels of his two favorite authors, Dickens and Thackeray. Dan called Erastus "Pendennis," after the title character in *The History of Pendennis* by English novelist and satirist William Makepeace Thackeray. Arthur Pendennis, known as Pen for short, was spoiled by his mother and breezed through the university, entered upper-class London society, wrote a successful novel, became editor of the *Pall Mall Gazette* and had many love affairs. He was steered awry by his cynical, materialistic uncle, Major Pendennis (read Parker Corning). After sowing his wild oats, Pen settled down and married his good and true love, Laura Bell.

In 1934, Dan was forty-nine-years-old, two years younger than Corning's father when he died, when he tapped Erastus (Pendennis), who was twenty-five. Those who were close to the two men politically and personally have likened their relationship to that of a father and son. It should be noted that Dan and his wife, Leta (nee Burnside), who died in 1963, never had children of their own. Dan brought Erastus into his family and into the machine, which were essentially one and the same. Corning didn't get to know Dan's oldest brother, Patrick ("Packy"), who died in 1933 and who had been leader of the First Ward, the guy to see about a job in the State Legislature where he worked as clerk of the Senate. But Erastus was acquainted with Dan's two other brothers, the rest of the machine triumvirate: Ed, the brilliant attorney, and John ("Solly"), the colorful street-level machine enforcer and CEO of its ancillary gambling operations. Erastus especially enjoyed Solly's company.

"You couldn't help but like Solly, who was everybody's friend," said the late Charlie Torche, born in 1911, lifelong Albanian, lawyer, lobbyist and partaker of the city's illegal pleasures. "Albany was an open town back in Solly's day, the '30s and '40s, and we'd hang out in the horse rooms and taverns. Solly controlled the numbers and the horse rooms. He was a big-time gambler, too. We played a lot of cards and lost a lot of bets on the ponies right in Dan's saloon."

The machine worked as a kind of political farm system similar to that of major league baseball. You paid your dues and followed protocol and executed Dan's orders and maybe one day you'd get called up to the show. Frank Cox, who came up through the ward ranks, was a printer at the *Times Union*. He finally had paid his dues to the point that Dan ran him for State Assembly in 1959 to fill the remaining term of Mayor Corning's brother, Eddie, who was still in a coma from an auto accident. Of course, Cox won. Harry Loucks, a longtime printer at the paper, recalled the backshop boys getting together at work to congratulate one of their own on becoming a state lawmaker. One printer piped up: "Hey, Frankie, now that you're a big-shot Assemblyman, whaddya gonna do?" Cox replied without missing a beat, "Whatever they tell me." Loucks roared with laughter over a story the printers have retold a thousand times hunched over their typographical work in the backshop.

Dan put Erastus Corning in the State Assembly in 1936, promoted him to senator and let him learn the political ropes. Corning was a minority member as a Democrat and didn't have much to do, but O'Connell watched and waited, wanting to see if the kid did what he was told or if he would screw up.

Dan's instruction of Erastus involved more than political strategy. There was time for drinking at Dan's saloon, for gambling with Solly, for the blood sport of cockfighting that brought the two families together. Those and other considerations contributed to the mayor's mother's opposition to her son entering Albany machine politics, a pursuit she considered below her class and stressful enough, at least in her husband's case, to lead to an early death. Erastus was torn, trying to play the swell even as he appeased his mother's concerns about class decorum and public appearances. "Twice while I was a state senator I went to cockfights with Dan," Corning told DeMare in her 1981 *Times Union* profile. "But he came to the conclusion once I was elected mayor that that was no longer suitable for a mayor, and he wouldn't take me any longer."

Eventually, Dan's age, changing times, and shifting public opinion about what constituted cruelty to animals merged to bring about the demise of Albany's golden age of cockfighting. "The last main I remember anyone talking about was a big gathering of gamecock owners in Wilkes-Barre, Pennsylvania in the 1960s," Holt-Harris said. "I didn't go, but Dan went with a group of local cockfighters. I never heard anything more after that." (Although cockfighting died out locally, it remained an active sport in New York City, despite its outlaw status. A *New York Times* article in April, 1995 on cockfighting cited the arrests of 547 people and the seizure of 1,600 fighting roosters to-date that year statewide by agents for the American Society for the Prevention of Cruelty to Animals. The *Times* noted that cockfighters pay as much as $300 a month to stash their game-cocks at out-of-the-way farms upstate to avoid arrest.)

Dan, a shrewd judge of character, had chosen well in Erastus, whose temperament was not afire with ambition. Trained in Grotonian reserve and deference to his father, Erastus would do what he was told politically, would be willing to wait in the wings with unusual patience. Most importantly, Erastus was a man who accepted the strictures of the secret society, various permutations of which he had belonged to since Wolf's Head. One of the rare personal letters from Corning to Dan O'Connell was written by the mayor on April 21, 1954. They were discussing the management of the New York Central Railroad, founded by Corning's great-grandfather. "Dear Dan," Corning wrote. "The quotation that appealed to me was the following sentence: 'One of the first things I learned is that a man in politics has only his word to sell.'" The quote is from Tammany Hall operative Jim Farley.

In Erastus, Dan found his perfect political protégé, his understudy as the machine boss. The feeling was mutual. "Dan and Erastus just seemed to fit together," said Martin Schenck. "They greatly admired each other." O'Connell family friend John Treffiletti concurred, recalling being at Dan's house on Whitehall Road with the two men, and, when the mayor left, Dan frequently turned to Treffiletti and said: "There goes the best mayor the city of Albany ever had and ever will have." Even their political rival, Albany County GOP chief Joseph F. Frangella, had to concede Dan and Erastus made beautiful political music together. Frangella said in 1974: "Erastus Corning is an expert second fiddler to the oldest one-man band in America. He has played his fiddle on Whitehall Road for so many years that even Jack Benny took lessons from him."

There was a sense of belonging in being Dan's boy that brought comfort to Erastus Corning 2nd, innately shy, a loner by disposition, considered by his closest friends as distant and aloof. Among Mayor Corning's extensive collection of Albany political memorabilia, donated to the Albany Institute of History & Art after his death, was a rare O'Connell For Assessor election card from 1919. It was a totem of sorts for Corning, as was his connection to cockfighting. In a hutch in the living room of the mayor's home on Corning Hill, where he stored important papers and mementos, he saved a *Life* magazine pictorial on cockfighting. The *Life* spread included glossy photographs of fighting cocks and a political cartoon that drew the analogy between politics and gamecocks. The mayor, who had a penchant for earthy humor, certainly didn't miss the off-color connection between cocks, the slang term for men's genitals, and what it takes to succeed in politics – although, at least publicly, Erastus Corning 2nd never fit the crude cliché of a ballsy ward leader.

And, despite the stereotypes about Dan's coarse style and gutter-level qualities, those who knew him well say his private interests complemented Corning's sensibilities. They both loved fishing and hunting, particularly bird hunting in the Helderbergs. The two hunted and fished together in the early days and, as Dan grew old and frail, Corning continued to hunt and fish with some of O'Connell's old codger pals from the Hilltowns. They both liked to have a drink, but Dan preferred beer (he ran a brewery, after all) to Erastus' taste for top-shelf Scotch (Dewar's White Label). They were both heavy smokers, too, plagued by emphysema at the end, although they disagreed on their tobacco choice. Holt-Harris remembered Dan razzing Erastus often when he'd light up: "What are you doin' smokin' them goddamned women's cigarettes?" O'Connell asked. Erastus smoked Kools. Dan smoked Camel non-filters. They shared a passion for history and literature, too, Corning's dual major at Yale. Dan's knowledge in those areas was self-taught, but no less impressive.

"I remember Dan reciting entire poems by Longfellow from memory," Treffiletti said. "He had an unbelievable mind. I needed a dictionary to keep up with Dan's vocabulary. I don't think Dan had to take a back seat to Erastus when it came to intelligence." A Thursday night read-aloud book club developed in the late-1960s to offer companionship and intellectual stimulation to the failing Dan, in his eighties and in declining health, with his wife long deceased. Living alone, aside from nursing assistance, O'Connell was a virtual recluse in his house. "We'd read mostly Civil War books, but also Thackeray and Dickens, who were Dan's favorite authors," said Holt-Harris, who was joined by Corning, Judge Bergan and Harold Blodgett. "Dan could quote long passages from every Dickens novel and he often talked about how he agreed with Dickens' social commentary and his championing of the little people."

Dan also had cronies and friends like Treffiletti who engaged the boss in conversations about sports to vary his diet of politics, history and literature. "Dan loved to talk about boxing and baseball, his two favorite sports," Treffiletti said. Treffiletti also watched Monday night football with Dan in his waning years. "He'd call me up and say come on over to watch the game and get away from all those girls [Treffiletti has five daughters]. At half-time, we'd have tea and pie. Dan always fell asleep in the second half." Treffiletti would help the old man to bed and also helped him take care of his personal hygiene when Dan no longer could do that for himself, including giving him showers. "I'd known Dan since I was five-years-old and there weren't many people he'd allow to give him that kind of help," Treffiletti said.

The machine was such a seamless apparatus of raw political power because it reached down through past generations, and each new crop of loyalists, like Erastus, was groomed from within machine families who had been raised in the system. Such was the case with Ray Kinley Jr., born in 1944, whom Corning made election commissioner. Kinley was Corning's golf caddy at Schuyler Meadows as a boy. His father, Ray Kinley Sr., was drafted into the Army the same time as Corning and was part of the mayor's reunion group. The senior Kinley was the mayor's golfing buddy and a political consultant to Corning who went on to became a senior vice president in Corning's bank, State Bank of Albany. Kinley's grandfather, Dan Kinley, was a machine lieutenant and Dan made him operator of the water filtration plant. His grandmother, Nellie Kinley, was given a job processing traffic tickets at City Hall. "They worked so well together because they had complementary talents," Kinley said of Dan and Erastus. "Dan knew the people. He never lost touch with the little people. Erastus was a wizard at math and he knew the election numbers like nobody I've ever seen. They instilled loyalty and rewarded those who were loyal and took away rewards from those who weren't."

Martin Schenck, a fellow Yalie two years behind Corning at New Haven, had several deep ties with both Corning and O'Connell. After law school, Schenck was hired by the [Ed] O'Connell and Aronowitz law firm where his dad practiced. Dan wanted Martin to follow in his dad's footsteps and made Schenck a judge, where he spent twenty-six years on the bench. His father, Gilbert Schenck, was a decorated World War I combat veteran, a close friend of Dan's and a football teammate of Ed's at Union College. Gilbert Schenck was Mayor Hackett's corporation counsel and moved up the machine's court hierarchy as a judge, eventually to the State Supreme Court where he was censured during the Dewey investigation of

1943 for conspiring on cases with Dan. Despite his Ivy League education, Martin Schenck received a continuing education from Dan. "Even though Dan didn't get past the fifth grade, he was amazingly well-read and had a large library," Schenck said. "He'd loan me books, everything from Shakespeare to the Civil War. Dan got me interested in the Civil War, about which I knew next to nothing."

Dan, who corresponded with Civil War scholars around the country, taught Schenck about the Civil War from his own encyclopedic knowledge and vast library on the subject. "It's the only war I could get interested in," Dan once said. Dan encouraged Schenck to write a biography of Confederate commander A.P. Hill, *Up Came Hill: The Story of the Light Division and Its Leaders*, published in 1958. Schenck dedicated his book to his wife, Barbara, and to Dan, his first reader and editor. "I'd take a few chapters of the manuscript to Dan and he'd read them and comment and offer suggestions," Schenck said. Schenck remembered how Dan would take trips to Florida, where the Ryans had a home, stopping at Gettysburg and other Civil War battlefields along the way. Jimmy Ryan would drive Dan – who had a fear of flying – to and from Florida as Dan offered a running commentary on Civil War history and extensive biographies of its major figures, all by memory.

Dan maintained a clear line between personal friendship and political business, however, and always chose politics if the two clashed. Schenck learned this rule following a falling-out with Dan when Schenck requested early retirement from the bench in 1972 when he turned sixty. Schenck was burned out after twenty-six years as a city and county court judge, but Dan wanted him to run again. You turned down Dan at your own peril. "I'd had enough of the bench and told Dan I wouldn't run again and I got a harangue from Dan like no other I've ever heard from him," Schenck recalled. "Things were never the same between Dan and me after that." That's the way the game was played in Albany machine politics, the price you paid to remain king of the mountain, a lesson Dan repeatedly drove home to a willing Erastus. "Erastus was a lonely man deep down and so was Dan," Holt-Harris said. "One of the political axioms Dan mentioned often was this: you can't have a friend in politics. Either you have to turn him down or you do him a favor that could get you both in trouble."

Holt-Harris also was taught about Dan's hidebound ways and demand for absolute loyalty. Holt-Harris was ecstatic when Gov. W. Averell Harriman personally selected Holt-Harris and offered him the position of counsel for a new state authority Harriman was establishing to develop an Olympic-caliber, state-run ski center at Whiteface Mountain near Lake Placid. Holt-Harris went to see Erastus. Erastus said they had to go see Dan. The boss asked Holt-Harris if he wanted the job. The answer was yes.

> Dan: "Then you'll have to resign as judge of recorder court and from the school board."

> Holt-Harris: "I don't understand."

> Dan: "It ain't got nothin' to do with you, Welshman (Dan's nickname for Holt-Harris). Harriman can't come into my county and pick one of my people without asking me. If you take it, you're one of Harriman's people. You ain't one of my people anymore."

Holt-Harris turned down Governor Harriman, the dashing jet-set millionaire, and stuck with the crotchety old man with thick bifocals and ill-fitting out-of-date clothes who rarely left his house. So went another tutorial on Albany machine power.

Dan was a man of his word and he kept it, a trait witnessed often by Erastus. Jake Herzog, whose father and uncle were important figures in the machine, was appointed by Dan as election commissioner in 1939 at the age of twenty-eight. As reward for his loyalty, Dan met with Herzog before he went off with the Navy to fight in the Pacific in World War II (he was injured in Okinawa). Dan asked, "What do you want when you come back?" Herzog replied, "I want to be a judge." Dan said, "You will be a judge." After returning to Albany in the fall of 1945 to recuperate from his wounds, Dan summoned Herzog to his camp in the Helderbergs. Herzog said he had forgotten Dan's pre-war promise, but Dan hadn't. "When you went away to the service, you told me you wanted to be a judge," the boss growled in typical gruffness. "I've got it all arranged. Truman will appoint Bucky Kempf to federal court, Burns will go to city court and I'll make you police court judge." It was Dan's chess board and he moved all the pieces at will, yet, within Dan's own inscrutable moral code, it was a political game with a heart and compassion. Erastus conducted the 1946 swearing-in of his buddy Herzog, age thirty-five. "I didn't get a swelled head," Herzog said. "Dan thought the world of my father and he made me a judge to thank my dad."

Rev. Joseph Romano, a Catholic priest assigned to Dan's parish, Saint James, had a beleaguered history with the political boss. Romano was appointed chaplain of the Albany Fire Department and became chief spokesman and organizer when the department battled the machine in the 1970s in an acrimonious struggle over unionization. Dan, rabidly anti-union, referred to Father Romano in a radio interview as "that dago son of a bitch." The quote brought the wrath of "every old lady with a rosary" down on Dan, increased sympathy for the union and helped turn the tide in the department's favor, Romano said. "Corning told me years later that was the dumbest thing the Party ever did, letting the press get to Dan for that comment," Romano said. Romano took communion to Dan, a shut-in in his later years, at his house on Whitehall Road once or twice a week. He also heard Dan's confession. "It was very childlike and he was in and out of reality at that point," Romano said. "We'd talk about the past, about people from the old neighborhoods and the kidnapping [Dan's nephew John Jr. was kidnapped in Albany in 1933 and later released after the O'Connells paid a ransom] and other history. We'd shoot the breeze about the Civil War. Dan actually left me some of his Civil War books and memorabilia when he died," Romano said. On one visit, Romano remembered Dan kept U.S. Sen. Henry "Scoop" Jackson (D-Washington), a presidential hopeful, waiting in the sun room of his Whitehall Road house for nearly one hour while Dan rambled on with Romano. "Jackson was an important man and I was embarrassed, but Dan wasn't," Romano said. Dan's message to Jackson through his housekeeper: "Tell him I'm with my priest." Dan told Romano stories of the times Joe Kennedy stopped by the house campaigning for his son, Jack. Dan referred to Joe Kennedy as "a bootlegger and a pimp," Romano said, and made him grovel for the machine's backing, including, according to Romano and several other sources, Joe Kennedy's gift of the county office building at 112 State Street.

In the fall of 1994, I took an open house tour of Dan's place at 142 Whitehall Road – a side-hall Colonial at the corner of Holmes Court and Whitehall a few blocks west of Delaware Avenue, near School 23 – to see if there was a palpable sense of hallowed ground as described by machine loyalists. Dan's house is within the solidly middle-class neighborhood of Saint James parish, the same section of the city where Dan's three brothers once lived. The ordinariness of Dan's house confirmed the notion that the boss, like his protégé, Erastus, was not covetous of material wealth or personal luxury. The house was for sale in September, 1994, having been bought and sold by a couple of owners since Dan died in 1977. The asking price was $134,900. The four-bedroom Colonial has a detached two-car garage and sits on a typical city lot, forty-four feet by 143 feet. The taxes, though, a legacy to Dan perhaps, were a relatively low $1,809 per year.

One entered the house, as Erastus did each morning, along with a steady stream of supplicants ranging from machine hacks to presidential candidates, from a postage stamp-sized covered front porch. To the left of the entry foyer and staircase was a small sun room where Dan kept his VIP visitors cooling their heels, a show of power for the lowly and mighty alike. To the right of the stairway was the living room with brick fireplace – where Dan hung a portrait of Harry Truman, his sole political idol. Off the living room was a kitchen and pantry, as well as a dining room, where a full bath had been built into a corner. Dan's bed was installed in the dining room when he grew too frail to make it upstairs to the bedroom. In good health and bad, Dan's throne of power was a well-worn Naugahyde recliner in the living room where he sat, enveloped in cigarette smoke, rasping out orders laced with profanities in his croaky voice, a stack of $20 bills in the drawer of a small lamp table at his side, where he reached with practiced smoothness for anyone down on his luck needing a little touch to tide him over.

Upstairs, Dan's master bedroom was large enough for a king-size bed and ensemble, which Dan had, plus a sitting area and walk-in cedar closet. There were three more bedrooms, including one with stairs to a full, finished attic. The attic was lined with homemade bookshelves where Dan kept the overflow of his vast Civil War library. The house had some unusual features. The upstairs bathroom was fitted with an odd custom ceramic shower, with a stainless steel wraparound apparatus with numerous spray heads that provide a full-body wash – head to toe, front and back, and sides all at once. Nothing like coming clean. Also, as a safeguard against his enemies, perhaps, Dan installed a professional-grade burglar alarm system and a fire alarm sprinkler system throughout the structure, the ceilings dotted with dozens of commercial sprinkler heads of the sort normally found in office buildings, not private homes. The biggest surprise of all was in the basement. Past a homemade wine cellar and the control panel for the sprinkler system rested a large, extremely heavy, bank-quality stand-up safe measuring about four feet by four feet. More intriguingly, the safe had a fist-sized hole of shredded metal blown in the upper left-hand side of the door. Someone had obviously wanted something in that safe rather badly; presumably, they didn't know the lock's combination. The blown safe in the basement is fact. The stories, legend and conjecture about the safe are not. One strain of rumors has it that the safe is where Dan kept the machine kickback loot before it was transferred to Party headquarters at 75 State Street. Another theory suggests the safe was purchased to hold the $250,000 demanded as ransom money by the kidnappers of Solly's son, John O'Connell Jr., who was nabbed in front of his family's home at 14 Putnam Street on July 7, 1933. The young O'Connell boy was held for twenty-three days in an apartment house in Hoboken, New Jersey as Dan and his brothers negotiated with the kidnappers. The O'Connell brothers first offered $20,000, which was rejected, and the payoff price inched up to $40,000, which the kidnappers eventually accepted. They released the kid unharmed, but the bills were marked and eight men were eventually convicted of the kidnapping. "I asked the owners of the house about the safe and they told me they'd always heard thieves blew it open and made off with $250,000 during a heist," said realtor Maria Martin, who gave me a guided tour. "I don't know what to think. All I can tell you is what I hear."

Dan's summer house on Beaver Dam Road in the Helderbergs is similarly utilitarian, a modest brick bungalow of three bedrooms, sturdy and unpretentious. What makes it special is its perch atop a cliff that affords a panoramic view, a sweeping vista that seems to encompass all of Albany, city and county. One can imagine Dan stringing a hammock between two trees in the backyard and gazing contemplatively out upon his kingdom, satisfied beyond anything money could buy of his creation and his absolute control over it. For that's what thrilled Dan and Erastus about politics, the blood sport aspect, the cockfighting part, imagining themselves the victors left standing triumphantly atop the heap of corpses after each election. The two men enriched themselves through their positions, certainly, with business flowing through Erastus' insurance company and customers to Dan's Hedrick Brewing Company because of their positions of influence. And maybe they even made a tidy profit directly from political gifts or, in Dan's memorable phrase, "honest graft," or whatever else one might like to call it. And why not? Both men dedicated their lives to the machine. What's wrong with a little off-the-books pension plan? They didn't get obscenely greedy about it, the way Curley of Boston and Tweed and his Tammany bosses did. You didn't see Dan or Erastus living in a mansion, chauffeured around in a limousine, with yachts and other expensive playthings to draw the unwanted attention of investigators and prosecutors. No, sir, Dan and Erastus lived relatively simply. Dan's summer home did have an in-ground swimming pool, a luxury in those days, but he also grew vegetables for the table there and dressed three decades out of fashion. You might mistake Dan for a plumber if you passed him on the street. His relatives recall Dan as a rather prosaic old man and the O'Connell clan as prototypically middle-class.

"Growing up as kids, he was just my uncle and he'd come to visit and we'd think nothing of it," said Mary Anne Grassie, Dan's grandniece and granddaughter of Dan's brother, Solly. She was born in 1938 and grew up on Summit Avenue, the daughter of John Jr., the kidnap victim, who became vice president of the family business, Hedrick Brewing Company. "We walked to St. James school (her friends and classmates were Polly Noonan's kids, who lived a block away) and rode the bus. My dad drove a Studebaker. We were just an average family. Dan never showed any sense of wealth, either. He usually gave us a sweater or hat and gloves for Christmas or our birthday. And when we went to Dan's house, he gave us chocolate cake and ice cream."

Grassie remembered spending summer days at Dan's summer home in the Helderbergs. There was always a gaggle of kids and they'd swim in the pool and ride Dan's brown-and-white spotted pony. Sometimes, Dan's niece, Leta Lynch Boyle, wife of machine lieutenant Don Lynch, would drive the kids in a little buggy pulled by the pony. Dan treated Leta like a daughter and bequeathed the Helderbergs house to her. The house wasn't winterized in Dan's time, though, and family gatherings wound down there each year after Labor Day. "It was always a thrill to get invited to go swimming at Uncle Dan's and sometimes we'd go from there over to his brother Packy's camp on Thompson's Lake," Grassie said. "But summer passed too quickly."

Grassie remembered visits to the family brewery on Central Avenue, near the city's public bath on the corner of Central and Ontario. "It was good ale and lager, but we never had a free supply at the house," Grassie said. "We were taught to pay for everything. I guess that was our moral value growing up. There were no freebies." The Little Sisters of the Poor, whom Dan had supported in a major way anonymously for years, got the property after the brewery was torn down in the 1960s.

Grassie saw a lot of Mayor Corning growing up. He visited Dan every day, even in the Helderbergs, she said. "What I really appreciated about Erastus is that after my father died, he came to visit my mother and us kids and was very kind and personable and like part of our family," Grassie said.

Corning did one more lasting kindness for Grassie. After she tired of Florida, Grassie moved back to the area, settling in Glens Falls. She wanted a job as a teacher. Corning knew the mayor of Glens Falls, Ed Bartholomew, and put in a good word for Grassie with him. Grassie got an interview and a job teaching in the Glens Falls school system. "It's all about who you know and Erastus made the call that got my foot in the door," Grassie said. "I got the job myself from there."

There were other perks to being born into the machine. Grassie was part of a large O'Connell contingent that was invited to President John F. Kennedy's inaugural and the festivities that followed, at which she met JFK's siblings. "From what I could see, Dan ran things as old-fashioned Irish politics," Grassie said. "It started in the saloons, expanded block by block into the neighborhoods, and grew into a shared sense of belonging and helping each other."

"I was always mistaken for Dan's grandson and everybody talked about him as larger-than-life, some kind of legend," said Daniel O'Connell, a grandnephew of Dan's and grandson of John "Solly" O'Connell. He lives in Albany, works for the state and he and his wife have two children. "To me, Dan was like any other elderly relative, happy to see you, kindly, hard of hearing."

O'Connell said his uncle Dan was very generous financially to his parents when they were first married. His father, John O'Connell, lives in Voorheesville and works for Niagara Mohawk Power Corp. "Dan was very shrewd and knew a lot about human nature and the needs of the people," O'Connell said. "Dan and Erastus worked together to achieve their common goal, which was to stay in power. Erastus was the active, out-front partner and Dan was the silent partner pulling the strings behind the scene."

Many have suggested Dan was a political genius. If he was, he stored the strategy all in his head. When Dan died in his sleep at the age of ninety-one on February 28, 1977, the monolithic political machine he had created began to vanish with him. Dan left almost no paper trail. He wrote very few letters, did not keep a diary or produce memoirs. He gave no extensive interviews. He conducted business face-to-face, rarely even over the phone. He didn't keep records. But a few insiders gained entree into Dan's template for Albany politics. One of them, State Supreme Court Judge Edward S. Conway was, ironically, an Irish-Catholic Republican. But Conway's father, John J. Conway, was a close personal friend of Dan's. He read Dickens with Dan, who gave Conway the nickname "Mr. Wickfield" after the kindly lawyer in Dickens' novel, *David Copperfield*.

The elder Conway would become Dan's personal lawyer for thirty years, after Conway sold Hedrick's Brewery to Dan for $25,000 in the early 1930s. The Conways bought a big house in Cohoes with the cash, where Edward grew up. The elder Conway had been elected Albany County District Attorney in 1923, defeated by the machine the next election and the last Republican to hold that post for fifty years. Conway's father took the brewery in lieu of legal fees after representing bootleggers who were secretly piping beer underground illegally from the brewery during Prohibition. Conway estimated the brewery earned Dan a few million dollars' profit during three decades of operation. Dan extended his loyalty to Edward Conway, the son, despite his GOP status. Dan made Conway a judge – largely to remove Conway from his position as Albany County GOP chairman, where he was making gains, Conway believed – confirming for Conway Dan's cynical world view.

Conway said:

> Dan's fundamental rules were these: the cop on the beat takes care of the Jews and lets them know their shops will be safe if they vote Democratic. They're so scared, they do. The Italians are run by matriarchs, so Dan knew to talk to the women there and got those votes. He knew never to have a Catholic mayor. Let the Protestants run the city and that's all they get. The Irish get the rest. The Jews get city judge. The Italians get county judge. The cops make out on their own beat with whatever graft comes their way. The firemen he called 'pinochle players' and they get a meal and a place to sleep and that's good enough for them. Don't fix the potholes because they're the best deterrents to speeding. Let the public schools rot and the private and Catholic schools would thrive and the Democrats didn't have to pay for them. Keep school taxes at a minimum, just enough to keep the schools from crumbling down. Uncle Dan had a way of taking care of everybody. Everybody got a little bit. That was the secret. Spread it around.

Conway also caddied for Dan's brother, Packy, and his father was one of Dan's lawyers during the baseball pool scandal. Conway knew Dan's brother, Solly, too, and wasn't unfamiliar with Solly's gambling operation.

"After Solly died, Dan didn't want anything to do with gambling and he let it go, but he always kept organized crime out of Albany," Conway said. "I know for a fact about the time a Chicago mobster named Syracuse Kelly was hired to knock off Dan. Dan's henchman, Walter Hickey, who had served time in Dannemora under an assumed name, headed off Kelly just below my dad's office, at Child's Restaurant at 50 State Street. Hickey knocked Kelly out and gave him a 'hot ass,' which meant putting a bullet hole through both cheeks in his ass and then Hickey dumped Kelly on a train with a one-way ticket. The big Chicago gangster never came back to Albany again."

"There were never any mobs in here. Dan wouldn't let them organize," said Alfred Bremm, born in 1904 and a South Ender who was a cop for thirty years, beginning in 1928. Bremm was hired as Johnny O'Connell's bodyguard after he was released by his kidnappers. "Wherever Johnny went, I went. I made sure nobody bothered him. I just got my wages as a cop for doing it, nothing extra. Johnny was in the office at the brewery most of the time anyway, so it was no big deal. The O'Connells ran a good, tight ship and did the right thing and were very popular. They all had a role. Solly controlled the numbers. Dan and Ed took care of politics. Johnny was the quiet one who ran the brewery and stayed out of the limelight."

Father Romano said Albany remained an open city long after the days of Prohibition and Legs Diamond. After Solly died, Dan gave the gambling operation to other machine lieutenants, Romano said. "You didn't open a card room in the city without their say-so," Romano said.

Romano saw in Dan and Erastus both the bright and dark sides, the good and evil, the complex mix of competing motivations. When Romano was spearheading the drive to unionize the fire department to provide better wages, benefits and working conditions, he observed firsthand nasty tactics and hardball actions as vicious as a fighting cock. But he also saw the anonymous kindnesses. Romano was assigned to St. Ann's parish in the South End and said Dan practically subsidized the entire budget of the church, even after he moved up to Whitehall Road into the St. James parish. Romano watched Dan hand out stacks of $20 bills to people down on their luck who streamed to his home. Romano said of Dan: "He always spoke of Italians and blacks in derogatory slang, but he also used that for his own Irish. In that sense, he was always a South End bartender. On the other hand, he was very much a Renaissance man and genuinely sensitive and concerned about the poor. It wasn't only for the votes, but a deep paternalism. He was critical of Irish bishops who had lost their empathy for the poor. He was the softest touch in the world to a person in need."

The same went for Erastus. Romano watched the mayor execute down-and-dirty, bare-knuckle politics during the fire department's drive for unionization. But Romano also remembered numerous random acts of kindness by Corning. "I'd get a call from the mayor that some old man was dying in the South End with no money and he'd ask me to arrange for the burial and Erastus would take care of the cost," Romano said. "Erastus never missed a wake of machine old-timers. I remember Corning paid for me to bury an old double-amputee, wheelchair-bound lady from the South End whose husband had taken care of Dan's fighting cocks. Covering the burial costs was in addition to Erastus putting in a wheelchair ramp at her house." The generous acts for the poor and forgotten were continued by Erastus after Dan died. His mentor had taught the mayor more than politics, after all.

Judge Koreman, whose parents grew up in the South End and attended grade school with Dan before he dropped out, understood the worlds of both Dan and Erastus. "They were two strong personalities raised in very different situations, but they were close because they had the same goal of preserving political power," Koreman said. "Hell, there must have been some arguments between them, but I never knew of a major disagreement they had all those years."

Both Erastus and Dan possessed not only exceptional intelligence, but extraordinary memories. The two men seemed to have photographic recall when it came to people and politics, which, in their minds, were one and the same. Ward heelers said Dan would sit in the recliner in his living room on Whitehall Road, rarely leaving, and run through his own internal electoral street map, as efficient as a computer database and spanning three generations. Nobody could track it or steal it, either, because Dan never wrote it down. "Dan would go street by street, block by block, ward by ward, and tell you who lived in each house, where they worked, what their relationship was to other people in the neighborhood and how they would vote. He had that knowledge of the entire city in his head," said Ray Joyce Jr., member of a longtime machine family, "and Dan's election estimates were right on the money. Always within a few votes." Joyce said Dan taught his father this mental technique. The senior Joyce won Dan's confidence and undying loyalty because he was an Albany cop who was on duty the night of the Johnny O'Connell kidnapping. The senior Joyce chased the kidnappers in a patrol car south on Route 9W toward Ravena where they were last seen heading south. Joyce and his wife raised twelve kids in Albany's west end, near Swinburne Park, and Dan helped get him off the force and into a better-paying job as a foreman at the New York Central Railroad's west Albany shops. Ray Joyce Jr. said he was rewarded politically by Corning for two things, as a World War II vet and because Dan respected the hard work of his father as committeeman and ward leader for Dan. Corning made the son, Ray Jr., born in 1923, his city treasurer and his brother, Harold Joyce, was given political posts as well. The political blueprint remained the same across the decades. Said Ray Joyce Jr.: "The foundation was keeping in close contact with the people. The committeeman was expected to be out year-round, not just around election time, ringing doorbells, going door-to-door and asking how he could help. The structure was almost like the military in which Erastus and Dan trained. The hierarchy went from the committeeman to the ward leader to Dan. It all ran on loyalty. If Dan asked you do to something, that was it. You did what you were told. No questions asked. There was the Party and the Catholic Church. In that order."

Both involved ritual observances. It has been suggested the voting booth was more important than the confessional to an Albany Democrat. "I know that my father would go into the voting booth with my mother, because he didn't trust her to vote Democratic," said Kate (Walsh) Grober, whose husband, George Grober, worked as an office assistant for Mayor Corning from 1976 until his death. Walsh's family members were loyal Democrats. Her dad, Michael Walsh, was given a job in the city streets department. Her uncle ran Kelly's Grill at Orange and Swan. "It was a way of life," she continued. "At our bar, they only served Hedrick's beer on tap. The Corning wealth was something that people like my family in Arbor Hill didn't mind as long as he got the job done, kept taxes low and gave the people decent city services."

The old-time ward heelers, like Ruben Gersowitz, born in 1913 and a South Ender who knew the O'Connells growing up, lamented that the machine's tactics of yore won't work anymore. "In hard times, the $5 vote and helping people out to lower their assessment was pure gold," said Gersowitz, whose loyalty was rewarded by Corning with a job as manager of the city-owned Wellington Hotel. "The public is much better educated nowadays. This new crop of intellectuals won't go for the old methods. And the people in the Party are too independent. They don't do what they're told. Corning and O'Connell meshed and everyone followed their orders. That won't happen anymore."

O'Connell's political genius reached its apex with his grooming of Corning and installing him as mayor in 1941, shortly after the Pearl Harbor attack. Wartime, as it had with O'Connell, would shape in important ways Corning's political dynasty. Three years after his inauguration, Corning passed up deferment possibilities and enlisted as an Army grunt at Dan's urging. It was that persona of Corning as an across-the-classes mayor who could mingle equally with blue collar or blue blood, encouraged and nurtured by the boss, that was one of Dan's greatest political insights. In their shared goal of holding onto power at all costs, the two men became inextricably linked; over the decades it became difficult to tell where Corning left off and O'Connell took over. For thirty-six years, Corning played the urbane alter-ego, the aristocratic mayor, to O'Connell's coarse and street-smart political boss – the longest-running performance anywhere on the American political stage. It is an act that is unlikely ever to be repeated. The charisma of Corning and the deep reverence Albanians felt for their perennial mayor has not been replicated in his successors, Tom Whalen and Jerry Jennings. How could it be? "Mayor Corning maintained his popularity over such a long time, when the world was changing drastically around him, and he remained constant as a larger-than-life figure," said Vincent McArdle Jr., corporation counsel under Corning and the city's lawyer since 1971. "Corning had an extraordinary presence and you knew you were with someone special that only comes along once in a long while."

In 1997, Leonard Weiss, a judge backed by the machine from City Court to State Supreme Court, is retired from the bench and is trying to resurrect the glory days of the machine as chairman of the Albany County Democratic organization. He tries to follow the lead of his mentor, Corning, whom Weiss considers almost a father figure, but people don't respond in the same way to the old rules of loyalty and hard work and eventual rewards for dues paid. In his office at the organization's headquarters, Weiss hung two portraits: Dan and Erastus. The pillars of the machine look down at him all day and he said he tries to borrow inspiration from their strength as he slogs through the daunting task before him.

In 1996, the machine notched a few victories to brighten the gloom of 1995's infighting and public squabbles, including an FBI investigation for financial irregularities, as well as a string of losses to insurgent Democratic and Republican candidates. Worse yet, the city and county are struggling to stay afloat financially, remaining in a downsizing mode as a Republican governor in the Executive Mansion, Gov. George Pataki, shipped jobs out of the region and shut off the spigot of Democratic state patronage jobs they had enjoyed for years under Democratic governors. "O'Connell and Corning had lots of jobs to give out. They could put people to work," Weiss said. "I don't have the jobs. It's hard to be chairman without jobs."

Harry Maikels, born in 1929, longtime committeeman for the machine, a county legislator and former commissioner of public works, knew the O'Connells growing up in the South End. Before his political jobs, he ran a dump truck and trash removal company. In the mid-1950s, Dan asked him for a favor. "I sent Dan up a couple truckloads of topsoil to his summer house in the Helderbergs," Maikels recalled. Dan was about seventy at the time. "I remember my driver coming back, shaking his head. Dan told him how he was planning to plant fruit trees, but my driver said there was no way he'd live long enough to see the trees mature. Well, Dan lived to the age of ninety-one and he did see those trees bear fruit."

In another fertilizer analogy, Polly Noonan told a story about learning the lesson of political physics and opposing forces while handling patronage jobs for the machine as a Senate staffer. "I'd tell our Democratic members if they wanted to put their girlfriend on the payroll, fine, but only do it after a Republican senator put his girlfriend on the payroll," Noonan said. "Then each one has something on the other and neither one will tell. I had to keep repeating that message all the time: Don't shit where you eat." Somehow, despite the harsh realities Weiss faces in 1997, the machine lives on and on and on, longer than any political scientist could have predicted, still bearing fruit in the orchard planted and fertilized by Dan and Erastus.

Chapter 6:

*From Albany to Germany: The G.I. Mayor Defends
Democracy and Boosts the Democratic Machine*

**"Don't call me Mayor Corning anymore. I'm just
'Rastus now. We're all in this together. We're all the same,
all brothers now."**

*Mayor Erastus Corning 2nd to his fellow Army draftees on
the train to basic training for World War II.*

April 13, 1944. The day to go off to war had arrived for the mayor.
Just ten days before, an induction order was delivered at City Hall for
Erastus Corning. He doodled on the back of his order with a pencil, made
some mathematical calculations regarding fuel oil, which was being
rationed at that time. A few men tried to get out of the draft in Albany, but
the vast majority, including Corning, accepted their military service as
required duty to their country – not happily, perhaps, but resignedly.
Corning kept busy in the nervous time leading up to the induction day.
Besides running the city, preparing for his departure by getting his political house in order, and spending time with his family, the Cornings were
selling off their livestock and hunkering down for the sacrifices of wartime.
Hundreds of fliers were distributed for the Corning Farms Dispersal Sale
of Holsteins on April 8, 1944, a large auction of cows to settle Parker's
estate. The mayor's uncle had died three years earlier and Erastus was helping to wrap up loose ends on the estate.

In April of 1944, the mayor was thirty-five years old, with a wife and
two children – a son, Erastus III, eleven, and a daughter, Bettina, age six –
and a job running New York's capital city and a prosperous insurance company. Corning could have received a deferment, as other mayors and
elected officials did, but Erastus would have none of it. "I'd never asked for
a deferment for anyone in the city, so I would have looked like a damn fool

if I had asked for one myself," Corning told Judith Morrison Lipton in a 1974 interview for a local magazine, *Insight*. He said he declined an opportunity to enter officer's candidate school, too. "I wasn't going to run away and take a commission," he said. Corning was notified by order number 2668 on April 3 by the Albany County Draft Board No. 342 of the U.S. Selective System, a draft board he controlled as mayor. Corning was to report for induction at eight o'clock on the morning of April 13, to Room 1001 in the building at 75 State Street, a familiar address to the mayor since it was Democratic headquarters. Civilian life had come to an end for Corning. In the small print of the induction order was this: "Willful failure to report promptly to this local board at the hour and on the day named in this notice is a violation of the Selective Training and Service Act of 1940, as amended, and subjects the violator to fine and imprisonment."

At 75 State Street, the inductees posed for an amateur filmmaker, stripped to the waist and joking with each other as they were examined by doctors for blood pressure and eyesight. Corning and more than sixty other men from Albany were reporting for induction into the Army. For the most part, these were men in their thirties, with jobs, wives, and children, and they had no choice. One of them, thirty-one-year-old Jake Carey, had to quit his job in the bakery at Freihofer's and as he marched from the Washington Avenue Armory to Union Station on induction day, his wife, Alice, lay in Albany Medical Center Hospital nursing their five-day-old baby. "We joked that they had finally reached the bottom of the barrel when they drafted us and that's what we called ourselves, The Bottom Of The Barrel," said Stanley Zimmer, who was inducted with Corning. "The war was almost over by then, we were older guys with families and we knew they must have been reaching way down to get us."

While Corning's patriotism ran high, as it always had, so too did his equally fervent desire to do the best thing politically. Corning was first sworn in as mayor three weeks after Pearl Harbor after winning election by a landslide, 57,938 votes to Republican Benjamin Hoff's 11,172 votes. During the campaign and throughout 1942, his first year in office, Corning beat the drum for America's war effort and pledged to do all he could as mayor to support his nation's armed forces. "Our country has been savagely and treacherously attacked . . . by the ruthless tactics of Japan's allies," Corning told the Albany Chamber of Commerce in his first public address as mayor-elect. "There is no question of the nation's unity and its determination to protect American interests and the principles of

American government at no matter what cost. The job is for all of us as individuals and as Albanians as well as Americans. The city must and will play its part to the utmost." Furthermore, political boss Dan O'Connell had counseled Corning to join the Army and not seek a deferment. The political dividends for a mayor who served his country would be astounding for many years to come. O'Connell knew this; he had used his own military service to utmost political advantage. In fact, O'Connell's return as a Navy war hero at the end of World War I gave a big boost to the O'Connell and Corning brothers' efforts to establish a Democratic political organization that could finally defeat the dynasty of the Barnes Republican machine. O'Connell appeared in campaign banners in his Navy uniform in 1919, a tactic that proved hugely popular with Albany voters. O'Connell was elected city assessor, his first and only elected office, and the O'Connell-Corning machine had established a foothold.

There was one other item of political expediency for Corning's Army induction: Gov. Thomas E. Dewey, the Republican governor of New York State. Dewey was elected in 1942 by unseating Democrat incumbent Gov. Charles Poletti, who completed the unexpired term of Gov. Herbert Lehman after Lehman resigned to take a federal post. Poletti served just twenty-eight days as governor, the shortest gubernatorial regime in state history, before Dewey won back the Executive Mansion for the Republicans and held it for eleven years, one of the longest tenures. As the new Republican governor, Dewey immediately grew obsessed with toppling the O'Connell-Corning machine. He launched in 1943 the first investigation into political corruption in Albany (mostly unsuccessful) and a second probe in the spring of 1944 in a renewed drive to pin corruption charges that would stick to Albany's fabled Democratic organization. Corning ripped into Dewey, comparing him to Hitler, in a radio speech on April 3, 1944, allowing the mayor to leave Albany as a conquering hero, not a corrupt politician: "In recent months Albany has been turned into an occupied city by the Governor of the State, a small man with a violent and burning desire to be the Republican candidate for Presidency this fall.... Terrorism, intimidation, smearing by innuendo and cleverly designed half-truths, threats that almost border on blackmail, are the weapons used by this small-sized counterpart of the European Dictator, and his satellites and subservient underlings. . . . I am sickened by this small man's disregard of human rights and human decencies." A brilliant strategy for Corning. Sucker-punch Dewey and then exit, treading the moral high ground. How do you investigate an absent mayor, let alone a heroic Army infantryman headed off to fight the Nazis? Another frustration, *investigatus interruptus*, for Dewey.

On the home front, Corning's wife, Betty, who was not the least bit interested in politics and did not care how the mayor's induction solved the machine's political problems, was not eager to see her husband go off to war, but the mayor would not be swayed. The sense of duty to country and the potential political benefits outweighed the sense of danger and fear of what the mayor-elect in a speech at Christmas time in 1941 had called "a war of frightful possibilities." It was sunny and brisk on April 13, 1944, the dreaded day of induction. "I hated like hell to go in," James Tortorici said. Tortorici was thirty-four years old at the time, with a wife and two-year-old son. He owned an Albany barber shop and was inducted alongside Corning. "I remember wishing I had a heart attack during the physical. None of us wanted to go in. I tried to get out of it, but there was no way out."

Corning passed the mayoral torch to Acting Mayor Frank S. Harris at a meeting of the Common Council on April 12 with this bit of legalese: "Pursuant to the provisions of Section 105-B of the New York State War Emergency Act, being Chapter 445 of the Laws of 1942, as amended by Chapter 544 of the Laws of 1942, and Chapter 421 of the Laws of 1943, I, Erastus Corning, 2nd, Mayor of the City of Albany, New York, having entered upon military duty, do hereby appoint Frank S. Harris temporary Mayor of the City of Albany, effective this date, for the unexpired term of my office as Mayor, or until I shall return, if the date of my return be prior to the expiration of such term." In conclusion, Corning offered these heartfelt remarks to the Common Council: "My prayer now is that I may return soon to our fine old City of Albany. I leave with my heart full of pride and love for it, a deep feeling that I will always have, wherever I may be."

Corning joined the other inductees the next morning as they reported to the Armory, on the corner of Washington Avenue and Lark Street, for their induction instructions. Tortorici was friendly with several of the other men since he cut their hair at his shop at 210 Central Avenue or knew them from around town. There was Otto Fausel, the insurance agent; Joe Barbagallo, who ran a dry cleaning business on Lark Street; Thomas Prime, who had a tavern, Prime's Grill, on Broadway in North Albany; and Stanley Zimmer, who had a barbershop next to Prime's. Corning did not move in their circle, inhabiting his own orbit as mayor. Still, Corning effortlessly and immediately became one of the boys at the Armory.

Arthur O'Keefe, an amateur filmmaker and member of the Albany Amateur Motion Picture Society, captured the induction of the "April 13th Group," as they called themselves. O'Keefe made a thirty-minute silent black-and-white documentary called *Wartime Albany*, with footage shot between 1941 and 1945. The film captured the combination of bravado and fear that gripped Corning and the other men on their induction day, a mix of emotions plainly visible on their faces. In one shot, O'Keefe zoomed in for a long, tight close-up of Corning smoking a cigarette, a brown manila envelope tucked under his left arm. The envelope contained the official papers of each man reporting for duty. The others had elected Corning keeper of the dossier, their leader. In the film, the mayor stood with a knot of men outside the Armory, smoking, shaking hands, smiling shyly for the camera. He was a head taller than the rest and looked heavy, almost paunchy, with a jowly looseness around his face. The G.I.-Mayor wore a tweed suit with vest, a pocketwatch, a crisp white shirt and tie, a brown fedora and camel hair overcoat, its collar turned up against the chill. He was better dressed than the other men and tried to assume a nonchalant air, but his darting eyes belied an edginess. Corning led the pack of men as they walked from the Armory, down Washington Avenue and toward Union Station, where they boarded a train for Fort Dix in New Jersey. Corning was their chief, clearly in command, comfortable with being in charge. He smoked a cigarette and strode purposely and forcefully down the avenue, alone. Curiously, Corning was one of the few men among the inductees who was not accompanied by a wife or girlfriend or mother. The mayor walked on by himself, stoically, without benefit of a loved one to share his fears. The others followed him.

Some days before, on April 4, Corning's colleague from the Legislature, Sen. William Bewley, Democrat from Middleport and chairman of tax and finance, wrote to the mayor: "No telling what the future has in store for you but I am sure you are the type who will face it with the spirit that 'America – Your Country' comes first," Bewley wrote. "I know that you have that in mind when you are leaving your family and all that you are leaving behind to take the steps that you are taking." Although none of several other letters, similar in tone to Bewley's, explicitly mentioned the danger of Corning becoming a casualty of war, the possibility that the mayor might never return was in the sub-text. If he was afraid, Corning managed to mask his fear on camera. As he marched off to war, leader of the pack, Corning must have been mulling over letters offering godspeed from friends, such as the one from March 14, 1944 from a Yale classmate, A. Augustus Low of New York City: "We want to warn you not to get lost in no-man's land and to come back safe and sound and successful."

"I can remember how scared I was, hugging my little boy. He was clinging to me and I was choked up, almost crying," Tortorici recalled. "The other guys were all saying their goodbyes, too, and there were a lot of hugs and kisses and women were crying and waving as we walked down Washington Avenue." Zimmer remembered Bill "Buck" Connally being so afraid he was rooted to the sidewalk and couldn't move. "He was a big, tough guy, a truck driver, but he was crying awfully bad," Zimmer said. "It was a shame to see that, but there was nothing we could do. We all just kept walking." They traveled quite a distance that day, from the Draft Board at 75 State Street, up the hill to the Washington Avenue Armory and back down Washington Avenue they walked – march would be too strong a word for this motley assemblage of men going off to fight the Germans. The citizens of Albany stopped on the street, stood in front of their shops and watched from stoops, waving and cheering these soldiers-to-be. Anti-Nazi sentiment ran high. One of the film's strongest images was of a little girl with a button that depicted Hitler being hanged from a noose, with appropriately moving parts, and the words, "Let's Pull Together." The destination for Corning and the sixty-odd inductees was Union Station and the train to Fort Dix for orientation. In the film, Corning was once more the focal point, waiting at the train ticket counter, smoking and smiling for the camera below a sign for the USO Lounge hung from a balcony. The mayor held court for a cluster of Army soldiers in uniform, apparently returning after leave, who basked in Corning's electric smile and the glow that seemed to emanate from him.

The film cut to a scene boarding the train. Corning lighted another cigarette, nodded and exchanged a few words with the conductor, who gave the mayor a farewell wave. Corning moved aside to let a few more men board before him and then stepped aboard. Inside the train, the mayor was tall and gangly and had to squat and duck under the overhead racks before taking his seat. That was the final image of Corning. The filmmaker cut away to a shot of a homemade sign that read, "So Long Mayor, Take Keer Yerself!" The scene ended with a long, lingering shot of the train, belching black smoke, chugging across the bridge over the Hudson River toward Rensselaer, the smoke hovering like a passing storm cloud over what is now the Corning Preserve, before disappearing from view.

1) *Erastus Corning (1794-1872), the Mayor's great-grandfather.*

2) *Erastus Corning Jr. (1827-1897), the Mayor's grandfather.*

3) *Parker Corning (1874-1943), the Mayor's uncle.*

4) *Edwin Corning (1883-1934), the Mayor's father.*

5) *Rear Admiral Albert Smith Barker, second husband of Ellen Maxwell.*

6) *Ellen Maxwell, the Mayor's grandmother.*

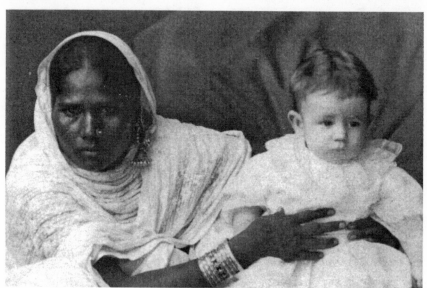

7) *Louise Maxwell, the Mayor's mother, with nurse in Lucknow, India in 1887.*

8) Louise Maxwell Corning on her wedding day, November 25, 1908, in Washington, D.C.

9) *Erastus Corning 2nd with mother in his christening outfit, Albany, 1909.*

10) *Louise Corning with her children, Erastus and Louise, Albany, 1915.*

11) Erastus and his sister, Louise, in Northeast Harbor, Maine, 1917.

12) Erastus at Albany Academy, 1922.

13) *Erastus, seated far right, in a Groton School play, 1928. Joseph Alsop is seated far left.*

14) *The board of the 1928* Grotonian. *Erastus is in the front row, second from left. Alsop is in second row, middle.*

15) *Erastus in his Groton class photo, 1926.*

16) The Corning children, from left, Louise, Erastus, Harriet and Edwin Jr. in 1928.

17) Betty and Erastus on their wedding day, June 23, 1932 in Philadelphia.

18) *The Mayor at Fort Dix, New Jersey, on April 14, 1944.*

19) *Albany's G.I. – Mayor is greeted at Union Station by his wife and Acting Mayor Frank S. Harris.*

20) *Erastus and Betty at Corning Hill in the late 1940s.*

21) *The Mayor and his wife in a 1964 photo.*

22) *The Mayor and boss Dan O'Connell in 1961.*

23) *Dan O'Connell's house on Whitehall Road.*

24) The Mayor attends the funeral of Dan O'Connell on March 2, 1977.

On the train, the men masked their fears by talking tough and cutting up. One of the guys shouted over to Corning, "Hey, Mayor!" Tortorici said he'll never forget Corning's reply. "Listen. Cut that shit out right now," replied Corning, who was known for his earthy sense of humor and salty tongue. "I'm 'Rastus. You're Larry. You're Otto. You're Jimmy. We're all in this together. We're all the same, all brothers now." The train car grew silent for a moment, Tortorici recalled, before the guys resumed talking. Corning had made his point. Nobody in the group called him mayor after that. They chose their group's moniker on the train shortly after it got underway. "We were all talking together and Corning was kind of the leader and we decided we'd call ourselves the April 13th group and we promised we'd get together every year for a reunion after the war," Tortorici said. They picked up nicknames on the train, too. The mayor became 'Rastus and insisted on the dropped "E." James Joseph Tortorici went by J.J. or Jimmy. Nicholas Maniscalco was stuck with the rather unflattering moniker of "Fish Face." J. Otto Fausel, who went by just Otto, was known to some of the guys, including Tortorici, because he was an agent for Stark Insurance. Corning at this time had been running his own insurance firm, Albany Associates, for twelve years, since graduating from Yale. Fausel, a top agent, was Corning's direct competitor and the mayor was savvy about how to beat the competition. Tortorici recalled, "I was there and heard it when Corning said on the train that he wanted to hire Otto to run Albany Associates after the war. I remember Otto saying he'd have to think about it. Corning said it again, "Otto, you've got the job if you want it." Fausel did, indeed, later join Albany Associates and had a lucrative and fruitful partnership with the mayor in the insurance business (Fausel was listed as vice president beside Corning the president) for more than forty years.

The four-hour train trip to Fort Dix passed slowly. Some men slept. Some played cards. Talk faded out and the men were left alone with their thoughts. When they arrived at Fort Dix, their initiation into Army life was swift. The forty-five soldiers in the April 13th group from Albany were placed together in the same barracks, but split up between two floors. Tortorici was next to Corning's bunk; Joe Barbagallo slept on the top bunk above Corning. "He was just a regular guy, no two ways about it," recalled Barbagallo, twenty-seven at the time, eight years younger than Corning.

The routine at Fort Dix grew numbing during the three-week Army orientation. They were up at dawn, whipped through a quick breakfast, did their morning marching, came back to the barracks for chores and other busywork, and then followed more marching, physical training, dinner and chores. "It was a lot of made-up work, like sweeping your area, picking up trash and cigarettes, but it didn't matter, Corning was right there doing his chores with the rest of us," Tortorici said. Occasionally, Corning attracted attention. Phil Scott of Brooklyn wrote to Corning on January 22, 1976, recalling an incident at Fort Dix on the mayor's first day there, April 14, 1944. "The mail clerk carelessly tosses out the mail to the new inductees, until he comes across one addressed to Mayor Erastus Corning of Albany with a return address, Franklin D. Roosevelt. The White House. Then, with preferential treatment, it was handed to you, Pvt. Corning. At that time I recall you remarking that if anyone of us would be around in the future, to drop a line to Mayor Corning, Albany, New York and remind you of this particular time."

The Army inductees were tested at Fort Dix to determine their mental aptitude, the first stage in categorizing them for future assignments. Tortorici said he scored in the seventies, which was about average, but Corning had one of the highest scores, close to a perfect 100. "I know Corning's score was one of the best and it was good enough to get him assigned to officer's training school right then and there, but he didn't take it," Tortorici recalled. "It was just like the way he didn't try to get out of going. He was a common guy when you got down to it. He told me the officer's thing was bullshit. That was his word." Corning and Tortorici made quite a pair. Corning, aristocratic in bearing, Ivy League-educated, six-feet two-inches tall, suave and sophisticated. Tortorici, five-feet six-inches tall, grew up poor on Colonie Street in Albany's North End and left school after twelfth grade. Corning didn't seek the center of things at Fort Dix. "He was a leader in some ways and not a leader in others," Tortorici said. "He just blended in from what I saw. At night, he'd go out and have a drink with us. He was no different than the dumbest guy there in that he fit right in. He had a good time when we went out and we'd come back to bed feeling pretty good and 'Rastus would too."

When their three weeks were up at Fort Dix, the April 13th group from Albany was split up and sent to three different camps for basic training: Camp Barkeley in Texas, Camp Swift in Georgia and Camp Blanding in Florida. Corning was assigned to Camp Blanding. Barbagallo was with Corning at Blanding, as were Lawrence Barry, Terrance McNally, Jack Calaverne, Stanley Potzruski and Jake Harris. One of Corning's closest friends during the long, hot summer of basic training was Harris, a big, strapping fellow, who had been a carpenter in Albany before his induction. He was a great athlete and had an easygoing nature. The extra pounds that showed in the slight pudginess of the mayor as he walked toward the train station on induction day were quickly worked off at Blanding, where basic training ground on for seventeen weeks, from the end of April until the end of August. The Florida heat was searing that summer and the added weight Corning had picked up as insulation against the cold Albany winters was a liability at Blanding.

"Jake used to tell stories about the mayor in basic training and he said Corning lost about fifty pounds and passed out twice during drills, but he got right back in line when he came to," recalled Alice Carey, widow of Jake Carey, Corning's good pal at Camp Blanding. Another close friend of Corning's during basic training was Ray Kinley, whom Corning would later reward with a political job; the mayor also would make Kinley's son, Ray Jr., election commissioner. Stanley Zimmer went through basic training with Corning, a thirty-four-year-old barber from North Albany at the time. While the two men didn't know each other before the war and their backgrounds couldn't have been any more divergent, they shared the bond of Albany and April 13. "I got put in a different company from the mayor at Blanding, but I saw him quite a few times," Zimmer said. "I remember he lost quite a bit of weight because of what they put us through, but so did most of the rest of us. Corning was a good athlete and tough. He was a very rugged soldier who could do everything better than most of the rest of us. They made him platoon leader at Blanding. He was big and tough and they only picked the best out to be platoon leader."

The schedule at basic training was intended to break down weak or willful individuals and to rebuild them as loyal members of a unit that followed orders without question. The men were up at four o'clock each morning for a four-mile "speed march," which meant double time. They marched and did physically rigorous drills all day long under the scorching Florida sun. "The routine at Blanding was tough, but Corning did it all," Barbagallo said. "We had to run several miles with a full pack, climbed walls with ropes, ran obstacle courses. Corning wasn't nothing but a buck private and had to take orders like everybody else, but I never heard him complain. He was friendly. We'd play cards in the barracks at night and he liked to drink with us."

Corning could have gotten out of this whole ordeal, remember, or whisked off to a cushy officer's training program – "ninety-day wonders" the foot soldiers derisively dubbed them – but more than anything the mayor wanted to be one of the grunts. He seemed to thrive on the great social equalizer quality of the Army, where he could shed the Groton class pretension he loathed and become just another infantryman with no special privileges. "He just wanted to be a regular soldier," Zimmer said. "We had a million ninety-day wonders and with his education and ability and connections, he surely could have been more than a private. But he wanted to be one of us. I remember once a general called Corning in to see him at Blanding. After he came out, I asked him what happened. Corning said, 'That bastard talked to me for an hour and never offered me a goddamn drink.' He could use some rough language like the rest of us. He might have been mayor, but he could swear as well as any of us."

In his desk at City Hall, Mayor Corning kept a quote from General Omar Bradley: "But Pearl Harbor and the subsequent lessons we learned, day by day, until September 1945, should have taught all military men that our military forces are one team – in the game to win regardless of who carries the ball. This is no time for 'fancy dans' who won't hit the line with all they have on every play, unless they can call the signals. Each player on this team – whether he shines in the spotlight of the backfield or eats dirt in the line – must be an all-American."

Despite the hardships of Camp Blanding, it was a pale prelude to the cataclysm of war. The successful completion of basic training in late August was rewarded with a ten-day furlough over Labor Day. Corning and his Albany contingent had one last reprieve before being sent into battle. They took the train up from Florida and ostensibly were supposed to spend time with their families before being shipped across the Atlantic. But Erastus had a bit of wildness left in him, according to a wartime story he told on more than one occasion to his deer hunting buddies during an annual hunting trip to the Adirondacks. According to Peter Noonan, the mayor told this story: "He got a leave from basic and was coming up on the train from Camp Blanding and he hooked up with some other Army guys and they were drinking pretty hard," Noonan said. "Well, Corning got so drunk he passed out and slept so long, the train passed through Albany and he missed his stop. So he just continued on up north and ended up in Sabattis and went fishing for a few days without telling his wife."

Corning was assigned to the 38th Regiment of the 2nd Infantry Division and sent by troopship to the European Theater. It was October, 1944, when they arrived in France, six months after the decisive, but devastatingly deadly, D-Day invasion at Normandy. Corning did not make a triumphant landing. He was sick as a dog, according to Larry Barry, a member of the April 13th group, who saw Corning in action on foreign soil. Corning was suffering from a stomach virus and was too weak to do much when he first landed in France. Barry scared up some chicken, made the mayor chicken soup and helped nurse him back to health. Barry said Corning later rewarded his kindness through small patronage jobs with the city and county.

After regaining his health, Corning's first task in the war theater was administrative, for which his mayoral job had prepared him. Attached to a headquarters group, he helped to re-establish some semblance of order and government in the towns and villages of France that were liberated by the advancing American soldiers, chasing across northern France in hot pursuit of the Germans. It was a fortuitous assignment that kept Corning out of some of the fiercest and deadliest fighting of the bloody Battle of the Bulge, though he had some involvement. Corning's combat came after the worst of the fighting from Hitler's counter-offensive attack in the Ardennes Forest was over. His 38th Infantry Regiment fought on the periphery of the Battle of the Bulge and the unit was tapped by General Patton for his dramatic dash into Czechoslovakia in the spring of 1945. After their successful mission chasing the straggling Germans out of the region, Corning was stationed in Eunojovice, Czechoslovakia, twenty-five miles southwest of Pilsen.

The Battle of the Bulge, which raged from December 16, 1944 until January 25, 1945, was a month-long offensive by the Germans that would become the largest single battle ever fought by the U.S. Army, ensnarling more than a million men. It was a last-gasp gamble by Adolph Hitler, a final attack designed to turn back the Allied armies that had gained a foothold on German soil. The Germans had secretly massed tanks, guns and twenty-five assault divisions along an eighty-mile front of the Ardennes Forest of eastern Belgium and northern Luxembourg.

The German army's attack through the Ardennes – a region of dense forests, rugged terrain and nasty weather – caught the Americans off-guard. The 275,000 German soldiers launched a cataclysmic artillery salvo at 4 a.m. on December 16. U.S. Army intelligence had failed to provide advance warning of Hitler's bold stroke on the quiet "Ghost Front," resulting in heavy American casualties. Furthermore, the G.I.s lacked proper winter gear, faced a shortage of ammunition and the 83,000 scattered troops were spread out too thinly to halt the attack. Of the four U.S. divisions, two were battered by recent combat and two had no fighting experience. The German blitz was Hitler's grand scheme to split the American and British forces and capture the port of Antwerp, where troops and supplies streamed through on their way to Berlin. Despite the surprise element, the German assault foundered after just nine days and was stopped short of the Meuse River, about sixty-five miles from the Nazi goal of Antwerp. It took several weeks more for American troops, however, to push back the Germans and realign the sixty-by-forty mile "bulge" in Allied lines. The American infantrymen proved their mettle in repulsing their German attackers. Winston Churchill called the Bulge "undoubtedly the greatest American battle of the war" and "an ever-famous American victory." Still, the U.S. Army paid a terrible price. Almost 9,000 Americans were killed in the Battle of the Bulge by mid-January, after the first month of fighting, and tens of thousands more were wounded. More than 10,000 troops were taken prisoners of war. There were some deserters. Many others suffered frostbite or succumbed to exposure.

For his part, Corning, the G.I.-Mayor, had small tastes of battle, but managed to escape the fiercest fighting. The images of war that he did experience apparently were too painful to recount. The mayor never spoke even to close personal friends about combat or the death and destruction he witnessed during the war. He occasionally let slip a glimpse of his World War II terror, though. For instance, the mayor gave this account to Jack McLean, Peter Noonan's cousin and a longtime hunting and fishing partner of Corning's. "He said he was in the Black Forest in Germany and he jumped into a foxhole, looked over and there was a German and he had a gun," McLean said. "All he said was, 'I ended up with his gun.' He wouldn't elaborate when I asked him to know more. And that's the only story he ever told me about the war."

John Polk Jr., who went through basic training at Blanding with Corning, was unexpectedly reunited with the mayor after the American soldiers took Leipzig and called in replacements. "My captain said we were getting the mayor of Albany in our unit and asked if I knew him," Polk recalled. "I couldn't believe it, but there he was the next day, radio operator for his unit, carrying a radio on his back that must have weighed forty pounds. There wasn't much unusual after that, other than the everyday battle of survival we'd been fighting for months. Corning was a good soldier, always willing to do whatever he was told. And he was an excellent rifleman."

Corning related one defining moment to Otto Fausel. Fausel told it to Peter Noonan on more than one occasion. "It happened in France at the tail end of the Battle of the Bulge," Noonan said. "It was a cold night and Corning and his partner both wanted to sleep in a barn to get warm, but one of them had to take the first watch. So, they flipped a coin. Corning lost the flip and was pretty upset about it as he watched the other soldier go into the barn to sleep. Corning staked out a spot in some cover across a field and watched for Germans. After a few minutes, all of a sudden the sky lighted up and there was the roar of a mortar shell exploding, destroying the barn. Corning made a quick search of what was left of the barn, but couldn't find any remains. Then, as Corning liked to say, 'I took off like a big-ass bird, running as fast as I could. And it was all because of a flip of a coin that I'm alive today.'"

A few members of Corning's April 13th Albany crew weren't so lucky. They were sent into the heaviest fighting of "Hitler's last gamble." Tom O'Neil was the first casualty of their close-knit group. "He was killed just a few days into his first overseas mission and it was a tragedy because he left a widow and several young kids," Zimmer said. Carey, one of Corning's closest pals from basic training, was sent directly into battle. During the Battle of the Bulge, in early January, 1945, Sergeant Carey, a squad leader in the 3rd Division, was hit with shrapnel from a tank mortar that exploded nearby. His head was bleeding heavily and his right leg was hit badly. He had no feeling in the left side of his body. Carey's injuries required many operations, including putting a metal plate in the right front portion of his head. He became a paraplegic who used a wheelchair for the rest of his life. Bobby Richmond, another member of their April 13th group, was captured by the Germans and held as a POW. Tortorici, of Albany, the medic, helped take care of Richmond in a field hospital after he was released.

From the front, Corning managed to write often and to keep in touch with developments back at City Hall. He corresponded frequently with Acting Mayor Frank Harris, a seventy-six-year-old machine regular and veteran of two wars, and his office manager, Bernard "Benny" V. Fitzpatrick. Both men wrote frequently to Corning to boost his spirits and to keep him up-to-date on developments in Albany. On May 23, 1945, Harris wrote to Corning: "I cannot give you any additional news that Benny has not sent because he doesn't give me a chance to read the headlines in the *Times Union* before he has it out of my hands and is cutting it up to send to you. So if you get his letters, you must feel that you are keeping right up to date with what goes on in Albany. We are getting along very nicely here in the office, and I feel that when you return and sit in the big chair that you will never know that you have been away, as you will find things going on just as you left them . . . But we will all be mighty glad to see you when you return."

In a letter dated December 21, 1945, Corning reported the cigarette ration had improved and that he was forwarding a pipe he no longer needed to James J. McGuiness, corporation counsel. In his characteristic dry wit, Corning wanted it known that he had been promoted in the Army. "Corning Wins Promotion" was the headline in the *Times Union* on January 15, 1945. "Writing from France . . . the soldier-mayor said he was made a first class private January 1, which means $4.80 a month more."

Similarly, Corning was a master of understatement when describing the wartime devastation during the Battle of the Bulge. "Took part in the American defense against von Runstedt's attack," Corning wrote on January 3. Gerd von Rundstedt was the field marshal of the German forces in the Ardennes region during the Battle of the Bulge.

Even though he was engaged in combat, Corning continued to run a certain amount of the major policy decisions at City Hall, and he also kept a tight rein on his insurance company from the war zone. Corning wrote often to Julian Erway, his buddy in the Senate and a prominent Albany attorney, who counseled the mayor on business deals. On January 24, 1945, Corning wrote to Erway about acquiring a rival insurance business and other financial matters. "See if you can get Mr. Towner [the head of Erway's law firm, Neile Towner] to pry Ponderous Pete loose from some more of the Traction Co. business. In the meantime, my very best to Mr. Towner and to Gene. All the luck in the world with the new job. I have the greatest confidence in the world that you will work it out in swell shape to the annoyance, anger and confusion of those charming souls who take such a great interest in things that are none of their goddamn business."

Corning rarely showed emotion in his letters from the front, despite the gruesome images he surely saw all around. He did express a note of homesickness in a letter he wrote in March, 1945 to Fitzpatrick, the mayor's office manager. "We are now across the Rhine and while it was quite a thrill to cross it as you can well imagine, crossing the Dunn Bridge would make that feeling amount to next to nothing," the mayor wrote. After Pfc. Corning had been in the European theater for nearly six months, he was scheduled for a brief leave. He wrote that he expected to be assigned to the American military government in Germany following his work for the headquarters group. Instead, Corning was returned to his infantry outfit following the leave and sent into battle once more. "Have seen a touch of combat," Corning wrote on April 25 from Germany. The *Times Union* – which called Corning "Albany's Army-going Mayor'" or "The G.I.-Mayor" in its headlines – said the letter "reveals for the first time that he is not with the military government section but with a strictly combat infantry outfit." Following the combat action, Corning and his outfit were given a few days rest, "which is very pleasant indeed," the mayor wrote.

Corning managed to find pleasure and enjoyable interludes in between the hardships of war. Corning sounded quite comfortable in correspondence with the Colinets, a French family that he befriended while stationed in Givet, a town in the Ardennes region of France. He spoke of playing cards, drinking wine, eating French cuisine and hunting duck and partridges. In a July 29, 1977 letter, Corning reminisced with Army pal Howard H. Lasker of Clinton Corners, New York. "Just a note from your old buddy and bridge partner at Givet," Corning wrote. In a January 23, 1970 letter to another war buddy, the company's armorer, Julius Soule, of Roseville, Michigan, Corning recalled: "I do remember the cook, Bing Crossler, and I think he will remember cooking all those fish that we got out of the Mulde River with hand grenades." Corning wrote home often to check on the condition of his buddy Jake Carey, who had been sent stateside in May to receive further treatment for the serious head wounds he suffered from the tank mortar shrapnel.

Corning's letters to Albany also discussed political strategy, particularly his upcoming re-election. The November election date was drawing near and Corning was still fighting the Germans. His wartime service was being viewed by O'Connell, at least in part, as re-election insurance. But Corning didn't appear to need much help. His quiet charm and the way he could connect with all classes made him a proven vote-getter. In 1941, the thirty-two-year-old former state assemblyman and senator had won his first term as mayor by a majority of 46,766 votes. Still, the machine took nothing for granted. It gave O'Connell pause when Corning wrote he had no firm assignment after an early-summer furlough in the States, but that he expected to be sent to the Pacific after that – right around the time of the election. Corning was an Army private in the war, but he was the Democratic machine's captain in Albany and boss Dan O'Connell and his underlings were eager to get the G.I.-Mayor back in time for the election in the fall of 1945. For now, though, Corning was in the midst of war. On June 5, Corning received a coveted pass to travel from Czechoslovakia, where he had now been moved, to Germany because of his political connections. Edward N. Scheiberling, who was from Albany and national commander of the American Legion, was making a tour of American war cemeteries in Europe. "Scheiberling is in Germany and some way arranged it, so that I am taking off on a pass to see him. It sounds like a good deal as it's the first pass I've had since I came across the Big Pond. It was darn nice of him to arrange it and I'm anxious to see him," Corning wrote on June 4 to Fitzpatrick, office manager.

Even in absentia, thousands of miles away, fighting a war, Corning was picked by O'Connell to run for re-election. The machine had a long reach. The absent Corning received a rousing ovation at a meeting of the city and county committees of the Albany Democratic organization in Odd Fellows Hall on June 14. Acting Mayor Harris told the capacity crowd: "I know our soldier-mayor candidate serving somewhere overseas is going to go over in a big way in the election." First, they had to have a candidate to run. Corning was in a war zone. He might be injured or killed. Even if he made it through unharmed, there was no guarantee Corning would be discharged in time for the November election. O'Connell and the Democrats "are watching the newspapers closely for a clue as to whether the soldier-mayor will be able to make a campaign appearance before election," according to the *Times Union*. The Democrats were benefiting enormously from the publicity of the mayor's war exploits and the buildup of the will-he-or-won't-he scenario the citizens of Albany were playing out regarding his return in time for the election. The *Times Union* and *Knickerbocker News* began tallying Corning's numbers under the point system of soldier discharges, and their readers followed the war service of the G.I.-Mayor as if it were the daily baseball box score. The stats were these: Corning entered April 13, 1944, giving him thirteen credits for thirteen months of service; eight for eight months overseas; five for participation in a major battle; and twenty-four points for two children. That's a total of fifty points. Army watchers predicted that would be enough for discharge, but all bets were off if Corning was reassigned to the Pacific theater. The Democratic machine made a practice of beating the odds, though.

The first break in news of Corning's furlough came on June 16, when a loyal Democrat, a former Albany policeman serving with the military police in Germany, Lt. James J. Corrigan, reported that Corning's division moved out of Czechoslovakia and was heading west, passing through Nuremberg, Germany the day before, en route to France and, eventually, the United States. "It is my opinion you can expect the mayor back in the States about the middle of July," Corrigan wrote, a prediction that proved to be on the mark. Corning arrived on a troopship in New York City on July 20, 1945 with the 38th Regiment of the 2nd Infantry Division. From New York, the soldiers took a train to Camp Kilmer, New Jersey. Meanwhile, vacations were being cut short to prepare for Corning's return. His wife, Betty, and their two children, who were at the family compound in Northeast Harbor, Maine, were heading back home. Acting Mayor Harris canceled the rest of his stay in Lake George to await his boss at City Hall.

Corning spent the ten-day furlough in late August with his family at Corning Hill in Glenmont. He had no public schedule and did not conduct mayoral business at City Hall. By September 1, Corning's leave was over and he took the train once more to Camp Dix, New Jersey. From there, Corning was sent on to Camp Swift, Texas, where he was reunited with buddies from the 38th Regiment. The newspapers surmised the mayor would be sent to the Pacific for further duty with the 38th. Corning himself wrote that he was ready to "beat the Japs in a hurry" and get back to Albany as soon as possible. Corning's political clout certainly enhanced the attention his military record review received. His credits for discharge, once thought to be borderline, somehow had edged above the magic number. Albany's G.I.-Mayor was coming home! Just in time for the election! What remarkable timing, the cynics said, hinting that the discharge had the smell of Dan O'Connell calling in some favors from people in high places. The rumors were lost in a swirl of civic boosterism for their native son. Corning's homecoming was front-page news in the *Times Union*. "He'll don civvies and bid farewell to the military at Camp Swift, Texas after seventeen months of duty which took him overseas and into France, Belgium, Germany and Czechoslovakia. He will be back as mayor before the week is out," the paper reported in its September 17, 1945 editions.

There had been speculation that the Democrats, who had already nominated Corning while away at war, might have to run his re-election campaign without the candidate or choose someone else. "Now he will be able to conduct his campaign in person," Acting Mayor Harris told the *Times Union*. "The people need him. I will automatically retire when the mayor returns." The soldier-mayor returned to ride a wave of publicity even a Corning – with his magisterial family name and sterling political breeding – could only have dreamed about. Uncle Dan was right once again. Military service had laid the foundation for Dan's own political dynasty and so it would do the same for Erastus Corning. The mayor had matured immeasurably from his war experience, too. Perhaps seen as something of a silver-spoon prep schooler going in, he came out a tough and decorated soldier, still a month shy of his thirty-sixth birthday, father of two, healthy and bearing no apparent wounds of war, with a lock on the mayor's office.

Corning employed the theatrical training from his Groton days to set the stage for his return to City Hall; the victorious war hero's appearance couldn't have been scripted better by a Hollywood screenwriter. Corning had sent word ahead that he did not want any big to-do for his homecoming, no pomp and circumstance. On September 20, 1945, precisely one year, five months and six days after he made the long march from the Washington Avenue Armory to Union Station with his fellow April 13th inductees, Corning returned to City Hall. He arrived at Union Station shortly after midnight and was at his City Hall office at 10:30 a.m. the same day to relieve Acting Mayor Harris of his interim duties. Pfc. Corning, No. 118241-9, reporting to duty, sir. A consummate showman. "The Mayor, still in uniform, said he planned to change to civvies as soon as he could be fitted for new clothes," The Knickerbocker News reported. Wearing the uniform didn't have anything to do with showing off his medals, of course. Corning had learned well O'Connell's lesson. Corning's uniform was decorated with the European Theater badge replete with two battle stars, the Presidential Citation awarded to his battalion, the Good Conduct medal and a Combat Infantryman badge. Corning settled into his unadorned brown chair behind his utilitarian gray metal desk, as unpretentious as ever, and went right to work on a full slate of postwar projects.

"Mayor Corning, still wearing Army service boots, appeared like any other soldier – lean, mustachioed and weathered," the Times Union reported. Corning greeted a steady stream of visitors, but in his typical laconic manner, diverted attention from himself and praised his stand-in. "Acting Mayor Harris told me on parting that he had tried to carry on the policies he believed I would want him to follow. He carried on a lot better than I could have done myself. He did a wonderful job and I thank him from the bottom of my heart," Corning said. Corning did not like to talk about himself and would not go into detail about his combat experience.

He did give his thoughts, however, on world peace and post-war Germany. "Their attitude must be changed so they will not be so susceptible to leaders who think only of war and conquest," the mayor said. "How long it will take to change that attitude and how it is going to be done, I do not know, except that it is a long-range program."

Corning was forty pounds lighter than when he entered the Army and was nicknamed "Slim" by his staff. The mayor was only half-joking when he said he needed a new wardrobe. Corning didn't get to the tailors on his first day back at work, but he did make time in his busy schedule to meet with his mother, who had just returned from Maine and stopped by City Hall first thing to see her son. Corning wasted no time in reclaiming control of his city and he undertook a broad range of projects: comprehensive survey of the entire sewer system as part of a long-range improvement plan, engineering study of the riverfront arterial highway, street re-pavings, expansion of Albany Airport, a new swimming pool at Swinburne Park and other park upgrades and a study of bus versus trolley transportation. "The hope of four years ago that we would be able to remove the trolleys from our streets now appears to be one that can soon be realized," Corning said. In addition to showing how he had reduced the city's debt by six million dollars over the last four years, improving the city's credit rating, Corning managed to turn the fiscal rundown into a flag-waving session. "I am proud to be an American," he said. "My military service has given me a broader and deeper understanding of my American citizenship."

At war, Corning remained much like the boyhood collector he had been growing up at Corning Hill. Despite the fact that he was in combat conditions and had heavy gear to lug, he brought back unusual rocks he had picked up in his marches across Europe. He donated the specimens to the State Museum's rock collection in the old State Education Building, but they were lost in the shuffle of the transition to the new facility in the Empire State Plaza, according to Dick Patrick, the city planner with whom Corning shared his rock story.

Corning took one last pause before the campaign by taking a brief vacation in Maine. He went without Betty and the kids to see his mother, but also for a reunion with his younger brother Eddie, a lieutenant in the Navy. The two brothers, who were very close growing up, hadn't seen each other in more than a year. Corning had pulled strings, including with the governor, to get Eddie into the Navy and keep him out of the front lines. "I enclose herewith a copy of the letter which I have written to the

Secretary of the Navy with regard to your brother Edwin," Gov. Herbert H. Lehman wrote to Corning on January 10, 1942. "I hope that it may be of some use." Corning sought assistance on Eddie's behalf with U.S. Rep. William T. Byrne, too, in a March 10, 1942 letter. "The thought I had was that if you felt it proper you might care to see Commander Lemeer," Corning wrote.

After returning from the war, Corning and his wife, Betty, kept in contact with the Colinets, the French family the mayor had befriended while stationed for a few months in the summer and fall of 1944 in their hometown of Givet, a small village along the Meuse River in north central France near the border with Belgium. Givet was a mustering-out encampment behind the lines where Corning was stationed for a few months before being sent to the front in Germany. In Givet, Corning found time to indulge his hunting and fishing passions with Mr. Colinet and their correspondence was filled with hunting and fishing news, as well as Corning's inquiries about Colinet's hunting dog, Rex. Corning wrote to the Colinets from Czechoslovakia in early June, 1945 to say that the war was over. "We were so happy to hear from you, knowing that you are in good health and the war is finally over," Mr. Colinet wrote in French on June 6, 1945. "We were worried, while waiting, knowing that you were in the battles. . . . Givet went back to its simple way of life since the American troops' departure. The repatriation of military and civil prisoners brings a little action here." On January 20, 1946, Mr. Colinet wrote in reply to a Christmas card Corning had sent. "Congratulations on your new election as mayor of your city, which shows the respect and confidence that the people have in you. At Givet, all is calm, waiting for better days, for the situation is not improving much, the supply of food and other needs is still precarious. After eliminating the bread ration card, it has been re-instituted for the new year, with a lesser amount than it was before. The financial situation is not good either because of the francs' devaluation."

Corning and his wife had discussed a trip to France and a visit to the Colinets in Givet, planned for the opening of hunting season the first Sunday of September, but the mayor felt he had too much work to do in Albany and they never went. This workaholic pattern continued throughout his mayoral career; Corning rarely took a vacation with his wife, always citing the workload. The Givet and Albany couples continued their correspondence and friendship. On May 3, 1946, the Colinets wrote again, thanking Betty Corning for a generous gift package of food. "We are very embarrassed and we really do not know how to thank you for your kindness," Mr. Colinet wrote. "Givet, dear Mr. Corning, represents for you a halting place on French ground, which left you with a good memory, a glorious stop of the American army. What have we done for you to deserve such generosity? We simply did our duty towards our liberators. The great torment which so upset and distressed the world will not soon return to the tranquillity and well-being of our good old Europe. The real peace is still very far away. . . . We have had a quantity of Polish prisoners. Actually, the Romanians are occupying the military posts for several months now and, because the Russians are in Romania, it's not an easy task for their return to their country." Betty Corning wrote to the Colinets in her finishing school *lingua Franca*, which they described as "good French." "You are really too kind," Mr. Colinet wrote on July 1, 1946. "We cannot refuse what you are offering so kindly. You are aware of the scarcity of food supplies all over Europe. We are lacking coffee, cocoa, rice, tea and soap."

Even after he returned safely home, Corning could not put the war behind him. He did much from City Hall to help rebuild the Dutch city of Nymegen, declaring it a sister city to Albany and spearheading a drive to assist in the rebuilding. Nymegen had been battered by American bombers in September of 1944 as they drove the Germans out of their last line of defense. The battle for Nymegen was a bloody one, with more than 800 U.S. casualties and thousands wounded during the first three days of fighting. Nymegen, with a population of 120,000 people, suffered a horrible loss in the battle: 2,200 citizens killed, 5,500 critically injured, 2,260 homes destroyed, 1,300 homes damaged, 400 streets destroyed. Although they had little food themselves, the citizens of Nymegen used the last of their depleted stores to keep the fighting Americans fed in spite of intense bombardments. Nymegen, an inland seaport much the same as Albany in geography and population, is situated on a broad river. Some of Albany's founding fathers came from Nymegen and none could know that nearly 300 years later, some young men from Albany would be the ones to liberate their native city.

Corning led the effort of his citizens to help reconstruct Nymegen's bombed-out Town Hall and to ship the needy Dutch vitamin capsules, cod liver oil for medicinal purposes, clothing, pots and pans and hospital supplies. The project caught on. *Time* magazine ran a picture in its December, 1946 issue beside the heading, "Albany Adopts Nymegen." Albany gained national attention for collecting 300 tons of food, clothing, medical supplies, window glass and other materials between January and April, 1947. The goodwill shipment was sent to Nymegen aboard the cargo ship *Westerdam* of the Holland-American Line. "This campaign was undoubtedly a unique success from the point of view of one town in this country adopting a town abroad," *Time* magazine said. Throughout the Nymegen drive, Corning was the cheerleader and chief motivator. For his efforts, Queen Wilhemina of Holland conferred on Mayor Corning her country's highest citizens' honor, making him an officer in the Order of Orange. "I feel greatly honored by the gracious action of the Queen," Corning said in a telegram. His work for Nymegen did not erase the mayor's troubling recollections about the war, nor the painful memory of his fallen comrades. In O'Keefe's documentary, *Wartime Albany*, Mayor Corning, recently returned from the front, was filmed conducting a burial service in late fall 1945 for soldiers killed in the war. The trees were bare and an icy wind scattered leaves at a small park across from the New Scotland Avenue Armory. A convoy of military vehicles proceeded up New Scotland Avenue, carrying a half-dozen flag-draped coffins, which were unloaded by Navy officers and placed upon makeshift sawhorse stands for the ceremony. There were about 150 mourners in attendance, including many in full military dress, and a brass band played. The mayor was bundled up in a heavy overcoat against the chill. He did not wear a hat. His hair had receded several inches from when he left for war on April 13, less than two years ago, and his face looked older, somehow harsher, with deeper lines than before. Corning read a speech during the military burial service from behind a solemn face with a grim, tight mouth that appeared to fight back sobs as he spoke. The filmmaker cut away to a shot of a statue of the Virgin Mary and then zoomed in on a lone bugler who blew what one assumed was "Taps." The camera found Corning once more, his moist eyes downcast, as he laid a wreath atop each coffin and brushed back tears.

Corning's grief was deep and heartfelt for lives lost, families shattered by the war. And yet, even in his despair, the reality was that his war experience provided a political payoff with a long shelf life. The papers now called him the "ex-G.I. Mayor" in nearly every reference and his sphere of influence reached beyond Albany as his political stock rose sharply. Suddenly, Corning was being mentioned as a possible candidate for governor. "Mayor Corning, previously mentioned in Democratic speculation as a candidate for state comptroller, is now listed among the possible candidates for nomination as Governor," the *Times Union* reported in January,

1946. Corning wouldn't run for governor that year, or any year, but he would be drafted into running for lieutenant governor in 1946 with U.S. Senator James M. Mead of Buffalo. The Mead-Corning ticket was defeated by popular incumbents Gov. Dewey and Lt. Gov. Joe R. Hanley. It was the only loss in Corning's political career, a crushing defeat Corning softened by joking about it; he liked to say he lost the lieutenant governor's race by more votes than all the votes combined that had been cast for him in eleven victorious mayoral elections.

While he continued accumulating power in politics and wealth in business, Corning never forgot his pals in the April 13th group. They were comrades-in-arms and maintained a bond for life. His buddy Jake Carey, who had a plate put in his head, was paralyzed on his left side and wheelchair-bound because of injuries sustained in the German mortar attack, was a typical case. "I remember Mayor Corning came to see Jake in the hospital in his uniform when he had a brief leave and he visited Jake lots of times in the hospital," recalled his widow, Alice Carey. Two years after the war was over, Carey's widow remembered the difficulty she encountered trying to get her husband discharged from the V.A. Hospital in Framingham, Massachusetts. He had been through numerous operations and had been hospitalized in three different facilities for more than a year after his combat injuries. "The doctor wasn't going to let Jake go if he didn't have a job, so I asked the doctor to call Mayor Corning, who had visited Jake in the hospital and offered his help," Carey recalled. "Mayor Corning asked, 'Can he sit on his ass?' The doctor said, 'Yes he can.' Then Mayor Corning said, 'Then send him over and I'll find him something.'" This was 1946 and Corning got Carey a job as a clerk in the Albany County tax delinquent department. Carey drove a car with hand controls to the office, where he used a wheelchair. His job involved answering phones and filing. Carey was well-liked around the office because he volunteered to work Saturday mornings in the summer if pain from his injury didn't prevent him from working. He held that job for ten years, until a fall sustained while getting in and out of his wheelchair fractured Carey's good leg. He couldn't get to work anymore and he was put on disability. The county paid him twenty-six dollars net each week and Corning made sure nothing held up those payments for his war buddy. In the summer of 1949, Corning took part in a house painting party among the April 13th gang to help the Careys out and to spruce up Carey's half of a Judson Street duplex with a fresh coat of paint. Another member of the April 13th group, Larry Barry, lived in the adjoining duplex and he had organized the house painting. "I remember Mayor Corning painted along with the other guys and they drank beer and I made them sandwiches and stuff to eat," Alice Carey recalled. "Mayor Corning always seemed to enjoy being just one of the guys. Maybe he didn't really like all that society stuff."

Corning also helped get a job for Carey's wife, Alice, by asking a favor of his buddy Judge Harold Koreman in Surrogate Court. Koreman hired Alice Carey as a clerk in Surrogate Court in 1947. "But I was certainly qualified," Alice Carey said. "I was a good typist and could run the copy machines." Her main job was to climb ladders, retrieve files and make photocopies. A hysterectomy in 1964 meant the end of her ladder climbing. She went out on disability, too, and also collected twenty-six dollars net pay each week from the county, which Corning made sure she received. "It was barely enough to live on and to buy food for our two kids, but it's all we had," Alice Carey recalled. "We never could have made it without Mayor Corning." After he broke his leg in 1956, Jake Carey couldn't get around and spent the next twenty-five years confined to his bed, cared for by his wife. At one point, she broke her leg and took care of her husband from her own wheelchair. Corning kept in touch over the years, visited Jake, gave the Careys money and gifts and helped out in whatever way he could. Jake Carey died on Dec. 13, 1979. Mayor Corning attended the funeral with the rest of the April 13th group. Corning also stopped by Carey's house for the wake. "We lived in a cold-water flat on Bradford Street at that time and it was pretty rough, but I remember the mayor walked right in and sat down and didn't look at anything around him," Alice Carey said. "And when he left the house, he blew a kiss to me. That made me feel so special."

The Army private made all his Army buddies, many of whom outranked him, feel special. For Tortorici, the Corning kindness came in the wake of a family crisis. His brother-in-law, a World War I vet, suffered a nervous breakdown and was about to be committed to a psychiatric facility in Poughkeepsie, when Tortorici asked the mayor to intercede. Corning's connections secured a bed and special care in the Albany V.A. Hospital, where the man made a steady recovery, remaining close to his family. Some months later, when Tortorici was alone with the mayor, he broached the matter of Corning's assistance. "I tried to thank him, but he said, "What are you talking about? I never helped you." That's the way he was," Tortorici says. "He never wanted credit for what he did."

Some took advantage of the mayor's largess. In addition to installing Otto Fausel to run his insurance business, Corning gave at least one other World War II buddy down on his luck a job with Albany Associates. In a 1990 interview with John Curley, Fausel recalled that one of the April 13th group, whom Fausel declined to name, was given a job as a cashier by Corning at the insurance office. Fausel later discovered the man had been embezzling money from the company. Fausel said he called Corning at City Hall. Corning listened quietly, without interrupting, according to Fausel. Corning said, "I'll be right down" and hung up. A couple of minutes later, Corning appeared in the office a few blocks down State Street hill. He summoned the cashier. Corning asked, "Where's your hat?" The man pretended not to know what Corning was getting at, Fausel said. Corning said in an even voice, "Put it on and don't come back." And that, by Fausel's account, was that. Later in his conversation with Curley, Fausel said, "He [Corning] was generous, but not that generous." Others among the wartime crew abused Corning's assistance. One of the April 13th group, a North Ender, was given a substantial loan by the mayor, but never repaid it. "When we found out about it, we cut him right out of our group," Tortorici said. "Corning never said anything about it. But we didn't like anyone treating our 'Rastus like that."

Corning's vow of assistance worked on a small scale, too. Zimmer and his son were building a house in East Greenbush and they needed a certain type of crushed stone to meet the specifications for the septic system. "We couldn't find it anywhere and someone said to call the mayor and I said no at first, but then I said why not and called Corning," Zimmer recalled. "He said he had the stone and would send someone right over. It wasn't a giveaway. We paid fair market price. But he did me a favor and it sure was nice to have an Albany Public Works crew bring me up a load of stone. When you called the mayor, he came through."

Frank Verenini, who served in the Navy, was twenty-seven years old and his third child was born the night before he marched off to war on April 13, 1944. After the war, Corning got Verenini, who was working for a dry cleaner, an extra job as a janitor with the Albany fire department to help him make ends meet. Verenini said Corning's job service reach was wide and deep for his April 13th crew. "I know he got some of the boys jobs with the state and federal government because of his connections," Verenini said. "And I know he paid taxes for some of the group until they got on their feet after the war. He was always there for us." Verenini credited Corning with much of the camaraderie and closeness among the group. "The mayor was the kind of guy who would slip $20 bills to the boys, but he never made you feel like he had helped you," Verenini said. "I think that way the mayor had rubbed off on us. We're still close fifty years after the war and we volunteer at the V.A. Hospital, make birthday cakes for the vets and are active in our American Legion posts. We always took care of each other."

Thomas Prime, who ran a family saloon, Genesee Tavern, on Broadway in north Albany for fifty years, served in the Navy. After retiring as a bar owner in 1974 at age sixty-five, Prime went to see his ward leader and asked for a part-time job. The ward leader said he'd ask the mayor, but never did. Prime called Corning, who said the job was his. Corning dashed off a letter to the errant ward leader. "The next day, I had my slip from my ward leader to go to work with the Parks Department," said Prime, who worked for the city parks crew in spring and summer for ten seasons. He made about eighty dollars per week for raking around St. Joseph's Church and the park at Ten Broeck Triangle in Arbor Hill. Corning stayed close when Prime moved his tavern to Sand Creek Road in Colonie in the early 1970s. "The mayor would stop by at my tavern and have a beer or Scotch and soda," Prime recalls. "He'd drink and sing with us, like a regular guy. Boy, that sure put me in good with the contractors who stopped by. They were impressed I knew the mayor." Others who never sought a favor from the mayor knew he was there. "He called me up and told me I could come down to City Hall anytime I needed help, but I never went," said George Louis, a Navy veteran from the April 13th group who ran a grocery store on Clinton Avenue in Arbor Hill. "I'm sorry now I didn't go down to see him, because I knew he would have given me some help."

It was Corning who led the oath among the inductees on the train down to Fort Dix on April 13, 1944, promising that all the survivors would gather each year for a reunion after the war. He was true to his word. It was during these gatherings that Corning proved he was one of the boys. Although he was a stalwart of the group, Corning missed the very first reunion in the summer of 1946 because he was in Maine at the time. "The mayor felt so bad he couldn't make it, he asked to have another get-together right away and he paid for it, $150 out of his pocket," Prime said. The earliest reunions were clambakes at Prime's family's camp in the Helderbergs, outside Berne, which had a pond and vast acreage. They were loosely organized affairs, with lots of food and drink. The boys would play poker, shoot craps, play softball. Mostly, they were there to get roaring drunk. The mayor had an appetite for all of it during those lost weekends. "We had a lot of food and the mayor always finished everything on his plate," Prime remembered. Steak on a hard roll in the morning, ushering in an endless feed through the day and night of hamburgers, hot dogs, fried chicken, steamed clams, baked potatoes, corn on the cob – the works. The parties started Friday evening and went through Sunday night or right into Monday morning sometimes. They'd get twenty to thirty guys camping out, including Corning. Craps and poker, along with kegs of beer and a solid supply of liquor, kept the weekend moving along. Corning loved to gamble with his buddies; craps was Corning's favorite and the game of choice at the reunions. They didn't have a table, just two dice tossed against a log on the ground. Eight or ten guys would start out playing. Corning was always in the game. A seven or eleven on the first roll won, a two, three or twelve lost. Anything else became your number and you tried to match it without hitting seven. The game would go on for hours and hours. They cut their teeth on craps in the Army: "A lot of us would go into town from Blanding on Sundays to shoot craps," Zimmer remembered. "Corning came with us, but Jake Harris was the real craps shooter. If Jake hit real good at craps, he'd be buying everybody drinks in town."

They recaptured that Army camaraderie at the reunions, especially at the never-ending craps games. "Them games could get rough," Zimmer recalled. "It usually started with a one dollar bet, but you could be shooting for twenty dollars a throw real quick. The ten guys who started would get down to three or so who still had money." Zimmer remembered the mayor's luck was lousy at craps one year up in the Helderbergs in the late-'40s. "He kept playing, but he lost real big that night and he ran out of money," Zimmer said. "I loaned him some money so he could keep throwing. The very next day, a car pulled up to my barber shop in Rensselaer and it was the mayor's driver with my money." Zimmer won't say how much he loaned the mayor, but admits "you could lose $200 to $300 easy in some of those games." Tortorici and Prime, who confirmed the story, believe Corning's losses that night were in the neighborhood of $500, still small change to Corning. The mayor told a few of his Army buddies he played high-stakes poker at the Fort Orange Club, but that's where the social class line was firmly drawn. The mayor never invited his blue-collar pals from the April 13th group to play cards with him there.

At times, Corning appeared to be a blue-collar guy trapped in a blue-blood background and he seemed to connect more with the working class than his own aristocratic class. Corning never pulled rank when it came to social class on the boys, but others did. Corning's insurance associate, Otto Fausel, lived in a large home on New Scotland Avenue and owned a Cadillac and fancy Chrysler. "You could tell Otto made big money and he stayed a little above us because he never gambled with us," Zimmer said. Similarly, fellow inductee Ray Kinley Sr., a close Corning friend, dropped out of the April 13th group after he became a senior vice-president with State Bank of Albany. "He was a big-shot bank executive and stopped mixing with us, but not Corning. He always stayed with the boys," Zimmer said.

At the reunion bashes, when they ran out of money or tired of craps, they switched to straight poker. "The poker games weren't that steep," Zimmer said. The games had a quarter limit and the pots rarely exceeded ten dollars. The same hard-core crew played craps and poker. It was Corning, Zimmer, Harris, Prime, Joe Barbagallo Sr., Tommy Richmond, Francis Brino and Larry Barry. Corning had his winning streaks, but losing big didn't rattle the mayor. "It never bothered him when he lost," Zimmer said. "I took a couple hundred bucks off Corning at craps once, but that was nothing to him," Barbagallo said. "The mayor was a sport," Tortorici said. "Some of the guys took Corning for quite a bit of money, but I think he might have even let them win sometimes."

They took gambling road trips in search of a game. Zimmer said that he, Corning, and several other guys from the group would charter a bus and head over to Pittsfield, Massachusetts where one of the cooks from Camp Blanding – a guy named Martin, who wasn't from Albany – owned a tavern. "Those were some wicked craps games," Zimmer said. "You could win $300 easy in a night at those games." Corning and a few guys would also shoot craps in the mid-1950s at Carmen's Hall on Clinton Avenue aside from the reunion action, recalled George Louis. "But we found out the guy running that game was crooked and used loaded dice, so we never went back there again," Louis said.

Corning drank with the boys as hard as he gambled. "We had lots of booze and got really drunk and nobody gave a damn he was mayor," Joe Barbagallo Sr. said. Barbagallo remembered one of the Helderberg bashes that started after work Friday and didn't stop until his work at Metropolitan Cleaners on the corner of Lark and Spring streets beckoned

Barbagallo at 5:30 Monday morning. "We'd been drinking straight through the weekend and it was three in the morning Monday and Corning wanted to drink some more," Barbagallo said. "What a pisser he was. He knew how to party. I remember him driving his car down the hill from Thacher Park and his head was bobbing back and forth as he took the turns. He was stinking drunk and I was thinking the car was going to go off the road. We got to the bottom of the hill and Corning stopped at the first gin mill we came to and we drank there some more," Barbagallo added. "Then we drove into Albany and we stopped at another bar. He was like a kid, ready for anything. He was drinking Dewar's Scotch. He could afford top shelf. He bought a lot of rounds for the boys, too. Well, it was 5:30 Monday morning and I had to get to work and I told the mayor to drive me to Lark and Spring," Barbagallo said. "We got there and I practically had to jump out of the car, because he was trying to get me to hit one more bar. Jesus Christ, the guy was something. He could hold his liquor. Even when he was drunk as a loon, he was a nice guy and a gentleman. I never saw him lose control."

Barbagallo said he and the mayor kept their minds, and eyes, on their drinking at the bars. "I can tell you for a fact Corning wasn't a womanizer," Barbagallo said. "I went drinking with him a lot and we got awful drunk, but I never saw him chase women." As Barbagallo told his story, he retrieved his military medals from a bedroom. There were two service medals and a Purple Heart for the staff sergeant with the 12th Infantry, 4th Division. Barbagallo was badly wounded from mortar shrapnel during a skirmish in the Battle of the Bulge. He was hospitalized in Paris and England for several months and was made a member of the military police after his recovery. He was discharged from the Army on January 12, 1946. He died from lung cancer in 1995. Race or religion didn't seem to be an issue at the reunions. Several members of the group were Jewish. At the 1956 gathering, Corning was pictured next to a black man. "We had two colored guys in our group," Zimmer said. "They got along with everybody." It was telling, however, that nobody remembered their names.

The drinking and gambling were tempered by age among the World War II buddies; advancing years also curtailed the softball games at the reunions by the late-1950s, when most of the men were middle-aged. Softball was replaced by horseshoes and the drunken weekends in the Helderbergs became a distant memory as the reunion group started gathering for dinners in local restaurants and invited their wives, all of them except

Corning, who never brought Betty. Neither did he bring Polly Noonan, but always came alone, a solitariness that did not go unnoticed. "His wife never went any place with him that I know of," Prime said. "He never brought Polly with him, either. I did see the mayor and Polly at parties at the Elks. That was their business."

Likewise, they never discussed the war at the reunions, nor did they reveal their fears and emotional wounds from the conflict. "We didn't have to," Tortorici said. "It was all part of us. We didn't need to mention our experiences to each other." Verenini put it this way: "We never talked about it, because we were all glad to have it behind us." Tortorici remembered coming back from the war on a train headed for Fort Dix when an oncoming train passed so closely and quickly that the violent suction sounded like an explosion. "All the soldiers in our car hit the floor at the same time, the way we did with incoming artillery," Tortorici said. "You just did it automatically. Nobody talked about it on the train, but we were nervous and jumpy. We didn't know how to feel. We didn't think we'd make it home. And it was hard not having anyone to talk to, because we left as a group and came home alone."

Tortorici recalled returning to Albany's Union Station in late May, 1946, two years after he had headed off to war. "It was like a dream because I had given up hope of ever getting home so many times," Tortorici said. His wife and five-year-old son, Jimmy Jr., were at the station. Tortorici ran up to sweep up his son in a wave of hugs and kisses, but the boy said, "Men don't kiss. We shake hands." Said Tortorici, "That nearly killed me. I was all nervous and afraid coming back and didn't know how to act or think I could do anything."

The last reunion Corning attended was in the spring of 1982, just before the mayor's health took a turn for the worse and he was admitted to Albany Medical Center Hospital on June 5. About twenty-five of the guys had a cookout at Schutzen Park, a German picnic area and dance hall in Colonie. "He wasn't well, but he was there," Tortorici recalled.

The surviving members of the April 13th group, numbering about twenty, attended Corning's funeral. They were seated in a place of honor inside All Saint's Cathedral. They have continued to gather for an annual dinner since Corning's death in 1983. There were eight members still alive for the fiftieth anniversary on April 13, 1994. There is a ritual to the reunion dinners. They light candles and say a prayer for the deceased members as a memorial tribute. They offer a special salute they call

"Albany, My Albany." It speaks of their loyalty to each other, to their hometown, to the memory of their fallen comrades. Perhaps no member epitomized those sentiments better than the G.I.-Mayor, Pfc. Erastus Corning. "You couldn't help but like that man, God bless him," Tortorici said. "He was a beautiful man. I'll never forget the way he always used to tell us: 'You're my boys. If you ever have a problem, just come to my office at City Hall and to hell with the guys out front. You tell them you're one of the boys and just walk right in.'"

Chapter 7:

From Dewey to DWI:
Investigations Against Corning and the Machine

"Any time it's bad weather and they [state officials] want to investigate something, they do it in Albany because they don't have to travel."

Mayor Erastus Corning 2nd to an audience at Carnegie Hall on the campus of Union College in Schenectady, April 23, 1981.

When it came to the Republican Party on the city and county levels, the Albany Democratic machine knew how to play go-along, get-along politics. Arrangements were made so each side could avoid self-destruction. The Democrats would throw the GOP a few judgeships, say, or strike up a truce not to challenge Republican control in suburban towns for similar *laissez-faire* in the cities, and, maybe, slice the state job patronage pie in such a way that left a few crusts for the GOP. "The Albany County Republican organization is unimportant. It lived for years on crumbs given it by the O'Connells, plus hopes for a bigger share," wrote Warren Moscow, *New York Times* political writer and dean of the Capitol press corps, in his 1948 book, *Politics in the Empire State*. That's the way things had worked for a generation, and worked well, for both parties. Until, that is, Thomas E. Dewey came to Albany in 1943, seized power at the Capitol for the Republicans and promised to make life hell for the Democratic machine running the capital city.

Dewey was the epitome of a politically ambitious prosecutor, a lawyer with good timing who rode a crime wave and the public's obsession with it to elective glory. The wiry little man with the tight pencil-thin mustache and even tighter law-and-order platform – who came to occupy the governor's seat in Albany during wartime after bringing New York City's underworld to its knees – wasn't about to cut a deal with the O'Connell-Corning machine. That wasn't the way damn-the-torpedoes Dewey played the political game, that wasn't the way he had been elected to rid the Empire State of corruption and vice, and it wasn't the way he was planning to parlay his reputation as a take-no-prisoners reformer all the way to the White House.

Dewey was born in 1902 in Owosso, Michigan above his grandfather's store on Main Street, on the west bank of the Shiawassee River. Owosso is something like Albany, at least in size. Lined with porches flying American flags and porch swings quivering in the breeze, and a Protestant church practically on every corner, Owosso has been called the "perfect location for a remake of any Andy Hardy movie" by essayist Thomas Mallon. Owosso's other famous son, James Oliver Curwood, an early adventure novelist, said of Owosso: "It's American, and it makes you feel at home." Dewey cloaked himself in the flag and engineered his celebrity as "Racket Buster" of New York City. But now he was in Albany, a long way upriver from the metropolis. An archetypal showdown was imminent, a piece of American political brinkmanship reminiscent of Dodge City. Albany was the O'Connell-Corning machine's town and the counselor from Owosso was about to meet a foe even tougher than Charles "Lucky" Luciano. "The Tammany machine braves are pikers compared to this machine," Dewey said in a gubernatorial campaign speech in 1942, making one of his central pledges the destruction of the Albany machine. Dewey singled out Dan O'Connell for annihilation, ensuring enmity between the two camps. Dewey, a Republican, was a source of rancor to Albany's new mayor, Erastus Corning 2nd, for reasons beyond party affiliation. Dewey broke twenty years of Democratic control of the Executive Mansion for starters. He also swept into the governorship after Corning's close friend and provider of much Democratic political patronage, Governor Herbert H. Lehman, resigned to take a federal appointment, leaving Lieutenant Governor Charles Poletti to serve the shortest gubernatorial term in history – twenty-eight days. In the vacuum left by Lehman's departure, Corning, elected mayor for the first time in 1942 after a career as a state legislator, was mentioned in the local press as an attractive Democratic candidate for governor. Corning never fanned the flames of that speculation, but it's clear from his comments in the Albany papers that he was flattered by the attention. Dewey's election not only overshadowed Corning's rising political star; it also cut off at the knees the mayor's influence up State Street hill at the Capitol. Corning had been a frequent social guest at the Executive Mansion during Lehman's term and his father,

Edwin, frequently attended high-level Cabinet meetings at the Eagle Street residence as Al Smith's lieutenant governor. Mayor Corning wasn't expecting a social invitation from Dewey, and, furthermore, could bid goodbye to the sympathetic ear he had at the Capitol on Albany matters.

This was the climate in which Dewey took up residence in Albany. He would have been *persona non grata* regardless to Corning and company had he chosen to seek peace and the path of least resistance with his new Democratic neighbors. Instead, Dewey wasted no time firing the first salvo in the war against what he saw as a corrupt Democratic organization. His real motivation was a desire to put another scalp on the political wampum belt he planned to use to trade his way from the Hudson to the Potomac. Dewey hadn't even had time to repair the oatmeal wallpaper that hung in shreds from the walls of the governor's study in the Mansion or to replace tattered draperies held together with safety pins in the official residence or to have the leaks in the roof fixed or to chase the bats out of the bedroom when he set his sights on a different kind of demolition.

On October 8, 1943, less than a year after taking office, Dewey made front-page headlines in an afternoon extra edition of The *Knickerbocker News* by seizing the election registration books of 1943 for Albany, Watervliet and Cohoes, together with other election data. "Records Seized," blared the seventy-two point banner headline, with an ominous tone in the text that hinted at the beginning of the fall of what had been believed to be an impenetrable political fortress the O'Connells and Cornings had built. The machine had impressive battalions of loyal soldiers at its beck and call, but Dewey had a formidable army of his own. Dewey suddenly formed as part of the New York State Law Department a new unit: the Albany County Board of Elections Fraud Bureau. It was the only county in the state that received such special attention. Erastus was not flattered.

Dewey let O'Connell and Corning and their ward heelers sweat a bit before following up the records seizure with an undercover investigation at election enrollment sites and a letter to the mayor, a copy of which the governor kindly provided to the *Times Union*, which ran the correspondence on the front page on October 15, 1943: "I have today directed the district attorney and the sheriff to take appropriate measures to enforce the Election Law," Dewey wrote Corning. "I have told them I shall hold them personally responsible for conditions which prevail in the remaining two days of registration and on Election Day. Surely you must be aware of your duties and responsibilities for the enforcement of all laws." Dewey said he found "flagrant violations." These included investigators who found in polling places "crimes" such as no enrollment booths, no doors in booths, booths folded on the floor, booths "hidden" behind the voting machine, voters unable to place by themselves their enrollment papers in the box provided, booths used for coat racks. Dewey didn't stop there, launching a three-pronged attack. On the same day, October 15, 1943, Dewey ordered twenty investigators from the State Department of Audit and Control to move into the comptroller's office in City Hall "to examine the accounts and fiscal affairs of the city," according to State Comptroller Frank C. Moore, Dewey's attack dog. The next day, on October 16, 1943, the news broke that Moore and his auditors discovered "a shortage" of $1,664,328 in capital funds of the city. "These moneys, raised through bond issues by the city for specific purposes, were illegally diverted to other uses in violation of the provisions of the general law," Moore said. Dewey thought he had his prey in the cross-hairs.

The scalp Dewey wanted was Uncle Dan's, who, in Dewey's mind at least, was from the same genus as Luciano and his ilk in the way O'Connell controlled his turf. Dewey had beaten one kind of mob and he was ready to try to extend his streak by taking on a political machine. Dewey first would have to go through Corning, though, who towered physically over Dewey, though seven years his junior. Besides possessing a keen intellect, Corning had learned a thing or two about composure and grace under fire. In every photograph from the Dewey probe, Corning appeared cool and collected. You never saw him sweat. Corning had only to hearken back to his days as a first former grinning and bearing the hazing dished out by upperclassmen at Groton; or, to the times he bluffed his way through the stern questioning of professors at Yale when he hadn't read the assignment after a night of drinking bathtub gin; or, to his years as a greenhorn state legislator in the minority party graciously accepting scraps from the Republican table. Most importantly, Corning was wickedly smart and about as quick on his feet and possessed of a razor-sharp wit as any front man O'Connell could ever hope to have in his corner.

Corning made the usual denials about the $1.6 million discrepancy, of course, producing city records to bolster his contention that what the state comptroller called "a shortage" was actually "a temporary loan" to meet current expenses pending receipt of other revenues. Corning said the idle bond issue balances had been temporarily used to tide over the city until more taxes arrived, saving interest charges so that the city didn't have to borrow again. Corning made it sound as if he deserved a fiscal good house-keeping seal of approval, not an indictment. Corning was at the top of his semantics game when it came to the opening of Dewey's inquiry into Albany city finances. The Groties from the speech team would have been proud of their rascally 'Rastus, that ol' dissembler.

Dewey's grand inquisition began officially on October 19, 1943. Corning arrived at the State Office Building (now the Alfred E. Smith Building) twenty minutes ahead of time for the hearing. Very cool. Corning was accompanied only by Corporation Counsel James J. McGuinness, whom it was ruled could stay only as a spectator and not as the mayor's lawyer. That was fine with him, Corning agreed. More cool. No sweat, gentlemen.

The press ate up every word of Corning's Oscar-caliber performance. The *Knickerbocker News* described the "fireworks this afternoon" and "the intensity of the struggle" between Corning and Comptroller Moore. Corning immediately put Dewey's pit bulls off balance, and had observers chuckling, when he resolutely refused for the first fifteen minutes of the hearing to sign a waiver of immunity. First Moore, and then his counsel, Robert Lansdowne, tried to prevail upon Corning to sign the waiver. Corning politely declined. Moore and Lansdowne finessed the point further. Corning was a balky cow refusing to go placidly into his stall for milking. Moore and Lansdowne pushed some more. No go. The prosecutors had grown visibly flummoxed by Corning's calm refusal to play by their rules. The *Knick News* reporter wrote: "Throughout the verbal exchange, Mayor Corning preserved a smiling exterior, insisting he had 'nothing to hide.'" At one point during the to-do, Lansdowne said that "if the witness does not sign the waiver we will not be able to proceed with this inquiry." The mayor, reiterating his refusal to sign, reached over and picked up a Bible saying, "I will take my oath on this Bible."

Point, game, set, match to Erastus. The Bible! How rich. Smashing. Better than the way he'd explained himself to the headmaster, since Corning likely hadn't cracked a Bible since mandatory morning chapel at Groton. In one bold, masterful stroke, though, Corning had set the tone for the Dewey hearing. The mayor would take the moral high ground, Bible under his arm, and reduce Dewey's henchmen to a comical kangaroo court. Corning's work as a thespian and his association with the drama club at Groton was paying off. This was theater and he had the hometown audience in the palm of his hand. (On the heels of his brilliant Bible remark, the mayor followed up with a reporter after the hearing by saying his offer to take his oath on the Bible "had behind it all the Christian belief that is in me.") When Moore and Lansdowne couldn't make Corning sign the waiver of immunity, they gave up in disgust and amended the hearing's rules to say Corning could testify under oath, without reference to the waiver. But Moore and Lansdowne were damned if they'd let Corning off the hook when it came to admitting the $1.6 million "shortage" in capital funds of the city Dewey's investigators had uncovered. Let the mayor try to wriggle out of that one. They had the numbers down in black and white, irrefutable evidence. Or so they thought. It was show time once more. Corning refused to let the word "shortage" pass his lips. Bullheaded, the prosecutors tried to bully the mayor. He would not say "shortage." Lansdowne lost it. He angrily dispatched an aide to get a copy of *Webster's Dictionary* and he read into the record that he found the word "shortage" on page 1,946 and he read its definition.

The *Knickerbocker News* reporter wrote: "The Mayor pointed out – 'regardless of what *Webster's* says,' Corning noted defiantly – the definition meant 'shortcoming' as well as 'deficiency.'

"Shortage connotes to me a defalcation," said the mayor. "There is none and there never has been any defalcation." The mayor said short-coming might mean failure to perform a duty. "We are strictly grammarians here,' interpolated Lansdowne sarcastically."

The opening Corning gambit had legs. Two days later, Moore called off the hearing when two city officials refused to sign waivers of immunity "after an exchange of bitter remarks," according to a *Knickerbocker News* account. Albany Corporation Counsel James J. McGuinness stalked from the hearing room, shouting, "This is not an inquiry! It's an inquisition!"

Dewey took to the airwaves on October 20, 1943, in a radio speech ostensibly to support the candidacy of Sen. Joe Hanley, GOP candidate for lieutenant governor. Dewey quickly strayed into a screed against the Albany County Democratic organization. Transcripts of the speech reveal Dewey at one point stumbled in his delivery and, consciously or subconsciously, said: "It took five years to break the power of the organized criminal underworld in the city of Albany." He quickly corrected himself and said, "I beg your pardon. I meant in the city of New York." And he went on to add: "But it won't take quite that long in Albany." Dewey, speaking in Schenectady, also referred to "the despotic rule of Dan O'Connell across the river."

This was decades before 1990s sound-bite politics, but Dewey and Corning knew the power of spin. Corning fought back and delivered his own radio address a few nights later, on October 26, 1943. Corning saved a draft of the speech in his personal papers, with his own underlines for emphasis and notations in the margins. Corning reached for the purple prose and laid it on mighty thick, pandering to the wartime paranoia of his listeners and the real terror of the driving Nazi invasion: "Mobilizing the State Police in their barracks at night under secret orders to march on Albany did not terrify Albany," the mayor said. "It merely brought to them thoughts of the castor oil days of the defunct Mussolini, and the putsch days of the soon-to-be defunct Hitler. While Albany became an occupied city in all the implications of that term, the temporary conquerors found just a peaceful people minding their own business, carrying on their American right of franchise legally and openly and honestly." Corning continued:

> Governor Dewey, Albany today stands unafraid. We have nothing to conceal and I as mayor would not tolerate for one moment any action on the part of any city official who would show any disposition on his part to withhold any information honestly and legally sought by the state in any one of the three investigations now under way under your directions . . . I am strongly of the belief that not only Albanians, but all the people of New York state regard as inexcusable and indefensible the spending of thousands of dollars of New York state money in Thomas E. Dewey's campaign to increase his stature as a presidential candidate.

In tandem with the public propaganda campaign through Corning and other officials, the machine took out full-page newspaper ads that pushed the hot buttons of wartime: "Terrorism . . . Foreign-inspired methods . . . The New Gestapo" the ad copy blared. It played well in Albany, although Corning was preaching to the choir while Dewey was after a statewide audience. Corning was right. Dewey was prosecuting for points in his popularity ratings as governor as much as anything else. Although the mayor managed to take a bit of wind out of his sails, the governor changed tack and stayed the course. Dewey was hidebound to see this through. He wanted to topple the machine and he'd use all the vast state resources at his disposal to do it. Corning, fond of bird hunting, liked to use an apropos political adage: "Shoot at anything that flies. And claim anything that falls." Now, that scattershot strategy was being used against him.

O'Connell was quarterbacking the machine's defense from behind the scenes and he had the best front man and counter-puncher in the business in Corning. O'Connell paid an anonymous consultant, probably a lawyer, to prepare a twenty-five page white paper for Corning. Entitled "In The Matter of Privilege of A Witness," it was meant to sharpen the mayor's arsenal of obfuscation and variations on pleading the Fifth Amendment. In his handwritten notes in the margins of the document, Corning displayed his tactic of turning the tables. In reference to charges of assessment tampering, Corning scribbled, "What does Dewey think the Republican cities and towns do to Democratic property?"

Corning may have won the first skirmish by turning Dewey's hearing into a comedy of errors, but the tough little fellow from Owosso wasn't conceding the battle. Dewey rolled over the machine's legal maneuvering to halt the grand jury and on March 1, 1944, twenty ward leaders were summoned into the grand jury room. George P. Monaghan was appointed by Dewey as Special Prosecutor and he brooked no machine interference. Dewey's incisive stroke had been to do an end run around the machine's control of the grand jury by impaneling his own special grand jury outside the machine's purview. First on the stand was John J. O'Connell Jr., chairman of the Albany County Democratic Committee and president of the organization in the First Ward. The grand jury also heard from Marguerite O'Connell, widow of Patrick J. O'Connell and office secretary for the county Democratic organization. Dan O'Connell, the real target, remained safely outside the fray. A month later, in April, State Police took into custody thirty-seven people indicted on charges of illegal voting and registration. Bail was set at $1,000 in all cases. The only charges that stuck were against twelve men, each with convictions for felonies that stripped them of their voting rights. Each pleaded guilty to a misdemeanor count of illegal registration. As part of the plea bargain arrangement, charges of illegal voting were dropped. The following month, in May, Dewey's investigators subpoenaed the business records of O'Connell's Hedrick Brewery and Albany Packing, which had ties to the machine.

Corning delivered one of his finest political haymaker speeches to the Albany County Democratic committee in the spring of 1944. The only thing was, Corning didn't write it. The mayor learned to be an effective speaker, but this engaging, potent and bare-knuckled piece of propaganda could not have come from Corning's more cerebral and subdued pen. This stem winder was drafted by freelance writer Abbett Pulliam of Altamont, whom Corning hired, according to the mayor's records. The speech was meant as a kind of machine manifesto and aspired to Marc Antony's "Friends, Romans, Countrymen . . ." Here are a few excerpts from Corning's annotated, revised draft:

> It might well be said that the people of Albany are wise beyond the average in their ability to evaluate political personalities. They quickly distinguish between the all wool and the shoddy. . . . We are a politically conscious people and we quickly separate the sheep from the goats. . . . Every theorist, every experimenter, every dreamer with new ideas and new programs to make government Utopian, has at some time or another stood at his Capitol window and said to himself: 'Ah, here's the very place; we'll try it out on the dog right here.' And Albany has been the innocent whelp compelled to take the beating. . . . And in conclusion let me say to you who are the active political workers of our party, that I am certain that your confidence and courage, your pride in our accomplishments, your contempt for the methods and motives of this political persecutor, will bring us all in closed ranks side by side for a gallant and successful battle. The victory will be ours. We cannot fail.

The speech stirred up the machine's drone bees. Outside the hive, though, it looked as if Dewey's aggressive investigation was beginning to inflict lasting damage on the supposedly indomitable machine. But Uncle Dan had another trick up his sleeve. It was wartime, after all, and even a political town like Albany was focused far more intensely on Hitler's march overseas than a grand jury probe at home. At the urging of O'Connell, who had turned his own service with the Navy in World War I into his greatest political asset, Corning marched off to fight the Nazi threat on April 13, 1944, although he could have gotten a draft deferment or a stateside officer's appointment. Instead, he went in as a buck private with the Army infantry. Take that, Dewey. A Bible-toting, G.I.-Mayor. Not even the famous prosecutor who cleaned up New York's mobs could trump that card in the fearsome climate of World War II. Corning smiled confidently as he marched off to war. You wonder if he wasn't thinking of Dewey and his henchmen and saying to himself, *hasta la vista* suckers.

Consider what Dewey had achieved by the summer of 1944, nearly a year after he started his expensive and controversial investigation of the machine: a few misdemeanor charges for illegal registration against ex-felons. Not exactly blockbuster stuff. And nothing to rouse public support. Uncle Dan seemed untouchable. Corning was gone and fast becoming a war hero, a political sacred cow. Against the backdrop of the Battle of the Bulge, at least on the home front of Democratic stronghold Albany, Dewey's inquisition seemed mean-spirited and misdirected at best and criminally wasteful at worst. O'Connell's strategy to delay, deflect and dodge was beginning to work. The longer this thing dragged on, the better it was for the machine. And at the one-year mark, the machine shifted gears, moving from a dance-around-the-ring defensive mode to a stick-and-jab offensive posture.

On September 20, 1944, former Albany County District Attorney John T. Delaney, a machine man, announced in the press he knew "of bold conspiracies to smear the names of Albany officials and business men and women" by the Dewey administration. Delaney addressed an overflow crowd at Odd Fellows Hall of the Democratic county committee meeting and received a rousing ovation when he said Dewey's estimated $500,000 investment in its investigation "is a lot of money to provide a Roman holiday for the Republican organization of Albany county." Also, Corning's fishing buddy and the machine candidate picked to fill Corning's Senate seat in 1941 when Corning became mayor, Sen. Julian B. Erway, got mileage out of the mayor's war service. Dewey appeared to be getting desperate when he indicted the mayor *in absentia*, and Erway jumped on what he derisively labeled "a political indictment," according to a *Knickerbocker News* article on October 4, 1944. Erway said, "I speak out in the face of public demand that the respected and beloved wartime mayor of this city be granted his constitutional right to an immediate trial of the indictment which has been made against him." Pvt. Corning was otherwise occupied, fighting on the fringes of the Battle of the Bulge at the time.

Corning gloated in a letter to Erway on October 10, 1944 from the war zone in France: "I am so sorry Monaghan burned his little fingers on our books. I wish he had taken a good look. They would have disappointed him. In any event, thanks for taking care of the matter. As you know, if the S.O.B. wants me the Army is very courteous and will honor any civil subpoena, so if the guy wants to do me a favor all he has to do is call me back for the grand jury and I'll get a free pass as well as transportation off the State."

Back in Albany, Dewey at least had a smaller fish in his skillet to fry, Frank J. Cassidy, Albany's superintendent of water rent delinquencies. William Kennedy took up the matter in O *Albany!*:

> One city water inspector was arrested passing out envelopes to voters at a polling place, and when searched he had forty-five envelopes in his pocket, each containing four dollars. This looked rather like a man purchasing votes. But he said he was contributing to a charity fund to buy food and shoes for needy folks and the polling place was the best spot to find them. He was released, probably because such ingenuity could not go unrewarded.

O'Connell called in a major chit at this point, taking advantage of Dewey's declining fortunes in the probe. The machine's control over every level of the judiciary was its ace in the hole. When things got hot and the boom was about to fall, a judge might simply wave a hand and make machine indictments disappear. Dan's *deus ex machina*. On October 13, 1944, Supreme Court Justice Murray ruled that Dewey's grand jury was illegally chosen and all indictments, including the one against Corning, should be thrown out. Former District Attorney John T. Delaney, perhaps the most quotable machine organ, came up with a doozy when he described "the whole desperate attempt to smear Albanians into a rubble of slander has been the sleaziest burlesque of popular government ever staged," a direct quote from the *Knickerbocker News*. "Dan O'Connell told me that when that verdict came down, Dewey smashed thirteen chairs in the Mansion," Polly Noonan said fifty years after the fact, as if the incident had happened only last week. Think of it as the Albany two-step: in vote-rigging it was known as "making the machine dance;" in the influencing of grand juries it might be called "making the machine walk."

Dewey would be damned if he was going to abandon his crusade, regardless of the fact his window of opportunity was shutting fast. Dewey reached for his strongest weapon. Public sentiment chastised the move, but Dewey was within his legal rights under Section 813-A of the Code of Criminal Procedure. The little terrier of a prosecutor had used it against organized crime in New York and he used it in Albany now. He got a Supreme Court justice, one not beholden to the machine, to approve the action. Dewey ordered the telephone wires of Daniel P. O'Connell and his "private, special unlisted" telephone to be tapped. In the capital city, this amounted to heresy, but Dewey was desperate.

O'Connell received interesting callers in December, 1943 and January, 1944 when Dewey's investigators were listening in. One of the most noteworthy exchanges, a transcript of which Corning kept in his personal files, occurred between Dan O'Connell and Supreme Court Justice Gilbert Schenck on January 18, 1944, as follows:.

Schenck: "Hello."

O'Connell: "Hello."

Schenck: "Dan?"

O'Connell: "Yes."

Schenck: "This is Gil Schenck."

O'Connell: "How are you, my boy?"

Schenck: "Oh, I have been having one hell of a time since – well, since two o'clock, we have had that case before our court."

O'Connell: "Umh'm."

Schenck: "I would have had three votes tonight, except your little boy out in Schoharie – even when I got him in his own room, and tried to pin him down he wouldn't go with me."

O'Connell: "Umh'm."

Schenck: "So . . . "

O'Connell: (interrupting) "You got to be careful with the phones."

Schenck: "Yeah, I know. So I told him – put it over till tomorrow, and I'll do the best I can. One fellow's all right, I'm all right, but it takes three to do it."

O'Connell: "Umh'm."

Schenck: "Yep. We won't talk about it, I just want to tell you, Dan."

O'Connell: "You got the law with you all right, you think?"

Schenck: "Got the law with me, and I am perfectly satisfied, and so is the fellow that granted the order."

O'Connell: "Yep."

Schenck: "Yep."

O'Connell: "Looks like they are going to gang up on us around here, don't it?"

Schenck: "What?"

O'Connell: "It looks . . . the attitude of that big bum Hill."

Schenck: "Oh, it was terrible."

O'Connell: "Truculent . . . You would think . . . "

Schenck: "Oh, it was terrible, worse than anybody ever told you."

O'Connell: "Yeah."

Schenck: "His performance there today was the most embarrassing thing I ever heard of."

O'Connell: "What the hell did we ever do to bring on this animosity?"

Schenck: "Oh, the only thing I thought, if you wanted to do it – but I don't think it would do a damned bit of good – I thought you might call Whalen, and I could get this young fellow to go and see Whalen tomorrow morning before we make any . . . "

O'Connell: "He might get some law down there."

Schenck: "What?"

O'Connell: "He might get some law down there."

Schenck: "God, he got it from me tonight. I was well primed, I had every case laid out, laid it down to him, and he still says 'Well, I want to be right' and that highbrow stuff. But I did the best I could, Dan, anyway."

O'Connell: "O.K."

Schenck: "And it looks as though the other fellow will be with me, but I don't know."

O'Connell: "Yes . . . "

Schenck: "But this fellow won't . . . "

O'Connell: "Yes . . . okeydoke."

Schenck: "Hate to bother you, but it's the fortunes of war, that's all there is to it. We just left down there. First chance I've had to telephone."

O'Connell: "Okeydoke."

Schenck: "O.K. big boy."

The discussion between the political boss and the judge involved the case of William Shea. Shea was indicted by Dewey's grand jury on charges of multiple voting, arrested on Election Day, 1943, and brought before a judge in Albany. His bail was fixed at $2,500. Early the next morning, Shea was bailed out by James S. Collins, night chief of police of Cohoes, who was on duty but left his post and drove ten miles in an official police car to the Albany County Courthouse, where Collins, a convicted bootlegger who went way back with the O'Connells, deposited $2,500 in cash as bail for Shea. Chief Collins was later indicted, but that's another matter. O'Connell was nothing if not loyal and he tried to pull judicial strings to beat the rap for Shea. O'Connell hired Albany attorney Robert E. Whalen, a politically connected lawyer whom Dan referred to as "Sir Robert."

Here's another conversation intercepted from the wiretap on O'Connell's phone between Judge Schenck and Dan. It took place on January 27, 1944

Schenck: "Hello, Dan?"

O'Connell: "Yeah."

Schenck: "This is Gil, Gil Schenck."

O'Connell: "How are you, my boy?"

Schenck: "Well, they kind of threw me to the wolves, Dan."

O'Connell: "Yeah."

Schenck: "Well, it's all we could do."

O'Connell: "Yeah."

Schenck: "How's everything?"

O'Connell: "Oh, I see Whalen's judge became leader of the Bar Association."

Schenck: "Yes."

O'Connell: "That's all he needs."

Schenck: "And the leader of the Judicial Section."

O'Connell: "Umh'm."

Schenck: "If I had had his vote, there would have been no appeal, you know."

O'Connell: "Uh?"

Schenck: "If I . . . If he had given me his vote, there would have been no appeal."

O'Connell: "I know it."

Schenck: "You couldn't have had an appeal."

O'Connell: "I know it."

Schenck: "Bob will tell you all about it."

O'Connell: "Yeah, well I am going to see him tomorrow."

Schenck: "Well, I did the best I could, and there were two good fellows with me."

O'Connell: "Okeydoke, big boy."

With such explosive, damning and irrefutable evidence of manipulation of judges, the reasonable reader might assume Dewey finally bagged his quarry. But Dan was a wily old fox. He'd been hit, but he crawled off, licked his wounds and regained his strength. And plotted his counterattack. In his stage play, *Grand View*, William Kennedy makes this political blackmail by Dan a central theme of his drama. In his non-fiction book, *O Albany!* Kennedy wrote that his interviews with Charlie Ryan – a key machine official who was working in the state comptrollers' office during the Dewey investigation – revealed that some top Republicans in the Legislature were receiving checks from a western New York firm that was performing contract services for the comptroller. Ryan told Kennedy the people who were getting the checks did not always live or work where they said they lived or worked and sometimes names of relatives such as children were on the checks. Ryan said he had a stack of the checks, complete with signatures of major Republican players in Dewey's inner circle. Ryan said O'Connell told him to call O'Connell's house, knowing the phone was tapped, and lay it on thick for Dewey that the machine would start their own investigation of the fraudulent check kickback scheme. Shortly afterward, according to what Ryan told Kennedy, Dewey and Dan agreed through intermediaries that each would call off their respective investigations and a truce was declared.

Leo O'Brien, syndicated political *Times Union* columnist and the dean of Capitol Hill reporters, told Kennedy a different version. O'Brien was well connected to state politicos and a close personal friend of Dan O'Connell's who covered Dewey as a newsman and was on a first-name basis with the governor. He also happened to live next door to Jim Hagerty, press secretary for Dewey. O'Brien's allegiances were divided. "The worse thing you can imagine is two people you think a lot of, out to crucify one another," O'Brien told Kennedy in March, 1982. "And then to find yourself in the middle is not a happy situation. But it got to a point, at the most delicate time, they had to have somebody both sides would trust, and I happened to be the guy. I wanted the damned investigations ended, not only of the O'Connells but of people on the other side." O'Brien related to Kennedy how he was dispatched to meet Dewey at the governor's private residence in Pawling, New York, driven by troopers in a state car, for a top-secret negotiating session in late fall, 1945. Dewey said he wanted to end the investigation "on condition that Mike Smith and Jack Murphy [party officials under indictment for misappropriating party funds] plead guilty and take suspended sentences," O'Brien said. O'Brien told Kennedy he countered to Dewey that Murphy was sick with cancer and Smith was outside the machine's control and also mentioned Dan had the dope on one of Dewey's investigators who held a no-show state job while in law school. Then, according to O'Brien, Dewey said: "I don't want to drop one investigation and have another one pick up." O'Brien said that was fine with O'Connell and rushed back to tell Dan of the deal. O'Brien met Dan on the steps of the Albany Elks Club. O'Brien said, "The investigation is over – provided, if the one is closed you won't keep the other one going." Dan replied, "That's easy enough."

Kennedy reported that the gist of this story wasn't made public until after Dewey died when Dan O'Connell, in a rare interview, recounted for Ernie Tetrault of WRGB-TV in 1971 the Dewey deal this way: "O'Brien came in after the investigation with the proposal that if I got some of 'em to plead guilty . . . he'd close the whole thing up. I said I wouldn't ask anybody to plead guilty to anything. We're not guilty of it anyway. So Dewey said . . . if I didn't back into his legislature with my district attorney he'd drop the whole matter . . . I said that's all right with me. I ain't got no ax to grind with the legislature or anybody else. So we got along fine from then on." Kennedy later asked Dan what he thought of Dewey. "He's a tough little bastard," O'Connell said.

O'Brien's take on Dewey dropping the investigation had less to do with fear or intimidation from O'Connell and more to do with the fact that it had gone on too long, produced too little, cost too much, and that the public tide had turned completely against it. Also, O'Brien said Dewey's P.R. men and his advisers on the presidential trail were counseling him to drop the Albany investigation. "You're riding a pretty tired horse," one of Dewey's advisers said.

On August 18, 1945, even before the deal was cut, the handwriting was on the wall when the state's highest legal tribunal, the Court of Appeals, by a vote of four to three, dismissed indictments against Corning, Acting Mayor Harris and other top Albany officials. James J. McGuinness, Albany corporation counsel, cleared of all charges by the vote, turned to Latin. "*Res ipsa loquitur*," he said of the ruling ("The thing speaks for itself.") Also cleared were Whalen ("Sir Robert" to Dan), the Albany attorney, and Frank J. Cassidy, superintendent of water rent delinquencies. The trio said in a joint statement: "After ten months of futile occupation of their community by invasion forces, the taxpayers of Albany may well regard this as V-A, Victory in Albany, Day." There was rejoicing in the streets and in the ward leader warrens. The celebration reached new heights when Albany's beloved G.I.-Mayor made his triumphant return to City Hall, still in uniform, on September 20, 1945, combat decorated, coming out as a private, the same rank he went in, having served with distinction in the Army's infantry for eighteen months. Corning held his head high and made no reference to the investigation, as if it never happened, but certainly relished rubbing the governor's nose in his war hero status. For his part, Dewey tucked tail between legs and beat a hasty retreat, de-fanged, a bulldog no more. Dewey pulled the plug on the machine investigation and also the probe he had simultaneously waged against corruption in the Legislature. Three days after Corning's return from the war, The Gannett News Service announced on September 24, 1945 the curtain's fall on Dewey's drama: "With their funds, which have aggregated nearly $600,000 practically gone, the two special prosecutors and their grand juries ordered by Governor Dewey to expose and punish the iniquities of legislators and public officers are about ready to fold their tents, which have been pitched in the shadow of the state Capitol for two years, and move away." Further vindication for Corning and the machine arrived on November 23, 1945, when the truckload of official records seized by Dewey's investigators was returned to the mayor at City Hall. Although the official expenditure of Dewey's attempt to break the power of the machine was tabulated at about $350,000, Kennedy, citing unspecified sources, said the cost, when factoring in Dewey's use of state services, workers and police, surpassed $1 million. The quarry Dewey bagged for this bounty was abysmal: fifty-two indictments of which thirty-eight people – all small fry and mostly jailbirds already – pleaded guilty, but only to misdemeanor election-law violations. There were no, zero, nada, zip jury convictions. All the big fish got away.

Special Prosecutor Monaghan made a half-hearted attempt to save face with a parting shot across Dan O'Connell's bow, but Dewey's investigation of the machine was an unmitigated disaster, going out with a whimper instead of the bang Dewey envisioned. Monaghan said: "The jury system of Albany County was found to be completely under the control of the dominant local political machine, which has been in power for nearly a quarter of a century. It was so contrived as to ensure that the judicial system could be made to serve the machine's purposes as occasion arose." Monaghan was making excuses for why he failed to get any major convictions. The scalps of Dan and Erastus and all the rest remained intact. John J. Murphy, treasurer of the Albany County Democratic Committee, indicted on twenty-nine counts of embezzlement, had his case postponed because of sickness. Murphy died of cancer on October 15, 1945. On January 15, 1946, the Judiciary Committee rendered its report, severely censuring Judge Schenck for his conduct. The "big boy" caught consorting with the boss on the O'Connell wiretaps got off with a wrist slap when the committee failed to recommend impeachment or removal. In an attempt to police its own, the New York State Bar Association formed a special committee to investigate Judge Schenck. The internal probe ruled the judge had breached his judicial privilege in his conversation with O'Connell. The committee found in Schenck "political passion burning most fiercely" and a judge neither independent nor unbiased in the Shea case he discussed with his political boss. "The strength of our judicial system is public confidence. The conduct of Judge Schenck was peculiarly of a kind to weaken and impair," the State Bar Association committee concluded. A second verbal wrist slap, as it were, but no formal action was taken to censure Judge Schenck and the machine continued to manipulate the judiciary with impunity. Business as usual.

Surprisingly, after years of hunkering down in their bunkers during Dewey's relentless assault, the machine's lieutenants were gracious in victory. They didn't crow in the press about their successful defense against Dewey's dogs of war. They accepted their stunning win in restrained silence. *Res ipsa loquitur.* Dan O'Connell issued the only statement: "If the city wasn't well administered they would have shouted it – but they found nothing." Corning recognized the historical importance of the Dewey investigation. He saved fourteen folders of Dewey material in his personal papers donated to the Albany Institute of History and Art. By the way, after Dewey had shot his wad, Corning was reelected mayor in 1945 with a plurality of 36,122 – the biggest victory of his career. *Res ipsa loquitur,* indeed.

The machine was at the height of its power after World War II. Dewey arrived in Albany in wartime with extraordinary momentum, riding a national wave of publicity, and it looked like nothing could stop him. Dan and Erastus did. Other reformers in the capital city would try over the years to chop down the machine's broad, mighty branches of power. But none matched the intense attack of Dewey, and the machine, realizing it had faced down its most formidable foe in the little man from Owosso, sensed they had little to fear from future prosecutors.

One of the machine's claims to fame and a matter of pride on which they campaigned was their assurance that they had kept organized crime out of Albany. Never mind that Solly O'Connell controlled the numbers, horse race wagering and other gambling opportunities for the machine. That seemed like splitting hairs to the O'Connells and Corning. Mayor Corning wrote to U.S. Sen. Estes Kefauver (D-Tennessee) on August 12, 1950 when Kefauver had solicited a statement from Corning as chairman of the Senate's Special Committee to Investigate Organized Crime in

Interstate Commerce. Corning wrote: "Twenty-six months of intensive, ruthless and bitterly partisan 'investigation,' instigated by Governor Dewey, have demonstrated that Albany is exceptionally free from organized crime. . . . It is my considered opinion that organized criminals seldom carry on their activities in Albany. I am confident that if any such activities do ever occur they are vigorously hunted down by our law enforcement agencies, and that there is no connivance whatsoever on the part of our police."

In 1959, state Comptroller Arthur Levitt, a Democrat with a reputation for bipartisan scrutiny and investigatory toughness, stuck his nose into Corning's business and the mayor bit it off. Corning wrote to Levitt: "In the first place, it wastes the time of public officials. In the second place, it casts doubts on their integrity where no such doubts should exist. In the third place, it tends to destroy the confidence in your office that has been built up over many years by former state comptrollers."

Corning may have put Levitt in his place, but the mayor's old nemesis from Maine, Nelson Rockefeller, would be a different opponent. When Rockefeller won the governor's seat in 1959, knocking out Gov. W. Averell Harriman after just three years of Democratic control, Rockefeller almost immediately went after his Northeast Harbor chum. Corning and Rockefeller had known each other since boyhood, playing tennis and sailing at the same private Maine club. Rockefeller set the State Investigation Commission (SIC) onto Corning's tail and never let up, although during Rocky's fifteen-year occupation of the Executive Mansion, the SIC was more like a pesky schnauzer nipping at Corning's heels than like Dewey's pit bulls. Rockefeller and Corning had common ground, after all, compared with Dewey's visceral hatred toward the Albany machine. Both Nelson and Erastus were bluebloods and even when they were doing battle politically, there was an undercurrent of civility and class simpatico. Still, Rocky wasted no time. Corning appeared before the SIC on December 1, 1960 at the Capitol. It was a public hearing into unspecified allegations and was never acknowledged by the mayor or reported in the press. Corning did reply to SIC chairman Jacob Grumet, however, prior to a second public hearing on December 14, 1960. Corning said he'd gladly send Grumet a copy of the mayor's annual budget if Grumet sent him a check for ten dollars to cover the cost of photocopying and handling. Take that, Nelson.

Corning couldn't keep the SIC's probe private for long. Grumet told the press the SIC investigators were looking into "the extraordinary real estate tax delinquencies on the Albany County tax rolls, as well as the policies, procedures and practices by which county real estate taxes are compromised." Specifically, real estate tax delinquencies in Albany County at the end of 1959 totaled $7.9 million, greater than the entire collected 1959 county general tax roll of $7.3 million. Back to you, Erastus. Corning had to fire off some response, even the inane we've-always-done-favors-for-our-friends rationale. Corning said in a statement: "I wish to reiterate that this program of handling tax delinquency in Albany County is a program of some fifteen years' standing. It is a program that is progressing in an orderly fashion. It is a program that I heartily recommend being continued as a good program." And besides, Corning added, other counties across New York state had delinquent tax rolls of comparable size. Go investigate them was the unspoken admonition.

This SIC deal was beginning to take on the tones of a bad Northeast Harbor badminton match. Indeed, the long, drawn-out, back-and-forth shot making would stretch out as long as Rockefeller occupied the Executive Mansion, from 1959 to 1973. The SIC probe also coincided with Corning's lengthy challenges and roadblocks put up to stall Rockefeller's grandiose concept for the South Mall. Corning fought the governor over the project and Rockefeller returned the favor with the continuing SIC investigation – a couple of outsized political shuttlecocks being slammed back and forth. The SIC wasn't just lobbing soft shots at Corning, who took the SIC investigations seriously enough to keep files on each one. The 1960 inquiry also centered on Corning's insurance firm, Albany Associates, and its role as stockholder in the development of a parking garage, Albany Parking Inc. at 536-538 Broadway, which won a tax delinquency compromise. Corning sidestepped questions about the Albany Associates linkage, but defended the parking lot as "a genuine community effort which saved the taxpayers of Albany from erecting this garage at a cost of $600,000."

Furthermore, the SIC pointed the finger at high-ranking machine officials. Donald L. Lynch, county treasurer, formed the Erly Development Corp. with the family of state Senator Julian B. Erway and through it compromised a $6,438 delinquency on Washington Avenue extension land for $3,850. On a $15,000 investment, the corporation realized in 1960 a $29,000-a-year income by leasing land for the Thruway Motel and Hellman Theater. Nice deal, if you can get it. Other friends of the machine did. Albert J. Field received tax compromises on parcels of land leased for a parking lot held by Field's own Fromfield Inc. and on Jolbar, the corporation of County Judge Martin Schenck, who had been Field's attorney. Grumet's SIC report also cited "evidence which indicated inefficiency, laxity and incompetence in the administration of the Purchasing Agent's office." Those called before the SIC, pleaded the fifth and declined to give testimony. They included: William Cronin, president of Colony Market Inc.; Edmund D. Kenny, president of Kenny Paper Supply Co.; George B. Beatty, Beatty Supply Co. and John Dawson, deputy purchasing agent.

Corning's own conflicts of interest were sometimes so extensive and transparent as to be absurdly comical. One such instance was a historic preservation battle that began heating up in the spring of 1968. Three historic buildings on Elk Street were to be torn down to make way for new headquarters for the New York State Bar Association. Mayor Corning grappled with competing loyalties regarding the project. Corning's mother, Louise Corning, led the charge to preserve the early nineteenth-century structures and appeared at public hearings. Mrs. Corning had reasons close to her heart for pushing for preservation, since this was the famous stretch of Albany's elegant townhouses where the Pruyns, Cornings, Parkers, Rathbones, Lansings, Van Rensselaers, Thachers and others of the city's ruling elite lived in nineteenth-century splendor. Also, one of the buildings, 4 Elk Street, was built by former President Martin Van Buren. Its historic importance was lessened since Van Buren never lived there, renting it out instead as an income property. The building was known as "Marty's three-walled building" because the wall of the structure next door was used as the building's fourth wall. The mayor appointed his wife, Betty, to look into preservation issues as a special adviser to the Albany Housing Historic Commission. On the other side of Capitol Park, however, Rockefeller's cousin, Alexander Aldrich, executive director of the Hudson River Valley Commission (which Corning had begun as a state senator in 1936), pushed for action on behalf of the Bar Association and said any delay of demolition plans could only last for thirty days. Corning said: "I believe public opinion can and should be marshaled to save these three buildings. What we have here is something we must preserve at all costs. The old buildings we have in Albany are very few. We must do what we can to save them."

Corning's longtime pal and political associate, Jake Herzog, was hired to represent the Bar Association, which was evicting the tenants in those Elk Street buildings. Also, Herzog said in an interview that the Bar Association paid him a fee to lobby Corning about the assessment. "I met with Erastus and he said he was friends with a lot of lawyers and judges and he didn't want to screw the Bar Association. We ended up agreeing on a total of $175,000 for the assessment for a building worth a couple of million dollars when it was all done," Herzog said. The assessment sailed through and, as a compromise, the Bar Association preserved the Elk Street building facades and demolished and overhauled the back space for offices. In fact, the view from Columbia Street on the east side reveals a modernistic jumble of geometric forms for the New York Bar Association's law center. These days, the gray stone exterior of the new portion looks serene enough, but it wasn't always so. Herzog recalled that a few months after construction began, trouble walked in. "The SIC guys appeared in my office one day with ledgers and badges and wanted to know about the assessment on behalf of Gov. Rockefeller," Herzog recalled. "So, I called up Erastus and he told me to come right over to his office. We sat there a couple of hours and planned our answers to the SIC and worked out a five-page answer sheet. When we were done, Corning said, 'Jake, you created a masterpiece' He didn't give out accolades easily, but we never heard another word about it from the SIC."

The SIC quietude was short-lived. In 1972, Rockefeller directed his investigatory arm to reach more strongly and more deeply into the O'Connell-Corning machine than ever before. They went digging for dirt. Literally. "SIC Quiz Broadens To Landfill" was the headline in the *Times Union* on June 23, 1972. The article noted that the SIC probe of Albany's City Hall was now "a far-reaching affair that will include examination of most city purchasing and operation of the controversial landfill." Investigators thought they had a smoking gun in Corning's relationship with Albany Supply & Equipment, which was found to have made "inordinately high" markups on goods it sold the city. The smoking gun came in the form of a little black notebook with coded entries kept by the company's president, William M. Graulty, whose markings next to the names of present and former city officials were said to represent the amounts of cash gift kickbacks, according to press accounts of the charges. Graulty retained the Albany law firm DeGraff, Foy, Conway & Holt-Harris.

At this juncture, Rocky seemed to have Erastus on the ropes. The SIC had evidence of 500 percent markups on some goods, with one contractor charging $232,000 above list price during a three-year period and another contractor awarded $700,000 without competitive public bidding. Jimmy Ryan, county purchasing agent, took the brunt of the SIC attack, including one investigator branding Albany County "the worst-run county in America." Those words were seared into large type on the front page of both Albany dailies. Corning made his own headlines when he testified once more before the SIC on December 21, 1972. He'd used the strategy to perfection with Dewey and he'd try it once more. He played dumb. And dumber. "Corning: It's News To Me" was the *Times Union* headline on December 12, 1972.

Corning set the tone at the outset. The investigator asked: "Mr. Mayor, what is your position?" Corning responded, "In what fashion?" To the question as to how the Democratic Party raised its funds, Corning answered, "I don't know." To the query of whether city street workers only put in abbreviated days, Corning answered, "I don't know." When asked if it was true, as the newspapers had reported, that many vendors kept their city bills under the $500 non-bidding maximum, Corning answered, "I don't know."

The irony hung as thick as cigar smoke in the packed gallery of the Court of Claims hall in the South Mall where Corning delivered his umpteenth SIC performance. Represented by Assistant Corporation Counsel, Polly N. Rutnik, daughter of Polly Noonan, Corning's longtime political associate, the mayor gave another Oscar-caliber performance. Corning wore his typically somber gray wool pinstriped suit, but it might just as well have been made of Teflon. Nothing stuck that afternoon.

Some of Corning's testimony has gone down in the annals of Albany political history in the glibness hall of fame. When the investigator asked, "What is Mr. O'Connell's position at this time in the County of Albany?" Corning said, "He is a citizen." When Corning was asked how city catch basins were cleaned before a no-bid contract was granted, the mayor replied: "Not very well." Then came the James Ryan passage that Corning elevated to the level of sublime comedy, worthy of the mayor's own pat phrase to clear his office of a person pitching an idea. "Elegant!" the mayor would say, tipping off the visitor his audience with the king was over. And elegant the Ryan parry and thrust was, as inspired as Abbott and Costello's Who's On First? routine.

Q: "Mr. Mayor, do you know James Ryan?"

A: "James Bryan?"

Q: "Ryan, R-Y-A-N."

A: "Yes, James Ryan; yes, I do."

Q: "How long have you known James Ryan, Mr. Mayor?"

A: "Oh, I would say perhaps twenty years, perhaps twenty-five."

Q: "What does Mr. Ryan do for a living, Mr. Mayor?"

A: "I don't know."

Q: "You have known this man for twenty years, Mr. Mayor, and you are not aware of what he does for a living or a livelihood?"

A: "I don't know."

Another favorite Corning ploy, honed during the Dewey investigation, was the splitting of semantic hairs as a way of keeping the inquisitor off balance and sputtering like a fool. The SIC probe had turned up astounding cost overcharges and the suggestion of kickbacks to machine officials by letting the no-bid contracts to pet contractors. There was the case of Albany Supply & Equipment's $1,200 broom ($224 retail) sold to the city; and a battered Jeep valued at $800 used by North End Contracting Co. at the city's landfill rented to the city at a cost of $988 per month. Corning, a one-man City Hall, professed to know nothing of this, of course, despite the fact that he micro-managed every single department in the city and knew where every fire hydrant and manhole cover was located. The transcript revealed the mayor's classic obfuscation:

Q: "Mr. Mayor, were these not, in fact, cost-plus contract arrangements?"

A: "Would you please repeat that question? I don't know. You are getting this double negative in, and I don't know whether to answer that question yes or no."

Q: "The question was: Were they cost-plus arrangements?"

A: "He said, 'Were they not.'"

Q: "Let's try this question. Were they cost-plus arrangements?"

A: "Yes."

Q: "Is it not a fact, Mr. Mayor, that as a result of increasing his costs, the contractor we are referring to would increase his profits?"

A: "This is the same question, Mr. Curran. He puts through another not in here and I don't know whether to answer him yes or no."

Q: "Does the cost increase the profits?"

A: "That again. You are doing the same thing."

Q: "As the costs increase, do the profits increase?"

A: "I don't know."

Corning was at his most obstreperous when the questioning turned personal and investigators tried to nail the mayor on the matter of personal income and conflict-of-interest. So entertaining were these exchanges that they were excerpted in both the *Times Union* and *Knickerbocker News.* Corning, as he had done with Dewey, won over the partisan gallery viewers with his saucy sarcasm.

Q: "Mr. Mayor, how much income did you receive from the insurance agency of which you are president?"

A: "I have no idea."

Q: "Are you sure you have no idea as to how much income you receive?"

A: "You asked me at the private hearing. I didn't know then and I don't know now. I didn't look."

Q: "Mr. Mayor, you are unable to tell me how much income you received for the year 1971 from Albany Associates?"

A: "That is correct."

Q: "Have you had an opportunity between the time of your private hearing and today to look this fact up?"

A: "I could have looked if I wanted. You didn't ask me to find the information."

Q: "Could you give me the total amount of salary and other payments that you received during the year 1971?"

A: "No."

Corning's performance drew thumbs-up reviews from spectators. The *Times Union* headline was, "Corning Fan: You're A Cool Cat, Mayor." A man had walked up to the mayor outside the hearing chambers afterward and chuckled as he shook Corning's hand and said, "You're a cool cat, mayor. You're okay." That was the general consensus. "At least ten different times during the testimony laughter rocked the gallery," according to the *Times Union*. "Most of the time the mayor and his two lawyers were laughing with the crowd. The sixty-three-year-old star witness held his eyeglasses in his hands for part of the question-and-answer period and sat with folded hands twirling his thumbs for the remainder."

Corning left the hearing in the South Mall, returned to City Hall and went ahead with his weekly press conference as scheduled. For the reporters, he compared the SIC affair to a "one-way street . . . they can attack you, but you can't answer." But Corning was about to turn those tables. A month after the hearing, in January, Corning said, "I think the nicest thing you can say about the SIC is it's a benign sort of parasite." A year later, in the fall of 1973, Corning was ripping the SIC as "a poor circus, a second-rate circus" and SIC Chairman Paul C. Curran as "a professional hatchet man." The SIC made a half-hearted attempt at looking into alleged corruption in the Albany Police Department, but their efforts were stonewalled every step of the way. All chairman Curran could do was to whine in the press. "Mayor Corning is in the wings and orchestrating an effort to obstruct" the SIC probe, Curran said, accusing the mayor of "dilatory tactics" and "bad faith."

Corning dropped the petty name-calling phase in favor of legislative action. He wrote to Governor Rockefeller on October 14, 1973, calling the SIC "un-American" and proposing six changes to the investigatory body the mayor claimed he would take up with Albany legislators and urge them to sponsor as bills. Furthermore, Corning said he planned to challenge the constitutionality of the SIC, which he characterized as "an unnecessary fifth wheel."

Rockefeller's SIC probes never managed to strike down Northeast Harbor foe Corning and boss O'Connell, which is what Rocky, like Dewey, so fervently desired. But it did manage to cloud City Hall for several years, hanging on like a bad flu that seemed, little by little, to infect the loyal electorate with seeds of doubt. The Rockefeller crew did manage to slap egg on Corning's face in regard to the Albany Supply overcharges and the notebook's secret codes, as well as for the sweet deal given ward leader William Carey and his North End Contracting Co. for running the city landfill. Carey was charged with grand larceny and offering false instruments. In exchange for Corning agreeing to terminate North End's contract for the landfill (as well as North End's deal for snow removal and sewer cleaning work) and the company reimbursing cost discrepancies and paying fines, Carey would walk. That was the deal. Everyone walked, eventually. But enough damage had been done to give Corning his first real scare in thirty years as mayor. Republican political newcomer Carl Touhey, an articulate, intelligent millionaire businessman with Ivy League credentials and a well-financed campaign for mayor, rode the SIC clouds of aspersions to within an eyelash of a stunning, historic upset over Corning in 1973. Actually, under vote fraud allegations, Corning defeated Touhey by just 3,500 votes, the smallest margin of victory for Corning in eleven terms. The relentless grind of the SIC probe had apparently worn down some voters and the machine seemed less invincible. Outwardly, the king retained his self-assured smugness. Corning delighted in clipping and saving ads for his campaign against Touhey positioned in the *Times Union* next to an ad for "Ex-Lax. The Chocolate Laxative. No Better Laxative At Any Price!" And, in another suspiciously juxtaposed advertisement in the *Times Union*, Corning's campaign ad ran next to one for Niagara Mohawk with the copy line, "Change Over To Natural Gas." Having survived the unthinkable – defeat – Corning was back to his old earthy humor. Life went on for the mayor, despite Rockefeller's, and Touhey's, attempts to topple him from power. Corning was still at the old stand in City Hall when Rockefeller and his extravagant modern art collection moved out of the Executive Mansion after the governor resigned on December 18, 1973, retiring to private life – a retirement interrupted eight months later when President Gerald Ford appointed Rockefeller Vice-President.

However, what Dewey and Rockefeller couldn't accomplish, namely enough public disgrace and negative opinion to cause Albany voters to turn Corning out of City Hall, the mayor nearly brought upon himself. Multiple SIC investigations could not compare to the negative publicity Corning received for the largest personal misstep of his political career, an arrest for driving while intoxicated that made headlines across the country in 1967. The mayor's DWI arrest was big news, a series of events shrouded in mystery and reconstructed as follows.

Mayor Corning, ever the consummate politician, put on his charming patrician poker face and displayed his usual gallantry at an obligatory appearance he wanted to skip on October 28, 1967, yet another Saturday night gala. The job required him to attend dozens of these functions each year. This endless grind of political appearances, forty-two years worth, three or four nights a week without fail, kept him away from his wife and children and took its toll on the mayor. This gala at the Thruway House on the Washington Avenue Extension – Corning's dream road, the project he pushed through, bringing development to the city's once-wild western border on the edge of the Pine Bush – was a particularly onerous affair. It was the annual Page One Ball of the Albany Newspaper Guild, attended by the reporters and editors of the *Times Union* and *Knickerbocker News*, which had been taking potshots at Corning and launching their own investigations into his administration all year long in an attempt to pin charges of corruption on the Albany Democratic machine. Corning, as the official mouthpiece of boss Dan O'Connell, had been feuding openly with the Hearst papers for years, pulling hundreds of thousands of dollars of city legal ads in a hardball move when relations grew more strained than usual. Despite the battles with the press, Corning apparently tried to heed his father, the lieutenant governor, who gave this political advice to his son: "Never pick a fight with someone who buys ink by the barrel." And so, here was Corning at the Page One Ball, which must have approximated the feeling of undergoing root canal for the mayor. And, before the night was over, it would place the only public smirch beside Corning's reputation in a long run of political life.

To such events as the newspaper gala, Corning generally went alone, or was accompanied by Polly Noonan, but never with his wife, who had refused from the beginning of their marriage to play the role of trophy wife at political functions. The Newspaper Guild gala was another routine mayoral ritual for Corning: don a subdued business suit, arrive fashionably late, pretend not to hear the buzz sweep through the room at your arrival, paste on a warm smile, press the flesh for thirty minutes or so, sip a Scotch and nibble on the hors d'oeuvres, listen to requests for favors and stay positive without committing, and, finally, try to glide out unnoticed before the sit-down dinner and dreary speeches began. This night, since he was facing his tormentors, the press, he sought moral support.

"He had asked me to go that night, but I was tired and didn't feel like going," recalled Polly Noonan. "He came over to our house that evening anyway. . . . He and Peter [Noonan's husband] had a couple of Scotches and watched a ballgame on TV. 'Geez Erastus, don't ruin that damn Scotch with water,'" Peter Noonan told Corning as the mayor fixed himself a tumbler of Dewar's with a splash of water for himself and one neat for Noonan, recalled Polly Noonan, who said that was her husband's standard joke when Erastus did the drink making. Noonan remembered that Corning's allergies and longtime lung problems had flared up that night. He was still smoking at that point, three packs a day, usually Kools. He carried an inhaler in case his lungs gave him trouble. Noonan believes Corning also was taking a prescription drug for the lung problem. "He said he was very tired, that he'd had a strenuous day and had been going to events for several nights in a row," Noonan said. "He said he had to go, though, and asked me to go once more. I said no, so he left and went to the party."

Francis "Doc" Rivett, a *Times Union* reporter who had covered everything from sports to politics at the paper since 1943, was president of the Newspaper Guild and had invited Corning. Rivett felt oddly protective of Corning that night, seeing him cornered at a table with Gene Robb, the hard-driving publisher of the Hearst papers who had taken off the gloves for the first time in the city's checkered history of newspaper *laissez-faire*, and had mounted a relentless campaign to pin evidence of corruption on Corning and the machine. "I caught the mayor's eye at Robb's table, saw he was ill at ease and brought him over to our table in a gesture of rescue, for which he thanked me," Rivett recalled. "He was drinking pretty good. I saw him have a couple of Scotches, but he really didn't show anything. After a while, he finally got up to leave." The mayor announced, "Gentlemen, it's time for me to go home." Jack Cassidy, who handled public relations for Albany Medical Center Hospital at the time and was known for his sarcastic wit, muttered in reply: "Which home, mayor?" There was a tense moment of silence, Rivett recalled, when those at the table waited to see the mayor's reaction, anticipating an explosion or rapier-quick counter strike, for the mayor surely had registered Cassidy's quip. Instead, in classic Corning style, he turned, nodded and smiled, pretending he hadn't heard, and left. Rivett figured it was around 10 p.m.

Rivett watched him leave the Thruway House, but what Corning did immediately following his departure is unclear. If he planned to return home to Corning Hill in Glenmont, the easiest route at that hour would have been to drive downtown on Washington Avenue and then cut over to Route 9W or Route 32 along the Hudson River. Or, Corning could have driven one-half mile west on Washington Avenue Extension to get on Interstate 90 and then I-787 to Route 9W. Instead, for reasons unknown, Corning drove well out of his way if Glenmont was his intended destination, and ended up on Albany-Shaker Road, between Miracle Lane and Shaker Elementary School in the vicinity of Osborne Road in the Town of Colonie. It was 11:40 p.m., nearly two hours after he left the Thruway House. Trooper A.F. Crary of Troop G of the State Police in Loudonville, spotted the mayor's personal car, a nondescript green Buick sedan, pointed eastward on Albany-Shaker Road, pulled over to the shoulder, not completely off the roadway, with the motor running and the mayor asleep at the wheel. The car was stopped along a dark, deserted stretch of the road with a ravine and woods on either side. "It was a routine traffic arrest in the normal course of duty," Trooper Crary told reporters. But there was nothing routine about the fact that the prominent mayor was charged with driving while intoxicated. Corning did not resist. "There were no incidents connected with the arrest," Crary said. Corning later submitted to a blood test at Memorial Hospital which was, by law, supposed to be taken within two hours of the arrest. It is unknown how much time elapsed between Crary's arrest and the blood test for Corning's blood-alcohol level. The presiding justice in the case, Colonie Town Justice Harry D'Agostino recalled, "He told me he had been at the newspaper party, he'd had a few drinks and that was all. I believed him. He did not appear drunk." D'Agostino asked Corning how he pleaded on the driving while intoxicated charge. "Innocent," Corning said. The mayor was released without bail in the custody of Julian Erway, the former senator and the mayor's fishing buddy. A hearing was set for November 9.

"We sort of made a game out of trying to guess the blood count on DWI arrests, but it wasn't easy," D'Agostino said. "I saw people I swore were dead drunk who, it turned out, were not and then I saw some I thought were sober and they were over the legal limit." If D'Agostino was taking bets on Corning, he would guess from observing him that night that the mayor wasn't legally drunk. But it would take the State Police laboratory a few days to analyze Corning's blood sample. Given the highly charged political matter – Corning was a kind of demigod in the Albany Democratic machine and he was now at the mercy, it would seem, of the Republican machine in Colonie – everyone bent over backwards to go by the book and to remove any hint of political hanky-panky. Corning's blood test was handled personally by the State Police laboratory director, Captain J.N. Cesaro. Cesaro signed Corning's evidence sheet, lab case 32-DD-2385, State Police Case No. 1808650 on October 30, 1967. A Dr. Orofino was listed as having taken the blood specimen.

Still, rumors of the all-powerful Corning and Democratic machine pulling strings and putting in the fix with the blood sample persist. Twenty-eight years after the incident, which D'Agostino remembered clearly, the former judge scoffed at rampant speculation that Corning's blood sample – which came in just barely below the legal limit – was doctored. "There are so many levels of checking and security on that blood work, so many people would have had to be in on something, I just don't see how tampering was possible," D'Agostino said of the rumors.

The Colonie Republicans would have exulted in something as politically devastating as a DWI conviction for Corning, but the arrest was closely scrutinized and was done by the book. "The whole thing was straightforward," D'Agostino said. "We treated the mayor like we would treat any other individual." Corning's DWI arrest, however, was covered by the Associated Press and put out on the national news wire, with the damaging allegations ending up in newspapers around the country. "I realize you have a job to do, but I have no comment," the mayor, who spoke in a calm voice according to the report, told an Associated Press reporter.

Curiously, Corning's nemesis, the *Times Union* and *Knickerbocker News*, downplayed the story – it was suggested they had a pang of guilt that it was their party at which Corning had done his drinking. The first story of the Saturday night arrest appeared in the Hearst papers on Monday. Corning was lucky the bust occurred too late to make deadline for the *Times Union*'s Sunday edition, nearly double the circulation of the rest of the week. When the story broke in Albany, it wasn't even front-page news. Both papers played it inside, on the cover of the local section, below the fold, lower right, in a place of moderate prominence. Neither of the papers mounted a serious investigation into the arrest, reporting only the routine court news and letting it drop after a total of four brief items on the arraignment and hearing.

But Corning took the matter with utmost seriousness. He had switched his legal representation from his buddy Erway to an expert in DWI cases, Earl H. Gallup Jr., a member of the Albany law firm of Whalen, McNamee, Creble and Nichols. Gallup had to sign a sworn deposition that

Erway went to the arraignment but wasn't Corning's attorney to meet legal requirements. Gallup's strategy was to get out front in the court of public opinion and push the mayor's innocence by calling a press conference five days after the arrest. Gallup said State Police laboratory analysis indicated the alcoholic concentration in the mayor's blood was eight hundredths of one per cent (0.08%). "That is less than sufficient to constitute *prima facie* evidence of a violation of the law," Gallup said. "Under the law, there must be at least .10 alcoholic content in the bloodstream to establish impairment and more than .15 to presume intoxication." "Blood Test Indicates Mayor Wasn't Tipsy, His Attorneys Say" read the *Times Union* headline.

Slick legal maneuvering by Corning, all right, and it sounded convincing, but the hearing was a week away. The mayor was unable to go about business as usual at City Hall as he had hoped. From his mailbox to his telephone to passersby on the street, Corning was reminded repeatedly of the arrest, both by supporters and detractors. For someone as guarded as Corning, a shy and profoundly private person, reliving the ordeal must have been excruciatingly embarrassing. Worst of all were notes from old pals, who read about the arrest in out-of-town papers. "'Rastus! What are you doing?" wrote Rev. Pierce Brennan, of Brooklyn, a fellow Yalie, on November 3, 1967. Many missives were sympathetic. "Re: Fate. There, but for the grace of God, go I and many others," wrote J.J. Lyons on October 31, 1967. In his letters to friends, Corning tried to appear nonchalant, shrugging off the matter as routine political harassment by Republicans in Colonie, acting as his own spin doctor in off-the-record conversations with the press.

The November 9 hearing finally arrived. A knot of reporters was staked out in front of Colonie Town Hall when Corning arrived with Gallup, his attorney, a few minutes before the 9 a.m. opening of court that Thursday. The mayor smiled at the assembled journalists, bid them a warm "Good morning" and refused to comment on the case. Corning and Gallup went into the courtroom and took their seats. Gallup made a motion to dismiss the charge on the grounds that the alcoholic concentration in the mayor's blood was .08, two hundredths of one percent below the legally allowable level of .10. "In light of the notoriety concerning this case," D'Agostino said he would make a statement. "The mayor was entitled to be treated like any other individual. In every case before me, in which a blood test has indicated less than .10 alcoholic content in the blood stream at the time of arrest, I've dismissed a charge of driving while intoxicated, either upon a motion or at my own discretion. If the alcoholic content was not sufficient to substantiate a charge of impairment, it is ridiculous to assume the defendant could have been driving while intoxicated." D'Agostino said a notice of motion for dismissal had been served by the district attorney on the commander of State Police Troop G and no papers were filed in opposition. D'Agostino then asked Trooper Crary, the arresting officer seated beside the judge, facing Corning, if he wished to oppose the motion. "No, sir," the trooper replied. D'Agostino asked Crary if he wanted to make a statement. The trooper looked directly at the mayor and said, "No, sir." D'Agostino dismissed the charge. Gallup and Corning walked out of court. The mayor told the reporters once more he would have no comment and Gallup drove off in his car with the mayor.

For Trooper Crary, the story didn't end there. He was reassigned to Malone in Essex County in a remote part of the Adirondacks near the Canadian border. Reporters immortalized the trooper who arrested the mayor in a jingle: "It's a long way for Crary to Tipperary." Corning wrote back to the Rev. Brennan on November 13, 1967, enclosing a newspaper clipping about the dismissal, "As you can see, this problem had a happy ending." But the case wasn't closed, for those who looked back on it with unanswered questions for three decades. What was Corning doing that night after the Newspaper Guild ball anyway, driving miles out of his way, getting arrested on the DWI charge two hours after he left the party? Rivett, the newspaperman, who was at the same table as Corning during the party, is certain the mayor had several drinks at the Thruway House. "I'm surprised they even found blood in the sample. He'd been drinking a lot that night," Rivett said. D'Agostino surmised, "All I can think is he got on the I-90 arterial like he was going home, apparently got fouled up, got off on Everett Road, made a wrong turn and ended up on Albany-Shaker Road." D'Agostino had no theory for a two-hour detour, however.

Polly Noonan wasn't surprised by the notion of Corning's drunkenness. "I saw Erastus drunk many times," Noonan said. "He was a happy drunk, a sleepy drunk. He'd fall asleep. He never got nasty. Up in Maine, he'd have a glass of Scotch for breakfast and I'd say, 'Erastus, you better watch out. You'll rot your liver.'" Noonan said her husband quit after a couple of drinks, but Corning kept on tossing back the Scotch and, years later, because of allergies and respiratory trouble, switched to vodka.

Rev. Joseph R. Romano, a Roman Catholic priest who was close to Dan O'Connell and was the political boss's confessor and pastor at St.

Ann's, said he has irrefutable evidence that Corning met up with a young woman that night after he left the newspaper ball. "There was a girl in the car," Romano said. "I know that for a fact. I know her family. They're in my parish. She's married now, but he picked her up that night. She had gone out with him a couple of times." Romano had no solid explanation for what happened to Corning's alleged female companion when the mayor was arrested. The DWI arrest and the notion of a young woman in the car – if, in fact, that was the case – normally would have meant the end of someone's political career once Dan O'Connell got wind of it. According to Romano: "Dan was very critical of Erastus boozing it up and womanizing, because Dan was actually straitlaced and kind of prudish when it came to church teachings. He truly considered marriage a sacrament forever and he'd kicked guys out of the Democratic Party for divorce. But Dan liked Erastus."

D'Agostino remains doubtful of Romano's scenario. "I never heard of any girl in the car and I figure I knew everything about the case," D'Agostino said. When pressed, D'Agostino conceded anything is possible, including the cover-up of a girl in the car. Polly Noonan posed a murky picture on the womanizing question. "He was a woman's man," she said. "I know he caught the eye of several women and ladies were interested in him and he in them. But I know there wasn't a woman in the car with him that night of the arrest, because he came back to my house afterward."

Noonan said she had seen Corning drunk many times, but he was not drunk that night – at least not several hours after being pulled over. The mayor told Noonan he felt lightheaded and dizzy, because of the medication, he figured, and pulled over his car to steady himself. He also told Noonan he was tired from several late nights of numerous functions and that he had a couple of drinks at the newspaper ball but was not drunk when he dozed off at the wheel of his car on the shoulder of the road.

"He stayed here a long time that night," Noonan recalled. She had him call a physician, Dr. Michael Blaise, who said Corning did not need to go to the hospital and could go home. Noonan, her husband and the mayor talked late into the night. It was perhaps 2 a.m., Noonan figured, when the mayor left, presumably for his home a short distance away. Except for the DWI arrest, it had been a typical night for the mayor, whose wife and children formed only thin bookends to his public life.

Still, to the outsider, and the voters, the Cornings lived a life of regimented upper-class domesticity. The mayor rose each morning at 6:45 a.m., listened to the 7 a.m. news on WGY radio station, perused the *New York Times* and *Times Union*, fed the family's cats and dogs and then drove to City Hall, arriving between 8 and 8:30 a.m. each morning. He went through the same routine on the morning of October 31, 1967, Halloween, when the news broke in the *Times Union* about his DWI arrest. Soon, it was all over town and around the country.

Not only was he mayor longer than anyone else in the history of American politics, but Corning was the archetypal artful dodger when it came to surviving the slings and arrows of personal indiscretion and political animus. For four decades, stretching from the Dewey probe across numerous state investigations to the DWI arrest, the mayor for life saved his elective hide on countless occasions with a masterful array of ways to wriggle out of the nooses his enemies devised for him. With his keen intellect, dry wit and *savoir-faire*, Corning sailed through troubled waters that would have capsized the careers of less seasoned skippers. Above all, Corning survived on his cult of personality and that ability to deliver to the people of Albany the government they deserved: the longest-running situation comedy in the land, on display daily at City Hall.

Chapter 8:

An Open Door to All: Mayor Corning at the Office

"I'm still at the old stand."

Mayor Corning in a letter to World War II buddy Julius Soule of Roseville, Michigan, after a thirty-five-year hiatus in their correspondence.

The old stand was a gray metal desk, a piece of generic office furniture you could find at a garage sale today for twenty dollars – or best offer. It was a World War II-vintage block of steel, with vinyl top, seven drawers, battleship gray finish, heavy enough to sink a ship. The man who sat behind that desk transformed it into a throne of power, a textbook case of urban machine politics as practiced by an undisputed master. To this humble desk arrived a steady stream of people each day for an audience with the king, from folks down on their luck seeking a few bucks, to retired machine loyalists wanting a patronage job, to presidential candidates begging for an endorsement. Behind the desk was the mayor's chair, a standard-issue, straight-backed steel structure covered in a rough, durable brown nylon tweed. The chair's vinyl-covered right armrest had worn through to the white cotton stuffing at the precise spot where Mayor Erastus Corning 2nd leaned his elbow while taking telephone calls from a black rotary phone that seemed to ring incessantly from the desk top. On the desk, Corning kept a brass desk calendar, an "In" basket in matching gray steel and a white marble pen holder. Taped to the left pull-out writing tray was a list of frequently called telephone numbers Corning had scribbled down in pencil: Doug Rutnik, Aurora Insurance, Bettina Corning Dudley, Alcove Reservoir, Maine caretaker Tom Pollard and others. Taped to the right pull-out writing tray was Corning's scrawled population statistics and tax rates for Albany compared to surrounding communities. On top of the desk, Corning kept a yellow legal pad for his correspondence.

Aside from the telephone, this notepad was the mayor's most powerful political tool.

Every year, on Christmas Eve, the mayor's secretaries, Thelma Dooley and Roberta "Bobbi" Miller, offered a Christmas gift to their boss in his City Hall office. The secretaries took a folder, walked with pomp and circumstance from their desks in the outer office to the mayor's desk in the inner sanctum, took their seats with great purpose, and began the ceremony. Thelma took the lead and spoke first. "Mayor Corning," she began, which is how Thelma always addressed him, compared to the more formal "Mister Mayor" for Bobbi. And then Thelma offered their gift: "You dictated 6,894 letters this year, Mayor Corning." The mayor smiled and discussed the number, compared it to past years. Recalled Thelma, "He was very interested in the annual tally of letters and he treated it like a record, the way he kept track of his days, months and years in office."

Each year, between 1973, when the two women were hired by Corning, and 1983, when he died – still dictating letters to Dooley and Miller surreptitiously from his intensive care unit hospital bed in defiance of doctor's orders – Mayor Corning dictated between 5,000 and 7,000 letters annually. Year after year, Dooley and Miller typed every word onto carbon paper, in triplicate. Their dueling IBM Selectric typewriters clattered through City Hall with the rapid-fire report of machine guns. The familiar staccato sound symbolized Corning's legendary punctuality in replying to queries of every stripe, with dispatch. It sounded like a downpour of metallic raindrops echoing off the barren walls of the outer office. Music to the mayor's ears. "It didn't matter who the letter was from, he'd answer it," Dooley said. "And his reply went out almost without exception the very next day after he received the letter." Corning's correspondence became the stuff of legend.

Factoring in weekends, holidays and vacations, when the mayor regularly worked but the secretaries weren't available for dictation, that was an average of twenty-five letters per day that were dictated, typed, signed by Corning and mailed – two carbons of each filed. Day in and day out, week after week, month following month, the years flowing like an endless stream of correspondence. Figuring his forty-two-year historic span in the City Hall office, the nation's longest-tenured mayor also may have been its most prodigious correspondent. That's a whopping 250,000-plus letters, more than one-quarter million missives that, laid end to end, surely would have stretched the 315-mile length of the Hudson River from its source at Lake Tear of the Clouds in the Adirondacks to its mouth in New York Harbor.

One year, the annual Christmas tally reached an all-time high, for the first time crashing through the 7,000-letter ceiling. Dooley remembered that Corning heard this miraculous number, leaned back in his chair, looped his hands behind his head in smug satisfaction, grinned broadly and told the women: "Whew! No wonder you're tired." The three marveled at this record-breaking effort a little longer before the mayor reached into his desk drawer and presented Dooley and Miller with their Christmas present. It was a check for ten dollars, the same amount the frugal mayor gave them every Christmas.

City Hall was not known for its generous remuneration. Dooley and Miller both started at an annual salary of $4,500 in the early 1970s, substantially lower than the going rate for secretaries or clerical workers in Albany's private sector, or public sector for that matter. The mayor himself was not adequately compensated. At the time he hired Dooley and Miller in 1973, Corning was making $12,500, a pittance compared to other mayors or members of the State Legislature, who were, despite their claims, part-time employees. But Corning learned from Dan O'Connell the golden rule of civil service as it related to machine politics: a thousand small, low-paying jobs spread around to voters (and by inference whole families of voters) were infinitely more useful when it came to self-preservation than controlling a dozen high-paying executive appointments. The average salary among City Hall employees, including department heads, in the early 1970s was between $7,000 and $8,000.

Working for Mayor Corning may have looked to the outside world like a seat of power and prestige, but to the employees it was their own kind of salt mine. The mayor did not engender a sense of camaraderie or playfulness in the office. He was all business and treated the work of running the city with stern efficiency, never attempting to create a mood of motivational joviality among his staff. He didn't need to groom loyalty or a sense of commitment among those who worked for him. They gave it willingly. Even the smallest nods to office etiquette common among most bosses were not followed by Corning. For instance, there was no office coffee pot. The mayor never brought in food or goodies to boost staff morale. Birthdays or holidays were not celebrated in the office. It was not a place of cookies, brownies, cakes; of office outings and lunches to mark a special date; of idle chatter around the water cooler. It wasn't that

Corning couldn't be generous. Those who worked for him suspected it was more a matter of the mayor's innate shyness. Despite the way he could charm a crowd like the most masterful politician at an official function, Corning lacked a certain social grace when it came to the small intimacies of interacting with his staff on a basic, personal level. Instead, he kept everything on a professional, aloof footing.

Not that Corning was some sort of modern-day Scrooge. He showed kindness in his own way. "He was very compassionate to me as a mother," Dooley said. "If I got a call from school to say my child was sick, the mayor would say, 'You go home, Bobbi. Your place is with your children.'" The mayor was liberal when it came to time off for his secretaries, too. If the mayor was going to be out all afternoon at a meeting or public function and Dooley and Miller were done typing the letters, Corning told them they were free to knock off early. He also gave them time off in addition to their regular vacation days if he was going fishing in Maine or on an out-of-town trip. "He said if he wasn't in the office, we didn't need to be and we liked that," Dooley recalled.

Other times, Corning asked Dooley and Miller to stay on the job when he went away and warned them to be ready to take dictation every morning. No matter where Corning went, be it fishing in Maine or to national Democratic conventions or to the hospital in the months of his long decline, Corning never failed to get in the last word. "He dictated from the Duke University Hospital as he was being prepped for his hip operation," Dooley recalled and both secretaries took dictation from the mayor at Corning Hill while he was recuperating from a 1977 hip replacement. Miller remembered taking dictation often from Maine. "He'd call us right before he got in the boat to go fishing every morning," Miller said.

The letters were in addition to hundreds of official mayoral proclamations – mostly boiler plate material, written to fit certain occasions – that Dooley and Miller typed each year. The mayor did not embrace modern technology that would have made his staff's work easier, however. Corning produced his flood of correspondence without benefit of a computer. Even in the early 1980s, when offices in Albany were routinely computerized and automated, each letter from the mayor's office was dictated directly by the mayor, signed by him, mistakes corrected with white-out, each envelope licked by one of Corning's senior citizen office fixtures, many of whom stayed longer than the furniture, those old men who inhabited the outer office and whose function, besides being envelope and stamp lickers and mail stuffers extraordinaire, was not always evident.

But like his ancient and humble office furnishings and the creaky, labor-intensive methods of his operation at City Hall, Mayor Corning had established a workaday ritual rooted in forty-two years of daily minutiae and tedium. His basic principles and work ethic never wavered. An apt job description can be found in Corning's comments at a testimonial dinner in 1966 to mark the mayor's twenty-fifth year in office. He said: "No one who wanted to see me was turned away. Never was a letter addressed to me not read by me and answered by me. I never failed to talk to someone on the phone. I have done my best within my ability to recognize the problems of the people of this city and to work with the people to solve their problems."

He stayed true to that guiding philosophy by an almost mulish devotion to routine and sameness without end. This is how it went day in and day out at Mayor Corning's office. The mayor was often the first one to work, arriving a little after 8 a.m. most mornings. Dooley and Bill Keefe, Corning's executive assistant, got in around 8:15 a.m. Miller came at 8:30 a.m. "The men," as they were called, appeared a little after 9 a.m. Corning never allowed a coffee pot in the office, so if you needed a quick java fix, you bought a cup of joe from the blind man with the snack stand in the City Hall Rotunda. His business came from untold senior citizens with hard-luck stories Corning put on the payroll and allowed to linger around City Hall without purpose. As soon as Miller arrived, the mayor summoned the two secretaries for the morning's dictation. It was 8:30 a.m. and Corning had his battle plan already laid out for the day.

"His ritual was always the same," Miller remembered. "On the right hand side of his desk was a yellow legal pad. Next to that was a stack of mail. He'd dictate a response. Flip over that letter he was replying to. Cross the name off his list on the legal pad. Dictate. Flip over another letter. Cross a name off the list. This went on and on. The dictation lasted an hour or more. And when he got through the pile and crossed off the last name, he'd look up at us and say, 'OK, I'm done.'" After he announced he was finished, the mayor often would stand up and lace his thumbs through the belt loops on his suit pants. "He liked to do that with his thumbs when he was satisfied or just thinking hard," Miller said. There were other signals the secretaries knew to read and heed. Recalled Miller, "If he looked up over the top of his reading glasses after you were done talking, gave a little smile and said, 'Elegant!' you knew that you were done and he meant for you to leave."

There were times when Miller and Dooley doubted the accuracy of their shorthand, no matter how many "elegants" the mayor tossed their way. Dooley remembered noticing a $2,000 donation to a certain social services organization, the same group to whom the mayor had sent a similar amount a few months before. Figuring there might be a mix-up, she brought the duplication to Corning's attention. "Thanks for saving me some money," Corning told her after consulting his checkbook ledger. "Do I get a cut?" Dooley asked. "Not on your life," replied the thankful, but ever-frugal Corning.

Dooley and Miller, who had alternated during the dictation round, took their steno pads with the letters copied down in shorthand, returned to their desks and started their IBM Selectrics hammering through the stack of correspondence. The typing usually consumed the entire afternoon. The workload would have been even heavier if they didn't escape speech duty. "He didn't have us type many speeches, because he had been giving so many speeches for so long, he usually just said something off the top of his head," Dooley recalled.

Even in the fiercest stress of the job – being mayor was only one of many balls he kept in the air at once, from the insurance business to machine politics, from his family and private affairs – Corning never lost his cool at the office. "Things could get very stressful around the office and he never raised his voice to me once," Miller said. "Never," Dooley concurred. "He was wonderful to work with even under the most intense pressure."

Corning remained grounded in an earthy sense of humor that could make the women blush. The mayor took great delight in allowing the women to examine his natural history collection courtesy of his longtime Maine fishing guide, Gary Cobb. They looked like half of a turkey's wishbone. They were bones, all right, the infrastructure that maintained erections in wild animals such as raccoons and woodchucks. "My pecker bones," Corning used to tell startled visitors with the self-conscious chuckle of a Grotonian pulling a third form prank that would earn a black mark from the masters. "Oh, sure, he could be raunchy," Dooley said. The same man who carried pecker bones, including a couple of tiny ones in his wallet, also on special formal occasions wore his Phi Beta Kappa key on his pocketwatch chain. A study in contradictions.

After the morning's correspondence was finished, Corning made his daily phone call to Otto Fausel at Albany Associates, Corning's insurance firm. He was briefed on the day's business by Otto and gave orders to the Army buddy who had marched off to World War II with Corning. The mayor directed from City Hall all the major transactions and important deals at Albany Associates, a multi-million dollar insurance firm that was prosperous in large measure because of its contracts with Albany County. Otto Fausel ran the day-to-day operations with Corning's morning guidance. After taking care of the insurance business, most days Corning had his driver – first, Russ Endres, and, from 1973 on, John "Dusty" Miller – drive him up to Dan O'Connell's house on Whitehall Road, the machine's unofficial headquarters. In the summer months, Dan held court at his camp on Beaver Dam Road in the Helderbergs just outside Thacher Park. After giving orders for his Albany Associates employees each morning, the roles were reversed and Corning was on the receiving end from the boss. "Sometimes, as he was heading out, the mayor would mutter something like, 'I'm going to get my orders,'" Dooley recalled.

Uncle Dan was not verbose, the meetings often lasting just five or ten minutes. But these brief, face-to-face political strategy sessions were necessary. Dan didn't like doing political business on the phone after being burned during the Dewey investigations of 1943 by phone taps. "Dan never came into the mayor's office and he never called," Dooley said.

After the quick run to Whitehall Road, Corning was driven directly back to the office. It was mid-morning. He'd take some phone calls; see some visitors; give his commissioners, little more than departmental figureheads, their marching orders; perhaps put in an appearance at some ribbon-cutting or smile for a ceremonial photo opportunity at City Hall. At precisely ten minutes to noon, the mayor would summon his driver. "You could set your watch by it," Dooley recalled. That time was sacrosanct. Nothing, not even pressing city business, got in the way of the dutiful son making his daily visit to his sickly mother, Louise Corning, in Eden Park Nursing Home on Holland Avenue, just off Delaware Avenue. Erastus Corning had always been close to his mother and he stayed that way during her final months in convalescence before her death in 1976. The mayor did it quietly, never making a fuss of his daily devotion. After his visit with his mother, Corning usually had his driver take him to the Fort Orange Club, where he ate lunch most days. He enjoyed the company of judges and business leaders, legislators and the Albany elite – a formal dining milieu Corning had become comfortable with since his days at Groton and Yale. Corning often sought out the openness of the "long table" at the private men's club (women weren't allowed until the mid-1980s, after Corning's death). The long table was a communal setting that could accommodate ten or twelve men, out-of-town guests or local club members who didn't have a lunch date – not that Corning would have to look far to find lunch partners. The long table was located in a casual rear tap room, off the formal dining area, where Corning preferred being part of the more freewheeling and unpredictable exchange between a table of strangers that might include Republicans and Democrats, Jews and Christians, blacks and whites, the very-rich and not-so-rich, young and old. After lunch, Corning's driver brought the mayor back to City Hall.

As the secretaries typed up the stack of dictation, the mayor's afternoon was consumed with a steady stream of walk-ins, punctuated by scheduled meetings with politicians or department heads. Betty Corning sometimes called her husband at City Hall, generally about home matters and gardening details. "She was involved in so much having to do with gardening and we typed up a lot of her work for flower shows," Dooley said. "We came to curse all those Latin plant names." Staff and visitors remember Corning taking frequent late afternoon calls from Polly Noonan. Before leaving the office, Corning would turn contemplative with his executive assistant, Bill Keefe. "He was a workaholic in a sense, and at the end of the day, he'd come stand in my little office, look out the window up Washington Avenue and we'd talk about who had come in to see him that day and what we'd accomplished," Keefe recalled. "He always liked to feel like we'd accomplished something."

Keefe, a Troy native and loyal Democrat, came to work for Corning after retiring at age fifty-seven as purchasing agent of Watervliet Arsenal, where he had worked for one-quarter century. Keefe lived on Albany's Orange Street as a young man, a neighbor of Bill Devane, the city's water commissioner. "I got to know guys in Democratic politics through Bill and one day he told me to go down and see the mayor," Keefe recalled. That was 1971 and Keefe was hired on the spot. Keefe was fifty-nine and celebrated his seventy-first birthday in the mayor's employ. Corning offered his new executive assistant a word of advice on his first day of work: "I hope you get a federal pension, Bill, because you'll need it if you work for me." For the next twelve years, until the mayor's death in the spring of 1983, Keefe was Corning's point man around the office. Keefe observed more closely than anyone else how the mayor worked. Said Keefe, "He could charm the birds out of the trees. And he could cut you in half with a raised eyebrow. I know. I got the eyebrow a few times."

Keefe developed a deep and abiding loyalty for his boss, even when Corning was critical of his executive assistant's work. "In twelve years working for the mayor, he chewed me out only three times," Keefe said. "I'll tell you one thing about Corning. He could chew you out on something you did wrong and that was it. You didn't hear about it again. He didn't hold a grudge." Keefe came to know the Corning nuances of dealing with the steady stream of people who trooped through the office, all wanting something from the mayor. Corning was ever the diplomat. He'd listen, appear interested, wait for the person to finish his or her pitch and proclaim, "That's interesting" – without giving the person a definitive answer to the requested favor.

Corning also showed Keefe a rare glimpse into his political vulnerabilities. "We went through some tough economic years in the 1970s and he was really feeling the pressure to provide services without raising taxes," Keefe recalled. "A few times he'd be looking out the window up Washington Avenue and say, 'Bill, we're holding it together with baling wire.' And he'd remind me you had to look a long way up the hill from the mayor's office to find a building that was paying any property tax. There is so much tax exempt property in Albany it made his job that much harder."

The mayor's office decor in Room 102 of City Hall did not match the soaring elegance of the H.H. Richardson-designed brownstone edifice Corning's grandfather, Erastus Jr., helped commission in the early 1880s after the previous City Hall was destroyed by fire. Mayor Corning's office bore none of the grandeur of the imposing, Moorish-influenced facade of City Hall. One might expect a large, richly carved antique mahogany desk for the nation's longest-tenured mayor. For all his forty-two years in office, Mayor Corning did business from behind a pedestrian, gray metal desk on which he placed a homemade spindle, with a nail driven through a wooden block that had all the grace of a junior high school shop class project. "It was an awful-looking thing he'd spike papers or bills down onto and we were kind of embarrassed that he kept it there," Dooley said.

Corning was a packrat in every place, from his Corning Hill home to his Maine camp on Webb Pond. His office desk was no exception. Of course, he had four decades "at the old stand," as he liked to call it, in which to accumulate junk. The complete list of objects taken from the mayor's desk at the time of his death in May, 1983, by archivists of the Albany Institute of History & Art ran to seven pages, single spaced. More than 400 individual items were catalogued. The surfeit of objects serves to illustrate several facets of the mayor's personality among his hodgepodge repository, items tossed into drawers willy-nilly, the organizational logic, if there was any, apparent only to Corning. The brief sampling from the archival list that follows highlights aspects of the mayor's *modus operandi*.

He had a sense of humor, at once naughty, sophisticated and sophomoric, raunchy and intellectual: two Naked Woman coins . . . coupon: good for one anything . . . Hagar the Horrible cartoon . . . I'm a Sullivan County Woodchuck button . . . cockroaches cards . . . mailing labels Erastus Corning, City Hal (sic) . . . .

He was a political junkie, collecting campaign paraphernalia from buttons to bumper stickers: Cuomo for Governor button . . . three Jimmy Carter White House matchbooks . . . framed ticket: Daniel O'Connell Assessor . . . collection of political cards: Boyle (2), Burns, Byrne, Coleman, Edwin Corning (5), Parker Corning (2), Delaney, Duncan, Ehrhardt, Happ, Hackett, Hastings & Morrison, Hayes, Hein, Keeler, McCabe (2), Merrigan, Neubauer & Fleming, Skelly, Snyder, Stanton, Wilson, Wolbert. . . .

He was a collector of curiosities, a chronicler of human foibles and a believer in the notion that fact is stranger than fiction: four programs on the Corning, Arkansas centennial, 1973 . . . bluefish and eel recipes . . . key to city of Beer-Sheva in wood case . . . City of Albany, California card . . . four Albany Tulip Festival coins, 1963 . . . Neiman-Marcus padlock . . . dog license . . . Keeler's folding paper cup . . . .

He was a devoted student of history, saving a wide array of scholarly historical articles that deepened his vast reservoir of historical knowledge: "The Last River Drive" by John N. Cole in *Horticulture* magazine with letter from Corning to Cole, 12/15/75 . . . "The Function of the Goldcrest's Crest" by David Lach in *Natural History* with notes from Corning . . . "Personal notes on sun density and volume" . . . Vol. 1, No. 4 of *The Cultivator*, Albany, June 1834 . . . *Earth Without a Moon* by Immanuel Velikovsky and *Giordano Bruno's View on the Earth Without a Moon* by A.M. Paterson . . . photocopied page from *Notes on Virginia* by Thomas Jefferson . . . .

He was a deeply committed environmentalist decades before it was politically correct: *A Chief's Lament* by Chief Seattle . . . personal note on

Alcove Reservoir polluters ... topographical maps of the Capital District area (31) ... topographical maps of the Adirondacks (9) ... personal notes on rainfall and area reservoirs ... "Prophecies on Man and Nature" by Paul B. Sims in Yale alumni magazine ... newsletters of the *Wildlife Society News* (3) ... copies of poems about the Northern Lights (2). ...

He had a deep affinity for the legacy of his family and the Albany Democratic machine, which, in a way, were one and the same: Vote for Corning necktie ... Re-elect Corning matchbook ... Hedrick Lager and Ale Coaster ... The Mayor plaque and wood box filled with 24 pens ... "Pictorial Review of Corning's Political Life" in the *Times Union* 1959. ...

His fear of destruction of the material world bordered on paranoia: "The Despairing Optimist" by Rene Dubos in *The American Scholar* 1979 ... several issues of *The Bulletin of Atomic Scientists* ... "The Other Energy Crisis: Firewood" by Erik P. Scholm in *American Forests* 1975 ... "A Fox Among the Hens: A Microcosm of Civilization" in the *Ellsworth American* 1975 ... "The Automobile Is Here To Stay – Or Is It?" speech by Mayor Corning 1969 . . . "Wastes Offer Answer for Forthcoming Protein Shortage" in *The Catalyst* 1974 ... "The Sky May Be Coming Unstitched" in *Environment Weekly* 1974. ...

And yet, despite his sincere concern about pollution and its effect on the environment, Corning could turn a blind eye to his own health. The walls of the mayor's City Hall office were oak panels, stained a blackish hue from decades of the mayor's heavy cigarette smoke. The mayor quit cold turkey in 1973 after more than forty years as a three-pack-a-day smoker. The threadbare burgundy carpet and musty burgundy draperies also picked up the deep, smoky essence of the mayor's cigarettes. The stale smell of smoke got into the very pores of the office and remained there, even after Corning quit the habit he had picked up at Yale in the early 1930s. "I remember the mayor came back from lunch at the Fort Orange Club one afternoon in 1973 and said, 'I'm quitting smoking right now,'" Dooley said. "He didn't explain why or say anything more about it, but he threw his pack of cigarettes away and that was that. As far as I know, he never smoked again." By the time he stopped smoking, however, it was too late. A debilitating condition brought on from complications due to emphysema led to his death a decade after he gave up cigarettes.

Corning did not go in for modern conveniences. He eschewed air-conditioning and refused A/C in his office and in his official city car. "We were ready to drop dead in the summer heat," Miller recalled. "And in the winter, the mayor would keep a window open in his office and we were freezing, but he said he liked it that way." Nothing about the office, or its operation, would be misconstrued as modern. "The mayor never wanted to throw anything out," Miller said. "We had files everywhere, stacked in the conference room so you couldn't move. There were rooms all around City Hall full of boxes and files. We even had police files. I don't know why. But one day, the mayor got up on a chair and then was standing on top of a filing cabinet looking for something and the cabinet started teetering and he almost fell and killed himself. That's when the mayor said, 'Gee, I guess it's about time we cleaned out some of these files.'" Dooley and Miller made a perfunctory effort, but the mayor, inveterate packrat, soon stopped them. Even amid such seeming chaos of files and records, Corning displayed legendary recall. "He had an incredible memory," Miller said. "If he said he did a speech or wrote a letter on such a such a day, it didn't matter if it was thirty years before. When we went to the files to find it, it was right there where he said it would be, down to the exact day."

Corning hired his trusted aides, Dooley and Miller, on the basis of a personal recommendation from Polly Noonan. Dooley, born in 1925, was fifty-eight when she started with the mayor and had been a clerical worker for the Democrats in the State Legislature, where Noonan worked and wielded considerable clout because of her closeness with the mayor. When Corning needed a secretary to fill in for Jen Ward, his longtime assistant who fell ill on a trip to Scotland, Polly Noonan sent over Dooley. A two-week temp job turned into more than two decades as Dooley worked for Corning's successors, mayors Whalen and Jennings. Curiously, Corning never held family political matters against Dooley. Although Dooley was a loyal Democrat, her brother, Thomas E. "Ed" Mulligan, was a Republican who ran against Corning for mayor in 1953. Corning didn't make the connection until 1977, four years after he hired Dooley. Corning made the discovery during funeral home calling hours for Dooley's deceased mother. Dooley's brother, Ed Mulligan, Corning's former challenger for mayor, was there. Dooley made the introduction. "Mayor Corning, you remember my brother, Ed?" The mayor didn't miss a beat and was gracious and kind and never mentioned the connection. Of course, Corning had obliterated Dooley's brother at the polls, 54,690 votes to Mulligan's 17,617. The mayor wouldn't let the matter go entirely, though. Dooley learned Corning later confronted Polly Noonan: "Why the hell didn't you tell me Thelma was Ed Mulligan's brother when I hired her?" Corning demanded. Noonan replied, "I didn't think it was important. She was a good worker and loyal Democrat." Dooley felt she had to break the silence with the mayor some time later: "I'm a loyal Democrat, but you know, Mayor Corning, I am not my brother's keeper." That seemed to satisfy the mayor. It was never spoken of again.

Miller started working for the mayor when she was thirty-one and was known as "the young kid of City Hall." Miller had been home with her children and out of the workforce for many years when Polly Noonan called in December of 1973 and said Corning needed a secretary. Miller and her husband, a Democratic committeeman, were actively involved in city politics. In the job interview, Corning said, "Bobbi, give it a try. If I'm not happy, I'll let you know. If you're not happy, you let me know," Miller recalled. She never needed that out. Miller started work January 7, 1974 and continued working after Corning's death for Mayor Whalen.

The office staff marveled at the stream of odd characters who flowed through the doors of Room 102 at City Hall and were welcomed into Corning's inner sanctum at the insistence of the mayor, who seemed to relish the visits of Albany eccentrics. Just in case things got out of control, Bill Keefe kept an emergency button beneath his desk in the outer office that rang an alarm at the police station. Keefe needed to use it one day when an agitated fellow in a red-checked hunting jacket planted himself in the office and reached in a threatening way into his jacket pocket. The mayor, who had come out to see the commotion, said quietly to Keefe: "Bill, call the cops." Then the mayor calmly told Dooley: "Thelma, go in the back of the office." The cops were there in a flash, handcuffed and took away the man, who, it turned out, had cigarettes and not a gun in his pocket. Dooley said it was the only time she saw the mayor shaken up.

Robert Hogan, who was reportedly mentally unstable but whose father was an Albany cop, became a regular at the office and was deemed harmless. Hogan wanted Corning's job and the mayor never discouraged the gentleman's ambitions. Hogan dropped in the first time and Keefe asked him: "Who are you?" Hogan replied: "I'm your new mayor, Robert Hogan." Dooley remembered Hogan fondly. "He wasn't playing with a full deck and he had this thing about being mayor of Albany," Dooley said. "He wrote the mayor often, long and crazy letters. The mayor always replied."

Keefe remembered showing a smartly dressed woman in to see the mayor. She had introduced herself as Mrs. Winthrop Rockefeller and tossed off seemingly inside information about the Rockefellers and Cornings and their connection through Maine. After a long time, the mayor emerged from his office with the woman and politely showed her out. Corning told Keefe, "I've just had a very interesting conversation with that lady. But I know Mrs. Rockefeller and she was not Mrs. Rockefeller. She said she wanted to open a bank and needed a million dollars." Those were just a couple of a vast collection of characters who appeared at the mayor's office, always receiving a warm reception from Corning. He collected eccentric people like so many coins, but he also seemed to have a genuine empathy for the most troubled and helpless among those who shuffled through City Hall. Corning not only replied to their letters, he often gave them a little cash when they came to him in need of a handout.

Visiting groups often proved equally quirky. Once, Corning was informed that a group was coming to watch him proclaim National Poetry Week. Keefe showed the visitors into his office and the mayor looked up from his desk with considerable surprise as several individuals carried a live, twenty-one pound, white turkey into his office. The proclamation, he was told, was to mark National Poultry Week. Corning went on with the show. But the bird broke loose during the ceremony. Turkeys are notorious for their messiness when frightened and this bird was no exception. "The keeper chased it and cleaned up after it as best he could," Corning recalled for a reporter. The following year the same group brought another turkey "killed, cleaned, plucked and frozen," recalled the mayor, who sent it to Child's Hospital.

Another unexpected visitor entered Corning's office through the chimney. Corning remembered coming into work one morning to find a young red-tailed hawk in the office fireplace. Corning called it a "tired-looking hawk," took it out and released it. He reminisced with a newspaper reporter that he'd seen a few mice scoot across his office floor during his four decades in City Hall, too. In 1979, the mayor, then seventy, went into the nuisance animal business briefly. Corning stalked a bat around City Hall with a fishing net he pulled from the trunk of his official car. "I was defending innocent women and small children," Corning said. Eyewitnesses described the mayor's bat-hunting style as "powerful, but controlled." Corning eventually tracked the frightened intruder to the second floor where he trapped it in his fishing net, but the bat broke free and the chase was on once more. Albany Traffic Court clerk Frances Meyers said she was startled when she stepped from her second-floor office and found Corning leaning over the balcony and flailing at the bat with his net. Meyers, whose son Richard was Democratic majority leader in the county legislature, said Corning pursued the bat as though it were a Democratic vote. Corning disagreed. "In that case, I would have used a smaller mesh net." The bat eluded Corning. Two days later, it reappeared outside the mayor's conference room where Charlie Reynolds, an elevator operator, killed it with a swipe of a mop. When asked about the fishing net he kept in his city car, Corning said, "You never can tell when you're going to need it." Corning also kept a fishing net in his desk drawer.

The follies were occasionally followed by tragedies. T. Garry Burns, the city clerk under Corning, was considered unorthodox, to say the least. The mayor was known to allow, even nurture, non-traditional behavior in his staff, despite the way he ruled with absolute control. But Dooley remembered how the mayor had had his fill of the antics of Burns when the city clerk wrote to Ayatollah Khomeini on official city letterhead asking for an autographed photo of the Shah. Corning found nothing humorous in the request. "He waited until everyone was out of City Hall and then the mayor just pulverized Garry," Dooley recalled. "The mayor really liked Garry and he did it quietly and didn't make it a public discipline." After Corning died and Thomas Whalen stepped into the mayor's job, Burns was removed from the job.

The mayor's driver, Russ Endres, who chauffeured Corning around town for twenty years, beginning in the late-1950s, was a character straight out of *The Last Hurrah*. Corning not only seemed to tolerate eccentricity in his staff; he appeared to cultivate it. Russ was not only the mayor's driver. He was allegedly a drunk driver. Staffers lost count of the times that a kindly cop picked up Russ, passed out from booze, deposited him in a drunk tank for the night, then dropped him off at City Hall in the morning in time for work. Or how many times Russ was considered a danger behind the wheel by Corning, who let Russ sleep it off in the back seat while the mayor himself assumed the driving duties.

John "Dusty" Miller (no relation to secretary Bobbi Miller) – who took over as the mayor's driver in 1973, when Endres's drunkenness finally got intolerable even for Corning – had seen the end coming and tried to warn Russ. Miller, born in 1914 in the same Second Avenue multi-family house where Dan O'Connell was born, grew up in the South End and knew the O'Connells from the neighborhood. A loyal Democrat, Miller was a highly decorated combat veteran in World War II. After the war, he was the manager of an Albany ambulance company and later an Albany police officer. His work on behalf of the machine was rewarded with a job in Public Works under Harry Maikels. Miller was a street inspector. He didn't like what he saw in Russ, the mayor's driver. "I'd see Russ with the mayor's "A" car parked out in front of a bar on Green Street or a tavern on Watervliet Street," Miller recalled. "I said, 'Jesus Russ, you gotta watch it.'" But Russ paid no heed. Corning had a phrase for it when Russ, who lived with his mother on Central Avenue, was out drinking and went AWOL. "Russ left the reservation," Corning said. "Someone go find him." And the mayor dispatched one of the outer office boys to scour the local gin mills until they rounded up Russ. Once caught, he was penitent. "He'd always say, 'My throat got dry. So I stopped for a ginger ale,'" Dooley recalled. "The mayor loved the guy. He literally took the wheel away from Russ when he was drunk and put Russ in the back until he sobered up." The mayor considered Russ's driving while intoxicated to be protected by some sort of divine intervention. Dooley remembered Corning often remarking: "God is with Russ when he drives.'"

But Russ's string of otherworldly luck eventually ran out. Several bad incidents led to the demise of the mayor's driver. Miller recalled one day Russ was waiting in the mayor's car on Broadway in front of Union Station for Corning to finish business. "The cab drivers came and told Russ he would have to move out of the parking spot, which was reserved for cabs," Miller recalled. Russ had been drinking. Russ also kept a pistol in the glove compartment. Russ got the handgun, brandished it at the cabbies, began yelling obscenities and caused quite a scene. Strike one for Russ.

Another situation arose some months later. Corning told Russ to bring the car up to the public works garage. Miller, who worked there, noticed a big traffic tie-up nearby. When he got closer, Miller spotted the mayor's "A" car plowed into a truck, badly damaged. No Russ. Corning's driver had fled the vehicle and bolted across the street. The police were in pursuit. He was arrested and charged with driving while intoxicated and leaving the scene of an accident. Strike two for Russ.

Nobody remembered what constituted strike three. But Russ was always behind the count. Miller recounted stories of Russ clashing with fellow employees. Bill Healy, the mayor's executive assistant, once had to lock himself in a storage room downstairs because Russ was chasing him, screaming and threatening bodily harm to Healy. Luckily, Russ' pistol was back in the glove compartment of the mayor's car. "I know the mayor hated to do it, but he finally had to let Russ go," Miller recalled. That was 1973. Miller drove Corning after that and also drove mayors Whalen and Jerry Jennings. But Corning was his favorite boss; it was no comparison.

Corning's official car was a standard black Buick Electra with a special "A" license plate for Albany and no air-conditioning or special options. "We had A/C in one car, but once when we hit a pothole, the damn unit dropped right down onto the mayor's feet and he refused to have it after that," Miller said. Each morning, at a little after 8 a.m., Corning would park his personal car, a green Buick Century in front of City Hall, the only vehicle allowed beside the traffic island. The car was stolen from that spot on a Saturday morning, a typical workday for the mayor, in March, 1977. Vermont police recovered the mayor's undamaged car five days later in a Manchester, Vermont garage – keys in the ignition, which is how the car was stolen in the first place. Corning entered a guilty plea and paid the fine for a violation against leaving ignition keys in an unattended vehicle. "I don't do that any-place but in front of City Hall," Corning said, because Miller often had to move the car due to traffic congestion. "I will make a definite point to lock up, of course, from now on," the mayor promised. The car was insured by Corning's own insurance company, Albany Associates.

At a little after five o'clock each evening, Miller parked the "A" car and went home. "I can't remember a single time in ten years that he used the "A" car for his own business," Miller said. "He drove himself in his own car to all the evening functions. He was absolutely clear on that." But Corning had a selective policy when it came to separating official city use from per-sonal use in the perks and trappings of power that came with City Hall. His secretaries typed Betty Corning's flower reports at the request of the mayor; they also typed the mayor's myriad orders for personal items from fishing and hunting catalogs; they typed reams of personal correspondence with fishing buddies in Maine and scientists around the world with whom Corning corresponded on personal matters. Even use of the mayor's car and his driver were not as etched in black and white as Corning claimed. Corning was not averse, for example, to summoning Dusty to drive him on an extracurricular activity during the workday. "He'd say, 'Let's take a ride, Dusty. It's a nice spring day.'" Miller remembered drives to the Ann Lee Pond in Colonie to observe black ducks. Or up into the Helderbergs to scout grouse prior to a hunting trip. Or along the Normanskill for a bit of birding. He was away from the old stand and off the reservation and loved every minute he played hooky. "He knew everything there was to

know about birds and animals and spent as much time as he could outdoors," Miller said.

These afternoon naturalist wanderings followed the mayor's sunrise
rambles on his property in Glenmont, fishing the Alcove Reservoir or
hunting grouse in the hilltowns of Albany County – all before work. "Most
days, he had already done a lot by the time he came into the office in the
morning," Miller said. Aside from having Miller drive him to meetings and
speeches and other official functions, Corning kept his driver busy with
personal errands. A regular trip for Miller was to the Lobster Pound fish
market in Latham where he'd buy one hundred dollars worth of fresh
Maine lobster for Corning. Or, out to nurseries to pick up special plants
and shrubs the mayor's wife had ordered.

All his life, Corning retained his childlike wonder of the world around
him. He was interested seemingly in everything. There weren't enough
hours in the day for him to read, to learn, to experience, to do all the things
that excited his active mind. Sometimes, his restlessness caught up with
him. "I remember many times I'd be driving him back from a speech in the
afternoon and he'd have been working so hard, he'd just fall asleep in the
car next to me," Miller recalled. "He was like a big kid that way."

Corning kept his golf clubs in the trunk of the "A" car, including his
prized hickory shaft putter. Corning was a member of the golf team at Yale
as a freshman and once played to a seven or eight handicap, but the demands
of politics and running the city left little time for golf. "He liked to play golf
when he could, but that wasn't often," Miller said. Still, Corning could
shoot in the mid-eighties despite long layoffs from the game.

Aside from an occasional round of golf, the springtime asparagus runs
were among the mayor's favorite excuses for going AWOL from City Hall
on a sunny afternoon. "We'd drive over to Bob's Farm Stand in Delmar
because the mayor loved to pick his own asparagus," Miller recalled. "He
was very particular about his asparagus." Some of the trips mixed politics
with pleasure. Miller remembered frequent summertime trips over to
Morton Avenue where families, mostly black families, were out on the
stoops. The mayor would get out of the car and say, 'Catch up with me in
a couple of blocks.' He'd stop and talk to everyone on the stoops, ask them
if they needed anything," Miller recalled. It was the sort of campaigning
disguised as a goodwill visit Corning pulled off with utmost genuineness.

Corning also loved the act of research, of poring over scholarly articles, combing reference books, scouring footnotes in the hope of turning

up the shred of information that would make his case. Corning particularly relished legal research in an attempt to one-up his own legal staff in the corporation counsel's office. Corning confided to friends he sometimes regretted not having gotten a law degree. The mayor wasn't about to let this deficiency stand in his way of doing battle with lawyers, a profession he loved to hate. Miller recalled: "The mayor would be in his office, preparing for a meeting with the lawyers, get stuck on a legal problem and say, 'Dusty, take me to the house.'" Miller knew the drill. It meant driving Corning to his house in Glenmont, where, among his broad library, he kept a collection of his own law books for legal research. Miller would wait in the car as Corning pored over his law books for a few hours before returning to City Hall, ready to take on the lawyers.

One such legal research run stood out in Miller's mind. It was a windy spring day, with heavy gusts that buffeted the Buick as Miller drove the mayor to Corning Hill. Corning went inside the house. An hour passed. Two hours. Three hours. Miller was waiting in the car. He dozed off for awhile and thought nothing of it. "It wasn't that unusually long and I figured he had a lot of reading to do," Miller said. All of a sudden, in the rearview mirror, Miller saw one of Corning's office assistants, Bill Toomey, who was concerned about the long absence and figured there was a problem, come tearing down the gravel driveway to where Miller was parked. Toomey was agitated. "Where the hell is the mayor, Dusty?" Toomey yelled as Miller rolled down the window, expressing his confusion as to what was going on. Miller trotted after Toomey, who raced around the house to the greenhouse in back. A wind gust had blown the greenhouse door shut, locking the mayor inside. Toomey opened the door, granting freedom to the mayor. By the time he got out of the greenhouse, where he had been imprisoned for hours while Miller snoozed, Corning was not smiling: "Christ, Dusty, I was yelling and yelling like a son of a bitch. Goddamn it, didn't you hear me?" Miller, who is hard of hearing, confessed he hadn't. "I was just waiting in the car like I was supposed to do, boss," Miller replied. It didn't take long during the drive back to City Hall for Corning to joke about the incident. The mayor and his trusted driver shared a lot of laughs about it over the years.

Even in private, Corning displayed a deep and abiding concern for the simplest, the lowliest, of Albany's citizenry. Miller remembered the mayor had a favorite saying for the elderly and infirm. "He never made fun of people," Miller said. "If he saw a crippled old man having a hard time crossing the street, the mayor would tell me to wait until he got across. Then he'd turn to me and say, 'There goes an old settler.'" Corning made an Easter visit one year to a homeless woman, Lulu Robinson, who had previously lived as a squatter in the bowels of the abandoned rubble that was the derelict Whitney's Department Store on North Pearl Street. After her story of life on the streets was published in the *Knickerbocker News* on April 2, 1980, Robinson was taken to a halfway house run by the Capital District Psychiatric Center, where Corning visited her on Easter and brought her a ham. "I found Ms. Robinson working away, washing dishes as hard as could be," Corning said. "She seemed a highly intelligent person."

The secretaries did not keep a book of the mayor's appointments. Corning preferred to schedule all his own appointments with pencil on his small desk calendar. Dooley and Miller didn't answer the phones, either. That was the men's job. Keefe or Frank Schreck or Joe Healy or George Hettie or Bill Toomey or Paul Duran or George Grober. Or others. Corning always kept a half-dozen or more retired men around, guys who needed a little income supplement to their pension, and, more importantly, a reason to get up and go out of the house each morning, a sense of being useful and needed. Corning's largess may have only meant a low-paying part-time job that brought in a few thousand dollars extra each year, just enough to put the men and their families over the hump, but it offered much more in the intangible realm of self-worth.

George Grober was typical of the outer office men, the good soldiers to Keefe's lieutenant role. The military metaphor had currency in the office, because the mayor's brand of in-house welfare for his contemporaries centered largely on veterans of World War II. Grober, born in 1918, was nine years younger than the mayor and both served in World War II. Grober, a Democrat born in Troy, built bridges with the Army combat engineer corps and later became a driver. Grober told great war stories. His best involved acting as chauffeur to Humphrey Bogart for a week through Italy while the actor entertained the troops. "Bogart showed up with two cases of booze and stayed drunk the entire week. Stinking drunk," Grober said. "Bogart didn't know where he was half the time and neither did his wife. I remember she fell out of the car once trying to get out and rolled down a hill into a ditch. We had to go down and pull her out and carry her back to the car." Corning liked Grober's war stories. After the war, Grober worked for the Internal Revenue Service for thirty years. After retiring from the IRS, Grober got a job in the Albany Water Department. It so happened Grober's cousin was Harry Maikels, Corning's commissioner of Public Works. Grober and his family also lived on Brookline Avenue in Albany, two doors down from Ray Joyce, a close Corning political adviser, and a few blocks away from the Whalens – young Tom Whalen, whom Grober watched grow up, would one day succeed Corning as mayor. Grober's wife, the former Kate Walsh, was the daughter of Michael Walsh, an employee in the city street department; her uncle ran Kelly's Grill at Orange and Swan, where the only beer on tap was O'Connell's Hedrick's. Grober's wife got a job working for the city's civil defense program and on a couple of occasions had to pinch hit and take dictation from the mayor. In Albany politics, it paid to have the family connection or to come from a staunchly Democratic neighborhood.

"After I retired from the IRS, I got tired of just hanging around the house," Grober said. "So Harry got me a job at the water department. Bill Keefe saw me hanging around the water department one day. I'd known Bill from the Watervliet Arsenal where Bill had worked. Bill asked me if I'd come work for him in the mayor's office. I said, 'Sure, why not?' I thought it was temporary, but I ended up working for Corning for seven years, until his death."

Grober and Keefe traded off working Saturdays, when the mayor without fail kept morning office hours and greeted an endless stream of visitors and residents with problems. "The mayor would talk to anybody. You never needed an appointment," Grober said. Grober answered the phones in the outer office and acted as a screening device who could put people off if the mayor didn't wish to see them – which was exceptionally rare. Besides answering phones and giving visitors the once-over, Grober had an important daily task. "It was my job to wind the grandfather clock," Grober said proudly. "Bill gave me that job when I started and told me the mayor loved that clock and I had to keep it in good working order. So, I did all the winding and made minor repairs and hired a clockmaker to do the maintenance."

Corning, whose family had anchored the city's banking institutions for generations, was a kind of automatic teller machine for Albany's street people. "They'd come in off the street, ask to see the mayor and the mayor would have us send them in," Grober recalled. "I know for a fact he gave them cash loans. I saw the mayor give out lots of money." There were limits to Corning's generosity, despite the fact he seemed to embody an exuberant good will toward the citizenry that matched the cinematic version of Spencer Tracy portraying Boston boss Mayor James Michael Curley in the film *The Last Hurrah*. Grober recounted, "I remember one woman came in, he gave her some money and she said, 'I promise I'll pay you back.' The mayor said, 'Fine, fine, I'll be here.' A few weeks later, the same woman comes in with her husband, looking for more money. I heard the mayor tell her she didn't pay back the last loan, so, he was sorry, but he wasn't going to give her any more money."

Mayor Corning had his sartorial oddities at the office. He always wore green socks, dark green socks every day without fail, no matter what his suit or shoe color was. "Personally, I think it was a great idea so he never mismatched them," said Grober. Actually, Corning was color-blind, according to city planner Dick Patrick, who was showing the mayor a multi-colored land use map when Corning conceded his malady.

The extended family of the paternalistic Corning was vast, his *ex officio* children numbering all the residents of the city of Albany, certainly, and probably most of the county – save for the staunch Republican pockets of Colonie and Bethlehem. Of course, the favorite children of the mayor, embraced by Corning's absolute micro-management and refusal to delegate even the smallest detail, were his staff. A few days after the mayor's death, Betty Corning had her husband's successor, Mayor Tom Whalen, call the staff into the mayor's office. Betty Corning presented each staff member with a small photo of their beloved late mayor, shook each person's hand, and thanked them for their years of loyal service to her husband. For the first time in forty-two years, Erastus Corning 2nd, only by dint of death, had relinquished his mayor's seat. Someone else would be taking over "the old stand." But no one would ever fill the chair with Corning's magnanimity.

On July 12, 1982, Bobbi Miller sent Mayor Corning a note and a memento at Albany Medical Center Hospital, where he had been admitted the month before. Miller clipped and attached to the letter a copy of "Ripley's Believe It Or Not" that appeared in the *Times Union* the day before, Sunday, July 11, 1982. The Ripley's cartoon bore a sketch of Corning and his record as the nation's longest-tenured mayor. The same edition of Ripley's that heralded Corning's milestone included a notation on a "super chicken" that laid an egg a day for 448 days, a record that appealed to Corning's earthiness. Under the Ripley's cartoon and Miller's words of congratulations, the mayor, in shaky cursive, wrote this reply: "Bobbi. I finally made it. Hurrah."

In *The Last Hurrah*, the novel based on Boston's mayor and political boss James Michael Curley, the Curley character, Skeffington, who is in poor health and barely hanging on for one last campaign, confided to his nephew, Adam Caulfield, the newspaper cartoonist: "I suppose," he said reflectively, "that I'm about the last of the old-style political leaders who's still alive and moving around. All the others are dead or in institutions, held together by adhesive tape, bits of wire and plastic tubes. When I join them, the old campaign will vanish like the Noble Red Man. There simply won't be anybody around who knows how to run one."

For Erastus Corning 2nd, mayor for life, alpha and omega mayor, the record and recognition he had been gunning for were finally his. Even though he didn't get to finish out his eleventh term, the Ripley cartoon was read by millions of Americans along with their Sunday funnies. The super chicken and the mayor's last hurrah. Miller had the letter and the Ripley cartoon framed. It hangs in her house and the same cartoon probably was saved in the homes of countless other Democratic loyalists around Albany as a kind of enduring political epithet. *Requiescat in pace*, Erastus. The beginning of the end for the fabled O'Connell-Corning machine. Last hurrahs all around.

Chapter 9:

A Big Fish in a Little Pond:
The Politics of Mayor Corning

**"If Mayor Corning wanted to destroy someone or take him
out, he likened the process to killing a fly. He'd seal the
windows, seal the doors and eventually the fly would
asphyxiate. Corning could be controlled and patient that
way, as opposed to other politicians, who'd try to kill
a fly with a hammer."**

Corning protégé and political adviser Doug Rutnik.

The monstrous blue Plymouth convertible, all chrome and fins,
lumbered down State Street in the five o'clock swelter of a late-August day
in 1977 and swung left on Pearl Street, revealing a sign on the car's door
that read: "If Anyone Knows More About Albany, Vote For Him." High
above the city's busiest intersection just crossed by the Plymouth, a huge
billboard was erected atop a building with a campaign slogan visible clear
across town. It proclaimed: "Keep The Mayor Mayor." The sixty-seven-
year-old inside the gleaming convertible flashed a familiar, winning smile –
the "million-vote smile" it was called – and pedestrians along Pearl Street
turned to bask in the powerful glow of that gaze. They pointed and waved.
An elderly woman mouthed the words, "God Bless You, Mr. Mayor." The
clipped, aristocratic voice boomed out of the back seat above the traffic
noise. "Hi! How are you?" "Hi there!" "Hi! How are you?" – over and
over again, an endless loop tape. At the corner of Clinton and North Pearl,
the car pulled to a stop under the Palace Theater marquee. The most powerful man in Albany, Mayor Erastus Corning 2nd, grimaced with pain as he
stepped out of the car and moved to shake hands with a knot of people just
off work, waiting for their bus. Corning walked with a pronounced limp,
his right hip flaring into an aching stab with each step, despite prescribed

painkillers. The hip's ball and socket had been destroyed by arthritis, worn bone grinding on worn bone, making it painful even to stand, and doctors, unbeknownst to the public, had determined the mayor needed an immediate right hip joint replacement. Corning informed his doctors the operation would have to wait until after the election. This was more important. It was nothing less than his political life at stake. "He was out every night campaigning in addition to all his other duties and the schedule was enough to kill a person half his age," said Harold Greenstein, an alderman and Common Council member who campaigned for Corning. "His hip was killing him, so he used the convertible so he didn't have to walk as much. That name Corning was pure magic. We'd run in front and say, 'Mayor Corning is coming!' and people would run out from their houses to shake his hand."

Fresh in the memory of the mayor, and the electorate, was his unforgettable match-up with Republican Carl Touhey in the 1973 election, four years earlier, when Corning campaigned on cruise control. He sounded and looked tired against Touhey, was bothered by nagging lung ailments and let slip that the term, his ninth, would be his last. Corning escaped with a shockingly close 3,500-vote win over Touhey, which served as a wake-up call to Corning and his machine cronies that the old complacency would no longer carry the day. Losing, once incomprehensible, was suddenly in the realm of possibility for the mayor with the historic tenure. Re-election had gone from being a formality to something Corning would have to earn with solid organization, hard work and rewarding loyalty – back to the old reliables, the machine's meat and potatoes. Despite the searing hip pain, Corning was running, as he told a reporter, "hard and scared." It was the summer of 1977 and Corning was facing the unthinkable: a primary challenge by a fellow Democrat, State Senator Howard C. Nolan Jr. It was Corning's first primary in nine terms as mayor. Never mind what the mayor said last time around. He wanted a tenth term and wanted it badly, but was being tested by an upstart state senator twenty years Corning's junior who coveted the mayor's throne and played the age card in his campaign slogan: "A City With A Future Needs A Mayor With A Future."

Corning campaigned harder than ever because his future was now. The mayor worried enough about the challenge from Nolan to loan $10,000 of his own money to his campaign organization, People for Corning. All that was past – four decades as mayor in the shadow of Dan O'Connell, the boss to whom Corning acquiesced – was prologue.

Corning was at an age when most men retired, but he was running the show in Albany, city and county, for the first time since O'Connell died on February 28, 1977 at ninety-one. Age and natural causes had finally felled the invincible political boss and now it was time for his surrogate son, O'Connell's urbane alter-ego, the mayor who had paid his dues for a lifetime, to ascend to the ultimate throne of power that had been Dan's. Corning had first entered the mayor's office at the age of thirty-two, three weeks after Pearl Harbor, and had spent his entire adult life in the job, evolving from "boy mayor" to "G.I.-Mayor" to "dean of American mayors" behind a plain gray metal office desk in City Hall. John Gunther had called Corning "one of the best mayors in America" in his *Inside U.S.A.* guidebook series. Following Dan's death, Corning got his first taste of total control of the political game in Albany and he liked its sweetness. Corning had no intentions of giving up that delicious pleasure and heady power, at least not without a fight. Nolan also was breaking machine protocol of paying your dues quietly for a few decades and hoping Dan gave you a judgeship, say, or a seat in Congress. In spite of the renegade nature of Nolan's primary challenge, there had been rumblings over the summer of 1977 that Nolan had picked up considerable support during the splintering of loyalties and maneuvering for position within the machine amid the power vacuum left by O'Connell's death earlier that year. Without Dan, a kind of paternalistic glue who bound the machine together, factions were arising along the organization's fault lines of age and ethnicity and economic class and Corning worried that Nolan's candidacy might gain momentum as a result of internal disarray.

The banner headline in the *Times Union* on September 1, 1977, a week before the primary election, confirmed Corning's worst fears: "Nolan leads Corning, poll shows." The independent newspaper survey gave Nolan a commanding nineteen percent lead over the incumbent mayor. Corning's response was to hobble faster on his pain-wracked hip, campaigning door-to-door for the first time in recent memory. The mayor hadn't liked the omens: a month before, when Corning cut a red, white and blue ribbon on July 29 for the official opening of his campaign headquarters on Central Avenue, as a brass band played a Sousa march, "The Thunderer," Corning's campaign hit a sour note. Media reports of the event focused on an embarrassing disclosure that the property was $33,731.53 in arrears for combined delinquent city, county and school taxes. "I was unaware of it," Corning said. But the damage had been done. The mayor couldn't afford to stumble again with Nolan breathing down his neck.

Corning, a history major and voracious reader of history, was thinking at this point in terms of legacy and wanted to set a record nobody could touch. He wasn't about to be denied his place in the history books by the upstart Nolan. Corning took this "longest-tenured mayor of any major city in America" business seriously. It was what had come to define him. Corning had a powerful sense of his place in political history, as great-grandson of a mayor of Albany, son of a lieutenant governor and nephew of a longtime Congressman. Mayor Corning had his secretaries track his longevity and he could rattle off his term as mayor by years, months and days.

Corning had only two challengers in the country to his claim of longest-tenured mayor. Mayor F. Edward Biertuempful, although he first took office in 1938, three years before Corning, was mayor of Union Township, New Jersey, more comparable to a village or small town in upstate New York. Since the bedroom community was not a city, Biertuempful, who referred to Corning as "that youngster up in Albany," was out of the running on a technicality. Corning eventually surpassed Biertuempful anyway. In early August, 1977, Corning's major rival for longest-tenured mayor of a major city was Orville Hubbard of Dearborn, Michigan, but that year Hubbard dropped out of a six-way primary race (including a challenge by his son, Frank Hubbard) and Corning surpassed the Dearborn mayor's tenure. Corning's eighteen-month absence for duty in World War II was counted, since he technically was mayor on leave during that time. Hubbard and Corning had corresponded over the years, but their rivalry was fierce. Like Corning, Hubbard could not give up the power of the mayor's seat and had run the city of Dearborn for three years from his wheelchair after suffering a stroke that robbed his speech and left Hubbard able only to utter one of his favorite expletives to get his point across at cabinet meetings over which he presided. Expletives of joy could certainly be heard from beneath the gilt curtains in Mayor Corning's newly redecorated office when he surpassed Hubbard. The record was finally Corning's. But he wanted to extend his streak, make it an untouchable mark.

And so the wizened old warrior, mayor for life, hobbled on, the scant hair left on his leonine head gone white with age. Not only was Corning's hip wracked with pain, but his lungs, weakened by childhood asthma, allergies and four decades of heavy smoking recently ceased, were beginning to fail in the searing heat and humidity of August as the primary campaign ground on. "The mayor was in a lot of pain, but he struggled through it," recalled Thomas Brown, a State Assemblyman and a Corning campaign coordinator. "He wanted to be the mayor of Albany forever. Who else could there be? Nolan's move was a streak of impetuousness not unlike a knight going against his king."

Corning assembled his own Round Table to lay out a battle plan to turn back the rising Nolan tide. Brown was joined by Ray Kinley Sr., Doug Rutnik, John Holt-Harris, Tom Whalen, Leo O'Brien, Vincent McArdle and Harold Koreman. The group of lawyers, judges and politicos met weekly at the Fort Orange Club to plot strategy. Holt-Harris, a judge and Corning's longtime friend, took charge and massaged the healthy egos in that circle into consensus for Corning. Whalen recalled, "Tom Brown and I were the outspoken minority in that we didn't think some of the old-style, bare-knuckles Democratic maneuvering would be accepted by voters in that era and Corning took our suggestions very seriously." Old-time machine hands pulled for Corning. U.S. District Court Judge James T. Foley wrote in August, a week before the 1977 primary: "Dear 'Rastus: Stay cool, calm and collected. Dan was always proud of you as Mayor of Albany."

Nolan's primary challenge represented only the most pressing political concern on several fronts of simultaneous attack against Corning, the first person in Albany's history to be both mayor and chairman of the indomitable political machine. Many were taking aim at once, trying to gang up and topple Corning from this pinnacle of power. A major internal rebellion was brewing. The powerful Ryan brothers, Charlie and Jimmy, were busy building up their own factions of O'Connell loyalists, preparing a grab for some of Corning's control. Sheriff John J. McNulty and his Green Island gang also were looking to carve away at Corning's base of support. The papers were referring to it as "the biggest intra-party struggle for power in more than five decades among Albany County Democrats." Chicago's late mayor and political boss Richard Daley, a personal friend of Corning's, held both positions as mayor and Democratic chairman and the combination made him unbeatable. That lesson had not been lost on Corning, who was attempting to establish himself as the once and future king in the post-O'Connell era. Corning convinced himself that a new day had dawned for himself and Albany with a symbolic re-decoration of his utilitarian City Hall office. The mayor's executive assistant, Bill Keefe, remembered the occasion. "It was the day after Dan O'Connell's funeral, which seemed like strange timing back then," Keefe recalled. "The office had burgundy drapes that must have been sixty years old. They were musty and tattered and crumbled when we took them down. The mayor had ordered material in France, had new drapes made from the fabric in New York City and paid for it all himself."

Election commissioner and architect Ray Kinley Jr., whose father, Ray Sr., was one of Corning's campaign coordinators in the 1977 Nolan primary, was summoned by Corning that spring after O'Connell was buried and Corning asked Kinley to submit a detailed estimate for a total renovation of his City Hall office. Corning had left the place in a tattered state out of deference to Dan, whose own taste in furnishings could best be described as early Salvation Army. Kinley's office renovation estimate came in at $330,000. "Infinitely more than I wanted to spend," Corning wrote back to Kinley. Corning did splurge on luxuriant drapes, however, crowned with 18-karat gold braid. "The mayor refused to skimp on those, because he paid for the drapes out of his own pocket," Kinley said, estimating the window treatments cost in excess of $10,000.

Corning would be damned if Howie, as the mayor had always referred to Nolan, was going to get those kingly drapes and all the reflected glory that shone through them. Corning went way back with Nolan and had been watching with wariness the ambitious politician unwilling to wait his turn and play by the machine's rules. Before they engaged in hardball politics in 1977, it was simply a matter of hardball in the 1940s. Howard Nolan first met Mayor Corning when Nolan was in fifth grade. Nolan and a couple of his buddies from the neighborhood, including Mark Heller, who is now Nolan's law partner, went to City Hall to ask the mayor if he would help them build a baseball diamond in their neighborhood on Colonial Avenue along upper New Scotland Avenue. With a call from Corning, it was done. Say no more. "We were awed by the mayor's power," Nolan recalled. Nolan saw more of the mayor's power as a youngster when he caddied for Corning, who unleashed long drives at Albany Municipal Golf Course in between discussions of power politics.

In his youth, Nolan never envisioned that, thirty years later, the junior state senator with major political desires would test Corning's power as Albany's perennial mayor. An epic showdown loomed. Nolan's primary was seen as political effrontery, a usurper to the throne Corning seemed assured of occupying for as long as he desired. But Nolan was eager and picked his opening wisely, attempting to fill the vacuum left by

O'Connell's death and to capitalize on the machine's internal squabbling. For Nolan, his challenge to Corning was seen as biting the hand that had fed him. No neophyte, Nolan had worked on campaigns for Jack and Bobby Kennedy and Nolan's father was a state employee, active in politics, who counted among his close friends Russell Hunt, a lawyer and machine candidate whom O'Connell had moved up from city corporation counsel to county district attorney to State Supreme Court justice. After a stint in the Marines, Nolan returned to Albany and worked in the law office of Jim Drislane, a politically connected attorney. In 1962, Hunt offered Nolan a part-time job as an assistant corporation counsel. Nolan took it and went to work for Corning. His work caught the mayor's attention, especially when Nolan won annexation cases that brought Albany new citizens – and Corning new votes. "I was Corning's fair-haired boy at the time, because I was winning cases in which the mayor took a great interest," Nolan said.

Nolan remembered an indelible impression of brilliance Corning stamped upon the young lawyer's consciousness at weekly meetings in the mayor's office when he worked as a corporation counsel in the early 1960s. "Mayor Corning was absolutely brilliant, as knowledgeable about the law as any lawyer, and he had an astounding grasp of municipal law," Nolan said. But the mutual respect society ended there. Their political philosophies were antithetical. Nolan was impatient for change. Corning sought to preserve the old-fashioned winning ward structure Dan had built. "Corning was like Dan in that he didn't want young people moved up too fast. I guess Corning forgot Dan made him mayor at age thirty-two. The mayor knew all the power would be his one day and he didn't want any dynamic, young challengers," Nolan said.

Against Corning's wishes, Nolan took off two months in 1964 from his corporation counsel's job to campaign for Bobby Kennedy's successful bid for the seat of U.S. Senator from New York. "The mayor thought Bobby was a smart-aleck and wise guy and never liked him," Nolan said. Nolan committed other transgressions in Corning's mind, including a proper lack of respect for the mayor's omnipotence and not-so-subtle critiques of Corning's status quo style. "Corning was a brilliant politician, but I thought he was a lousy mayor," Nolan said. "He'd been in the office way too long and he never changed with the times. He was an underachiever. He just sleepwalked through the job."

The power of Corning that had so impressed Nolan the boy distressed Nolan the man. In the late-1960s, Nolan quit the machine and left town to represent the developer Norris McFarland in projects in Detroit, Memphis and the Carolinas. Nolan returned to Albany several years later when McFarland proposed to build at 41 State Street the first substantial office building in downtown Albany in three decades. Nolan discovered numerous legal roadblocks thrown up by the machine, impediments to a developer or entrepreneur who might challenge the machine's power. "It was the same status quo I left," Nolan recalled. "You needed variances to build anything, which was the way the machine kept control by forcing you to go to them for a favor. I remember an examiner asking McFarland why he wasn't using Carnegie Steel in his building. Carnegie Steel went out of business in 1937. That's how incredibly behind the times they were."

Nolan rankled Corning anew with his independence in the Legislature following his 1974 come-from-behind win against GOP candidate Carl Touhey for the State Senate. Corning didn't want Nolan to get the nod and never backed him, but Dan prevailed and gave Nolan his support. The newly installed freshman senator gloated in his freedom from Corning's control. When Senate Democrats gathered in January of 1975 to choose their new majority leader that year, Corning lobbied Nolan hard to vote for the mayor's friend, Sen. Jeremiah Bloom of Brooklyn, whose secretary happened to be Corning confidante Polly Noonan. "Corning was calling me daily, really leaning on me to vote for Bloom," Nolan recalled. Nolan went to see O'Connell. "Dan told me to vote for whomever I felt would be in the best interest of the Democratic Party," Nolan said. Nolan cast his vote for the eventual victor, the new majority leader, Sen. Manfred Ohrenstein, a Manhattan liberal. It was a public nose-thumbing at Corning. "I've never seen anyone as mad as Corning when you voted for Ohrenstein," attorney and Corning protégé Doug Rutnik told Nolan in confidence. Corning's enmity toward Nolan was, by now, deep and profound. "Corning never forgave me for that," Nolan said. "He wouldn't even talk to me. I was the senator representing Albany and he gave me the complete cold shoulder."

In December of 1976, when Nolan was contemplating a mayoral primary challenge against Corning, he went to see Jimmy Ryan, who had just come from a visit with Dan O'Connell in the hospital. Nolan had known Ryan, a friend of Nolan's father, since he was a kid. "Jimmy told me Dan didn't want me to run against Erastus, that it would hurt the organization," Nolan recalled. "I told Jimmy to go back to Dan and say as long as Dan was alive, I won't run against Corning if that's what he wanted." Dan was buried on March 3, 1977. Nolan declared his candidacy four days later, on March 7. The king maker was dead. The king breaker was alive and well. Nolan vs. Corning. The press was treating the primary with all the hype of the Joe Frazier-Muhammad Ali epic heavyweight title boxing match, The Thrilla in Manila.

An editorial in the *Times Union* on March 11, 1977 said: "We couldn't be happier. Nothing could be healthier for Albany politics than some genuine competition. For more years than most residents have been alive, the Democratic machine has exercised monopoly politics in the city, arrogantly disregarding the public interest. If nothing else, a hard-fought primary by Nolan should put the machine on notice that its cheating ways are going to be challenged not only by those outside the party, but also by bright, energetic people within it." A *Knickerbocker News* editorial on June 2, 1977 put it this way: "We are glad to see the Nolan challenge and interpret it as one more sign that this arrogant political machine does not have the power it used to have."

And then, one week before the primary, the bombshell exploded across the front page of the September 1, 1977 edition of the *Times Union*: "Nolan leads Corning, poll shows." And a commanding nineteen point lead, no less – a jolt of adrenaline for the Nolan campaign, a flutter of fear in the gut of Corning and grist for the Albany political mill. Could the perennial mayor actually lose? The city was abuzz with the unprecedented possibility. But behind the scenes, Nolan's and Corning's own pollsters were at work. The Corning camp showed the mayor up by ten percentage points, fifty-five to forty-five, but Nolan was closing fast. To Nolan's own strategists, Nolan's numbers looked very bad. "We got pretty sophisticated with our polling and knew we were never close, but we didn't want to tell Howie," said Heller, Nolan's law partner and campaign manager. "We were certain the *Times Union* poll was way off, but we took advantage of the momentary doubt it planted in people's minds."

Primary day, September 8, 1977, proved anti-climactic. Corning liked what he saw as he watched early results roll in from his traditional spot alongside ward heelers fielding tallies by phone in a back room of Democratic headquarters at 75 State Street – a scene straight out of *The Last Hurrah*. With only five wards reporting, Corning had seen enough. After nine elections, the mathematical whiz had the numerical patterns down cold. Corning emerged from the back room at 9:32 p.m., thirty-two minutes after the polls had closed, grinned broadly and told a *Times Union* reporter, "I've been around awhile, and the people like a little bit of what I've been doing." Corning was driven to his campaign headquarters on Central Avenue several blocks away. At 10:30 p.m., ninety minutes after the polls closed, Nolan conceded defeat. He shook the mayor's hand and said, "It was a great victory, and I'll tell you right now, you've got my complete support in November."

A throng of Corning campaign supporters erupted into jubilant applause at the headquarters, plastered with signs and bumper stickers with the ubiquitous slogan, "Keep The Mayor Mayor." In private conversation, the mayor's supporters admitted they suffered anxiety attacks over the Nolan challenge right up until the first results began to flow in. It was a Corning landslide: Corning 16,139 votes to Nolan's 9,605, or 62.7 percent for the mayor and 37.3 percent of the vote for the senator. More than forty-eight percent of the 42,000 enrolled Democrats in the city had voted, better than twice the national average for primaries. Corning held the controls with a firm grip and the machine still worked. It could get out the vote like no other political organization in America. Corning was the once and future king. There was life for the mayor after Dan, after all.

After Nolan's concession, Corning spoke to his supporters at headquarters. The raucous victory celebration hushed to a reverential silence. The mayor invoked the patron saint and conferred upon himself status of heir. "This is the first time since Dan O'Connell died at the end of February that there was any opportunity for anybody to express how they felt about the Democratic organization in Albany. This has been a great example of what that feeling is. It's been well done, a vote of confidence," Corning said.

The headline in the *Times Union* the morning after the primary was, "Corning rebuffs challenge." The story said: "Erastus Corning II, the nation's longest-serving mayor, has done it again. Another in the long series of challenges to his rule over the City of Albany was fended off Thursday. The eyes of the state and nation were on Albany to see if Corning and the seemingly indestructible political machine fashioned shortly after the turn of the century would survive . . . About the death of the political machine so often predicted by critics, Corning would often say, 'The wish is father to the thought.' Primary night proved Erastus Corning right once again."

On Friday, September 9, 1977, the morning after his crushing defeat of Nolan, Corning came into his City Hall office – early, as usual. His secretary, Thelma Dooley, noticed the boss was smiling and his walk seem less labored, with only a slight limp. His mood appeared light as air, almost giddy, Dooley remembered thinking. As he strode to his desk, the mayor stopped, turned to Dooley in the outer office and said, "You know, the best thing about this job is that nobody comes in second place."

News of Corning's defeat of Nolan reached far and wide, resulting in a long profile in the *Washington Post* by William Claiborne. "I never realized how many former Albany residents now live in Washington until that story ran and people began recollecting happy acquaintances with you over the years," Claiborne wrote to Corning on October 31, 1977, a few days after his Corning profile was published in the *Post*. Corning's old Yale chum, William J. Vanden Heuvel, American ambassador to Geneva, wrote to the mayor on September 12, 1977: "The news of your victory has brought joy and elation to this international city. By its very nature, politics is brutal and unappreciative. It is therefore with special pleasure that your victory vindicates a great public record and makes it possible for you to continue your unparalleled contribution to your city and state. Remembering our long friendship with appreciation and mindful of your loyalty and support in crucial times . . ."

It took a long time for the *Times Union* to wipe the egg off its face over its wildly inaccurate poll. During his victory celebration, Corning tweaked the newspaper by beaming and posing for a picture while holding aloft, in Trumanesque fashion, the *Times Union* headline, "Nolan leads Corning, poll shows." Corning was strong and defiant when he met with the editorial boards of the *Times Union* and *Knickerbocker News* for more than an hour on October 12, 1977 to assess his hard-fought primary win over Nolan. "I have no apologies for Albany," Corning said and defended his administration's long years in office. "The services are very nearly as good as we can have, given our taxpayers' ability to pay." As the interview session wound down, the big question was put to Corning: would he leave office after his tenth four-year term? "Enough is enough," Corning told the editors and reporters of the newspapers. They had their headline and thought they had finally pinned down the elusive *major domo*. A month later, Corning had amended that answer to say, "At this time it certainly will be my last term. But you never can tell." Corning held all the cards and he was keeping them close to his vest – he always was a good poker player, according to his card buddies. It was a foregone conclusion that Corning would wipe out his unknown Republican opponent, Michael Ruberti in the November general election, which he did. Corning: 30,812, Ruberti: 6,970.

Corning's political celebrity as the longest-tenured mayor of any American city was being carried in news items from coast-to-coast. Mayor Corning received congratulatory letters from national political figures, including San Francisco Mayor George Moscone. "Looking forward to seeing you in San Francisco for the annual meeting of the National League of Cities," Moscone wrote on November 9, 1977. Corning's old Senate colleague, Bernard M. Bloom, now a Surrogate Judge in Brooklyn, wrote on November 10, 1977: "Dear E: Why by only 80%? I thought you would have 99%?" U.S. Sen. Henry "Scoop" Jackson sent his warm wishes for another term. Baltimore Mayor William Donald Schaefer wrote on November 11, 1977: "Many of your fellow mayors would be interested in learning the secret of your success." Gordon Ackerman wrote to Corning on November 10, 1977 after returning to Albany from Europe as a reporter for *Time*, *Life* and CBS News. "It was a pleasure to find you still at the helm here and to see how Albany has maintained its fine image throughout the country as a clean, modern and very lovely city under your guidance." An editorial in the *Times Union*, which had endorsed Nolan in the primary, said of Corning the morning after his election to a tenth term: "The Democrats should get on their knees and thank God for Erastus Corning. He kept the party going for the past six or eight years because of O'Connell's failing health. He has been the sole motivating factor and brains." Corning didn't let the national media attention and the praise from colleagues regarding the political benchmark he had achieved distract him from his desired revenge. In his private files, Mayor Corning kept a copy of signatures of people who signed designating petitions for Nolan. Corning had made cryptic checks and marks in the margins, as if he had pored over the list of names line by line and was bent on vindictive strikes against those who supported Nolan, his sworn enemy.

The grueling primary had taken a heavy physical toll on the mayor. Corning was scheduled for right hip replacement surgery the week after the election, but it was delayed due to Corning's hospitalization from bronchitis and lung complications. It was Corning's first surgery since a tonsillectomy at the age of nine. Bad lungs had been a chronic problem for Corning, going back to his Groton days when he had to miss several weeks of school for asthma-like ailments. Corning's doctors kept the mayor in Albany Medical Center Hospital from November 29, 1977 until the actual operation date, December 7, 1977, while waiting for his lung condition to improve. The headline in the November 30, 1977 *Knickerbocker News* – "Mayor operates City Hall from a hospital room" – was a dark foreshadowing of his long illness and hospitalization at the same hospital in 1982. Keefe shuttled municipal paperwork and political business to Corning at his hospital bed in another eerie harbinger. Finally, on December 7, the mayor's lung problems had cleared up and the three-hour right hip reconstruction was a go. Dr. Manir Jabbur and a team of resident orthopedic surgeons were done by 10:30 a.m., on schedule, and the mayor's disintegrated socket and femur were replaced with a one-half ounce polyethylene cup for the socket and a four-inch metal head weighing nine ounces for the ball, along with a tapered metal shaft. The shaft was held in Corning's right femur by methyl methacrylate cement. All traces of Corning's extensive arthritis were removed. The mayor was reported in good condition after the operation. His recovery was slightly slower than average, but eighteen days later, on Christmas day, Corning left Albany Med on crutches. The promise of another term as mayor, extending his historic streak, gave the mayor strength. Lazarus-like, he dropped his crutches and walked unaided to the swearing-in ceremony on the afternoon of New Year's Eve, 1978, number ten, same as it ever was. Corning was flanked by family and friends and posed for the familiar quadrennial photo under an oil portrait of the city's first mayor, Peter Schuyler. "This will be my last term," Corning vowed, but nobody believed him. Corning's macabre humor was back in form as he brought a model of his fake hip and proudly displayed it on his mayoral desk as a conversation piece and an unspoken warning to any young upstarts like Nolan on the horizon. He may be a political dinosaur, a metal-hipped, wheezy-lunged urban machine boss, an endangered species, but Mayor Erastus Corning 2nd could still vanquish all foes.

Within weeks of securing his tenth term and recovering from the hip replacement and lung ailments, Corning went to work with a surgeon's precision to remove the political threat of the renegade machine factions represented by the Ryans and McNultys. Corning, the newly ascended political boss, was as deliberate as a master chess player in setting up the moves that cut his rivals off at the knees. It was a gradual, almost imperceptible, power play by Corning, but no less deadly for those who dared challenge his leadership.

Corning could be vengeful, too, and played cutthroat political payback when it came to evening the score with Nolan. One such casualty was the mayor's accountant, Howard Kahn, a friend of Nolan's and a founder of the prestigious Albany accounting firm Urbach, Kahn & Werlin – one of the top twenty-five accounting firms in the country. Kahn's transgression? In June of 1977, Kahn's daughter was married. Kahn invited his longtime friend, Nolan, during the bitter Democratic mayoral primary that summer. Another wedding guest was Richard Meyers, Democratic majority leader of the county legislator commonly described as Corning's political "hatchet man" and a distant relative of Kahn's. The wedding was on a Sunday. On Monday morning, while he hosted a brunch for family and close friends, Kahn got a call from Mayor Corning. The mayor was livid about Nolan's presence at Kahn's daughter's wedding. Corning hung up before Kahn could explain himself. "Corning never spoke to me after that," Kahn said. "After thirty years working together and becoming friends, I was suddenly dead in the water. I blame Richie Meyers more for being a spy than I do Corning. One thing I refused to do was apologize for my friendship with Howard Nolan."

And one thing Corning refused to do was to apologize for playing politics the way he was taught by Dan O'Connell, who played hard and for keeps. This take-no-prisoners attitude was a learned behavior that ran counter to Corning's innate personality. By nature, he was passive rather than aggressive. He rarely provoked a confrontation, although he would defend himself forcefully if attacked or challenged. He was not driven by a lust for power or blind ambition. He waited patiently until Dan died and then enjoyed the authority he felt he had earned after four decades of faithful service to his political boss. He did not possess a burning drive to reach the top in business or in politics beyond being mayor. The time greedier men would have spent devising their next moneymaking opportunity or plotting a political promotion, Corning spent reading or studying one of his arcane fields of interest or fishing and hunting. Corning was, above all else, a go-along and get-along kind of guy. Left to his own devices, he would rather have studied art and become an artist or pursued a career in conservation or as a naturalist, he told friends in rare confessional moments. But politics was a foregone conclusion. Erastus' father would have it no other way. Although his mother and wife were at best ambivalent, and at worst opposed, to Erastus embarking on a career in politics – the family believed that the strain of politics had contributed to the early death of his father, Edwin Corning – the young man's fate was sealed. Erastus was only twenty-seven when first elected to the New York State

Legislature in 1936, where he spent six years, one in the Assembly and five in the Senate. No heavy lifting required. As a Democrat and member of the minority party at the time, Corning was allowed to introduce only a dozen or so bills each year, a couple of which were passed and signed into law – all inconsequential – such as: change Highway 508 to Highway 1468 in Coeymans (1936); decorate Capitol and office buildings at Albany during Christmas and appropriate $1,000 (1937); require time lost by highway workers due to bad weather to be made up within three weeks (1937); change name of St. Vincent's Asylum in Albany to St. Vincent's Child Care Society of the Albany Diocese (1940); create committee of three senators and three Assemblymen with a budget of $250 to look into getting replacement portraits of former governors missing from walls in executive chamber of Capitol (1941).

Corning very likely was growing more and more frustrated with the monotony of each passing legislative session, but he kept his boredom in check. Spurred by the rebukes of Dan O'Connell, Corning put aside his initial wildness as a freshman legislator and accompanying bouts of post-session boozing on the town and learned to settle comfortably into the glacial pace of the Legislature. He became a thirty-year-old senator with the gravity and bearing of a seventy-year-old statesman. Youthful folly and recklessness behind him, it was in the Senate that Corning perfected the art of looking and sounding good, but doing little. His considerable charm, a sincere enjoyment of people, and a commanding aristocratic air proved enough to see him through as a lawmaker even without solid accomplishments. Corning did what he was told, even if that meant being a stooge for Tammany Hall, as the *New York Times* reported on March 26, 1941: "Senator Erastus Corning, a Democrat from Albany, sponsored a bill in the state Senate protecting the tenure of Tammany Hall district leaders at a cost to New York City of $1.5 million. The bill was sent to Mr. Corning by the Tammany Hall Committee and it specifically protects Tammany ward leader John J. Kelly by avoiding a primary in the fall as required by law. It will also benefit Tammany boss William Solomon. Mr. Corning declined comment on the intent of the bill." Despite his blind allegiance to his own machine and connection to Tammany's corrupt organization, Corning's reputation in the Legislature was of a quiet plodder. "Not a shouter or a desk thumper" is how a *Times Union* reporter in 1941 described Corning's six years as a lawmaker. "Patient and hard-working, when he addressed his colleagues, he did so briefly, with his facts and his arguments marshaled carefully in advance. He proved himself as a regular fellow who refuses to coast on the reputations of his ancestors." Corning learned to play the role that had been scripted for him. The state Capitol was merely a training ground, a time for seasoning. Corning's late father and Dan O'Connell had been grooming Erastus for a position far more powerful and vital – running City Hall as the machine's mayor. Corning accepted his destiny with the same sense of predictability that others viewed it. "Erastus Corning II, Democratic candidate for Mayor of Albany, turned to a career of public service as naturally as other men take up banking, journalism or the law," the *Times Union* wrote in an election advance profile on November 4, 1941. "He was bred in that tradition. He could not have avoided a career of public service."

His father and Dan had chosen wisely. In his first election in 1941, Corning demolished his Republican opponent, Benjamin R. Hoff, 57,946 to 11,477. It was the most smashing victory in a mayoral race in Albany's history. The machine delivered. Edwin's boy finally had his political patrimony, the prize the father had imagined for the son since Groton. The silent misgivings of Erastus' wife and mother were too little, too late. When first elected mayor, at thirty-two, Corning became the youngest chief executive in the city's history and one of the youngest in the state. His great-grandfather, Erastus Corning, was elected the thirty-ninth mayor of Albany 107 years prior, serving from 1834 to 1837. Corning, the seventieth mayor of Albany, took office exactly twenty years after the O'Connell-Corning machine's first victorious mayoral candidate, William S. Hackett, was inaugurated. No one could have guessed, in 1941, that he'd be mayor in 1951 and 1961 and 1971 and 1981, too. Mayor for life. The signs that Corning was something special, one-of-a-kind, were evident at his first public reception on January 2, 1942, the day after his swearing-in. Corning's appeal was immediate and huge. When the mayor, his wife and mother arrived at City Hall at 9:30 a.m. on New Year's Day, a large crowd was already waiting for him. For the next three hours, Mayor Corning met a steady stream of well-wishers described as a "vast throng" by the *Times Union*, an unusually large outpouring of support for a company town in which a Democrat mayor was as certain as death and taxes. The paper reported, "More than 6,000 persons filed through the executive offices to congratulate the youthful mayor at the start of his four-year term, including Gov. and Mrs. Herbert H. Lehman . . . It was a huge cross-section of the city's residents from all walks of life."

Mayor Corning swept into City Hall just three weeks after the catastrophic surprise attack on Pearl Harbor on December 7, 1941. The massive Japanese air assault was a defining moment in United States history, causing a devastating loss of 2,397 lives, 1,143 wounded, and eighteen ships destroyed. President Roosevelt called it "a date which will live in infamy" and, with the approval of Congress, declared war on Japan. Corning, suddenly a wartime mayor at an age some men were going off to battle, sought to inspire and rally the citizens of Albany with a maturity beyond his years. "I will enter upon the duties of mayor of the city with the determination that my first thought will be to meet the demands of the nation, to be ready at all times to keep Albany in the forefront of the municipalities of the nation, to keep its citizens ever conscious of the tremendous duty that confronts them and of the sacrifices that they may be called upon to make," Corning said in his first public speech as mayor. "I will do my utmost to keep our affairs on an even keel and the daily life of our city as normal as the abnormal condition of the world will allow." Just sixteen months later, on April 13, 1944, Corning, who oversaw the draft boards, was drafted into the Army, declining a deferral and brushing aside opportunities for an administrative officer position far from combat. Instead, with the blessing of Dan O'Connell, who convinced the mayor of the political payoff of such a move, Corning left his wife and two young children and his desk at City Hall behind. He served as a private, a combat infantryman, until his discharge in September, 1945. He returned to Albany just in time to roll over his Republican challenger, Harold J. Murphy, in a landslide re-election victory.

To consider Corning's political career is to observe a remarkable streak. Alongside his three undefeated runs for the Legislature without a loss and his perfect 11-for-11 record in mayoral elections, Corning had only one defeat in fifty-seven continuous years in elected public office – his unsuccessful 1946 race for Lieutenant Governor. Corning hadn't wanted to be tapped as the candidate, since he had no passion for statewide office, but he ran out of deference to Dan and to honor the memory of his father, who was Al Smith's second-in-command in 1928; it was a campaign of commemoration for Corning. Tammany Hall's James A. Farley wrote to Corning from New York City on September 5, 1946 to congratulate him for the lieutenant governor nomination:

> I was a great friend of your father and your uncle, both of whom
> I knew intimately and had not only an extremely high regard but

a real affection. They were kind, considerate and generous to me at all times and I shall always recall most pleasantly the fine association I had with them. You bear an honored name and you made a splendid record in your services to your city and state, and in the recent war. There is no doubt but that you would fill the office of Lieutenant Governor with a credit and distinction and give to it the dignity and intelligence so necessary in that most important post.

Corning was paired on the Democratic ticket with U.S. Senator James M. Mead of Buffalo as the gubernatorial candidate. Corning and O'Connell realized early on in the campaign that he was a sacrificial lamb being offered for slaughter to the jaws of the extraordinarily popular and powerful Thomas E. Dewey ticket. But it was the O'Connell-Corning machine's turn to fall on its sword. For the first and only time, Corning knew what it felt like to be one of his Republican mayoral opponents as Corning was crushed by GOP incumbent Joe R. Hanley in the Lieutenant Governor's race of 1946, losing by 1.4 million votes. "More votes than all my victories for mayor combined," Corning was fond of saying, a way of lessening the embarrassment with humor. Still, Corning had a graciousness in defeat. He wrote a letter of congratulations to Lieutenant Governor Hanley. "Thank you for your letter of November 7," Hanley wrote back to Corning. "It was just like you. I did appreciate the way you conducted the entire campaign, and I can say to you, regardless of what happened at election time, that you have grown in stature throughout the entire state."

Salt in the wounds of the decimated Corning came in the form of a letter from Glenwood J. Moeller, of North Tonawanda, New York, on November 16, 1946. "Congratulations to New York State on your defeat, Mayor Corning! The inane, simple, poppy-cock dribble which you drooled during your vicious campaign was the depth of a distorted mental capacity, moral turpitude and dishonest American citizenship. (Signed) An Honest American Citizen." Corning never met a crank he didn't like and, without fail, responded, as he did with every letter that came across his desk. Corning replied the following day, on November 17, 1946. "I also am glad to know that you consider yourself to be an honest American citizen. I'm hoping to have the undoubted pleasure of meeting you sometime in the not-too-distant future."

The people of Albany didn't hold it against Corning that he was a loser in his only try for statewide office. He was re-elected to his third term as mayor in 1949 by one of his largest margins. It's instructive to observe all eleven of Corning's elections for mayor in a single block and to chart the occasional blips in his otherwise solid pattern of popularity – notably the 1973 squeaker against Carl Touhey that coincided with damaging revelations of mismanagement and cronyism by the State Investigation Commission (SIC). Here is the elective record of Mayor Corning. 1941: Corning, 57,868; Benjamin R. Hoff, 11,087. 1945: Corning, 50,868; Harold J. Murphy, 14,313. 1949: Corning, 60,497; Charles E. Walsh Jr., 16,215. 1953: Corning, 54,690; Thomas E. Mulligan, 17,617. 1957: Corning, 57,129, Edward Ray, 9,321. 1961: Corning, 49,192; Rev. Robert Hudnut, 15,112. 1965: Corning, 45,637; Jacob Olshansky, 10,995. 1969: Corning, 37,644; Al Hartheimer, 14,981. 1973: Corning, 25,390; Carl Touhey, 21,838. 1977: Corning, 30,812; Michael Ruberti, 6,970. 1981: Corning, 29,713; Charles Touhey, 13,709.

When it came to such a string of numbers, Corning was adept at reducing complexity to a simple theorem. For instance, by way of explanation for his historic forty-two-year tenure as mayor, Corning said, "I like being mayor." The elaborately and exquisitely detailed organization of the machine could, in Corning's mind, be viewed with utter simplicity: "I like doing business with my friends." Corning also was a pragmatist. Although political positions such as State Senator or United States Congressman have an impressive sound and connote power to the general public, Corning understood they were, in actuality, large titles with small authority. The real power, he saw, resided in the mayor's office at City Hall, where Corning only had to place a phone call to make anyone do anything he wanted. That was raw, unadulterated control. It was omnipotence, really, and Mayor Corning had it. Senator Corning, which he had been, or Congressman Corning, which he could have been, did not begin to approach that kind of potency – beholden as those positions were to numerous special interests and political benefactors. Mayor Corning had only O'Connell from whom to take orders and, after Dan died and the usurpers to the throne were subdued, the kingdom and the power and the glory were Corning's and Corning's alone.

Corning's control reached beyond City Hall. He had influence with patronage positions on the state level and ordered his political foot soldiers to rat out their friends and acquaintances all over town. "I would appreciate your checking on Mr. Martin J. Goodman, 66 Pheasant Ridge Drive, Loudonville," Corning wrote to Charles Hall, chair of the Democratic Party in Colonie. Goodman was an attorney with the state Department of Motor Vehicles and was shown to have Republican leanings, so Corning turned thumbs down on Goodman. The same went for scores of others, including Environmental Conservation department attorney Marc Pellegrino, of Guilderland. Corning wrote to banker Andrew Andersen: "I would appreciate if you would check on Mr. Pellegrino . . . he seems to be antagonistic to the Democratic Party." Corning submitted dozens of names of state Office of General Services (OGS) employees, where the mayor controlled the valve on a pipeline of patronage jobs. Corning held the destinies of hundreds of state workers in his hands. A letter or phone call from the mayor could mean the difference between being hired or fired, promoted or demoted. On October 28, 1975, for instance, Corning wrote to OGS commissioner James O'Shea. "In connection with Donald Miller, of 61 South Lake Avenue, Albany, he is an insurgent Democrat, a poll watcher for Theresa Cooke and a Cooke worker in the general campaign against the Democratic candidate. He, in no way, could be endorsed here."

Two decades after Corning wrote that letter, Miller was told of this secret backstabbing by the mayor. Miller, a retired mechanical estimator with twenty-eight years' service at OGS, was not promoted to the ranks of state engineering administrator during his career. Miller spent several moments in stunned silence when told of the letter Corning wrote clandestinely to Miller's boss. "At first I thought it was funny, but then I became outraged," said Miller, who was still living in the same South Lake Avenue house in 1996, not far, ironically, from the mayor's "official" residence. "I can't believe he'd try to hurt me that way. I was such a little fish. I was no threat to Corning. He had no idea even who I was." Miller said he and his wife, Rita, whose politics also were investigated by Corning's aides, are enrolled Democrats. Miller was a career, low-level state worker not actively involved in politics. One day, after being asked to assist, Miller helped out on the campaign of Theresa Cooke – a Democratic insurgent whom Corning despised. "I was a poll watcher for the Cooke campaign one day and that was the extent of my political involvement," Miller said. "It's unbelievable that Corning took the time and effort to go after me. It shows you the scope of the mayor's power and something of his paranoia, too."

Corning became obsessed with retaining control over every facet of his kingdom and keeping the machine in power. The man beloved as "the people's mayor" wasn't above using brutal purging tactics to cut down enemies. In Corning's voluminous files marked "Politics" and preserved in the archives of the Albany Institute of History & Art – those documents that survived the days of shredding by Corning's secretaries after the mayor's death – a portrait emerges of a mayor as ruthless political boss. Corning had his spies out in the community, watching for lapses in loyalty among Democrats, eager to report transgressions to the mayor. Corning's reprisals were swift and forceful. The scenario worked like this. Corning would get a call from a snitch ratting out a Democrat who had strayed. Corning would write to his assistant, Bill Keefe, to start an investigation. Dozens of notes from Corning to Keefe are in the file with the same wording: "Bill: I would like you to quietly and confidentially get me the political picture of . . ." Keefe would write back in a couple of days with a full run-down of the indictable offenses by the person on Corning's hit list: campaigning for a Republican, fraternizing with insurgent Democrats, failing to contribute money, time and effort to machine candidates, etc.

Here are a few representative samples. Corning to Keefe August 1, 1975: "It is my understanding that Richard Edward Damm signed a petition of Betty Gross on Line 6, Page 15. Mr. Damm indicated that he was a resident of the 15th Ward, 4th District. I would like to quietly investigate this to see if Mr. Damm who signed the petition is the same Mr. Damm who is Director of Planning for the County of Albany." Keefe responded that they were one and the same. Damm's rise in county government was about to come to an end courtesy of Corning. John Jennings wrote to Corning on December 4, 1975, looking for a job for his friend Thomas J. Callanan, of Delmar. "This is just a note to say that we checked on Thomas J. Callanan," Corning responded a few days later. "He apparently worked hard for the Republican ticket last year." Nothing more needed to be said about Callanan's job prospects.

Corning was the conduit for an enormous amount of political patronage, at city, county and state levels. After the mayor's death, his secretaries, Miller and Dooley (who knew how to keep a secret as well as they typed) presided over a great shredding marathon. They won't say who gave the orders – they're too loyal for that – but they were told to shred all of the political patronage files at City Hall. The secretaries knew which ones. They were spread out among the mayor's office and several nooks and crannies around City Hall. "There were six to ten cabinet files full," Dooley recalled. "That was a lot of documents to shred. It took us a couple of weekends, shredding hour after hour." Corning's confetti. The tales of many careers made or killed were buried in that avalanche of shredded paper. *Requiescat in pace.*

Corning's network was broad. He got notes from Homer Perkins informing the mayor about the activities of Nebraska Brace. Perkins, long the lone black Democratic county legislator, also was given a job as a city building inspector by Corning; some in the black community openly referred to Perkins as an "Uncle Tom" for the way they perceived that he had sold out to Corning and the machine. Perkins was able to parlay his city job into ownership of a dozen properties in the city. One hand washes the other, the mayor liked to say in private. Perkins reported on Brace, a black political maverick among Democrats, for attending a meeting with Nolan and later supporting the mayoral challenger. When Brace defied Corning – the mayor had said "it's not your time" – and ran for alderman in the third ward in 1977 against the machine candidate, Corning loosed the wrath of the organization. "They threw everything at me, from trying to kill my petitions to putting up a lot of money for my challenger," Brace said. "I beat them three times against all odds without ever getting an endorsement from the Democrats. I won because the people in the black community wanted change. They felt the machine wasn't moving with the times, blacks weren't getting opportunities and Homer Perkins was too much in Corning's pocket." Still, when Brace prevailed by thirty votes in the 1977 election to his first term as alderman, Corning called him the morning after to offer congratulations. The mayor was always willing to turn an enemy into an ally. Brace's harsh rhetoric against Corning and his policies softened over time and the two began to help each other out. "I remember there were a few times the mayor would call and say he wanted to have a few black faces at an event, so he would give my wife and me a couple of $125 fund-raiser dinner tickets and ask us to go to represent the city," Brace said. The spell of Corning's charm was potent. "I'd still fight with him on issues, but I really got to like the guy," Brace said. After being voted out of his aldermanic position in 1989, Brace had a job with Nolan in the State Senate and now works with the Albany Housing Authority. The machine has a way of wearing down even the fiercest opponent.

The finesse of the machine was something to behold. Corning and O'Connell knew when to back off and not gird for a battle it had no chance of winning or a war in which the political casualties would be too high even if the machine might emerge victorious, as was the case with the hands-off policy against the Republican dynasties in Bethlehem and Colonie. That *laissez faire* strategy became a blueprint for other challengers, including Corning's relationship with the immensely popular hawkish Democratic Congressman from Schenectady, Sam Stratton. "Corning never liked Sam because Sam was anti-establishment and bucked the Democratic machine," said William Murphy, a retired English professor at Union College in Schenectady who was Stratton's campaign manager and his political consultant for thirty years. Stratton also was enormously popular, widely admired and won re-election by stunning margins, a rival to Corning's reputation as political master of the Capital Region universe. Murphy recalled how Corning directed machine operatives to gerrymander Stratton's district several times, without avail. "Sam was the most dynamic politician and vote-getter around and they couldn't beat him," Murphy recalled. "Finally, they called a truce. Dan O'Connell met with Sam and said they wouldn't do anything to try to hurt him anymore. Corning had his power base over in Albany and Sam had his in Schenectady." Before the truce, however, Corning submarined Stratton's high hopes to receive the Democratic nomination for governor in 1964 at the party's state convention in Syracuse in the days before statewide primaries, according to Murphy. "Sam was the front-runner and was eager to face Rockefeller, but Corning, who was chairman of the convention that year, was against Sam," Murphy recalled. "Corning wouldn't even bring up Sam's name on the floor. Robert Morgenthau was nominated, Corning pushed him through the seconding process, banged the gavel and said the convention was adjourned. I remember Sam's daughter crying, 'It isn't fair. It isn't fair.'" All's fair in love, war and in politics – at least in Albany.

Corning thrived on the power that came with being one of the last of the dying breed of old-fashioned urban machine bosses. At the 1972 national Democratic convention, Corning ripped into Howard Samuels, a veteran politico, as unfit to lead the McGovern campaign. Samuels dashed off an angry letter on August 22, 1972. "I never thought I'd see the day when Erastus Corning would publicly create division after a divisive primary when unity is so necessary," Samuels wrote. Corning liked to hold the destiny of so many men and women in his hands, their fate awaiting his political whims. State Supreme Court Judge Joseph Hawkins of Poughkeepsie wrote to Corning pleading to be given an opening on the state's highest court, the Court of Appeals. "It was good to get your resume, and your kind note," Corning wrote in reply to Hawkins' bid on March 21, 1972. "You never can tell what will happen in this game of picking candidates."

From Dan O'Connell, Corning inherited deep connections to national politicians, including President Harry Truman, to whom O'Connell delivered Albany County by a huge plurality. That political favor had a long shelf life, providing Corning entree to the White House and a sympathetic ear from Truman when the mayor lobbied the president for federal aid for Albany. Corning wrote to Truman on May 28, 1949. "Dear President Truman: I want to thank you very much indeed for your courtesy and consideration to me yesterday during what must always be an extremely busy schedule. I am enclosing a memorandum prepared in part by the Albany Port District Commission and in part by me on my request for funds to complete Stage One of the survey looking towards deepening the Hudson River. Anything that can be done to hasten the appropriation of funds for this survey will be greatly appreciated."

Corning went to the well again with Truman two months later, in July of 1949, seeking federal approval and funding for the construction of a new dam and reservoir on the Sacandaga River that would prevent the perennial springtime flooding of Broadway and parts of downtown Albany along with other riverside communities along the upper Hudson. Truman's secretary Matthew J. Connelly responded to Corning on July 6, 1949. "The President asked me to check into the above matter very carefully and we have been advised that it appears no further action by the Federal Power Commission is necessary in order for New York Power & Light Corp. to proceed and to apply for a license to build a new dam on the Sacandaga River."

The mayor also had many opportunities to participate firsthand in the hurly-burly of national politics. Beginning with Dan O'Connell's naming Corning a replacement delegate for Corning's deceased father at the 1934 Democratic National Convention, Erastus Corning participated in eleven national conventions – a string broken only by his service in World War II. The mayor's political savvy served him well on the larger stage, as he negotiated behind the scenes at conventions and leveraged his support of a candidate for future political favors. Rarely, it appeared, was Corning outfoxed. Reportage on the conventions by the local press portrayed Corning as a dignified statesman above the fray, rather than the backroom political power broker he was. Corning scored prestige points and burnished his political image with his attendance at the conventions. Only once did Corning seriously misjudge public sentiment and end up losing favor with his constituents, a misstep that occurred at the turbulent 1968 convention in Chicago.

Corning went to Chicago that long, hot August during the great national divide over the Vietnam War in the company of Arthur Kirwin, a party operative. Corning was a supporter of Hubert Humphrey, although he let the wooing by Senator Eugene McCarthy play itself out in hopes of goodies to come. Humphrey gained the presidential nomination by more than 1,100 votes on the first ballot that night and chose Edmund Muskie as his running mate. Still, the mood at the convention was one of highly charged anarchy. The Democrats were deeply splintered by a move to draft the slain Robert Kennedy's younger brother, Ted; by George McGovern's anti-war campaign; and by the platform committee's refusal to insert a plank urging a halt to bombing in Vietnam. Corning did not support that anti-war plank. Nothing of the chaos on the floor of the convention hall's Amphitheater approached the cataclysm in the streets outside, however, as anti-war demonstrators engaged in a titanic clash with 20,000 police, National Guardsmen, and soldiers assembled by Mayor Richard Daley, who had promised to preserve law and order in his city. The streets near the convention Amphitheater were spattered with blood from the melee as an estimated 10,000 young people who had come to protest in a non-violent way America's involvement in the Vietnam War were rushed by baton-swinging cops. The police charged the crowd, shouting "Kill 'em! Kill 'em!" The demonstrators yelled back, "Pigs, pigs! Oink, oink!" The frenzied, brutal scene was captured by television news cameras as protesters chanted, "The whole world's watching! The whole world's watching!" Before it was over, more than 700 demonstrators were injured and 650 arrested; police reported eighty of their men injured. A stunned American public expressed outrage at Daley's strong-arm methods, called "Gestapo tactics."

Over the years, Daley and Corning, who shared common ground as Democratic machine mayors, had corresponded and become friendly after meeting at the 1956 convention. In Chicago twelve years later, although public opinion was running in strong opposition to Daley's forceful repulsion of the demonstrators, Corning made a point of walking to Daley's office from his room at the Sheraton Chicago Hotel to congratulate the mayor personally. Daley was gone, but Corning left a note with the mayor's secretary: "I wanted to congratulate Mayor Daley and members of the police department on a wonderful job and true sense of responsibility. I believe they kept a violent element from destroying a good part of the city of Chicago." Corning told a *Times Union* reporter that "large groups of people wanted to cause confusion and disruption in downtown Chicago. These groups deliberately tried to get arrested and get others arrested. I applaud Mayor Daley's response. I consider the police heroes."

Back home in Albany, Corning's praise of Daley deeply divided the citizenry. A *Times Union* editorial on September 3 criticized the mayor for commending "the brutal bullies of the Chicago police department" and posed the thought: "One might wonder what Mayor Corning has in mind for Albany." Two weeks later, on September 19, the Albany branch of the NAACP called a press conference to lambaste Mayor Corning for his praise of Mayor Daley. Corning received dozens of letters from residents of Albany, both in support and in opposition to his stand on Daley's police action, although the negative view held a slight majority. A few letters offer the flavor of the reaction. From retired Sgt. Major Jack Cogan of Albany: "Congratulations on your firm stand in Chicago for law and order. Your willingness to stand against popular opinion of the moment is outstanding." From D. Arthur Leahy of Albany: "I am not against the colored, the hippies or the yippies or any other minority groups – but these are crucial times in America. You have shown not only in works but in actions your determination to mean what you say. This takes courage." From Madeline Kellogg of Watervliet: "As a taxpayer, I would like an explanation on this shameful act performed by you." From A. Youngerman of Albany: "This was the most brutal, calculated police action I had ever seen and comments of eyewitnesses confirmed my opinion. I consider it both strange and unfortunate that you should congratulate Mayor Daley for this exhibition. I have always thought better of you." Corning wrote back to Youngerman to defend himself: "I think my position on the matter was arrived at from talking to hundreds of people and from personal observation."

After a few weeks, the matter began to blow over in Albany, but Corning was stung by the criticism; his skin wasn't as thick as he professed. A presidential panel, headed by Milton Eisenhower, chided the Chicago Police for having used "unrestrained and indiscriminate" violence in its report at the end of November. But the Chicago boss remained unrepentant. Mayor Daley sent out a form letter on October 25, 1968 to his supporters, Corning among them: "Dear Friend: It was most heartening to read your kind words of support for decisions I made only after thorough and deliberate consideration of all the facts at hand . . . The right to dissent is what makes our country great; disruption and divisiveness are threats to that greatness." Two years later, the "Chicago Seven" were found not guilty of conspiring to incite a riot – Corning's footnote in that historic event long forgotten by then.

Mayor Corning played a more prominent, albeit less controversial role, in an earlier Democratic convention in Chicago, the 1952 edition. Corning the war hero and exceedingly popular mayoral vote-getter was at the height of his powers. Leading up to that convention, in the 1950 election for Governor of New York, Corning was prominently mentioned among the short list of Democratic contenders and the mayor issued a statement that he would not accept the nomination, if offered, "under any circumstances." Corning also ran the 1950 New York State Convention as chairman. Manhattan Borough President Robert F. Wagner Jr., a future New York City mayor, a longtime friend and Yale colleague of the mayor, wrote Corning on September 8, 1950: "Dear 'Rastus: Just a note to congratulate you on the splendid job you did as Chairman of the State Convention. Such an undertaking will often-times have its heartaches, but you handled each situation just the right way. Many of the delegates from New York County on the way down in the train expressed themselves along the lines that you were as good, if not better, than many other persons they had seen in that spot. I thought you ought to know this, and hope to see you soon." Despite his own rejection of Democratic party leaders who tried to draft him as a gubernatorial candidate, Corning's personal political stock remained at an all-time high in Chicago in July, 1952.

Corning went to Chicago to push the nomination of Oscar R. Ewing for President at the urging of Dan O'Connell, a friend of Ewing's, who was head of the Federal Security Agency and a New Dealer who was a key ally to President Truman. Corning had sent a letter to Truman at the White House lobbying for Ewing. Corning himself, privately, seemed to be leaning toward Adlai Stevenson, but the ever-diplomatic and loyal machine mayor was in Chicago to do Dan's bidding. Corning, the team player, gained national publicity by delivering the nominating speech for Ewing on the convention floor on July 25, 1952. At the time, O'Connell was feuding with state Democratic chairman Paul J. Fitzpatrick, who was marshaling his forces to nominate New York Gov. W. Averell Harriman. The convention was contentious and split along special-interest lines. Even though

Corning liked what he saw in Stevenson and there was a surge of support behind the Illinois governor, Corning stuck with Ewing on all ballots out of loyalty to Dan. Finally, after a rowdy floor session that lasted past 2:30 a.m. on July 26, the Democratic Party nominated Stevenson, an admired intellectual. His running mate was Alabama Senator John J. Sparkman. The cerebral Stevenson said: "Eggheads of the world unite. You have nothing to lose but your yolks!" Corning liked Stevenson's brainy, highbrow style and worked hard to elect him. Corning secretly got a kick out of the assessment of Stevenson by Richard Nixon, running mate for Republican presidential candidate Dwight D. Eisenhower, who called Adlai "the appeaser who got his Ph.D. from Dean Acheson's College of Cowardly Communist Containment."

After the '52 Chicago convention, even though the machine backed Ewing and feuded with state Democratic leaders, O'Connell and Corning pledged support for Stevenson. Corning drafted a letter at the request of O'Connell, a kind of declaration of independence sent on August 18, 1952 to Stephen Mitchell, Chairman of the Democratic National Committee: "Albany County will give Governor Stevenson a majority of over 15,000 in the coming election. If past elections are any criterion, Albany will be the only Democratic county north of the Bronx in spite of the fact that Stevenson and Sparkman will carry the state by over 300,000. We have not had assistance from the New York State Committee under its present leadership, would not have welcomed it at any time, and, in the light of its actions in recent years climaxed by the National Convention, reject its leadership completely and will have nothing to do with it. We take full responsibility for Albany County and a substantial Democratic majority. We are Democrats and as Democrats we will not be found wanting." In the end, however, the Stevenson campaign foundered and Eisenhower won in a landslide. Corning wrote to Stevenson at the State Capitol in Springfield, Illinois on November 5, 1952, the morning after the Democratic washout. "Needless to say, I am sorry about the outcome of the election, and also that the estimate I gave you on Albany County was so far off [only about half of Corning's promised 15,000-vote plurality]. The compensations to me, however, were great, as your running gave me the honor and pleasure of meeting you, and also your wonderful sister. I want to tell you that, in my opinion, you conducted the finest campaign in my memory, and I believe of all time."

Even though his Party and, by inference, he, too, came out a loser in 1952, Mayor Corning managed to soar above the political wreckage and came away with an enhanced national reputation. Oscar Ewing wrote to Corning on May 4, 1954. "Dear Erastus: Just a day or two ago I received a bound copy of the proceedings of the Democratic National Convention in 1952. I re-read the speech you made nominating me for President and I want to tell you again how good I thought the speech was and how much I appreciated you making it. I know Dan asked you to do it, but I cannot refrain from telling you again how splendidly you did your part. I have been away much of this winter and this has prevented me from going up to see Dan. With his operation and slow recovery, I dare say it was a relief to him not to have too many visitors. P.S. Those of us who are working on the dinner for President Truman Saturday night appreciate very much your taking a table." In subsequent years, Corning received personal congratulations on his re-elections from Stevenson, President John F. Kennedy and other national political figures.

Corning used this political stature to identify and support up-and-coming candidates well ahead of the curve, enhancing his own reputation for political acumen. For example, secretary Bobbi Miller remembered taking dictation from the mayor shortly after she arrived in 1974 as the mayor replied to a letter from Jimmy Carter. Miller, who was active in local politics herself, prided herself on keeping on top of politicians Corning frequently wrote to, but this Carter was a new one. "Mister Mayor," Miller said. "I've never heard of this name. Who's this Jimmy Carter?" The mayor smiled his sly little grin and replied, "Oh, he's just a peanut farmer. But you'll be hearing about him." The political oracle had spoken. Corning's prediction came true, with Carter's name splashed across headlines and television newscasts a year later; Corning delivered Albany County solidly for Carter in '76. Carter was deeply appreciative of Corning's help and he tapped Corning to serve as upstate campaign director in his re-election bid against Republican Ronald Reagan in the 1980 election. Carter invited Corning to join him in Pittsburgh aboard Air Force One to fly along on a leg of the campaign trail, ending at a Carter rally in Rochester. Corning delivered Albany County to Carter by 22,000 votes, but Carter was beaten elsewhere in a Reagan landslide. Carter showed his gratitude by inviting Corning and his daughter, Bettina, to a small farewell dinner party at the White House.

At times, Corning's participation on the periphery of presidential politics surprised machine loyalists. Although he almost always remained on the machine track and stayed the course Dan O'Connell laid out for him, Corning occasionally strayed from the straight and narrow. A case in point was the mayor's breaking with O'Connell and the machine in the 1972 presidential election. O'Connell, eighty-six and infirm, wanted Hubert Humphrey or Washington State U.S. Senator Henry "Scoop" Jackson, both personal friends of the boss, as the Democratic nominee. Corning backed the liberal, anti-war Democratic candidate George McGovern and became co-chair of the McGovern campaign in upstate New York. Out of spite, O'Connell went to the convention as the head of Albany's uncommitted delegation, the only city in the state that didn't elect a McGovern delegate. Even after McGovern won the nomination, O'Connell wouldn't back the liberal senator from South Dakota. Corning's McGovern campaign co-chair, Sarah Birn, a lawyer who lived in Delmar, recalled the mayor's stand. "Mayor Corning caused a genuine split in the organization by backing McGovern. It surprised all the old-timers, but McGovern was concerned about the environment and so was Corning," Birn said. "More than that, it was an anti-Nixon effort. He told me he was going to do everything possible to defeat Nixon because he detested him and didn't want him to become President. The mayor said Dan's policy was not to get involved in national politics, but he felt this was different." Birn and Corning hosted a McGovern strategy dinner with campaign manager Pierre Salinger at the Fort Orange Club for Democratic county chairmen throughout the region. Birn said Corning worked hard for McGovern. "I wouldn't say he was a true McGovernite, like I was, but he thought McGovern the only Democratic candidate with a chance of beating Nixon," Birn said. Corning's support was decisive as McGovern carried Albany by 12,000 votes – the only city in the state the Democratic candidate won. Nationally, Nixon rolled up the highest winning percentage in history by a Republican, 60.7 percent of the vote. McGovern carried only Massachusetts. Corning voiced no regrets for his support of the overwhelming loser.

Despite such defeats of Stevenson and McGovern during forays into national politics, Corning never lost his confidence in identifying and supporting candidates he believed in even if it meant risking his own political capital. The mayor's greatest discovery was Mario Cuomo, in whose career Corning played the role of kingmaker. In the 1982 New York gubernatorial election, Corning was the earliest and most ardent supporter of long shot Cuomo, who was Carey's Lieutenant Governor and had scant statewide name recognition. The smart money and power brokers in the Democratic Party were lining up behind the popular New York City Mayor, Ed Koch. The nomination appeared to be Koch's for the taking, but Koch made some disparaging remarks about Albany – calling the city "sterile" and without decent restaurants or culture and filled with pickup truck-driving rednecks who shopped at Sears. Koch's put-downs of Albany infuriated Corning, who threw his support behind Cuomo with vigor. In fact, Corning convinced Cuomo to abandon any fears and to run.

Matilda Cuomo, the candidate's wife, remembered Corning calling her husband. "Mario, will you run?" Corning asked Cuomo. Cuomo and his wife demurred, saying Koch had all the organization and money and Cuomo had no chance. It would be political suicide. Corning grew adamant. "We don't want Koch," the mayor said. "Will you run?" Cuomo recalled, "Corning kept saying to me, 'Listen to me. You will win. You will win.'" Cuomo added, "Nobody thought I could win. Corning called me into his office and went through the numbers with me and he was a brilliant mathematician. Corning had done the analysis and it was remarkable. More importantly, Corning saw something in me he liked. I was plain and hard-working and I was willing to live in the city's hotel, The Wellington, which was nothing to write home about." Cuomo finally relented, heeded the command of Corning and entered the gubernatorial race. Corning was hospitalized during Cuomo's campaign. "My husband and I went to see the mayor a couple of times in the hospital because he was such a great help to our campaign," Matilda Cuomo said. "We felt terrible when he died, but we were glad he lived long enough to see my husband inaugurated as governor." Cuomo's wife said her husband learned a political lesson he never forgot from Corning. "He told Mario never to lose touch with the people. Even though the mayor was from the upper-class, people from all classes loved him."

Cuomo said he came to consider Corning his mentor, although the mayor had died before he could witness the rise of his protégé, who was pushed perennially as presidential timber. Cuomo had first glimpsed the political power of Corning when Cuomo was a young law clerk in the state Court of Appeals in the 1950s. "I've never found anybody else like him in American politics," Cuomo said. "He's certainly one of the most unusual politicians we've had, along with the Huey Longs and all the other remarkable personalities. I can't imagine any politician being brighter or more imaginative than Erastus Corning. I don't regard the political games he played as venal or significantly corrupt. He played the game his way, with extraordinary personal and professional integrity." Cuomo liked the way Corning surrounded himself with what Cuomo called "old Fishhooks McCarthy politicians." Cuomo explained, "Fishhooks McCarthy was Al Smith's right-hand man. He went to church every day of his life and offered the same prayer: 'O, Lord. Give me health and strength. I'll steal the rest.'"

Former Albany County Executive Jim Coyne, the fallen golden boy of the machine and deposed Albany County Executive who served a prison term for accepting kickbacks and bribes, included an incendiary anecdote about the Koch-Cuomo race in his political memoir, *Questions That Bother Him So*. Coyne was quoted in the *Times Union* as supporting Koch and was considering giving Koch his endorsement. Corning called Coyne the morning the story broke. The mayor's tone was angry and threatening. Coyne wrote, "He said to me that many of my programs had been approved in the past year by him and that he felt that we had a good relationship. However, if I were to endorse 'that faggot son of a bitch' you will never again get a program through the [county] Legislature and there will be a war!" Coyne had visitors in his office and called Corning back a short while later. Coyne said, "Mr. Mayor, when, where and what do you want me to say when I endorse Mario." Coyne said in his book that he told his staff, "I just ate crow for Mario." Cuomo challenged the veracity of Coyne's anecdote. "I just can't believe Mayor Corning used the term faggot," Cuomo said. "That was not his style. He was earthy, but he was not a bigot and would never use a term like that. I had many conversations with Corning and he didn't like Koch and used a lot of terms to describe him, but never vile ones."

Closer to home, Corning enjoyed special status with a succession of New York governors at a level far exceeding that of the state's other mayors. Historically, the governor's office in New York had been a stepping-stone to the White House and holders of that title received immediate national stature. Corning became a fixture at the Capitol for political functions and at the Executive Mansion for social gatherings. "Mayor Corning was in the Mansion quite often," recalled Robert Bennett, butler and superintendent at the Eagle Street governor's residence for thirty-eight years and six governors, from Dewey to Cuomo. "He was a true gentleman. If I needed something taken care of or some service from the city, I just called the mayor and he took care of it regardless of whether a Democrat or Republican was in the Mansion." At social functions at the Mansion, Bennett tried to give Corning special treatment, but the mayor refused. "I'd try to take the mayor to the front of the line, but he said he would wait his turn like the rest," Bennett said. "He didn't want any special favors." During Nelson Rockefeller's fourteen-year tenure at the Mansion, Corning was a frequent guest, despite their different political affiliations and their battles over the South Mall, an elected school board in Albany, and other issues. "The mayor's mother was a close family friend of the Rockefellers from Maine," Bennett said. "I remember the mayor's mother going for rides in Mary Rockefeller's Austin to search for wildflowers in the Helderbergs."

In June of 1978, when Rockefeller's second wife, Happy Rockefeller, joined the former governor to help dedicate the State University Plaza, Mrs. Rockefeller enjoyed a reunion with Corning. "Erastus, it's so good to see you!" she said, rushing up to Mayor Corning and giving him a hug. "Do you remember when Nelson and I were first married and no one here would talk to me? You were the only one at those parties who would talk to me. Do you remember, Erastus? I'll never forget it." The exchange was published in the *Knickerbocker News* on June 6, 1978. "I remember," Corning said, with an austere, aristocratic smile as he and Mrs. Rockefeller linked arms and walked up State Street to a private dinner at LaSerre Restaurant.

During the four decades of his mayoralty, Erastus Corning had opportunities for other political jobs dangled before him: Congressman, State Environmental Commissioner, State Democratic Party chairman, Governor. He turned his back on all of them. Perhaps Corning's most curious turn-down was an offer from President Harry Truman for Corning to become a member of his cabinet. "Truman offered Corning the job of Secretary of Commerce, but the mayor turned it down," said Mark Heller, a law partner of Howard Nolan. "I know that's true. My father [Julius Heller, a longtime newspaperman with the *Knickerbocker News*] was in his office at City Hall when Corning took the call." Heller said he had never made that story public before. Heller's revelation helped explain a cryptic scouting report on Mayor Corning from an anonymous political consultant. The unsigned, typewritten memorandum was sent to President Truman on February 8, 1952 and was contained in the collection of Frances

Perkins of Washington, D.C. and housed in the New York State Library Archives. The unknown author critiqued Robert Wagner Jr. ("appears to be almost illiterate although he is a graduate of Yale College and Yale Law School") and Franklin D. Roosevelt Jr. ("young and a very poor record of attendance in Congress") and others in addition to Corning. The report on Corning is informative for its political astuteness and unvarnished view of the mayor.

> With regard to Erastus Corning, Mayor of Albany, I personally have been much impressed with him on the few occasions when I have seen him but I learn from those who have had an intimate opportunity to observe him as Mayor that he has been completely under the thumb of the O'Connells and that Dan O'Connell ran the city of Albany from the Federal Penitentiary where he once resided. The O'Connells have, as you know, always been regarded as the less desirable type of Democratic bosses. Al Smith definitely broke with them, but that was a good many years ago. There is also a wide difference of opinion as to whether Erastus Corning's father, Edwin, who was Lt. Governor under Smith, was a desirable character. I was reliably informed that Governor Smith told he would never permit him to be Governor because Corning would turn the State of New York over to be looted. This statement was said to be a direct quotation. And I do now recall that Smith felt very doubtful and suspicious of Edwin Corning. An uncle was also not much, I am told, and was given to helping himself. Two Erastus Cornings have been physicians and have had an admirable background. Elting Corning, who is an uncle of the present young Erastus, is a very fine man. It appears that Elting and Dr. Erastus recommended that young Erastus be trained for a profession like medicine or law or even the Church, and not be allowed to go into politics. Young Erastus is very bright, had excellent academic marks at the Academy and at college, and some of the older friends of Dr. Erastus regretted the fact that he ever went into politics, thinking it would ruin what might otherwise be a good person. I am sorry to report this, for I have been very well impressed with him, and his popularity among veterans is astonishingly good.

That intriguing synopsis touched upon the essential enigma of Erastus Corning. So much promise, so little progress. It is no small feat to get elected eleven times to any position, be it dog catcher or mayor. But in the symphony of Albany politics, Corning played second fiddle to Dan O'Connell for thirty-six of his forty-two years in City Hall. The job remained interesting for Corning because of his close interaction with a wide range of people and the way he controlled the destiny of so many in his hands.

But what did Corning do with all his local power and extraordinary access to state and national political arenas? Sooner or later, whether political allies, friends from his social class, or blue-collar city employees, everyone voiced the essential Corning conundrum: Why did he stay mayor of Albany for so long? With all his intellect and ability, why did he not reach for higher office? Where was his political ambition? There were as many interpretations as people who knew Corning. The mayor himself used a simple analogy: "I like to be a big fish in a little pond." Many friends believe that went a long way toward answering the question, but other motivations were ascribed to what some view as Corning's record as an underachiever. Thomas Brown, the State Assemblyman, remembered Corning's reply to his question about the mayor's apparent lack of political ambition. "Well, Tommy," the mayor began. "To ascend to something you assume is high but which has no real power is one thing. But to be in the center of a whirlwind every day and to be able to control the storm is another." As Mayor of Albany, Corning could be king. But as Congressman or State Senator or, even, Governor, his powers were more princely in their scope. By moving up he would inherit layers of superiors to whom he would have been beholden in higher office, be it statewide or national. In Albany, he answered only to Dan O'Connell and when Dan died, he called all the shots himself. The power at City Hall was pure and undiluted, a potent drug.

Close associates, such as Judge Francis Bergan, offered a more pragmatic reading of the flat line of Corning's political career. First of all, the power in the mayor's office was more centralized and intense than perhaps any other elected position. Secondly, the lucrative insurance business that flowed to Corning's Albany Associates would dry up if he left City Hall, and that conduit of cash was Corning's primary means of support. Thirdly, the Polly Noonan factor was an Achilles heel political opponents would exploit if Corning tried to move up to statewide or national office. Finally, Corning really did enjoy direct contact with the gamut of people he saw and

helped as mayor and his mastery of the job left time for pursuing his myriad intellectual and outdoor sporting interests. That's the way Bergan saw it
and many Corning associates agreed with the sage judge's summation.

Some saw Corning's role as Albany's mayor for life as a symbol of
Dan O'Connell's political genius. "Erastus never sought the job. Dan had
to talk him into being mayor," Polly Noonan said. "It turned out that
Dan's instincts were perfect, because Erastus ended up loving the job and
didn't want any other. Erastus told me early on that his philosophy was
that he is mayor of all of the people all of the time. His door was always
open at City Hall, his home telephone number was listed in the phone
book and you could call him anytime if you needed something."

Over the years, Corning answered the question of political ambition
to a certain extent. Why did he never go higher than mayor of Albany? Jack
McLean, a cousin of Polly Noonan's and the mayor's hunting buddy
recalled: "He told me he never had any desire of going higher than State
Assemblyman, which was a part-time, three-month job in those days,"
McLean said. "He could run his insurance business, work in the Legislature
and pursue his many interests. He said Dan made him mayor and once he
got in the job, he decided he really loved it. The job was different from day
to day because the people and the issues changed all the time." Polly's son,
Peter Noonan, said Corning would get irked if asked such a pointed question. "I won't say he was lazy, but the Mayor's job was safe and too many
demands went with higher office," Noonan said. "He had everything
knocked as mayor and did whatever he wanted. I think he took more pride
in making kings than in being one himself."

Corning never provided a complete, satisfactory answer to his closest friends regarding the essential political riddle that defined him. That
didn't stop journalists, pundits and politicians from attempting their own
plumbings of Corning's motivation. Generations of reporters put the
question to Corning. Veteran *Times Union* political writer Joe Picchi
thought Corning was just being honest with himself. "After his run for
Lieutenant Governor, I think he recognized he didn't have statewide
appeal," Picchi said. "I don't think he could have won anything outside
Albany County. He was the big fish in the little pond like he used to say.
He liked to be talked about for higher positions, but I think he knew none
of them was really going to happen."

Thomas M. Whalen III, Corning's successor as mayor, formed his
own opinion after campaigning and working in Corning's shadow for sev-

eral years before the mayor's death. "He was a patrician to the manor born and Albany was his manor," Whalen said. "His family's heritage and roots were here. He was lord of the manor, a big fish in a small pond. He was also intensely people-oriented. He came to enjoy the job because of its interaction with people. He liked the power, too, but I think the daily interaction with people was the key. If you become a U.S. Senator or a Governor, you lose that direct connection with people."

Corning protégé Jack McEneny, a State Assemblyman and former city official, said the mayor told him he didn't feel challenged by, and didn't particularly enjoy, being a state legislator. The job of mayor seemed to be the position to which his talent and temperament were best suited. "It was a job he was comfortable with and he never felt like a slave to his job," McEneny said. "Corning's job as mayor opened up all kinds of doors he couldn't have opened otherwise. And he knew how to do the job so well that he had the time to pursue other interests."

The stories of Corning's power in Albany are legion. It was that omnipotence that lay at the core of his wanting to remain in the mayor's seat, refusing to give up its privileges even from his death bed. A few anecdotes will suffice. For instance, Donald McKay, chairman of Tougher Industries on Broadway in north Albany, knew Corning from business dealings and from membership at the Fort Orange Club. McKay was a pilot who owned a small private plane. One night at the club, McKay told the mayor that he was fed up with the fact that there was no covered hangar space at Albany County Airport and he was going to move his plane to Schenectady County's covered hangars. Corning said he'd have county attorney Bob Lyman call McKay. A few weeks later, back at the club, Corning asked McKay if Lyman called yet. McKay said no. The next day, Lyman called, apologetic, and determined what McKay wanted at the Albany County Airport. "And, just like that, because the mayor said so, it was done," McKay said. "The county built indoor hangar space. That's the way the mayor was. He'd say make it so and it was done." As another example, "Adirondack" Dan Malmed discovered the potency of a call from Mayor Corning when the bank was foreclosing in the 1960s on the building Malmed leased for Adirondack Dan's Army-Navy Store downtown. "Lew Swyer told me to buy the building that was being foreclosed on and I went up to the mayor to ask what my bid should be," Malmed recalled. "Corning made one call to Lieutenant Governor Malcolm Wilson, who was a director at the bank that was foreclosing on the building. Corning spoke to Wilson and the bank took my bid. That's all it took. We've owned the building ever since."

Despite an almost blind reverence by Albanians, such incidents added to the humanness of Corning, who used his power for good and ill, revealing a character of shadow as well as light. A personal act of financial intercession by the mayor disclosed for the first time by Corning's accountant, Howard Kahn, is revealing on this point. Corning hired Kahn in 1965, after his audit exposed corruption that helped bring down a Democratic machine in Cohoes, a rival to the O'Connell-Corning Albany machine. The Cohoes political scandal diverted attention from crusaders looking at the Albany machine. Corning, a math whiz himself, came to appreciate Kahn's brilliance with numbers. Kahn, born in 1915 and a lifelong Albanian, also was a loyal Democrat. In 1965, Corning gave Kahn an important assignment. Albany Castings, a manufacturer of malleable castings in Voorheesville, was broke and on the verge of going under. The steelmaker Cornings had known the owners of Albany Castings, the Blumenower family, since the early part of the century. Corning was also a poker-playing buddy of Henry Blumenower and handled his insurance through Albany Associates. Corning stepped in and offered to help the Blumenowers during their financial dire straits. The mayor asked Kahn to conduct a thorough audit of Albany Castings and to reorganize the company under Chapter 11 of the bankruptcy law. Kahn determined that Albany Castings required an immediate cash infusion of about $300,000 to stave off creditors, meet payroll and remain solvent. But the company's credit was not good enough to secure a loan through its bank, National Commercial Bank & Trust [now Key Bank], of which Corning was a director. Albany Castings needed a white knight and they found one in Corning. "Mayor Corning stepped in and personally guaranteed the loan with the bank," Kahn said. "Within six months, Albany Castings folded up like an accordion and Corning paid the whole loan he had guaranteed. He came up with something in the neighborhood of $300,000 out of his own pocket. He was as good as his word." Kahn never fully understood Corning's motivations for bailing out Albany Castings to the tune of six figures. While Corning was comfortably wealthy, $300,000 represented more than a year's income combining his mayor's salary, the insurance business and investment dividends. "There was the family connection with the Blumenowers. But he also told me that Albany Castings employed a few hundred laborers, mostly inner-city black men from Albany, and they were his people and he wanted to save their jobs as mayor," Kahn said. "If you want to be cynical, you can say his motive was to keep those men voting for him. I honestly believe it was done out of altruism." It wasn't the first time Corning had made ill-advised business loans – a euphemism for charitable donation when it came to the mayor. Kahn said Corning similarly bailed out failing lumberyards in Maine in which he held financial interests. "He wanted to keep those folks up in Maine employed, keep them out of the woods, in his phrase," Kahn said. There is a post-script to the Albany Castings saga. In auditing Corning's income tax return, an Internal Revenue Service agent disallowed Corning's claimed deduction for the bad loan to Albany Castings. Kahn helped Corning challenge the write-off and won a partial deduction. "He got a consolation prize, but he still lost a couple of hundred thousand dollars in the deal," Kahn said. Kahn fretted over his bill for the Albany Castings work. "We considered waiving our fee because he's the mayor," Kahn said. "I finally decided we did a job for him and we're entitled to get paid the full amount without any discount for being mayor. I sent him the bill on a Monday, and I got the check Wednesday with a nice thank-you note. And for years afterward, we got customers who said the mayor referred them to us."

Kahn also handled accounting for Corning's insurance business, Albany Associates, and helped the mayor out of a political sticky wicket on more than one occasion. One politically sensitive assignment was Kahn's 1972 audit of North End Contracting Co., whose no-bid contract to operate the city's landfill was being investigated for irregularities by the State Investigation Commission (SIC). North End, owned by William Carey, Ninth Ward Democratic leader, got the landfill contract and Corning's insurance company got North End's insurance business – worth an estimated $40,000 per year in 1971. SIC investigators disclosed Carey's million-dollar, cost-plus arrangement made Albany's refuse costs many times higher than other cities. SIC accountants determined North End overcharged Albany $450,000 over an eighteen-month period, including a yearly charge of $13,000 for the rental of a twenty-year-old Jeep worth $800. The damaging SIC allegations were being splashed across the newspapers and the negative publicity was hurting Corning as he prepared for what he knew would be a tough election in 1973 against Republican Carl Touhey. Corning hired Kahn to perform an independent audit of North End's books. The mayor's caveat: "Howard, I want this all put to bed before the election." North End handed back a hefty six-figure check to the city as reimbursement for the overcharges and Kahn's firm contributed $1,000 to Corning's campaign against Touhey.

Even those defeated by Corning admired the wit, intelligence and finesse with which the mayor played the political game. Carl Touhey, the Republican-Independent candidate for mayor in 1973, remembered a board meeting during their campaign of the National Commercial Bank & Trust, to whose board both candidates belonged. "I was sitting next to Erastus and I had a hole in the sole of my shoe," Touhey recalled. "The president of the board said, 'Gee, Carl, you've got a hole in your shoe, just like Adlai Stevenson.' Without looking up, Corning muttered, 'He didn't get elected either.'" Touhey laughed at the recollection. It was that sense of playfulness in politics that caused Touhey to continue his cordial encounters with Corning at the Fort Orange Club, where both were members and where the two talked over glasses of Scotch and occasionally shared a table at dinner.

Touhey was Corning's toughest and most memorable opponent in eleven mayoral elections. The two men were well matched. Touhey was an Ivy Leaguer from a wealthy Albany family that had established a Ford dealership, Orange Motors, in the city in 1917, the year before Carl was born. Touhey had taken over the car business and expanded into real estate development, the soft drink industry, and other companies. When Touhey challenged Corning in 1973, his political inexperience was mitigated by other factors: Touhey was bright and savvy in business, he was wealthier than the mayor, and he could call upon the same upper-class connections.

Touhey separated Corning the convivial fellow club member from Corning the machine mayor. It wasn't a single incident that pushed Touhey into the political arena for the first time in 1973, but an accumulation of disgust. "Corning had this aura of being a great mayor, but Dan ran the show and the city was a dump, a rundown pothole of a place at that time," Touhey recalled. "Half the city owed their jobs to the machine and you better never forget to be grateful and show your loyalty because they could take away the job at anytime." Touhey was tired of being cut out of legitimate business opportunities, too. "We're the oldest and biggest Ford dealership and the city never bought a single car from us all those years," Touhey said. "One year they bought the police Packards and then Hudsons and then Buicks and then Dodges. It depended on who had an in with Dan that year. The thing was rigged and we knew Dan was getting some kind of kickback, but we didn't lower ourselves. We refused to bow and scrape before the machine to get their handout, because that meant you owed them your vote and more."

Finally, in 1973, Touhey's anger was converted into action. "I was fed up and decided to run for mayor for the hell of it," said Touhey, who had never run for any elected office before. Touhey's announcement that he was entering the race coincided with news of a bid by insurgent Theresa Cooke, Corning's loudest critic, for city comptroller. At his weekly press conference on February 21, 1973, Corning dubbed the Touhey-Cooke candidacies "a double-decker Danzig special with tastefully arranged mushrooms." That was Corning's witty rejoinder to imply that Capital Newspapers publisher Robert Danzig and Albany County GOP chairman, Joseph Frangella, a mushroom farmer, were pulling strings behind the scene. Nonsense, Touhey claimed. He started out as an independent and only accepted the Republican nomination much later in the campaign. "I had my own money and picked up probably ninety-five percent of the campaign costs out of my own pocket," said Touhey, who estimated he spent about $70,000 on the mayoral race. He abandoned efforts to raise money, Touhey said, "because people were afraid of reprisals from the machine." One contributor to the Touhey campaign was a close personal friend of Corning's, the developer Lew Swyer, who gave Touhey $500. Touhey never made Swyer's support public until now. "It took a lot of guts for Lew to give me money and it symbolized discontent over the lack of progress in the city under Corning," Touhey said.

Touhey's financial independence bought him political freedom, too, and he spoke his mind. His campaign picked up steam as he hammered away at Corning's record of broken promises. Touhey the businessman cut through Corning's subterfuge in handling city finances with no oversight. Touhey offered convincing, critical interpretations of financial information and the mayor's secretive budgets. Touhey was smart, he was tough, and he knew the numbers. His message was that taxes were going up without anything to show for it. On the election stump, Touhey was convincing in holding Corning's feet to the fire over what he considered gross mismanagement and mounting city debt. At the same time that Touhey was scoring direct hits on the mayor's empty promises, Corning was being called before SIC investigators and grand juries investigating police corruption and city purchasing improprieties. Polls showed Touhey's support on the way up and Corning's approval rating plummeting.

Corning had to find a way to distract voters from Touhey's solid and convincing attacks on the mayor's financial mismanagement of the city. Corning needed comic relief and a distraction from the issue; he found it in Vincent Bytner, the third candidate in the 1973 mayoral race, a self-styled Independent Democrat. Bytner was a kind of working man's Ross Perot, colorful and quotable and a diversion. Bytner, who ran an Albany travel agency, knew Corning from booking the mayor's flights and from asking the mayor for favors as president of the Central Avenue Civic and Merchants Association. Bytner remembered Corning taking him aside at the Polish Community Center just after Corning's campaign against Touhey had gotten underway. "I like the way you handle yourself. You're not afraid to speak up," Bytner remembered Corning telling him. "Why don't you run for mayor? I'll take care of getting you on the ballot." Bytner found himself in the race and played his role as buffoonish distraction even better than Corning could have anticipated. Bytner dressed up a donkey, put a fedora on the animal's head and marched it down to City Hall to symbolize his Democratic endorsement. The mayor came out of his office and enjoyed a belly laugh over Bytner's antics. "I'm the type of guy some people call a loose cannon," Bytner said. "I know that's why Corning wanted me in the race. That was fine with me. I'm not afraid to be outrageous." Corning rewarded Bytner's grandstanding by removing objections to a large Bytner campaign sign across the front of his Central Avenue travel agency; Corning personally called Bytner to say his sign permit was waiting for him at City Hall. At Corning's suggestion, Bytner had a small slogan painted in a bottom corner of the sign. "Bytner. A gentleman and a scholar."

During a candidates' debate in the dignified environment of the Albany Institute of History & Art, Bytner incited an argument over Christopher Columbus' ethnic lineage. Touhey was reduced to raving and sputtering as he clashed with Bytner. Touhey said Columbus was Spanish. He's Italian, Bytner said, pounding the table and demanding an apology to all Italians. Corning stood safely to the side, laughing at the fireworks. "That debate just fell apart," Bytner recalled. "To me it was a lot of fun. Afterward, Corning just winked at me. I was having a great time."

On election day, Bytner hired an airplane to tow a banner across Albany that read, "Vote Bytner." The night of the election, Bytner recalled he got a call from machine lieutenant Charlie Ryan. "Vince, whatever you do, we don't want you to impound the ballot," Ryan told Bytner ominously. "I'd never do that. What's the matter? Is Erastus losing?" Bytner asked. Ryan was silent. "He's in trouble, but we'll be able to pull it out," Ryan told Bytner. "How many is Erastus going to win by?" Bytner asked. "It will have to be a couple of thousand votes," Ryan answered.

Down at Democratic headquarters, on the tenth floor of 75 State Street, whispers were running through the room. "The mayor ain't running too well," was the way one longtime committeeman put it to a *Knickerbocker News* reporter when returns were about half in. The machine had been predicting a victory margin for Corning of 20,000 votes and something had gone terribly wrong. "How'd you do in your ward?" one ward leader asked another. "Terrible," was the reply. "And you?" the second asked the first. "It was a disaster." At 9:40 p.m., Corning called his eighty-seven-year-old political boss, Dan O'Connell, who was at his home on Whitehall Road. "Things look pretty good," the mayor was overheard to say, but his usual rock-ribbed election night confidence over the outcome was missing. The longest night of Corning's political career wore on. The returns showed that Corning and Touhey were running neck and neck in a virtual dead heat. Bytner hung up the telephone after talking to Ryan and watched the returns on television at home, beginning to piece together his theory. "Charlie said Erastus would win by a couple thousand votes and I had 3,500 signatures on my petition from people I knew supported me," Bytner said. "I'm convinced they took my votes and gave them to Erastus. I have no proof, but it all added up." At 1:15 a.m., with all the returns in, Touhey's remarkable challenge – he beat Corning in ten out of nineteen wards – had come up 3,552 votes short of victory. The count was Corning 25,390, Touhey 21,838 and Bytner 320. In his concession speech, Touhey called his showing "a milestone and a breakthrough in Albany politics. We showed that the people of Albany henceforth are going to demand and get good, clean government or else."

The unprecedented tightness of the race prompted Frangella, the county GOP leader, to call on Governor Rockefeller to impound the ballots. Frangella's call came late and was mostly a symbolic move. Rockefeller complied, ordering the State Police to round up and place under their care the voting machines. Hours passed. By then, if, indeed, there was vote tampering, it easily could have been committed and completed. The impoundment effort lost steam in subsequent days, mainly because Touhey didn't force the issue, and it was eventually dropped. No election irregularities were charged. Touhey has heard the rumors about how the machine stole the vote and denied him the election. He doesn't doubt they were capable of such shenanigans, but it's a moot point to Touhey. "I wasn't ready to be mayor and didn't want to be mayor," Touhey said. "I ran out of personal principle. If I would have won, I would have called for a recount."

Bytner had no direct evidence to support his conspiracy theory that the machine stole the election from Touhey by transferring Bytner's votes to Corning, thus enabling the mayor to squeak by for a ninth term. Bytner offered the following as circumstantial evidence. Less than six months after the election, Corning called Bytner personally to say the building permit that had been denied Bytner for three years had been approved – after the request to build an in-ground swimming pool on a tiny vacant lot Bytner sought to purchase from the city next to his home at 70 Marsdale Street had been tied up in bureaucratic red tape for years. The obstacles suddenly vanished shortly after Corning's narrow win over Touhey. "You can put two and two together and see it any way you like," Bytner said. "I say it was a political payoff. I was their dupe and I didn't even know it. I wouldn't have run if I realized they were going to use me as a stooge and steal the votes out of my column. I don't think Erastus was directly involved. But there were plenty of insiders with utter loyalty to the machine who could have pulled it off."

The day after the election, Touhey received an unexpected visitor at his office at Orange Motors. Mayor Corning had come calling. "I thought it was quite strange, but he congratulated me for my campaign and we talked a little bit more," Touhey recalled. "And then he said, 'I want you to know all the things you pointed out about the budget didn't go in one ear and out the other. I'm going to make some changes.'" Touhey said he waited and waited but nothing changed.

Touhey even visited the man he considered the true Albany power broker, Dan O'Connell. "Dan's big Irish wolfhound plopped its huge paws on my lap and Dan said, 'Hell, you must be OK. My dog likes you.'" And so it went. Touhey harbored no animosity toward Dan, nor to Erastus, with whom he continued to share genial hours over Scotch and scuttlebutt at the Fort Orange Club. What Touhey saw as his contribution to Albany was the fact that his strong showing in 1973 broke the logjam of fear over challenging the machine. Hence Nolan's primary in 1977 and the credible campaign for mayor in 1981 of Touhey's son, Charles, who got almost 14,000 votes.

Mostly, though, Corning's mayoral elections were a blur of landslides. Few gave Corning even the slightest scare, although, in 1969, architect and political neophyte Albert Hartheimer received a sizable 14,981 votes. That was newsworthy for a Republican in Albany, even when one considers Corning pulled in 37,644 votes that year to swamp Hartheimer. "Nobody wanted to take on Corning," Hartheimer said. "It was like going up against the firing line." Hartheimer had grown up in the stranglehold of Mayor Frank Hague's political machine in Jersey City and decided to challenge Corning out of a sense of democratic principles. He campaigned on a slogan borrowed from Joseph Stalin's renegade daughter: "I prefer the chaos of democracy to the order of a dictatorship."

The O'Connell-Corning machine enjoyed long stretches of tight-fisted order marked by brief moments of chaos when small threats to unchecked power managed to break the stranglehold. One such glimmer of opposition came in 1961 – years before the Hartheimer challenge – in the form of a new political party called Citizens United Reform Effort (CURE). Led by an idealistic, twenty-seven-year-old assistant pastor of the Westminster Presbyterian Church, Rev. Robert K. Hudnut, as mayoral candidate, CURE and its slate of Charles Liddle for council president and Stanley Ringel for treasurer campaigned on an eight-point "Bill of Rights for Albanians." The reformers offered an indictment of the two-decade rule of Mayor Corning: for being hostile to new business entrepreneurs; for poor public services and deteriorated city facilities; for giving no-bid contracts to his friends; for not allowing an independent, elected school board; for punishing dissidents with reprisals. "We believe that control by fear, control by favor, control by boss are a continuing insult to our dignity as human beings," the CURE statement concluded. Hudnut received 15,756 votes to Corning's 49,406. But a few bricks had been chipped out of the monolithic machine and what began as small ripples of dissatisfaction were beginning to build into a tide of opposition.

CURE's effectiveness was limited by the fact that it was a small, poorly financed, grass-roots movement that failed to gain the full support of the Republican establishment in Albany County. The lack of institutional backing by the GOP raised anew in some political observers' minds the longtime rumor that there had been a deal cut between O'Connell and Corning and the then-Albany County GOP bosses, William K. Sanford and Joseph Frangella. The rumored arrangement was that the Democrats got Albany without challenge and the Republicans got Colonie and

Bethlehem without a fight. Theories of a political deal are nonsense, according to Harry D'Agostino, who now runs the GOP organization in Colonie, which has controlled town politics since 1895. "Sanford was a lot like Corning, both were tall, aristocrat Ivy Leaguers from prominent families," D'Agostino said. "They belonged to the same clubs and social circles and they got along. People saw them together and started talking. But there was never any deal." There was no need to play ball with the GOP, since the O'Connell-Corning machine enjoyed a strong edge in the balance of power in Albany County. "Dan knew he could control the county with Albany, Cohoes and Watervliet," D'Agostino said. "The other towns were just trouble because you'd have to promise jobs and there weren't enough jobs to go around. He didn't need their votes and he saw them as not in his best interest and just a lot of headache."

D'Agostino conceded there was a political allocation system in effect between the suburban GOP bosses and the urban Democratic leaders on the matter of judgeships. "An election costs a lot of money," D'Agostino said. "So the leaders would get together, pick a candidate, cross-endorse, agree that the other party would get a judgeship next time around and both organizations saved a lot of campaign money." Corning was so assured of his political abilities that he could separate political from personal endeavors. "Nobody ever got really pissed off at the mayor because he was such a classy guy," D'Agostino said. "He had political opponents, not enemies. When Joe Frangella was GOP chairman, he took his shots at Corning, but they remained friends and got along outside politics."

The Republicans seemed to adopt two attitudes toward Corning: to go along to get along, or to directly challenge and risk the consequences. One who chose the latter, more dangerous course, was John W. "Jack" Tabner, who had battled the O'Connell-Corning machine since the early 1950s, first as a GOP Assemblyman and later as the Albany County Republican Committee's attorney. Tabner, an Irish-Catholic who grew up in Cohoes, broke with his Democratic genetic markers in the early 1950s and embraced the underdog Republicans. "It was a little like the Polish militia fighting the German Wehrmacht," Tabner said. "But I was sickened by how the Democrats used their power against outsiders. They controlled everything and only helped their insiders. It was like a tribal religion. I knew Corning for thirty years and I consider him a great waste of talent who let the city go down the tubes because all they cared about was staying in power."

Tabner worked as legal counsel to the Colonie planning board through the 1950s and 1960s and watched how Corning's inflexible machine tactics hampered economic development in Albany's deteriorated downtown. "Sears and Macy's originally wanted to go into downtown Albany, but Corning put so many political stipulations on the deal that they left Albany and came to us," Tabner said. "It was a piece of cake taking business away from Albany, because Corning and O'Connell were out of touch. Dan was a nineteenth-century man. Corning was the king going through the city scattering coins and crusts of bread when he's at the Fort Orange Club eating cake." Tabner represented a widely held view of Corning, that he and the machine acted as a brake that slowed progress in Albany and turned away many potential business developments for the city.

Corning's own cousin, John "Jack" McElroy, a Republican businessman, was eventually driven out of Albany by machine politics. McElroy was president of Central Warehouse Corp. in Albany, but he sold the Albany facility, built a freezer warehouse in Colonie and eventually moved to Florida because of political impediments. "The machine made it difficult for most businesses, which is why Albany never reached its full potential and is the way it is today," McElroy said. "New businesses didn't want to move in here. I had a big out-of-town outfit that wanted to make a huge freezer warehouse complex in conjunction with our building in Albany. After doing a detailed business analysis, they said they couldn't come to Albany because of the machine politics."

Retired bank president Gerald Fitzgerald, a Republican, had a unique vantage point from which to witness the regressive quality of Corning's politics when it came to the business community. Fitzgerald was president of the former National Commercial Bank & Trust Co. and Community State Bank, on whose boards Corning sat. "I separate my views of Erastus Corning as a bank director and a mayor," Fitzgerald said. "He did an excellent job for both banks." When it came to running the city of Albany, though, Fitzgerald faulted Corning for sacrificing progress and the common good for the benefit of the machine's chosen few. "Any new project in Albany first and foremost had to be something the machine wanted and if it conflicted with a greater need for the people of Albany that was immaterial," Fitzgerald said. "Corning's management style was to control everything, down to the smallest detail, so that he could preserve his power." Fitzgerald criticized Corning and the machine for what he termed the "massive stagnation" of Albany. "The machine was only interested in maintaining the status quo and as the world grew and changed, those in the young generation with education and ambition moved out and left a blue-collar city subject to the domination and the dole and the patronage that kept the machine in power. History has a way of repeating itself and that's the classic machine situation."

This growing criticism of Corning's policies among the city's business leaders dovetailed with the gains Republicans made with the CURE reform effort in the early 1960s – exposing the machine's vulnerabilities by the end of a turbulent decade in the nation's history. Dan Button, the former *Times Union* executive, had pulled off a stunning upset in 1966 in the race for U.S. Congress over machine candidate Richard Conners, who had been expected to be a shoo-in replacement for the retired Leo O'Brien. But an increasingly dissatisfied electorate, coupled with the machine's growing arrogance and lackadaisical campaigning, began to point out the fault lines along Albany county's political landscape. "Dan O'Connell was so sure Conners was going to beat me he said, 'Don't worry. We don't have to run for office. We stand,'" Button recalled. "The public decided I wanted the job the most, I was willing to work hard for them and I wouldn't be a machine yes man in Washington."

Button proved himself a solid, hard-working representative in his first term in Congress. Furthermore, Button's well-organized and strongly financed re-election campaign in 1968, which swamped machine candidate Jake Herzog by a 31,000-vote margin, provided the impetus for unprecedented Republican inroads. Though Corning remained untouchable, the king of the hill in City Hall, throughout Albany County, the GOP, behind a newfound vigor and combativeness in party leader Frangella, ripped a few holes in the heretofore impenetrable Democratic machine's wall of dominance. In 1968, the Republicans swept into power with a force that political pundits did not think possible. The margins were wide and the machine candidates knocked out of office were longtime incumbents: Arnold Proskin beat Joseph Scully for district attorney; Walter B. Langley turned aside Senator Julian Erway; Raymond Skuse defeated Assemblyman Frank Cox; and Fred Field crushed Assemblyman Harvey Lifset.

At times, Corning was something of a hindrance to machine candidates as much as a help. He had bucked popular opinion by supporting Mayor Richard Daley's crushing police response to demonstrators at the 1968 Democratic National Convention and remained in favor of the increasingly unpopular Vietnam War. Sensing a chink in Corning's armor,

Frangella, the GOP leader, acted like a bear awakened from hibernation. He took to the TV airwaves in the 1968 campaign with this message for Corning: "Albany's mayor is a leader of a nineteenth-century machine which pretends to support Democracy, while the capital city rots in its grasp. For too long he has sought to be a dictator of this city and county. Mr. Mayor, we promise you that Albany County will keep a free press and that you and your kitchen cabinet of outdated cronies will be retired before too long. Do not try to frighten us with the United States District Attorney. You've tried to use the Albany County Grand Jury many times for political purposes. I know. I've been subpoenaed myself."

The Republicans were young and hungry and the Democratic machine candidates were old and stagnant and beginning to be viewed as party hacks by the voters, among whom a tentative streak of independence was widening. Corning appeared flustered by this turnabout and began lashing out at the press, which was publishing reports critical of the mayor's administration and of machine tactics. Corning resorted to typical intimidation. On November 1, 1968, Corning announced at a press conference that he had asked U.S. Attorney General Ramsey Clark to investigate Capital Newspapers (publishers of Albany's *Times Union* and *Knickerbocker News*) for alleged violations of federal anti-trust laws.

The mayor was willing to find allies wherever he could, despite the quickness with which political allegiances could turn sour. Nolan, who became Corning's nemesis in the 1977 primary, had actually been a loyal spy for the mayor in 1968. Nolan wrote to Corning on March 27, 1968 with campaign advice that turned out to be prophetic. "You are making the biggest mistake of your life by trying to put Joseph Scully in as D.A.," Nolan wrote. "He is nothing but a playboy and the papers are waiting for you to make this appointment. Take your time and investigate what I am trying to tell you. If you don't, you will have a Republican D.A. next year. Get Pinckney or somebody else that you can handle." Corning did not heed Nolan's advice. The 1968 election turned out to be the worst overall upset for the O'Connell-Corning machine since it seized power in 1921. The machine operatives were stunned. "We were a bunch of nuts with a Rube Goldberg contraption compared to their organization and we knocked them off," Skuse said. "It was an absolute shock for O'Connell and Corning. Of course, we awakened the sleeping giant. I didn't have any illusions of a long tenure." Mayor Corning was chastened, but defiant in the aftermath of the Republican explosion. "I know that, when a circumstance such as this comes along, you just work that much harder," Corning told the *Knickerbocker News*. "Everybody works that much harder and you look the thing over carefully and just buckle down and go to work."

As a result, Corning micro-managed the 1970 elections himself. The machine ran Thomas Keegan to try to unseat Proskin from the D.A.'s office. Corning the Yale math whiz wrote to candidate Keegan on October 28, 1970 and offered a tutorial in nitpicking. "I heard one of Mr. Proskin's radio ads this morning in which he said that the backlog of cases had been cut 200%," Corning wrote. "This, of course, is an utter absurdity, as there is no cut possible, mathematically, more than 100%. If you had 100 cases and a 50% cut, you would have fifty cases left. If you had a 100% cut, you would have no cases left. I presume that if you are going to talk about a 200% cut, it would mean that you would have eliminated 100 cases before they started."

The taste of the power of incumbency was short-lived for the Republicans. The Democrats managed to pull off some slick gerrymandering in re-drawing election districts, but they also practiced what Corning preached: they cast aside their complacency and went back to what had proven successful for them in the first place. They re-committed themselves to the hard, painstaking work of street by street, block by block, ward by ward organizing. They retired old machine hacks and replaced them with qualified, intelligent young candidates. They buckled down and went to work and the GOP fell like a tree with weak roots in a wind storm. "The GOP victories had a signal effect on the quality of all Democratic office seekers after 1968," Skuse said. "They put up dramatically improved candidates after that and we Republicans can be proud of creating that change."

Skuse was defeated in the Assembly in 1970 after a single term by Thomas Brown, but not before Skuse managed to introduce legislation that challenged Corning's dictatorial control of his appointed Albany school board, a patronage mill for the machine. Corning used his power to hold off for a few more years a change in the law that would force him to hold school board elections for the first time in Albany's history. Skuse, who was hired as chief lobbyist for the New York State United Teachers Federation (NYSUT) after losing his Assembly seat, remained a thorn in Corning's side on the issue of educational reform in Albany. "I chose to live in Albany, but the school system really irritated me," Skuse said. "The mayor appointed three friends to run the school board and the school system was filled with more part-time patronage workers than teachers and the teachers were not allowed to organize, so education in Albany was a fallow field."

Corning used his clout with Rockefeller to kill Skuse's elected school board mandate, although Skuse came back the next year to use his connections with the Republican Speaker of the Assembly, Perry Duryea, to pass it. "I knew that was political suicide for me at the time and that I had deeply offended the machine," Skuse said. "It was a brutal hit and started to break down the patronage in the school system and it opened the door for the teachers to organize."

Skuse used his two years in the Assembly to embarrass Corning and the machine politically, helping to organize a legislative hearing to investigate the sleight-of-hand financing practices of Mayor Corning: underestimate city expenses, bond out the deficits on twenty-year issues and, on paper, keep taxes low with a pending financial disaster for the next generation to face. "I remember I kept going after Corning, asking him how he could justify bonding out for an extended period to cover everyday expenses," Skuse said. "He was evasive and cold. I finally had enough and asked straight out, 'Mayor Corning, come on, why did you do it?'" Corning replied, "Because I wanted to." Skuse was dumb struck that the citizenry was not outraged with such effrontery. "Corning got away with that answer because people were afraid to challenge him," Skuse said. "The man had ultimate power and his answer effectively brought the hearing to a close. We got the truth, but it had no effect." After two years in the Assembly, Skuse was knocked out by Brown in 1970. "The great majority of people in Albany were satisfied living with low taxes and poor services in a pre-Depression atmosphere and that was a very strong thing to break."

The Republican reformers of the 1960s and early 1970s may have bent the O'Connell-Corning machine out of shape for a time, but they were not able to break its utter domination. The Republican breakthrough was not unlike the Battle of the Bulge in which Mayor Corning fought. The machine swiftly and forcefully repelled the enemy. They regained their seats with energetic, bright and young Democrats. The new crop was typified by Tom Brown, an Albany Law School graduate who also was a classmate of Howard Nolan's at Christian Brothers Academy. Brown was one year shy of his fortieth birthday when he defeated Skuse and put the Assembly seat back in Democratic hands. Brown credited Corning's political acumen: "He was a master of the political process. He advised me to go out to meet the people, listen carefully to what they want, try your best to give it to them, but avoid making a lot of big promises you may not be able to keep." Brown was elected to three terms in the Assembly and often sought Corning's counsel at City Hall on Saturday mornings. "I had gone to Dan a few times, but he always said, 'Listen to Corning. Listen to Corning.' The mayor understood the mystical ways of state government. His advice was to do my homework, be in the chamber to vote, keep in touch with him and Dan and keep close to the people. He also had a saying about political squabbles. 'Tom, don't trip over a pebble.'"

Corning heeded his own advice. He seemed always to be in complete control of himself and the situation, no matter how strong the pressure of politics. That was a lasting image of the mayor, protector and shepherd of Albany, smoothing out rough edges, blanketing the city from the jagged peaks and valleys that affected other American cities during the turbulent social upheaval of the 1960s and other times of uncertainty. Mayor Corning was a permanent presence, a steady hand on the tiller, steering Albany around shoals and other trouble. Constituents revered Corning with a mixture of awe and fear and hope that flecks of his power would rub off on them. On his birthday each year, October 7, Mayor Corning received dozens of cards and gifts from strangers to close friends to contractors offering thanks for work to job seekers hoping to prime the pump of patronage. A brief sampling from Corning's 1979 birthday: John Clyne (card); Becker Wrecking & Salvage Corp. (turkey and ham); Carosello Bakery (cake and cookies); Stulmaker's Ltd. (tie); Picotte Realty (azalea); Kasselman Electric (azalea and floral arrangement); Gary Becker (cake); James Tully Jr., state tax commissioner (cake); Mrs. Anthony Paolucci (handmade scarf); James Germano, state corrections services (slippers); Harold Gabrilove (clock); Wadie F. Hermina (card and calendar); George DeWitt (painting); Joseph Gulley (plant); Cossie DiPierro, Teamsters president (ham); Dott's Garage (card); Joseph Valenti (fruit basket); Vartan Tchekmeian (fruit basket); John Holt-Harris (trout and pheasant); Judge Lawrence Cook (subscription to *Sports Illustrated*); Richard Salomon (corned beef); Luigi Serafini (bread).

From his City Hall office, laden with gifts, Corning kept a firm hand on the doings of the machine's legislators up the hill at the Capitol. Harvey Lifset, a World War II hero elected to the Assembly for the first of six terms in 1956, remembered weekly visits to the mayor for political advice. "The mayor understood how the Legislature worked and he'd have suggestions for new legislation, for bills pending, how the electorate might react to cer-

tain votes coming up." When the Democrats gained control of the Assembly
in the mid-1960s, Lifset was named chairman of the powerful Ways & Means
Committee in 1966. That gave Lifset far-reaching control of legislation and
money, the twin engines that drove the state house. Lifset remained respectful of Corning's power. "I never took the position that I was chairman now
and Erastus should come up to see me," Lifset said. "I'd still go down to see
the mayor. It wasn't a matter of getting my orders. It was a discussion, but I
had the utmost respect for his opinion. But if he used the phrase, 'I've been
talking to Dan and Dan says,' . . . then you knew you it was something you
were being told to do." Corning adopted the machine's paternalistic pattern
of taking care of the little people and that extended to his brother, Eddie,
whose reputation in the Legislature was one of being a likable fellow with
limited ability. "Everyone knew Eddie rode in on the mayor's coattails, but
people still liked him anyway," said Lifset, who served in the Assembly alongside Eddie Corning. "He wasn't given much to do in the Legislature."

Corning worked his behind-the-scenes political influence on the local,
state and national levels. Although he was fiercely loyal to his Democratic
Party, Corning cut deals with Republicans when it suited his purposes. For
example, Corning did business with Schenectady Mayor Frank Duci, a
Republican who spent sixteen years in the office. Corning even attended a
testimonial dinner on behalf of Duci, a reward for Duci's going along with
Corning's plan to transfer garbage from Schenectady and neighboring
municipalities to ANSWERS, Albany's waste-recovery facility. "Politics and
running the city was Mayor Corning's twenty-four-hour-a-day business and
he loved it, from the people who came to his office to the deals to getting
patronage jobs for loyal Democrats," Duci said. "He operated by one hand
washing the other. I had several meetings with Governor Rockefeller and I
know Rocky was making deals with Corning and each one did the other
favors. There was a harmony there, despite the fact Corning was a
Democrat and Rockefeller a Republican. Mayor Corning did whatever it
took to get things done."

Sometimes, that meant quelling dissent within his own Party.
Insurgent Democrat Theresa Cooke got under Mayor Corning's skin perhaps more than any other political challenger in his forty-two years. Cooke
was anathema to Corning. Part of the reason was because she was a woman
and Corning, according to several women, including Polly Noonan, possessed a broad streak of chauvinism. Cooke, a housewife, also had paid no
political dues and had absolutely no experience. But apparently nobody told

Cooke you can't fight City Hall. She started poking around Corning's administration and dug up damaging information in the early 1970s. Cooke wasn't afraid to sling mud at the mayor and his cronies in front of the press. Cooke was a bright, attractive, vivacious woman and although he despised her politics, Corning made a few offhand remarks to friends that he admired her figure. Meanwhile, Cooke hammered away at Corning whenever possible. She held press conferences outside Corning's vacant home and official voting address at 116 South Lake Avenue in Albany as a way of focusing attention on the mayor's deceits. In January, 1972, in front of one hundred people at Chancellor's Hall in the State Education Building, Cooke charged Corning with "outright fraud" and "kickbacks" and coercion on behalf of his insurance company. She proposed a movement to impeach the mayor. Cooke offered analysis that she said proved that the 1972 city budget of $33 million included more than $14 million, or forty percent, of political patronage waste. Cooke gave a list of abuses: nine people on the payroll of the outdoor swimming pool at Lincoln Park in winter; twenty-seven people on the payroll of Albany Municipal Golf Course in winter; sixty-two employees allegedly working in Washington Park in winter; fifteen people for Swinburne Park's skating rink in addition to a twenty-three member grounds crew for the tiny park; forty-eight employees to tend Bleecker Stadium which had no winter schedule. "This city of Albany is among the most corrupt in the entire nation," Cooke charged. "And there's nothing in this city that Erastus Corning does not personally approve." In his speech to the Albany County Women's Democratic Club in the fall of 1972 Corning defended his fiscal practices with the claim that he and the machine undertook "the most careful husbandry of every single penny of every single dollar of the taxpayers' money throughout almost half a century."

If one needs confirmation of the extent to which Cooke managed to infuriate Corning and the machine, look no further than the old assessment tactic. The assessment was changed in 1971 on the property Cooke owned with her husband, Peter, at 164 Manning Boulevard in Albany, a two-story frame house the Cookes bought in 1970. In the span of one year since the Cookes moved in, the assessment was raised from $9,000 to $21,000, a hike of a whopping 133 percent. Cooke went to the press and got the assessment reduced to its original level of $9,000, but not before causing considerable embarrassment for Corning.

Corning's rhetoric began to ring hollow to Albanians, although this subtle shift portended no change in his lock on City Hall, while Cooke's rigorous analysis brought the machine's featherbedding ways into sharp focus. After a narrow defeat for city comptroller, Cooke came back a few years later, in 1974, by winning election to the post of county treasurer – a single-term passing annoyance to the mayor for life.

Aside from the power and the glory that came with being mayor for so long, Corning was in his milieu in Albany. Along with his family having been its leading citizens heading a small elite who ran the show in the city since the middle 1800s, Corning knew the texture of Albany, the stories of its families, the layout of its streets, the makeup of its neighborhoods, the intrigues of its history, the way it worked. It was a local knowledge he took to heart. He loved the city and the people who lived there. An illustration of the unfettered pleasure he found in being mayor is the saga of Chris and Betsy Mercogliano's house. Chris and Betsy came to Albany in 1973, youthful hippies who settled in as teachers at The Free School, an alternative school in a run-down neighborhood near the Executive Mansion. The Mercoglianos and their hippie friends ran the school and formed a community, or commune, in which they purchased gutted row houses, renovated them, and held them in common ownership. In June, 1980, the Mercoglianos, both twenty-six at the time, paid $2,000 for a condemned shell of a house at 3 Wilbur Street, just off Grand Boulevard and around the block from The Free School on Elm Street. The owner of 1 Wilbur Street happened to be Art Giguere, Polly Noonan's uncle. Giguere was concerned that the 3 Wilbur Street property was going to collapse onto his house, so he went to the mayor's office and asked to have the house torn down and Corning said he'd schedule the razing. "We raced up to City Hall Monday morning to stop the demolition," recalled Mercogliano, at the time a long-haired hippie with torn jeans, no money, no political clout and no idea how machine politics worked. The Mercoglianos pleaded with building commissioner Floyd Planz, who said to avoid demolition the building would have to be renovated to strict code. The Mercoglianos didn't have the necessary resources and took their case to the Capitol Hill Improvement Corp., where the couple was told to write a letter to Mayor Corning. In Albany politics, a letter to the mayor provided the key that unlocked many doors previously shut to citizens. As usual, Corning replied to the Mercoglianos the next day, June 12, 1980. "Many, many thanks for your note," the mayor wrote. "It was so thoughtful of you to write and I am so glad you are going to be neighbors to the Gigueres. If there is anything I can do to help either of you, please let me know." On a follow-up visit with Planz, the

Mercoglianos dropped Corning's name and said the mayor had written them a reply, offering any help he could give them. "The change in Planz was unbelievable," Mercogliano said. "The gruffness, the crazy code requirements, the ultimatums were all gone. The building department was totally supportive of us after that." The Mercoglianos secured a federal HUD grant for renovations and started work to shore up 3 Wilbur Street that summer. "It was open to the elements on three sides and was totally rotten, a non-house," Mercogliano said. "We went one sill and section of foundation at a time. It was slow going."

One of the aspects of the house that attracted the Mercoglianos to the property was the garden space behind it on which they planned to grow their own vegetables, raise chickens and goats, and practice a self-sufficient, sustainable, organic lifestyle. After the Mercoglianos were deep into the house renovations, they discovered their garden belonged to Albany County. They went to see John Lynch, head of the county's real property division and a machine operative. "He was a mean bastard and told us to get lost, we were nobody, he wasn't going to bend, the county wanted the property," Mercogliano said. The Mercoglianos went to city planner Dick Patrick, who told them to write the mayor a letter. Mayor Corning replied the next day. "Many thanks for your letter of Aug. 1. My guess is that we can work this out, but it will take me a few days to be sure. In the meantime, I visited Arthur Giguere and Mrs. Giguere yesterday and was so very pleased to see how much work you have done already. It looks great. I will be in touch with you again soon and I am returning the map."

Corning had learned from Dan O'Connell that a politician has nothing but his word to sell; the mayor was as good as his word with the Mercoglianos regarding the garden plot. Corning wrote to the couple on September 9, 1980. "We have appraised the property at $500, which seems to me to be modest. If you would like to have this property put up in auction, with little chance for anyone outbidding you, please let me know." Mercogliano, still a political neophyte and fearful somebody might steal his garden out from under him, called the mayor. Mercogliano said he told Corning he was afraid he'd be outbid. And then, as Mercogliano recalled, Corning paused for a very long moment. Finally, the mayor broke his silence: "Listen, Mr. Mercogliano. I can only tell you this one time. In order for every auction sale to be finalized, it has to be approved by a special committee of the Common Council, of which I am the head. Do you understand? No one else will get this property." The Mercoglianos got their lot for $500 and they have a lovely garden and goats and chickens in a small outbuilding behind their house at 3 Wilbur Street, where they've lived for eighteen years. The house is fully renovated and they live there with their two daughters, Lily and Sarah, who are students at The Free School a block away, where Corning was instrumental in assisting school founder Mary Leue by holding at bay city building inspectors who were ready to shut down Leue for code violations. Corning allowed Leue to make the code improvements in time, when she could afford them, given the school's shoestring budget. "None of us with The Free School were from Albany, we had no political connections, no clout," Mercogliano said. "We were hippies and radicals with this little off-beat school working with poor kids using unusual teaching methods. The mayor made his own assessment and decided we were worth helping to survive."

Betsy Mercogliano raised honeybees in the garden in the spring of 1981, and that Christmas, Betsy and Chris took a jar of honey from 3 Wilbur Street to Mayor Corning at City Hall. The mayor invited them to stay. "We sat there for a half-hour and we chatted about everything, from the progress on our house to The Free School to raising honeybees to the Gigueres," Mercogliano said. "He was the king archetype with profound paternal feelings for his city and its people." Mercogliano's fifth-grade students at The Free School interviewed Mayor Corning in his City Hall office on May 26, 1982 for their school newspaper, the *Classic*. Corning was gracious with his time among the students and generously expansive in his answers. The interview concluded with Corning's answer to the question, "How long do you plan to be Mayor?" Mayor Corning replied, "Well, I was re-elected last fall and I took another oath of office on January first of this year for another four-year term. I am seventy-two-years-old now and you don't look as far ahead at seventy-two as you did at thirty-two. So, I am living every day by itself. I hope to finish this term out, and if by some chance, I feel as good as I do today, maybe I will try again. But, I just don't know . . ."

The staff of the student paper returned to City Hall two weeks later to present Mayor Corning with a copy of the *Classic* in which they published his interview. They were told by Corning's assistant, Bill Keefe, that the mayor had to leave work early. The TV broadcast led off its report that night with the news that Mayor Corning had been rushed to Albany Medical Center Hospital with lung complications. He remained mayor from his hospital bed and died one year later.

Chapter 10:

Feeding His Soul: The Mayor in Maine and Afield

**"As you know, my main interest is to have the camp at
Floods Pond good and strong so that it will last a long time.
I am not so much interested in the finish of it."**

*Mayor Corning to Maine caretaker Leroy Dority on
March 10, 1948. Dority was building Corning a
Thoreau-styled log cabin in the wilderness.*

The two-lane country road wended its way past Fletchers Landing and skirted Graham Lake as shafts of light flickered through a cathedral of pines. The road dipped and curved, passing a scattering of shacks. "Bait" read a sign on one tumbledown bungalow. "That's where we used to buy our worms from a nice, old man my father called Mr. Worm," recalled the mayor's daughter, Bettina Corning Dudley. "Even if we weren't buying worms, my father always stopped there to talk to Mr. Worm and Mrs. Worm, as he called them." Ours was the only car around on a sunny, windless April morning. Spring comes late to Maine and remnants of the winter of 1995's record snowfall in excess of ten feet could still be seen in shaded ravines as the lake lapped at the shoulder of the roadway. "I've never seen the water this high," said Dudley, fifty-nine, who first came to Maine with her father just after World War II. The canopy of pines gave way to open fields of wild blueberries as the road dropped down a long, steep hill. As we began to climb up the incline, the view on both sides was of boulder-strewn swales of ocher-colored blueberry shrubs slowly returning to life. "Now, this is the game my father taught us to play," Dudley instructed as we continued driving up the hill. "Look off to the right as we reach the crest of the hill and the first one to spot water shouts, 'I spy Webb Pond!'" There, nestled into an emerald bowl of conifers, was a glint of sunlight on indigo. "I spy Webb Pond!" Dudley shouted with girlish glee.

Spring runoff had made the steep gravel drive impassable even for a four-wheel drive vehicle, so we parked the Pathfinder just off the roadway at the edge of a blueberry field. It's a one-half mile hike down to the Corning camp at Webb Pond, which the mayor's father built in 1928, the year of his heart attack and stroke that left him an invalid. Meant as a simple and quiet retreat far from the social whirl of Stoney Point, their lavish estate in Northeast Harbor, Edwin Corning never saw the place of solitude and curative refuge he created, which became for his family a powerful emotional touchstone and the most sacred place on earth for Edwin's son. "We're almost there," Bettina said. "My father's *sanctum sanctorum*." The harsh winter had left in its wake many blown-down trees, one of which tore out the single utility line serving the camp, knocking out power that had not yet been restored. This was Dudley's first visit to the camp since late the previous fall. As we reached the back door, we trudged over a large hump of wet, sandy soil. "Frost heaves," Dudley said. "Every spring, the camp gets knocked off a few of its pilings by the frost. But it rides out the waves and somehow, it's still standing every year when we return."

The seasons and cycles of the Corning camp at Webb Pond over the course of seven decades mirror the phases of the human experience. It was here, inside the rustic, cedar-shingled cabin that Bettina and her husband, Ted, spent their honeymoon, as did her parents, Erastus and Betty. And it was here in the summer of 1994 that Bettina brought her husband, suffering from an advanced inoperable brain tumor, for life's final chapter. But the camp was not winterized and fall's chill descended, so she moved her husband into a nearby nursing home, where he died early in 1995. Ted Dudley, the mayor's son-in-law, was cremated and his wife and their two sons scattered his ashes on Webb Pond. Spring brought many changes for the recently widowed Dudley, who decided to leave Maryland, where the couple had lived, and relocate to Maine. She bought a small house in the woods on Mount Desert Island. Dudley received good news in the spring of 1996, that she was a grandmother for the first time. Her son, Erastus Christopher, named his firstborn Christopher Erastus. "There's a new Erastus in the world," said the proud grandmother. "The cycle of life goes on." She talked about her hopes of spending a few weeks each summer with her grandson, Christopher Erastus, here at Webb Pond, which would be the fifth generation to do so.

The camp at Webb Pond is quintessential backcountry Maine, covered in weathered cedar shingles that are streaked with moss and a patina of gray. The trim is painted forest green, the front of the cabin is ringed with a deck stained red and thick cedar branches fashioned into railings. Towering pines ring the house, resting on pilings a stone's throw from water's edge. On this April afternoon, the only sound was the soft burble of a spring that supplies the camp with its water. The docks had been pulled ashore for the winter and a pair of wooden 1928 Old Town canoes were being restored. The Cornings own about 100 acres and nearly the entire southern shore of the three-mile long pond. Their shoreline has remained wild and undeveloped, although the opposite shore is being rapidly subdivided and built up. A pair of loons floated on the pond. They dove and resurfaced a few moments later, never far from one another, mates for life.

Inside, the camp is filled with artifacts of the mayor's life in the Maine woods. It is a veritable museum of natural history, a larger version of the playhouse the mayor used as his boyhood retreat behind his home at Corning Hill, a magical place stocked with discoveries of nature from his ramblings through the wilderness. Above the large stone fireplace at Webb Pond hangs a moose head, with one of the mayor's battered brown felt hunting hats perched at a rakish angle between the palm-like racks of antlers. The mayor made a list of the dozens of artifacts in the camp, six pages of handwritten notes, along with the story of how they came to be. A brief sampling paints a portrait of a man for whom the Maine woods were a kind of cathedral, a refuge that fed the soul, a place to which he could escape the pressures of politics and bask in the restorative power of wilderness:

> 1 skunk & 1 white weasel caught by Edwin Corning Jr. . . . 1 bobcat allegedly trapped by Francis Wilbur seventy-five feet west of camp winter of 1926 or 1927 and killed by him with a knife . . . 1 goshawk shot by Erastus Corning 2nd in Schoharie County about 1954 . . . perch Erastus Corning 2nd 4 lb. 9/1/46 . . . coon skin shot by Edwin Corning at Zabel's about 1948 . . . deer feet shot by Erastus Corning 2nd Bull Hill 1935 . . . black bear trapped by Kingman 1926 or 1927 . . . 1 snapping turtle shell Alcove Reservoir about 1953 . . . rocky mountain sheep shot presumably by father in 1905 in British Columbia . . . seal head of above referred to skin . . . moose head presented in 1958 by H.G. Batchelder . . . immature eagle feathers shot by Erastus Corning 2nd hunting ducks with Ben Hower on Frenchman's Bay 1934 or 1935 . . . fish hawk shot by Erastus Corning 2nd on flowage

about 1933 . . . alleged Spanish pompano given by Dr. Ned Cox 1928; unknown black bear head . . . albino English sparrow shot by Eddie at Farm about 1934 . . . 69 birds mounted and identi- fied . . . lady's-slippers [a variety of orchid] found between miles 40 & 41 just north of 2 Rod Road. . . .

Perhaps more than any other place, Maine was where Erastus Corning 2nd felt happy and at peace, truly at home. It was where he developed his lifelong love of the outdoors and honed his precise skills as hunter and fish- erman. Maine informed the mayor's character and touched his soul, yet it was a place and a lifelong refuge he kept separate from his political associ- ates in Albany. In the divided lives of Erastus Corning, Maine represented a special slice of his private experience he shared with family and very few others. Those glorious summers spent growing up in Maine were where the four Corning children were, for a time, immersed in the pure joy of youth and play and were unfettered with the sadness that marked the brief, tragic lives of the mayor's brother and two sisters – all three of whom died before age fifty, plagued by health complications due to alleged alcoholism. And Maine was where Erastus first began a romance with the woman who would be his wife for fifty years.

Elizabeth was the youngest of three children whose father, Charles Platt, a Philadelphia insurance executive, died when she was a young girl. Her mother, Dorothy Falcon Sims Platt, an artist well-known for her needlepoint designs and paintings of flowers, raised the children as a single mother – never remarrying. They received a large insurance settlement and were well-off financially, living in the exclusive Chestnut Hill section of Philadelphia, where the Platt children attended the exclusive Springside School. Elizabeth spent her senior year abroad at a finishing school in Florence, Italy, called the School for American Girls. "I just loved Florence and spoke French one week, Italian the next," Betty Corning recalled.

The summer of 1930, after returning from Florence, Betty, as she was known, and her best friend, Mary Fel Jordan, went to Northeast Harbor together. Jordan's family, also members of Philadelphia society, had a sum- mer home there. "I was just coming out in Philadelphia society and it was a perfect age to be," Betty Corning said of the summer of 1930. "And Northeast Harbor was the place to be for an eighteen-year-old girl from Philadelphia." Jordan and Platt joined loads of friends at Northeast Harbor, which they dubbed "Philadelphia on the rocks." Betty Corning said, "There was always a Philadelphia contingent up there and I thought of it as the domain of Philadelphians, but then I discovered there was a group of Albanians there as well, led by Bishop Doane." Corning's grandfather, Erastus Corning Jr., had helped William Croswell Doane, the Episcopal bishop, build All Saint's Cathedral in Albany. Both men bought property in Northeast Harbor in the 1870s – the first of the summer people – and were responsible, along with Harvard University's President Charles Eliot, with establishing an Episcopal chapel there and developing Northeast Harbor into an exclusive WASP enclave.

Erastus and Betty were not strangers when their paths crossed in Northeast Harbor. The Cornings had relatives in Philadelphia and Erastus had visited the city while he was in Groton and, later, while a student at Yale. "I remember seeing Erastus and his sister, Louise, at parties in Philadelphia and I had known him somewhat from those social affairs, but not well," Betty Corning said. But in Northeast Harbor, Betty's best friend, Jordan, played Cupid and fixed Betty up with Erastus. "I remember she put us together at a picnic and I was quite taken with Erastus right away," Betty Corning recalled. "He was just two years older than me. When I talked to my mother, I told her I had met this handsome gentleman from Albany named Erastus. I'm sure she expected him to be a black man because of his name and Albany was considered so remote and wild compared to Philadelphia."

Their first dates were among Erastus' beloved outdoors in Maine. "He taught me to love Maine, the camp, the birds, the outdoors," Betty Corning said. "He taught me to fish and I loved it. We fished on the Maine ponds every chance we got. Those were our common bonds." They shared a strong interest in art, too. Betty's mother was an artist and Erastus fantasized about traveling with Betty to Florence, where Erastus envisioned studying art and learning to be a painter. They daydreamed about Florence on their dates, Betty remembered, and never stopped talking about tomorrow. For one of their early dates, Erastus took Betty to the 1932 Yale-Harvard game and afterwards to dinner at Lochober's, a landmark restaurant in Boston. Soon, Erastus was inviting Betty home to meet his family and to have dinner at their estate, Stoney Point, in Northeast Harbor. "There were always large groups there for dinner, fifteen or twenty people around the table," Betty Corning recalled. "Mr. Corning was quite an invalid at that time after his heart attack, but I'd talk with him and I liked him greatly." Betty Corning remembered the Corning compound at Northeast

Harbor as a hub of activity: Erastus and Eddie would go out fishing or compete in sailboat races; Louise and Harriet would plan parties with their mother; a steady stream of relatives and friends would drop by. "Northeast Harbor could be very hectic with all the social events and you practically needed to go away from there just to get a vacation," said Betty Corning, who was introduced into the Northeast Harbor social circle that included the Cornings, the Kents, Daurences, Rockefellers and Pulitzers, whose rounds of formal parties spun on throughout the summer without pause.

The Cornings were a relatively inconspicuous family compared to the other socialites on Maine's Gold Coast. "They built their camp on Webb Pond so they could escape the Northeast Harbor scene and have a little peace and quiet," Betty Corning said. Of course, this imposed solitude amounted to a less ostentatious, rustic version of the Northeast Harbor social scene, since the Cornings bought property on Webb Pond along with at least three other Northeast society families.

The Corning family's connection to Maine reaches back more than a century, a bond that was formed most intensely with Mayor Corning, who sought the refuge of the Maine woods whenever he could. The family estate was located on Mount Desert Island, in the northeastern, or Down East part of the state, in the wealthy community of Northeast Harbor – summer home of the Rockefellers in nearby Seal Harbor, among others – on the fringes of Acadia National Park. The mayor's grandparents, Erastus Corning Jr. and Mary Parker Corning, purchased in 1886 the Northeast Harbor property, a five-acre parcel that contained more than 300 feet of frontage on Northeast Harbor with a small rocky peninsula that jutted into the mouth of the harbor. Hence the Cornings' name for their estate: Stoney Point. Here, four generations of Cornings spent the summer months in the luxury to which they had grown accustomed. "I remember the Cornings arriving just after school was out in June in a limousine driven by their chauffeur and all of them piling out with their luggage and they'd pack it all up again and drive back to Albany after Labor Day," recalled Clifford Manchester, whose parents, Russell and Mona Manchester, were the Cornings' caretakers at Northeast Harbor for more than fifty years beginning in 1923. Stoney Point was laid out for comfort and privacy, designed to resemble the Adirondack Great Camps built by millionaire nineteenth-century industrialists – the Whitneys, Vanderbilts and Durants. The Corning estate included five main structures. The main house was a large, gabled three-story structure with a Great Camp-styled sprawling living room, formal dining room, large kitchen and vast play-room for the kids. The upstairs contained rooms for the live-in domestic servants. An addition was built in the front of the house on the main floor in 1929 to accommodate Edwin Corning, the mayor's father, left an invalid the year before from a heart attack and stroke and advancing diabetes that necessitated a leg amputation. "Mr. Corning had his special room and he would sit there hour after hour, looking out the window at the water," Manchester recalled.

His wife, Louise Maxwell Corning, was an iron-willed matriarch who anchored the family during her husband's long decline. "Mrs. Corning def-initely ran the household, but there was no doubt Edwin still made major decisions even though he was bedridden," Manchester said. Sprinkled around the main house were three sleeping cottages: one for the boys, one for the girls and one for the adults. Each cottage had a living room and playroom area, as well as three bedrooms and two bathrooms. The Cornings did not sleep in the main house, except for Edwin, whose illness and frailty made it difficult for him to move between the houses. Another cottage, attached to a four-stall garage, was where the caretakers and chauf-feur stayed. While the Corning's main house was substantial and luxurious, it was not ornate by Northeast Harbor standards and was dwarfed by Rockefeller's Seal Harbor mansion. Still, the Cornings owned the premier piece of real estate in the area. "The view is one of the best and the house one of the most admired in all of Northeast Harbor," according to Dwight Carter, a real estate agent in Northeast Harbor.

Clifford Manchester recalled the magical mood created by the sibilant sound of the sea as it crashed into boulders a few yards from the front deck at high tide. "I remember lying in bed at night with the light of the Bell Island Lighthouse sweeping across the windows and I could hear the bell clanging at night and almost feel the salt sea spray." It was amid this idyllic seaside landscape that Erastus Corning 2nd came of age and developed his lifelong love of the outdoors.

The Cornings had five boats docked at Stoney Point: a twenty-foot open launch, *The Maybe*, for fishing trips to Frenchman's Bay and picnic runs to Mt. Desert Rock; *The Buzz*, a twenty-foot Chris-Craft mahogany runabout with a powerful engine and square bow for stability that helped it out-race the competition; a forty-foot cabin cruiser they'd take on overnight cruises along the coast to Dock Harbor during sailboat races; and the Corning pride and joy, *Polly* (named before the mayor knew Polly

Noonan), a graceful wooden A-class thirty-foot sloop. The *Polly* was one of a popular racing class of identical sailboats owned by the wealthy summer residents of Northeast Harbor, including Gov. Nelson Rockefeller. Growing up, the future mayor of Albany and the eventual governor of New York – both of whom would end up anchored in Albany – raced along the coast to Dock Harbor, concluding with floating parties aboard their various motor yachts that followed the sloops.

Erastus and his three younger siblings – Louise, Harriet and Eddie – all sailed, although they learned without the help of their father, who had sent his children off to boarding school while he was consumed with his political and business careers. The father had limited contact with his children as they grew up and then he suffered a catastrophic stroke when Erastus, the oldest, was nineteen and Eddie, the youngest, was only nine. As a result, the Corning children had a succession of surrogate fathers, one of whom was Maine caretaker Russ Manchester, Clifford's father. "My father spent a lot of time with Erastus especially and his main job through the summer was to keep the kids entertained," Clifford Manchester recalled. His dad was a native Down Easter, who grew up in Northeast Harbor, six-foot two-inches tall and wiry, a man of few words, a handyman who could fix just about anything and seemed to know everything there was to know about sailing, fishing and the outdoors. His main job was owner of a garage storage business in town, where he would store the limousines of the wealthy summer residents. Between Memorial Day and Labor Day, though, Russ Manchester was hired to be a kind of camp counselor to the Corning children. Manchester taught the kids to sail, to catch cod and other saltwater fish, as well as to take them on excursions to inland ponds for trout fishing. They tried a few times to accommodate Edwin the invalid by carrying him into the ponds and strapping him into a canoe with an ultra-light fly rod, but Erastus never got the chance to experience the wilderness with his father. His father unavailable, with only an occasional male father figure guiding him in self-discipline, the young Erastus had a tendency to run wild. In his later years, Erastus enjoyed telling stories about his out-of-control phase. He spun this yarn often for Peter Noonan, Polly's son. During a summer break from Yale, probably 1931, before the start of Corning's senior year, his father bought Erastus a Packard roadster. "The mayor recounted how he was up in Maine, had gotten drunk, and was driving like the devil down a country road in the middle of the night when he lost control of the Packard, which went off a bridge, rolled over and ended up stuck in a creek. The mayor wasn't injured seriously, but that beautiful car was totaled. The mayor said he never got over it and his father never forgave him because the Packard was never fixed," Noonan said.

In addition to acting as surrogate father and attempting to calm some of Erastus' wild ways, Manchester also taught Erastus how to hunt. In a technique called driving, now illegal, they'd round up a half-dozen to a dozen men to flush the deer for waiting hunters to shoot. "I went hunting with Erastus a few times and he knew what he was doing and he'd talk about hunting with my father," Clifford Manchester said. Corning gave Manchester two hunting rifles as gifts, including a Savage 44/40, which Manchester still uses. There were other gifts and acts of kindness from the Cornings to their employees over the years, such as presents for the five Manchester children at Christmas and on each of their birthdays. "I felt like they treated us almost like members of the family," Manchester said. "I never felt any animosity between the summer people and the locals. There wasn't much else in Northeast Harbor and we realized these people were our livelihood and we needed them." Mutual appreciation ran deep between the Cornings and their Maine servants. A Manchester daughter, Elizabeth Louise Johnston, was given her middle name in honor of the mayor's mother. "I thought of her as a grand lady," Johnston said. The mayor's mother was something of a mentor to Johnston, encouraging the young woman to enter a nursing program at St. Margaret's Hospital and House for Babies in Albany, where Corning was a trustee and used her position to gain Johnston's admission in 1955. "It was my first time away from home and she was very kind to me," said Johnston, who stayed overnight at the Upper Farm estate at Corning Hill in Glenmont when she first arrived in Albany. She was a frequent guest there and Mrs. Corning would send a driver and car to fetch Johnston when she fell ill so the young woman could be pampered by Mrs. Corning, whose daughter, Louise, had died the year before. Mrs. Corning also would stop by the hospital to visit Johnston. "Everyone was so impressed that I knew the great Mrs. Corning and that made me feel special," Johnston recalled. Flora Gray, Johnston's sister, was struck by how well Mrs. Corning bore up under the sadness of her life, the long, slow decline and early death of her husband, as well as the troubled lives ravaged by alleged alcoholism that led to early deaths of both daughters and one son. "There sure was an awful lot of tragedy in her life, but she never let it show," Gray said. "I can't remember her complaining and she was a delightful, old-fashioned lady who was liked and respected by others."

Mrs. Corning remembered the caretakers' children, particularly at their weddings. When Clifford Manchester was married in 1952, the mayor's mother let them use the Corning camp at Webb Pond for their honeymoon. When Flora Gray was engaged, Mrs. Corning invited her to Stoney Point for a formal tea in her honor and presented Gray with an heirloom silver tray and a cash gift for her wedding. Mrs. Corning also offered this advice: "Whenever you go away on a trip, bring home a tree to plant as a remembrance of that happy time."

Betty Corning, too, bestowed gifts and kindness upon the Manchester children, including boxes of clothing her own children had outgrown. "That really helped us because we didn't have much money," Johnston said. "The Cornings paid us well compared to other caretakers and gave us a bonus at Christmas, but it didn't go far with five kids." Betty Corning gave Johnston a black fur coat she still wears. "Betty sent it to me with a note saying she thought of me and how the coat could keep me warm in the cold Maine winters," Johnston said.

Gray was friendly with the mayor's sisters, Louise and Harriet, and recalled them both as tragic figures. "They both had troubled marriages as far as I could tell and died young," Gray said. "I never saw them much after they married. I felt bad about how their lives turned out because they were nice girls." Gray remembered Louise bringing her books each summer. "She gave me wonderful books. I remember *Heidi* and the Hans Christian Anderson books," Gray said. "She was nice to me." Despite their close and long relationship with the Cornings, Johnston said her family was very conscious of class distinction growing up in Northeast Harbor. "We were the natives and we felt jealous of these summer people with all that money coming to our town for the summer and staying in those fabulous mansions," Johnston said. The Manchesters lived on the Corning estate over the winter. Mona Manchester, Johnston's mother, cooked for Mrs. Corning in her later years after she sold off most of the estate and built a smaller home by the bay, where Nelson Rockefeller was an occasional dinner guest, Johnston said. "She'd ask my mother to come over and cook something special because Nelson was coming to dinner. It was just Mrs. Corning and Nelson, not Erastus." Gray remembered working in the kitchen for the mayor's mother at large dinner gatherings. "Nelson Rockefeller was very pleasant," Gray said. "Erastus didn't come to those dinners much. He preferred the camp at Webb Pond to the social scene of

Northeast Harbor. Erastus told me he knew Nelson well because they went to the same swimming and tennis clubs and both sailed."

Erastus maintained a friendship and correspondence with his mentor, Russ Manchester, and visited his surrogate father in the hospital in Bar Harbor on several occasions, the last time shortly before his death in 1975 after a lengthy battle with cancer. They never talked politics. "My father was a staunch Republican and that was a source of amusement to him and Erastus over the years," Johnston recalled.

A few years after her husband's death in 1934, Mrs. Corning sold off the Stoney Point estate, retaining one acre and the most desirable frontage, where she built a cabin overlooking the water and continued to spend summers there by herself. The buyer of Stoney Point was William A.M. Burden, a friend of Nelson Rockefeller's who had spent summers in Northeast Harbor since childhood. Burden had met Rockefeller's close associate, the architect Wallace K. Harrison, during wartime service in Washington, D.C., where Burden served as deputy secretary of the Commerce Department and ambassador to Belgium after a career as an executive with the Defense Supplies Corporation. In 1946, Burden hired Harrison, a modernist architect who designed the United Nations complex in New York City, to create a modernistic summer house on the former Corning estate. Harrison designed for the Burdens a low-slung, single-story undulating wooden structure anchored by two massive fieldstone chimneys – turning on its head the Corning style of quiet, old-money, WASP traditionalism. The jarring change surely bothered Erastus, who, as the invincible mayor of Albany with national political clout, would have something to say three decades later regarding the colossal Rockefeller-Harrison project in Albany, the South Mall. Maine was simply the latest chapter in a prickly past between the Cornings and Burdens, reaching back to the middle of the nineteenth century, when Henry Burden, owner of the prosperous Burden Iron Works in Troy, battled the first Erastus Corning and his Albany Iron Works in the courts. Burden charged Corning with patent rights infringement, which wound up in a case that spent many years bogged down in the courts. Another aspect of the families' feud stemmed from a dispute over accessibility and control of Wyants Kill, a creek that drove their manufacturing operations.

"The Burdens were very different from the Cornings and seemed so odd to us," Johnston recalled. "They had a big bomb shelter built on the estate in the 1950s when I was in high school. They were showy, too. They would have a caretaker get two seats on a jet to Washington just so they could bring large boxes of fresh Maine lobster and hand deliver it to them so it would be nice and fresh. They built a large saltwater swimming pool in addition to an indoor pool on the property and had lots of big political people there for parties. They named the Corning children's cottages Ambassador I and Ambassador II." From the sweeping terrace in front of their sculptured house, the Burdens, prominent Republicans, and their guests, could look down the hillside to water's edge and the mayor's mother, staunch Democrat, alone in her cabin. The irony wouldn't have been lost on her son, the Democratic machine mayor, an image he surely stored away in his young mind. History was the mayor's passion, and he couldn't help but be stung by the knowledge that Burden's mother was a member of the Vanderbilt family, who stole the New York Central Railroad away from its founder, the mayor's great-grandfather.

Since boyhood, Erastus Corning 2nd loved the backcountry of Maine, especially the inland ponds when the trout were hitting. Corning's family also built a camp on Webb Pond at North Ellsworth, about twenty miles inland from Northeast Harbor on the mainland off Mount Desert Island to the north. Webb Pond, where newlyweds Erastus and Betty Corning spent their honeymoon, was where the mayor returned every summer to fish and spend weeks of meditative solitude. He maintained lifelong friendships with Maine guides and caretakers; it was a friendship of equals he forged with these rustic outdoorsmen. Al Martin, a Maine painter, wrote a story about his first encounter with the mayor, who possessed a Maine native's reticence. "For eight years, I had known this friend only as Erastus and I hadn't the slightest idea where his home was," Martin wrote. "I knew he owned a camp on a Maine lake somewhere in, or close, to Hancock County and because of the woodsy clothes he wore I had the thought he was a Maine guide . . . Erastus Corning 2nd? But he's the Mayor of Albany, I said. 'That's me Al,' Erastus said. Our Boston friend looked as if he had a fish bone stuck in his throat. He stammered a little then said: 'I'm sorry, Sir. I meant no offense when I called you a farmer.' Erastus said, 'I took it as a compliment, sir.'"

Corning was especially close to Leroy Dority, who lived in North Ellsworth near Webb Pond, a guide Corning had fished with since the 1930s and with whom Corning maintained a lifelong correspondence. On June 18, 1943, Corning wrote: "Dear Roy. As I told you last fall, the fellow that I hunted with since I was a kid, died while I was out hunting with him.

He has a very nice five-year-old English setter, well trained, with an excellent nose, though a little bit inclined to be headstrong . . ." [Corning became guardian of the dog for a time, but Betty demanded it be returned and Dority took it back.] Most of their letters pertained to the rhythms of the outdoors: what date the ice went out, whether the silver trout were biting, how much the biggest landlocked salmon weighed, how well the deer and partridge hunting had gone. With Dority, Corning sought a more authentic wilderness experience, moving from the pampered luxury of Northeast Harbor to the rustic comfort of Webb Pond to an isolated inland body of water, Floods Pond, deep in the forest of the mainland off Mount Desert Island, west of Bangor. Corning bought Lot No. 4 on Floods Pond in August of 1947 and hired Dority and a crew to help him build a simple cabin there. Corning paid twelve dollars to Raymond Sargent to bulldoze a road into the site; sixteen dollars to Malcolm Salsbury to pave it with gravel; seven dollars to Thomas Pollard and twenty dollars to Dority to clear the site. Corning hiked into his Floods Pond lot over the Thanksgiving weekend of 1947 to do some ice fishing. "I don't think there is any need of doing anything more on the site," Corning wrote to Dority. "I will be glad of a little hard work."

Floods Pond, a man-made lake formed in the 1920s with a hydroelectric dam, is about twenty miles long and more than one hundred feet deep in spots. It was at this hideaway that Erastus and his brother, Eddie, indulged their dual obsessions for binge drinking and extreme fishing, packing in cases of booze and fishing from sun up to sun down – for spring salmon as soon as the ice was out, through the summer and into fall when they'd switch to hunting. Their quarry at Floods Pond was the mysterious silver trout, a large species that is stout, square-tailed and silvery in color, a rare type of landlocked salmon that has been confirmed only in one other place, a pond in New Hampshire. The silver trout weighed three pounds or more in Floods Pond, and were terrific fighters, a deep-water fish difficult to catch outside of their early spring heavy feeding season when they were shallow and would hit bait and lures. Corning, a devoted trout fisherman, was obsessed when it came to catching the elusive silver trout on remote, isolated and undeveloped Floods Pond. In the winter, it was a two-mile slog by snowshoe through thick forest to the cabin. Having grown up amid the social whirl of Northeast Harbor – a scene and its devotees Corning found shallow and tiresome – and seeking to move outside the neighborly obligations of Webb Pond, Corning wanted to be left alone to fish in peace.

In sports as in politics, Corning preferred the path of the loner. For Corning, building a rustic structure in the Maine wilderness became an exercise in persistence and self-reliance not unlike Thoreau's Walden Pond. On a scrap of paper, Corning sketched his own crude log cabin, a one-room shelter measuring twenty-five feet by seventeen feet – a solid structure that would last, the simpler the better being Corning's directive. The single room was unfurnished save for four bunks and a wood stove, within a structure built of hemlock logs caulked with oakum to block out drafts, and unfinished spruce boards for flooring. There was no electricity or running water. It was here, in the wilds of Maine, that Corning learned how to harvest edible food from the underbrush, such as leafy plants, roots, berries and mushrooms that grew wild. All his life, Corning practiced the odd rituals and quirky tastes of the woodsman. As some sort of forgotten old-fashioned potion, Corning sometimes boiled skunk oil on his mother's stove at Corning Hill. From wholesale grocer John Treffiletti, Corning ordered smoked pig jowls by the case, along with fiddlehead ferns, the only such order the grocer received for those unusual foodstuffs.

As in Albany, Corning remained a bundle of contradictions in Maine. Even as he went to great lengths to certify his Thoreauesque experience in the woods with an almost monastic reverence, his means to that end seemed contradictory. In traveling to Maine in the early years for fishing trips with his brother Eddie and buddies Sen. Julian Erway, Albany Associates manager Otto Fausel and others, Corning would have his City Hall driver chauffeur them to the train station with suitcases of gear, including a folding poker table for games on the train. The men transferred to a luxury sleeper car in Boston – after a lavish dinner – and the train would continue on to Bangor, Maine, where Corning would have a hired car and driver waiting to shuttle them to Floods Pond. "Mayor Corning was very much a traditionalist," Fausel said. "The whole Corning family was like that. When they latched onto something and made it their tradition, that's the way it was done." In later years, however, with mayoral and political duties making his time tight, Corning chartered a private plane to fly him and his buddies to Maine. In addition to these indulgences, more contradictions surrounded the experience of Floods Pond, where Corning's camp was situated adjacent to a camp owned by Polly Noonan and her husband, Peter. The mayor was a workaholic at City Hall who rarely took vacations, and even less frequently went away for an extended period with his own family, but he enjoyed spending time with the Noonan family at Floods Pond. "Erastus talked my husband into buying the lot next to his," Polly Noonan said. "He said he liked my kids around. Our two little log cabins were the only ones on the pond and they sat side by side. I went up there for a month every summer with the kids and my father. Peter would come up on weekends or for a few days that he took off work and then go back to Albany. Erastus did the same thing. They were both workaholics. Even though they enjoyed getting away, Peter and Erastus would sneak into Ellsworth to call their offices to check up on what was going on. They couldn't leave work behind." Noonan's son, Peter, remembered "wonderful times at Floods Pond, ice fishing with the mayor and him taking all us kids out for hikes in the woods." Those times ended when the Noonan camp, which was not built as sturdily as Corning's structure, was destroyed in a heavy snowfall that caused the roof to collapse during the winter of 1962.

Ironically, local politics, a game the Corning family had mastered over the generations, doomed the mayor's idyllic fishing retreat at Floods Pond – paradise lost. A friend of Corning's on the City Council in Bangor tipped off the mayor in 1948 that the city planned to take over the pond for its municipal water supply, meaning the end of fishing and their camps. (Corning's favorite fishing spot in Albany County was the Alcove Reservoir, the city's water supply and officially closed to anglers, although it actually was used by the mayor as his private fishing haven.) Still, Corning told Dority, his guide, he would sit tight at Floods Pond and try to use his political influence if push came to shove. "They wouldn't be able to do anything on it until 1949 at the earliest, so I am going to take a chance and hope they never do," Corning wrote, although his optimism ended when Bangor took the pond for its water supply two decades later. During the protracted hearings, Dority acted as Corning's spy, attending meetings of the Bangor Water Company and reporting back to Corning, such as this February 28, 1958 dispatch: "There was nothing on the blueprint that showed they were going to build any dam and overflow the cottages." Dority and the mayor also discussed strategies about protesting the dam proposal and Corning hired a lawyer, who negotiated and managed to delay the inevitable, allowing the mayor to fish there a while longer if he stayed away from the municipal water intake pipe. Finally, after Corning's orchestrated delays, in the early 1970s the Bangor Water Company seized control of Floods Pond, compensated Corning and Noonan for their property and ordered the removal of the log cabins – ending the mayor's pursuit of the mysterious silver trout and his contradictory wilderness experience. The mayor's longtime friend and guide, Leroy Dority, did not live to see the resolution of the Floods Pond saga; he died in the summer of 1965. The mayor's Floods Pond cabin was dismantled, transported over frozen ponds and through the woods on snowmobiles, and reassembled on nearby Pierce Pond, where Corning made a yearly fishing pilgrimage. Pierce Pond fishing camp owner, guide and friend of the mayor's, Gary Cobb, renovated it with a few thousand dollars Corning donated and turned it into a wilderness tribute by naming it Mayor's Cottage and the small island on Pierce Pond where it stands, Mayor's Island.

Corning was deeply saddened at the death of Dority, another surrogate father figure with whom he had fished for more than thirty years. Dority died suddenly in his pickup truck, slumped over the wheel, as he prepared for a daily drive into town. Corning struggled to express his feelings, mixed up with unresolved grief over the death of his own father thirty years earlier. "Your letter came as a great shock to me, as I had not heard at all about Roy's passing away," Corning wrote to Dority's son-in-law, Thomas Pollard. "The only thing I can say is I know he would have hated to be an invalid, and that this is the way he would like to have died. If you will please give my regrets to all the family, I surely will appreciate it. It is hard to think that it was more than thirty years ago that I first met Roy, and rented his boat on Memorial Day. If there is anything that I can do for Mildred, or any of you, please do not hesitate to let me know, because I feel that I have lost a very real friend." Pollard was four years younger than Corning and a lifelong Maine resident who had fished, hunted and learned to be an outdoorsman at Dority's side. Since the 1920s, Dority, and later Pollard, worked as guides, camp builders and caretakers for the Cornings on Floods and Webb ponds. "It was about 1924 when Erastus [then fifteen] came up duck hunting for the first time and his blind was near my father-in-law's. We got to talking and it mushroomed from that into fishing and everything else," Pollard recalled. "He was a true fisherman. He enjoyed any kind of fishing, ice fishing or fly fishing or spin casting, just as long as it was fishing. Some people fly fish and won't do anything else. The mayor wasn't like that. You name it, the mayor would go fishing for it. He had an obsession for fishing. He was ardent about it. His composure was excellent and he hated to lose a fish."

Gradually, as was happening to the thinning ranks of his hunting companions in Albany – mostly Dan O'Connell's political cronies – Corning's old-time Maine fishing buddies were being lost to age or infirmity. Corning and Pollard tried to keep the past alive through their correspondence, swapping yarns about the old days and crusty hunters and fishermen they had known.

A hidebound traditionalist who resisted change and tried to keep his rituals the same year after year, Corning let nostalgia get in the way of his good business sense when it came to commercial dealings in Maine. The Corning family's sawmill operations in Maine, first purchased by Edwin Corning and preserved by the mayor, despite a flow of red ink, illustrate the mayor's big heart and desire to hold onto a way of life that was passing. The Cornings, together with the Zanzingers and the Reaths – wealthy families from Philadelphia who owned summer homes in Northeast Harbor – became partners in several small sawmills on the mainland north of Mount Desert Island. The sawmills employed about a dozen people generally and made lumber of the spruce and pine cut in the surrounding forests. "That was a depressed area, and still is, and there were a number of the old sawmills going out of business in the 1930s and '40s and the locals were left unemployed," said Austin Goodyear, of Ellsworth, Maine, who purchased Ellsworth Falls Lumber and Supply and a sawmill from the mayor. "The summer people bought up several of these sawmills and operated them on a break-even basis to help out the locals and keep them employed," Goodyear said. "It was a rather romantic notion. The reality was that they were little operations, very tenuous, and closed one by one after they had lost money year after year."

In a kind of personal welfare program that mirrored the practice of the Albany Democratic machine, Mayor Corning paid out of his own pocket to keep these dying operations running as long as he could, supplying his own Ellsworth Falls Lumber Company in Ellsworth (population 4,500). Corning's was the last sawmill remaining in operation when Goodyear bought it, along with the lumber company, from the mayor in 1968 for $200,000. "We went back and forth for a long time, because I don't think Corning really wanted to sell. He had a soft spot in his heart for those people who worked in the sawmills," Goodyear said. A longtime friend of the mayor, Dorcas Dickens, widow of blueberry grower and logger Reg Dickens, said, "The mayor wasn't like the other people from away. He really cared about the natives and tried to take care of them. He only kept the sawmills going so the men could put food on their tables." After buying out Corning, Goodyear shut down the antiquated sawmill, putting its fifteen employees out of work in a struggling economy where jobs were scarce. He replaced the mill and lumber company with a hardware store, Ellsworth Builder's Supply. Corning refused to yield all his interest in the company. "He put in the agreement that he retained some shares so he could keep a hand in the business and try to get his longtime employees a job at my store," Goodyear said.

Maine was a place of serendipity and unusual alliances, where Corning liked to revel in the strange coincidences, his own intertwined career with Nelson Rockefeller chief among them. Another was John Quine, whose family owned a camp on Molasses Pond. Quine recalled going to the Corning camp on nearby Webb Pond with his grandmother for formal tea at the invitation of the mayor's mother or meeting the Cornings at Saturday night baked bean suppers in Eastbrook. Quine, twenty-five years the mayor's junior, didn't know Erastus while growing up, but met the mayor after the *Ellsworth American* newspaper wrote an article about Quine, who was elected mayor of Meriden, Connecticut in 1974. Corning sent Quine a letter, remarking on the fact that they were both mayors, both had spent summers in Maine since boyhood and both had politics in their blood. Quine's grandfather, Albert Day, was mayor of Bangor, Maine in the 1920s and had made an unsuccessful run for the governor's seat. After politics, Day went back to running his business, Adams Dry Goods Co. in Bangor. That's where the similarities ended, however. Corning served eleven terms compared to a single term for Quine, who also happened to be a Republican. "I'm a Republican in a Democratic city, which is why I only served one term," said Quine, who later was elected to the city council. "You learned early on when you get up fishing on the lakes of Maine, nobody mentions politics." Quine managed to lure away from Albany one of Corning's top budget officials to work for him in Meriden. But Corning had the last laugh. Quine was out of his mayoral job two years later, in 1976, while Corning was entering his thirty-fifth year of his mayoral career – a fact Corning didn't mind reminding Quine about.

After being forced to give up his fishing camp on Floods Pond to the Bangor Water Company, the mayor sought a replacement wilderness experience on Pierce Pond, one hundred miles inland from Webb Pond. The fishing camp on Pierce Pond had been run by two generations of the Cobb family when Gary Cobb, thirty years the mayor's junior, became the fishing guide for Corning during annual pilgrimages to Pierce Pond begun in 1958. Cobb was also the guy who got Corning started collecting the pecker bones he kept in his City Hall office. "He was my favorite guest without question out of hundreds of guests over the years," Cobb said. "We formed a deep friendship, almost a father-son bond, that lasted right up until he died." The annual summer fishing trip to Pierce Pond was a sacrosanct ritual for the mayor, who kept a diary of every visit there with a record of the weather, what fish he caught and the news around the camp. For the first seven years, until his death, Eddie accompanied his brother to Pierce Pond for a week in late June or early July. "Eddie was the little brother who listened to Erastus, the one in charge," Cobb said. "Eddie drank a lot. He didn't make a spectacle of himself in camp, but he had a drinking problem. Erastus was bigger, taller, more important, more successful. Eddie was smaller in every way and that might have had something to do with it." Corning also returned to Pierce Pond each August for a time with his wife. "Betty fished some, but mostly she just came to observe the wildlife," Cobb said. "They both knew an awful lot about wildflowers and things. He was especially knowledgeable about the birds and their songs." Cobb said he noticed trouble in the marriage right away, as early as 1958. "I could see for myself there wasn't much love between the mayor and Betty," Cobb says. "I felt something was wrong, because I didn't have the sense that they really enjoyed doing things together. There was a tension there. There was never a lot of conversation or good-natured chatter between them. It was very quiet if they were together in the boat."

Corning preferred to come by himself, though, which he did for a week at the end of September for hard-core fishing – always alone after Eddie died in 1964. The mayor had a profound need to experience what for him was the pure balm of the outdoors. For starters, the mayor was superstitious when it came to his fishing hat, always wearing the same old, beat-up, wide-brimmed brown felt hat with a red bandanna tied around it that he had found years ago in the woods. At Pierce Pond, Corning stopped shaving and assumed the guise and attitude of a true Down Easter. "He'd let his whiskers grow out when he came to Maine and dress like the rest of us and cuss a lot, too," Cobb recalled. "After two days, you'd think he was a guide. No one would ever know he was the mayor unless he told them. He could walk into the general store around here, sit down and play cards, shoot the breeze about local stuff and tell a joke to get all the old-timers laughing."

Cobb said Corning, thirty years his senior, wore him out on their fishing expeditions as the mayor went out fishing before sunrise, stopping only for breakfast, and continuing until nightfall.

Nothing seemed to bother the mayor when he was out in the woods. "I remember one time we camped at a remote pond and the mosquitoes and no-see-ums were unbearable," Cobb said. "I couldn't sleep a wink, but somehow the mayor slept soundly. Of course, the mayor was a terrible snorer and a heavy sleeper who could sleep through anything." Cobb described the mayor as restless, always searching for better fishing and eager for new experiences, a tendency that invited trouble and caused the mayor to get lost once while heading to a remote pond. "He was lost for a few hours, nothing serious," said Cobb, who found the mayor near an abandoned mining camp, where he uncovered an antique pot he dug up and saved to remind himself of the adventure.

Cobb said Corning was one of the best anglers among dozens of serious fishermen who stayed at Pierce Pond each year and vied for bragging rights over biggest fish caught. Each year beginning in 1952, the guests competed to have their name engraved on the Perry-Doris Cup, a silver Paul Revere bowl. Corning was the only one who came out on top three times: in 1965, winning with a seven-pound, two-ounce salmon; in 1968 with a four-pound twelve-ounce salmon; and, in 1971 for a salmon that also weighed four pounds, twelve ounces. Cobb was with the mayor when Corning caught his record seven-pounder and Betty sent the mounted fish to Cobb as a gift after the mayor died.

The mayor rewarded himself for a hard day fishing. Back at camp, Corning enjoyed a few cocktails before dinner. "He liked Canadian Club and water," Cobb recalled. "He'd pour the whiskey in and then add a little pond water and he was happy. We'd build a fire in the ground and let it build up with coals and put on a big pot of baked beans we called baked-in-the-ground beans. We'd have it with salt pork. Or fish that we caught that day or a big steak. He loved to eat. Really laid it on."

For Cobb, Corning was an important surrogate father figure, and, for Corning, Cobb offered a second chance at the opportunity missed with the mayor's own estranged son. "He was definitely a father figure to me and I got the sense he was looking for something in me, because he wasn't close with his own son and he never talked about him," Cobb said. "When you sleep in a tent with someone night after night for all those years, you get to know them well and you talk about everything, but he hardly ever mentioned his son. The mayor never talked much about his own father, either. He spoke the most about his mother."

Corning was generous to the Cobb family over the years. "He took a lot of interest in our family and sent presents on our birthdays and at Christmas and kept up with what my children were doing," Cobb said. "He did it because he wanted to, not because he was trying to score points. He always told me if I needed financial help of any kind, he was always available if I needed him." When the mayor died, Cobb felt as if he had lost a father. He chartered a plane and flew to Albany for the funeral. He was seated in a place of honor, not far from Gov. Mario M. Cuomo and other politicians. "It was an honor for a fishing guide from Maine to be there with all the other dignitaries, but I really wanted to pay my respects for my favorite guest, the man who made the biggest impression on me," Cobb said. "He's got an island named for him now. I think he'd like that."

As for the future of Mayor's Island and Pierce Pond, Cobb is trying to raise funds for a trust to protect the land around the pond from potential development that could compromise its wilderness character. "The mayor's son called to say he wouldn't be involved with the trust fund project in any way," Cobb said. "It's kind of sad. I know how much it would have meant to his father. The mayor really loved it at Pierce Pond and he'd stop shaving on each visit until it was time go to back to Albany. Then he'd go down to the pond with a little shaving cream and razor and scrape the beard off." Back to Albany, to the family ghosts and his old, patrician self, mayor for life.

There were two antidotes that retained their potency for Mayor Corning throughout his life as he sought to relieve the burden of a largely joyless marriage and the grind of politics: drinking, and fishing and hunting with the boys. The former became a nightly refuge that took the socially acceptable form of Scotch at the Fort Orange Club. The latter was the mayor's periodic forays to Maine, the Adirondacks or the Alcove Reservoir. It was in the woods, free from his public political persona and far from the smothering tightness of home, that Mayor Corning could indulge both desires to the fullest – binge drinking with the boys marked by long days of hunting and fishing. It was during these brief episodes that punctuated the seemingly endless and stultifyingly mundane routine at City Hall that Corning broke away from the patrician persona his father preordained for him, and he gave vent to the more natural and freer elements of his personality that he generally held so thoroughly in check. For instance, in advance of the mayor's annual weekend ice fishing trip to Maine over the Washington's Birthday holiday with his brother, Sen. Julian

Erway and Otto Fausel, Corning wrote to Pollard and requested the usual staples year after year: five bottles of vodka, five bottles of Canadian Club and two bottles of Scotch. "Eddie has been off the hard stuff and actually isn't drinking anything anymore, so we won't need too much beer," Corning wrote in 1960, the year after his brother sustained critical injuries and lapsed into a lengthy coma following a car accident on the way back from a fishing trip at Moose Pond in the Adirondacks. Eddie was a passenger in a car driven by Les Knapp that ran off the road and struck a tree along Route 9 near Boght Corners in Latham in May, 1959. "Eddie is improving all the time, although his memory is pretty faulty on a lot of things before the accident," Corning wrote to Pollard in February of 1960. "The doctors are still not certain as to the extent of his brain injuries so that what we must do is hope and pray . . . Barbara [Eddie's wife] and Mother are both holding up very well." Pollard was in a good position to observe the dynamic between the Corning brothers. "They were two different people," Pollard said. "The mayor had more patience and could carry off almost any situation. If any decisions were to be made, Erastus made them. Eddie was not as big a man as Erastus physically, but Eddie was easy to get along with and very genial. I never heard Eddie lose his temper and lots of times he had reason to. The only flare-ups I had with him were when he had been drinking some of that high-potency 100-proof stuff they had around there. Eddie was a drinker."

In 1964, Corning had to break sad news to Pollard once more. "Friday, Eddie went home from work perfectly normal, changed his clothes and did some chores, and about six o'clock, when Barbara and the children came in, he was half-lying on the sofa and apparently had been dead only a very few minutes. He certainly didn't suffer at all, and the autopsy showed that he died of a cerebral hemorrhage, which was almost certainly connected with the accident of five years ago," Corning wrote Pollard on February 5. The two men, friends through the experience of fishing in Maine, struggled to express their emotions and feelings over the unexpected death of their brother and friend at the age of forty-five. Pollard replied, "Sure was a shock to hear about Eddie passing so quickly, it's hard to believe even now that he won't be in the boat fishing with me again. Well, he left many pleasant memories here over the years and we're sure going to miss him. Also, I have the feeling too, how much he enjoyed and looked forward to the trips to Maine, and like to think I helped make them a little better especially the last few years." Corning wrote back to Pollard and his wife, Velma, on April 12,

1964: "It is very hard to realize that Eddie is no longer with us but one of the satisfactions that we all can have is that in spite of the accident, he enjoyed so much fishing and hunting in these last five years."

Even as he watched his father, his two sisters and his brother suffer the ravages of alleged alcoholism – observing firsthand the heart-wrenching effects on his mother of her loved ones dying before their time – Corning continued to engage in heavy drinking and dangerous stunts while drunk that seemed to give the mayor the rush that comes with cheating death. Polly Noonan's son, Peter, recalled one of the mayor's drunken episodes in Maine in the mid-1940s when Noonan was a boy: "Erastus had a Model A that he'd drive out on Floods Pond in winter. My dad, Eddie and Erastus would get roaring drunk and drive around out on the ice totally loaded, ripped out of their minds. I remember being scared to death, thinking they'd die driving out there. They were so drunk they thought nothing of it. They were just lucky nothing ever happened."

Fishing the remote lakes in Maine, Pollard remembered they'd drink the water without filtration except for Mayor Corning, who had his own method. "The mayor used to put vodka in his water each morning. He said it was to kill off the germs," Pollard said. Drinking and fishing went hand-in-hand and took several forms. "The mayor also used to bring some kind of high-potent rum and drink it with milk and everybody stood back and waited for him to fall down," Pollard said. "He never did. His eyes shone a little bright, but that was all."

The mayor's annual fall deer hunting trip to Sabattis in the Adirondacks was another opportunity for Corning to cut loose with the boys and the booze. Sabattis was a railroad station in the Adirondack rail network established in the late-1800s by the Durants and Whitneys and other wealthy New York City industrialists who wanted a wilderness experience that promised luxury without hardship. Sabattis, near Tupper Lake on the edge of the Five Pond Wilderness area, is situated on the border of Hamilton and St. Lawrence counties in the northeast corner of the Adirondack Park. Despite various crises at City Hall over the years, nothing was ever going to stop Mayor Corning from taking an annual powder to Sabattis. The hunting trip became a deeply ingrained tradition Corning refused to abandon, despite the hobbling pain just before hip replacement surgery, or the severely weakened lungs from emphysema shortly before his long and final hospitalization. The Sabattis trip, however earthy and profane, was as close as Corning – who eschewed church in rebellion against the forced feedings of morning chapel and evening prayer at Groton – came in adulthood to participating in a spiritual ritual. For a man whose entire upbringing and the inherited traits of his social class had taught him to bury his emotions, to sublimate his demonstrative side, to hide rather than reveal his deepest feelings, the Sabattis experience contained elements of catharsis for Corning. He was assisted in this opening up, of course, by copious quantities of Scotch, a surefire social lubricant for the naturally shy Corning.

The mayor traveled to Sabattis well stocked: an armful of bottles of Dewar's White Label, and several cartons of his favorite smokes, Kools. As a drinker and a smoker, Corning had a prodigious appetite. He smoked three packs of Kools a day at one point, and the Dewar's was never far from Corning's lips at Sabattis. Tony Monticup has a picture of the mayor passed out on a couch in the lodge, so ripped on Scotch he never woke up while the other guys horsed around with a large deer antler rack around his crotch for flash snapshots. "He could drink a lot before he got really drunk," said Peter Noonan, who saw Corning drunk countless times. "He didn't really taper his drinking down until the end when his health was failing." The mayor was legendary for his snoring, too. "He'd fall asleep loaded and it would just make it worse," Noonan said. "Boy, could he saw wood. When he and my dad got snoring at the same time, the walls actually shook."

It was in the boozy camaraderie of the hunting lodge with the boys that the mayor never had to grow up – free from worries professional, personal and political for a time – and reveling in the kind of sophomoric pranks he pulled at Groton. For instance, the mayor saved this letter burned with a cigarette into white birch bark, dated July 8, 1950 and placed in Corning's bound volumes of the *New York State Conservationist* magazine: "My Brother: Now that you have successfully completed the test put to you, and having smoked the pipe of our tribe, we hereby confer upon you the name of Chief Poking Fire. With full rights and privileges of this tribe. *Na-Go-Ga-Gis-Da-Yong-Duk.*"

Sabattis meant more than another excuse to get drunk with the boys and go hunting for Corning, though. It is the place where Corning's father and mother met in 1908, two years after Edwin Corning had graduated from Yale, and began their intense courtship that resulted in marriage a few months later, followed, in 1909, by the birth of their firstborn, a son, Erastus 2nd. "The mayor always said he had a special place in his heart for Sabattis because of its connection with his mother and father," said Jack

McLean, Polly Noonan's cousin and a longtime hunting and fishing partner of the mayor's. In preserving the Sabattis hunting trip as a ritual that endured four decades, Corning managed to maintain a link to a father he hardly knew growing up.

There were other strands of historical interest for the Cornings at Sabattis. The Cornings' initial tie to Sabattis was through the Low family, which had business interests with the Cornings in shipping and railroads during the nineteenth century. The Lows came by their wealth by developing Consolidated Edison, the hydroelectric giant. At the turn-of-the-century, the Low fortune was such that they owned a private railroad car that would be hooked onto the Adirondack train on Friday night in Manhattan for a luxurious ride to Sabattis, where the entourage transferred to horse-drawn coach for the final leg of the journey to the Low's posh camp on Lake Marian. The Lows had plenty of room for company; they owned approximately 90,000 acres of forest preserve in the Adirondacks surrounding Sabattis, including a 5,000-acre private hunting preserve. Their property included Lows Lake, a large body of water several miles long, and a sprinkling of smaller ponds: Grass Pond, Long Pond, Trout Pond, Hitchins Pond and a sprawling wetlands along the Bog River flow. The Low holdings are deep in the interior, ten miles from Route 30, the nearest highway, and twenty miles from the closest town of any consequence, Tupper Lake. The Cornings had been friendly with the Lows beginning with the mayor's grandfather. When the mayor's mother and father met, they both were staying in Sabattis as guests of the Lows. Their son, Erastus, continued the connection to the Lows by befriending in New Haven fellow Yalie Gus Low, a couple years behind Corning.

The mayor brought with him annually to Sabattis male members of his adopted family, the Noonans, and surrogate sons who shared the mayor's own passion for the outdoors and the earthy life. The mayor began deer hunting at Sabattis before World War II, but transformed it into an annual symbolic escape with the boys beginning in the late-1950s. Corning's Sabattis crew included: Polly Noonan's husband, Peter Noonan Sr.; his sons, Peter Jr. and Brian; Noonan's cousin, McLean; Noonan's sons-in-law, Joe Montimurro and Doug Rutnik; the mayor's brother, Eddie; Andrew Pinckney Sr., a World War II POW and political associate of the mayor's; Tony Monticup, son-in-law of the mayor's friend Judge Mike Tepedino; Eddie Miller, husband of the mayor's secretary; assorted political and personal buddies, including John Knox, Ed Bartley and John Treffiletti.

Corning's own son never went on the Sabattis trip, a conspicuous absence the boys never asked about and the mayor never offered to explain.

After much anticipation, the chosen weekend arrived in late November. "It never varied," Peter Noonan said. "The mayor wanted it the same every year." The ten or twelve young men, mostly twenty to thirty years the mayor's junior, would meet after work Thursday evening over at the Noonan compound, either at Polly's house or her son Peter's. There, they'd pack their rifles and hunting gear and split up into four or five cars. The caravan set out. Their first stop was Potter's Diner in Warrensburg for dinner. "The mayor always had the same thing," Peter Noonan recalled. "A big, greasy plate of fried eggs, bacon, home fries and toast." The crew would wolf down their gargantuan portions and wash it down with beer – the mayor would take the check and do the math in his head, figuring what each person owed, including tip – before continuing on. Next stop was Farrell's Tavern in Indian Lake for shots and beers. "Sometimes we had to wake up old man Farrell to come down and open up the tavern," Peter Noonan said. "The mayor liked Farrell and they'd swap stories as the mayor took his shots of Scotch with beer chasers."

Their bellies full and their minds swirling with the quick infusion of alcohol, the caravan would lurch ahead. One final stop at the Long Lake Hotel to relieve themselves, a quick pop of booze for the road, and then on toward Sabattis and their home base for hunting. Corning had arranged for use of the private camp because of his connection to Low and was clearly boss of the outing. They stayed at the Low lodge on Hitchins Pond, a ten-bedroom facility powered by a hydroelectric plant the Lows built on the Bog River Flow at the mouth of Lows Lake. The focal point of the lodge was a vast, sparkling kitchen, with large electric ovens, stoves and walk-in coolers. Mission control for the gathering was a sprawling kitchen table, which seated twenty comfortably. It was around this table that the mayor and his crew experienced a rare closeness and community and sharing.

As a gesture of respect, the other men christened Corning White Eagle at Sabattis. "It was because of his white hair, but it was more. We all looked up to the mayor. He was the heart and soul of our group," Peter Noonan Jr. said. "In his later years, after he lost his hair, we jokingly renamed him Bald Eagle. He didn't like that."

Noonan remembered his father, Peter Sr., Polly's husband, didn't much like to hunt, but he went to Sabattis anyway, to read and cook and drink and enjoy the community of the table. "There was always someone at the kitchen table," McLean recalled. "If you didn't want to go out hunting, you'd sit at the table telling stories, reading, drinking, playing cards or eating." Noonan added, "I remember the mayor loved to hear stories. He'd soak up everyone's tales like a sponge. He had an odd sense of humor. He'd laugh hysterically at things nobody else thought was funny. Maybe that's why he couldn't tell a joke worth a damn. He'd start out all right, but then he'd always screw up the punchline."

Although it was clear Corning was in charge and he could never quite shed his essence as a political boss or his air of inviolable authority, Sabattis, unlike the city of Albany, was a truly democratic society. Inhibitions removed by the steady flow of liquor during the hunting trip, Corning was no longer a sacred cow. "All bets were off on this trip, nobody was nobody and there were no holds barred," McLean said. "We razzed the mayor mercilessly, but he could take it as well as he could give it out." And when his turn came to cook dinner, for instance, or wash the dishes or stoke the fire, the mayor never pulled rank. "He did his share. It didn't matter what it was, the mayor pitched in," said McLean – shades of the G.I.-Mayor's days at basic training during World War II.

Despite his wealth, Corning was no spendthrift. "He was very frugal and there were no luxuries on the Sabattis trip," McLean recalled. "The year I got married, he paid my way as a wedding gift, but that was it. Each year, a few weeks after the trip, you'd get your per diem bill from the mayor. He had it all tallied up and we were expected to pay it right away." During poker games at the kitchen table, Corning, despite smoking like a chimney and drinking like a fish, was a formidable foe. "He was a good poker player who liked to bluff a lot," McLean said. It was dealer's choice and the games were low-stakes, mostly dime and quarter bets. Nobody got hurt badly; one player might lose thirty dollars over a weekend if he had a streak of rotten luck. The mayor didn't need luck at the poker table, at least in his mind. "The mayor had a lot of experience at poker, but he drank too much while he was playing to be a great player," Noonan said. He remembered Corning's knack for counting cards, for memorizing what had been played, for knowing the odds and for retaining the details of at least two dozen obscure card games in his head.

Given the emphasis on camaraderie, the stated purpose of the Sabattis trip, deer hunting, seemed almost secondary, although Corning was careful, and superstitious, when it came to his hunting preparations. He wore an ancient outfit that never changed: patched and re-patched wool pants in his favorite color, green; a tattered Pendleton plaid shirt; oddly outdated lace-up boots with rubber soles that McLean remembered as "damn ugly;" and, on his head the woolen helmet liner from his World War II infantry-man-issue combat gear. "It was a smelly, awful thing he wore for more than thirty years, until the moths finally devoured it," McLean said. "It wasn't just a matter of being frugal. Everything had a meaning for the mayor and I think the helmet liner was one way he kept in touch with his war experience. Going hunting was in some way like going into combat for him." Another hunter's spoil Corning treasured was the liver, heart and kidneys of a fresh kill. "He loved cooking and eating the deer innards right after it was field dressed," McLean said, apparently some sort of tribal virility rite for the mayor.

Corning always brought to Sabattis his trusty Remington .35, a rifle he bought himself in 1946, just after he got out of the Army. Each time he bagged a deer, Corning put a notch on the stock of the Remington. The Remington had twenty-six notches after thirty years of hunting with it when Corning took a large, eight-point buck in November, 1976 at Sabattis. It would not be overstating it to say that to the mayor, his rifles were possessed of an almost spiritual significance. They were among his most prized possessions and he gave them as gifts to the men he loved most. He owned several vintage Parker shotguns, for instance, and gave them as gifts to Peter Noonan Jr. and Doug Rutnik. Corning presented to Brian Noonan a rare, beautifully scrolled old German weapon the mayor liked to say he "liberated" from a German soldier during the war, an unusual over-under weapon – twelve-gauge double-barreled shotgun on top, with a six-millimeter rifle barrel underneath. Corning gave McLean the first shotgun he ever owned, a 1930 vintage Remington twenty-gauge double-barrel pump shotgun that had been a gift from Corning's father. "I was just out of Vietnam, I didn't have any money to buy a gun to hunt with and the mayor gave me that. I'll always treasure it," McLean said. His son, Erastus III, was not a hunter and did not get any of his father's guns as gifts. What remained of his father's beloved hunting collection, including valuable wildlife art, sentimental trophies and gifts from old hunters, as well as hundreds of books on hunting, was sold at public auction by Erastus III after his mother's death.

Sabattis, so resonant and rich as it was with Corning family connections, naturally became a wellspring of amusing hunting anecdotes about the mayor. Unlike the younger men on the trip, the mayor was known as a dignified deer hunter, displaying none of the machismo of Tony Monticup, owner of a construction company, who would tramp twenty or thirty miles around the Low property in a day of hard-core hunting in order to bag a deer each year. "The mayor would rather take it easy and drive his car back into the woods on some old logging road," Peter Noonan Jr. said. "He had that little green Chevy Citation, stick shift, no radio, no air-conditioning. He loved a stripped-down car and he really beat them. He'd drive way back into the woods at Sabattis and knock off the oil pan on a rock. He got stuck more than once and we'd have to take a truck miles back in there and tow the mayor's car back out."

The Low's hunting preserve was rugged, mountainous terrain, utterly isolated with only a rudimentary trail network. When the hunters dispersed at daybreak on their quests for deer, it would be easy for an unskilled woodsman to get lost. Corning, who prided himself on his backwoods sense and reconnoitering skills honed during a lifetime spent in the forest, did manage to get lost one year. That time, McLean and Corning set out on a hunt together, eventually deciding to split up and rejoin each other at Otter Pond. Both had maps and a compass and knew how to use them. Corning went tramping up Iron Mountain and was supposed to come down the other side and meet McLean at Otter Pond, but the mayor never showed. McLean waited ninety minutes. Still no Corning. McLean hiked back to Corning's car and waited until dusk, but the mayor still didn't show. McLean was growing worried because the mayor was a heavy smoker and drinker who was in his late-sixties. McLean feared a heart attack. When McLean got back to the lodge, it was dark and getting quite late. Corning had just arrived, safe and sound. It was later determined the mayor turned left at Silver Lake Mountain by mistake and had to hike around a cliff face, a six mile detour, before making his way back to the lodge. "I was misdirected," was how the mayor put it to McLean and the guys over Scotches at the kitchen table. Said McLean, "We razzed him about that for the next five years. He would not admit he got lost. Misdirected. That's all he'd say. He was an excellent woodsman who knew every plant and he would not say he made a mistake in the woods."

Another incident that stuck in Corning's craw was the saga of Buttons the deer. By the mid-1970s, the Lows had sold part of their property to a Boy Scout troop from Long Island and the mayor had obtained permission from the Scouts to continue to hunt that area. The Scouts had been feeding a partially tame deer that had buttons instead of spikes, a type of deer whose stunted antlers makes it a "button buck". The Scouts nicknamed him Buttons. Since a button buck is unusual and deer remain in a relatively small home range area, the caretaker, Armand Vaillancourt, had come to recognize and enjoy the company of Buttons. Vaillancourt told the Sabattis crew to look out for Buttons, to protect it for the Scouts and, under no circumstances, were they to shoot the beloved pet deer. McLean continued: "The next year, the mayor was up on the high line over by the Boy Scout camp, shot a nice four-pointer and was quite proud of himself. When we got the deer back to camp, Armand took one look at it and said the mayor had shot Buttons. Armand really gave the mayor the business. It wasn't the mayor's fault, of course, since the buttons had grown out into points, but from then on the mayor was known as the cruel killer of Buttons."

Never-before-published stories of Corning's wild ways abound. One fall in the 1960s, the Sabattis crew made a side trip to Lake George, where longtime Albany Democratic machine lieutenant Mary Marcy's son, Bill Marcy, owned a camp at The Hague. The camp's boathouse had a large deck that hung out directly over the water. It was early morning following a night of heavy drinking and the men were slowly waking up, stumbling out onto the deck. Marcy's housekeeper was taking breakfast orders from the hungry hunters. The mayor – who had been watching with considerable interest large trout swim lazily in the crystalline water beneath the deck, drawn by the slatted sunlight – announced he had a hankering for a trout breakfast. "I'm sorry, mister mayor, but we don't have any trout," the housekeeper told Corning. "I'd really like some trout," the mayor repeated, eyeing the shadows below. "We don't have any trout," the housekeeper said once more, shaking her head. "But if you get a trout, I'll cook it."

The mayor quietly got up from his chair, went inside the house and returned with his trusty .35 Remington, the one with twenty-odd deer notches. The men on the deck watched silently; Noonan and McLean recalled that it all happened as if in slow-motion. The mayor clicked off the rifle's safety, lowered the barrel until it rested in the gap between the deck's planks and pulled the trigger. There was a sharp report. The men joined Corning as he walked around the side of the house, down to the shore and retrieved a fish, floating belly up on the surface, a fine fourteen-inch brook trout. With a touch of the dramatic learned on stage at Groton, Corning marched with ceremony back into the kitchen, extended the fish to the housekeeper and said, "Here's a trout. I'd like you to cook it for me now." "Yep," McLean said. "He barked that trout. It had a little life left in it, but we couldn't revive the brookie. We all gave the mayor hell for shooting it." Said Noonan, "Here was the mayor of the capital city of New York, who always called himself a devoted conservationist, breaking at least a half-dozen New York state conservation laws. We never let him forget that one."

It was in the woods and on the waters that the mayor managed to break out, and, where, aided by alcohol, Erastus the man found his salvation and, perhaps, even achieved a kind of epiphany of the soul while flushing grouse or tracking deer, hunkered down in a duck blind or casting a fly to entice a trout to rise. Corning was a passionate reader of literature pertaining to hunting and fishing and he once remarked in a letter to a friend how much he was moved by the book, *A River Runs Through It*, with its powerfully drawn symbolism between fly fishing and spirituality.

Polly Noonan's former son-in-law, Douglas Rutnik, Albany lawyer and political adviser to Corning, was also a hunting buddy for twenty years. The two men spent most of their time together bird hunting, particularly ruffed grouse (known generically as partridge) in the hilltowns of Albany County. Corning hunted grouse with his first shotgun, a double-barrel Remington twenty-gauge that was a gift from his father in his final year at Yale. As with all his hunting and fishing trips, grouse involved ritual to hunt the birds the way Corning preferred. Corning and Rutnik were generally joined by Polly Noonan's son, Brian. They hunted each Sunday during the fall season, often from near Dan O'Connell's summer home. On the way to hunting, Corning would stop in to confer with O'Connell on Whitehall Road in Albany, the mayor's way of mixing business with pleasure.

The mayor and the men flushed and chased the grouse, with three hunters driving the grouse out of hiding for the hunter to shoot. It involved a lot of hiking, perhaps ten miles in an afternoon. The mayor was an excellent shot, but he preferred to chase the grouse. "He invariably ended up where he shouldn't have been, up above us, maybe twenty yards away," Rutnik recalled. "BOOM! BOOM! BOOM! Our shots whistled just over the mayor's head on more than one occasion. There were a lot of close calls. The mayor almost got killed several times while grouse hunting." As it was, as time went by, Corning outlived many, watching a lot of his old hunting partners die off. "He used to hunt with his brother, Eddie, but Eddie died. And then the old-timers like the brewer at Hedrick's Brewery passed away and he found young guys like me to fill in," Rutnik said. Others among the grouse pack were McLean and Polly Noonan's son-in-law, Joe Montimurro. Rutnik said Corning routinely broke hunting laws himself and encouraged the men with him to do the same. "He'd say I'm going to go road hunting up in the hilltowns and he'd drive around, looking for grouse off the side of the road," Rutnik said. "One day, he got so excited driving along when he saw a big grouse just off the road that he reached for his shotgun across the seat and blew a big hole in the roof of the car. BOOM! I swear. It was a green Chevy like he always bought. He used to beat his cars so bad the hole in the roof didn't really bother him because it had a lot of miles on it, was in really rough shape and he was going to trade it in soon anyway." After blasting the hole in the roof, Rutnik continued, "the mayor had the peace of mind to stop the car, get out and kill that grouse with the second shot from his double-barrel Remington," Rutnik said. Corning, the celebrated conservationist, was once more breaking state conservation laws: "road hunting," the discharging of firearms from a vehicle, was both illegal and dangerous given the chance of a round striking a nearby house or passing car.

The mayor was never injured or arrested while road hunting, and managed to maintain a record of hunting on Election Day for each of his eleven mayoral elections. Corning's routine was to vote early, as soon as the polls opened, and then go duck hunting on the Hudson River. Corning's fascination with eccentric folks and colorful personalities was well established and on Election Day he combined two joys, duck hunting and the irrepressible Perry Peloubet. Peloubet, who lived in Athens south of Albany with his wife, was a bred-in-the-bone Hudson River rat. Peloubet had commandeered in the 1940s a derelict oil barge run aground on the western shore of the Hudson between Athens and Coxsackie. Peloubet pirated electricity, fashioned a water system and turned the wheel house, somewhat slanted given the pitch of the beached vessel, into his private weekend retreat and duck hunting headquarters. Peloubet had lived in the wheel house with his wife for a time, but had since moved to less rustic quarters in nearby Athens proper. "Perry was a great old guy whose family had been hunting ducks on the Hudson River for generations and he told great stories," Rutnik recalled. "We'd go down there Election Day morning, Perry would have a big breakfast for us, and he'd have the decoys out on the river for the mayor."

The mayor brought his Old Town canoe or a ten-foot collapsible rowboat he kept at the Alcove Reservoir to Perry's place, along with a Parker double-barreled twelve-gauge shotgun he favored for duck hunting, or, after the strong kick of the Parker started hurting his shoulder in later years, a three-shot sixteen-gauge shotgun. Duck hunting was usually successful with Perry, who knew how to bring in a wide variety of birds from the Hudson flyway: teals, pintails, mallards, black ducks, goldeneyes, buf-fleheads. "The mayor was a great shot," McLean said. "He cleaned and ate every duck he shot. He never shot anything he wasn't going to eat." While Corning had a lot of experience duck hunting, he deferred to the expertise of Perry, a good twenty years older than the mayor and who continued hunting into his late-70s. The drill began as the decoys were placed out down river. Corning and Perry would huddle in Perry's skiff turned into "sneak boat," camouflaged with cattails and river grasses. They'd slide into the sneak boat upriver, drifting with the current down to the decoys to set up a good shot. They also used duck blinds along the shore if need be. "Perry could talk to those ducks like nobody I've ever heard," McLean said. "He didn't need a duck call. He used his own voice and he'd draw all dif-ferent varieties onto our blind."

As with political cronies, when it came to a hunting buddy like Perry Peloubet, Corning was intensely loyal. The mayor always sent the Peloubets Christmas gifts and generous checks on birthdays and special occasions. McLean and Noonan also recalled that the mayor never failed to bring along a gift of food for the couple and presents for the Peloubets' numerous foster children when he came hunting. The mayor also came to the aid of the Peloubets with his political muscle, in the 1970s, when the oil company that owned the beached derelict barge was going to evict the Peloubets from the vessel they had been squatting on for more than thirty years. "The mayor stepped in," Peter Noonan recalled. "He hired Rutnik to represent the Peloubets in court and the mayor used what influence he could. In the end, Corning stopped the eviction and they were allowed to continue using the barge. That's the way the mayor was. He would always go to bat for his friends."

Corning had his own, private ethical standards – double standards, some might say – when it came to using his political power to reward friends and punish enemies. At the Alcove Reservoir on Route 32 in south-ern Albany County, he routinely and frequently broke the law by fishing and hunting in the well posted, no-access water supply for the city of Albany. What's more, Corning not only kept a canoe and a collapsible row-boat on the Alcove, illegally, of course, but he compounded the infraction by operating it with a gas- and oil-belching outboard motor. "It was an ancient Johnson, probably from the '40s, a two-horsepower and it smoked like hell," McLean recalled. Right into the drinking water supply of his citizens the oil and gas poured. Granted, Corning possessed a proprietary interest: his father, after all, along with the O'Connell brothers, established the Alcove Reservoir system and developed it as a good drinking water supply, which for decades they held out to voters as a shining example of the positive leadership brought about by their Democratic organization. And it was Corning's great-grandfather, the first Erastus, and grandfather, Erastus Jr., who established Albany's first reservoir in the 1800s at Six-Mile Waterworks on Washington Avenue Extension and laid pipes for the inaugural municipal drinking water network.

With such a deep reservoir of family history associated with Albany's water, the Alcove in essence became the mayor's own 1,500-acre private hunting and fishing preserve. Outdoorsmen got to calling it Corning Pond. It served as a getaway escape from City Hall for the mayor. It was against the law to hunt or fish there, but the mayor's lawlessness was a well-known fact among hunters and anglers, a nudge and wink secret among the guys. It's easy to find other illegal sportsmen who willfully violated the no trespassing signs at the Alcove, too, with the mayor's blessing. In fact, Corning made the Alcove a kind of private preserve for himself and close friends. Corning also proudly brought out-of-town VIPs to the Alcove. For several years in the 1950s, when pro golfers Sam Snead and Gene Sarazen came to Schuyler Meadows to play a benefit tournament for cancer research, Corning and pal Judge Martin Schenck played with the golfing legends. "But what Snead and Sarazen really wanted to do was to go fishing, so Corning took them to the Alcove," Schenck said. The mayor eventually created the Corning Memorial Forest and Wildlife Demonstration Area at the reservoir and instituted his own permit system that rewarded political allies and shut out foes. It was run as a cooperative venture between the city's water department and the Capital District Chapter of the Ruffed Grouse Society.

Nearly every week, no matter the season, year in and year out for his entire life, Corning drove out to the Alcove. Corning especially liked to introduce children to the sport of fishing with a brief outing there. In a rare foray afield with his own children, the mayor took Bettina and Erastus III and his wife, Betty, fishing at the Alcove on occasion. Mother and daughter enjoyed fishing, Bettina recalled; Rasty did not. The Noonan kids all loved to fish. The mayor had what he wanted. "Erastus called them 'official inspection trips,'" recalled Polly Noonan. "He'd pack up Peter, me and our kids in his car and drive to the Alcove. He had a canoe there, which we have on our pond now. We'd have a picnic lunch and Erastus would teach my kids to fish. He always said he loved to have my kids around. His own were never around, you know." Polly's son, Peter Noonan, remembered as a boy waiting with great anticipation for the arrival of the mayor in his trusty green Chevy pulling up Noonan Lane each Saturday. Adventure had arrived. "On Saturdays, the mayor would work at City Hall until noon and then at about 12:15 he'd show up at our house. It was like clockwork," Peter Noonan said. "We'd sit around the kitchen table and all talk for awhile and then we'd make plans to go out hunting or fishing." As with the rest of his sporting life, Corning had a favorite ritual at the Alcove. "He would always drive quite a bit out of his way to park in the same little old lady's yard," Peter Noonan recalled. "He'd knock on her door, she'd welcome the mayor in and they'd sit down and chat for a little while. And then the mayor would always leave a gift, a couple of jars of jam or a ham or some fruit. He always brought something for her. And she'd usually have a pie she baked for us. He could have parked anywhere, but he chose to be kind to her. I never knew her name, but that impressed me. It was a big thrill every time she got a visit from the mayor. I think that was the personal touch that kept him getting re-elected."

The mayor, who possessed an insouciant charm seated behind his mythic desk at City Hall, maintained it while casting a spinner on the Alcove. Bob Denney, a retired steelworker in his seventies who lived his entire life on the shores of the Normanskill in a farmhouse directly below the Delaware Avenue bridge on the outskirts of Albany, recalled: "I'm duck hunting on the Alcove real early one fall morning. It's dark and foggy and the first light of daybreak is beginning. I'm on the shore, hunkered down, waiting, and I see some shapes on the water. As the sun rises a little more, I can just make out the forms of a grouping of ducks that have landed. I take aim and fire away with my shotgun. It's completely silent and I'm looking to see what I hit, when I hear this voice from the fog, 'Congratulations. You just shot my decoys.' It was Mayor Corning," Denney said, throwing his head back in laughter at the recollection. "The mayor wasn't mad or anything, but he came over to me and we had a good laugh about it. We became friends after that. I used to hunt with the mayor on the Alcove for years. Great fella, the mayor. A real sport."

Chapter 11:

Paving the Pine Bush and Burning Garbage for Profit: Corning and the Environment

---

**Men's conception of themselves and of each other
has always depended on their notion of the earth.
When the earth was the World – all the world there was –
and the stars were lights in Dante's heaven,
and the ground beneath men's feet roofed Hell,
they saw themselves as creatures at the center of the universe,
the sole, particular concern of God –
and from that high place they ruled and killed
and conquered as they pleased.**

*Opening stanza of "Riders on Earth Together" by
Archibald MacLeish, a poem Corning often recited publicly
to explain his environmentalism.*

In the minds of many environmentalists, the Pine Bush is Albany's crown jewel, a unique and vast pine barrens that offers urban dwellers a piece of wilderness within the city. To them, it is a place of incomparable natural beauty and a window through which to glimpse rare flora and fauna. The Pine Bush is a sanctuary for thousands of species of plants, animals and insects, including one found in very few other places, the Karner Blue butterfly, an endangered species named to both the state and federal protected species list. More importantly, the Pine Bush is a one-of-a-kind ecosystem. Nothing precisely like this accident of geology, geography and ecology exists anywhere else in the world. Located on the western edge of Albany and also partly in two neighboring suburban towns, untouched and ancient at its core, it is the largest inland pine barrens in the world and the only one located on sand dunes. To the eyes of developers, though, the 4,000-acre undeveloped portion of the forty-square mile Pine Bush repre-

sents a wasted swath of sand mounds and scrub pines, a pointless emptiness unless paved over, covered with strip malls and corporate parks and
condominium clusters – anything that generates jobs, tax revenue, profits
and progress. The developers had history on their side, for Albanians had
ignored the Pine Bush over the centuries and, when they thought of it at
all, it was viewed as an ugly bramble on the outskirts of the city. "Not even
a diseased dog ought to be allowed to die and be buried on the premises,
out of respect for the dog," was how the Pine Bush was described by influential nineteenth-century Albany publisher and historian, Joel Munsell,
who wrote the definitive multi-volume history of Albany. Following a trip
that took him through the Pine Bush in 1798, Timothy Dwight observed
he had "passed over a hard pine plain, and presented nothing agreeable. The
plain is uninhabited, the soil lean, and the road indifferent."

The dawn of the back-to-the-land urge and attendant environmental
movement coincided with the height of the counterculture revolution in
the late-1960s across America, even in machine-subdued Albany. Although
it lagged a few years behind most national trends, the enthusiasm for environmentalism ran high. In Albany, a focal point for land conservation was
the Pine Bush. In particular, an environmental group called Save The Pine
Bush became increasingly active and vocal in the debate over the fate of the
pine barrens. By the early 1970s, the battle lines – environmentalists represented by Save The Pine Bush, who appreciated its unique beauty, versus
developers who considered it a worthless piece of land unless it was built
up – were clearly drawn. The fight over the Pine Bush divided the citizens
of Albany in a way few issues ever had and it put Mayor Corning precisely
in the middle, astride an isthmus separating the warring parties.

Corning, the king of all he surveyed in the city, wanted it both ways on
the Pine Bush – known historically as the King's Highway. The mayor had
a dilemma with the incompatible interests in this corner of his kingdom. On
one hand, Corning wanted to be true to his interests and to enhance his reputation as an environmentalist ahead of his time, possessed of a profound
passion for the land and for preservation of rare natural history. On the
other hand, Corning was a political animal who owed loyalty to machine
operatives pushing for development so they might profit handsomely on
their land speculation deals in the Pine Bush. Furthermore, the mayor was
tied to pro-development forces through personal connections to lawyers
representing the developers and the land speculators. In many things,
Corning managed to have it both ways, but when it came to the Pine Bush,

the lines seemed more sharply drawn; the issue tested the limits of Corning's creative governance and resolution of conflict.

Corning expressed the clash of his competing agendas in his foreword to a book by Don Rittner, *Pine Bush: Albany's Last Frontier*, published in 1976 when Rittner served as city archaeologist, after having been hired by Corning and appointed by the mayor as de facto Pine Bush ombudsman. In the book's foreword, Corning wrote: "The Pine Bush is an ancient area that is precious and beautiful, almost unique in its fauna and flora . . . Recognizing the vast changes that have taken place and also recognizing the recent tremendous upsurge in interest in preserving the Pine Bush, it is essential to find the best balance between protection and progress, the best balance between land owner and nature lover. This is not easy, but a start has been made."

Conveniently, Corning adopted the impersonal tone of the past tense in the foreword when describing the degradation of the Pine Bush's wilderness character: "A quarter of a century ago the Thruway split the Pine Bush in half and then came . . . the Washington Avenue Extension. Sewer and water lines were installed and the landfill was placed in operation. Over ten million dollars were spent in federal, state and local funds. In addition, almost a million dollars has been obligated for sewers by Pine Bush property owners." The mayor neglected to mention that he was the driving force behind those irrevocable changes and that it was his hand – the hand of the king – more than any other that transformed the Pine Bush from a wild place into a manmade infrastructure that set the table upon which large-scale development would feast.

The mayor neglected to mentioned in the book's foreword, too, that his forebear, the first Erastus Corning, a mayor of Albany, was responsible for the single largest manmade alteration that changed the face of the Pine Bush in the nineteenth century. In 1850, led by Corning, the city's richest and most influential person, Albany dammed up Patroon's Creek and created Rensselaer Lake, known today as Six-Mile Waterworks, where Washington Avenue Extension and Fuller Road intersect. With the construction of that 200-million gallon reservoir, drinking water was pumped from the Pine Bush to downtown. Corning's conduit, a four-foot high brick tunnel beneath what is Washington Avenue today, ran four miles to Bleecker Reservoir (now Bleecker Stadium) and further to another containment area called Tivoli Lakes (now Tivoli Park). The Pine Bush continued as the fresh water supply for Albany residents until 1875, when the

Hudson River was tapped for a growing population. Later, with the creation of the Alcove Reservoir under the second Corning to be mayor, Erastus 2nd, that source was abandoned. Corning's foreword also conveniently forgot to note the fact that he was the man who had not only built the infrastructure that allowed development of the Pine Bush, but that he had also built the city dump there in 1969.

To an objective outsider, Corning's position on the Pine Bush seemed transparent and hypocritical, but the majority of the voting citizenry, meaning Democratic loyalists, refused to see the contradictions. Even in February, 1970, while Corning was building the dump in this environmentally sensitive area he had so often praised as a naturalist treasure, the mayor offered testimony before a state legislative environmental committee that proposed a law to ban internal combustion engines in all cars by 1975. "The state of pollution is critical," he said, "and there is very little time left to clean up the environment." Corning, not a church-goer, concluded his testimony by quoting from the second chapter of the Bible's Book of Genesis: "And the Lord God took the man, and put him into the Garden of Eden to dress it and keep it." In the final analysis, Corning, disingenuous about his involvement in the building up of the Pine Bush in his foreword for Rittner's book, shrugged and said he couldn't halt progress. "We cannot roll up the roads, nor can we dig up the sewers and water lines. They are going to be used; there is no way I know of that we can go back," Corning wrote.

As a Phi Beta Kappa history major at Yale, Corning was not unaware of the Pine Bush's past; he simply chose to ignore it. Corning's great-grandfather wasn't alone in the exploitation of the environmental treasure. In the early 1600s, the Dutch deforested the Pine Bush to use its pine trees for the stockade walls and the structures of Fort Orange on the Hudson River, four miles to the east of the pine barrens. Throughout the colonial era, the Pine Bush was a heavily traveled shortcut for fur traders crossing between the Hudson and Mohawk valleys. By the end of the seventeenth century, a sixteen-mile road linking the two river valleys was a lifeline of commerce between frontier settlements in Schenectady and Albany. The route went by a number of names, including the Albany Road and the Schenectady Path. In the end, the moniker that endured was the King's Highway. It became a strategic military road during the French and Indian War, By the 1760s, several taverns opened along the King's Highway to slake the thirsts of travelers kicking up dust on the sandy plain, including one owned by Isaac Jacob Truax. Corning, who possessed a comprehensive library of books on local history, including volumes about the Pine Bush, knew all this, of course, and yet he chose to continue in the tradition of his great-grandfather by laying the infrastructure that created a seedbed for development. Nonetheless, he attacked development there by those outside his control. Corning took a backhanded swipe at Gov. Nelson Rockefeller at a luncheon at the Thruway House while making a push for more development in the Pine Bush. "This hotel where we're having lunch today was once Pine Bush," Corning said at a gathering in January, 1979. "The State Office Campus and the State University complex were part of the Pine Bush, too. But when Edward Durrell Stone took over as architect of the State University campus, he leveled every dune and took down every tree. I didn't want to see the State University take this and I opposed the governor on it."

When it came to the Pine Bush, Corning – who talked environmentalism out of one side of his mouth and cut sweetheart deals for developers who were personal friends out of the other side – faced a crucible of sorts in the matter of Neil Hellman, dubbed by the local press as "the race horse magnate." Hellman obliged their hype and liked his thoroughbreds fast, his development projects glitzy and his philanthropy outsized. In the Pine Bush, Hellman saw a blank canvas upon which the multi-millionaire businessman could create a lasting image that would enlarge his already epic stature in Albany. Hellman proposed for the Pine Bush nothing less than "a city within a city." A visionary entrepreneur, Hellman had purchased development rights to 390 acres in the center of the Pine Bush just as Corning was making development possible in the late-1960s by constructing Washington Avenue Extension that fed into the state Thruway. The extension and its water, sewer and power suddenly made Hellman's vision possible. Corning's Washington Avenue Extension, the environmentalists would later say, was like a "knife through the heart of the Pine Bush." Others, notably entrenched Democratic ward leaders, tipped off by the mayor in a bit of insider trading, also snapped up Pine Bush parcels in rampant land speculation just as Corning was unveiling his own twentieth-century version of the King's Highway. Hellman was a shrewd speculator and saw opportunity himself in the Pine Bush, expecting the mayor to play ball with him. Corning was king, after all, and Washington Avenue Extension was his highway. Washington Avenue Extension promised to open up Pine Bush development the way the Adirondack Northway caused a development boom in Saratoga County after it was built in the 1950s. When it came to transforming sand dunes into a profitable business venture, nobody thought as big as Hellman.

Hellman's imagined "city within a city" was no hyperbole. It was a 390-acre megaplex, four times the size of Rockefeller's phantasmagoria, the Empire State Plaza, and bigger even than the downtown Albany core from the Capitol to the Hudson River and the commercial district flanking each side of State Street Hill combined. The entirety of Hellman's grand scheme was never made public, but he envisioned apartment complexes, stores, an office park, a school and municipal services such as its own fire and police stations. It seems probable in hindsight that years before it was unveiled, Hellman had been talking with Corning and sketching out for the mayor the possibilities of the "city within a city." The mayor's first published remarks about development in the Pine Bush came in January, 1967 during an annual interview with *Knickerbocker News* reporters and editors. "There will be a school, probably two schools. There'll be a police station, a firehouse, a shopping center. It'll be a complete community. I'd say that, within five years, you'd have a population of 10,000 to 15,000 in the Pine Bush." Corning took the words right out of Hellman's mouth, as it were. Later in the same newspaper interview, however, Corning expressed the essential contradiction at the center of his policies regarding the Pine Bush. The mayor said, "It is an example of a natural area – a pine barren – that exists in no other place in the world. The various agencies in Washington and in New York who are interested in preserving unusual natural areas are enthusiastic about this and they were the ones that suggested and pinpointed the area."

Because of the explosive nature of Hellman's proposal, as well as persistent opposition by Save The Pine Bush forces, the development project was kept under close wraps while Hellman went about building movie theaters and other structures around the city. By early 1975, however, Hellman was ready to move ahead on his "city within a city" when the newspapers broke the story that Hellman had purchased options on nearly 400 acres of land in the sensitive core of the Pine Bush. "The environmentalists jumped on that, because that was the core of the Pine Bush and they knew if Hellman got it through, it was essentially the end of the Pine Bush," Rittner said.

The Save the Pine Bushers got busy and organized students from the State University of New York at Albany to march in front of City Hall; they conducted a letter writing campaign to the newspapers and the Common Council; they enlisted the assistance of prominent scientists to plead their case, including a stirring missive on behalf of preserving the Karner Blue butterfly from famous novelist Vladimir Nabokov, author of *Lolita* and an internationally recognized lepidopterist whose specialty included the Karner Blue. It was shaping up into a battle royal. Corning had one foot in each camp, but both sides were pulling and the mayor's have-it-both-ways position was beginning to look untenable. A *Times Union* front-page headline on March 26, 1975 read: "Albany's choice: Hellman development or butterfly haven." The story began, "Butterflies are not free when they live in the middle of a tract of expensive, developable land, says entrepreneur Neil Hellman." Further complicating the matter was the fact that Hellman's attorney was none other than Richard Meyers, a Corning protégé who had risen through the ranks of the machine, got elected to the Albany County Legislature where he galvanized his power as majority leader. And there were more conflicts of interest for Corning buried within the sands of the Pine Bush. Albany County Clerk Donald Lynch – executive secretary of the Albany County Democratic Committee and a close ally of boss Dan O'Connell, who also happened to be married to O'Connell's niece – owned acreage in the Pine Bush he wished to develop and had already built the Town House Motor Hotel in that area in the mid-1960s. Moreover, Douglas Rutnik – Albany County public defender, political adviser to the mayor, and well-connected in the law firm he ran with his then wife, Noonan's daughter, Polly – represented Pine Bush developers, including BPS Management Corp., Anderson Development Corp. of Albany and Mid-Atlantic Land Corp., builders of the Point of Woods condominium complex.

Rittner was privy to other, private conflicts. Rittner said the mayor's wife, Betty Corning, was writing generous personal checks, anonymously, and having Rittner funnel them to environmental groups waging battle for preservation of the Pine Bush against the mayor and pro-development forces. "It was a bizarre set of circumstances for the mayor," recalled Rittner, who, himself, was part insider as city employee and also fighting City Hall in his environmental activism. "While Corning was publicly supporting preservation of the Pine Bush and development, his wife was trying to stop development." Betty Corning, for whom politics was anathema, nonetheless broke tradition by attending meetings to preserve the Pine Bush. City planner Dick Patrick remembered seeing Betty Corning at one such meeting at the State University of New York at Albany. Theresa

Cooke, an outspoken critic of the mayor, had recently called Corning "a liar" in the press. Said Patrick, "Nobody else would have noticed it. But when Cooke started to speak, Betty Corning quietly got up and left. It was her silent protest, in a very restrained way like she was. But she would not sit there in front of someone who had called her husband a liar. She had that kind of loyalty."

Corning's fence straddling would not play well for the public indefinitely. The mayor finally made a public remark on May 6, 1975. He told the *Times Union* that development of the Pine Bush had been "guaranteed" by construction of the State Thruway – conveniently laying blame at the feet of the state, as usual – without mentioning the metamorphosis wrought by his own Washington Avenue Extension. Corning also said Hellman's compromise proposal to donate a small piece of land at the edge of his development for a city park seemed reasonable. But two men whose counsel he respected on such matters, Rittner and Patrick, broke ranks with Corning and openly opposed Hellman's plan. The newspapers picked up on this rare challenge to the mayor's absolute authority over staffers. "City planner Dick Patrick surprised many at a public hearing on the rezoning Monday when he spoke in opposition to the rezoning for the Hellman development," the *Times Union* said on May 6, 1975. "Corning said that 'on the face of it' he disagreed with some of Patrick's comments, which warned against development of the area."

Patrick, after all, who had a degree in landscape architecture from Syracuse University, had been hand-picked by the mayor as Albany's first city planner in 1966. Patrick was working for New York State at the time when Corning interviewed him. "I sent the mayor my resume and I listed my hobbies as bird watching, stamp collecting and Oriental rugs," Patrick said. "I got a note back right away from the mayor, who said he was glad to see that I shared some of his hobbies, meaning stamp collecting and birding. And he ended the letter with this exact quote: 'I would be happy if you would come in so we could pass the time of day together.' After working for the state bureaucracy, I never imagined I'd find a politician with that kind of eloquence." After their passing the time of day together, Corning offered the job to Patrick, who was twenty-nine at the time. Patrick worked up the original land-use plan for the Pine Bush in the late-1960s, shortly after arriving. "It wasn't controversial at that time, because, frankly, nobody really cared about the Pine Bush then," Patrick said. "And the mayor maintained control and picked out the parcels himself." Patrick remembered that Corning knew the Pine Bush terrain intimately from firsthand experience. "He invited me to go bird watching in the Pine Bush with him once," Patrick said. "There had been a fire, but that didn't bother the mayor. He trudged right through and his clothes were all black with soot. He obviously knew the layout of the place and took us into some remote areas. He had these pocket field glasses he had picked up overseas during World War II and he could also identify birds by their calls. His knowledge of birds and nature was impressive."

Similarly, Rittner, the city archaeologist and Pine Bush consultant, has a quirky story about how he got hired by Corning. Rittner was completing his bachelor's degree in environmental studies in 1972 at the State University of New York at Albany and he needed an archaeological project for his last nine credits to graduate. "I said I'd save the Pine Bush. That sounds like a good nine-credit project," Rittner said with a laugh. Encouraged by his SUNYA professors, who also happened to be Pine Bush preservationists, Rittner called City Hall on a whim. It was late on a Friday afternoon. Corning answered the phone himself. Rittner paused, stammered, was not prepared to speak directly to the mayor. Corning gently coaxed the tongue-tied caller and suggested Rittner drop by City Hall tomorrow morning, a Saturday. "I was a hippie with hair down to my ass, wearing the one pair of jeans I owned and some ratty shirt and I'm in the office of the king," Rittner said. "I mean, you can smell the political history in that office. I looked at him leaning back in his chair and realized that man had been sitting in that chair since before I was born. That hit me like a rock." Rittner recovered enough to stumble through the pitch he had been rehearsing in his mind, explaining he wanted to map the historic route of the King's Highway through the Pine Bush and to excavate the eighteenth-century Isaac Truax tavern as a tie-in to the upcoming Bicentennial celebration in 1976. "I go through this long spiel, very nervously, and the mayor listened in silence and when I was all finished, he opened his desk drawer, pulled out his checkbook and said, 'Now, how much would you like to get started?'" Rittner was stunned. And speechless. Corning answered for him. "How about $500 to start?" the mayor offered. "And how do you spell your last name?" Corning handed over his personal check. "I was totally blown away," Rittner said. "I'm this hippie college kid who spoke to him for the first time the day before and he's giving me a check. I just sort of floated out of there and as I got to the door, the mayor said, 'When you spend that, just come back for more. And let me know how it's going.'"

Rittner, who was twenty-two that summer of 1972, rounded up a couple dozen SUNYA student volunteers, borrowed archaeological digging equipment and went to work trying to unearth the Pine Bush's past as a way of ensuring its future. "It was a really hot, humid summer and the mayor came out to our dig site a couple of times in the sweltering heat of the afternoon," Rittner recalled. "The mayor would arrive in his black Buick, driven by Dusty Miller, and he'd walk around the dig site in his dark business suit. He must have been broiling, but he spent quite a bit of time with us and was obviously very interested and shared with us his vast knowledge about the history of the Pine Bush."

Rittner and his band of volunteers managed to make substantial progress on the Truax dig, using only Corning's $500 donation. The gist of their research was that the Truax tavern, dating from the late-1750s, and situated in the Pine Bush along Corning's Washington Avenue Extension near the city's western border, was a fairly sophisticated structure catering to a sizable clientele. The project's findings disputed the conventionally accepted historical view that the King's Highway and taverns along its route were primitive and unremarkable. "The mayor really liked the fact that a bunch of hippie college kids had proven the historians wrong," Rittner said. "He could see the person for who he was, rather than the way he looked." Rittner wrapped up the project by sending the mayor a one hundred-page report on their findings, which provided the germ of the later book. After graduation, Rittner wrote the mayor and asked for a job with the city in January, 1973. Corning told Rittner to write up a job description; that's how easy it was for Rittner to be hired at an annual salary of $8,500 as the city's first, and perhaps the nation's first, municipal archaeologist. Said Rittner, "I learned time and time again, if Corning wanted something to happen in Albany, it just happened."

It was a lesson Patrick and Rittner were taught again perforce two years later, in the spring of 1975, when Hellman's "city within a city" proposal arrived at its moment of truth. Again, the mayor tried to buy time. On April 17, 1975, an Albany city planning board hearing on Hellman's proposal was abruptly canceled because the hearing had been illegally set, according to Corning and Hellman's attorney, Meyers, who, conveniently, were in agreement. Two months went by, a decision delayed by more technicalities, before Hellman's proposal wended its tortuous way to the

Albany Common Council for a vote. The Common Council, maligned as a "rubber stamp" for Corning – its long string of unanimous approvals of the mayor's initiatives rarely broken – was giving indications in the press that it would vote in favor of Hellman's proposal. Those rumblings sent shivers up the spines of Save the Pine Bush activists, who viewed Hellman's development as a line drawn in the sand that would in perpetuity judge how well they had achieved their preservation goals. To the minds of the Save The Pine Bush activists, this was nothing less than the mother of all Pine Bush projects and they rallied their forces to undertake a media blitz.

A few days before the Common Council meeting at which a vote was to be taken on Hellman's proposal, Corning called Rittner into his office. The mayor said, "That was quite an effort by the Save The Pine Bush people, Don. I wonder who was behind it?" Rittner said Corning had a gleam in his eye and the two shared a moment of realization that the mayor privately supported the group and Rittner's covert actions on their behalf. Still, Corning remained poker-faced regarding his position on the Hellman project. A few days later, on June 16, 1975, the Common Council postponed its scheduled vote, citing a letter from Corning calling for the creation of a special area with new zoning guidelines that the mayor had just presented to the Council. They said they needed time to review it; Hellman's meter was running out. The options he held to purchase the 390 acres were to expire on June 30. The pressure was growing intense. A trickle of speculation leaking out from the Common Council still pointed to approval.

On June 22, 1975, the day before the vote by the Common Council, Rittner asked for a meeting with the mayor to make a last-ditch plea. "Mayor, you have a reputation as a historian and an environmentalist who was out front on saving the Pine Bush in the mid-1960s, before anyone else, but if this Hellman deal goes through, it's all over. We've lost the Pine Bush. If you don't stop it, the Pine Bush is lost. It's history," Rittner said. As Rittner described it, the mayor grew silent, leaned forward in his chair, rested his arms on his desk and peered over the tops of the half-spectacles he wore for reading, a stare he used when he wanted to make a point with special forcefulness. Rittner recalled he thought he detected the trace of a smirk on Corning's lips. The mayor finally spoke in soft, measured tones, Rittner recalled.

Corning: "Don, don't worry about it. I don't like Hellman."

Rittner: "Are we going to preserve this area, then?"

Corning: "Is that the best part?"

Rittner: "It's the best."

Corning: "OK, then, we'll buy it."

The following night, in a stunning reversal of what they had been indicating, the Common Council voted against Hellman's project. The headline in the *Times Union* the next morning read, "Hellman's Pine Bush Project Legally Dead." Hellman tried to up the ante by offering to donate twenty-five acres for a nature preserve near the Guilderland-Albany border and to scale down his project by selling up to one hundred acres of his parcel to the city for use as an ecological park. Corning let Hellman squirm as the deadline on his options to purchase the acreage owned by Muncie Construction Corp. of El Paso, Texas ran out, and the landowner declined an extension, saying it was time to "fish or cut bait." Corning's actions suggested another analogy; the mayor had allowed Hellman's "city within a city" to sink to the bottom, never to be heard from again, the lost Atlantis of the Pine Bush, a mythical community that never was.

Speaking two decades after the fact, some Corning watchers wondered aloud if the mayor's *ad hominem* overturning of the project by Hellman, who was Jewish, might be construed as a sign of Corning's anti-Semitism. It seems unlikely for a number of reasons. One of Corning's close personal friends was Lew Swyer, a major developer who also happened to be Jewish, and the two had worked in tandem on a number of development projects in Albany, including some in the Pine Bush. Corning was a buddy of Al Hessberg, too, a prominent attorney and also a Jew. It was Corning who sponsored Hessberg's membership in the Fort Orange Club, making Hessberg the first Jewish member of the private club. And there were other Jews whom Corning counted among his friends and whose political careers he had championed within the machine hierarchy, such as State Supreme Court Judge Leonard Weiss. If it wasn't anti-Semitism, then, what was it that caused Corning to scuttle the biggest development project on the drawing boards for Albany at the time? Was it a combination of a deep desire to preserve something of the Pine Bush, of a supreme arrogance that demanded absolute control, and of an allegiance to Dan O'Connell (approaching ninety and on his deathbed when Hellman's project was killed, but still the boss)? Regardless of the mix of motives that played into the final decision, Corning could lay claim to his cherished reputation as conservationist in the Hellman deal. Corning had not only blocked the race horse magnate from getting out of the gate and becoming the supposed despoiler of the Pine Bush, but Corning had, significantly, quietly acquired more acreage in the pine barrens for the city. In 1978, Albany owned 649 acres of pristine Pine Bush property, forever wild – at least for the time being – and all of it rescued from the developer's bulldozer by none other than Mayor Corning. The King's Highway, to be sure. Such environmental altruism was short-lived, however. By March of 1978, the mayor went on record in full support of three proposed developments in the Pine Bush, including 218 single-family lots for condominiums and thirteen commercial building sites. "It's all part of the plan we've been following all along," Corning said. "To protect everything we could north of the Thruway and develop south of the Thruway, with the exception of the waters of the Kaikout Kill."

Exceptions would be made in the name of political expediency, however, for Corning loyalists and friends of the machine, who sidled up to the Pine Bush trough to consume sizable chunks of billable hours and hefty commissions at real estate closings. Many enjoyed a piece of the windfall, not the least of whom was Corning. He cemented his power base by his favorable dispensations on Pine Bush projects. Investigative reporting conducted by both the *Times Union* and *Knickerbocker News* staffs discovered evidence that Corning profited personally by Pine Bush development through construction liability policies and other coverage underwritten by the mayor's insurance business, Albany Associates.

All the while, Corning liked to hold his Pine Bush cards close to his vest. A *Knickerbocker News* article, citing unnamed sources, on June 20, 1978 reported that Corning "has endorsed an unpublicized land use plan that provides for continued moderate development of the Pine Bush through 1990." At the same time, Corning brushed aside a U.S. Department of the Interior designation of the Pine Bush as a national "Natural Landmark," saying the honor was a nice thing, but that such a designation would not cause the city to defer its present or future plans for development there. Absolving himself from responsibility, Corning kept returning to a familiar mantra: The city had sunk ten million dollars into the Washington Avenue Extension infrastructure and it would be irresponsible not to go along with development to recoup on the investment by enlarging Albany's tax base. Corning proved to be a master strategist in the Pine Bush, having it both ways, the fiscally vigilant mayor and the committed conservationist.

In truth, he was fundamentally neither the former or latter, a sham duality in the minds of environmentalists. Previously splintered and unorganized activism by environmentalists was galvanized in 1978 with the formation of Save The Pine Bush, a group whose roots began in 1972 with a Protect Your Environment (PYE) Club at the State University of New York at Albany. One of Save The Pine Bush's first moves that year was to challenge Corning's absolute authority in controlling Pine Bush development by bringing to light legalities surrounding the city's planning board. They hired a lawyer, Lewis Oliver, a criminal attorney newly arrived from New York City where he worked with social activists and grass-roots groups. Oliver recalled when he first arrived he was amazed at how brazen Corning's manipulation and control of development in the Pine Bush had been. Oliver set out trying to repeal a legal loophole that stemmed from slick maneuvering in 1957 by Corning's Common Council, circumventing two 1929 ordinances that set up an oversight planning board. The 1957 legislation took away from the planning board its power to approve, modify or disapprove subdivisions. Corning would be the sole arbiter on proposals for housing developments, with input from O'Connell, of course. This smacked of a dictatorship and the Save The Pine Bush people, represented by Oliver, were determined to have this practice overturned in court. Corning cagily made an end-run at this point, establishing the city's Environmental Quality Review Board by statute. It was set up much like the city's school board before becoming an elected body. Absolute authority for subdivisions and development rested with the Environmental Quality Review Board through mayoral appointment. The three-member board included Corning, Corporation Counsel Vincent McArdle and Common Council President James Giblin. Said Oliver, "This centralized all the environmental projects and Corning ran them the way he ran the school district and everything else in the city. Of course, every development was approved if they wanted it approved. Eventually, I won a case that invalidated Corning's Environmental Quality Review Board, but that was many years after it was established and, by then, the Pine Bush was substantially built up."

Corning played a convenient shell game during meetings of his Environmental Quality Review Board. They'd meet at a certain time one week, a different time the next week, switching hours and venues to limit public scrutiny of the Pine Bush political sweetheart deals sailing through City Hall. "The change in meeting rooms was not an effort to keep the meeting secret, but I would agree it was hard to find," Corning told reporters. Save The Pine Bush spent months exposing Corning's sleight of hand, going to the courts and the press – the lack of public notification of the meetings was a running controversy in the papers for weeks – before everyone lost interest and the city's traditional process of backroom deals continued, according to Oliver.

Another lawsuit Oliver handled beginning in 1978 was against condominium developments, The Dunes and Pinehurst, both in the Pine Bush. The developers were represented by Rutnik & Rutnik attorney Peter Lynch, whose family had strong ties to the Democratic Party and land holdings in the Pine Bush. The crux of the suit brought by Oliver was this: that the city fronted the money for developers to put in roads, water and sewers, including more than one million dollars in improvements in The Dunes. The cost was then passed on to the condo buyers with a surcharge assessed on each lot. "This was a huge savings for the developers," Oliver said. "It was really an early form of corporate welfare. The developer didn't need capital or up-front money because the city posted bonds for the improvements. In essence, Pine Bush development flourished because the city was subsidizing it." After more than a decade of delays and lengthy challenges by the city, The Court of Appeals ruled in favor of Oliver's clients, owners of condos in The Dunes. The city paid a large settlement. But by then, Corning was long dead.

Corning was very much alive, however, when investigative reporters and the State Investigation Commission caught the mayor in a compromising position with regard to the city's Pine Bush landfill. The Rapp Road dump in the Pine Bush had been operated since the late-1960s by a friend of the party, ward leader William Carey, president of North End Contracting Company. Carey was the son of Eddie Carey, a Ninth Ward committeeman, known as "the Squire of North Albany" and landlord to the family of writer William Kennedy. In *O Albany!* Kennedy summarized the landfill problems: "The State Investigation Commission noted in 1972 that the firm overcharged the city by $450,000 on a landfill contract. One specific overcharge concerned the rental of a used Jeep the firm had bought for $800 and rented to the city for $23,408 for one year, a somewhat heftier fee than usual for used Jeep rentals in cities other than Albany. Carey's firm repaid the $450,000 overcharge, plus a fine, and remained in the city's good graces, which is how it is done in Albany."

After the SIC launched its probe of impropriety, months of obfuscation and created obstacles for the press and state investigators – courtesy of the mayor – ensued. Corning was trying to delay the SIC's final report and any indictments until after his tough 1973 mayoralty campaign against Carl Touhey. Finally, Corning quietly conceded the rip-off and the *Times Union* headline on December 20, 1973 read: "North End to Repay Landfill Overcharge – Corning." Still, the master side-stepper managed to distance himself from the reek of the dump scandal and declined further comment. Never mind that Carey's low-budget and low-tech operation may have been polluting the Pine Bush through inadequate sanitary landfill procedures, exacerbated by the high level of leachate in the sandy soil. Such possibilities were inconsequential when everyone was getting a piece of the action, from Carey to Corning to the machine. In the end, Carey paid a hefty six-figure fine and the political embarrassment was quickly buried in the sands of the Pine Bush. Or so the mayor thought. But Touhey came within an eyelash of defeating the supposedly invincible Corning, a wake-up call to the mayor that an increasingly restless citizenry would no longer tolerate the machine's past arrogance and corruption.

A few years later, starting in the late-1970s, Corning faced additional public discontent for his peripheral support of the Crossgates Mall in Guilderland. This Pyramid Corporation behemoth, the largest mall in the region, was being built not only on environmentally sensitive Pine Bush property, but the mall also threatened an aquifer from which Guilderland residents drew their drinking water. Bumper stickers that said "Don't Mall Our Water" became familiar sights on cars throughout Albany and the region. The proposed construction of Crossgates was highly controversial and spawned marches, pickets, boycotts and an extended public relations campaign. But the mayor, the esteemed environmentalist, remained silent. Corning hid behind the smoke screen that the mall was a Guilderland matter and not an Albany issue. As a result, he declined comment on Crossgates, the biggest development to compromise the Pine Bush he professed to love and wanted to preserve, a project that would forever transform the pine barrens. Moreover, Corning traditionally opposed suburban malls because they sucked out life and commerce from dying downtown Albany merchants. But on Crossgates, Corning was silent. The mayor certainly knew that Richard Meyers – Albany attorney, party loyalist, majority leader of the Albany County Legislature – was hired by the Pyramid Corp. of Syracuse to represent them locally in their development of the eighty-five million dollar Crossgates Mall. "Richie made more off that one closing than both mine and the mayor's salaries combined for several years," said city planner Dick Patrick.

There were potholes lurking for Corning on the King's Highway, however, when it came to Crossgates. A Federal Bureau of Investigation probe involving Corning, Meyers, Crossgates and hardball machine politics delineated a fragment of the sub-text of the controversial mall deal. The *Knickerbocker News* broke the story in June of 1981 that some dubbed "Crossgate/Gaffneygate." The general outline was thus: In the winter of 1981, John "Jack" Gaffney, a party loyalist, was fired for unspecified inadequate performance from his job at the State Department of Motor Vehicles in Albany; he went to see the mayor for help in securing a new patronage position. Gaffney's wife, Anne Gaffney, was making headlines at this time for her strident opposition to Crossgates Mall and had recently been elected to the Albany County Legislature as a Democratic insurgent on the strength of her anti-mall stance. Jack Gaffney wanted evidence and brought a concealed pocket tape recorder to his meetings between January, 1981 and May, 1981 and secretly recorded six hours' worth of conversations between himself and Corning, Meyers and legislative aide Dennis Ryan. According to published reports, the Democratic leaders spelled out three conditions Gaffney had to meet in exchange for a new patronage job. First, that his wife vote with the regular machine-backed Democratic members of the county legislature when her vote was needed and that she must inform the party leadership if she planned to vote against them. Second, that the Gaffneys cease participation in Guilderland town politics. Third, that the Gaffneys stop publicly opposing the Crossgates Mall. Gaffney went to the FBI on March 30 with his testimony and the tapes. On the basis of that evidence, the FBI launched an investigation into possible bribery and conspiracy charges against Corning, Meyers and Ryan.

The *Knickerbocker News* editorial on June 26, 1981, took the mayor to task while acknowledging the political realities of Albany. "Providing jobs for loyal party members is an accepted political practice. They help cement the power of those in charge, and sometimes put highly qualified people in jobs they wouldn't ordinarily get. But when the awarding of a patronage job is tied to something else – such as ending political activism, voting a certain way, and backing away from a point of view which runs counter to the private endeavors of a political leader – we have a different matter entirely."

The strong-arm tactics apparently were all right with the mayor – a political source called them "vintage, old-fashioned politics" – but the third condition for Gaffney regarding Crossgates made Corning livid. "Corning denied that a rift has developed between himself and Meyers over the Crossgates condition," according to a *Times Union* article. "Several political sources said the Crossgates condition was thrown in by Meyers unknown to the mayor, and that Corning was extremely upset over it. Sources said the mayor was furious to have his name linked with Crossgates, because he's never had anything to do with Crossgates and has never taken a stand on Crossgates. Corning is a self-proclaimed environmentalist with a fondness for the Pine Bush . . ." Corning laid back on the controversy. "The matter is not of the slightest concern to me," Corning told the *Times Union* on July 4, 1981. Meyers went on the offensive: "You must consider from whence the allegation comes," he told the *Knickerbocker News*. "A person with a rather serious drinking problem."

Meyers kept slinging mud and eventually some stuck. Corning played the patrician, seemingly above the fray. The Gaffneys tried to keep the issue alive in the press, but after months and months of delays and a reluctance on the part of the FBI to move the matter to a resolution, the stalled Crossgate/Gaffneygate matter faded away and was forgotten. A brief news item appeared on July 13, 1982 in the *Knickerbocker News* – more than a year after the matter became public. The FBI had turned over the investigation to the U.S. Attorney's Office. A formal written report was promised. You could almost hear the sighs of relief by Corning, Meyers and Ryan. Ahhhh, a nice, safe political haven where the machine could work its old magic and get the investigation to disappear – reminiscent of their tactic against Dewey. So it came to pass; the probe died and did not make the papers again, and the tapes were never made public.

But that wasn't the last word on Crossgates and Corning. "I talked to the mayor a long time one afternoon about Crossgates and he said he didn't like the mall being built there, but it was going to go through," Rittner said. "He said he was going to do his best to get something out of it for the city." Shades of the South Mall? He did get a few hundred thousand dollars for Albany out of the deal, which he used to purchase more Pine Bush land. How much, if anything, Corning derived for himself through his insurance firm or how much political capital he gained by Crossgates is impossible to measure. Corning was in conflict about Crossgates, according to Rittner. The mayor urged Rittner to represent the city at Crossgates public hearings, knowing Rittner would be pro-environment. "Corning was between a rock and a hard place on Crossgates," Rittner said. "He was against it, but he was getting intense pressure from the party to support it." When Rittner sent a scathing letter on official Albany letterhead to Filene's opposing Crossgates and asking that the Boston store not come to Guilderland, Corning had to act. The mayor called Rittner into his office. "Don, I'm getting my ass kicked by the party," Corning told Rittner "I've got to let you go. It's strictly a political move to get these guys off my back. It's not a personal thing, Don, you know that." Corning had his sacrificial lamb. Rittner finished his six-year tenure as city archaeologist. It was 1979.

Corning nonetheless admired Rittner's chutzpah on behalf of preserving the Pine Bush. In the spring of 1978, when Corning was on a Maine fishing trip, Rittner filed formal applications in Washington, D.C. to make the Karner Blue butterfly a federally listed endangered species. "The designation would have halted Pine Bush development in its tracks," Rittner said. When he returned from Maine, Corning caught wind of Rittner's sneaky end-run and called him into his office. "He was really pissed. He had fire in his eyes and he ranted and raved for a good ten minutes," Rittner said. "He was yelling and swearing. 'What the fuck is this, Don? I couldn't shit out there in the Pine Bush without an environmental impact statement if this goes through!'" Rittner replied, "You know, mayor, even Rome fell." Rittner said Corning paused, looked out the window, gazed up toward the Capitol and stared in silence for several long moments. Rittner thought the mayor had intimations of his and the machine's mortality. "You can leave now," the mayor finally told Rittner in a soft voice. Rittner retained no animosity toward Corning and, instead, possessed something close to reverence for him. "He was a genuine environmentalist and was trying to do the right thing before anyone was formally interested in the environment," Rittner said. "But he was also a politician and he had to take care of business in the Pine Bush." Rittner said he lost his political naivete at City Hall. He was puzzled to find that a forty dollar surcharge was tacked on by the city purchasing agent to the cost of every item Rittner ordered for his job, such as shovels. Rittner brought this discrepancy to Corning, who smiled as if to say you poor, naive boy and responded, "Just do what you were doing, Don. I'll take care of it."

Rittner remembered sitting with Corning for untold hours in discussions about history, during which time the mayor was continuously interrupted by phone calls. He'd listen to the caller and then cut a deal. "Make it so," was what the mayor always said before hanging up, the king running his kingdom. Rittner also developed an awe for the long arm of Corning's authority. He remembered whispering with environmentalist Victor Lord in the men's restroom of the Albany Public Library, plotting strategy, surreptitiously they thought, prior to a Pine Bush meeting. The next morning, Corning called Rittner into his office. "Don, I want you to stop telling Victor Lord everything," Corning said. Rittner said he was certain there was nobody else in that bathroom because he checked and, besides, the two men were whispering. "I don't want to sound paranoid," Rittner said, "but the only explanation was that Corning had that bathroom bugged." Rittner said he felt close to Corning, attributable partly to the fact that they shared the same passions for the natural world and enjoyed discussions about arcane fragments of Albany history. But there was more to the relationship. "I felt like he was a father talking to a son with me," Rittner said. "I think I was something of a surrogate son because his own son wasn't around and the two were not close."

Why didn't Corning just say "make it so" when it came to preserving the Pine Bush? The Pine Bush offers historians a litmus test on Corning's environmental legacy. From Oliver's vantage point, Corning was at best a conundrum in his stance toward the pine barrens. "The mayor truly considered himself an environmentalist, but I never saw him that way as I fought him all the time on environmental issues," Oliver said. "He was a complete contradiction, the man who bought the most Pine Bush land for the city to retain as a preserve, on the one hand, and the man who also put the dump there and created the infrastructure for development and let all the building projects go through."

Reszin Adams, a Democratic insurgent and longtime activist for a range of social causes, was one of the earliest and most involved members of Save The Pine Bush. "I think Corning was a hypocrite who was saying how much he was doing to save the downtown of Albany and he was developing the Pine Bush out in what I consider the suburbs at the same time," Adams said. "I hold Corning directly responsible for what happened in the Pine Bush. When his citizens started protesting it, he should have listened to them. He liked to call himself an environmentalist, but his record showed him to be something different."

John Wolcott had been involved with the Pine Bush since 1971, when he began attending meetings of the Environment Club at SUNYA. He was in his late-thirties at the time and had worked as an amateur archaeologist trying to save important historic artifacts at downtown construction sites. He also worked for the alternative weekly newspaper, The *Washington Park Spirit*, which made no secret of its aggressive opposition to Corning and the machine on issues of the environment and open government. Wolcott remembered an Earth Day rally in 1972 at the SUNYA Campus Center that Corning attended, at which Wolcott publicly accused Corning of selling out the Pine Bush to Donald Lynch for political reasons. "The mayor looked flustered, but he didn't say anything, didn't have a comeback," Wolcott recalled. "I saw Corning as a dictator who wore his conservation and environmental work on his sleeve. He held incredible power and it was autocratic to give all that power to one person. When push came to shove, he went along with political and business friends in allowing development of the Pine Bush. I was in a few meetings on the Pine Bush with him with other environmentalists and it was very much thrust and parry. He was evasive and tried to sidestep our direct questions. He'd never give a straight answer."

Wolcott said he was once in the office of city planner Dick Patrick when a business person was seeking a bit of guidance on the best way to approach a development project in the Pine Bush. Wolcott said Patrick answered that question in two words: Rutnik & Rutnik.

Wolcott said he also observed Corning using his clout with established environmental groups in order to spread his dominance. For instance, in the fall of 1971, when Wolcott was a reporter for the *Washington Park Spirit*, he tried to obtain a copy of the much-anticipated Pine Bush preservation proposal from the Nature Conservancy. Staff members with that long-established non-profit group devoted to land preservation and open space conservation stalled and evaded Wolcott. Finally, Wolcott pinned down a Nature Conservancy staffer who apologized and told Wolcott, "I can't release it because Mayor Corning is on our board and he got involved and made us take back the proposal for revisions before we can release it." Wolcott said it was the Nature Conservancy's revised preservation proposal in part that removed sweeping restrictions on development and preservation and paved the way for almost no opposition to Corning's efforts to improve the Washington Avenue Extension infrastructure.

By 1997, preservation of the Pine Bush was in pretty good shape, with the total amount of protected land at 2,290 acres. Much of that acreage was preserved after Corning's death, however, through the foresight and leadership of officials in Guilderland and Colonie, strongholds of the Republican Party, which isn't generally associated with being pro-environment. Much of the Pine Bush conservation effort was spurred by activist groups like Save The Pine Bush, the Nature Conservancy and other open space advocates who worked to purchase the land outright or to obtain easements for public use and agreements that it would not be developed. Corning's contribution of protecting 640 acres of Pine Bush during his forty-two year tenure seemed modest by comparison. On the other hand, by 1997 Washington Avenue Extension was coming into its own as the corridor of commerce Corning envisioned. Crossgates Mall completed a major expansion. A huge strip mall went up across from the mall, with national chain stores that sucked even more business out of dying downtown Albany: Wal-Mart, Sam's Club, Home Depot, Media Play, Old Navy and MJ Designs. At the corner of Washington Avenue Extension and Fuller Road, one of the largest public construction projects in recent years, a sleek research center for the State University of New York at Albany's atmospheric sciences department and the National Weather Service was built. Also on Washington Avenue Extension, across from the SUNYA campus, two new motels and a gas station were constructed in 1997. Furthermore, the interstices between corporate parks and parking lots were being graded, paved and filled in with more of the same brick, boxy, faceless office facades forming an almost unbroken wall of commercial space on both sides of Washington Avenue Extension from the University campus to its end two miles west at New Karner Road (Route 155). Zoning regulations kept development low-slung and close to the ground, but Corning had trumped them all, personally guiding construction of two nursing home high-rises – Daughters of Sarah and Teresian House – a great vantage point for the king to survey The King's Highway and his kingdom.

Let us take the long view of a fundamental question: what of Erastus Corning 2nd's reputation as a great environmentalist? Truth or political propaganda? Let's inspect the record from the beginning. In 1936, Corning's first year in elective political office, having won a seat in the State Assembly, Corning was named to the committees of villages, canals and conservation. As a freshman minority party member of the lower house, Corning introduced just six bills, none of much substance. In 1937, with his machine-backed elective promotion to the upper house, Senator Corning chaired the commerce and navigation committee and continued to serve on the conservation committee. His legislative initiatives tended to remove restrictive policy so that it would be easier for hunters and anglers to pursue their sport. Corning, of course, was an enthusiast of all sports afield. One bill introduced by Corning and passed into law in 1937, for example, removed restrictions against taking mink, raccoon, otter, fisher, martin or sable with traps in Albany County. A bill from Corning that died in committee would have permitted Albany County hunters to kill with a shotgun deer with horns not less than three inches between November 1-15. Another bill that went nowhere would have dropped the requirement for New York State residents to purchase a New Jersey fishing license in Hudson River waters between the two states if the agreement was reciprocal. Corning did, however, sponsor three pieces of legislation in the 1937 session for which he earned a nod of approval from conservationists. One bill would have appropriated $100,000 from the state's conservation fund to acquire land for game refuges and hunting and fishing programs. It was progressive for its day – it also extended the happy hunting grounds for Corning and his pals – but the bill went nowhere. Another dead-end bill was the creation of three new seasonal game managers at a cost of $10,500 a year (more patronage jobs for Democrats, surely). Finally, at the end of the session, Corning managed to get passed the most meaningful initiative of his six-year state legislative career. Corning called for the creation of a nine-member Scenic Hudson Commission to "survey scenic, historic and commercial assets of the Hudson Valley." The appropriation was $15,000 and the report was due February 1, 1938. In that era, the Hudson River was slowly sliding into cesspool status, a dumping ground for the toxic chemicals of manufacturing plants that lined its shores and for discharge of raw sewage from dozens of communities. Also, continued degradation arrived in the form of a development hodgepodge unbridled by stringent zoning regulations. Amid this climate of disdain and abuse for the Hudson River, Corning's call for an official stock-taking of this precious resource could be seen as the vision of a conservationist before his time.

In the mind of the citizenry, particularly loyal Democrats, Corning was a conservationist practically worthy of canonization. Even the press, which held Corning up to close scrutiny for his political machinations, seemed to accept the conservationist tag without question. In an editorial on February 12, 1970, the *Knickerbocker News* said: "While many politicians are currently jumping on the environmental bandwagon, Mayor Corning has publicly worked in this field for over thirty years. Drawing on a life-long interest in conservation, which he terms 'part of the Corning family tradition,' and extensive reading on environmental topics, the mayor enters into talks on pollution with knowledgeable fervor." Yet, when the *Knick News* editorial writers had to come up with a list of Corning's environmental accomplishments to support their claim, the pickings were slim. They cited his open-space lands legislation for the Alcove Reservoir (all the better hunting and fishing for Corning, who made the Alcove his personal, albeit illegal, fish and game preserve); Tivoli Lakes Nature Center (a grim and little-used ravine that is home to large-scale dumping and violent crime from adjacent housing projects in Arbor Hill, pushed by Corning because it contained the one-time rail bed of his great-grandfather's New York Central Railroad); and the Pine Bush. Legitimately, to give Corning his due, the editorial noted that Gov. Nelson Rockefeller rightly praised Corning for providing the impetus for the state's Pure Waters Program by leading the way with Albany's sewage treatment plant and urging neighboring communities up and down the river to stop discharging raw sewage into the Hudson.

The *Knickerbocker News'* editorial writers were less impressed by Corning's record on the environment in his backyard. "The mayor doesn't appear to have done too good a job on conserving the environment of his own city," the *Knick* said. The newspaper faulted Corning for selling out the Pine Bush for political advantage. Still, there was speculation in the winter of 1970, as Governor Rockefeller announced that he was creating a new state agency called the State Department of Environmental Conservation (EnCon), that Rocky would appoint Corning as EnCon's first commissioner. Political columnists discounted the fact that Rockefeller was a Republican and Corning a Democrat and focused, instead, on their similar patrician upbringings; acquaintance since boyhood from summers spent in Maine; the deal they cut to finance construction of the South Mall; their *laissez faire* attitude toward each other in campaigns; and, the mayor's long-held interest in the environment. "Mayor Noncommittal on State Post" read the *Times Union* headline of February 2, 1970. Corning played coy and got political mileage out of the conjecture, a common ploy of his. "While Mayor Corning declines official comment on reports that he is under consideration for appointment as commissioner for the proposed State Department of Environmental Conservation, he does not rule out taking the position if it is offered."

Corning, of course, didn't get the commissioner's job, yet that didn't stop political pundits from taking the bait and floating Corning's name once more for EnCon commissioner when Democrat Hugh Carey was elected governor in 1974. The speculation seemed more of a stretch, though, and the *Times Union* headline was phrased as a question: "Corning as Carey environmental chief?" This time, the bait was being dangled by Corning's friend and Democratic Congressman, Leo W. O'Brien. "For years Erastus Corning has been a bug almost on the environment," O'Brien told the *Times Union*, meaning that as a compliment. O'Brien went on to say that Corning called him frequently at his Capitol Hill office to propose environmental legislation. O'Brien apparently meant that as a compliment, too, but it merely confirmed the machine's control via Corning and O'Connell on Washington politics from their seat of power in Albany.

Despite the efforts of O'Brien and others, Corning did not receive the appointment as EnCon commissioner. Corning saved face by making his own announcement on November 15, 1974 that he would not accept a cabinet appointment in the Carey administration – even though none had been offered. Commissioner of EnCon was the only cabinet post Corning was ever interested in, his political advisers liked to say, but they doubted Corning would have given up being mayor for life for any job.

Congressman O'Brien got it right when he called Corning "almost a bug on the environment." At his essence, Corning remained throughout manhood a perpetual boy in the woods of Corning Hill, never outgrowing his enjoyment of naturalist ramblings and childlike fascination with nature's quirks and oddities. Witness his "pecker bone" collection, for instance. Corning's wallet also contained a tiny compass and pencil shavings. The mayor said he carried those oddities so that he could build a fire to keep warm in case he was ever lost in the wilderness and then he would find his way out of the woods with the compass.

Another environment-related curiosity of Corning's was his lifelong involvement with the "monster" phenomena. Corning saved boxes of correspondence and research material, purchased books and sent personal checks to groups attempting to prove the existence of "Nessie" in Loch Ness, Scotland; "Champ" in Lake Champlain; and "Big Foot," the giant of mountain lore. He bought every book available on those subjects and had a large section of his home library devoted to an area of study many legitimate scientists consider quackery. Not the mayor. Corning was a card-carrying member of the Lake Champlain Phenomenon Investigation (to which he sent a check for $250 to help finance a study of the sea monster dubbed "Champ") and of the Loch Ness Phenomena Investigation Society (to whom he sent yearly dues of ten dollars to Scotland). The mayor occasionally wore to work a Loch Ness society tie with sea serpent logo. While on a trip to Scotland in 1961 to visit his daughter, Bettina, and son-in-law, Ted Dudley, who was working on his Ph.D. in botany at the University of Edinburgh, Corning made special trips to meet with authorities on Nessie and was disappointed that his travel plans precluded a visit to Loch Ness. John McEneny, a close aide to Corning in City Hall and a historian, spoke with the mayor on several occasions about sea monsters and was convinced Corning truly believed in them. Joseph W. Zarzynski, a high school teacher and scuba diver who headed the Lake Champlain Phenomenon Investigation and organized special sonar studies of the lake bottom, was impressed with Corning's knowledge on the subject. Zarzynski once referred to the mayor as "a walking encyclopedia on lake monsters." Corning told Zarzynski his fascination dated back to childhood and, as mayor, he had even attempted to get governmental grants to support research into these paranormal creatures, without success. Corning wrote to Robert Flacke, the EnCon commissioner who got the Carey appointment the mayor privately coveted, on December 19, 1980 in an attempt to get action at the state level. Corning wrote, "Through over twenty years, I have built up a substantial file on this whole, general subject and am still of the belief that there is a real possibility that these lake monsters do exist. It seems to me that it would not be stretching the imagination to provide some State Legislative protection. I would like to visit with you on the subject as it really is intriguing."

Corning was an unrepentant packrat of naturalist minutiae. That's putting it kindly. In today's parlance, he was a science geek. He retained the glee of a kid with a chemistry set and transferred it to strange ends as an adult. James Lenden recalled a lunch at the Fort Orange Club when the talk turned to plants. It was August 23, 1978, to be exact. Lenden knew this because of the mayor's correspondence. At lunch, Corning mentioned the species Fringed Gentian, and told Lenden if he looked along the Massachusetts Turnpike in late September, he could see this lovely, short-lived wildflower. Corning even mentioned certain mile markers where

Fringed Gentians could be found and Lenden rolled his eyes, figuring Corning was enjoying a joke at Lenden's expense. The next day, August 24, Corning sent Lenden a letter with an enclosure. It was Corning's scientific survey of Fringed Gentians on the Mass Pike. The mayor's list went from 1964 to 1978, one listing for westbound and another for eastbound, during annual week-long fall trips to Maine. Corning noted the mile marker sightings of Fringed Gentians and made notations about the presence of hobble bush, birdsfoot violets, Quaker ladies, laurel, aguewood and bottle gentians. "That was vintage Corning," Lenden said. "That's the way he was with everything, an absolute stickler for detail."

Lenden was too polite to suggest that Corning was, in Freudian terminology, anal retentive, but the mayor's behavior suggests that sort of compulsion. When the mayor called the Albany newspapers, for example, it often had nothing to do with municipal affairs. *Times Union* columnist Barney Fowler wrote in his column on March 16, 1982 that Corning "had a bone to pick" with the papers. Fowler had figured it was a budget matter, because Corning was under fire for withholding information about his budget from the public. Instead, Corning chose to scrutinize and criticize the eye-straining daily weather information compiled by wire services and published in both the *Times Union* and *Knickerbocker News*. "It occurred to me that you couldn't have an excess of that size in a year, and a deficit of that size in a month," the mayor told Fowler, after the mayor noticed the weather box in the *Times Union* was reporting more than an inch of "excess" precipitation for the year but a "deficiency" of nearly .75 inches for March. That couldn't be right, the mayor thought, so he called the paper and asked for a correction. Then, as Corning put it, "the infection spread" temporarily to the *Knickerbocker News*, which previously had been reporting a precipitation excess in both categories. The mayor called the *Knick News*, as well. "It's one of the statistics I'm always interested in because I'm always interested in the Alcove Reservoir," Corning explained to Fowler. Corning told the columnist he had been getting the precipitation count from the papers only because his own rain gauge – yes, he kept a rain gauge – isn't much use in snow, and the water measurement device at the city reservoir had been malfunctioning. The mayor faced a crippling, multi-million dollar deficit in the city that he couldn't remedy, but he set the papers straight: the error of .75 inches of rain was duly noted and corrected.

These few examples among many reveal Corning as something of a frustrated scientist. The mayor maintained long, detailed scientific correspondence with his son-in-law Ted Dudley, a botanist. Corning also wrote frequently to experts in a variety of scientific fields, a prolific correspondence all done at City Hall – at taxpayer expense, letters typed and mailed by his civil servant secretaries. Throughout his political career, Corning made time during his workday to follow his intense, if scattershot, intellect wherever it might lead him. One of Corning's deepest and lengthiest obsessions was finding an answer to the question: did salmon ever spawn up the Hudson River? In trying to answer that question, Corning amassed boxes full of research material and correspondence with leading ichthyologists across the country and throughout the world. "He [Corning] probably knew as much about where salmon were and weren't in U.S. waters as any man alive . . . he studied the subject all his life," according to Art Lee, a fishing partner of Corning's and former Albany newspaperman who wrote a lengthy article on Atlantic salmon for the April, 1996 issue of *Fly Rod & Reel* magazine that prominently mentioned the mayor. Corning maintained that the Hudson was a salmon-free water and gathered scientific evidence to support his position, "There were no salmon in the Hudson River, then or afterward," Lee wrote, "except during a very brief period of stocking by Corning's father (New York's Lieutenant Governor) and some of his angling cronies in hopes of establishing a run." One can imagine Erastus as a boy going with his dad and some of his buddies – toting buckets of fingerling salmon they raised in ponds on his family's Upper Farm – down Corning Hill to the shores of the Hudson River at the mouth of the Normanskill where it flowed through Corning's property. That must have been a powerful boyhood image and Corning never forgot it, wondering if the salmon ever took – deciding after lifelong researching that the fish never survived. Lee also noted that Corning's research showed that there were never any salmon in the Delaware River system, either. "He did know chapter and verse, however, about the stupendous runs of Atlantics that migrated annually up the St. Lawrence, through what is now a maze of locks and other manmade blockages, the length and breadth of Lake Ontario, and ultimately into such streams as the Salmon River, the New York fishery . . ." Lee wrote.

Corning's tastes ran from salmon to paranormal phenomena to futuristic inventions. In the 1960s, Mayor Corning proposed for Albany a moving sidewalk, a "people mover" as he called it, that would transport pedestrians up and down State Street Hill from the Capitol to Broadway – an enhancement to tourism and development, plus no pollution from cars, in Corning's mind. It never came to pass. "The People Mover was a serious pursuit for the mayor, but the technology just wasn't there and it never went anyplace," city planner Patrick said. Patrick said Corning went so far as to ask renowned engineer and architect Barton Ashton of Washington, D.C. to study the feasibility of a People Mover for Albany. What some viewed as a loopy Corning idea had a few supporters elsewhere. In the fall of 1979, the *Knickerbocker News* ran a sarcastic piece on a Los Angeles Project. "The people mover concept was joked about, especially when mentioned along with an age-old dream of a booming downtown retail center," according to the *Knick News*. "Well, Los Angeles approved of a 2.9-mile concrete guide-way for 75,000 riders a day computer-run system costing about $132 million and $43 million for parking garages."

As a politician on the periphery of professional scientists, Corning relished the role of being a self-taught authority among a gathering of scholars. For example, Corning delivered a thoughtful, well-researched treatise entitled "The Automobile Is Here To Stay – Or Is It?" at the annual convention of the New York State Highway Engineers on April 17, 1969 at the Concord Hotel in the Catskills. In his speech, Corning talked knowledgeably about scientific concepts not yet widely reported in the popular press of that time – automobile carbon monoxide emissions, the greenhouse effect, radioisotopes, unsustainable population growth. "If our population continues to climb at its present rate," Corning said ominously, "we are not going to have room for both people and automobiles as we know them today." He used a local analogy: "Looking at the State Campus office complex in Albany, one is overwhelmed by the vast sea of automobiles covering a far greater area than all the office buildings." Corning quoted from Barry Commoner's book, *Science and Survival*. "We are stealing from future generations not just their lumber or their coal, but the basic necessities of life: air, water and soil. A new conservation movement is needed to preserve life itself."

Corning laid blame partly at the feet of the greedy industrialists of the past, neglecting to mention that's where the source of his family's wealth came from: railroads, steel, industrial felt, lumber – land plunderers and polluters all. But Corning looked to the future and envisioned "great breakthroughs in mass transportation . . . monorails, moving sidewalks, mini-buses, high speed trains." Corning predicted private ownership of automobiles would become a thing of the past in our cities, replaced by "a fleet of mini-autos, self-driven taxis, owned by the city, autos without keys that can be driven by anyone to anywhere he wants to go and then left for the next person who wants to go someplace else." Corning wound up his speech by saying the job of highway engineer was growing more challenging all the time and those working in the field would need to develop new skills. "The job of selling a highway location is getting tougher every day," Corning said. He wound up by reading a lengthy poem by Archibald MacLeish, "Riders on Earth Together," which begins: "Men's conception of themselves and of each other has always depended on their notion of the earth." MacLeish, like Corning a Yale grad (1917), was one of the mayor's favorite poets and he tracked MacLeish's varied careers as soldier, lawyer, editor, historian, professor and civil servant. In the best environmental tradition, Corning recycled his speech to the highway engineers. "The Automobile Is Here To Stay – Or Is It?" was reprinted in its entirety, covering a full page, in the *Knickerbocker News* on October 3, 1970, several copies of which he proudly clipped and saved in his files.

Buoyed by that experience, Corning took his environmentalist speechifying on the road, traveling to Toronto, Canada, in 1971 with engineer Pat Mahoney to discuss an idea that the mayor was beginning to formulate on a waste-energy recovery plant that a decade later would become Albany's ANSWERS project. The Toronto gathering was the inaugural World Conference of the Future sponsored by the World Future Society, of which Corning was an early member. Corning also addressed a symposium of the esteemed American Association for the Advancement of Science (AAAS) in Boston on December 27, 1969. The mayor, moving into the big leagues of scientific endeavor, felt comfortable in this learned realm. "All of you know why you are here," Corning began. "You know that the paper-thin film that is the surface of the earth, the biosphere, or as we so presumptuously call it, our environment, is in imminent danger of complete destruction. It can cease to exist almost overnight, at least as to its ability to support life as we know it. . . . You must work for the broadest possible knowledge. It must be spiritual, scientific, economic. . . . I pray that you may have the insight and the intelligence and the drive to save the world. I mean that literally. I pray that you will save the world so that future generations may enjoy it, may continue to realize that it is a very beautiful world and that it is the only one we've got."

From the vantage point of 1997, some might consider Corning's message extremist and unnecessarily apocalyptic. But in 1969, environmentalism and the conservation movement were developing strength and causing some, Corning among them, to believe in a kind of coming environmental Armageddon. They were unrestrained in their excitability. It's important to note that Corning in the late-1960s was deeply immersed not only in his usual slew of technical and journal reading on a broad range of scientific disciplines, but he was devouring everything written by Immanuel Velikovsky, one of the most controversial figures in modern science. Velikovsky is best known for his books *Earth in Upheaval* (1955) and *Worlds in Collision* (1950). Corning's copies were well-thumbed and he kept Velikovsky's books both in his home library and at the office, where he saved a file with related articles and reviews about Velikovsky's works. One of these, a 1975 column by Stephen Jay Gould in *Natural History* magazine titled "Velikovsky in Collision" summarizes the controversy. Gould said *Worlds in Collision* continues "to engender intense debate" twenty-five years after it was published following a drive by his academic enemies who sought to suppress its publication. The book theorizes that the earth's passing twice through Venus's tail in 1500 B.C. (at the time of the Jewish exodus from Egypt) and near collisions with Venus and Mars and then Mars and Earth about 700 B.C. were such terrors that we'd like to forget them, but that they left an indelible mark on humankind. "They lurk in our inherited and unconscious memory, causing fear, neurosis, aggression, and such social manifestations as war," Gould wrote explaining Velikovsky's point of view. He went on to discuss how Velikovsky rejected plate tectonics and proposed a radically new cataclysmic theory of human history. Gould, a respected geologist and evolutionist at Harvard University and an award-winning science writer, credited Velikovsky with being a persuasive and engaging writer and a scientist who is "neither crank nor charlatan" but "gloriously wrong." Gould ended his critique of Velikovsky thus: "We sing praises to the unorthodox hero, but for each successful heretic, there are a hundred forgotten men who challenged prevailing notions and lost." Gould considered Velikovsky one of those losers. Not so Corning. The mayor remained a devoted reader of Velikovsky's works and champion of his controversial theories.

Corning possessed a restless mind throughout his life when it came to scientific inquiry and the natural world. He was one of the founding members of the local chapter of the Eastern New York Solar Energy Society and gave the keynote address at the inaugural meeting of that group on February 13, 1976 in Albany. The mayor also was a founding member of the Solar Energy Organization in the United States long before it was fashionable to be interested in the field. Corning had shelves of books on solar energy in his home library and subscribed to several industry periodicals and kept voluminous files of technical articles on solar energy applications for everything from homes to cars. The mayor also was a founding member of the Weather Modification Society, joining a group of scientists associated with the New York State Atmospheric, Science & Research Center at the State University of New York at Albany, and he regularly attended their meetings. Like his grandfather, Erastus Corning Jr., who amassed a world-renowned butterfly and moth collection housed at the New York State Museum, the mayor was passionate about winged insects. Corning corresponded with and occasionally joined in late-night forays in the field with moth experts from the State Museum staff and maintained a membership in the local chapter of a national lepidopterist society. In his micromanagement mayoral style, Corning enjoyed studying a particular scientific field, attaining what he considered a level of self-taught expertise, and then setting city policy without outside recommendations. Take botany, for instance. Corning almost single-handedly controlled landscaping and plantings in parks and public spaces across Albany and fancied himself a landscape architect and botanist. A letter Corning wrote on July 10, 1964 about Washington Park to his son-in-law Ted Dudley, a Ph.D. botanist, is indicative: "My own thoughts are to point the development of the trees in Washington Park along the line of those that are native to the northeastern part of the country, with one or two sections of the Park not limited to such trees. In these sections, trees of unusual beauty or interest could be planted. . . . I don't know if this map and my ideas are in any way new. . . ." Patrick, the city planner, remembered Corning refusing to relinquish control on something so seemingly minute as the Washington Park plantings. For instance, the wall of evergreen shrubs by the Shakespeare stage in the park was originally going to be an arc shape because that's what the mayor wanted. Patrick argued for a straight line, which is what grows today. "The mayor let me win one every once in a while," Patrick said. Around the Moses statue, Patrick proposed a median of high, arching trees. Corning wanted small, flowering trees. Corning prevailed. "The mayor often brought home the plans to his wife, who was an expert in gardening, but I don't think he always took her word, either," Patrick said. "He liked to get his way."

Patrick learned to read Corning's moods, botanical and otherwise, at City Hall. "If he was fairly pissed off at what you were telling him, he'd swivel around in his chair, look up Washington Avenue and let a long pause hang there so that you could repent your sins," Patrick said. "If he was extremely pissed off, he would slowly tear a page from his yellow legal pad and rip it slowly all the way down lengthwise." The sense of dread Corning could instantly impart to his staffers often just as quickly slid into humor, such as the practical joke the mayor pulled on Patrick. Each winter, Corning would send Patrick out to Washington Park to check on the dawn redwood trees. Patrick would return to City Hall with dismal news. "I felt terrible, but I told him the dawn redwoods had dropped their needles and appeared to be dead," Patrick said. Corning would send Patrick back out to check in the spring. "I couldn't contain my excitement when I came back to report they'd made a remarkable recovery," Patrick said. He learned later that this species of trees do that naturally each year, only after the mayor had gotten much mileage out of tricking his city planner.

Corning's environmentalism sometimes took the form of publicity-seeking gimmicks. For example, in the spring of 1970, Corning asked for citizen volunteers to participate in Project Help Your Environment (HYE) that attempted to hand out 5,000 air test kits to capture air particles for later evaluation within a fifteen-mile radius of Albany County Airport. Corning called it the first such partnership between citizens and scientists; it never got off the ground. Neither did Corning's ecology panel, which the mayor brought about through a change in city ordinance in 1970. The mayor envisioned the new panel set up in a similar way to his appointed school board, offering total control, but, sensing a threat to his omnipotence from grass-roots environmental groups, Corning dragged his feet for fourteen months on an ecology panel. When he finally acted, late in 1971, it was laughable. Corning appointed nine city residents, all high school students, to run the City of Albany Committee for Conservation of the Environment. That group died within four months after accomplishing nothing. Teenagers made good photo opportunities, after all, but never challenged Corning's iron fist. In the summer of 1971, Corning also sent forth Albany's "Hudsonauts," a flotilla of sixteen high school kids in canoes whom the mayor said were going to clean up pollution along 160 miles of Hudson River.

Anonymously, Mayor Corning contributed his own money and energies to a number of worthwhile environmental efforts, including the launchings of new environmental magazines, many of which survived only a few issues. Corning studiously avoided publicity for his participation, often asking that his name not be mentioned as a contributor. Corning did not seek attention either for his assistance to the experimental rice farmer, Hugh Ferguson, keeper of the region's only Hudson River rice paddy. The press found out about it, however, and wrote feature stories about Ferguson, a native of Jamaica, who moved to the area in 1957 to marry his American pen pal. Corning loved that tale, as well as the fact that Ferguson, who grew rice as a kid, staked out a rice paddy in his Arbor Hill backyard by flooding the small plot and harvesting the crop in 1979. Ferguson wanted to expand and asked the mayor for permission to use city land. Corning walked right over to Ferguson's backyard and, after a brief discussion and inspection of Ferguson's garden, proposed the Corning Preserve along the Hudson. The mayor said, "Ferguson, take whatever plot you want, just don't take the picnic grounds." Ferguson flooded five acres along the river, courtesy of Corning, free of charge. Corning even helped Ferguson market his crop – about one ton of all-natural rice from a Chinese variety that thrives in this northern climate – to local health food stores. In 1996, at the age of sixty-eight, Ferguson was still growing riverside rice in his sixteenth season thanks to a boost from Corning. "Oh yeah, he liked surprises," Ferguson said of Corning, who granted the farmer growing rights for Ferguson's lifetime.

On more substantive environmental issues, one of Corning's regrets was his failure to create a nature trail and wildlife sanctuary along the Normanskill Creek in Albany that he began talking about in 1961 and included among his campaign promises every four years. Corning did manage to see a piece of his Normanskill vision realized when, in the summer of 1980, the city acquired the historic 230-acre Stevens Farm, formerly Normans Kill Dairy, along the creek in the shadow of the Delaware Avenue Bridge. Corning secured a $140,000 federal matching grant to complete the acquisition. "A jubilant Mayor Corning described it as a perfectly beautiful piece of land with a mile of streamfront" at a press conference covered by the *Times Union* on July 17, 1980. Corning described ideas for its use ranging from a city park to cross-country skiing and hiking trails to the site of an old-fashioned English brew-pub. None of these came to pass. In 1997, the Stevens Farm was used only as stables for the six horses of the Albany Police Mounted Unit. It is not open to the public and has not been utilized for recreational opportunities. Another environmental project Corning backed that never came to fruition when he was mayor was a planetarium and natural science center for Albany, an idea that died in the mid-1970s, expiring in a flood of lip service from the mayor, but starved of cash.

On the state level, Corning knew well the political advantage of commissions appointed to study an issue – giving the appearance of action with plenty of patronage opportunities. Corning backed a state study similar to the one he headed forty years earlier, a 1977 Hudson River commission established to examine the estuary from its origin deep in the Adirondacks to its mingling with the Atlantic Ocean in New York Harbor. Corning had the power to "make it so" when he wanted. One wonders why he didn't wield that power more often on behalf of the environmental initiatives he professed to desire so passionately. He did manage to save the immensely popular Five Rivers Environmental Center with a call to Gov. Hugh Carey in the spring of 1980 when proposed state budget cuts would have shut down the center, suspending popular programs for children and families. "Mayor Corning picked up the phone and did what a good mayor should do and called the governor," Carey said at a press conference announcing that Five Rivers would survive on May 2, 1980. "Corning is not just my mayor; he's my landlord." Carey was referring to Corning's financing scheme for the South Mall that gave Albany County ownership until the state repaid bonds the county issued to build it.

The largest environmental project Corning undertook, and one of the accomplishments the mayor put near the top of his list of achievements as mayor, was the ANSWERS plant. It took an entire decade to bring the plan from conception to completion, but it was a visionary project for which the mayor deserved much of the credit. Pat Mahoney, an engineer and Corning protégé who built his business, Smith & Mahoney P.C., with city contracts, was a young civil engineer just out of Rensselaer Polytechnic Institute in 1964 with a specialty in water and water supply when he was hired by Ben Smith, an engineer friend of Corning's and Dan O'Connell's who was the architect of the Albany water system beginning in 1927. Smith gave Mahoney his blessing, which put him in good stead with Corning, and the two men grew close professionally and personally over the years, which is bound to happen, Mahoney figured, when you tramp around in dumps together, which is what he and the mayor often did. In Mahoney's telling, the colossal ANSWERS project took root during something as mundane as a visit to the old McCarty Avenue landfill in Albany in the late-1960s when Corning was mulling his decision to move the dump to the Pine Bush. On this particular day, Corning witnessed an entire truckload of blemished billiard ball rejects being dumped into the landfill by workers for the Albany Billiard Co. What a waste, Corning thought, turned to Mahoney and asked, "Pat, don't you think there ought to be a better way to recover all these valuable materials being dumped into the ground and wasting all this land?"

Mahoney shrugged and concurred. It made good common sense, although the engineer forgot about it until another visit with Corning to the McCarty Avenue dump one evening a few weeks later. "Corning was driving his old Chevy and the guys who lived off the dump, known as pickers, had gleaming Chryslers," Mahoney said. "These guys were making a good living by salvaging the copper pipe and other valuable materials being wasted and buried in the ground. Corning kept saying, 'There must be a better way. There must be a better way.'" Mahoney knew that tone in the mayor's voice. Corning was a dog with a bone when he got such a notion in his head. The next thing Mahoney knew, the mayor had commissioned him to do an analysis of the city's solid waste stream at the landfill. Mahoney's report showed that roughly seventy-five percent of the stuff Albanians were throwing away was combustible material. Ergo, if you burn that junk you save valuable land, you do the earth a favor and you create energy: a savings all around in Corning's mind. There was only one problem. Fuel oil was still ridiculously cheap and it wouldn't make economic sense to burn garbage until later, when oil and gasoline prices rose. The energy crisis and long gasoline lines of the early-1970s gave Corning the footing he needed to go ahead with his waste recovery dream and present his proposal to the public.

The news on ANSWERS broke in understated fashion on September 7, 1973 in the *Times Union* long before the acronym was in circulation. "Albany Eyes Garbage Use To Fuel Mall" the headline read and insiders might have been thinking here we go again, another Corning People Mover. In an era when garbage was still buried, for the most part, this was futuristic stuff. Corning proudly proposed at his press conference a $5.9-million project to be financed jointly by the city and the state to process the garbage of Albany and neighboring communities that would heat and cool the South Mall and other state buildings in the area. "This will be seen as an example for the state and the nation to follow," Corning said in tones of high drama. "The costs of energy are soaring. The time is right for us to be going into the steam business." This was a radical notion, indeed, getting the state to finance a large project that might not even fly in the city –

an intriguing reversal on Corning's financing scheme that allowed the city to bail out Rockefeller and the state at the South Mall, newly dedicated when the mayor unveiled ANSWERS.

Three months later, after intense lobbying, Corning received backing from top officials at the State Department of Environmental Conservation. With that first hurdle cleared, ANSWERS went for a vote up the hill from City Hall at the Capitol. The mayor again lobbied hard for passage in the State Legislature and by the summer of 1974, in the waning days of the legislative session, Corning, having called in favors, pushed his ANSWERS into reality. "State Will Burn Trash To Power Its Offices" was the headline in the *Times Union* on July 21, 1974. The garbage burning plant was estimated to take eighteen months to complete. An added benefit to the city was extension on the life of the Rapp Road landfill in the Pine Bush. The plan was set: garbage would be burned at the state Office of General Services' Sheridan Avenue plant and the steam generated would be used to heat and cool the Capitol, South Mall buildings, the Alfred E. Smith building and the State Education Department building. It seemed so pure. So simple. So brilliant. A win-win-win situation. It sounded almost too good to be true, which should have been a tip-off to anyone willing to give the project the sort of intense scrutiny that was lacking. But Corning was the emperor, remember, and who in his kingdom was going to say the emperor had no clothes?

Corning's credibility as elder statesman was so high that he could convince the citizenry that his ANSWERS plant was the savior to the garbage dilemma faced by municipalities from coast to coast. A Schenectady neighborhood group that had done its homework put Corning on the spot at a meeting on January 26, 1981. They wanted to know how Corning could be so sure about ANSWERS when a resource recovery garbage plant in Hempstead, Long Island was ordered shut down by the federal government a few weeks before when it began leaking toxic chemicals. "If our solid waste project was even remotely like that of Hempstead, I can assure you I wouldn't be mayor today," Corning said on January 27, 1981. He did not elaborate on the specific differences between the two plants. Now, watch Corning's hands closely. Here goes the shell game again. The Albany ANSWERS plant – whose price tag now had doubled from its original cost, to $11.7 million, the mayor blithely noted – was a minor-league operation compared to the $130 million Hempstead plant. Observe Corning's logic here. "Our plant is far less sophisticated and expensive and therefore more reliable," Corning said. To use the mayor's own favorite expression of satisfaction: Elegant!

In simplest terms, the Albany ANSWERS process worked like this: garbage was "dry shredded" in huge hammer mills at the Rapp Road plant, passed under magnets to separate metals, and compacted for shipment to the state steam generating plant on Sheridan Avenue. Harmful chemical dioxins like the ones spewed from the Hempstead facility, which led to its closure, couldn't happen in Albany, Corning's hired experts said, because the flame temperature in the Sheridan Avenue plant would be higher than at the Hempstead plant. The Albany plant was one-tenth the price of Hemsptead and it was going to have a better burner was what they were saying. The carcinogenic byproducts at Hempstead resulted from incomplete burning, but the large dioxin molecules can't survive the higher temperatures at Albany, the experts said.

Despite the cloud of concern that was beginning to settle over Corning's ANSWERS plant, the mayor announced he was pushing ahead on other experimental energy projects. These, too, grew out of Corning's voracious reading of scholarly literature on alternative energy sources. The mayor ordered studies made to determine if waste paper could efficiently and economically be transformed into ethanol, apparently eventually to be used as alternative automobile fuel. Another project involved an investigation into whether installing heat exchangers in the city's sewer treatment plant could harness heat produced during sewage treatment to heat water in boilers for warming buildings. Finally, on a third front, Corning had his engineers study whether recovering methane gas from sewer sludge for possible conversion to gasoline was feasible. The short answer to all three studies, alas, was no, no and no.

Such setbacks hardly dampened the mayor's boundless enthusiasm for searching for energy alternatives and trying to stay ahead of the curve of new technology. One of Corning's favorite energy experiments was the planting of two five-acre plots of poplars in the spring of 1981 to determine if the trees could become a good source of ethanol. Ethanol, an alcohol-based fuel, made mostly from corn, was beginning to be used at that time as an additive in gasoline for automobiles with some encouraging results. What Corning liked about the poplar experiment was that it didn't use feed that could have gone to animals or humans. The mayor's plan was to let the poplars grow for three years, cut down the saplings, put the branches through a chipper and ferment the poplar bits to make ethanol. It was meant to be a sustainable source because the tree roots were left to produce new shoots, and, eventually more saplings. Corning admitted the poplar technology was at least twenty-five years away from being an economically viable source of energy, but the mayor went ahead anyway and directed city workers to plant poplars at the city's Stevens Farm along the Normanskill and at the state's Five Rivers Environmental Education Center in Delmar – two sites Corning acquired or saved with a wave of his hand. Corning did not live to see the outcome of his poplar experiment. The trees were planted, but after the mayor's death the plan was forgotten and virtually nobody remembers it today. But the poplars are out there, if you know where to look, growing into maturity, offering beauty and shade for anyone who happens upon them. They may never produce an ounce of ethanol, but they've made some of God's creatures great and small a fine home.

Corning's passionate embrace of experimental, environmentally benign technologies and his tireless quest for alternative energy sources were not widely known among the general public. Like other aspects of Corning's complex personality, this pursuit of progressivism might seem to some contradictory, given the mayor's hidebound political traditionalism and regressive machine governance. Others might consider the mayor's investigation of alternative energy sources as a case of the boyhood collector and tinkerer who never grew up and indulged his hobby at taxpayer expense. But there was a truly visionary aspect to Corning's yearnings for energy breakthroughs that might be likened to Don Quixote tilting at windmills. In fact, Corning read broadly on the topic of harnessing wind to be converted into energy and, given Albany's Dutch heritage, seriously investigated the possibility of erecting windmills around town as both energy source and tourist attraction. He eventually abandoned this idea. Even a quixotic dreamer like Corning couldn't realize all his fantasies.

But the ANSWERS project was shaping up to be all that Corning ever wanted on the experimental energy front. It did the right thing, the mayor believed, down the line. It salvaged waste and turned it from a negative into a positive. It extended the overburdened landfill. It heated and cooled state buildings and saved on their energy bill. And, best of all, it brought money into city coffers at a time when Albany was facing mounting deficits. In other words, Corning would balance his in-the-red budget on garbage. In ANSWERS, it seemed, the king would have it all. If this didn't top Corning's complicated financing scheme that allowed Rockefeller to build the South Mall, the mayor didn't know what did.

Mahoney, the ANSWERS engineer, said the mayor was involved at every level of planning of the plant and made all major decisions from the outset. "Corning determined early on that he didn't want to spend six to seven times the cost of a gallon of No. 6 fuel oil, but he wouldn't mind doubling the cost to build a waste-to-energy facility," Mahoney said. Despite Mahoney's technical work and pulling other experts into the ANSWERS project and Corning's shepherding of the plan through sticky political wickets, there were signs of trouble from the beginning. The commissioner of the state Office of General Services, John Egan, the state's landlord and the project manager for the state's portion of ANSWERS, was getting cold feet. The cost continued to mushroom and eventually rose to four times the original estimate, to twenty-two million dollars. This at a time when New York State was in dire financial straits itself and was tightening its belt all around. Corning didn't particularly like Egan, according to Mahoney. "Governor Cuomo had great respect for Mayor Corning's judgment and asked Corning what he thought about each one of his cabinet appointments," Mahoney said. "Corning wavered on Egan and expressed some concerns, but when Cuomo put Egan in, Corning stayed loyal to one of the Party's old friends." Mahoney said the agreement between Corning and Egan concerning millions of dollars and a complicated arrangement was done in typical Corning fashion. "The agreement was always only a handshake," Mahoney said. "That was as good as any contract with Corning." But Corning eventually wanted to protect himself and the city from what he considered an increasingly obstinate Egan. "I had grave reservations about the design because the state wasn't taking our new requirements into consideration and Egan said he'd correct the bids, but never made any of the changes we asked for," Mahoney said. "Corning decided he wanted a contract after all with the state. He asked me to negotiate the contract and said: 'I'm trusting you, Mahoney. If you're wrong, get the hell out of town.'"

Egan and Mahoney had a clash of personalities. The OGS commissioner met privately with Corning and asked the mayor to dump Mahoney from ANSWERS. Corning related this to Mahoney and the mayor's answer to Egan was this: "As far as ANSWERS is concerned, Pat Mahoney speaks for me and anything he says goes." Egan and Mahoney didn't speak after that and the breakdown in communication between city and state also contributed to the project's growing problems, not the least of which were huge cost overruns and delays.

Even after ANSWERS was up and running, it was plagued by inefficiencies and nagging doubt. Mahoney recalled taking a group of potential Japanese investors through the ANSWERS plant in the mid-1980s to convince them to invest in a waste-energy recovery facility Mahoney had on the drawing boards for southeastern Massachusetts. "Nobody was in the control room when we got there and the plant was running," Mahoney recalled. "The guy in charge was asleep in a conference room and I had to shake him awake to tell him we were going on a plant tour."

Mahoney blamed the state for the troubled ANSWERS project. As soon as Corning was hospitalized in 1982, when the controversy spread to the public and a grass-roots environmental movement began to call for its closure, the state blamed the city. This was Mahoney's take: "It was poorly designed from the start because the state wouldn't change the design specifications the way we wanted. It was undersized, in the wrong place and the pollution systems were overloaded. The boiler was too short. The feed system was all wrong. No dust controllers were installed. It could only handle 350 tons a day when it was supposed to do 600 tons a day. The state fought requested air pollution controls every step of the way. It never did proper air testing after 1987. I could go on and on."

The last impression Corning had of ANSWERS was a positive one. In a letter Mahoney sent to Corning in the Boston hospital on January 2, 1983, Mahoney was upbeat. "ANSWERS has been running well since last July when OGS began burning almost all of the fuel we were producing at our Rapp Road plant," Mahoney wrote. "This will become one of the most successful in the world. It is the most efficient and well managed facility of its kind. You've created a model for the waste processing industry." From his Boston hospital bed, on January 7, 1983, Corning, failing badly, wrote back to Mahoney in shaky penmanship. "We make quite a team and I know in my heart of the great all pervading confidence I have for you as a dedicated engineer and a goddamn stubborn Irishman," Corning wrote. "Water was our early and great love and now ANSWERS. As you say we can both of us get down on our knees and thank Ben Smith. God bless you, Pat."

A decade after building ANSWERS, Mahoney and his firm completed in the early-1990s a $400 million waste-energy recovery facility in the community of Rochester in southeastern Massachusetts, known as SEMASS. That plant handles 3,000 tons of garbage a day, five times larger than the capacity Albany estimated but never attained. SEMASS received awards and plaudits from environmental groups. "We know what we're doing and

Albany could have had a great facility like SEMASS if we'd done it our way without the state," Mahoney said.

The debate is now moot. The state's Sheridan Avenue incinerator and steam generating plant is idle; ANSWERS is dead. The incinerator was shut down in 1994, following months of protests from residents who lived downwind of the towering smokestack, especially people in the Mansion and South End neighborhoods. Those two urban neighborhoods are home to a largely black population of mostly low-income families or people on public assistance. Residents had been complaining about air pollution for years, without much interest paid from the powers that be. But the evidence was mounting. The residents awoke some mornings to find their cars and stoops covered with a fine black soot containing harmful dioxins and potentially carcinogenic particulate matter spewed from the smokestack in the garbage burning process. They said their babies and children seemed sicker than most. Their lawns and gardens failed to thrive. Those with breathing difficulties or lung ailments complained of problems. They went to the newspapers and lodged protests with the city and state and asked state Health Department officials to investigate, but their voices lacked political clout and were not heard. Their rallying cry became one of "environmental racism," arguing that the city and state were polluting poor people willy-nilly. This would never happen to the rich folks uptown in the mansions of Manning Boulevard and other affluent neighborhoods of the city, they charged. Eventually, their persistence paid off. Public sentiment swung their way. A round of testing, though inconclusive, proved there might be a public health threat. So, in 1994, the late Mayor Corning's ANSWERS plant, his great vision for the city and his beloved Albanians, was shut down amid a cloud of controversy. The bitter taste left in the mouths of downtown residents who fought for closure was this: their revered mayor, the longest-tenured in the nation, had been unwittingly polluting and perhaps contributing to the early deaths of those who kept him in power for so long.

Mahoney can't argue with the outcome, but he adamantly opposed the leap of conjecture that posthumously tarred and feathered Corning for the controversial demise of ANSWERS. "The mayor did it for all the right reasons and he was convinced it was a sound concept and he was right," Mahoney said. "It really works and should have worked here as well as it works elsewhere. Recovery rather than disposal is the only sensible solution to the solid waste dilemma and Corning was way ahead of the pack on it.

Corning died expecting ANSWERS to do great things. I'm glad he didn't live to see how badly it turned out. Not only was that technology the right way to go, it made economic sense. The city of Albany made more money off garbage than any city its size. Albany hasn't paid for waste disposal for many years and it actually made about four million dollars a year profit between landfill tipping fees and ANSWERS and that's what kept the city with a surplus. The city balanced its books on garbage." Or, as the skeptics might re-phrase the headline, "Polluting for Profit."

A post-script to ANSWERS: a *Times Union* headline from March 8, 1996 read: "Albany wants to build another dump in Pine Bush." The article detailed Mayor Jerry Jennings' solid waste dilemma. An interim landfill in the Pine Bush was filling up fast, with less than one year capacity left, and a new landfill proposed for Coeymans in southern Albany County was stalled in a lawsuit brought by that community. Jennings was seeking state approval to build a third landfill (Jennings') in a valley between the former Rapp Road dump (Corning's) and the interim landfill (former Mayor Thomas Whalen's). More trashing of the Pine Bush. On another garbage front, Jennings, faced with looming red ink, announced he was shutting down in the summer of 1996 Corning's Rapp Road ANSWERS waste-shredding facility – which looked like the equivalent of one hand clapping following the shutdown of the ANSWERS state incinerator in 1994. The shredding plant amounted to a $2.5 million-a-year patronage pit run by the politically connected Energy Answers Corp. that employed thirty people, who also happened to be Democratic Party loyalists. Many of those shredder operators were members of Jennings' biggest campaign contributor, Laborers Local 190. The *Times Union* article suggested that Jennings had kept the patronage mill running as long as he could, but he was drowning in debt and had to cut the white elephant loose. A prior investigation in 1994 by the *Times Union* found that many experts questioned the benefits of a shredding operation like Albany's for a landfill. The consensus was that shredding offered some compaction improvements, but over time the settling that decomposing garbage normally undergoes would equal the short-term compaction gained from shredding. With such limited space left in Albany's landfill, many questioned whether the compaction gains were worth the cost. Jennings said he was going to close the shredder, purchase a heavier tractor to roll over the trash to increase its compaction and save the city about $750,000 a year in the process. Jennings expected a battle and political fallout from machine holdovers.

All things considered, there is no clear-cut analysis of Mayor Corning's legacy as environmentalist, complex and contradictory as it was. The Atlantic Chapter of the Sierra Club announced in the spring of 1982 it was going to present Corning with its prestigious Distinguished Environmentalist Award. The *Knickerbocker News*, which had been critical of the mayor's environmental record, wrote a laudatory editorial about the award on June 21, 1982 under the headline, "Mr. Corning as Guardian of the Environment." The editorial summarized the Sierra Club's citation, which gave a long list of Corning's accomplishments: Hudson Valley Survey Commission; park lands acquisition along the Hudson; open space ringing the Alcove Reservoir to protect the city's water supply; Tivoli Lake, Buckingham Pond and Washington Park pond improvements; the experimental rice paddy along the Hudson River; ANSWERS; purchase of Stevens Farm along the Normans Kill; community gardens and expansion of city parks. The award "is doubly merited," the editorial said, because "the mayor would not exploit the environment, and neither would he seek to exploit his environmental record for political advantage." Some, no doubt, saw an irony in this. Nonetheless, Corning was scheduled to receive the Sierra Club honor on the evening of June 21, 1982 at the Erastus Corning II Riverfront Preserve. But Corning was in Albany Medical Center Hospital with lung ailments, the ceremony was postponed and was never rescheduled. Perhaps just as well. Corning's moment in the sun would have been overshadowed by clouds of discontent. Activist Reszin Adams said Save The Pine Bush members along with people from several other grass-roots environmental groups planned a demonstration at the Sierra Club award event. Adams said the protesters saw Corning less as a guardian of the environment and more as an opportunist. In the final analysis, perhaps all the closer one got to verity regarding Corning and the environment was a wide divergence of opinion, and no consensus – one group offering him an award that others planned to protest. The essential contradiction of the mayor's divided stand on the Pine Bush was played out again and again, a broken record.

Chapter 12:

The Great Manipulator: Corning and the Press

"I wonder really whether or not a source can say anything.
The reporter in effect is saying I believe, I guess, I think,
I want you to believe, I heard, someone told me or I dreamt
it up out of whole cloth. It is offensive, lousy reporting
and bad English. I don't know why, but in thinking about
your letter over a drink yesterday evening, all of a sudden
the song 'Who Threw the Overalls in Mrs. Murphy's
Chowder' came to mind."

*Letter from Mayor Corning on September 18, 1979 to
Cary B. Ziter, a former* Schenectady Gazette *reporter living
in Colorado Springs and conducting a national survey of people
in power, how they dealt with the press and how they felt
about the use of "sources said."*

In 1960, the Hearst Corporation, a multi-billion dollar media empire, consolidated its control of the Albany newspaper market with its acquisition from the Gannett chain of the *Knickerbocker News*, an afternoon daily. At the same time, Hearst's morning paper, the *Times Union*, was on the rise with an expanded Sunday edition that was enjoying robust circulation growth. A dynamic publisher, Gene Robb, had arrived at this apogee of local journalism following a standoff against a wily adversary, the Democratic machine, which had played Hearst and Gannett off each other for years. One of the machine's favorite tactics was to threaten the two competing, and financially struggling, newspapers with the loss of hundreds of thousands of dollars in legal advertising if they took off the kid gloves with which the Albany papers had coddled the machine for decades. It was essentially the corporate version of the carrot-and-stick assessment ploy the machine worked so successfully against Albany property owners who didn't toe the line. Now, with the consolidation into Hearst's Capital Newspapers – "a monopoly" in the mind of Corning, who refused to categorize his own party's control of Albany politics as such – Robb had achieved a level playing field and was preparing for a showdown. The incomparably brilliant Corning may have finally met his match: a pair of Phi Beta Kappas were set to square off.

Robb had graduated Phi Beta Kappa with a degree in journalism from the University of Nebraska and worked as a reporter briefly before his executive potential was recognized and he was groomed by Hearst in a succession of managerial positions. Robb, who also held a law degree from George Washington University, was unabashedly ambitious. He was elected in the mid-1960s to the prestigious positions of president of the American Newspaper Publishers Association and a director of Associated Press, the wire service that operates as a newspaper cooperative. Moreover, in Albany, as publisher of both the *Times Union* and *Knickerbocker News*, Robb enjoyed prestige and moved in similar social circles as Corning, including membership in the Fort Orange Club.

In 1967, Robb and corporate executives at Hearst headquarters in New York City decided Albany was poised for growth and profit as a newspaper market and developed a multi-million dollar plan for modernizing and expanding their presses at the newspaper plant at 24 Sheridan Avenue – two blocks below City Hall, within earshot of the toll of its carillon and within range for Corning, a right fielder with a decent arm at Groton, to shatter the plant's vulnerable window-lined walls with hurled brickbats. Corning may have contemplated such tricks on Halloween in 1967; that's when the news broke in Robb's newspapers about the mayor's arrest on a charge of driving while intoxicated (DWI). It was Corning's only brush with publicized personal scandal in his forty-two years as mayor and it stung him deeply. The DWI bust occurred on Saturday, October 28, three days before the papers published the story, when Robb showed restraint and positioned the article on an inside local page in both the *Times Union* and *Knickerbocker News*. Ironically, the drunken driving charge followed Corning's leaving the annual Page One Ball thrown by the Albany Newspaper Guild at the Thruway House, where Corning drank at Robb's table. Despite Robb's downplaying the DWI story, it went national, was sent out on the AP and UPI wires, and picked up by newspapers across the country. Corning was beyond angry. Reporting on the DWI arrest concluded a year of penetrating coverage by Robb's papers that began, for the first time, to break through the wall of inscrutability that the O'Connell-Corning machine had erected around itself. Corning seemed suddenly vulnerable to a tough, probing press and yet former Private Corning, the combat-decorated World War II infantryman, had saved some ammunition.

The planned press expansion at the Hearst plant offered an unexpected target for the mayor. Robert Danzig, Robb's protégé who went on to become publisher of the Albany newspapers and later head of the entire Hearst newspaper group, took up the story. "We had entered into a contract to buy an additional press line, but our property boundary did not run straight to the street and we needed a teeny V-shaped lot next to us for the press expansion," Danzig recalled. "We went about trying to acquire that parcel, which was of no value to anybody, and was too small to be built upon. We eventually discovered the city owned the wedge of land after seizing it for unpaid back taxes." The Hearst papers' managers at the Sheridan Avenue plant may have been able to hear the mayor's certain howls of glee just up the hill at City Hall: Gotcha, Mr. Robb! Over brandy and fine cigars, the boys at "The Fort," as the Fort Orange Club was known, surely mulled that one across the green of the billiard table. Ol' 'Rastus had Hearst snookered, after all. Said Danzig, "We tried to negotiate, but the city refused to sell that piece of property to us. There we sat with this expensive press expansion and not enough room to install it."

Robb ceded that round of their ongoing battle to Corning, but the war had just begun. Erastus' arrogance appeared to be a chink in his armor. Robb didn't take his eyes off the enemy as he secretly tapped rising star Danzig to scout alternative locations for Albany's Hearst newspapers. If Robb couldn't topple Corning from his City Hall throne, he'd go around the mayor for life. Danzig located a pumpkin farm in Colonie, adjacent to a pig farm, along an altogether unimpressive stretch of suburban scrub land. But it was hard by the Adirondack Northway, offering important interstate transportation access, and the Colonie address dovetailed with the long-range strategy of Hearst executives to transform Capital Newspapers from an Albany paper into a regional information source. In a prescient purchase, Hearst bought the property at the precise spot that would, many years later, evolve into one of the busiest and most valuable commercial intersections in the Capital Region. The modern newspaper plant, built in 1969, had plenty of room for the new presses and additional expansion. The newspapers' substantial investment at the corner of Wolf Road and Albany-Shaker

Road set the stage and became a catalyst for the explosive development of Wolf Road as the region's premier commercial strip.

Back in Albany, Sheridan Avenue was becoming a ghost town. The newspaper plant sat vacant and forlorn, home to vagrants and vermin, several of its windows shattered by vandals. The broken windows were reminiscent of a bitter labor strike at the paper in 1964, when Corning had refused to send in police to quell the violence, resulting in costly property damage that was another spur for the paper's flight to the suburbs. In downtown Albany, where Henry James and Herman Melville had once lived and where the newspaper – the first draft of history – continued that literary line, suddenly there was a void. Just up the hill, in his City Hall office, was Erastus still gloating? He had just lost a prime indicator of any viable city, a daily newspaper with an address inside city limits. Not only that, but the tens of thousands of dollars Hearst paid in Albany taxes dried up and flowed into Colonie's Republican-controlled coffers instead. Perhaps more importantly, Capital Newspapers' payroll in 1969 when the paper moved from the city to the suburbs stood at 972 employees. That's nearly 1,000 people who came to downtown Albany every day and spent money there. They ate lunch at neighboring restaurants, bought personal and gift items at nearby stores, and made downtown a more vibrant place all-around. Being newspaper people, most likely they single-handedly accounted for the solvency of any saloon within a five-mile radius of the plant. All that gone. Erastus had won the battle, but how much had he already lost and was yet to lose in the war of Albany's economic viability versus continued Democratic machine dominance? "Mayor Corning lost 972 people on our payroll and everything that went with it at a time when the city was struggling," Danzig said. "All because of his petty enmity over a small slice of land. It's beyond belief and defies logic."

After more than a century, the capital city on the Hudson no longer had a daily newspaper within its city limits. Over a piece of sod just big enough to bury a man, the Albany part of the masthead had departed, at least literally, from the *Times Union* and *Knickerbocker News*. Robb could go to work on the machine now, free from fear of economic or assessment reprisals. But that opportunity was cut short when Robb – the man William Kennedy, a former *Times Union* reporter, credited as the single most influential person in making the machine accountable to the public in the history of Albany – died unexpectedly on August 18, 1969. "He was a capable

26) *The Mayor with fellow Albany April 13th draftees in 1944 at Camp Blanding, Florida. Erastus is in the middle, center row.*

27) *The Mayor at tenth annual reunion of the April 13th group in 1956 in the Helderbergs. Erastus is in the back row, third from the right.*

28) *The Mayor joins, from left, Sen. Estes Kefauver, Gov. W. Averell Harriman and Presidential nominee Adlai Stevenson during the 1952 Presidential campaign.*

29) *The Mayor with John F. Kennedy in Albany during the 1960 Presidential campaign.*

30) *The Mayor and machine cronies on the reviewing stand for Albany's Saint Patrick's Day Parade, 1960.*

31) *The Mayor with the Rev. Martin Luther King Jr. and Gov. Nelson Rockefeller in Albany, 1961.*

32) The Mayor in a familiar office pose, 1961.

33) The Mayor reviews a model for the South Mall with rival Rockefeller in 1963.

34) The Mayor displays a trophy salmon caught at Pierce Pond, Maine on July 16, 1965.

35) The Corning family's rustic camp at Webb Pond, Maine.

36) *Dedication of the Empire State Plaza on November 21, 1973. From left Lt. Gov. Malcolm Wilson, the Mayor, Attorney General Louis Lefkowitz, Senate Majority Leader Warren Anderson, Assembly Speaker Perry Duryea, architect Wallace Harrison and Rockefeller.*

37) *The Mayor gloats after defeating Sen. Howard Nolan in a 1977 mayoral primary that proved pollsters wrong.*

38) *The Mayor sports a t-shirt with a caricature of himself.*

39) *The Mayor at a 1977 Democratic picnic with, from left, Harold Greenstein, Gerald Jennings, Sol Greenberg, Leonard Weiss and Richard Haggerty.*

40) *The Mayor looks over an Albany community garden in 1979.*

41) The Mayor at City Hall in 1980.

42) *The Mayor holds a press conference in front of City Hall during the Springboks' rugby controversy in 1981.*

43) The Mayor's gray metal desk sits empty at City Hall in 1982. The Mayor continued to run the city from his hospital bed.

44) *The body of the Mayor lies in state at the Cathedral of All Saints.*

45) *The hearse carries the Mayor through Albany for the final time after his funeral on May 31, 1983.*

46) *Polly Noonan grieves after the Mayor's funeral.*

NEVER BE THE SAME

48) *The Corning family burial plot in Albany Rural Cemetery.*

and good newspaperman," Corning told Kennedy about Robb long after the publisher's death. "I liked him. A fine man."

One of Mayor Corning's greatest attributes as a politician was his extraordinary accessibility to his constituents. Corning's legendary open-door policy, in which any citizen could walk in off the street on a whim and receive a face-to-face session with the mayor in his City Hall office, was virtually unheard of among politicians of his stature. He was the mayor, in Gov. Mario Cuomo's ringing phrase, "of the capital city of the greatest state in the greatest nation on earth." And yet, Corning was easier to reach than the cop on the beat or the mailman on the route. Corning's availability was, in large part, what got him elected to an unprecedented eleven four-year terms, which the mayor realized accounted for his popularity. In reality, however, his highly touted openness was an illusion. For all his forty-two years as mayor, except for a few fleeting challenges by Republicans or reform-minded Democrat candidates, Corning did not have to answer to the intense scrutiny of a legitimate opposition force. Corning's claims and pronouncements were entered into the public record and the citizens' imagination as gospel, unchallenged, in the way that a demagogue or a dictator creates and controls his community's dialogue to such an extent that the line became blurred between the mayor's imagined reality and independently confirmed truth. The Republican Party in Albany County, for example, never mounted a credible, sustained challenge to Corning's autocratic leadership. Without political checks and balances on the mayor and the machine's absolute authority, it fell to the press to build Albany's last line of defense between democracy and oligarchy. In the capital city, the Fourth Estate had an unusual opportunity to perform its crucial role in a democratic society. To what extent did the Albany press, principally newspapers, uphold its journalistic mission to inform the public about the city's political process? Did the press do its job to keep Corning accountable to the people? Were the newspapers an adequate check and balance on the mayor's power? The quick answer is, at first no, and, much later, maybe. But it's a far more complicated and compelling matter than that. At least that's what extensive interviews with reporters and editors who covered Corning during each of his four decades in power suggest.

In the beginning of Corning's tenure, the 1940s and early 1950s, for all intents and purposes, the Albany newspapers were in the pocket of the machine. Critical coverage was generally non-existent. Before World War II, Corning was a young, dashing and handsome leader from one of

Albany's leading patrician families; some likened him to a matinee idol. After the war, Corning was the G.I.-Mayor whose patriotism-fueled popularity was nothing short of astounding. Corning proved a tough target for the press to hit. "I knew him since he was the boy mayor and he was ever the aristocrat, even though I saw a polite arrogance in him," said Duane LaFleche, who worked thirty-five years as a reporter and editor at the *Knickerbocker News* beginning in 1942, Corning's first year in office. "It was hard to criticize someone so charming. Women adored him and so did men. Of course, he was a rascal, too." LaFleche conceded that in the pre-Robb era at the *Knick*, despite the paper's professed Republican editorial stance, he worked under an unwritten code that he had to "pull punches" when it came to coverage of the machine. LaFleche said in those early years of Corning's reign, the papers cowered beneath the threatening shadow of the machine. "The machine was the kind of paternalistic system that seemed to create love by the people under it, but deep down it was fear," LaFleche said. "It took care of so many people, but you could never forget it controlled hundreds of city, county and state jobs and the machine seemed omniscient."

LaFleche remembered being summoned to Whitehall Road for his first and only audience with boss Dan O'Connell, in October, 1960. O'Connell gave LaFleche a Coca-Cola, the two talked casually for nearly thirty minutes, and just before LaFleche got up to leave, O'Connell inquired if there was any truth to the rumor he heard that the *Knick News* was being sold by Gannett to Hearst. "That rumor's been around for years and it's not going to happen anytime soon," LaFleche told O'Connell. The next day, the sale of the *Knick* to Hearst was announced. "You could say Dan had good sources," LaFleche said.

There was virtually no investigative reporting conducted on Corning and his policies during the mayor's first three decades in office. The reasons extended beyond Corning's stature as beloved *major domo*. William Kennedy wrote of the 1950s, when he was a *Times Union* reporter: "There were reporters on both papers, covering either City Hall or the County Court House or both, who moonlighted on the city and county payrolls; and it didn't make any difference to the editors of either paper, almost all of whom were Democratic boosters."

Francis "Doc" Rivett, who started as a reporter at the *Times Union* in 1943, does not equivocate in stating that the machine bought off reporters. "They put the old-timers who covered City Hall on the pad," said Rivett.

"It wasn't much from what I heard, beer money or a little help with their kids' college tuition. There was a clear agreement that they wouldn't write negative stories. The editors knew about it, but it was a different time." If reporters grew too independent and tried to roil the waters in Corning's placid pool of power, all the mayor had to do was make one call to the paper's top brass and that probing journalist would be reassigned – probably to Schaghticoke – recalled William Rowley, who started as a reporter at the *Knick News* in 1947 and later taught journalism at the State University of New York at Albany. In addition to the threat of retribution, Corning possessed a towering intellect and used it to intimidate new reporters on the City Hall beat. "It was a cat-and-mouse game covering the mayor and you were the mouse," Rowley said. "You couldn't dig out the good stories because he was impossible to pin down and everything in the city went through Corning."

There's a Corning press anecdote that has been told and re-told so many times by reporters – including in *O Albany!* by Kennedy – that it has taken on the air of historical truth. It goes like this. Reporters were commiserating about how well-nigh impossible it was to get Corning to take a position on an issue he didn't want to discuss. A reporter from the Capitol bureau of the *New York Times*, who had a high opinion of himself as a *Times*-man is wont to do, boldly proclaimed to those he considered minor-league journalists that he could get a straight answer out of the mayor. In fact, it was said he took wagers. At the end of a Corning press conference, the *Times* reporter, who had been silent until then, spoke up. "Excuse me, Mr. Mayor. What is your favorite color?" The other reporters watched the mayor expectantly. Corning paused and the reporters prepared to pay off their lost bets to the wily *Times* correspondent. Suddenly, Corning spoke. "Plaid," he said. The reporters roared. Corning went down in local journalistic lore for that brilliant rhetorical parry. The mayor later denied to Kennedy that he said such a thing, but by then the anecdote was firmly established as fact.

One more aspect of Corning's repertoire in keeping the press at bay was flattery. "He was such an aristocrat and always so gracious, it just didn't seem that he could be this backroom wheeler-dealer," said Shirley Armstrong, who covered the courts for the *Times Union* for thirty-three years, starting in 1955. She would see Corning occasionally out with judges, who were among the mayor's social friends and fellow Fort Orange Clubmen.

"Whenever you saw him, he was friendly and a regular fella, one of the gang. I think he disarmed reporters."

Rowley recalled a meeting in the late-'40s when the mayor invited the *Knick*'s editorial writer, who asked Rowley to come along, to lunch at the old Ten Eyck Hotel, a popular Democratic hangout at the time. "Corning explained how Dan and some machine boys were having some trouble with the State Liquor Authority," Rowley said. "The mayor was wining and dining this editorial writer, who was pretty much in Corning's pocket anyway. He finally asked him to write an editorial praising the virtues of old family saloons in Albany." That's when Rowley interrupted and said the paper couldn't be bought that way. Corning ended the lunch graciously and, as he left, turned and said: "Well, there's more than one way to skin a cat."

Even when the press did shake off its shackles and wrote stories that were critical of the machine, they landed on the doorsteps of Albanians with the proverbial sound made by a tree that falls in the forest with nobody around to hear it. "There wasn't a critical mass of liberal opinion in Albany at that time," Rowley said. "It wasn't until educated liberals came in with the growth of state government and the state university and new corporations that it began to change." Frank Robinson summarized the situation in his 1973 book, *Albany's O'Connell Machine*. Robinson wrote: "A strong political machine does not need a sympathetic press. People do not vote for machine candidates because they believe them to be embodiments of civic virtue; they support the machine because it has done them favors, or because they think it can do them harm if they balk, or because its nearest arm is someone in their own neighborhood whom they know and trust. As long as taxes are reasonable and the city is not going to pot, the newspapers can scream for reform until blue in the face without result."

The honeymoon for Corning was an extended one of about, say, two decades. But the climate of blind allegiance to Corning's rhetoric began to change in the early-1960s coinciding with the consolidation of the *Times Union* and *Knickerbocker News* under Hearst control, fueled by publisher Robb's aggressive editorial stance. Robb had promoted Daniel Button from chief editorial writer to executive editor of the *Times Union* in 1960; Button, a politically active Republican, was not afraid to show his dislike of Corning and the machine in print. Button's first transgression in Corning's mind was to back the GOP Congressional candidate, Irving Waxman, a friend of Button's, against the machine's man, Leo O'Brien, a former newspaperman. The *Knick News* also endorsed Waxman over O'Brien and, as the *Times Union*'s once-cozy coverage also turned critical toward the machine, Button earned himself a spot on Corning's hit list. "I didn't know it until several years later and it was never made public, but Corning went to Hearst headquarters in New York to protest what we were doing in Albany, which was finally reporting the news," Button said. Corning got no satisfaction with the Hearst brass.

With the support of his bosses, Button turned up the heat in the early-1960s, writing editorials criticizing the county election board as being a puppet of the machine and implying election fraud. A development deal to put a gas station on the corner of North Allen and Western Avenue had Corning's backing, but the *Times Union* opposed it in an editorial. Button got personally involved because he lived in the neighborhood and his kids went to School 16, a hundred yards away from the proposed gas station. The Pine Hills neighborhood association and parents of schoolchildren mounted a noisy campaign; Corning was forced to back down. The king was not used to losing in his kingdom and the defeat didn't sit well. "That really hurt Corning and he was very unhappy with me after that one," Button said. Eventually, a Mobil station went in a block away, on the corner of West Lawrence and Western.

Corning was angered further by the Albany newspapers' front-page coverage of the State Investigation Commission's hearings in the fall of 1960. That SIC probe centered on Albany County's policy of allowing millions of dollars in real estate tax delinquencies and then granting bargain-basement land deals to people politically connected to the machine. The following year, in the fall of 1961, the Hearst papers gave full (and, some would say, sympathetic) coverage to Corning's mayoral challenger, Rev. Robert K. Hudnut, a Presbyterian minister, and his fledgling political reform party, Citizens United Reform Effort (CURE). Hudnut was joined on the CURE slate by Charles Liddle for council president and Stanley Ringel for treasurer. The CURE candidates were trounced on Election Day, but Corning and O'Connell decided the series of uppity actions by Robb in the pages of the *Times Union* and *Knickerbocker News* demanded retribution. The reprisal was swift and decisive. The city and county's legal advertising was yanked from the Hearst papers, amounting to a substantial loss estimated at roughly $300,000 per year.

Corning gave a television address in early November of 1967, ostensibly an election speech, which turned into a venomous anti-Hearst diatribe meant to poison public opinion toward the papers. Corning said:

The local Hearst monopoly is called the *Times Union* in the morning and the *Knickerbocker News* in the afternoon. . . . We have been subjected to news being deliberately withheld, deliberately suppressed. . . . It is not news to anyone that there has been the most flagrant kind of editorializing in the news columns. Then there are the phony letters to the editor. They really are amusing. . . . The plain and unvarnished fact is that the taxpayers of the city of Albany and the county of Albany have been overcharged by Mr. Hearst's messenger boy, Gene Robb, to the tune of hundreds of thousands of dollars. Call it highway robbery if you will. Call it a high-class swindle. . . . The city and county sued the Hearst Corporation for charging fees of legal notices for two papers when they claim only one under Hearst . . . As I think the people of Albany know very generally, there is no greater champion for freedom of the press than I. . . . But the desperate and idiotic charge that the city and county took away the legal advertising from the Hearst Empire because of Hearst newspaper criticism is a barefaced lie.

The machine moved forward on other fronts to fight the papers, still their only opposition since the Republicans seemed to be pulling a political version of Rip Van Winkle. With control of the Albany County grand jury system, it was easy for the machine to harass and intimidate reporters and editors. Newspaper personnel, including Robb, were called before grand juries dozens of times in the early-1960s on what amounted to frivolous charges of conspiracy clearly meant to intimidate and to cause the Hearst executives to back down from damaging revelations against the machine raised by their investigative journalism. "Within my thirty-five years as a newspaperman, I have never heard of a comparable situation anywhere in the United States," Robb complained to a grand jury in 1963 during one of his own dozen appearances. Button framed as a memento his subpoena to appear before a grand jury on March 10, 1963, when assistant district attorney Ray Fisher grilled Button for more than an hour about his editorial critical of the county election board. "He went line by line and made me account for every word of my editorial," Button recalled. "It was clearly meant to menace and intimidate us."

Reporter Edward Swietnicki became a convenient whipping-boy, charged with perjury for conflicting statements to the grand jury about discussions he had with an editor about a story. The very real threat of a jail sentence hung over Swietnicki's head, but more than that was at stake. *Knickerbocker News* Executive Editor Robert G. Fichenberg, a fine writer and tough editor whom the machine considered another Hearst nemesis, summed up the grand jury situation in a column: "The basic issue is this. The attempt by a powerful, entrenched political machine to harass and intimidate a newspaper and its reporters in an effort to discourage public disclosure of any story that might not reflect favorably on the machine. Any newspaper that caves in under this type of threat betrays its public trust." On the perjury charge, Swietnicki was represented by an effective defense attorney, M. Andrew Dwyer, of Troy, who took the case to trial and got a jury to acquit the reporter. The papers had proven they wouldn't cave in. The technique of intimidation-by-grand jury long favored by O'Connell, Corning and their cronies began to wane after that, but the machine had other weapons in its arsenal.

"You can't imagine how tense the atmosphere was in those years between the newspapers and Corning, who was just a couple blocks away from the old plant," said Joe Picchi, a political reporter who started at the *Times Union* in 1959. "It seemed like hardly a month went by that the police or someone else from the city wasn't suing us. I remember hearing that in the early-1960s the paper had tens of millions of dollars in libel suits brought against us by the city, but they never went anywhere. It was a very strained relationship and Corning was behind it all."

The early-1960s were a time of elemental shifts in the political plate tectonics of Albany. Coinciding with the growing independence and tough political coverage of the newspapers, Gov. Nelson Rockefeller was pushing his vision for a South Mall that would alter irrevocably Albany's physical landscape. Robb and Corning were fellow members, coincidentally, of Rockefeller's temporary state commission headed by Lt. Gov. Malcolm Wilson, whose task it was to review proposals and offer recommendations for the South Mall project. Initially, at least, the mayor and the publisher were foes once more. Robb's papers backed the South Mall; Corning opposed it. Robb let his Republican leanings and admiration for Rocky show ever so slightly on his South Mall boosterism while Button, the *Times Union* executive editor, resigned in 1966 to accept the Republican nomination as a candidate for Congress – a seat left vacant by Leo O'Brien's retirement. Button stunned the machine by beating their candidate, Richard Conners, a shocking victory Button turned into a thumb gouge in the eye of the machine in 1968 when he cruised to an easy re-election against Corning's close friend, Jacob Herzog, whom Dan O'Connell hand-picked and figured was a lock. Losing to a Republican was bad enough in Corning's eyes, but losing to a former *Times Union* editor raised the mayor's hackles anew. The newspaper was just doing its job, according to those running it. Said Danzig, "We were not out to get the machine, but we were dedicated to digging out the information that would inform the people about what was going on in Albany. The machine had never encountered that kind of force before, or a newspaper that refused to give up after so much was thrown at it."

The machine had one more big play up its sleeve. The theory: if you can't co-opt the competition, buy your own mouthpiece. Corning and company supported a group of local investors who had acquired the Schenectady *Union-Star*, a small daily that was struggling financially, to gear up with the machine's backing for a launch of an Albany edition in the mid-1960s. Danzig recalled telephoning anonymously the *Union-Star*'s telemarketing operation, which was soliciting subscribers for its proposed Albany edition, and he got Polly Noonan on the phone. "It was just one more verification for me how heavily involved the machine was," Danzig said. That rival Albany edition fizzled, Hearst acquired the Schenectady *Union-Star* in 1968 from the group of investors and Robb tapped Danzig to run it. The *Union-Star* was eventually folded into the *Times Union*, long after the machine was out of the newspaper business – but its efforts at trying to strong-arm the press into submission continued.

Robb seemed an immovable object. "Gene Robb was the heartbeat of the newspapers and the symbol of its integrity and he was the difference between the machine's manipulation and control such as it was and total corruption," Danzig said. Danzig feels strongly that Robb paid the ultimate price for his firm stand on behalf of journalistic principles. Robb's sudden passing in 1969 by heart attack in middle age could be considered job-related, Danzig believes. "He gave his life for the newspaper and refused to compromise under tremendous personal pressure from the machine," Danzig said. "I saw the price he paid."

The machine tried to fill the vacuum left by Robb's death by sowing its old seeds of malice. Danzig succeeded Robb in September, 1969 and Corning announced the next month that the city was giving its legal advertising back to the Hearst papers. The implication was that the new publisher had cut a deal, which was news to Danzig. "The newscasts were using phrases like, 'A new rapprochement has been reached between City Hall and Capital Newspapers,'" Danzig recalled. "I was devastated by Corning's implication that I had chosen to sell the soul of the paper as the new publisher to get back the legal advertising." Danzig asked for a meeting with the newspaper's attorney, Samuel Aronowitz. In an ironic twist, Aronowitz had agreed to represent the Hearst papers despite the firm's history with the party. Aronowitz, after all, was the law partner of the late Ed O'Connell, Dan's brother and an architect of the Democratic political dynasty. Danzig vented his frustration to Aronowitz, informing the counselor that, as publisher, he was going to write an editorial refusing the legal ads and he planned to run it on page one along with his signature. The sage Aronowitz looked over the top of his *pince-nez* glasses and fixed Danzig with a stare. "How many editorials have you written since you've been publisher?" Aranonwitz asked. Danzig conceded that this would be his first and that an editorial had never run on page one. Aronowitz told the new publisher, "I think you ought to go ahead and run the editorial on the front page because it will make you feel better. But you should know it won't make a damn bit of difference. The real power is not what you as a publisher say, but what you as a newspaper do."

Danzig dropped his plans for the bombshell editorial, accepted the return of the legal advertising without comment and was guided by Aronowitz's wise counsel – saying little and acting forcefully. Danzig also took Aronowitz's advice to meet with Dan O'Connell. Danzig recalled the scene at Whitehall Road as "something out of a Woody Allen movie." O'Connell was cordial and displayed his photographic memory for detail, recounting stories of Danzig's wife's family, the Bradys, Irish-Catholic and Democrats – Dan's people. After an amiable hour's chat, Danzig got up to leave. The doorbell rang. Mayor Corning was at the door. The two men were still strangers. Danzig said on his way out, "Mr. Mayor. How interesting to meet you. I'm Bob Danzig." Corning turned "beet red," according to Danzig, whose gotcha inflection embarrassed the normally suave mayor.

In that fall's election, 1969, the papers refused to endorse for mayor either Corning or Republican challenger Albert Hartheimer, an architect by profession and a political neophyte. When the worst blizzard in a century hit Albany on December 29, 1969, dumping more than twenty-seven inches of snow, the city was paralyzed. Despite what Corning termed "the largest anti-snow armada in Albany's history," snow removal operations were abysmal. The crippling effects of poor plowing were felt for weeks.

The *Times Union* and *Knick News* lambasted Corning's efforts and their investigative reporting showed Albany's snow emergency operation was riddled with an ineffective network of no-bid patronage operators possessed of pickup trucks with jerry-built plows on the front, a hodgepodge of amateurs with inadequate equipment, rather than the armada in the analogy coming from the demagogue in City Hall. In a rare straight-out attack, Corning fought back.

"Mayor Corning staunchly defended the city's snow removal program and leveled a blast at recent sharp editorial criticism of municipal efforts to clear the streets of more than fifty inches of snow that fell during the month of December," the *Knickerbocker News* reported. "The editorials noted that the city had been on the brink of a disaster during the snowstorm and had not moved with sufficient speed to remedy the situation. The mayor termed the editorial 'completely erroneous' and 'a perfect example of my undying belief that the newspapers have a perfect right to be completely wrong.'"

At the same time, Danzig directed his editor to make a beat change in City Hall. Ed Fennell, the *Times Union* reporter who had covered Corning for many years, was, by the accounts of several of his colleagues, personally chummy with Corning and his soft coverage reflected that. John McLoughlin, an ambitious reporter who had left the *Times Union* in the mid-1960s after two years to work at a Rochester paper, was lured back to Albany in 1969 with a promise of covering Corning and having his own political column. McLoughlin wanted to shake things up. "I know there was a lot of talk going on behind the scenes because Corning was really pissed at Danzig for pulling Fennell out and putting me in," McLoughlin said. Danzig confirmed that Corning called a meeting with Hearst corporate executives in the wake of these changes by the new publisher. The mayor used all his leverage to push Danzig, a protégé of Robb's who was trying to keep the spirit of his mentor alive, out of the publisher's seat. "It was a Hollywood power scene beyond imagination and Corning was playing the lead," Danzig said. Hearst stuck by Danzig and Corning gave up. The aggressive coverage continued.

"I was never under any directive to get Corning or get the machine," McLoughlin said. "The stories were there to be had for anyone willing to go after them." McLoughlin set the tone for his tenure covering City Hall with a blistering column and series of follow-up articles on the routine practice of Albany's Common Council to suspend competitive bidding because they deemed it "impracticable" – a legal loophole that allowed Corning to purchase goods and services from the machine's friends with impunity. "This was an unbelievable abuse of power and I couldn't believe it had never been reported before," McLoughlin recalled. "They were suspending competitive bidding on every purchase for all those years and nobody ever called them on it."

As a result of McLoughlin's coverage, a newly elected crop of Republican state legislators – Raymond Skuse, Fred Field and Walter Langley – introduced legislation that tried to make Albany conform with the competitive bidding law in the same manner as all other cities in New York State. Corning had his hands full fighting these renegade Republicans on several fronts in the early-1970s. It was Skuse, Field, Langley and others who also forced in this era the issue of Albany's long-standing appointed school board, a city school board that was not freely elected – another Albany-only anomaly that set the capital city apart from all the other municipalities across New York State. Instead of open elections, Corning installed three of his friends as a titular board and then ran the entire school system the way he saw fit. Only in Albany.

Corning held weekly press conferences on Thursdays in City Hall in the early-1970s to put his own spin on stories. At the time, the mayor was taking flak for his hard-line position opposing competitive bidding, fighting the proposed elected school board and other staples of a free and open democratic society. Corning also was mired in controversy from the ongoing SIC investigations for allegedly corrupt city purchasing practices. The mayor had developed a method for influencing the press: he fixed their five-dollar parking tickets. It worked with the five-dollar vote. Why not with the five-dollar fixed ticket? This weekly ritual had gone on for many months, perhaps years, before the *Knickerbocker News* blew the whistle on Corning's legerdemain in an article on March 2, 1972. The story read: "There's a little parade in Albany City Hall most Thursdays before Mayor Corning starts his weekly press conference. And today was no exception. The parade ends at a small pile of blue five-dollar parking tickets in front of the assembled microphones on the mayor's desk. In a move almost too unobtrusive to follow, the mayor scoops up the tickets and deposits them out of sight in a suit pocket. From there, no one but the mayor knows what happens to them. But they're never seen again." The reporters who covered Corning during this time, the early-1970s, recalled the mayor's parking ticket prestidigitation with clarity. In fact, the mayor's smooth move from desk top to suit coat pocket with the tickets remains a lasting symbol of Corning's fluid control of everything in his kingdom, the reporters said. The ticket fix was just another example of Corning saying by his actions, "Make it so." And so it was.

"I never knew how the ticket fixing came about initially, but it went on every week," said McLoughlin. His editors at the *Times Union*, who knew of the practice but didn't publish a story about it, were adamant that reporters with the paper should not get their tickets fixed. In fact, McLoughlin recalled, when he left the *Times Union* in 1973 to work as a television reporter at Albany's WTEN-Channel 10, he had more than $300 worth of unpaid parking tickets. McLoughlin the scofflaw went to the court of Judge John Holt-Harris, the city traffic recorder and longtime friend of Corning's, whom the mayor had appointed to the school board and other politically sensitive positions. Said McLoughlin, "I went to pay off all my fines and the clerk asked, 'You sure you want to pay all of them? Nobody pays them all. The judge will pare them down for you.'" McLoughlin wrote a check for the full amount.

Carol DeMare, who joined the *Times Union* as a reporter in 1971, was assigned to City Hall the following year and recalled that the *Times Union* and *Knick News* had strict policies not to get their tickets fixed. But that didn't stop the broadcast media. "It was mostly TV reporters and some radio guys who did it," DeMare recalled. "There was a big stack of tickets every week. The TV people were shameless. The news editors and other staff from the station would save them up from their private cars and give them to the reporter to bring down to the mayor each week. It became so obnoxious and out of control, we blew the whistle on it." DeMare wrote a story outlining how common the practice was and quoted a radio station reporter, who produced a memo from his boss at the station that ended with the reminder: "And don't forget to take the tickets!" Herb Starr, who covered Corning from 1967 to 1975, first for radio and then TV, said the ticket fix was *de rigueur* among the broadcast ranks. "Oh, yeah, he just took them and made them go away. We all knew about it and took full advantage," Starr said.

The print journalists were pretty proud of themselves for exposing the ticket fixing practice. They couldn't dig up scandal, pin political corruption, or make any of the SIC investigations stick on Corning's Teflon-coated image, but with the parking ticket scam they thought they finally had the mayor in their journalistic cross hairs. Corning, of course, who had been a close observer of the animal kingdom since boyhood, would not allow himself to be cornered. The wily adversary had dug a couple of alternate escape holes long ago. Plausible deniability was the mayor's middle name, after all, and Corning explained the ticket fixing practice this way: TV reporters had asked if they could have special press parking spaces set aside for them in front of City Hall in order to have easy access for their heavy camera gear to the Thursday morning press conferences. Since that wasn't practical, Corning decided he'd take the reporters' parking tickets and, as he told the *Times Union*, "see if the judge [Holt-Harris] would excuse them." The force of Corning's personality was such that reporters understood that such a bogus explanation nonetheless would be the last word on the matter. The mayor would not apologize, would not deign to defend himself, would not elaborate. That explanation was the end of it. Period. The parking ticket fix practice ceased, as if it were only a mirage. No parking spaces were reserved for the press in the aftermath, of course, and there was not another mention of that chapter of Corning's guile in manipulating the press. Game, set and match to the mayor.

Regardless of how big or how small the matter, Corning controlled the entire flow of information at City Hall anyway, every single drop. Even the commissioner of each department, essentially a figurehead who deferred to the mayor on the most mundane decision, was not allowed to speak to the press. On even the most routine requests for information by reporters, the automatic response by all city employees low and high was the same: "Go ask the mayor." Reporters, as well, were soon trained as if they were a pack of Pavlov's dogs. They went straight to Corning, no matter what. The enterprising DeMare once reached by telephone a Maine sheriff's deputy who agreed to row out to the middle of Webb Pond, where the Cornings had a remote summer camp, to summon the vacationing mayor, who was out fishing in a canoe. Corning rewarded DeMare's perseverance with a call back and a comment on a breaking news story that gave DeMare a scoop. If you worked hard and were fair, Corning at least respected you, DeMare said. "If you were accurate in what you wrote about Corning and quoted him correctly, you had no problem," DeMare said. "But if you twisted his ideas or got a fact or single word in a quote wrong, he'd jump all over you. In a charming patrician way, of course, but you got the message."

Paul Vitello, who came to cover Corning for the *Knickerbocker News* in 1975 after a stint as the Chicago City Hall beat reporter for a wire service, was instantly taken with the parallels between Chicago Mayor Richard Daley's machine and the O'Connell-Corning machine. Vitello had to admit, though, that fixing reporters' parking tickets as routine business at the mayor's press conference was something not even the brazen Daley would dream up. "The feeling I had immediately with Corning was that he was a patrician and brilliant," Vitello said. "You knew right away he was several dozen IQ points above any reporter and that wasn't always the case with small-city politicians. Compared to Daley, who was rough-cut and had a hard time stringing two words together, Corning was suave and superior and that made him much more interesting, and difficult, to cover."

Starr, too, had a yardstick with which to measure Corning. He grew up in Boston in the vestigial shadow of political boss James Michael Curley, dubbed "The Rascal King" in a recent biography, and as a young man Starr had brushes with cronies from Mayor Curley's inner circle. Starr saw the power of the Albany machine as a combination of the brilliance of Corning, a WASP aristocrat, running City Hall and the political street smarts of the working-class Irish machine boss, O'Connell, behind the scenes – an added dimension Curley lacked. Starr, always more of a media personality than a journalist, was no threat to Corning and therefore was given special access by the mayor, who also enjoyed Starr's practiced roguery. Starr was the designated class clown among the press corps at Corning's press conferences. One such performance in the early-1970s is recalled fondly by Starr and his colleagues. "Corning was having his Thursday morning press conference and he was dodging the questions, as usual, so I asked him again and he said, 'Herb, you're a high-class jerk,'" Starr recalled. Normally, a reporter would have known enough to shut up at that point. Not Starr. He pressed on, trying to force a straight answer from the mayor, who fixed Starr with an icy stare and said, for all the reporters to hear, "Herb, you are an unadulterated fuckhead." Starr considers that his proudest moment in eight years covering Corning. The comment was never reported.

In fact, Corning's language commonly was raw and uncensored when he talked with reporters, on the record, but it was standard operating procedure not only not to print the mayor's profanity, but not even to make note of the expletives. The curses and coarse phrases simply disappeared from reporters' copy, reminiscent of the parking tickets. Make it so, as the mayor would say. And it was so. Remember, that was a different era in journalism, the reporters will tell you today, but there was also a sense of

Corning's press conferences being a kind of locker-room or extension of a men's club. That clubbiness was another way that Corning exerted subtle control over the press, drawing them into his little power play by making them, for a time, a journalistic version of Groton or Yale or the Fort Orange Club or other pockets of exclusivity that Corning knew so well.

Corning would curse openly with reporters and make disparaging, off-color remarks about his political foes that were never reported. Starr recalled the mayor musing about how he liked the "big tits" of a woman who ran an Albany non-profit agency and therefore as mayor did her favors. To McLoughlin, Corning called the marchers at a gay rights demonstration "fairies" and also said a woman Democratic elected official better get off the fence on an issue or her "fucking fat ass" would break it. Those few examples only hint at the decidedly un-patrician language of Corning that the public never read or heard.

The early press coverage of Corning's tenure was also exclusively male, which added to the locker-room tone, until Carol DeMare broke the gender barrier and became in 1972 the first female reporter to cover the mayor's weekly press conference. She was soon joined by Joann Crupi of the *Knickerbocker News* and subsequent women City Hall reporters who followed them. The beginning of the women reporters spelled the end of the profanity-laced sessions with the press. "I was told the mayor used to say fuck this and fuck that all the time around reporters, but he cleaned up his foul language as soon as I came to cover him," DeMare said. "I was actually a little disappointed, because the press conferences got very boring after that."

Corning's weekly press conference, Thursdays at 9:30 a.m. in City Hall, became a liability in 1973. It was a tough year for the mayor. He was under fire for yet another SIC investigation into purchasing practices, he was called before an Albany County grand jury regarding alleged election improprieties, and he was facing the toughest mayoral campaign of his career against Carl Touhey. When things got hot, as they had that year, Corning's best strategy from past experience was to lay low and let the political storm blow over. But the weekly press conference gave the reporters a chance to come loaded for bear and pepper Corning with their toughest shots. Corning, the consummate escape artist, never met an answer he couldn't wriggle out of, but his political Houdini act was wearing thin and reporters were finally pointing out Corning's obfuscations.

When Herb Starr got in a dig that Corning didn't like, inadvertently he may have speeded up the demise of the press conferences. Starr directed his videographer to get a close-up cutaway shot of Corning's hands. Said Starr, "The mayor had this habit of crossing his fingers, twiddling his fingers and twirling his thumbs faster and faster when he was nervously dodging questions," Starr said. The footage of Corning's manic fingers filled the TV screen over the mayor's voice hemming and hawing and avoiding a direct answer. Starr swore Corning hid his hands under the table and kept them still after that. Whatever the fingers were doing, the weekly press conferences certainly were an endangered species. Corning pulled the plug on his Thursday morning press conferences on November 15, 1973, five weeks after his squeaker of a victory over Touhey – a shockingly close 3,500-vote margin and the closest any challenger had come to knocking Corning out of City Hall in three decades. The mayor put a spin on why he quit the press conferences after more than two years: "It was a very enjoyable talk show on my part," Corning said, but added that he did not think it was an efficient way to disseminate information. "I heard from folks in Glens Falls, Troy, Pittsfield, Schenectady and down in Greene County. They created in their own minds almost a half-baked TV personality out of me. I'm not a TV personality but the mayor of Albany, and I'd like to do it [dispense news] a different way from now on."

Those who covered Corning after 1973 could no longer rely on a captive audience with the mayor at his weekly press conference and, increasingly, reporters found Corning, despite his accessibility, an exceedingly wary quarry. Although they couldn't prove it, the press came to believe that the Phi Beta Kappa mayor deliberately spoke in fog-shrouded sentences and non sequiturs, using diction meant to confuse, beginning one thought and segueing off on a tangent without completing the earlier notion, leaving half-finished phrases dangling, drifting from idea to idea without resolution. Call it Corningspeak. Said DeMare, "Because Corning didn't speak in complete sentences, he was extremely difficult to quote. After awhile, I figured that was his strategy to keep the press off-balance." "You'd leave a half-hour interview with the mayor, have pages and pages of notes in your notebook, get back to the office to write it up and you'd realize he hadn't actually completed a thought and you didn't have a single usable quote," recalled Nancy Connell, a *Times Union* reporter who covered Corning from 1981 until his death. "He had a way of starting out a sentence, getting a few words into it, then veering off somewhere else, then veering off again.

I've always wondered if this wasn't deliberate with reporters." It seems likely that Corning's convoluted interview sessions with reporters were a studied technique of obliquity since, by comparison, Corning's written articles, memos, letters and drafts of speeches were well-crafted and possessed a clear line of thought from beginning to middle to end. The same conciseness of ideas marked his public speaking engagements, which, although Corning was not a dynamic presence at the podium, were generally short, straightforward and coherent – even if, for political purposes, they were deliberately vague and devoid of specifics.

E.J. McMahon Jr., a reporter and political columnist who covered the mayor for both papers from 1980 until his death, theorized that Corning borrowed a page from the press conference script of President Dwight D. Eisenhower. Eisenhower's biographer, Stephen Ambrose, described the president's manipulation of the press corps through Tuesday morning press conferences. "Through the conferences, he could educate and inform, or confuse if that suited his purpose," Ambrose wrote in his biography, *Eisenhower: Soldier and President*. "The conferences helped him stay in control . . . despite the jeers of his critics, who had great fun with his jumbled syntax, his confessions that he did not know about this or that issue, and his often inappropriate or impossibly confusing answers." McMahon, who, like Starr, can do a dead-on vocal impersonation of Corning, noted that the mayor bore a striking physical resemblance to Ike – bald head; craggy good looks; round, deep-set eyes; erect bearing; authoritative air. "Just like Ike, Corning knew exactly what he was doing with the way he talked to the press," McMahon said. "He was exceptionally cagey." One of Corning's favorite quotes used to dodge a reporter trying to coax the mayor into speculating on an upcoming project was this: "I'm not a member of the bridge-crosser's club."

Corning also kept reporters on the defensive, even slightly paranoid, with his infamous calls to the newspaper to complain there was an inaccuracy in a story or that he had been misquoted. Ron Kermani, a *Times Union* reporter who covered Corning for the last three years of the mayor's life, has a story of a call from the mayor considered a classic by his peers. It involved T. Garry Burns, the city clerk, an admirer of the deposed Shah of Iran. Burns wrote the Shah a note of support on city letterhead and received an autographed glossy photograph from the controversial Iranian leader, which Burns framed and hung on a wall of the Common Council chamber beside Democratic Party icon, President John F. Kennedy.

Kermani got a tip, confirmed the photo and went to the mayor for a comment. Corning went, in Kermani's words, "absolutely ballistic, a face I'd never seen, totally out of control." Corning said of Burns, "He's a fucking idiot." Kermani went back to the newspaper office, wrote his story with great care and it ran on the front page of the *Times Union* the next morning. At about nine a.m., Corning called the *TU* city desk, early for the staff of a morning paper, and asked to speak to Kermani, who was there. Corning didn't hide his anger with the reporter.

Corning: "Ron, you misquoted me."

Kermani (nervously): "Mayor, I don't believe I did, but let me check my notes once more . . . .(He checks) . . . No, I believe I quoted you accurately."

Corning: "No, Ron, I called him a fucking idiot."[The *Times Union* had published only the "idiot" part of Corning's characterization of Burns, it being a family newspaper and all.]

Corning: "Ron, next time be more careful how you quote me."

To this day, Kermani is not sure how to interpret Corning's call. Kermani, an Albany native who had grown up being fed stories of Corning's fantastical powers and whose family wasn't overtly political, but remained respectful of the machine's long reach, believes the call served a dual purpose. "He was having fun at my expense," Kermani said. "But it was also a message of warning. Corning was telling me that just because I was a reporter who grew up here and thought I knew the place and had contacts and was out to prove himself, don't mess with the mayor."

Despite his supposedly cavalier attitude toward the press and their coverage of him – trying to give the impression that he was above worrying about criticism, untouchable – Corning was known among reporters to pore over every word they wrote about him. And he was a stickler for accuracy. If they committed the slightest factual error or misquoted Corning, they could expect a call at the newspaper. DeMare decided to test the conventional wisdom. It was in the mid-1970s and DeMare wrote a throwaway story about Corning's speech to the Urban League. Corning had said, "Albany is a nice place to live in." DeMare said she intentionally improved Corning's grammar and quoted him as saying, "Albany is a nice place in which to live." Corning called DeMare the next morning at the paper. DeMare told the mayor she made the change on purpose to see for herself if he really read every word in the paper as other reporters and Corning's aides had said. "It's the only time I've misquoted you, but I now know it's true what they say," DeMare said. Corning was not amused.

McMahon remembered a Corning call, too, in 1981, after the reporter had written a lengthy profile of the mayor following McMahon's shadowing Corning during an entire day of his official duties. McMahon described Corning listening to a Kiwanis Club anthem being sung and characterized the mayor as "gazing distractedly around the room." Out of an article that ran perhaps 3,000 words, Corning zeroed in on a single one, "distractedly." He called McMahon early in the morning at work with his *Webster's Dictionary* at his side. McMahon said, "He told me the fourth entry in his dictionary's definition noted that distractedly could mean mentally disturbed. And he did not appreciate being called a lunatic by implication." McMahon, stunned, sputtered some apology, which Corning accepted with a tone of Grotonian indifference. "He made it sound like he was just leafing through his dictionary and happened to call, that he didn't really care about this but he thought he should bring it to my attention," McMahon said. "It was another way of tweaking a reporter and laying down a groundwork of intimidation for next time."

Another favorite Corning call to the newspapers was to point out errors in arcane weather and recreational data published in a sea of tiny agate type. Invariably, Corning would call the *Times Union* city desk early Saturday morning and Kermani, who worked that shift, would answer. "He was always very polite and said he was calling only as a subscriber who wanted to point out an error," Kermani recalled. "And then he'd point out the tiniest discrepancy. It might be a minute off in the time of high tide or six inches off the wave height in the boating table or one-hundredth of an inch of precipitation. He watched the rain like a hawk. He'd remind us he had a rain gauge at his house and he checked it against our rain chart. He was fastidious, almost compulsive, about these weather data tables."

One line Corning never allowed reporters to cross was the one that demarcated his personal life. Not only did nobody write for the first forty years of his mayoralty about Corning's divided private life between his family and the Noonans, but the press also never wrote about Corning's estrangement from his biological family, particularly with his son, Erastus III. "He flatly refused to discuss his wife or children," DeMare recalled. "You almost forgot he had a family. He never mentioned them. Didn't display pictures of them. Nothing. Every four years, during the swearing-in ceremony, there was a formal picture taken and that's the only time we ever saw Betty and Bettina. But even at that function, Erastus III stopped showing up."

Ed Dague, the TV reporter and anchor, had been covering Corning since the late-1960s and had developed a special trust and rapport with the mayor. Corning opened up slightly once to Dague about his failings as a father and family man after Dague had asked the mayor the whereabouts of his son and Corning couldn't answer him. He wasn't being his usual elusive self; he was profoundly embarrassed that he didn't know. "He's somewhere between Moscow and Hawaii. We don't keep in touch," Corning told Dague. "I haven't been a very good father. I hardly know my son." Alan Miller, an enterprising *Times Union* reporter who was on vacation in Hawaii in 1980, tracked down the mayor's son, who had lived away from Albany and his famous father since boyhood at Groton. It was a brief interview. "His son didn't have much to say," Miller recalled. "He said they didn't have a relationship."

When it came to Betty Corning, she was off-limits to the press on any matter, including politics, for which she showed not the slightest interest. The mayor's wife neither campaigned for her husband nor attended political functions with him. She never discussed publicly any matter of city policy. The few brief interviews she gave all had to do with gardening, never speaking of her husband.

Beginning in the 1950s until his death, Corning chose his liaison in the press, notably Arvis Chalmers, *Knickerbocker News* political columnist and dean of the legislative correspondents, as a kind of ambassador between the machine and Capital Newspapers. Chalmers was given unusual access and socialized with Corning and Noonan and politicians of all levels, whether it was over drinks at a bar or cards across a poker table. Chalmers knew a lot, especially about Corning, but never betrayed that trust even a decade after the mayor's death. Chalmers died in 1996, holding his Corning confidences close to his vest to the end.

Corning occasionally would toss reporters small bones of intimacy. For example, the Albany County Legislature threw an annual Christmas party to which reporters were invited, and many went. The ground rule was that everything at the party was off-the-record, a condition the reporters accepted. The politicians let their guard down, even Corning, although nothing was ever published about the party. "I remember the mayor at the reporters' table one year and he drank a lot of beer that night with us," DeMare said. "The party hacks wanted to schmooze with him and they were pissed Corning sat at our table all night. The mayor was toying with us, as usual."

Such coziness ended with the arrival of Harry Rosenfeld, who came to Albany amid high expectations in October of 1978 as the new editor of the *Times Union*, riding the journalistic fame of Watergate. Rosenfeld was metro editor at the *Washington Post* on the night in June of 1972 when a routine hotel burglary news item broke, which soon exploded into the biggest story in modern journalism. Rosenfeld directed the reporting of Bob Woodward and Carl Bernstein on the Watergate story until editor-in-chief Ben Bradlee and other superiors saw how big the story was, craved the limelight and eclipsed Rosenfeld. Still, Rosenfeld had his assurance of fame – Jack Warden portrayed Rosenfeld with memorable crustiness in the movie *All The President's Men* – and his reputation as a tough and bright newspaperman from the big leagues preceded Rosenfeld's arrival in Albany. When Rosenfeld got here, Dan O'Connell had been dead for a year and the dust was only beginning to settle after a political power struggle for his position of dominance astride the machine. Corning had expended enormous amounts of political capital and physical energy – enduring a hip replacement and hospitalization from lung complications the year Rosenfeld arrived – as he crushed the attempted usurpation of his power by the Ryans, the McNultys and Howard Nolan. Now, Corning was finally omnipotent, no longer beholden to Uncle Dan, mayor and political boss in name and in deed. After thirty-five years as Dan's understudy, Corning stepped into the leading role. He was Albany's Julius Caesar, after all these years, but there were plenty of Brutuses waiting in the wings, knives sharpened, ready to lunge. Rosenfeld was perceived as one more conspirator, albeit an outsider, taking aim at Corning atop his pedestal of power. Corning had a message for Rosenfeld, but the mayor let the crackerjack new editor settle in first and then, a year after Rosenfeld arrived, in the fall of 1979, Corning called with an urgent message. The mayor's call came on Yom Kippur, the day of atonement, the holiest Jewish holiday, which Rosenfeld was spending with other observant Jews fasting and offering prayers of repentance at his temple, Congregation Beth Emeth on Academy Road in Albany. Rosenfeld recalled, "Someone came to me in the synagogue and said there was an urgent message. I was to call the mayor immediately. It disrupted not only my prayers, but those of everyone around me and I went out, got to a phone and called Corning. It turned out to be a minor matter on a Joe Picchi story he didn't think was right. It obviously could have waited until the next day or he could have taken it up with another editor at the paper." Rosenfeld said to this day he is unsure whether Corning was oblivious to the fact that it was Yom Kippur (which Rosenfeld doubts); or, since he had many Jewish friends, that Corning realized the significance of the holy day and was just being insensitive (which he also doubts); or, that he had chosen this opportunity with great care to show the hotshot editor who was boss (the most likely explanation in Rosenfeld's mind). "You never quite knew where you stood with Corning, which kept you off-balance and gave him the advantage," Rosenfeld said. "He cultivated that sense of being an enigma."

Rosenfeld's first hire when he arrived in the fall of 1978 at the *Times Union* was Alan Miller, an aggressive, young reporter who had worked in the *Washington Post*'s Tokyo bureau as a graduate student. Some of his colleagues considered Miller a hired gun, but those sentiments largely may be attributed to professional jealousy since Miller was a doggedly determined and brilliant journalist who did some of the finest City Hall investigative reporting the *Times Union* had ever seen. "Harry was new to Albany, wanted to make his mark and I pursued Corning very much with his support and encouragement," said Miller, now an investigative reporter in the Washington bureau of the *Los Angeles Times*. "The ushering in of the Rosenfeld era meant a much tougher approach to the mayor and the machine." In Corning, Miller found "a compelling, challenging, fascinating figure to cover. I was getting an education in urban American politics by focusing on one of the last great master practitioners."

Miller's first major investigative project on Corning was a five-part series titled "His Honor, The Boss" that ran in October of 1979 in the *Times Union*. The series ripped through the shroud of secrecy with which the machine had wrapped itself in order to conceal its inner workings. The series essentially was a political flow chart that mapped out, with remarkable clarity, who was feeding at the machine patronage trough, how much they got, and what they did to curry special favor. More importantly, Miller's probing reporting confirmed how cunningly Corning had galvanized his power after O'Connell's death by cutting off at the knees with surgical precision all political rivals. The series revealed what its title promised, that Corning was now "His Honor, The Boss," the king from whom all favors flowed, a single man controlling the city and county in its entirety. Miller named names, forcing into the light the shadowy machine lieutenants and Corning cronies. The series also broke new ground by specifying the hundreds of thousands of dollars that flowed to Corning's insurance firm through its monopoly of county coverage.

The series was followed up by an angry editorial from Rosenfeld meant as a wake-up call to apathetic Albanians, a rallying cry to all those who loved freedom and democracy and a truly representative government. The bluster fell on deaf ears. For all its weight and complex detail, Miller's series landed with a whisper, rather than a shout, and his months of labor were quickly forgotten.

Ironically, it was a single routine story by Miller about the night of the Jimmy Carter-Edward Kennedy primary in the spring of 1980 that Miller had spent at Albany's Democratic Committee headquarters on State Street that made the biggest splash and earned Miller the machine's enmity. Carter won the primary in Albany, but by a smaller margin than Corning and machine members had predicted. Kennedy put in an unexpectedly strong showing in the New Scotland Avenue and Pine Hills wards, despite Corning's backing of Carter. Miller quoted Noonan as saying, "It was those Jews again." That single remark, Miller said, caused more fallout than his five-part series. Noonan's comment stirred up Albany's Jewish community, prompting letters to the editor suggesting Noonan was anti-Semitic. Rosenfeld ran the letters and Miller wrote a follow-up reaction piece. Miller, who is Jewish, was told by inside political sources that Noonan wanted his hide. Miller watched his step. But neither he nor Rosenfeld backed down. Corning stopped talking to Miller at that point. The freeze-out of Miller was so complete that Corning would walk straight ahead, refusing to look at Miller and uttering "No comment" as Miller asked questions when the mayor emerged from City Hall to walk to his car. It go so bad that Miller sent Corning registered letters with return receipts at Rosenfeld's suggestion to get answers to Miller's questions. Corning put pressure on Rosenfeld to pull Miller off the City Hall beat; Rosenfeld refused. Miller has always admired Rosenfeld's tenacity. "Harry stood up for me against a very powerful man," Miller said. "Not many editors would do that."

While Miller had lost his access to the mayor, his investigative reporting on City Hall only grew more determined. In 1980, Miller published another multi-part series. Entitled "All In The Family," it chronicled the rise to political prominence of Polly Noonan and how her influence with Corning distributed patronage and power to her children, members of her family, her then son-in-law, Doug Rutnik, and other relatives. Miller broke one of Albany's most sacred taboos, linking the mayor and Polly Noonan personally and in business dealings that laid out in remarkable detail the long and complex relationship between the two. Miller also coined the term for that relationship that became part of Albany newspaper lore: he called Polly Noonan Corning's "confidante." The modifier stuck and became a lasting moniker for Noonan, who despised the nudge-and-wink connotation it carried for readers. "They really hated Harry and me after that, these outsiders coming in taking on their entrenched little group that had run Albany for so many years without much trouble from the press," Miller said. "There we were, laying out all the machine's secret deals for the people of Albany to see."

Despite the diligent digging of Miller and determination of Rosenfeld, ultimately the steady stream of probing articles – reporters with the *Knickerbocker News* also were publishing hard-hitting, investigative pieces on purchasing and patronage – caused no lasting change and seemed to have little effect on the way Corning and the machine operated. It was business as usual. "Those of us covering City Hall had no illusions we were going to take down the machine," Miller said. "But you'd hear all these rumors about corruption we tried to chase down. I kept hearing about a vault beneath Democratic headquarters at 75 State Street where they stored the kickback cash from no-bid contracts. I found not one shred of evidence for any of those rumors." "Corning was so cool and unflappable, he gave the impression that none of our stories ever bothered him," political columnist McMahon said. "And the reality is that we broke these terrific stories, but they had no legs. We kept shouting, 'Hey folks, your money's being wasted on the friends of the mayor!' But the people of Albany didn't care. Because they were in on it. Everyone got a little piece of the action from the machine."

McMahon went on to lobby at the Capitol on behalf of Republican politicians and causes, having left newspaper work chastened by the Corning experience. "It taught me the limits of journalism," McMahon said. "All your hard work is tomorrow's fish wrapper. You can't change people by what you write if they don't want to be changed." "The machine had a stranglehold on the city and people were truly frightened to challenge it," Rosenfeld said. "I'd hear little whispers about the machine's corruption, but never the details and there was nothing we could track down. We did a lot of stories pointing out the control and manipulation of the machine, but the people of Albany were terribly apathetic. Nothing we did seemed to shake them up enough to act. That's because Corning had cut so many of them in on it."

Doc Rivett, the former *Times Union* reporter and editor, went on to work in public relations for the State Public Service Commission, where he encountered Fred Dusenbury, a Corning challenger for mayor in 1981. Dusenbury was a political neophyte and a jokester from Schenectady who went nowhere with his Citizens' Party candidacy. But the goateed satirist embarrassed Corning with stinging attacks on the mayor's fictitious Albany address and other personal matters and referred to him as "Dr. Corning" because of an honorary medical degree the mayor had received. In October of 1981, two months before the election, Dusenbury raised a fuss over PSC documents he wanted that Rivett said were not public. Dusenbury got into a heated argument with Rivett in the PSC office. There were threats and counter-threats that led to shoves and fisticuffs. Rivett punched Dusenbury, who called the police and pressed charges. The fracas made the papers. Corning called Rivett the next morning.

Corning: "Doc, is that story accurate?"

Rivett: "Yes, it is. In fact, if anything, I'd say it's understated. I hit the bastard three times."

Corning: "I'm so pleased somebody finally gave that cocksucker what he had coming to him."

Rivett said he never revealed this before, but he learned later that Corning called up attorney Doug Rutnik and told him to have his firm represent Rivett. Rivett went to Albany City Court with his *pro bono* attorney and the case was heard by Judge Thomas Keegan, a friend of Corning's. The case was adjourned in contemplation of dismissal. "Behave yourself until Valentine's Day," Keegan told Rivett as he left the court. Said Rivett, "It was Corning's doing that I got off. I think it was Corning's way of rewarding me for doing to Dusenbury what he secretly wanted to do but couldn't as mayor."

Corning was not toppled by the *Times Union*'s most focused and potent salvo, an exhaustive investigative project called "The Machine's Expensive Friends" that ran December 5-8, 1982. City Hall reporters Nancy Connell and Ralph Cipriano spent months examining thousands of payment vouchers in the city treasurer's office. Their painstaking documentation paid off. The reporters were able to establish an irrefutable paper trail that linked the city and county of Albany's spending of tens of thousands of dollars of public money to reward the machine's friends. The series laid bare Corning's clear pattern of favoritism for machine loyalists and offered comparative analysis to see how much taxpayers overpaid through no-bid contracts. "I like doing business with my friends," was Corning's infamous reply. The series, follow-up articles and editorials were reprinted as a special supplement in February, 1983. Connell's and Cipriano's extraordinary journalistic package of articles received awards and thousands of copies of the reprint were distributed to libraries and schools throughout the Capital Region and beyond. What the groundbreaking series could not do was impeach Corning, mayor for life. Corning was in the hospital in Boston by the time the articles ran, and never commented publicly on them. For the mayor, who was in grave physical decline by then, it was as if they never were published. The paper may have finally nailed Corning, but it was too late. He was gone from Albany and never coming back.

Over forty-two years, Corning saw dozens of reporters, editors and publishers come and go from the mastheads and credits of Albany's newspapers, radio and TV stations. They turned all their journalistic powers on the man who occupied the seat in City Hall, the biggest story around, and their efforts managed to do little more than burnish the legend. The series and investigative articles and information attributed to sources did not shake Corning from what he liked to call "the old stand." Even in the mayor's final year of life – spent hospitalized and dying an excruciatingly slow death from lung ailments first in Albany and then in Boston – the press seemed outfoxed by Corning. He was in intensive care much of the time, sprouting tubes from all parts of his body, breathing with the aid of a respirator, unable to speak, his throat pierced by a tracheotomy, weakened from numerous surgeries, shrunken to skeletal proportions, pumped up with painkillers. And still Corning kept the press off-balance, frustrated, essentially powerless. The king still held the throne and all its power and glory.

It seems bizarre now, in hindsight, to go back to 1982 and 1983 and look at the newspaper coverage of Corning's long decline. It was a daily death watch, with almost no new information, but there it was, day after day, a brief news item saying Corning was still dying but still running the city with the help of his aides. Same as it ever was. Corning had no plans of resigning. Mayor for life. And a master manipulator of the press until he drew his last breath. Corning called Joe Picchi to the Boston hospital in November, 1982. "There were tubes everywhere in him, he had the tracheotomy and really couldn't talk and he had lost a lot of weight," Picchi recalled. "We talked for a few minutes. And then he said he wanted me to come work for him when he got back. He really believed he was going back to City Hall."

Corning called a few of his old adversaries from the press to his deathbed. One was Harry Rosenfeld, who visited the mayor twice at the hospital in Albany at Corning's invitation. They spoke of the long-ago past and how Corning wanted to write a book about history and the mayor talked about how he planned to launch new projects to re-invigorate Albany. "Harry, we're going to have some fun together," were the last words Corning spoke to Rosenfeld. But after Rosenfeld's father died in January, 1983, the mayor wrote a moving condolence letter in shaky, labored script from his Boston hospital bed where Corning lay dying. The note recounted details about Rosenfeld's father's immigrant beginnings in this country that Rosenfeld had forgotten he had even told the mayor.

McLoughlin interviewed Corning for the last time in his hospital room in Albany in August, 1982, just before he was transferred to Boston. "He didn't make much sense and was suffering from too much or too little oxygen," McLoughlin said. "He told me he was going to hook up a little motor in his boat in Maine to power the ventilator and then he got into a lot of rambling thoughts that went nowhere." It was the last contact McLoughlin had with Corning, except for a request via Bill Keefe from Boston that the mayor wanted videotapes of figure skating. "It was a request out of the blue and seemed strange, but we sent them," McLoughlin said.

Another journalist summoned by the mayor to Boston was Ed Dague, the TV reporter and anchor who had covered Corning since 1968. Corning wanted advice on how to present himself in his wheelchair and oxygen tank when he returned to City Hall. "I told him I was crossing an ethical line if I gave him advice," Dague recalled. "We talked some more, but he was under the influence of medication and not making a lot of sense. A few days later, he wrote me a little note that said, 'Dear Ed: Ethics are only for those not bright enough to know right and wrong.'" Dague's last interview with Corning was in the Boston hospital a few months before he died. Corning was very weak and could barely speak, but one portion of that taped interview made it into Dague's obituary on Corning. The mayor lifted a feeble arm and whispered, "See you shortly. Thank you. God Bless."

Corning died at 12:20 p.m. on Saturday, May 28, 1983 in his hospital room in Boston. DeMare was in the newsroom of the *Times Union* that afternoon, finishing up a Sunday story, when the call came in from the hospital's public relations director. It was just before 2 p.m. Joe Sharkey, city editor, took the call and stood up at the city desk and yelled out, "The mayor's dead!" DeMare immediately set to work getting the details and reaction. She had cultivated the Boston hospital public relations person for months and it had paid off. He called the *Times Union* before any other news organization. DeMare was getting a jump on the story. Other reporters were called in, of course, and they added to what's known as "B matter," background material previously filed in the computer system during Corning's long decline. DeMare remembered thinking, "Corning died on our cycle. We had enough time to lead the Sunday paper with the news. Dan O'Connell didn't cooperate. He didn't die on our cycle and we had to follow up a day later." Sharkey banged out a few paragraphs on Corning's death, something along the lines of "The nation's longest-tenured mayor, Erastus Corning 2nd of Albany, died Saturday...." The news went out on the wire services' "Bulletin" file, the file reserved for news of national significance and special urgency such as wars and assassinations.

Corning stories dominated the thick Sunday morning edition of the *Times Union* on May 29, 1983. The staffs of the *Times Union* and *Knickerbocker News* combined to produce a twenty-page special supplement on June 3, 1983. It was filled with dozens of photographs, illustrations and cartoons and many thousands of words of type. The back page contained a single image, the hearse bearing Corning's coffin parked in front of City Hall, just beyond the windows of the office he occupied since 1941. The photo caption said simply, "The End of an Era."

Even in death, Corning wanted the last word and got in one final manipulation of the press. For all of his seventy-three years of life and in dozens of references in the posthumous special supplement, he was referred to as Erastus Corning II in the press. Roman numeral. Inked on his will, chiseled on his granite grave marker and printed on all of his official papers is Erastus Corning 2nd. Arabic numeral. The peevish stickler for accuracy had allowed the press to wallow in their error all those years. The lifelong misidentification wasn't discovered until Corning's will was made public. The press had never accurately defined the mayor, after all. Following the discovery of the Arabicized preference, Rosenfeld decreed he would be Erastus Corning 2nd evermore. "That symbolized the way Corning felt about the press," DeMare said. "He was dead, but he was tweaking us one last time."

Chapter 13:

From Maine to the South Mall: Corning vs. Rockefeller

**"What do I want to be remembered for the most?
That I had Nelson by the balls."**

*Mayor Erastus Corning 2nd to Don Rittner and his wife,
Nancy, at University Hospital in Boston a few months
before the mayor's death.*

Erastus Corning 2nd and Nelson A. Rockefeller began competing against each other in the 1920s during the summers of their youth spent on Maine's Mount Desert Island. Although they traveled in separate orbits, the arc of their respective lives resembled twin parabolic curves, drawing away at one point only to intersect later at another position on their respective paths. From old money to adolescent rites of passage, from Ivy League to early society marriages, from a business base to political careers, Rockefeller and Corning exhibited strangely similar trajectories. What began as a boyhood sporting rivalry in Maine ended, nearly one-half century later, in an epic power struggle in Albany between two political warhorses battling over the most controversial and costly state government complex in America. Rockefeller got his monument. Corning earned his footnote in history. And New York's capital city was irrevocably altered. This political battle royal between Democrat and Republican was played out across Albany's urban stage, but it was rooted in an accident of geography along the Maine coast.

The Corning family compound, Stoney Point, was located in Northeast Harbor. By the standards of Albany society's summer homes, it was impressive: three hundred feet of frontage amid five acres of prime real estate with a main house, four cottages and caretaker outbuildings. The Rockefeller estate was at Seal Harbor, a few miles away from the Corning property to the east along the rocky, pine-covered southern shoreline of

Mount Desert Island. The Rockefellers set the standard for opulence and their summer retreat dwarfed the Cornings and all others in Maine. The Rockefeller family owned a 30,000-acre estate in Maine, 11,000 acres of which on Mount Desert Island they donated to the federal government between 1920 and 1950 – amounting to one-third of today's Acadia National Park. If land ownership was the game, the Rockefellers with their unrivaled wealth won the prize hands-down; neither the Cornings nor anyone else could dream of competing with Rockefeller money.

In 1941, Nelson Rockefeller commissioned architect Wallace K. Harrison – whose major works include Rockefeller Center, the United Nations complex, Lincoln Center for the Performing Arts and the Empire State Plaza in Albany – to build him a summer home in Seal Harbor. Rockefeller called the dramatic, cantilevered ode to modernism "The Anchorage." It was the talk of Mount Desert Island and is featured in glossy coffee table books on modern architecture. The Corning family's Maine camps, traditional and understated, were pedestrian by comparison. When the mayor's mother could no longer afford the cost or effort to keep up the Stoney Point compound, she sold off the buildings and most of the property in the 1940s. The buyer was Rockefeller's friend, William A.M. Burden – a member of the Vanderbilt clan, a wealthy banker and U.S. ambassador to Belgium – who had Harrison design for him in 1947 on the former Corning property a low-slung, modernistic structure with unusual walls suggesting the undulating curl of a breaking wave.

In terms of conspicuous wealth and avant-garde architecture, nobody in Maine came close to Rockefeller, but there was one place where Erastus could achieve a level playing field with Nelson, at least for a time. Both the Rockefellers and Cornings belonged to the Northeast Harbor Club, an exclusive private facility with tennis courts, a golf course, swimming pool and dockage. It was on Maine's bays, on the courts and on the links that the two young men from prominent New York families tested their mettle. The sport that captured the imaginations of the moneyed aristocrats who summered on Mount Desert Island was sailing. Fathers pushed sons to master the art of reading the tricky winds that swirled around the craggy coastline of Maine. Patrician pride, and substantial side wagers, were at stake. Winning the annual Northeast Harbor Regatta earned cocktail circuit bragging rights not even Rockefeller's fortune could buy. The Northeast Harbor Club's members raced identical thirty-foot sloops, graceful wooden A-class vessels designed for speed. Nelson Rockefeller's passion was sailing and he worked to excel at the sport, while Erastus Corning was a reluctant skipper. But Corning's father pushed his firstborn son to sail in hopes of one day competing in the regatta and upholding family pride. The mayor related his father's sailing obsession to his daughter, Bettina, decades later. "My father told me he never liked to sail, but his own father made him learn and hired men to teach him," Bettina said. "He hated it, but my father worked at it and ended up becoming an expert sailor." Erastus Corning and Nelson Rockefeller were among the competitors of the Northeast Harbor Regatta on July 4, 1928. Corning had just graduated from Groton and would enter Yale in the fall. Rockefeller, eighteen months older, had completed his sophomore year at Dartmouth. Against all odds, Corning won the regatta that year. He brought the trophy to his father – who was Lieutenant Governor of New York, the State Democratic Party chairman and a front-runner to become Al Smith's successor as Governor – and offered his victory over Rockefeller as if it were a spoil of war. The champion sailor had just raced in his last regatta. Erastus Corning announced to his father: "There, I've won. Now, I can quit."

Although he competed without much enthusiasm in sports at Groton and Yale, Corning was a gifted athlete and had the hardware at his camp on Webb Pond in Maine to prove it. Trophies he won at highly competitive Northeast Harbor Club events over the years included: mixed doubles tennis (1925), the speedboat race (1927), the annual water sports competition (1928), the golf course club championship (1930). Rockefeller, on the other hand, was athletically challenged. He conceded to a political associate that his athletic career at Dartmouth amounted to a single touchdown – for the opposing team. Rockefeller's biographer, Joseph E. Persico, attributed Nelson's lack of athletic skill to his father's attempts to "cure" his natural left handedness with a string and rubber band each time the boy reached for a fork with his left hand. Nelson was conditioned to eat, write and play sports unnaturally, with his right hand, according to Persico in his biography, *The Imperial Rockefeller*. Some historians have suggested that may have contributed to Rockefeller's dyslexia.

When it came to settling their competitive score, Corning won the rivalry over Rockefeller in sports. In other areas of their growing up, the two young men were evenly matched. The Cornings and Rockefellers were both good friends with Charles W. Eliot, president of Harvard University, who established Northeast Harbor as a bastion of WASP Ascendancy in the 1870s with Albany's Episcopal Bishop William Croswell Doane and the first

Erastus Corning. Corning was Phi Beta Kappa at Yale; Rockefeller was Phi Beta Kappa at Dartmouth. Nelson drove a Ford touring car around Northeast Harbor as a young man; Corning's father gave him a Packard runabout. Corning and Rockefeller both were married within weeks after their college graduations and both men wed Philadelphia Main Line women. Rockefeller married Mary Todhunter Clark, fresh from a Paris finishing school, in 1930 in a wedding ceremony in Philadelphia; Corning married Elizabeth Norris Platt, who attended a finishing school in Florence, in 1932 in a ceremony in Philadelphia. Both women were tall, lean and possessed of patrician faces that would not be described as beautiful. As a young man, Rockefeller was called off to Washington, D.C., where he began his political career as an administrator under the Democratic president Franklin Delano Roosevelt. Corning stayed in Albany, where he left a position as a state lawmaker to become mayor for life under the Democratic boss Dan O'Connell.

"We knew the Rockefellers well in Maine, and we sailed and went to parties and played tennis together," Corning recalled in an interview with *Knickerbocker News* columnist John Maguire published January 28, 1979. "Nelson was a year older than I, and Laurance, Winthrop and David were in about the same age range as my brother and sisters. Ours was not a close friendship, but as close as you get with someone you see only a few months a year." Two decades ensued in which Rockefeller and Corning were little more than two sloops passing in the night off the coast of Maine. They lost touch completely. No one could have predicted that the youngsters who battled it out in sports in Maine in the 1920s and early-1930s would meet again in Albany in 1959 when Rockfeller was sworn in at his inaugural in Albany as Governor of New York State. The stage was set for a showdown in the capital city on the Hudson: Mayor Corning versus Governor Rockefeller; Democrat against Republican; Yale squaring off against Dartmouth. Only this time, the two men were vying for something more substantial than the silver cup of the Northeast Harbor Club Regatta. They were locked in a titanic struggle involving hundreds of millions of dollars of taxpayer money and the heart of the capital city of New York whose destiny – architectural, cultural, social, political and psychological – rested in their hands. It was a war fought on a first-name basis between two silver spoon trust funders: 'Rastus meets Nelson.

Erastus Corning began keeping files on Nelson Rockefeller's megalomaniacal vision of immortality in Albany starting in 1962. He labeled these voluminous folders "Brasilia," after the futuristic capital of Brazil carved from the wilderness in 1960 as a symbol of the modernist architectural movement. Rockefeller had visited Brasilia on numerous occasions and had discussed with friends his admiration for the modernistic complex. As it turned out, Rockefeller sprung upon Corning without warning his version of Brasilia in Albany. The mayor, a traditionalist whose passion was preserving historic architecture, and who ran his city with iron-fisted control, was stunned when his lackeys informed him that state officials had filed a series of maps with the Albany County Clerk's office on March 26, 1962 in which Rockefeller, as the state's highest official, intended to take title to ninety-eight and one-half acres – forty square blocks, home to some 3,500 families – in the heart of downtown Albany's historic district. Corning had figured something was coming down the pike when Rockefeller appointed Corning to a spot on the governor's eighteen-member Temporary State Commission on the Capital City, formed in April, 1961 and headed by Rockefeller's loyal and stalwart Lieutenant Governor, Malcolm Wilson. Nobody on the commission quibbled with the reality that Albany – a shabby, dank and crumbling backwater in the early-1960s with about as much pizzazz as a Dutch wooden shoe – could use the boost of a facelift and downtown revitalization. But Wilson had not tipped his hand about the final report of the commission and its cataclysmic recommendation to demolish the center of Albany with its eighteenth- and nineteenth-century buildings and replace it with a modernist marble monolith that appeared to have been dropped down from some distant planet, perhaps Pluto. But for Rockefeller, the massive project to transform Albany was, in biographer Persico's words, "the ultimate example of his compulsion to construct."

After Corning recovered from his momentary paralysis at the audacity of the governor's revolutionary vision for the city, the mayor, a Groton boxer, counter-punched the governor, directing his lawyers to file suit against Rockefeller to cease and desist. The city's attorneys took a scatter-shot approach in an attempt to stall the condemnation proceedings. "There were more than one hundred court of claims actions filed before we even got started," recalled William C. Hennessy, former commissioner of the State Department of Transportation who helped oversee the massive land transfer for the state. "Eventually, we were able to acquire all the property without a single eviction and we kept the total claims settlements down to twelve." But the mayor was buying time to try to roil public opinion against the project in order to strengthen his negotiating position with

Rockefeller. "The State is planning to carve out from the heart of the city a large, sterile area for a monumental group of buildings which will look most spectacular on postcards all over the world but will, in fact, hurt the people of Albany," Mayor Corning told a gathering of downtown planners on March 31, 1962, an address that made front-page news of that afternoon's *Knickerbocker News*. "It is a ruthless takeover. The first I heard of the plan was Thursday [two days before]. If the governor thinks that's being well-briefed, that's his privilege. I don't. I don't think it's ever going to be built. It's going to fail. The people who established the program are going to realize that it is not a good thing, but a sterile monument."

Rockefeller countered by pronouncing the South Mall "the most spectacularly beautiful seat of government in the world" and "the greatest thing that has happened to this country in one hundred years." For his part, Corning likened it to "a sprawling colossus" and something "that might be expected of a dictatorship" – of course, that was the mayor of a political machine that had lasted longer than any dictatorship on the planet talking. Political boss Dan O'Connell – champion of the little people, backer of underdogs, whose idol, literarily and in terms of social criticism, was Charles Dickens – described the displacement of so many of Albany's working-class metaphorically. "It's a good thing Longfellow isn't alive today," O'Connell said. "He'd have written a poem about it." Corning saved his toughest jab at Rockefeller for the end of his speech to the downtown planners. "I find my dispute with the Governor's plan for Albany so strong that I may decide to run for Lieutenant Governor," Corning said. The ticket would be Corning and Democratic gubernatorial candidate Robert F. Wagner Jr., New York City mayor and fellow Yalie. "The challenge of the state's seizure of forty downtown blocks kind of whets one's appetite for an election battle," Corning said. Corning's candidacy never materialized, but Rockefeller got the message.

Later that year, September of 1962, Corning was at the height of his statewide political powers. He was voted permanent chairman of the State Democratic Convention in Syracuse and delivered one of the most memorable speeches of his career when he addressed 1,138 Democratic delegates in the War Memorial Auditorium and launched into a blistering attack on Rockefeller's ambitions that offered an intriguing resonance to Corning's own lack of resolve to move up in politics. "Fourteen years ago our great Democratic President, Harry S. Truman, said that everyone was against him except the people," Corning began. "Today we are almost suffocated by tons of Rockefeller handouts dutifully publicized by the newspapers in the State; newspapers almost without exception captivated by the power of money. . . . We have an opportunity to nominate a Governor who will be Governor – one who will not look at the Executive Mansion in Albany as a pleasant place for a short stay and his time there as an interlude, a pause on his travels to a far more exciting occupation on the banks of another river." After the convention, back at City Hall, Corning received a flood of wrenching, heartfelt letters – from children to senior citizens – residents of the nineteenth-century Albany row houses in the area that Rockefeller intended to bulldoze and build over. They wrote about why they loved where they lived, about the closeness of the neighborhood, and that they didn't want to see their lives uprooted while they were displaced by a Rockefellerian ego trip. Corning's reply to Miss Patricia Beaupre on April 2, 1962 was typical: "I will do everything I can to keep the Governor from being successful in his plan to tear down so many good houses here in Albany."

Corning viewed with rose-colored glasses the proposed ninety-eight and one-half acre site of the South Mall – so named because it was situated south of the Capitol, from State Street to beyond Madison Avenue, and from Swan Street east to Eagle. In reality, this area was a blighted, derelict red-light district and den of multiple vices known as "The Gut." Much of the place had the feel of a decaying slum, which in part set Rockefeller on his crusade in the first place. The South Mall's genesis was a 1959 visit to Albany by Princess Beatrix of the Netherlands for the Hudson-Champlain Celebration, at which the Governor gave Beatrix a tour of downtown Albany. "Rockefeller felt that the buildings the Princess and those with her saw were not as good-looking or as appropriate for a capital city as he thought they should be," Corning told the *Knickerbocker News* on January 28, 1979. Further solidifying Rockefeller's vision of giving the city a major facelift was a 1960 stop by the King and Queen of Denmark to celebrate the anniversary of the city's establishment of Fort Orange by the Dutch in 1624. To biographer Persico, Rockefeller described his embarrassment at having to drive with the Danish royalty through "The Gut." "The Queen was riding with Mayor Corning and myself. I thought, 'Well, it's his city so I'll ride up there with the security guys,' so I had plenty of time to observe the scene. I could see the way the city was running and what this lady might think. Here was a great Dutch city built in the New World, and then she comes to look at it, never having seen it before. My God!" Rockefeller claimed he vowed then and there to make Albany a suitable showcase as the Empire State's capital, worthy of visits by royalty – and temporary residence for a Rockefeller or two.

Still, "The Gut" was not home solely to putrefaction and depravity as Rockefeller would have people believe. Within those ninety-eight and one-half acres there was plenty of fine architecture worth preserving, not to mention a couple of churches, a brand new high school, a three-story state office building at State and Swan, saloons, grocery stores and even a police station. More importantly, there were thousands of Democratic votes residing there, a ward that solidly delivered for the O'Connell-Corning machine – especially if enough five-dollar bills were passed around. Where would that margin of electoral comfort for the machine go when the houses were torn down? Probably to Rensselaer or somewhere outside Albany, since low-income housing was scarce in the city thanks to the same machine that bought the poor folks' trust and loyalty for a fiver.

Corning continued his onslaught against the South Mall in a speech to the Democratic Party faithful in a meeting on April 26, 1962: "Either the governor's promises of the spending of money are phony, or his promises of no tax increases are phony. Not even a Rockefeller can have his cake and eat it too. . . . This land seizure will have the greatest effect on the people of Albany of anything in the memory of man. It will displace thousands of people who do not want to move from their homes. It will disrupt many small businesses. It will not help downtown Albany. It will be a tragedy. Do not build this magnificent monument on a foundation of human misery."

Not everyone was on Corning's side in opposing Rockefeller's South Mall. William J. Myers, an Albany resident and Yale student, wrote to the mayor on March 31, 1962. "You have become a laughing stock around New York State. I know I myself wouldn't want to be looked upon as the man who stood in the way of an improved capital city." Corning fired back a reply to Myers the next day: "I would think that a young man, a junior in the College I graduated from almost thirty years ago, would have an exploratory type mind, and would take the trouble to look up the facts."

Eventually, Corning won round one of his battle with Rockefeller. The city of Albany on September 22, 1962 was granted a court injunction that stopped Rockefeller and the state from proceeding with land seizure by eminent domain in preparation for construction of the South Mall. Instead of gloating, Corning tried a conciliatory tone with Rockefeller on September 28, 1962. "Dear Nelson: I am concerned with the possibility that many of the people now living in the South Mall area may be forced to move by action of the State, or fear of such imminent action in the month before election. This might cause them to be disenfranchised. I would appreciate your looking into this, and suggest that as few people as possible be forced to move during the month . . ." No reply from Rockefeller. Meanwhile, Corning was quietly working the Legislature as he had learned to do during his years as a lawmaker. He worked through the machine's man in the State Senate, Julian Erway, Corning's old fishing buddy, to introduce bills that would require the state to pay for loss of all tax revenues from the land seizure for Rockefeller's mall. Besides the potential loss of thousands of guaranteed Democratic votes, if the voters who were displaced moved out of the city, it meant fewer taxpayers and Corning was hyper-sensitive to further erosion of Albany's limited tax base. In 1969, the Conference of Large City Boards of Education estimated the total assessed value of property in Albany was about $577 million, $304 million taxable and $273 million exempt. The South Mall would tip that inequity even further toward tax-exempt property.

Corning – a good poker player who liked the high-stakes games at the Fort Orange Club – was not only holding his cards close to his vest during maneuvering to gain the upper hand with Rockefeller, but also was counting cards, dealing off the bottom of the deck, bluffing and talking out of both sides of his mouth, and upping the ante with the governor. This was more than power politics between Democrat and Republican: it was two rich boys from those Maine summers locked in a dead-heat sailboat race, running bow-to-bow, but this time they were playing with the capital of New York and with people's lives.

The field of their competition was immense, a project a half-mile long and a quarter-mile wide, and said to be the largest construction of marble ever pieced together, a complex almost unimaginably expansive, welded onto a platform driven five stories into the Earth: elemental and monumental in inexplicable proportions, a monolith to state bureaucracy. Specifically, the South Mall contained a forty-four story office tower, four identical twenty-three story buildings, a legislative building, a justice building, a headquarters for the motor vehicle department, a cultural center that included a museum and library, a convention center, a performing arts center with two theaters, a laboratory for the health department, and a platform with a 500-foot reflecting pool flanked by two smaller pools, as well as lawns, trees, fountains, promenades and extensive outdoor sculpture and art work. Some found symbolism in the fact that the South Mall site was an Atlantis of mud, gooey blue clay left behind by the last Ice Age, and also a stream bed through which flowed the Rutten Kill ("rat creek" in Dutch). There were other coincidences. Corning's great-grandfather, the first Erastus, championed the mid-nineteenth century public works project to level the stream's ravine with more unstable clay fill. The Rutten Kill was called "pestiferous . . . a dismal and unsanitary ravine" by Tip Roseberry in his Albany history book, *Flashback*. Corning's fill project required three years, sixty teams of horses and 250 laborers to peel down Madison Avenue to fill in the Rutten Kill ravine. For the South Mall builders, the fluid mound of clay left by the first Erastus required costly anchoring, namely 24,000 steel pilings driven deep into bedrock, a total of 304 miles of H-beam piles – stretching the entire length of the Hudson River from the Adirondacks to New York Harbor if laid end-to-end. The Mall contained 232,000 tons of steel, 900,000 cubic yards of concrete and 40,000 tons of marble. In all, it would take eighteen years and nearly $2 billion for Rockefeller to finish his Ozymandian monument. Each stage of construction was its own engineering hell, but driving the pilings was a particular nightmare. Because of the fluid nature of the fill, each time one piling was driven in, the piling next to it would pop back up like an arcade game; hence, the need for the excavation of some three million cubic yards of clay. Some original design features never made the final construction, the most significant of which was the "Arch of Freedom" Rockefeller wanted, a 336-foot version of the Saint Louis arch just behind where the State Library and Museum now stand.

Publicly, Corning and Rockefeller were consumed in a bitter feud, but privately they were discussing how to put a favorable spin on the story. When Rockefeller acquiesced to some of Corning's legislative efforts to get compensation in lieu of taxes for Albany, the governor's counsel, Sol Neil Corbin, wrote to Corning on March 27, 1963: "I assume that you will discuss directly with the Governor the matter of the news handling of the bill's introduction." Curiously, at press conferences and civic events during this time, Corning continued to blast Rockefeller's project as the governor's "Brasilia" – the mocking title the mayor continued to scrawl across the top of his South Mall files. Nonetheless, Corning saw fit to attend a cocktail party thrown by Rockefeller on March 27, 1963 to mark the first anniversary of the unveiling of the South Mall project. A month later, on April 23, 1963, Corning attended the unveiling of the South Mall architects' scale models with Rockefeller, Wilson and other members of the Capital City Commission. That was after Corning enjoyed a private lunch with the Governor amid Rockefeller's private museum of priceless modern art – Picasso, Mondrian, Klee, Miro, Matisse, Van Gogh, Feininger and Motherwell – at the Executive Mansion. The governor's residence was not slated for demolition, by the way, although situated mere yards beyond the gaping grand canyon the South Mall construction site would create in the heart of Albany. Corning's about-face from condemnation to support of the South Mall was praised by many and the mayor was perceived to be making history. "Most unique in all of this, and overlooked by even you, perhaps, is the historical fact that your very important contribution to the rebirth of Albany came exactly 150 years to the month after the arrival here in 1814 of Erastus Corning," George H.C. Farley of Albany wrote to Corning on April 1, 1963. "What an appropriate tribute for one whose successful life was concerned with politics, finance and the development of the greater Albany area!"

A major player in the development of the South Mall was architect George Dudley, who later retired to Rensselaerville in southern Albany County. Like Corning, Dudley was a Yalie (Class of '36), four years younger than the mayor. Dudley grew up in New Haven and his father taught mechanical engineering at the college. As a townie, Dudley harbored something of an inferiority complex among Corning and his "white shoe group" of wealthy out-of-town prep school types. Three decades after graduating from Yale, Dudley arrived in Albany, on Corning's home turf, as an assistant to architect Wallace K. Harrison, who had worked with Rockefeller in Washington in the Inter-American Affairs office and on numerous architectural projects. Dudley traveled frequently on Rockefeller's behalf to Venezuela and South America and knew how both Harrison and the governor worked best. Harrison, of course, was considered a kind of Court Architect to the Rockefeller family, responsible for Rockefeller Center and Lincoln Center and the United Nations complex (Rockefellers put up the cash), as well as Nelson Rockefeller's own homage to modernism, his summer retreat, The Anchorage, in Seal Harbor, Maine.

Harrison gave form to Rockefeller's driving ambition for immortality through monumental buildings. Rockefeller, who once confessed to having an "edifice complex," was a frustrated architect who spoke with regret that he didn't go into the field. His family, after all, helped build the World Trade

Center, museums, churches, hotels, foreign university buildings and other grand structures in addition to helping restore Rheims Cathedral and the Chateau de Versailles. The South Mall would be Harrison's last monumental commission and Rockefeller's architectural curtain call. They promised to pull out all the stops no matter how large the obstacles Corning threw up before them. "Rockefeller was dyslexic and Harrison never went to college and was too impatient to read, so they both liked a lot of maps and charts," Dudley said. "So, I was called up to Albany to set up a Chart Room to map out ways to streamline government and make it more efficient. That was the beginning of the New York State Planning Office."

Both Rockefeller and Harrison were visionaries, idea men, who left the scutwork of planning and tedious minutiae of executing their bursts of creativity to detail men like Dudley. "I remember working in Washington with Harrison, who was baffled by all the bureaucracy," Dudley said. "Periodically, he'd just dump some memos from his 'In' basket into the garbage can. Then he'd say, 'You see, George. If you leave these things long enough, they take care of themselves.'" It's been said that Rockefeller helped develop the initial concept for the South Mall while on an airplane with Harrison by sketching on the back of an envelope what Rockefeller could recall from visiting the palace of the Dalai Lama at Lhasa, Tibet, a sublime conceptual capital high atop a cliff. Harrison fleshed out Rockefeller's scratchings. The two men enjoyed a design simpatico. They had worked together since World War II.

Dudley came to Albany in 1959, shortly after Rockefeller took office, and was given a room at the Fort Orange Club, the mayor's daily lunch spot. One afternoon, Dudley, who knew almost nobody in Albany, took a seat at the long table where visitors or single diners eat. Dudley recalled, "I was sitting there and this tall, white-haired, patrician-looking gentleman came to the long table and asked, 'May I join you?'" The man sat down and began to chat with Dudley, who sketched out his background and why he was in Albany. The stranger was evasive about himself and didn't even give his name, Dudley recalled. Finally, after Dudley had completed his monologue, the man said: "All this talk of planning for the state. I'm not so sure you need all this planning as long as you have continuity of administration." Ah, continuity of administration. Dudley let that phrase swirl around in his mouth a few times like a fine Bordeaux. What a brilliant definition of the O'Connell-Corning machine. It wasn't until quite some time later that Dudley learned the identity of his unexpected lunch partner in

1959. "He never did introduce himself, but that was my introduction to the mayor," said Dudley, who later realized Corning was cunning enough to have been conducting a stealth covert action to glean secrets from the Rockefeller camp.

Dudley was a good source to try to tap for information. He attended numerous high-level secret meetings about the South Mall with Rockefeller and his top aides and lawyers at the Executive Mansion. Dudley was the person with the property maps always rolled up under his arm, coordinating architect for a vast army of people – politicians to pile drivers – involved in Rockefeller's version of Versailles on the Hudson. "Nelson talked slightly about his relationship with Mayor Corning, which I understand could be rather prickly," Dudley said. "Nelson did so many things that had a good effect on the city that the mayor went along. They needed to work with each other in Albany and they accommodated each other because of that."

Both Corning and Rockefeller were astute politicians who understood that the balance of power was such that neither one could halt or complete construction of the colossal South Mall without assistance from the other. The Democratic machine had proven itself a force to be reckoned with, even for Republican governors and their administrations, from Dewey on. The boyhood combatants from long-ago summer sporting fields in Maine had fought to a draw. The state defeated the city on appeal and Albany's lawsuit to stop the land seizure and building demolition was lost. For his part, Rockefeller knew that the project was so costly – hundreds of millions of dollars even by conservative initial estimates – that it would require a public referendum. New York City, overwhelmingly Democratic and home to the state's greatest concentration of population, would never vote for a marble monument to the Republican Rockefeller 150 miles upriver in the slums of Albany. Corning, meanwhile, realized that Rockefeller might be able to get something, perhaps a scaled-back version of the South Mall, built in Albany without mayoral support, and so Corning decided to cut the best deal possible for himself, his machine Democrats and his city. The only problem was, the wrecking cranes and bulldozers had already marched ahead and most of the buildings had been demolished. The heart of the city looked like a war zone, street after street sacked and plundered. A dust bowl was all that remained. "Several times, I met with Mayor Corning to talk about developments on the South Mall and he was always cooperative and piqued that Rockefeller would speak negatively about him because the mayor wasn't used to anyone challenging him," Dudley said. "The governor's feeling was that the mayor was cooperating as much as he could in his position without looking like he was acquiescing to a Republican."

And so came the fancy financial footwork of which Mayor Corning was most proud, the single stroke in all his forty-two years in City Hall that he considered his greatest contribution to Albany's (and his own) immortality. It was a legal loophole exploited by Corning, the cagey former lawmaker. Corning figured out in advance of Rockefeller – who felt stymied by upstate-downstate political realities – a way to circumvent New York State constitutional law. The law specifically prohibited the state's contraction of such a massive debt unless that debt was duly authorized by the State Legislature and put to the state's voters as a bond issue referendum. Such a bond issue could only take effect after it received a majority of the votes at a general election. In other words, to prevent state politicians from raiding state coffers or issuing bonds for massive capital projects like the South Mall, such an expenditure had to be put to a vote of the people. Such pure and public a form of democracy was not Rockefeller's, or the Albany Democratic machine's, *modus operandi*.

Corning liked to claim sole credit for devising the intricately crafted and finessed financing scheme that managed to sidestep state law and saddle state taxpayers with forty years of debt for a marble colossus they may or may not have wanted. This was the same South Mall, remember, that Corning had railed against as a destroyer of everything that was sacred in Albany when Rockefeller first proposed it. The power play of turning the project to his advantage became another matter for Corning. Yet, the stroke of underhanded political genius Corning takes credit for may not be his entirely. Perhaps it was recycled from an offer Corning made Governor Thomas E. Dewey in 1946 when Dewey wanted to build a costly state office campus on the outskirts of the city, an offer that Dewey rejected. In his book, *The Politics of Architecture*, Samuel Bleecker gave credit for the South Mall bonding plan to Joseph McGovern, a bond attorney with the New York City law firm of Sullivan, Donovan, Hanrahan, McGovern & Lane. McGovern's firm had done bonding work in Albany since the early-1940s. Corning called his old friend, McGovern, and the bond attorney worked out the specifics, according to Bleecker. In the margin of an uncorrected proof of Bleecker's book, in whose version of the South Mall story Corning found much to dispute, the mayor crossed out the McGovern section and wrote this notation: "No. Did not talk to McGovern till after gov. took the fly." In scores of interviews with Corning's political associates, a handful of names came up repeatedly as having been contributors, if not more, on the financing scheme: John Clyne, the attorney and judge; Frank Wells McCabe, the banker and vice-chairman of the state commission that recommended the South Mall; Lew Swyer, the developer; and Dan O'Connell. Whatever their input – three are long dead and Clyne isn't talking – at least publicly the deal was all Corning's, although the interpretations are numerous. Here are two examples of the range of scuttlebutt: Dan Malmed, owner of Adirondack Dan's Army-Navy Store and a personal friend of Corning's, who spoke with the mayor in depth on topics ranging from bonsai trees to the fish species splake, points the finger at Swyer. "Lew Swyer was the only guy who could sit on the desk and chat with both Corning and Rockefeller," Malmed said. "I know that Swyer was the go-between between Corning and Rockefeller during the South Mall negotiations." Gerald Fitzgerald, retired bank president and a colleague of McCabe's at National Commercial Bank & Trust Co., has another theory. "Rockefeller had a lot of clout with the bankers in Albany and he was pressing to rehabilitate the failing downtown, but everything was so tightly controlled by the Democratic machine he went on his own and tried to go around the machine," Fitzgerald said. "I know McCabe was involved in the discussions to bring the Corning and Rockefeller sides together. McCabe was on a first-name basis with both Corning and Rockefeller and he was from down near Rocky's estate in Pocantico Hills. McCabe was in the same social circle as Corning and was also Phi Beta Kappa from Yale several years before Corning. I believe McCabe's knowledge of banking and bonds planted the seed for the South Mall financing deal and McCabe let Corning take credit for it." In numerous interviews, however, Corning took credit for the plan and Rockefeller seconded that version of events, although doubts linger among those on the periphery of the deal cutting. Regardless, whatever the fountainhead for the financing scheme, Erastus knew he had Nelson "by the balls" as he told Don Rittner, city archaeologist and a Corning protégé. In essence, Corning became Rockefeller's landlord; that was a victory for Erastus sweeter even than beating Nelson in the Northeast Harbor Regatta.

The gist of the Corning financing scheme brokered in 1965 that broke through political gridlock and allowed the South Mall to move forward was thus: Corning would direct Albany County to sell a series of forty-year bonds to build the South Mall, then turn the money over to the state, which would take on construction as the county's "agent." The agent's service fees the state paid the county over forty years to cover the debt incurred by the sale of the county's bonds and as an indemnity in lieu of taxes would amount to roughly thirty-five million dollars. In this lease-purchase arrangement, when the county was paid off by the year 2004, the state then would retain legal possession and become sole owner. That was the tantalizing solution to Rockefeller's dilemma: an end-run around the Legislature and citizens of New York State, an arrangement so complex that the legal document spelling out the deal was thirty-three pages.

Corning, who had honed his fly fishing skills during summers in Maine, dangled the tidy financing plan in front of Rockefeller's nose like the master angler he was. Corning used an analogy that gave him great pleasure to recount over the years. This is how the mayor characterized Rockefeller's reaction to the lease-purchase plan: "He took to it like a trout rising to a fly," Corning said. Corning possessed the patience of an experienced fly fisherman and once he had hooked Rockefeller, Corning let the Governor run a while and he played out this powerful politician before netting him. The financing scheme bill devised by Corning overwhelmingly passed both houses of the Legislature on April 16, 1963. It was far from a done deal, though. Corning was just beginning to put on the table the cards he had been clutching to his chest. The mayor wanted Albany to get something substantial for all its trouble and the resulting displacement of so many thousands of its citizens. The poker game between Corning and Rockefeller began in earnest and, with each round, Corning kept upping the ante for Albany. In the end, Rockefeller, a far less disciplined and single-minded gambler than Corning, essentially threw up his hands. Rockefeller called Corning "a genius of creative financing," according to Persico. The mayor had prevailed over the governor once more. Rockefeller put a favorable spin on his capitulation. "This was a magnificent concept," Gov. Rockefeller told the *Wall Street Journal* in a front-page story on the South Mall on March 18, 1971. "I mean, this was new, it was fresh. I went for it right away." The *Wall Street Journal* continued, "But some others think the Governor had no choice but to take Mayor Corning's deal. The Governor wanted the Mall built very badly, and Corning set his price, says one."

What Corning got for Albany was nothing short of spectacular compared with what Rockefeller was offering in the beginning. The mayor managed to pry out of the state some thirteen million dollars for the city and county in lieu of lost real estate taxes – a very generous settlement, according to analysis by financial consultants. Corning also got Rockefeller to add to redrafted architectural plans the museum, convention center and restaurant, which were not included in the initial proposal. "I raised hell because I wanted it to be something that was good for the people, not just for the employees. And, we got it," Corning told the *Times Union* in a 1981 interview. Rockefeller didn't just roll over, though, and Corning had to raise hell for quite some time to get his way. The negotiations grew protracted, strained and occasionally bitter, but the mayor was confident he had the upper hand. Pat Mahoney, the engineer closely associated with city projects since 1964 and a Corning protégé, recalled hearing a phone conversation between Corning and Rockefeller in the mayor's office during a confrontation over the South Mall. Critics had been criticizing Corning for selling out the city and not getting enough in return from the state. Mahoney broached the topic. Corning said in a calm fashion: "You of all people, Pat, ought to know better than that. I'm not going to get out horse traded here by a goddamn Rockefeller. I'm a pretty goddamn good horse trader myself."

After nearly two years of Corning's horse trading, Rockefeller had reached the limits of his patience. Private correspondence between Corning and Rockefeller revealed the strained relationship. The mayor and Governor were sending a series of increasingly testy letters back and forth from City Hall to the Capitol via messenger. Here's Rockefeller to Corning on December 29, 1964: "The fact that, after twenty months of negotiations, we are still without execution of a final contract, has given me deep concern – particularly in view of the fact that two weeks ago you proposed to me as a condition of your approval completely new demands that would cost the State well over ten million dollars a year in payments to the city." Rockefeller's letter ran three pages and the governor promised he was going to play hardball by taking his case to the public and, perhaps, killing the South Mall project altogether. Take that, Erastus.

Corning shot back a reply the same afternoon. The tone was sarcastic, right from the opening smart-alecky salutation. There also was an undercurrent of two spoiled rich boys arguing over who had reserved the tennis court at the country club. Corning wrote:

Your Excellency: Your letter represents a complete misunderstanding on your part as to what I was endeavoring to get across to you. In paragraphs two and three of your letter, you state that you publicly gave credit to me for proposing this method of financing. By those statements you appear to imply that this financing was not proposed by me. This, of course, is not the fact as you very well know. You seem to have had a continuing lack of understanding of my role in this whole matter . . . In conclusion, permit me to say that I have probably spent ten times as much time on the South Mall as you have. I have a great deal of interest in it. I resent your statements as to procrastination, when such procrastination lies with the State and not with the City. I deny unequivocally your statements of my breaking faith, and of course I reject your absurd ultimatum.

While Corning was obsessed with the South Mall, he hadn't forgotten more mundane matters of personal importance. On the back of Rockefeller's cantankerous letter, the mayor had scrawled a list of reminders in his flowing penmanship: "rabbit repellent for shrubs . . . *Maine Times* . . . Davis at polls . . . brook trout . . . snow plows." Corning's obstinacy on the South Mall was a political counter strike against Rockefeller, whose SIC investigators were once again probing alleged irregularities in Albany County purchasing practices. One target of the SIC inquiry in May, 1964 was the exorbitant prices and sub-standard quality of food purchased for the Albany County nursing facility, Ann Lee Home. Rockefeller kept up the pressure as a state audit cited Albany as operating at a deficit of $3.1 million. Corning dismissed the report as "technical" and irrelevant. On another front, Rockefeller caught Corning in the wide net he cast with a new state "conflict of interest" law the governor signed in August, 1964, which made it mandatory for the mayor to notify the Common Council he was a director of the National Commercial Bank and Trust Co., which had already been made public and was permissible under the law. But it was another ongoing irritant for Corning, courtesy of Rockefeller.

The competition between the Yalie and Dartmouth grad could turn as petty as a fraternity prank. Consider the photo incident. At a press conference in the spring of 1965 to announce the agreement on the financing scheme – Rockefeller reluctantly shared the limelight with Corning and gave the mayor credit for the plan – the governor turned it into a photo opportunity. Rockefeller inscribed a large glossy of himself superimposed on the South Mall, crediting Corning for making the "South Maul" possible. Rockefeller was dyslexic and Corning made private, snide references to this learning disability on the part of the governor. Corning accepted the picture with the glaring spelling error with a deliciously obsequious tone mocking Rockefeller, who had no idea of his mistake. Corning wrote to Rockefeller on May 18, 1965: "Dear Nelson: Many thanks for the photograph of the signing of the South Mall Agreement. It is a good one, and I am very glad to have it." Corning had a place of honor in mind for the photo. The mayor hung Nelson in the crapper. Corning thought of Rockefeller each time he used the outhouse at his wilderness cabin on Floods Pond in Maine during their South Mall skirmishes. It gave him great pleasure to consider himself, a mayor of an unexceptional city of about 100,000, the intellectual and political superior of a Governor of the state's eighteen million residents and inheritor of one of this nation's greatest family fortunes. Corning had finally managed to put Rockefeller in his place: the outhouse, not the White House. Moreover, for posterity, the mayor had a snapshot taken of himself, a rascal king seated on his throne in the outhouse, gazing at the Rocky memento. On August 8, 1966, Corning wrote to caretaker Thomas Pollard with an important mission: "I would appreciate it, if you would, as soon as convenient, go over to the Camp at Floods and very carefully take down the photograph of Governor Rockefeller that is the one on the door of the outhouse," Corning wrote. "I would like it mailed to me flat, between two pieces of cardboard, as I have another useful purpose for it." Corning considered the Rockefeller photo such a great conversation piece that he filed it in his desk drawer at City Hall, producing it whenever a visitor doubted the story or needed a reminder of Corning's primacy over the almighty Rockefeller.

There were other examples of the depths of prep school spitefulness to which both men would stoop. City planner Dick Patrick said the Rockefeller-Corning tiff extended into landscape plantings. "They liked to pull each other's chains a lot," Patrick said. "Rocky planted the sycamores in front of the Capitol just to piss off the mayor. He knew Corning didn't think much of sycamores, because they have no fall color and are coarse and not highly regarded as trees. So Corning had to look out at those sycamores year after year from his City Hall window. Rocky must have taken great pleasure in that."

The mayor was incensed when Rockefeller bailed him out during an embarrassing incident that arose from labor strife with picketing Albany firefighters, who had been trying to unionize for years against a vehemently opposed Democratic machine. The scene was a dedication ceremony on December 21, 1970 for the twenty-four million dollar Parker F. Dunn Memorial Bridge over the Hudson River. The firefighters had set up a picket line at the ramp to the bridge. Corning's car was blocked, so he sat there as Rockefeller and other elected officials awaited the mayor at midspan for the ribbon-cutting ceremony. Rockefeller sent a State Police bodyguard to fetch the mayor, who refused to get out of his car. Rockefeller finally persuaded the firefighters to form a corridor to allow the mayor's car to travel out onto the span to join the rest of the official motorcade. Corning was livid at this point, but it got worse. The crowd heckled the mayor and cheered Rockefeller, who offered to act as intermediary. "I'll talk to the mayor and see if we can't get this thing moving again," the Governor told firefighters in response to stalled negotiations. "I have to be very careful not to intervene between a municipal employer and his employees, though." Privately, Rockefeller was filled with childish glee at this turnabout on Corning, who fumed and swore under his breath, according to Rev. Joseph Romano, the firefighters' union organizer. Credit that round of one-upmanship to Rockefeller.

It wasn't all personal ire between Corning and Rockefeller. There were other practical considerations for Corning's intransigence that caused the South Mall delays. He was holding out for a bigger piece of the pie for Albany, and for himself. After much wrangling, Rockefeller reluctantly gave in to a Corning demand that the South Mall contract spell out insurance arrangements. It read: "All construction contractors must furnish liability insurance covering both the county and the state, with coverage of not less than $100,000 for each person and $500,000 for each accident." The mayor executed another masterful stroke that left the Governor feeling like a dog chasing his own tail. The insurance liability windfall, estimated to be tens of thousands of dollars in premiums, went to Corning's firm, Albany Associates. That's not all. The contractors awarded the lucrative deal to haul bricks and demolition debris from the South Mall project to the McCarty Avenue landfill were none other than Becker Wrecking and MacFarland Construction Co. of Albany, proving that old machine magic was alive and well and still potent.

And there's more. When those dump trucks piloted by Corning's pals were filled with soil excavated from the canyon where the South Mall would one day rise, the mayor asked for a slight detour. If the loads happened to be clean fill, the dump trucks drove on past the McCarty Avenue landfill, their destination, and made a drop on Corning's property in Glenmont at Corning Hill. A little home improvement for the mayor, courtesy of Rockefeller, unbeknownst to the Governor. It's difficult to keep track of the multiple maneuverings Corning employed to take advantage of the state and his Republican rival. The mayor's insurance payday, patronage contractors' bonanza and free fill made it triple-dipping at least – shades of his great-grandfather the railroad baron. The mayor's plan was to fill in the steep ravines on the Corning Hill property, with an eye to subdividing it as building lots. In the spring of 1979, Corning asked Frank Leavitt, district conservationist for the Albany County Soil & Water District to make a survey of the Corning Hill property since the mayor was planning to sell off some acreage to developers. "Extensive area to the east of the gully is fill material from the South Mall construction," Leavitt wrote to Corning on May 8, 1979. "Some areas are actively eroding." Alas, the pirated free fill was mostly clay, thus unstable, and unsuitable for home construction. Tough break on Corning's part, but the price was right anyway. "I never heard that the mayor used some of the fill, but I can believe it," said John Byron, director of construction on the South Mall for the State's Office of General Services (OGS), an agency Rockefeller created to oversee the project. "It was all clay and was very poor soil to try to build on, so it wouldn't have done him much good. That dirt we excavated had very little value at all. It was a challenge just to get rid of it. The extra cost to drive some over to Corning's property wasn't much and some of the contractors were probably happy to give it away." The mayor shared the wealth. He requested excavation soil from the South Mall to be hauled over to Hackett Boulevard and Child's Hospital to fill in a gully for a planned expansion. Child's Hospital happened to be operated by the Episcopal diocese; the mayor's wife was a board member and the Corning family was a longtime major donor to the hospital.

In Corning's extensive dealings with Rockefeller during the decade of South Mall construction, the trout fishing analogy carried through. The mayor was careful not to give his catch enough slack to slip the hook and he kept the line taut. Corning wrote this to Rockefeller on January 15, 1965: "I think perhaps that it is time we cleared the air somewhat on the

South Mall. Statements emanating from your office have exaggerated the Albany proposals to the point where I find difficulty recognizing them. These outrageous statements were manufactured in your office, not in our conversations. There must come a point where the State will recognize that it cannot continue to take more and more Albany property off the tax rolls without making some payment for the services it requires and gets from both the County and the City." After the two old adversaries from Maine shook hands and smiled for the cameras at the signing of the agreement in the second week of May, 1965, Corning wasted no time in exploiting his role for all the political mileage he could get. It amounted to a canonization. Corning was given a standing ovation and thunderous applause and hailed as "The Hero of the South Mall" during a march and celebration of hundreds of union members for the Building and Construction Trades Union annual communion breakfast on May 17, 1965. Corning walked at the head of a procession from the Cathedral of Immaculate Conception, where union members attended Mass, past the South Mall site to the Ten Eyck Hotel. "It's a pretty nice thing to be a landlord for the Rockefellers," Corning said. The crowd cheered. "When you are right and united, you will win. The South Mall will be the greatest single governmental office complex history has ever known." The transformation of Mayor Corning was complete, from the most vehement critic of the South Mall to its patron saint and biggest booster.

On October 20, 1965, two weeks after his fifty-sixth birthday – spent, as usual, at City Hall, as a typical workday – Corning was talking of the South Mall in ecstatic tones one rarely heard the mayor invoke. He delivered this radio address: "We have worked closely with the state, doing our very best to make the state's plans the most satisfactory for all our people. To make the South Mall a living monument, a place for pleasure as well as work, a place for homes and music and beauty and culture as well as the most spectacular complex of governmental offices ever dreamed of in this world we live in." Say so long to Brasilia and all that sarcasm, Erastus, and say hello to Nirvana. What a difference cutting a few sweetheart deals makes. A year later, in December of 1966, Corning gushed at a Kiwanis Club luncheon that the South Mall would be the catalyst to make Albany "one of the most fantastic cities in the world."

Corning's sense of ownership of the South Mall was as overpowering as the prose he used to describe the project. This was his city, after all, and he ruled it completely and absolutely. At work the mayor was known as a micro-manager beyond compare, who handled every detail from paper clips to manhole covers. Corning prided himself on knowing where every fire hydrant, every sewer grate, every streetlight was in Albany at all times. Corning's obsession with such minutiae extended into his daily dealings with the state on the South Mall. Each morning, on his way to City Hall, Corning drove around the construction site and made mental notes. Later in the afternoon, Corning would direct his chauffeur, Dusty Miller, regardless of their destination, to drive him around the streets adjacent to the work zone. The mayor played mother hen to this monumental state government complex-in-progress. Widely known as a control freak at City Hall, Corning's attempt at riding herd on the South Mall megalopolis was almost comical. The stack of nit-picking letters and memos Corning sent to South Mall project managers filled an entire archival box. The steady stream of criticism began in the summer of 1964. A typical memo from Corning was dispatched on August 13, 1964: "The south side of Jefferson Street west of Eagle Street has not been cleaned up properly after demolition." Another from Corning on April 28, 1967: "There is one manhole cover with frame that is damaged on Swan Street, between Madison and Hamilton. It was damaged by some State contractor and I respectfully request that it be repaired."

The mayor appointed himself commander-in-chief of the construction crew police. On June 19, 1967, he was complaining about dump trucks driving too fast through downtown Albany. "These truck operators have got to realize that they DO NOT OWN these streets," Corning wrote. On September 7, 1967 Corning was at it again: "I have continued to look at Eagle Street each morning," he wrote in a memo to project supervisors. "It is still very, very dirty and the catch basins at the northeast corner of Eagle and Hudson are still full." Construction director Byron remembered well Corning's daily harangue. "The mayor kept us on our toes," Byron said. "A lot of his concerns were brought directly to me. I told our contractors to be more careful, to hose down the roads to reduce dust. But I also explained to the mayor that we were moving three million yards of dirt and his city was bound to get a little dirty."

Byron recalled Corning had the clout to go directly to Governor Rockefeller with concerns. "There were bound to be problems," Byron said. "It was an overwhelming challenge to manage the project, which involved sixty-three prime contractors and 270 subcontractors on the site at one time, as well as more than 3,500 construction workers." To make it more complex, some contractors were cost-plus, meaning they'd have to submit all their costs to the state for review and payment, locked in at a reasonable profit above their overhead. Alongside them were the "hard money" contractors working for a fixed bid price. To make matters worse, Rockefeller was in a big rush as he eyed the Presidency and wanted his monument completed as the icing on his political cake. The Governor cracked the whip and the clot of contractors stumbled over each other as they tried to build a dozen structures at once. It was construction chaos. Byron downplayed media accounts of a South Mall project rife with corruption among the contractors, sabotage, and an underlying element of criminality. "A lot of that was overstated," Byron said. "There was a fire in one of the towers early on and that remained suspicious and was never settled. That was one of the few unusual situations in my mind. We did have a twenty-four hour fire watch and fire standpipes all around the perimeter when the Egg was going up because there was a tremendous amount of wood in that building."

Meanwhile, the cost of the South Mall continued its steady climb. What began as the oft-quoted $250 million price tag had soared past $450 million and was headed up, up, up into the $1 billion stratosphere. The actual number was a Rockefellerian fiction; he just kept getting cash advances through the Legislature when he needed them. With each announcement of additional funding given, though, the public hue and cry rose several decibels. Corning, who kept Albany's budget scrawled in pencil in a suit coat pocket, was uncharacteristically glib in response to the cost explosion. "Albany's South Mall could cost up to one billion dollars," Corning told 250 members of the Building and Construction Trades Union of Albany on May 25, 1969. "I guess I was a poor prophet when I thought originally it would be fifty million dollars." Actually, Corning ran up on Rockefeller's tab a total of $985 million in Albany County bonding. The actual price, all told, was said to be in the neighborhood of $1.9 billion. On January 28, 1971, when the *Times Union* announced another legislative approval of $127 million more for the South Mall, the paper ran man-on-the-street characterizations of the project. A few examples: "Our Vietnam . . . Rocky's erector set . . . financial monstrosity . . . Rockefeller Center North . . . Taj Mahal . . . Albany Maul."

"Rockefeller just pulled that initial $250 million figure out of his hat," Byron said. "The increases were all reasonable. With a project that complex, delays were inevitable. Some of the early drawings involving the structural steel for the platform were done in a hurry and didn't represent how much steel was needed. The health labs added millions of dollars extra that hadn't even been considered. Early on, they were figuring the cost based on limestone and they ended up with expensive marble. That was another increase." The South Mall rampant cost overruns had a feeling of *deja vu* for those who knew the history of the adjacent State Capitol building's construction. After two controversial design competitions in the 1860s, Thomas Fuller, a Canadian, was named architect for the project. His neo-Renaissance design carried a four-million dollar price tag. By 1875, the budget had topped seven million dollars and the building was far from done, so an architectural advisory board yanked control from Fuller and decided upon finishing it up in a Romanesque style. After decades of controversy, the Capitol was completed in 1898 at a cost of twenty-five million dollars – the most expensive building on the North American continent at the time. A few details of the South Mall's extravagance can be seen in the two-million-square-feet of fine Vermont and Georgia marble used on the exterior of the buildings, said to be personally selected by Rockefeller and an upgrade that drove up the final cost tens of millions of dollars.

Rockefeller didn't mind that kind of cosmetic cost overrun, but when it came to following through on his promise to relocate the displaced residents from the South Mall to a new low-income housing project he proposed to build nearby, all the Governor came up with were financial excuses. Rockefeller canceled the housing deal because the projected cost rose from ten million dollars to about twenty million dollars, although it didn't seem to matter that the cost of the South Mall rose fivefold from its original projection.

During planning meetings with architect Harrison and Rockefeller, Byron recalled Mayor Corning was mentioned only for his ability to keep open the funding spigots. "Rockefeller and Harrison worked through give and take and reaching a consensus," Byron said. "I remember they'd get exasperated when we needed more bond money to continue and we had to deal with John Clyne, the county attorney, who was Corning's man."

Corning's intense desire to keep tabs on and control what happened at every storm sewer and curb cut of the South Mall project underlay his need for wider recognition for his role in this historic, internationally recognized governmental complex. Corning got that attention on June 16, 1968 in a front-page article in the *New York Times*, although it wasn't the kind of publicity he was seeking. "Political Patronage Rising at Fast Rate,

Study Finds," the headline read, and the *Times* called Corning's role in the South Mall *vis-à-vis* his insurance firm "the stuff of modern political patronage." The *Times* called the South Mall "a ninety-eight-acre ditch" and said "Mayor Corning is one of many political figures who has derived a profit from the ditch." The *Times* reported that Corning's insurance firm, Albany Associates, wrote insurance for heating and plumbing contractors working on the South Mall with premiums totaling $7,000 annually. That's in addition to the $100,000 in premiums Corning's company received each year for insuring the property of Albany County. "All this business was obtained without competitive bidding," the *Times* said. "Asked whether there was a conflict between his public and private offices, the Mayor replied in an interview: 'I'm in no way a county official. The question of conflict of interest has never been raised.'" The *Times* also reported that a good friend of Corning's and of the Democratic machine, Peter D. Kiernan, president of Rose & Kiernan of Albany, received $200,000 in annual insurance premiums on the South Mall project – also awarded without competitive bidding.

The *Wall Street Journal* shed a national limelight on Corning and the South Mall once more, albeit unfavorably, with a front-page article on March 18, 1971. "Whatever the state's troubles, the city of Albany stands to reap nice rewards. So, perhaps incidentally, do several businesses in which the city's mayor, Erastus Corning 2d, has an interest," the *Wall Street Journal* reported. "The state agreed to pay the city in lieu of taxes sums totaling $28 million by the year 2005, an amount that exceeds what the slums could have been expected to produce in taxes. The state also threw in a 300,000-square foot convention center, built nominally for state uses but open to the city when vacant." The depository of cash from the roughly one billion dollar Albany County Mall bond sales was none other than a bank to which the Cornings had a long association, National Commercial Bank and Trust Company – of which the mayor was a director and his family had long been associated. Its president, Frank Wells McCabe, had been involved in the discussions which created the original county bonding deal. The State Bank of Albany, where Corning's mother kept a substantial account, also got some of the Mall business.

In the spring of 1971, Corning put the political screws to Rockefeller by holding hostage for a time seventy million dollars in desperately needed bonding for the cash-strapped Mall project. Corning wanted the Governor to push for repeal of a new state law that required open school board elections and ended the mayor's authority to appoint the Albany school board himself, thus controlling millions of dollars in patronage. Rockefeller obliged in what Corning critics called political blackmail, but the legislation was defeated in the Assembly and the city school board remained an elected body. That was only the tip of the political corruption iceberg when it came to construction of the South Mall. Hard-hitting investigative pieces in the *Times Union* and a series in the *Knickerbocker News* by Scott Christianson chronicled the labor strife, theft, sabotage, arson, featherbedding and all manner of price gouging that conspired to create a project that was several years behind schedule and hundreds of millions of dollars over budget. A federal grand jury began investigating alleged improprieties, including a thriving bookie operation, in the South Mall project in the fall of 1970. Corning played dumb. "As long as rumors are rumors, they're rumors," the mayor told reporters questioning him about the federal probe on November 19, 1970. Mayor Corning, the old warrior, managed to emerge from the long-running debacle mostly unscathed. In the spring of 1971, despite persistent rumors, Corning said he had not been shown any evidence that alleged gambling and racketeering in connection with the South Mall project was taking place on city property. Asked about reports of illegal betting and gambling activities on city property near and around the ninety-eight-acre site, the mayor told reporters on April 29, 1971: "All property fenced in at the South Mall is completely in the charge of the state." The master of the non-denial denial had struck again.

State Comptroller Arthur Levitt, a Democrat, seemed like the boy crying wolf as he released periodic audits and harsh criticism of the "wasteful practices" surrounding South Mall construction. On January 28, 1971, Levitt told the *New York Times* the $250 million cost estimate had hit $850 million officially, but the state's chief fiscal officer said the final cost would likely be in the neighborhood of $1.5 billion. Corning said all the right things publicly, expressing concern about the rising cost and taking credit for getting so many gifts for Albany through his tough negotiating. Privately, in 1971, he changed the heading of his file folders from Brasilia to South Mall for the first time, signaling a fundamental change of heart. In public, Corning's favorite fall-back position was to blame the state. Rockefeller scrapped plans to build a 442-unit low-income housing project as too expensive in February, 1969. Any time the matter of housing to replace the inexpensive dwellings being torn down in the massive displacement was raised, Corning said it was the state's responsibility and not the city's to provide an alternative. While Corning and Rockefeller passed the buck, the uprooted families had no place to go to find affordable housing. Many ended up in the slums of Rensselaer.

Corning enjoyed being in a position of power that required the state and its Governor to come begging. When Rockefeller wanted the reflecting pools in pristine condition for the South Mall dedication celebration, he had his commissioner of the Office of General Services write to Corning asking permission to fill them up with city of Albany water. The Hudson River water the state had been drawing up to fill the pools was clouded with algae and the contaminants were clogging the filters. Corning granted the request, but he did so in a way that reminded state officials he now held a bargaining chip and that they owed him one.

Corning could, however, lay aside the pettiness of politics for the compassion of the personal. Corning, who had grieved over the loss of his younger brother, Eddie, dead before his time, empathized when Rockefeller felt the sorrow of the passing of his brother, Winthrop. Corning sent Rockefeller a personal letter of condolence. Rockefeller replied from the Executive Chamber on March 15. 1973: "Dear 'Rastus: Thank you so much for your most thoughtful note. It does indeed help to hear from friends such as you. Win was a wonderful human being and we all miss him terribly. Sincerely, Nelson."

In the fall of 1973, when Rockefeller was rumored to be the Republicans' replacement for resigned Vice-President Spiro Agnew, Corning seemed genuine about losing the thrill of challenging his old Albany adversary. "I feel Gov. Rockefeller would be a very able and capable replacement for Vice-President Agnew, but I would be sorry to see my old friend leave Albany," Corning told the *Knickerbocker News* on October 12, 1973. Some time later, Rockefeller would leave for Washington, D.C. and the vice presidency. Meanwhile, Corning was re-elected in 1973 to his ninth term by the narrowest margin of his long career, a winner over newcomer Carl Touhey by a mere 3,552 votes.

This was the backdrop for the final denouement regarding the lifelong competition between Corning and Rockefeller. The event was the November 22, 1973 unveiling of a marble plaque officially naming the South Mall the Gov. Nelson A. Rockefeller Empire State Plaza. Persico wrote Rockefeller's speech for the dedication, including the master builder's construction credo: "Mean structures breed small vision. But great architecture reflects mankind at its true worth . . . What we are recognizing in these buildings is that we have an aesthetic nature – that we have cultural values, and that these values are what lift us up above the scurrying ant heap of those absorbed only in survival, and make us a society touched with Divine Grace." Rockefeller also said, "You know, if there is anything more satisfying than dedicating a new building, it is dedicating eight new buildings." That same day, Rockefeller's closely held secret that he planned to resign as Governor – intended as a time-honored political stepping-stone to the White House – was beginning to leak out. Rockefeller's driving ambition to become President, the one thing he wanted more than all the marble monuments he erected, fell short.

Byron attended the dedication and recalled the buoyant mood on that blustery, cold fall day on the Plaza's windswept marble expanse. "There was a lot of back slapping and Wally Harrison talked and Rockefeller talked and then I saw a lot of laughing going on, but I was too far away to tell what it was," recalled Byron. The laughter was nervous. Corning's name had been left off the marble dedication monument. "Gov. Rockefeller apologized to the mayor at the dedication ceremony for the omission and added, since the lettering was only painted in gold and not carved yet, Corning's name will be included," according to a *Knickerbocker News* account. Byron remembered that there were one or two other misspellings of the names of individuals included on the stone. Perhaps it was Rockefeller's dyslexia again, perhaps it was an innocent error, or, perhaps, Rockefeller was looking to slight Corning one last time and used the other mistakes as cover. Nobody knows for certain. Regarding those questions there is only conjecture. What is certain is that when it came Corning's time to speak, the recently re-elected mayor said: "Since now I have a choice, I may simply have it inscribed E. Corning, financial architect." The press reported it as a joke. It's possible Corning was dead serious.

Corning conceded the testiness that existed between him and Rockefeller to *Knickerbocker News* columnist John Maguire in an interview that appeared January 28, 1979. "I used to get into arguments with him when he was new here," Corning said. "There was some confusion about nomenclature and I couldn't understand what he was talking about." Corning confirmed a long-standing rumor about Rockefeller's early unfamiliarity with the Albany scene and that the Governor got it wrong when it came to the Delaware & Hudson Railroad building (now administrative headquarters for the State University of New York), which Rockefeller confused with Union Station (now Fleet Financial Services). "Rockefeller didn't think the D&H was City Hall, but he did think it was Union Station. One day he said something about the railroad station and he meant the D&H building," said Corning, who never missed an opportunity to mention Rockefeller's learning disability and the Governor's occasional confusion as a result. Corning had lobbied hard for state assistance from Rockefeller to preserve Union Station. The Governor eventually acquiesced to Corning's requests, but Rockefeller saved the wrong building, the D&H structure instead of Union Station. "No, he didn't read well. He had dyslexia, you know," Corning told Maguire. "When he was reading his speeches at first, he had difficulty with them. But he was a very smart man, Phi Beta Kappa at Dartmouth, and when he threw out the prepared speeches and just talked, he was much better." Corning credited Rockefeller with great improvements in Albany. "The Empire State Plaza is Nelson Rockefeller's greatest achievement, as far as I'm concerned," Corning said to Maguire. "He helped greatly to make Albany the most spectacular capital in the world."

Corning read with great interest all of the newspaper pieces, magazine articles and book chapters that took a probing, critical look at the South Mall. The mayor challenged the accuracy of many of the accounts, particularly Bleecker's chapter on the Mall in *The Politics of Architecture*. Corning wrote to Judge Bergan on December 7, 1981 after marking up what the mayor considered inaccuracies on a draft copy of Bleecker's chapter: "I think you will see that there are a great many untruths in it and some almost unbelievably inaccurate statements about the history of the South Mall," Corning said.

Nobody was lukewarm about Rockefeller's monument. You either loved it or loathed it. Mostly, it was the latter. While Corning liked to claim credit for the financing scheme that made construction possible, he distanced himself from all criticism of the complex, be it architectural, social or economical. It was Corning's old trick of abdicating responsibility; the Teflon mayor was at his elusive, enigmatic best when it came to making sure none of the ill will directed at the completed South Mall stuck to him. Although Corning pretended not to care, criticism about the South Mall from architectural critics was particularly vituperative. The architectural writer Wolf Von Eckardt described in a *New York* magazine piece the South Mall's relationship to the rest of Albany as that of "a battleship floating on a lily pond . . . an ugly anachronism – the City Beautiful's last erection." Others were less abstract and laid the phallic symbolism squarely in

Rockefeller's lap. *Time* magazine art critic Robert Hughes featured the South Mall in his 1981 public television series, "The Shock of the New." Hughes called it "an architecture of coercion" and likened Rockefeller's vision in marble and mortar to the fascistic design favored by Mussolini, Hitler and Stalin. "One could see any building at Albany Mall with an eagle on top, or a swastika, or a hammer and sickle: it makes no difference to the building," Hughes said. The urban planner Jane Jacobs saw the South Mall as "planning insanity . . . only succeeding in destroying a good amount of viable housing and small business, and they are the base of a city's economy." "Foolish, silly and impractical" was what a *New York Times* architectural critic had to say. *Fortune* magazine called it "an imperial enclave, rising on a hill overlooking the Hudson River."

Furthermore, the architectural writer Carol Herselle Krinsky compared Rockefeller to Peter the Great in an article titled "St. Petersburg-on-the-Hudson: The South Mall." Krinsky wrote, "As Peter the Great and his imperial successors aggrandized a small riverfront outpost, Governor Rockefeller had a plan for aggrandizing a small riverfront city in decline . . . The entire Mall was developed in a way that suggests if not royal power, then at least that a strong will can still be exercised in a democracy, and what the consequences may be." In a May, 1979, critique by Martin Filler titled "Halicarnassus on the Hudson" in the trade journal *Progressive Architecture*, the South Mall was deemed "one of the most disheartening tales in the annals of public architecture in the country. . . .The Mall buildings loom menacingly, like aliens from another galaxy set down on this marble landing strip . . . leaving one not knowing whether to laugh or to cry. God only knows what future generations will make of all this." Filler reserved his biggest gripe for The Egg (the writer Isaac Bashevis Singer allowed it looked like a blintz). "Intended by Harrison to be a formal homage to the sculpture of Brancusi," the Egg, according to Filler, "more closely resembles a futuristic Italian bidet from the MOMA Design Collection." Filler concluded the South Mall was "a monstrosity of misplaced priorities, the built embodiment of government rampant, gorging on its citizenry for the benefit of its own growth and self-perpetuation. The Albany Mall stands as the ultimate cautionary evidence in this country of what can happen if the appetites of the beast go unchecked."

For his part, Corning wanted the citizenry to believe in his patrician persona, that he had demanded, and received, beauty for the city of Albany from the state beast that was Rockefeller. In her biography, *Wallace K.*

Harrison, Architect, Victoria Newhouse cast Corning as "the Great Compromiser" possessed of "apparently irresistible powers of persuasion." She painted Rockefeller as obsessed and out of control. "It was his baby, and his dominance of the project surpassed the behavior of the most possessive parent. . . . Harrison could not reconcile with his own beliefs the motives and means of self-aggrandizement that underlay Rockefeller's interest in the Albany Mall, and perhaps he was quietly expressing his change of heart when he observed later that the greatest problem with Albany was that nobody knew what they were building the Mall for."

In their Rockefeller biography, *I Never Wanted To Be Vice-President of Anything!*, journalists Michael Kramer and Sam Roberts wrote this about the South Mall: "However, for sheer extravagance and waste nothing compares with the Albany Mall. It is truly Nelson Rockefeller's monument." Rockefeller's biographer Persico said the Governor took criticism in stride and watched construction progress from his office in the Capitol "with a proud eye, remembering the naysayers who had disparaged Rockefeller Center long ago. A satisfied smile crossed his face the morning he spotted the words Rocky's Pyramid, which workmen had painted in huge, crude letters on the unfinished shaft of the main tower."

Assessments of the South Mall by hometown viewers, despite their allegiance to Albany's mayor for life, could be equally harsh. Joseph A. Brieg wrote in the Catholic diocese of Albany's weekly newspaper, the *Evangelist*, on October 3, 1974: "It is hardly possible to imagine anything in worse cultural, architectural and environmental taste, or more violently out of place . . . There in the midst of homey, venerable, folksy Albany, Rockefeller erected state office buildings which soar thirty or forty stories into the sky, as if a hunk of Manhattan had been torn loose, lifted and dropped there."

Native son William Kennedy weighed in with his viewpoint in a May, 1983 article in *Atlantic Monthly*, titled "Everything Everybody Ever Wanted." Kennedy wrote:

> If, then, we consider the Mall as the consequence of one man's political will, imposed upon our time and space in spite of its incredible cost, in spite of the arrogant wastry and duplicity that marked the manipulation of public money, in spite of the many construction scandals, underworld intrusions, and colossal thievery that went not only unpunished but un-investigated; if we

consider further the brilliant stroke by which the city's political leaders took the Mall away from Rockefeller even before he had begun to build it; and if, most important, we consider the transubstantiation the Mall effected in Albany – turning a slug of a town into a handsome and prancing dude – then I think we may safely agree with Rockefeller that it is indeed a beaut.

Although the impact of the Empire State Plaza on the city of Albany continues to be debated in 1997, Corning had plenty of thank yous to write with the ending of the chapter on the South Mall construction two decades ago. One such letter of gratitude went to Byron, the construction director, on June 14, 1978. "Again, my thanks for making the birth, growth and coming of age of the South Mall so much easier than it could have been," Corning wrote. Corning also thanked the unwitting catalyst of the South Mall when he wrote to Crown Princess Beatrix of the Netherlands to congratulate her on a promotion on February 1, 1980. "All of us in Albany had a great and very natural interest in your Mother's announcement yesterday and I hope you will be interested in what the newspapers in Albany have written in regard to your wonderful visit, unbelievably more than twenty years ago now. I know that you will most wonderfully succeed both your Mother and your Grandmother for the benefit of your people. On my part, I am very proud of our association."

Even Rockefeller was willing to bury the hatchet on the rivalry with Corning. The former Governor and Vice-President, retired to private life, wrote to Corning on November 6, 1978 from Rockefeller Plaza. "Dear 'Rastus: I thought you might like to have the enclosed souvenir which comes with my deep appreciation for all you did to make that day possible." Rockefeller sent the Mayor a framed state proclamation officially naming the South Mall the Nelson A. Rockefeller State Plaza. The ceremony one month before, on October 6, 1978, was the doing of Gov. Hugh Carey, not Corning, and there had been some friction between the Mayor and Governor over the function, despite the fact both were Democrats. In the end, Corning hung Rockefeller's souvenir not in a place of honor, but out of the way on a wall where his secretary worked. Three months after he sent Corning the framed commemorative keepsake, Rockefeller died. His passing was every bit as controversial as the erection of the South Mall and the sexual double entendres linking the two acts flowed freely.

The completion of construction was not the end of Corning's eagle-eye watchfulness on the South Mall, though; in many ways, it was only the beginning. The mayor was every bit as determined – as he had been in holding the state's feet to the fire to keep the construction site as tidy as possible – to make sure he controlled as much patronage as possible when it came to South Mall activities. In an intriguing twist, Barbara McNamee, who would become the wife of Dudley, the architect and Rockefeller appointee on the South Mall planning committee, was named by Corning as vice-chair of the executive committee of the Empire State Plaza Council.

Corning was strongly opposed to a law signed in 1979 that made the performing arts center, known as "the Egg" for its ovoid architecture, a separate corporation. "To put it bluntly, the $500,000 [the corporation's proposed annual budget] is beautiful; the structure stinks," Corning wrote to Assemblyman Dick Conners and Sen. Howard Nolan on May 24, 1979. "The Egg is such an integral part of the public facilities that to have it run completely separately would be an administrative nightmare." What upset Corning was that he would lose considerable control if the Egg's corporation, Empire State Institute for the Performing Arts (ESIPA), became autonomous. The mayor wrote to OGS commissioner John Egan on August 8, 1979. "I want to know when ESIPA becomes the law of the land . . . no request has been made of me as yet to make an appointment." Corning named an old buddy, Harold Gabrilove, chairman of the RTA Corp. (known as the Nipper building) on Broadway in Albany's North End. Corning also rode herd over the performers booked into the Egg, standing up like an overly protective stage mother for performing artists from his city. Although he was not much of a fan of the performing arts himself and rarely attended ballet, theater, opera or orchestral performances, it was all about control with Corning. The mayor wrote to his close friend Lew Swyer, ESIPA board member and a guiding force and patron for the performing arts locally, on July 22, 1980. "I have no desire to interfere with the operation of the Egg except when it comes to discriminating dollarwise against Albany artists. I would like to know if it does, and then we will see to it that it is discontinued." Swyer replied the next day. "I assure you, I have no intention of staying with this corporation unless it can be shaped up into a form we are both satisfied with." Corning had not received satisfaction when he wrote to Mark Tilley, executive director of the Egg, on February 11, 1981: "I still am completely at a loss to know the reason for subsidizing out of town organizations and charging local ones." When Tilley tried to give Corning two free tickets to Ernest Borgnine in "An Offer You Can't Refuse" at the Egg, the mayor declined the freebies, sent his check and went to the show with no strings attached. Swyer reassured Corning on March 31, 1981 that he was still the mayor's point man at the Plaza. "If I perceive no progress toward change, I will remove myself from involvement in the Corporation as I seem to be the only one that is minding the store," Swyer wrote.

Perhaps Corning's greatest achievement in the saga of the South Mall was his keen judge of character, namely Rockefeller's. It was a no-lose situation for Corning. The failures belonged to Rockefeller; Corning claimed partial credit for the successes. Biographer Persico put Corning's strategy aptly in his preface to *The Imperial Rockefeller*. Persico wrote: "To tie one's fate to the Rockefellers, particularly this Rockefeller, was to gain entry to a world of enlarged possibilities, the chance not only to realize one's potential but to lift that potential considerably by the booster rocket of the Rockefeller connection." Persico summed up the metaphor of the South Mall: "History may choose to remember or ignore the abstract ideals that move public figures, but the towering complex in Albany stands there unignorable and all but permanent. In time, the present cumbersome name will inevitably be shortened, and Rockefeller Center in the state's premier city will be balanced by Rockefeller Plaza in the state's capital." Persico got that last prediction wrong. In fact, twenty-four years after its dedication, the ninety-eight and one-half acre complex is not referred to as Rockefeller Plaza at all, either among locals or visitors. Common usage in and around Albany for those who have lived here for several years remains the South Mall, or, simply, The Plaza for newer residents. In 1997, the reality is that Rockefeller's name recognition is awfully thin around State and Eagle streets.

The one building given a name that has stuck in 1997 belongs to Corning, which happens to be the tallest structure between Montreal and New York City. Corning Tower. And therein hangs a tale. In weak, shaky handwriting from his Boston hospital bed two months before his death, Mayor Corning took notes from his stalwart assistant Bill Keefe regarding negotiations for naming the South Mall's tallest building. Corning's notes: "Gov. [Cuomo] talking with group. What are we going to do for Erastus? Dick [Conners] said Corning was tall – why not the Tower? McNulty also mentioned it. Cuomo looked out window at Tower, thinking . . . Tall in negotiations. Consulted Betty first. Conners sponsor in Assembly and

Anderson in Senate. Chap. 6, Laws of 1983. Passed Mar. 14 and signed the 15th." In an interview, Gov. Mario M. Cuomo recounted these details. "The Mall was very important to Mayor Corning and we did a lot of work to get the bill exactly right," Cuomo said. "The mayor regarded the Mall as his triumph. Some others saw it as Rocky's triumph, but that didn't matter. We worked it out with Polly Noonan and Bill Keefe and Conners and McNulty in the Assembly and Andy [Senate Majority Leader Warren M. Anderson, a Republican] in the Senate."

Hospitalized in Boston with chronic lung ailments and other complications, Corning was too ill to attend Cuomo's bill signing ceremony on March 15, 1983 in the governor's ceremonial Red Room on the second floor of the Capitol. Corning's wife, Betty, attended, as did Senate Majority Leader Anderson (R-Binghamton), Senate Minority Leader Manfred Ohrenstein (D-Manhattan), Assembly Speaker Stanley Fink (D-Brooklyn), Corning pal Judge John Holt-Harris Jr., Albany corporation counsel Vincent McArdle and Bill Keefe. An unusual guest who did not normally attend such public events was Cuomo's wife, Matilda, who had befriended both Erastus and Betty Corning. After signing the bill into law, officially naming the building Corning Tower, Cuomo said: "Mayor Corning's place as an institution is not just in the City of Albany but in the entire State of New York. Mayor Corning literally towers above us all now." Cuomo continued: "Mayor Corning has devoted his entire adult life to the people of this state, to public service. His dedication, his devotion to this city and state that he so loves, have blazed a trail which those of us in public service would do well to follow. Yet his greatest contributions have been not merely as mayor, but as a person. He is indeed a man of strength, stature, and splendid style. We salute and pay tribute to a very special man, a model public servant." Office of General Services Commissioner John C. Egan said: "It is fitting, indeed, that this outstanding structure, from which can be seen all parts of Albany, be renamed for the outstanding public servant who has for so long served all the people of Albany."

The Corning Tower is common usage today to designate the tallest building of the Plaza. One rarely hears Rockefeller's name attached to the epic building project anymore, other than as an off-color remark – Rocky's last erection. There was a fitting symmetry to the fact that the tower's observation deck, where more than 250,000 visitors gaze down on Albany each year, is located on the forty-second floor – one floor for each year Corning was mayor. From boyhood sailing and sporting competitions in

Maine to the marble monolith of the largest state government complex ever built in this country, even as he lay dying in Boston while the governor signed Corning Tower into law, Albany's mayor for life had topped his old rival Rockefeller once more. In death, as in life, it would seem, Corning had "Nelson by the balls," as he liked to say. Corning will retain that grip until the year 2004, when Albany County's term as the state's landlord is up and the state retains official ownership of the South Mall. That official deed transfer will come after the city and county received tens of millions of dollars in payments from the state in lieu of lost taxes. That transition year, 2004, will be about the time that the deteriorating mammoth marble complex will require untold millions of dollars in renovations, no doubt – paid for by state money, not city or county coffers. And the spirit of the rascally Erastus will be smirking atop Corning Tower, knowing he beat Nelson at the political game in perpetuity.

Chapter 14:

Long on Years, Short on Accomplishments:
The Record of Mayor Corning

"The political story of Erastus Corning is a tragedy in a way,
for it's the story of an unusually personable and able
politician – one of the most knowledgeable public officials
in the state in the field of municipal government – who
apparently chose to settle for the path of mediocrity in
office and subservience to a backward-looking political
machine, instead of the more exciting and productive
possibility of using all his knowledge and skills to the
fullest. The tragedy of Erastus Corning and of the city,
therefore, is in what might have been."

Editorial in the Knickerbocker News, *November 3, 1977,*
when the paper chose not to endorse either Corning or
Republican mayoral candidate E. Michael Ruberti.

More than any other accomplishment, Erastus Corning 2nd
wanted to be remembered in the collective memory of Albany and in history books across the land for his longevity: The Longest-Tenured Mayor Of Any City In America. Corning enjoyed wearing that designation on his sleeve as a kind of walking epitaph in his final years, and hardly a mention was made of the mayor in the media without that lengthy modifier. Sadly, it came to be his *raison d'être*, as if quantity equaled quality. Corning himself seemed unable to articulate what his epoch as Albany's mayor had meant other than to measure it as if it were some large appliance for which simply functioning was enough. "Durable is the word," Corning once said to a toastmaster struggling to find the right adjective to describe his mayoral record of forty-two years, a mark likely never to be broken in United States electoral politics. With Corning's national recognition, however,

must come an equally intense scrutiny of his leadership. What did he accomplish during that long stretch of years he spent controlling the destiny of Albany?

When one reviews the corpus of Mayor Corning's record, it is difficult to find a pulse. No theme emerges from his long reign except for stability, a numb sameness year after year that ultimately amounted to stagnation and decline. Corning was not a master builder for Albany as, say, Robert Moses was for New York City; the great public works projects in Albany must be credited largely to Gov. Nelson Rockefeller. Corning was not an inspirational or charismatic leader in the mold of President John F. Kennedy, either. Nor was the mayor a dramatic shaper of sweeping governmental changes in his Albany kingdom the way President Franklin D. Roosevelt and his New Deal were for the nation. Unlike most memorable elected officials, national and otherwise, Mayor Corning failed to outline and promote his own vision for a brighter tomorrow. The unspoken subtext of Mayor Corning's game plan, if ever there was one, revealed an implicit view that Albany was a city whose best days were behind it, rather than ahead of it. Corning, in keeping with O'Connell's political philosophy, ruled a backwards-looking administration that ran and won on the old verities of the Democratic machine: low taxes, marginal services, patronage rewards for loyalty to the Party, punishments for anyone who challenged the machine's manifesto.

The O'Connell-Corning organization swept into power in 1921 riding the popularity of reform. The Republican Barnes machine, which had reigned since 1899, had alienated Albanians with its anti-labor, anti-suffrage positions, through the mounting inflation caused by its policies, and by its handling of a divisive trolley strike. Voters turned against the Republicans further as a result of a coal scandal: a coal shipment worth $18,000 bought by the city failed to arrive at municipal buildings and yet free loads of coal were delivered to the homes of GOP officials. The O'Connell-Corning machine seized control by exploiting these misuses of power and by promising change. At first, it seemed, they kept their promises at City Hall with a responsive administration that listened to citizens who decried the condition of Albany's schools by building new school buildings and improving the formerly dismal high school graduation rates. Soon, though, as it dispensed patronage far and wide to solidify its control and awarded no-bid municipal contracts to friends of the machine at inflated costs, the reform-minded Democrats grew bloated and dysfunctional. Holding onto power was their obsession; improving the city became secondary. Eventually, the city's broken heart beat faintly if at all. Corning's lack of a blueprint for resuscitating Albany's moribund civic life, in a place where his family roots ran deep and proud, became painfully obvious. All things considered, the mayor for life left a legacy at City Hall of an EKG from a person whose heart has stopped beating. A flat line. There was nothing of the symphony in Corning's years in office, no movements or crescendos or grand finales. And, certainly, no surprises. The mayor hated surprises. Days melted into weeks into months into years into decades on Corning's watch without detectable change. All around him, the world experienced upheaval: wars were fought, great social movements were waged, economies rose and fell, vast cultural shifts occurred, technology expanded, generations were born and generations died. But Mayor Corning seemed immovable, monolithic, a permanent landmark on the Albany scene every bit as ageless as a granite monument, holding power during the tenures of seven Governors in Albany and nine Presidents in Washington, D.C. Corning answered every letter that arrived at his office in City Hall the very next day, offered an audience to all comers, and gave the illusion of action and progress when the city actually was constricted and choked off from civic vitality like clogged arteries that starve a pumping heart. Code blue. Corning's flatliner style must be seen in the context of political boss Dan O'Connell, however, and Dan's own hidebound methods and inherent contempt for all notions considered progressive. The machine's power rested in preserving the status quo and Corning's political record reflects his role as a product of machine politics and preserving its power at all costs.

In the final analysis, Mayor Corning helped create, and presided over, a city in decline, an Albany that would be unrecognizable to the first Erastus Corning, the empire builder. During the four decades that the railroad baron's great-grandson ruled Albany, the city was marked by deterioration and loss – the epic scale of Gov. Nelson Rockefeller's accomplishments aside. On Mayor Corning's watch, the city lost population; nearly 30,000 people, or slightly more than twenty percent of its residents, fled Albany. Downtown suffered a steady hemorrhage of commerce and civic vitality until its past vibrancy was gone, leaving only a husk of its former self. Albany's infrastructure – from streets and sidewalks to municipal buildings and parks – fell into severe disrepair from years of deferred maintenance and were sadly outdated and decrepit at the time of Corning's death. Municipal services in Albany, such as snow removal and garbage pickup, were shabby and inadequate and gave outsiders the impression of a city both politically corrupt and woefully unsophisticated. In objective terms, the draining away of population to the suburbs and loss of downtown business to large suburban malls was a trend cities all across America were experiencing along with Albany. But the other indictments fall squarely and personally on the shoulders of Corning and the Democratic machine. It has been said many times, and in many ways, including by Corning supporters, that his successor, Mayor Thomas M. Whalen III, did more in ten years to improve the quality of life in Albany than Mayor Corning managed to do in forty-two. A sad coda, indeed, to Corning's historic tenure, but an accurate assessment nonetheless.

As president of the Center Square Neighborhood Association and the city's leading homeowner activist, Harold Rubin became a nemesis to Mayor Corning by battling the machine's iron grip and lack of progressive policy. (Coincidentally, Rubin now owns the Albany row house where Mayor Corning was born, 156 Chestnut Street.) Rubin and a coalition of neighborhood groups fought the mayor on zoning ordinances, on lax building code enforcement, on the secretive budget process, on inadequate city services. Corning vigorously fought this grass-roots challenge to his authority and blocked their reasonable and valuable initiatives at every turn. "The horrible thing was that Mayor Corning was brilliant and knew the city better than anybody else and yet he let Albany go down the tubes," Rubin said. "That's inexcusable. Corning had the opportunity to do wonderful things for his city and yet he didn't do it. He had the ability and the power and he did not exercise it for the long-term good of the city."

"Basically, Corning was holding the fort together and making sure it was no worse from when he came in," said Paul Bray, son of the city's long-time school superintendent under Corning. Bray is a state legislative bill drafter and urban planning scholar who founded Albany Roundtable, a series of lectures on urbanism. "Corning wasn't worried about creating a better tomorrow. It was a little bit like Eastern European Communism. Let it be and don't intervene, don't anticipate crises, remain passive and just maintain the status quo."

Even diehard Democrats who idolized Corning, including State Assemblyman John McEneny, failed to compile a sizable list of major concrete Corning achievements. McEneny started out with the South Mall financing deal and then paused, searching for something definitively positive Corning could claim as his own. "He kept the city calm during the racial unrest of the '60s, he saw the need for regional planning, he protected the environment and he brought dignity to the office," McEneny said. "I don't think you can underestimate that notion of dignity. There was a need for the mayor to be a strong and intelligent person, because the office of mayor had decayed in a lot of cities. Corning brought prestige and stability to Albany. In many cities, the job of mayor was downgraded, but not in Albany under Corning." Another politician who considered Corning a mentor was Gov. Mario M. Cuomo. "Mayor Corning was one of the greatest mayors this country has ever had because he was gifted by God with a very special mind," Cuomo said. "He was smarter than everyone around him. He was well-educated by his experience. He'd been around forever in this town and knew everything about it. His absolute iron-handedness was a great, great asset. He sought to control things and was undeviating in his rule. He was boss and did everything his way. Period. That makes for efficiency. It may occasionally make for great unfairness, too. I wish I could have run the state the way he ran the city."

Ivan Steen, a State University of New York at Albany history professor, who wrote scholarly articles on the mayor and began an oral history project on the Corning years just before the mayor's death, recalled someone trying to pin down the mayor on the matter of his legacy during an appearance at the Albany Institute of History & Art. "What's your best accomplishment as mayor?" an audience member asked Corning. The mayor paused, apparently deep in thought, and then replied, "Cleaning up City Hall. It hadn't been washed in a long while." His answer brought down the house, of course, but it danced around the question. There he went again, Corning the artful dodger, forever dodging hard truths with humor, satire or cynicism. Maybe Corning's record was as puzzling as the Gertrude Stein image of emptiness: When you delved into it, there was no there there.

Within the enigmatic bundle of contradictions that comprised the cult of personality possessed by Mayor Corning, only on his deathbed did the man himself, and not the persona Albany's citizenry had created, allow a glimmer of self-criticism and begin to admit fundamental failings of the dictatorial political machine that had produced him. It was too little, too late, this professed desire to change to a more open and democratic form of government. He died before he could prove if he, machine Democrat, really had experienced a democratic conversion. Corning's politics and those of the machine were not a representative democracy but, in the phrase that has stuck with Albanians, represented "a benign dictatorship." Benign by whose measure? Another pet term used freely by O'Connell and others in his employ was "honest graft." Honest compared with what? Perhaps Dan and Erastus and their underlings did not loot the city blind in the method of Tweed and Tammany Hall. Or, maybe the mayor and the Party chairman did not build themselves mansions and ride in limousines in the manner of Boston's Curley. Dan O'Connell once showed Judge John Holt-Harris the spectacular view from his summer home on the Helderberg escarpment overlooking Albany, with a vista that stretched as far as the eye could see and said: "You know – they say that's the city I looted. I'll tell you: That's the city I loved." That's beside the point. With absolute control over the city for so long, what did Dan and Erastus accomplish on the matter of improving Albany and bettering the lives of its people? The answer is buried in the irrefutable details of the mayor's public deeds, regardless of the rhetoric and demagoguery that accompanied them. On that score, Mayor Corning himself recognized the shortcomings and lack of a far-reaching vision for which he must be held accountable. In his desk at City Hall, the mayor kept this quotation about politics from Andrew Oliver, an eighteenth-century Boston political leader so unpopular he was hanged in effigy and his house destroyed by an angry mob:

> Politics is the most hazardous of all professions. There is no other in which a man can hope to do so much good to his fellow creatures – and neither is there any in which, by a mere loss of nerve, he may do as widespread harm. There is not another in which he may so easily lose his own soul, nor is there another in which a positive and strict veracity is so difficult. But danger is the inseparable companion of honor. With all its temptations and degradation that beset it, politics is still the noblest career any man can choose.

Mayor Corning did not lose his soul right away in politics; he needed the full forty-two years to work on that. "Corning Wins In Landslide" was the banner headline in the *Times Union* on Wednesday, November 5, 1941, the morning after Corning was elected to his first term as mayor with a plurality of 46,469 votes over Republican Benjamin R. Hoff. "The most smashing victory in Albany's history," according to the story, which made note of the parallel with his great-grandfather's election as mayor 107 years earlier. "I have always felt that Albany is the greatest city in the world and I shall be happy to contribute what I can toward the welfare and progress of that city which is so near and dear to me," the mayor-elect, just thirty-two, youngest in the history of the city, told reporters. "Twenty or thirty years ago, Albany was a city that was stagnating. No improvements were being made. Albany's streets were in disrepair and its parks and schools were in bad condition. In the last twenty years Albany has been a better city each year than it was the year before because of the Democratic party." Corning took office three weeks after the cataclysmic surprise attack by the Japanese at Pearl Harbor, plunging the United States into World War II. Corning rode into City Hall on a wave of support. More than 6,000 people greeted Albany's 70th chief executive during swearing-in ceremonies on New Year's Day, 1942. One of the first things Corning took credit for as mayor – and an issue he and the other Democratic machine candidates campaigned on for decades – was the quality of Albany's drinking water. Before the O'Connell-Corning machine seized power in 1921, Albany drew its drinking water from the Hudson River. The machine built the Basic and Alcove reservoirs and relocated the water supply away from the pollutants of the Hudson to a pristine rural corner of Albany County. While a major public works project, the reservoir was a necessary and expected public health improvement rather than a benchmark of Democratic leadership. Albany's water supply was an enduring political touchstone for the machine that carried weight with voters, beginning with Corning's great-grandfather, a four-term mayor of Albany, who created the city's first municipal water supply in the mid-1800s with a reservoir at Six-Mile Waterworks and a brick culvert carrying water downtown. Erastus Corning 2nd exerted dictatorial control over the modern-day water supply, ranging from using Alcove Reservoir as his own private fishing pond to turning aside several attempts to fluoridate Albany's water. The mayor, an anti-fluoridation fanatic, broke rank with Gov. Hugh Carey's health program for fluoridating municipal water adopted by twenty-three cities across the state. "It is forced medication and I won't have it," Corning said in defying the Governor's initiative. "There are plenty of other ways to get fluorides without forcing it down people." Albany was the largest city in the state without fluoridated water when Carey initiated the plan in 1975. Cavities or not, Corning stood his ground and kept fluoride out of the water as long as he was mayor. To this day, Albany does not fluoridate its water.

In the early months of 1942, Corning was a compelling figure who led the wartime effort by personal action. He directed from the top of the Alfred E. Smith Building a ten-minute trial of night defense against air raids in which Albany staged the most successful practice blackout of the entire Northeast. Corning led the drive to raise donations totaling 90,000 dimes, or $9,000, in Albany's March of Dimes. He organized the MacArthur Day events, led thousands in a parade to Bleecker Stadium for "I Am An American" Day and was sworn in as director of civilian protection of the Albany War Council. There seemed hardly enough time to accomplish what needed to be done in the city, but his forward momentum was interrupted by the draft notice and his departure for Army service on April 13, 1944. After his return from World War II and an overwhelming re-election to a second term in the 1945 election, Corning displayed a restlessness and desire to launch new projects in Albany. He lost no time in laying out an ambitious post-war construction agenda for the city. "I am proud to be an American," Corning told an audience of downtown businessmen on October 1, 1945. "My military service has given me a broader and deeper understanding of my American citizenship." In the spring of 1946, dozens of streets were being re-paved, the Albany County Airport was being expanded, Swinburne Park was getting a new swimming pool. The city's transportation system was receiving an overhaul and Corning made a promise that trolleys would be gone from all of Albany's streets within four years – a time schedule the mayor could not keep. In addition, the biggest alteration to the face of the riverfront city lay ahead. In the decade following the end of World War II, engineers began design work on the arterial highway, Interstate Route 787, a plan applauded by Corning. By the time the highway was completed, Albany would be cut off from the Hudson River, the ties of its history severed, a gateway for its future development barricaded. With the pretzel illogic of multiple ribbons of asphalt thrown up between downtown and the mighty Hudson, Albany would be a riverfront city no more.

One of the mayor's most egregious shortcomings must be considered his lack of vision regarding the Hudson River – the most important commercial, cultural and scenic resource in the region – which Corning managed to tear away from the fabric of city life. It was a curious failure in the mayor's record, considering that Corning chaired the Hudson River Valley Commission in the late-1930s and was an ardent supporter of the state's Pure Waters Act in the late-1960s. Instead, Corning's legendary kingly authority was nowhere in evidence beginning in the 1950s when federal transportation authorities cut the city off from its river with construction of Interstate 787. Between downtown and the shores of the Hudson, Albany was left with a forbidding six-lane swath of concrete with metal guardrails and arterial eyesores comprising several unruly nests of on-ramps, off-ramps and merging lanes. "That was a bad plan in the first place," city planner Dick Patrick said. "The mayor wasted a lot of money trying to find solutions to the city being cut off from the river after the fact and there is none. The South Mall just made it worse because that was built without any idea how traffic would circulate around it."

These highway abominations could have been avoided with better planning and political will. Albany was a river town and its whole *raison d'être* was the Hudson, but where was Mayor Corning when I-787 was allowed to sever those historical ties? To excuse Corning by saying he couldn't stop a federal highway project is naive; the mayor certainly could have offered an alternative route away from the river and finessed his position. Corning had the power to turn night into day in his fiefdom and he let the feds come in and force Albany to turn its back on the Hudson River. Many residents of Albany have expressed these sentiments: Shame on you, Erastus. Shame.

Corning deflected questions throughout his career concerning this monumental dereliction of his mayoral duties. The mayor made a few half-hearted stabs at correcting the abomination of I-787, but it was generally political lip-service to answer his critics and always a case of too little, too late. For instance, Corning in 1969 pried loose city funds to hire the planning firm of Candeub, Fleissig and Associates to develop a riverfront development project. Corning said he couldn't find the money to fund his own project and the plan was never implemented. Five years later, in 1974, Republican state leaders, including Gov. Malcolm Wilson, and State Transportation Commissioner Raymond Shuler, took the planning firm's recommendations and said they were going to carry the ball that Corning had dropped. Corning had to eat political humble pie as he looked on at a Capitol press conference on November 25, 1974. Wilson and Shuler took the words right out of the mayor's mouth and announced the creation of a seventeen-acre recreational and commercial development along Albany's stretch of riverfront to be known as Fort Orange Village. The village was to be built on state and city land from the rear of the D&H Plaza to the Clinton Square interchange of Interstate 787. Plans called for a hotel, dining facilities and shops with a public marina, playgrounds, bicycle and pedestrian paths, picnic areas and other attractions. But by then, Wilson was a lame duck Governor, swept aside by Hugh Carey, who dropped Fort Orange Village when state money got tight. Ultimately, the grand scope of Fort Orange Village was reduced to a modest project worth $1.9 million, mostly federal money, which bought a narrow paved bike trail, a few picnic tables and benches and a couple of pieces of playground equipment. Against the backdrop of the colossal failure of I-787, the project – officially dedicated in 1979 as the Erastus Corning II Riverfront Preserve, a seventieth birthday present for Corning – looked like a paltry and pathetic backhanded dismissal by the mayor who could have done, and should have done, so much more for his city when it came to the Hudson River. A decade after the mayor died, Corning Preserve often looked like a forlorn, seedy place you wouldn't want to walk through at night. Homeless people, often drunk and unruly, congregate in its shadowy pockets and often sleep in a tumble-down brick structure on the river's edge. Several rapes have been reported there. The preserve gets some legitimate use during the day as a boat launch – the Albany Rowing Club stores its crew shells there – and from joggers, inline skaters, bicyclists and walkers. But there's no focal point, no attractions, nothing to eat, save for a greasy spoon hot dog and fast food vendor who parks a truck there on summer weekends. In 1997, the scene improved when a barge called The Riverfront Bar & Grill opened. But so much for Fort Orange Village.

Corning's missed opportunity on riverfront development is emblematic of his political approach to many improvement projects only dreamed about in Albany. Residents would shoot for the moon and Corning would, instead, give them a dim star and make them believe that they had just received the universe. The muscularity and vibrancy of Corning's post-war administration quickly dissipated into a dull, gray eminence. In his campaign for re-election in 1953, Corning's message was no longer one of the gung-ho master builder embarking on a half-dozen major initiatives at once. Instead, he had no agenda other than the status quo, which is synonymous with machine politics. "I will stand for re-election on the principle of careful, prudent and frugal government," he said in a campaign speech on September 29, 1953. "There must be as small a burden of local taxes as possible." The only specific accomplishment he cited in his previous two terms was the Albany water supply.

During what should have been the glory days for Mayor Corning, the late-1950s and early-1960s – a prosperous post-war era when other cities were tapping into a torrent of federal aid for urban renewal with the giddiness of children opening presents on Christmas morning – there was nothing under the tree for Albany. No money for downtown revitalization. No funds for public housing projects. Nothing for much-needed infrastructure improvements. It was a well-known political decision that Dan O'Connell would not accept urban renewal money from Washington, since he did not want to be beholden to anyone, not even the federal government. Period. End of discussion. It was an issue of refusing to relinquish an ounce of control. Albany was O'Connell's and Corning's turf and nobody from outside was going to put conditions on how jobs were filled there, what contractors received bids, where and when the renovations could be made. This hard-line position of isolationism on the part of the machine was a curse economically – but a strange blessing unintentionally in architectural terms. While downtown went to seed and plans for large-scale construction and improvements came to a virtual standstill in Albany without federal money, pockets of the city's historic housing stock escaped the wrecking ball. That doesn't account for the loss of some historic structures amid the decrepit rowhouses destroyed to make room for the South Mall, however, an architectural devastation of which Corning was a prime player. Corning wasn't particularly proud to have accounted for the irony that Albany's old buildings were saved because the machine was too hard-headed and hungry for total control to accept urban renewal money. It was the same mindset that blocked major retailers, such as Sears and Macy's, who initially wanted to build their department stores downtown. Sears and Macy's encountered so much interference from Corning and the machine that they opted instead to open in a suburban mall, Colonie Center.

A major paranoia on the part of O'Connell and Corning was fear of any challenge to their autonomy, be it the federal government, corporations or the state. Gov. Nelson A. Rockefeller's obsession to immortalize himself across Albany's skyline and his display of dazzling construction projects forced Corning and his cronies to come up with a few building initiatives to tout as their own. One such public relations ploy in the 1960s was Corning's downtown parking garage that the mayor said would utilize the natural slope between North Pearl Street and Broadway. Heralded as an antidote to Albany's chronic parking shortages, the mayor promised several levels of covered parking with space for 7,000 cars that would solve the parking crunch and lure shoppers to struggling downtown merchants. Corning talked up the $40 million mega-garage for months and got a lot of press and mileage from municipal leaders. "The garage will bring downtown back – and bring it back with bells on," Corning promised. Some years later, the mayor dropped the plan without explanation. The garage became a mirage. There was no bell ringing, only a hollow sound and a sour taste left in the mouth. There were other will-o-the-wisp projects from Corning. Who can forget his plan for a moving sidewalk that would shuttle a flood of shoppers to stores up and down State Street? The mayor's celebrated "people mover" turned out to be a fiction, too.

Meanwhile, Rockefeller dealt in fact, not only promising major economic development projects for Albany, but delivering on those promises. In fact, many political observers make the case that Rockefeller could claim far more concrete accomplishments for Albany in fourteen years from the Governor's Mansion than Mayor Corning did during forty-two years in City Hall. For example, Rockefeller transformed the city's economy and the face of its architecture with his construction in the 1960s of the new campus for the State University of New York at Albany. Replacing an archaic and tiny downtown campus for the original State College for Teachers, Rockefeller chose a striking modernistic design by Edward Durrell Stone that has gained national attention. The State University of New York at Albany brings more than 16,000 students, renowned researchers, international academic conferences and tens of millions of dollars in economic benefit to the city each year. Corning had almost nothing to do with the university construction, since he had no leverage with which to coerce Rockefeller to kowtow to him. If Corning couldn't have total control, he often withheld cooperation. In the 1970s, completion of the city's only major hotel downtown, The Albany Hilton – now the Albany Omni, improved from its struggling days – got its genesis from the governor because of his desire to provide his guests acceptable accommodations. For his part, Corning did push for demolition of the old Ten Eyck Hotel to make room for the new Hilton, got his close friend the developer Lew Swyer involved and convinced Rockefeller to include office and retail space along North Pearl Street as part of the design. In the end, though, it was the Governor and not the mayor who made the Hilton fly, with funding from the State Urban Development Corporation.

There were so many promises left unfulfilled on the part of the mayor. Corning's architectural obsession was the hulking shell of the derelict Union Station, where the last train stopped on December 29, 1968, leaving the structure abandoned, and slowly deteriorating into a huge eyesore for downtown Albany. Corning's attachment to its grand granite edifice was partly due to his sincere interest in preserving the city's historic architecture, but he also had an emotional connection since it had been part of the New York Central Railroad, founded by Corning's great-grandfather. Corning had the will to save Union Station, but not the means. Rockefeller stepped in and acquired the sagging structure with state money, but it sat forlorn for more than a decade, a magnet for ambitious ideas that never came to pass. Finally, after decades of failed attempts, Mayor Corning helped piece together the details that brought about the rebirth of Union Station, adaptively re-used as banking headquarters for Norstar (later acquired by Fleet). Although he worked energetically to save Union Station, Corning did not live to see the civic celebration surrounding the re-dedication of the graceful old depot as banking offices. If it were not for State officials, the station may have been lost forever. And then, of course, there was the South Mall, which brought an entirely new level of combat and collaboration between Rockefeller and Corning. From the State University of New York at Albany to the South Mall is not even an exhaustive list of what Rockefeller brought to Albany by wedding great personal wealth and ambition to the public works of state government. Corning possessed a similar kind of utter power, albeit on a smaller scale, but he used it to hold down and control the city in order to maintain its small-town, parochial sense of itself that gave the machine its authority. Think of what Albany might have looked like in 1997 without Rockefeller – a scary thought. "Governor Rockefeller was the best mayor Albany ever had," Albany County GOP chief Joseph C. Frangella quipped. Many who had watched the city declining in the shadow of the machine's lust for retaining power weren't laughing.

Many residents of the city, even machine loyalists who will speak their minds in meditative moments, agreed with Kennedy's assessment in *O Albany!* Kennedy wrote: "That Albany turnaround – from being an object of ridicule to being a city of quality – is a phenomenon attributable in large measure to one man, New York State's all-time master builder, Nelson Rockefeller." The press held the same view. In its editorial of November 30, 1965, the *Knickerbocker News* damned Mayor Corning with faint praise:

Let us say that the state led the way toward a new Albany with its construction of the campus site, the new State University, the mall and the arterial highway system. Let us say also that it was the first to translate plans into action. It has made the dirt fly. Governor Rockefeller's vision of a new Capital City has proven contagious with Mayor Corning. While the cynical might be inclined to view the administration's planning as nothing more than planning, even the cynical must sense in the mayor's answers to questions a willingness on the part of the administration to lead the city out of the morass into which it had allowed it to wander.

Aside from faulting Corning for a lackluster record in the realm of large public works projects, when it came to the small matters of municipal government, such as city parks, his efforts were deficient, too. Partly because of a brainwashed and co-opted citizenry, enfeebled by the patroon psychology that eroded any impulse toward protest, and an acquiescent press, Mayor Corning's demagoguery was accepted as gospel. For decades, the mayor took every public opportunity to expound upon how fortunate the city was to be graced with such lovely parks and the recreational opportunities they offered. As an example, Corning used such superlatives when he held a press conference and ribbon-cutting commemorating a new park in 1965 on South Allen Street a few blocks from St. Peter's Hospital and New Scotland Avenue. That "park" is a pathetic little patch cut out of a swampy gully that floods so badly each spring it is unusable for months. It consists of a couple of swings and a few rusty pieces of playground equipment, a site so unappealing that it is rarely used. It wasn't until 1968, after swallowing Corning's park praises blithely for decades, that the *Knickerbocker News* conducted a thorough investigation of Albany's park facilities and found that an oversight agency, The Council of Community Services, concluded that Albany was deficient by thirty-five acres in its parks and recreational land and failed to meet that group's minimal standards. Corning countered by dusting off his old plan to create a nature preserve and park along the Normanskill Creek between New Scotland Avenue and the Delaware Avenue bridge. Although the mayor promised it for more than thirty years, that Normanskill project never came to fruition. Another mirage.

A similar scenario of hollow promises littered the record of Mayor Corning when it came to basic municipal emergency services, such as flood control and snow removal that were both clearly inadequate. In the 1969 election, Republican candidate Albert Hartheimer directed public scrutiny for the first time toward such deficiencies, blaming Corning's foot-dragging on construction of new storm sewers for "the all-too-familiar scene of flooded streets, homes and parks after heavy rainstorms." The *Times Union* ran this headline: "Corning, 'Not God,' To Blame for Albany Flooding, Opponent Says." The mayor clipped and saved the headline. But the assault on Corning for not providing basic services required by inclement weather was not going to melt away like some April snowstorm. The city's dismal patchwork of snow removal, rife with political featherbedding, was a sloppy, loosely organized squadron of patronage jobs for any incompetent machine hack with a plow attached to his pickup truck.

Three years before Hartheimer's campaign, a column in the *Knickerbocker News* by executive editor Robert Fichenberg, brought this machine practice into sharp focus: "According to figures compiled by the non-partisan Citizens Public Expenditure Survey Inc., as of October, 1965, Albany had the highest number of city employees per 1,000 inhabitants in the state and it paid these employees the lowest salaries, by far, of any city. Albany municipal salaries are so miserable that experts who study such things say they're probably the lowest pay scales for any comparable city in the United States. The O'Connell machine loads the public payrolls with as many politically beholden people as it can and pays them wages so low most of them are eligible for War on Poverty aid. What this does for the efficiency of municipal services I leave to you." The practice of spreading around the patronage jobs may have cemented Democratic votes, but it made a horrible and dangerous mess of clearing away snow. The "Blizzard of '69" struck on December 29, dumping nearly three feet of snow on the city over the course of three days, crippling Albany and bringing the city to a virtual standstill. Corning was pilloried for unsatisfactory snow removal. Even the *New York Times* piled on and heaped criticism on Corning with a front-page story by Sydney Schanberg. "The snow and ice are still taken away by the same methods the city fathers used in centuries past – solar heat," Schanberg wrote. "There is a popular saying here: 'God brought the snow and God will take it away' – sometime around March or April." Corning fought back against Schanberg's sarcastic strike, confirming for those who still wondered that, indeed, Albany's mayor for life did not possess divine powers. "I know of no process of levitation that would raise parked cars on the streets so the city could take away the snow or sweep under them," Corning said. "The snow he [Schanberg] referred to was actually Gov. Rockefeller's snow."

But Corning's finger-pointing and deflecting blame onto the state as a way of masking the city's slipshod services had lost its political expediency. A *Times Union* editorial on December 30, 1969 expressed a new critical edge that would challenge Corning's smoke and mirrors long overlooked by the mayor's reassuring, paternalistic rhetoric. "He can make small accomplishments appear large," the paper said. "He can make the accomplishments of others appear to be his. One sometimes would be led to think the state's South Mall was being built by his administration. He makes plans appear to be realities . . . His faults are these: A party loyalty that he has permitted to limit his potentiality as mayor. An inclination to be a one-man city hall, in which even trivial decisions can be made nowhere but in his office." The micro-manager label, which would become an overarching criticism of Corning's administration, was being applied for the first time. And it stuck.

One perennial dilemma not even a vaunted control freak like Corning could bring under his command was a chronic shortage of parking in downtown Albany. In 1980, Corning reached for gimmicks that some considered as wacky as the mayor's plan for a "people mover" conveyor belt for State Street. Corning asked drivers to put cardboard clocks on their windshields to show when they had begun their free ninety-minute parking on Albany streets. Strictly on the honor system. Corning got the idea from a similar clock system used in Vienna, Austria. But downtown and Central Avenue merchants rejected the idea. It was the second consecutive parking scheme Corning proposed and had rebuffed. The mayor's pitch for a parking coupon plan borrowed from one used in Tel Aviv, Israel also was laughed out of town as a lame-brained idea. City-built and city-operated parking garages were the only serious solution, the merchants said, but Corning pleaded poverty and said there was no money for such large capital projects.

Who could argue? Corning was the only person who knew how much money the city of Albany had at its disposal and he craved the control such a dictatorial procedure provided. Corning, a brilliant mathematician, crowned himself a one-man budget division. He kept city finances handwritten in pencil on a single sheet of paper inside the breast pocket of his suit jacket. By 1980, when Albany was beginning to raise taxes to cover its mounting debts, this Corning routine of holding all municipal money matters close to his vest had worn thin and the newspapers mounted an all-out effort to pry open the budget process by publishing investigative articles and a relentless editorial attack. This editorial from the *Knickerbocker News* on November, 11, 1980 that likened Corning to Scarlet O'Hara in *Gone With The Wind* was indicative: "The problem is poor planning and a combination of falling revenues and extraneous money being used as a stopgap to plug financial holes . . . Which brings us to another concern: The lack of public scrutiny and input into the Albany budget. Mayor Corning presides over his city like a benevolent 19th-century father; how Papa spends his money is his business as long as he provides adequately for the kiddies under his roof."

The construction of the new Albany High School is an instructive example of Mayor Corning's failure as the city's administrator. The comedy of errors that this botched project became might have been funny as a piece of absurd theater, but millions of dollars of taxpayer money were at stake, to say nothing of the public trust and the education of the city's future leaders. The new Albany High School was supposed to open in the fall of 1968, but fell six years behind schedule and ballooned to four times the cost the mayor originally promised because of Corning's misuse of power and the inadequacy of his leadership. The $23.3-million high school boondoggle underscored rampant patronage in the Albany city school district and taxpayers paid a high price for that classic Corningism: "I like doing business with my friends." There were a lot of friends of the machine packing the school district payroll, including the architects originally hired to design the high school, whose alleged incompetence drove its cost millions over budget and caused the firm eventually to be forced off the job. "The ward leaders would come into the personnel department and ask for jobs for their people. That was no secret," said David Bray, superintendent of the Albany School District from 1975 to 1982. Corning broke with a long tradition of Protestant superintendents by appointing Bray, who was Jewish. Up until 1972, when a three-member school board of Corning cronies was appointed by the mayor, Bray recalled the mayor's power over the school district was total and absolute. And when Corning's power was challenged, he possessed the tenacity of one of Dan O'Connell's fighting cocks in the bloodsport. Albany was the only city in the entire state that didn't have an elected school board at the time. A broad-based, grass-roots effort of ordinary citizens began to complain and said the time for school reform was long overdue and they demanded that Corning open up the process with an elected school board. Corning made their simple request for a democratic system of governance sound like bomb-throwing anarchy. The machine's political paradigm, after all, more closely resembled Iron Curtain Eastern Europe at the time, and not the Eastern United States. But Corning was a relentless opponent to opening up the school board and blocked the grass-roots drive toward elections for years through a variety of underhanded power play tactics. The supreme cynicism of Corning shone through in his refusal to respond to the desire of his citizens, even as he gave the illusion of listening to constituent concerns by answering every call and letter immediately and maintaining an open-door policy at City Hall. That was political performance, though. The real Mayor Corning took the legal route, forcing the school board case all the way to the state's highest court, The Court of Appeals. The cost to the city in legal expenses and loss of faith of its citizens was high, another black mark on the record of Corning. A *Knickerbocker News* editorial on May 26, 1970 was blunt in its criticism: "The high school mess is the best argument yet presented for taking administration of the school system out of the hands of the politicians and placing it where it belongs, in the hands of an elected school board that knows at least enough to keep the public informed of what it is doing."

Even after the board was forced through state law to become an independently elected unit in 1972, Corning retained enormous control over the operation, Bray said. The mayor held power largely for power's sake, but he sometimes used his authority for purely altruistic purposes, Bray said, and offered this never-before-published anecdote as proof. In the early-1970s, Corning came up with his own plan to assist poor mentally retarded youngsters in the city schools. "I think we might be able to help these kids and improve their quality of life with early medical care, good nutrition and home health care," Corning told Bray. The mayor outlined the recommendations, adapted from Corning's lengthy discussions with pediatricians, State Health Department researchers, psychologists and nurses. Corning wanted Bray to chair the project, which included hiring a top-notch pediatric nurse to make house calls to these students' homes for early medical intervention. Bray also was charged with setting up a tracking mechanism to see if these children who worked with the nurse showed improvement. "This was a very progressive notion for its time and Mayor

Corning had devised it all himself," Bray said. "He had one mandate. He told me he wanted it kept strictly confidential. He said the fact that he was involved would make people think it was all political. I can tell you it was not." The pilot project got off the ground because Corning paid the nurse's salary out of his own pocket, about $25,000 annually, for two or three years. "The mayor never let that be known," Bray said. "It was never made public. Corning never got credit for the program, but it turned out to be very successful and we turned it over to the County and State Health departments after a few years." Such was the enigma of Mayor Corning, the sides of shadow and light, a leader capable of such private goodness for retarded children and such public obstinacy on the school board issue.

Early in the 1970s, concurrent with the school board brouhaha, Corning faced his most difficult challenge regarding city employees. The long-running labor feud between the city police and fire departments not only highlighted Corning's failings in labor relations, but it displayed Corning's willingness to sacrifice the public safety of his citizens on the altar of machine politics. It was a time-honored machine tactic to hire an exorbitant number of patronage employees for votes, but to pay them miserably low wages in order to hold down Albany's tax rate – a winning combination for the Democrats seven decades running. The strategy had sailed along smoothly from the 1920s through the 1960s, but then trouble arrived in the form of the city's fire and police personnel. Fed up with poor salaries and poor benefits, and unable to get Corning to the bargaining table, they voted in favor of union representation for the first time in 1970. Corning would not brook such effrontery; he was not about to see his absolute authority challenged by labor unions. The battle over unionization of the city's police and fire departments was among the most heated municipal issues of Corning's time in office, raging on for several years. The longer the issue went unresolved, the lower morale fell in these two critical public safety departments, and the retaliatory nature of the labor dispute created an unsafe and potentially dangerous situation in regard to response time to crimes and fires. The angry tenor of the struggle was set at the outset, when Corning refused on April 18, 1970 to recognize the Albany Permanent Professional Firefighters Association as the bargaining agent for the city's firemen. Corning was sending a message that public employee unions would not come to the city of Albany without a fight. Two days later, on April 20, a bomb threat to the mayor's home and car was called into the *Times Union*. A police search of Corning's car and both his houses, in

Albany and Glenmont, revealed no explosives. Although nobody overtly blamed the firemen for the bomb scare, at least not publicly, a line had been drawn in the streets: this was war. To the outside observer, the firefighters' main request for a $1,500 annual pay raise and reduction of required hours to a regular forty-hour weekly shift did not seem excessive, since in 1970 they were among the lowest paid in the state, earning just $7,500 annually for a forty-eight-hour work week with five years' experience. Corning considered the firefighters simply one more challenge to his authority at a critical juncture when he was facing threats to his power on several fronts: from a newly critical press, from reform-minded Republicans making inroads on the Democratic machine with election victories in the state Legislature, from citizen groups demanding competitive bidding and an elected school board.

A *Knickerbocker News* editorial on June 5, 1970 summarized the breadth of the negativity directed at Corning throughout the city:

> Recent events in Albany make it appropriate to give thought to what this Democratic administration of the city of Albany has proved itself capable of and, conversely, to consider the areas in which it has proved grossly incompetent. First, its capabilities. It has proved time and again its uncanny ability to win city elections. And that ends the listing of its capabilities. Second, the areas where it has proved incompetent. It has never learned how to plow snow. It doesn't know how to plan or build a school. It can't bring an urban redevelopment undertaking to fruition. It can't get state-assisted housing built. It can't operate the public housing it has in a decent fashion. It has proved its inability to provide leadership in sustaining the heart of the city, downtown. It has failed to give Albany a respectable image, one that would attract new business and new industry and new residents. It has ever been afflicted with procrastination and delay.

Meanwhile, Corning, unmoved by unfavorable public opinion, continued to block negotiations with the firefighters until a mediator with the Public Employment Relations Board (PERB) was called in. Before the fight was over, the firefighters had picketed Dan O'Connell's house on Whitehall Road and staged numerous demonstrations at City Hall and at events where Corning spoke. Rev. Joseph Romano, the firefighters' union organizer, said he was harassed by "machine thugs."

Corning was incapable of compromise, of cutting his losses on the labor issue, declaring victory and moving on. No matter how much suffering and damage his hard-line position caused, Corning would not concede an inch, even when he saw it was obvious the firefighters would prevail. In the final analysis, Corning and his stubbornness lost on all counts – although the city's residents lost more in a further erosion of public trust. The firefighters were unionized and they finally reached agreement on their contract on August 2, 1972 with a raise of $1,930 over two years, essentially what the firefighters sought since the outset of the acrimonious two-year battle with Corning; the settlement with the fire department cost the city about $650,000. That wouldn't be the end of Corning's bitter fight against the firefighters, though.

With the ink barely dry on the tentative firefighters' contract, still bitterly contested by the mayor, Corning waged another labor battle with the police department. The department's 335 patrolmen voted overwhelmingly to unionize as the Albany Police Officers Union in September of 1974, but Corning refused to recognize the new bargaining unit and threatened layoffs if the cops' demands required raising taxes. In a repeat of the firefighters' scenario, the standoff dragged on. In June of 1975, the police in retaliation began a parking ticket blitz job action that wreaked havoc with workers and merchants downtown. Mayor Corning's official vehicle was ticketed five times in three days for illegal parking in his usual spot at the circle in front of City Hall. Corning seethed, but paid the fines. A month later, the policemen were carrying signs and holding noisy demonstrations outside City Hall. One can easily imagine the decline in essential services to residents whom the police officers and firefighters were supposed to be protecting during their dispute with Corning, who was playing hardball with two bats. At the same time he was staring down the cops, Corning went to court in September of 1975 to overturn an arbitration award granting firefighters a twenty-percent salary hike – Corning's legal challenge being only the second time in the state's history that any mayor had fought an award granted under the Taylor Law. On September 24, 1975, the firefighters chanted "Scab! Scab! Scab!" at Mayor Corning, blocked his car and forced cancellation of the mayor's scheduled speech to a convention of state security officers. Corning lost in court when a unanimous decision by the Appellate Division upheld an arbitration award giving firefighters retroactive raises of nineteen percent, the end of four years without a pay hike. Corning earned the distinction of becoming the first person in the history of the New York State Firefighters Association to be officially "censured and condemned" at its annual meeting in the summer of 1976 for his protracted fight to block unionization of firefighters and the raises they won through arbitration.

As he grew more withdrawn at City Hall during the controversy, out of touch with his constituents, Corning patented the notion of a Teflon politician upon whom criticism seems never to stick, long before that image was used to describe President Ronald Reagan. Corning's supreme self-confidence as a politician was a key attribute to his success in the face of public excoriation, demonstrated by the mayor's agreeing in 1977 to a ninety-minute public inquisition by unionists, labor mediators and public employees – the very elements he had battled tooth and nail for the past eight years. "In a virtuoso performance of wit, charm and skillful dodging of some issues, the mayor gained several rounds of applause from the professional labor lawyers, negotiators and mediators and left unscathed," the *Knickerbocker News* reported. Finally, after many years of bitter labor strife, the police and firefighters got their raises in the spring of 1977, including $1.5 million in retroactive pay, although Corning did not officially sign the pacts – one last gob of spit in the face of the unions – until the fall of 1978.

The Teflon mayor could afford such contempt for due process because he faced no serious opposition. A statewide survey in 1978 showed that Albany led by huge margins every other city in New York in the percentage of Democrats enrolled, 78.4 percent of the total registration of 50,212 in Albany. Albany had only 2,399 enrolled Republicans, or 4.7 percent of the registered voters.

Republican Carl Touhey's near-upset of Corning in the 1973 election proved, however, that the citizenry was growing tired of empty rhetoric from the mayor. Touhey relentlessly attacked Corning's record and what he called "toying with the people of Albany" via the mayor's "litany of unkept promises." These Corning fictions included: a 1964 promise to reduce the city's $18 million indebtedness by one-third in the next decade (in reality, the city's indebtedness had risen to $72 million by 1973); a 1964 pledge to undertake a $50 million downtown renewal program (never materialized); a 1964 promise to begin construction of a new city water reservoir and to clean and modernize City Hall (both abandoned); a 1965 promise to build a new library for $1.25 million (long delayed, well over budget and inadequate).

There was no disputing the fact that Corning ran the longest and tightest one-man City Hall in the country, but his entrenched power caused many progressive ideas to die on the vine. The mayor killed several proposals to bring professional baseball to the city-owned Bleecker Stadium, for example, offering only empty explanations. Corning also rejected in 1974 a proposed $7 million sports arena downtown from Schenectady developer Wade Lupe on the site of the abandoned Union Station. Corning's only comment was that the construction timetable was "impossible and unrealistic" and he exercised his unilateral veto power. The bottom line on both baseball and the sports arena was that they weren't Corning's ideas, they weren't proposed by machine Democrats, and they couldn't claim credit. On the other hand, 1974 was the same year that Corning closed the deal on the joint city-state ANSWERS project, the waste recovery burn plant that generated heat for the Capitol, the South Mall and other nearby state buildings. This was the mayor's baby from the beginning, and he coddled the project from conception to completion. Seeming to solve several energy-related quandaries in one fell swoop, it sounded almost too good to be true, and it was. Corning was spared the ignominy of its closure after his death when the ANSWERS plant was shown to be polluting Albany's inner-city residents and shut down for good in 1995. ANSWERS was one of the mayor's proudest accomplishments, a project he held up as a shining example of the progressive leadership he showed during his historic tenure, and it will go down in history ultimately as a solid-waste energy recovery experiment gone awry.

Despite these obvious shortcomings, a major accomplishment Corning supporters point to in defense of the mayor's record is the fact that Albany managed to avoid most of the 1960s turmoil surrounding the civil rights movement. While other cities across America were burned and looted and irreparably damaged by the race riots of the 1960s, Albany remained a relative island of calm in a sea of racial strife. Through a reassuring, patrician personality and an iron grip on municipal affairs – coupled with a co-opting of high-profile black leaders through city appointments and political patronage – Corning was able to retain order in his city when angry, young, disenfranchised and enraged black men tore down cities elsewhere. However, even on this issue, Corning's record must be reviewed with scrutiny. On several occasions, Corning's relations with the black community – essentially two large ghettos, Arbor Hill and the South End – grew strained and broke down. One such moment of trouble occurred on

January 20, 1966, when Corning was being honored by pastors of black churches at a testimonial dinner marking his twenty-fifth year as mayor. Dozens of young black protesters picketed the dinner, criticizing Corning for a lack of physicians in Arbor Hill and the South End, "for rat-infested streets and roach-infested housing," for a lack of affordable apartments, for inferior inner-city schools, and for the refusal of machine leaders to accept federal money through Washington's War on Poverty program. "They use threats and fear tactics to keep Negroes in line and hand out their $5 bills in the slums for votes on Election Day," an unidentified protester told a *Times Union* reporter. The growing unrest in the black community didn't end there. On May 16, 1966, a group of activists from the South End blocked Corning from entering his driveway at his home on Corning Hill. The mayor sped off toward Albany without saying a word as the black people sang "We Shall Overcome" and carried signs that read "Erastus blast'us again" and "Cut the Corn Corning." A Bethlehem police officer arrived and the crowd dispersed. Corning maintained the charade of his bogus residency by saying they were at the wrong house; that he actually lived at his official residence of 116 South Lake Avenue in Albany. Nobody bought it, but the mayor stuck to the farce.

An ongoing and more pronounced sign of serious opposition to Corning's record on behalf of the city's poor black communities came on Election Day in 1966. Two dozen picketers from the militant black group, The Brothers, were arrested for demonstrations at polling places in Arbor Hill and the South End. The Brothers carried signs that read, "Don't sell your soul for $5." Corning drew criticism for ordering police to crack down on The Brothers; newspaper editorials labeled the arrests and arraignments "political bullying." The Brothers had other tactics up their sleeves to embarrass Corning. At a June 26, 1968 appreciation award ceremony in Arbor Hill honoring Corning, led by Homer Perkins and other black leaders, more than fifty placard-waving demonstrators disrupted Corning's speech and broke up the dinner by dumping jars of dead cockroaches on the stage. The protesters then stamped their feet and shouted "Uncle Tom" repeatedly when Perkins tried to speak. Corning said later: "The Negro has been moving forward in Albany for a long time and the question is one of degree."

Even while Corning was espousing sentiments for improving conditions in the black community, he was conducting his own J. Edgar Hooveresque surveillance of black activists, particularly the organizers of

The Brothers. Corning directed his own police department and State Police investigators to prepare for him a kind of spy file on each member of The Brothers. Corning kept in his personal records at City Hall mug shots, rap sheets, reports and surveillance information on the group's most active members, including Leon Van Dyke, Gordon Van Ness, Peter Jones, Robert Dobbs, Sam McDowell, Earl Thorpe, Leon Alfano Wood, John Joseph Rollins and James Pryor. Van Dyke, a founding member of The Brothers, recalled the genesis of the group that was the most militant and bothersome to Corning in the history of his mayoralty. Van Dyke grew up in Philadelphia, served in the Army in the early 1950s, came to Albany in 1960, worked at various restaurants as a cook, and then tried to get hired as a laborer on the South Mall construction. "I'd go down to the labor hall with a bunch of other black guys and we never got called," Van Dyke said. "Day after day we'd wait and all the white guys would get hired, but us black guys never did. The university and the South Mall were built by white hands. I organized a demonstration with pickets, we got some press coverage and that was the nucleus of The Brothers." The year was 1965 and Van Dyke and his band of black construction picketers began meeting in the South End. The core group consisted of fifteen or so black men, although as many as seventy-five people, including a few women, considered themselves members of The Brothers during the five years the group was active. The Brothers immediately aimed their sights on Corning as their main target. "Underneath that nice veneer Corning had, he was a bastard," Van Dyke said. "I believe Corning was a racist to the extent that he had no blacks in his administration. Whether he liked blacks or not personally, he didn't like us enough to give us a play in city politics. He might not have called us niggers to our faces, but he didn't have any respect for blacks, either."

The Brothers made their headquarters at Nebbies Shoe Shine Parlor at 170 North Pearl Street, where Van Dyke recalled meeting Nebraska Brace, who went on to win election as a maverick Democratic city alderman. "People were running numbers and playing cards. There was always a lot of action there," Van Dyke said. The storefront office was a focal point where national black leaders like Stokely Carmichael and Eldridge Cleaver stopped on their way through Albany. Van Dyke said The Brothers were continually harassed by the Albany police at Corning's urging. "The cops used to sit across the street from our office, taking pictures of who came and went, keeping an eye on us and they also tapped our phones," Van Dyke said. "The police harassed us, constantly threw us in jail on phony charges, kept us locked up on high bail and tried to break us up. Besides that, there was a real problem with police brutality against blacks in general. If you wandered out of the ghetto up beyond Bleecker Stadium, you could get your head taken off." The Brothers had bricks thrown through their office window, had their building sprayed with bullets from passing cars and their headquarters was routinely vandalized by graffiti and destruction of property. Several members of The Brothers were arrested during a 1969 State Street riot that temporarily brought downtown to a halt as police blockaded the rock-throwing fracas. "It was a big deal and very tense even though nobody got shot and there wasn't any burning and looting," Van Dyke recalled. "We went out into the street to try to calm down the situation and to get the kids to stop throwing rocks, but they arrested our guys anyway for inciting a riot. Same old crap from Corning's cops."

The Brothers had an agenda aside from pressuring Corning to adopt policies to improve conditions in the ghettos of Arbor Hill and the South End. They also demanded an end to police brutality, improvements in the schools, access to health care, city jobs, better representation in municipal government. In the final analysis, did their struggle for civil rights in Albany make a difference? Van Dyke said The Brothers at least demanded a voice for blacks in the public discourse, but actual gains their militancy achieved were less than inspiring. "Even though we didn't get everything we wanted, I still see The Brothers as heroes," he said. "They took a big risk, got thrown in jail a lot, hassled all the time and yet they kept fighting the good fight." A decade after The Brothers ended their most forceful acts of protest, little had changed. Brace, the maverick black alderman of Arbor Hill, again criticized machine policies toward minorities during the 1977 election. "Minorities in Albany had no political representation or power," Brace said then. "Minorities were systematically excluded from making decisions in government."

Corning's record on racial issues is a complex, contradictory one requiring close review. Two of the mayor's behind-the-scenes efforts generally unknown to the public are illustrative examples. The first involved Attorney General Janet Reno, a close personal friend of Corning's daughter, Bettina. Reno and Bettina were roommates at Cornell University, Reno was the bridesmaid at Bettina's wedding in Albany and Bettina later worked for the Attorney General in Washington, D.C. The Mayor Corning anecdote occurred when Reno was state Attorney General of Florida and is recounted in Paul Anderson's 1995 biography, *Janet Reno:*

Doing the Right Thing. Reno prosecuted the 1979 case of Arthur McDuffie, a black insurance executive, father of three and former Marine who died after being bludgeoned to death by white Miami police officers following a high-speed chase. McDuffie's murder ignited racial tensions and Miami was riddled by mob violence, looting and sniper fire for a week. Reno lost the trial against McDuffie's police killers and was labeled "anti-black." Reno apologized for trying the case badly, but the public insults and vilification continued with a relentless pressure. Reno's biographer wrote: "Friends and family rallied around her. She received a call from Erastus Corning II, the mayor of Albany and father of her Cornell roommate, Bettina Corning Dudley, who urged Reno to hang tough. He advised her to do the right thing, and she would survive." Corning's daughter said Reno returned the favor two years later with a similar call of support to the mayor, under siege for his unyielding position of allowing an all-white South African rugby team to play in Albany. "My father was many things, but he was not a racist. He didn't have a racist or bigoted bone in his body," his daughter said. "His openness was his greatest attribute. He was tolerant of everyone."

"I'll never forget how the mayor supported me in a very difficult time, and I tried to return the favor," Reno told me in a 1997 interview from the Attorney General's office. "I always looked up to Mayor Corning as a model elected official. He stuck to the work at hand and didn't jump ahead to the next job or office like so many politicians do."

Reno recalled meeting the mayor and his wife when they visited Bettina at Cornell and regularly took the two roommates to dinner at the Taughannock Inn. "The mayor told the most delightful stories that made us all laugh," Reno said. "The talk always came around to Albany and politics. And I remember the typewritten letters he sent Bettina at Cornell that contained bits of his political philosophy."

Another Corning action never made public was his championing and donation of several thousand dollars of his own money to bring about the publication of two autobiographies of black men. The first was the life story of a black minstrel singer the mayor had known since boyhood through his entertaining at Corning family functions, including at a 1926 New Year's Eve party and at the wedding of Eddie Corning, the mayor's brother, in 1950. The book's title was, *Tom Fletcher, 100 Years of the Negro in Show Business.* In the self-published book's acknowledgments, Fletcher thanked Corning for encouraging him to write down his memories and for donating the money that made the volume possible. The second was another small, self-published book on the life of a civic leader in Albany's black community, Edward Frasier Kennell. Corning shepherded the project and spoke at a memorial service for Kennell at Arbor Hill Community Center: "Our only safeguard against forgetting the accomplishments of Eddie Kennell is to publish an account of his life and times," Mayor Corning said. "Otherwise, he will have left nothing more than footprints on the sands of time, footprints easily washed away and lost forever." Corning was praised in the Kennell book's acknowledgments as catalyst for the publication, both conceptually and financially. Corning's support of those biographies of black men might be considered alongside charges by The Brothers and other black groups in Albany that the mayor's policies were racist and that he himself did little to overturn discriminatory practices, despite his power to do so.

Amid this conflicting view of Corning's record on the issue of racial equality, a singular event near the end of his career (and life) threatened to tear apart the city along lines of race. The 1981 rugby match in Albany by the South African rugby team, the Springboks, grew into one of the most difficult personal and moral dilemmas Corning faced during his decades as mayor. Because of apartheid, the official South African policy of racial segregation, the rugby match quickly exploded into a bitter, racially charged debate in Albany marked by demonstrations and lawsuits. The city was thrown into turmoil and into the glare of an unwanted national controversy. Other cities across the United States had banned the Springboks as representatives of an apartheid country; only Erastus Corning 2nd, mayor of Albany, was going against the national and international climate and allowing them to play in his city.

At the time, in 1981, few made the connection between the Springboks dispute and Mayor Corning's controversial decision in 1947 in which he denied the use of a city school for a concert by Paul Robeson, the black artist, scholar, civil rights champion and Communist sympathizer. The Robeson concert, which had been approved for Philip Livingston Junior High School in Albany, was later canceled by Corning because some citizens complained to the mayor about Robeson's Communist sympathies. Robeson also happened to be one of the earliest and most outspoken critics of South African apartheid. "That was thirty-four years ago and a person has a perfect right to change his philosophy," Corning told the *Times Union* in a September 18, 1981 article. "At that time I was just back from the war less than two years and you would have to look at the whole thing in the context of that time. Robeson's concert and speech was against the United States and the rugby match was not." Attorney Arthur Harvey called Corning's cancellation of the Robeson concert "a slur on the Negro people as a whole" in a 1947 newspaper article.

The Robeson affair stung Corning deeply and he was branded a racist by some in his hometown. Corning saved several file folders filled with letters and articles chronicling his Robeson decision, an action reported in the New York *Herald Tribune* on May 1, 1947: "A hastily-organized civil rights committee failed today to get Mayor Erastus Corning 2nd of Albany to retreat from his position of refusing to let Paul Robeson, Negro baritone, give a concert May 9 in the auditorium of Philip Livingston Junior High School. Mayor Corning told the civil rights committee he would have no objection if those sponsoring the Robeson concert were to hire an auditorium other than a public-school auditorium." The Associated Press wire service made it a national story, stirring up criticism aimed at Corning and Albany. The mayor was deluged with dozens of telegrams from artists, writers and advocates of free speech denouncing his decision. Many of the letters, which came from as far away as California, were angry screeds that labeled the mayor a racist. One letter came unsigned, mailed from New York City's Yale Club, with a special mark that signified it was from a member of Corning's secret society at Yale, Wolf's Head. "Dear Erastus: Please quit playing stupid Catholic politics. As you should know the Jesuits hate American democracy and will never help you politically, so don't truckle to Catholic bigotry."

Ultimately, State Supreme Court Justice Isadore Bookstein ordered that Robeson be allowed to sing in Albany with the proviso that he could not make a speech. "He may only sing in the high school and if he opens his mouth to start a speech, the Albany police have been authorized to stop the whole show," Corning said. The Robeson concert went off without incident. The New York *Daily News* praised the judge for striking down what it perceived as Corning's racism, and granting free speech a victory instead. "We'd like to ring up some applause for Justice Isadore Bookstein of the Albany, N.Y. Supreme Court," the May 8, 1947 editorial said. The Robeson concert and Springbok controversies troubled Corning perhaps more deeply than any other situations he encountered in his years as mayor. Both profoundly damaged Mayor Corning's reputation as a man of tolerance and diversity and left whispers about racist tendencies swirling around his legacy.

Meanwhile, on September 22, 1981, the Springboks' tour was bearing down on Albany for its scheduled match at the city-owned Bleecker Stadium like a juggernaut of mass destruction. The violence over the all-white team's link to apartheid in South Africa was erupting half a world away. In Wellington, New Zealand in July, the Springboks game went on despite widespread opposition and demonstrations. More than three hundred arrests were made and injuries were heavy, although a threatened sabotage plane crash into the crowded stadium of 27,000 people did not occur. The game in Hamilton, New Zealand was canceled after 5,000 demonstrators occupied the field and fought with fans and police in a mass riot. In Auckland, New Zealand, protesters fought police, slashed television lines and dropped flour bombs on the players from an aircraft that buzzed the stadium. At least fifty people were seriously injured.

Similar troubles and violence were predicted for Albany if Corning allowed the Springboks to play. Mayors in New York City, Chicago, Rochester and Los Angeles withdrew previously granted permission for the Springboks to play in their cities. A coalition group called the Capital District Committee Against Apartheid formed in Albany to organize protests against the Springboks match. The group turned up the heat on Corning as newspapers wrote strong editorials telling the mayor to cancel the game. The heads of six Albany religious denominations, including both the Catholic and Episcopal bishops of Albany, urged Corning to call it off. A statement from Catholic Bishop Howard Hubbard, Episcopal Bishop Wilbur Hogg and others said: "To dignify and to accept the South African rugby team on its own terms is to associate ourselves with racism, to reject our spiritual teachings and to forsake our historical memories. We urge Mayor Corning to revoke the permit for the rugby match."

At the height of the Springboks controversy, Mayor Corning was invited to appear on Ted Koppel's national newsmaker show, "Nightline." Corning didn't grasp the significance of the venue and secretary Thelma Dooley recalled the mayor's befuddlement. "He came in that morning and asked me, 'Thelma, who the hell is Ted Koppel?' But he said it like COE-pell. He mispronounced it. He obviously didn't know who Koppel was and hadn't seen the show."

The mayor later offered a classic Corningism during a news conference that brushed off the controversy and Koppel's interest: "I don't watch the show because it's past my bedtime." The press roared with laughter. Corning had given them their lead. And it put the lighthearted spin he desired in an effort to defuse the heated situation. In racial terms, it's difficult to fathom Corning's motives for allowing the Springboks to play. In part, he seemed out of touch and far removed from the groundswell of citizen anger and grass-roots social activism against apartheid. He also didn't seem to understand the sensitivity required of such an incendiary racial issue, attributable more to his sheltered, privileged upbringing than to any personal animosity toward black people. However, even though the mayor ascribed his actions entirely to the principle of upholding the First Amendment's right of free speech, his motives remained unclear and once more the enigma of Corning emerged.

Attorney Sarah Birn, co-chair of the McGovern presidential campaign with Corning in 1972, was running the Albany office of the New York Civil Liberties Union at the time of the Springboks' uproar. CNN, the cable news network, came to interview Birn at her Delmar home, but she did not reveal to the reporters that Mayor Corning had been privately calling her each morning for a bit of soul-searching. "He was genuinely upset and called me for long heart-to-heart talks," Birn said. "I think he needed some moral hand-holding. He said he was offended that his own Episcopal bishop and the Catholic bishop would imply that his position made him a racist. He said he was not a racist. He told me it was the most painful chapter in his life. Every day was bringing new pressures upon him. He couldn't come up with an ideal solution. He internalized the whole incident and said it made him very sad and his heart heavy."

Meanwhile, behind the scenes, machinations surrounding the FBI and the Springboks had the makings of a spy novel. The agent provocateur plant was Michael Kevin Fitzpatrick, an FBI informant who infiltrated the local anti-apartheid group and tried, without success, to turn the group away from its simple acts of civil disobedience such as picketing and a sit-in to sabotaging public utilities and a conspiracy of violence. Fitzpatrick's convoluted tale of snitching for the FBI in Albany in 1981 didn't come to light until 1995, when Fitzpatrick was discovered to be at the center of the alleged scheme by Malcolm X's daughter Qubilah Shabazz to assassinate Nation of Islam leader Louis Farrakhan.

Education professor Maggie Kirwin, now Dean of Education at The College of Saint Rose in Albany, was an active participant in the anti-apartheid group and met regularly in the Central Avenue apartment of organizer Vera Michelson. She recalled driving around Albany with an anti-apartheid sign on her car and being accosted. "Nigger Lover!" was the most common racial epithet hurled at Kirwin during those tense and dangerous days in 1981. In addition to angry public sentiment, the protesters had to endure the surveillance, intimidation and harassment tactics of Corning's police force. "The police followed us all the time, our phones were tapped, cops took pictures of us when we went to Vera's apartment, her apartment was broken into, many members in our group were arrested and it was all an FBI set-up," Kirwin said. "I'm reluctant to call Corning a racist because I didn't know him well personally. But I was appalled at the fact that Albany was going to be the only city in this country that allowed the game to be played. I blamed Mayor Corning for allowing that national disgrace, a slap in the face to every black person in the country."

Corning offered his most comprehensive public statement on his position regarding the Springboks' controversy in remarks he made at a news conference on August 25, 1981:

> The world-wide tour of the South African rugby team has brought far greater awareness and knowledge of apartheid than the total of all previous publicity ever. It has had a powerful effect, crystallizing understanding throughout the world and consequent outrage at its evils. I abhor everything about apartheid. Our Constitution guarantees an individual the right to publicly espouse an unpopular cause, and the same right to a number of individuals in peaceful assembly. For that reason, it is wrong to prohibit an individual or group from taking part in a public athletic event because of their beliefs or the policies of their government. There is a vast difference between a ban or prohibition and a boycott or peaceful demonstration. The permit for the use of Bleecker Stadium stays in full effect. Individuals are free to act as their conscience dictates, approve, watch or ignore the game, boycott it or demonstrate and protest peacefully.

Corning was unwavering in his position protecting First Amendment rights by allowing the Springboks to play in Albany. The mayor battled with Gov. Hugh Carey, a fellow Democrat, who tried to cancel the game on the grounds of "an imminent danger of riot." More than 10,000 angry demonstrators, including thousands bused up from New York City, were expected in Albany. The matter ended up in federal court before Senior

Judge James T. Foley of U.S. District Court, Northern District of New York. Lanny Walters, attorney for the Capital District Coalition Against Apartheid, called it "a constitutional case of mammoth proportions." At that point, Corning could have washed his hands of the matter and dropped the mess into Governor Carey's lap, or turned the case over to his lawyers. Instead, Corning himself went to Judge Foley's court. Lew Oliver, a civil rights and environmental attorney in Albany often at odds with the mayor, was working with William Kunstler in representing some of the anti-apartheid protesters and heard Corning's address to the judge. "Corning made an impassioned, impressive speech on behalf of apartheid," Oliver said. "That's the way I saw it. It was a personal commitment from Corning toward the racist policies of South Africa and he was seeing it through toward the end. It was one more instance of Corning playing the control freak and controlling everything." Although others saw it differently from Oliver, as yet another First Amendment speech, Corning's argument carried the day and Judge Foley ruled that the Springboks game could go on as scheduled. The protesters tried to stop the match at the last possible moment by a desperate plea to U.S. Supreme Court Justice Thurgood Marshall, but the nation's highest court would not hear the case.

On the night of the game, September 22, 1981, a wall of protesters chanted "One, two, three, four! Throw Corning out the door!" as they marched up Clinton Avenue from City Hall to Bleecker Stadium. The demonstrators numbered just 500, rather than the 10,000 that had been predicted. They walked beneath a canopy of umbrellas that offered little protection against a cold, driving rain that pounded the streets in sheets. The soggy protesters reached Bleecker Stadium and joined another 500 or so observers, bringing the total to about 1,000 people. Only two chartered buses arrived from New York City, not the dozens predicted, and the protesters' ranks were nearly outnumbered by hundreds of heavily armed police officers keeping a wary eye on the crowd outside the stadium. The low demonstrator turnout was blamed on the rainy weather. Corning joined city, state and federal law enforcement officials at a command center across from Bleecker Stadium, atop the roof of Central Towers apartments at 400 Central Avenue. Corning brought his close and longtime friend, Judge John Holt-Harris, and the new president of the Common Council, Thomas Whalen, whom some political observers thought Corning was grooming to be the next mayor. "Thank God it rained heavily that night," Whalen said. "If there wouldn't have been a torrential downpour, chances are there would have been a much bigger crowd and violence. Everybody was very concerned about what might happen. The police were on high alert. The mayor was anxious, but he also seemed confident that he had taken the right position. He never wavered in his position." A police officer assigned to crowd control told a *Knickerbocker News* reporter on the scene, "Every time they're afraid something big is going to happen in Albany, the mayor has a talk with the man upstairs, and then it either rains or it snows."

The game went off like clockwork amid tight security and the eighty-minute contest ended with the Springboks crushing the Colonials, an all-star team of the Eastern Rugby Union, by a score of 41-0. There were no major incidents reported and no injuries. "It went off without a hitch," a police officer said. The crowd quickly and peacefully dispersed after the game and, in all, nine people were taken into custody during the demonstrations, although none of the arrests were major – mostly minor drug possession charges brought against New York City residents. Police Court Judge Thomas Keegan dismissed the cases and told the defendants to "be in the car and get out of town by midnight, just like the Old West."

Afterwards, reporters tried to get a comment from Mayor Corning, the man who had made news around the world and somehow managed to avoid the riot so many had predicted. But Corning could not be found. At the start of the rugby match, he left the police command station atop the apartment building and was driven by his chauffeur a mile downtown to the Fort Orange Club, still men only and mostly white in 1981, where Corning, mayor for life, was ensconced in leather and oaken comfort, served a fine dinner by formally attired waiters, warmed by a fire and the slow burn of a double Dewar's on the rocks, safely out of the rain.

Chapter 15:

The Auction: Selling off the Memory of the Mayor

"It was upsetting to sell it all off, not for the things themselves, but more for the fact that it represented the end of my parents' life and the close of that chapter in our family's history."

Bettina Corning Dudley, the mayor's daughter, commenting on the auction.

"**N**ow, there's only one of these," auctioneer Dean Doin said, as he held aloft a shiny gold badge that looked like a police officer's shield. The badge bore the city seal and its blue lettering read, "Mayor. City of Albany. Erastus Corning 2nd." Although he rarely carried the badge in his pocket – Mayor Corning needed no introduction – and preferred instead to use his pant's pocket for something useful, like a pocketknife or compass, Corning laid claim to this shiny totem of political power longer than any other city mayor in the history of America. The family's shining legacy in business and politics had shifted to past tense, though, and the Corning's golden age had faded to a musty melancholy during the family's estate auction on New Year's Day, 1994. It was five months after the death of Betty Corning and a decade after the death of Erastus Corning 2nd.

Whispers filled the auction hall. There was something unsettling about watching the son watching the selling off of the mayor's prized personal possessions to the highest bidder. One of Albany's most beloved icons was being dismantled cuff link by cuff link, fedora by fedora, campaign button by campaign button, his wife's handmade tie by handmade tie. "It's all rather bizarre, isn't it?" mused Fred Cawley, historic preservationist and veteran auction goer, who considered the Corning antiques of mediocre quality for serious collectors. But Cawley, like so many others, had come here anyway to witness a macabre moment in Albany's political annals. The crowd joked, its mood buoyant, and treated the auction as a pleasant spectator sport as more than five hundred people packed into a space designed for perhaps one-third that many. All the seats were spoken for more than an hour before the first gavel banged, although little turf battles broke out between people saving seats for late arrivals and folks left standing, pressed four and five deep against side walls and in back.

The mayor's son, middle-aged, gone completely gray, bore an uncanny resemblance to his father, with that same aquiline nose, the deep-set, probing eyes, the high, handsome cheekbones and the gleam of an easy grin. Erastus Corning III, or Rasty, flashed the father's winning smile from the position of prominence where he posted himself – at the only entrance to the auction floor. Corning held a stack of his brochures for Corning Tours, his small business for which he led groups of tourists to Russia. As the hundreds of auction-goers – family friends, political cronies, collectors and the merely curious – filed into the auditorium, Erastus III smiled brightly and pressed one of his pamphlets upon them, and engaged in a bit of small talk if it was a person he recognized. "His experience, up-to-date knowledge, and contacts in Russia and Eastern Europe make him the ideal tour leader," Corning's brochure read. Then the auction began. To a Russian scholar, such as Erastus III, what transpired would be familiar terrain. A memory erased. A legacy sold off. Tear down the wall of Communism. Dismantle the Albany machine. Let the purge begin. Bye, bye Erastus 2nd.

"C'mon, what do I hear for the mayor's badge? Can someone start me off at $300?" The auctioneer Doin stoked the crowd, but he didn't need to, since an additional two hundred people who couldn't attend had left bids and other bidders were on telephones long-distance all afternoon bidding on treasures described in national antique trade newspaper advertisements. Fred Dicker, a *New York Post* Capitol correspondent, who once wrote about the Albany machine's corruption for the Albany *Times Union*, was in the bidding for the mayor's badge at $375, but Dicker soon dropped out as the price sailed past $400. There was back-and-forth battling as the price climbed higher. Finally, at $500, the ceiling had been reached. "Going once. Final call at $500. Going twice. Anyone else at $500 for the mayor's badge? Sold to #338."

The auctioneer's job was an easy one this afternoon. The mystique of the enigmatic eleven-term mayor and the myth of the urban political machine he controlled ensured intense interest, even for those nursing New Year's Eve hangovers, or for those who would rather be at home watching the college bowl games, but whose voyeurism proved stronger than their love of football.

Still, there was a strange sense of sport at work at the Albany Auction Gallery, located on River Road in Glenmont, a stone's throw from the fabled Corning Farm, where five generations of Corning glory in business and politics was drawing to a particularly un-aristocratic close. It was a distasteful thing to watch, in a way, not unlike the farm foreclosure auctions that swept the country like wildfire in the 1980s. The sterling Corning legacy as empire builders and railroad barons had come to this: putting the family heirlooms on the auction block and selling them to the highest bidder. There was an unspoken sub-text, with an element of Greek tragedy, that lurked just beneath the surface of the day's proceedings, but which few articulated – including media accounts of the auction – except in the whispers and muffled gossip passed behind auction programs. But there was something of tragedy's appeal, that evil pleasure in seeing the mighty broken and brought low that attracted hundreds to the Albany Auction Gallery.

Outside, temperatures struggled to nudge above freezing and several inches of snow blanketed the ground on New Year's Day, 1994, as the auction began. The gallery's small gravel parking lot had been plowed, but the cars kept coming and vehicles quickly overflowed into snowy, icy vacant lots on the other side of Route 32. Inside, it was stuffy and sweaty and the attendees spent the afternoon peeling off stifling woolen layers and trying to find a suitable place for their bulky winter coats. The auction began at one o'clock in the afternoon and continued for six hours, past dark, and still there was so much left to be sold it ran for two more days, January 15 and January 22. There were hundreds of lots as part of the Corning estate auction, including thousands of books sold by the boxful, and while the quantity was there, serious collectors were not impressed by the quality of the offerings.

"In terms of antiques, it's not a significant auction for us," Robert Meringolo, owner of the Albany Auction Gallery, said during a preview visit two days before the auction. "We don't expect it to top $250,000 in overall sales, but there is a lot of public interest just because these are items from Mayor Corning." While the Corning sale was just another auction among dozens Meringolo conducts each year, it divided Erastus III and his sister, Bettina, the couple's heirs. "The son was very unemotional about all this and was just interested in the bottom line," Meringolo said. "But the daughter was here for the planning stages and kind of broke down over selling it all. She was crying and very distraught. She didn't have the stomach to watch all her parents' things being sold off." Nearly a year after the auction, which she refused to attend, Bettina Corning Dudley struggled with an explanation for the public sale of family heirlooms. "Well, I can't speak for my brother, but my husband and I are of modest means," she began. "And what would I do with all those things? And even if I were to hold onto it for another generation, you can't hold onto it forever. All things must pass. Nothing is known of my grandfather [Edwin Corning] anymore, for instance."

Bettina Corning Dudley said both she and her brother, and their children, removed a few things they wanted from the estate prior to the auction. The mayor's daughter said she took some of her mother's jewelry and promptly put it in a safe deposit box. "I'll never wear it myself. It's for my kids," she said. And she took some of her father's books, particularly those on birds and natural history, a love of which he passed on to her. And she took a few pieces of furniture and representative silverware. And all the rest, hundreds and hundreds of items, going once . . . going twice . . . sold with a bang of the gavel. Gone forever. "Your heart wrenches," conceded Bettina Corning Dudley. "Maybe it was the wrong decision to sell off everything like that. I'll admit I felt uncomfortable with it. But you can't hold onto things forever."

Although there were no windows in the gallery where the Corning auction was taking place, I found myself gazing toward the southern wall and daydreaming about the Corning family's remarkable achievements in railroads, steel, politics and banking that put them atop the heap of the Albany aristocracy. In the seventh row, displaying that familiar Corning profile, Erastus III, fifth generation of his family in Albany, watched it all come to an end. Seated beside Corning was longtime family friend and director emeritus of the Albany Institute of History & Art, Norman Rice, keeper of Corning lore, expert on antiques and a reliable appraiser. Rice and Corning conferred quietly as the son wrote down the selling price of each item on a yellow legal pad. It was an arduous task as the auctioneer droned on and on, hour after hour, but Erastus III tracked the sales.

"I know people thought the whole auction was symbolic of me hating my father, but it was not," the son said two years after the auction. "It was no more symbolic than Jackie Onassis' things being sold at auction recently by her children. If I kept everything, I'd have had to build a new room on my house just for the strawberry china. What use do I have for all that? People also need to realize I felt nothing for my father. There was nothing there."

The irony of the auction scene was not lost on anyone with the slightest knowledge of Albany politics. Members of the Noonan family attended. The two strangely commingled families were never far apart in life either. Noonan Lane – a large parcel of land in Glenmont just over the Albany border where Polly and Peter Noonan and assorted offspring and relatives built numerous houses in a family compound – is located near Corning Hill, at the bottom of which sat the auction site of the Albany Auction Gallery.

Ironies abounded at the auction. Tammis Groft, curator of the Albany Institute of History & Art, which the Corning family supported in a substantial way for generations, was forced to bid along with the rest of the auction goers. Groft ended up shelling out $1,400 from the financially-strapped Institute – it had to trim its staff and reduce its hours later that year – for a watercolor of Albany's City Hall. It was painted in 1884 by Harry Finn, founder of the U.S. Watercolor Association. The painting hung in Corning's house. Groft opened up the Institute's checkbook on several other occasions that afternoon, too, paying $275 for a photo of Gov. Al Smith inscribed to the mayor's father, Edwin Corning, who was Smith's Lieutenant Governor in 1927-28. The Smith photo was discovered by the son buried amid the clutter of an attic in his parents' house. Groft also spent $2,000 to add to the Institute's collection a silver Tiffany bowl that was a wedding gift to the Cornings in 1932, inscribed with names of the thirteen ushers, Yale classmates and members of the same senior secret society as Corning, Wolf's Head. The bowl was identical to a wedding gift given to Corning's father, Edwin, and his wife Louise in 1908 from his father's fellow Wolf's Head members. "This is an important piece of Albany history," Meringolo told the crowd to heighten interest in the Tiffany bowl, as if they needed to be reminded of that fact. Everywhere they cared to look during the auction confirmed that. The bowl was an item one might have assumed the children of Erastus and Betty might have chosen to keep quietly in the family. It wasn't to be.

Instead, what would the exceedingly guarded, almost pathologically private Betty Corning, only recently buried, think of this public picking over the Corning carcass? The auctioneer pitched the personal selling points in a way that would have made Betty wither like a dying clematis.

"These were Betty Corning's mother's carved Philadelphia side chairs, which Betty placed in the foyer as the first thing you saw when you came to the Corning house," Doin the auctioneer gushed. The gambit worked. Bidding was brisk and the chairs sold for $750 apiece, but the pair was split up and went their separate ways to different buyers. More symbolism. "This is the silver tea set Betty used every morning for her breakfast," Doin said, before banging the gavel. Sold for $850. On and on it went like that. Every item told a story. The public humiliation of the jocular manner among the auction attendees would have caused a thousand deaths for reticent Betty Corning. When the three-carat emerald and platinum ring the mayor long ago bought for his wife went up for bid and sold for a lower-than-expected price of $2,900, Doin the auctioneer couldn't resist making a joke. "That's a great buy and it's sure going to make someone happy," Doin said, pausing for effect, rolling his eyes and making a face. "Or maybe not." On it went. Three afternoons of this sad spectacle before the hundreds of lots in the Corning estate were all sold off.

The auction took place five months after Betty Corning's death. It was only one day after the mayor's erstwhile and loyal assistant, Bill Keefe, had given the greatest gift one could have imagined for his old boss, a deeply personal and spiritual mass of remembrance for the mayor and Betty, that Erastus III was clearing out his parents' house with the auctioneers. The sentiment from the memorial service for the mayor and Betty Corning faded quickly. "I just can't imagine why he saved all this stuff," his exasperated son said, dwarfed by stacks of dozens of boxes. Several truckloads of furnishings and books already had been pulled out of the house in which Betty and Erastus had lived since 1932, the house where his parents had accumulated six decades of possessions. "It seems like he kept every padded envelope that ever came to the house, pieces of string too small even to tie a knot with," Erastus III said with a derisive shake of his head.

Corning had rented an industrial dumpster for throwaways and it was filling up with items such as piles of canned foodstuff that looked to be World War II-vintage, nearly rusted through now, but still stacked neatly in the basement. Even though the furnace had long ago been converted to oil, there was the coal bin, with some chunks of coal left, harkening back to the Democratic machine's halcyon days when they cemented their power throughout the Depression's devastation by promising, and delivering, a full coal bin to their loyal supporters. There were sentimental signposts at every turn in the house. No emotion registered on Erastus III's blank face.

When his attention was called to a height mark painted on a post in the basement – a time-honored tradition between father and son in the psychological dance of manhood and stature and measuring up – Erastus III merely offered a wordless shrug. He quickly moved past the white dab of paint and the inscription, "E.C. 1945" at about five-feet tall; Erastus III showed his father's tall height even at age twelve.

The son waded through his father's effects like some sort of emotional archaeologist, sifting and inspecting, trying to understand the man he said he hardly knew, a decade after his death now, the father he had never come to terms with in life. Erastus III looked baffled and a little embarrassed as he unearthed deeply personal possessions his father had saved – items such as the hand-embroidered ties, apparently never worn, that Betty had sewed for her husband, with scenes of Canada geese in flight, a trout rising to a fly. Erastus III seemed puzzled as he pulled down and discarded a large shelf fungus his father had collected on some long-ago ramblings through the woods and tacked up on the wall above his desk in what was called the "green room," a spare room outside his parents' bedroom that served as a study and Betty's library. The wall's accouterments also included assorted deer antlers, trophies from the mayor's lifelong love of hunting.

Downstairs, among the mayor's financial records and personal papers, was a small box of uncertain vintage containing what looked like some sort of antique golf balls. They were perfectly rounded and made up of bits of twigs and grasses and densely compacted loam. Erastus III displayed the curious objects as if they were valuable jewels and invited me to hold one. "Have you any idea what those are?" he asked me, clearly delighted at the mystery. I professed ignorance. "I didn't know either until I did some research. They're large twig balls that were coughed up by hawks or owls, something like cat hair balls." The son chuckled at his father's eccentricity, shook his head in puzzlement at the chosen talismans. "God knows when he found them. Maybe up in Maine when he was a boy. But they obviously were important to him. He saved them all these years."

So many nuances Erastus III hadn't known about Erastus 2nd. When he came across a rack of pipes, the son seemed surprised. "I only knew him to be a cigarette smoker, but I guess he was an occasional pipe smoker, too." More shrugs. So many gaps to try to fill in, much too late, by the son. He hardly paused at the photos of his father in adolescence, dressed as an adult, wearing stage makeup, and acting in a play. "That must have been from when he was at Groton," the son said. He had never been told by his father that the play was *Kathleen*, in which his father, then a Groton sixth-former, or senior, was cast as Johnny Blair, a Rhodes scholar from Milwaukee.

Near the drama photos in a living room hutch where the mayor stored papers and mementos particularly important to him was a period print of the Albany Iron Works where his great-grandfather, the first Erastus, had established the family fortune. Amid the same pile of ephemera was a *Life* magazine pictorial on cockfighting, the blood sport enjoyed by Cornings and O'Connells alike, the fight to the death that brought them together as a Democratic political machine in the first place. Layer after layer Erastus III peeled away, in the manner of Peer Gynt, but the whole of his enigmatic father's many parts never seemed to reveal itself fully to the son. "This is very strange for me and seems almost unreal," Erastus III said in a rare moment of exposure of his heart. "I never really knew my father and now I'm going through all his things, getting ready to sell them." After a reflective pause, all the son offered was this: "This is a lesson to me in getting all my affairs and things in order and not leaving such a mess for my children," Corning said.

The mood and sentiments expressed just the day before at the mass of remembrance for his parents, which Erastus III and Bettina attended, sitting together in the front row, seemed a kind of fiction in the house of sadness and regret. "In their own particular way, Erastus and Elizabeth lived in God's way," Bishop David Ball of the Albany Episcopal diocese had said in his homily the day before the son cleared out his parent's house. The memorial service was held in Saint Mary's Roman Catholic Church. Even though the Cornings were Episcopalians and built All Saints Cathedral, Keefe figured the mayor – who was not a churchgoer – spent as much time at Saint Mary's just down the hill from City Hall on official mayoral funeral duty as he spent up the hill at the Episcopal cathedral. Might as well hold it at Saint Mary's for convenience sake and because it was Keefe's parish. Nearly two hundred people, including Gov. Mario M. Cuomo, seated in the front row across the aisle from Erastus III and Bettina, were in attendance, joining family friends, former employees of the mayor's, political cronies, machine hacks, even some enemies. Ball continued in his homily: "For all those long years of public service, Erastus served this city with determination and intelligence. Betty was less publicly visible, but no less important. She possessed her own inimitable style. We thank God for Erastus and Elizabeth Corning." Some months afterward, Ball said in an interview that he chose his words carefully during that homily, conceding that his task was not an easy one, and that he struggled to strike a balance between truth of what the marriage between Erastus and Betty had been versus the overarching goodness of their contributions to the city and church and elsewhere both individually and together.

Bishop Howard Hubbard, leader of the Albany Catholic diocese, celebrated the Mass with Ball in a nod to ecumenism and also to reflect the reality that while the mayor was Episcopalian, his forty-two years in City Hall were marked by a close and mutually beneficial alliance with the Catholic diocese. During the prayers of the faithful, read by Robert Roche, the mayor's attorney and a family friend, Roche paid homage to the work of Corning's other family members, too, for their efforts "to lighten the burdens of others." The sign of peace, a kind of spiritual communal handshake, required some uneasy reconciliation's that would have tickled the mayor's acute sense of irony. There was Senator Howard Nolan in the second row, directly behind Cuomo – Nolan the man who would be Albany's king and the only Democrat ever to mount a primary challenge against Corning, and Cuomo, the grateful governor who had Corning the king maker to thank for a decisive blessing early in his political career. As Nolan and Cuomo shook hands, so, too, did Harold Joyce. Joyce, the tragic political figure who couldn't win the mayor's seat even with the machine's backing, grasped hands with some of the ward-level politicos who stabbed poor Harold in the back in his publicly humiliating loss to Jerry Jennings in the mayoral primary earlier that year. Thomas M. Whalen III was there, having arrived late and slunk into an obscure back pew, the Corning heir who angered the final remnants of Dan O'Connellites for changing the rules of machine politics late in the game. And on and on it went, the handshake of peace as political science symposium.

Gov. Mario Cuomo, New York's three-term governor and a much-discussed presidential candidate who never was, paused outside St. Mary's on the sidewalk alongside Lodge Street, nearly in the shadow of City Hall, where Corning was king. Cuomo, the great orator, was at a rare loss for words. He tried to sum up what Corning had meant to his own political career, when, in 1981, as an obscure Lieutenant Governor he went up against what looked like an unbeatable Ed Koch, the popular New York City mayor, when Cuomo could hardly get Democratic leaders around the state to return his phone calls. Against all odds and conventional wisdom, Corning went out on a limb to a rather dangerous degree and backed the dark horse candidacy of Cuomo. The rest, as they say, is history. "His legacy is so deep and long and can't be contained on some tombstone," Cuomo had finally managed to say in characteristic aplomb, searching for the right metaphors and images. "He is one of the nation's great public officials."

Cuomo related how he came to know Corning four decades earlier when Cuomo was a law clerk in the Court of Appeals and just a cocky, freshly minted lawyer while Corning was already into his umpteenth year as mayor. Cuomo recounted how Corning was way out in front of the curve, the most important guest to show up at Cuomo's modest and largely overlooked inaugural ceremony when he was sworn in as New York's Lieutenant Governor in 1979, deep in the shadow of Gov. Hugh Carey, the same thankless job as political water carrier Corning's father, Edwin Corning, filled beside the beloved Governor, Al Smith. Cuomo was stretching for superlatives by this point: "Mayor Corning was extremely well educated, very cultured, the classic politician of his time. He had more depth than Robert Moses. He could have been anything. I hope they write the book on Erastus Corning that says he could have been Governor or President or the head of the biggest company in the world."

Two weeks after Gov. Cuomo uttered those words following the mass in the Cornings' honor, the auction to sell off anything worth anything associated with the mayor packed them in. Many sentimental items were on the block: the mayor's brown fedora, in the iconic style of Dan O'Connell, made by Cavanagh Hats of New York, sold for $300. The mayor's never-worn Stetson cowboy hat with feathers, still in the box, needed some prodding from Meringolo, the gallery owner. "If this doesn't beat the price for Dan O'Connell's fedora [sold for $600 at auction a few years before], we want to know why," Meringolo said, although no explanation was offered when the Stetson brought just $200. On and on it went, for several hours that New Year's Day. The silver engraved tea set that was a wedding gift to the Cornings sold early for $3,100. An 1830s teapot, decorated with strawberries, Betty Corning's favorite china motif, went for $7,500, which was some sort of national auction record for that kind of teapot, according to Meringolo.

"There's still an enormous amount of respect and love for Mayor Corning and Mrs. Corning," State Assemblyman John J. McEneny, a senior staffer for Corning and political protégé of the mayor, told Joe Mahoney of the *Times Union*, who covered the auction. "Obviously, anyone who is going to bid on these items wants to hold something that belonged to the mayor and his wife."

"This is a piece of history," local antiques collector Pete Bishop told Mahoney. "The Corning family was a force in politics around here for 150 years." That's why prices were pushed well above what the same items might have brought at another auction belonging to an estate without such a powerful family name. The top price paid at the Corning auction was $9,000 for an 1869 oil portrait by Thomas Kirby VanZandt of Erastus "Tip" Corning, a great-uncle of the mayor's, depicted riding in a horse-drawn sleigh through wintry Washington Park. The crowd broke into applause when the gavel banged sold to a man who wore jeans and a flannel shirt and wiped away tears. "Will the painting be leaving the area?" Meringolo asked. The man shook his head no. The audience erupted into applause once more.

How could an auctioneer even calculate an opening bid on some items? Consider the certificate the mayor framed and hung in his study from the Maine Department of Fish & Game, "The One That Didn't Get Away Club." The paper certified Corning caught a brook trout weighing a whopping seven pounds two ounces and measuring twenty-three and one-half inches, on June 26, 1958 at Pierce Pond, Maine, a local record for that year. It was one of the mayor's proudest moments during a lifetime spent fishing and hunting, and he treasured the framed certificate. It brought $50. And whither Corning's Maine hunting licenses? The mayor saved them all, beginning in 1934. He stood six-feet two-inches and weighed 195 pounds – but had put on five pounds more by 1937, according to the licenses. A bag of political buttons the mayor had collected starting in the 1930s sold for $325. A large campaign poster of a beaming Corning running for Lieutenant Governor in 1946 – the only election he ever lost – went for $225. A duplicate of the poster, stained and slightly tattered, sold for $75 to McEneny, who keeps it propped against a wall in his State Assembly office. A large amount of Betty Corning's jewelry was up for grabs: a Victorian-era carved platinum pin ($1,900); a gold charm bracelet from her world travels ($500); a pearl necklace with diamond clasp ($550).

The auction was a voyeuristic experience, a public window onto the lives of the exceedingly private Cornings. Part of the appeal of the auction, aside from walking away with a piece of political history, was to view the Cornings' lifestyle – which mirrored the contents of their house, old money and established taste, traditional and understated. You could imagine walking through the Corning house in your mind's eye as the auction progressed. An 1830s banjo clock that hung in the front hallway, just inside the front door, sold for $1,100. "It was working when we took it off the wall just a few days ago," Doin reassured the buyer. Another clock from the entry foyer, an exquisite mid-eighteenth century John Pike grandfather clock with Westminster chimes, fetched $5,000. A nine-foot by twelve-foot Persian rug from the living room sold for $7,250. The mayor's Chippendale chest of drawers from his bedroom, an altered eighteenth-century high boy made of tiger maple, where he stored his underwear and all those green socks he favored, sold for $1,700 – the price would have been higher if the piece was in original condition. An early nineteenth-century double steeple clock that was in their living room brought $1,000. Four silver-plated candlesticks from the sideboard in Corning's dining room were sold for $300; the sideboard itself brought $1,000. A painted blanket box from 1824 that had been stuffed in the attic drew $2,600. A Houghton & Son English four-piece silver tea set from 1871 went for $1,300. The Cornings decorated their home with examples of the things they loved: nature scenes, birds and wildlife, flowers and plants. A nineteenth-century Harry Finn black-and-white watercolor of ducks in flight that hung in the upstairs hallway sold for $6,250. A Walter Palmer snow scene painting sold for $2,750. There were numerous flower paintings by Betty Corning's mother, a noted flower artist, that went to the highest bidder.

It was fitting that the Cornings – whose family fortune had its foundation in iron and steel – should have items of weight and substance. The nineteenth-century brass andirons that anchored their living room fireplace sold for $900. A pair of nineteenth-century cast-iron garden urns that Betty filled with petunias and other brightly colored annuals sold for $4,250. A cast-iron fern pattern bench that sat beside a gardener's shed near Betty's front yard vegetable and cutting garden – where Betty toiled for untold hours at her life's passion – ended up bringing $700. A framed needlepoint from mother to daughter sold for $175; various embroidered ties Betty made for her husband brought $55 apiece – two went to McEneny.

But that's only the beginning. The Corning auction contained an overwhelming number of items, particularly thousands of books. On the second auction date, box after box of books were sold as lots containing dozens of volumes each. Personal and professional interest drew Bob Falk, a collector and interpretive program manager at the Mills Mansion state historic site in Staatsburg, New York. Falk had met the mayor during Falk's days working at Albany's Schuyler Mansion. Both men shared a passion for history. Falk purchased several lots of books for five dollars apiece – the price paid for a vote by Albany's machine, ironically. In perusing the contents, Falk grew fascinated by the mayor's restless intellect. The titles only hinted at Corning's wide interests: *Morton's Book of Curing Meats*; Immanuel Velikovsky's *Worlds in Collision* and *Earth In Upheaval*; a copy of Baedeker's *Tyrol and the Dolomites* signed by the mayor from Munich on July 26, 1928 (during Corning's European tour with his Groton drama teacher); and, perhaps Falk's favorite find, Frank R. Kent's book, *The Great Game of Politics*, published by Doubleday in 1926. The book was subtitled *The Necessity For Party Machines – The Good & Bad Sides*. The book's title page was signed: "Erastus Corning 2nd. Nov. 7, 1928. #385." Kent, author of *The Story of Maryland Politics*, described the work thus: "An effort to present the elementary human facts about politics, politicians, and political machines, candidates and their ways, for the benefit of the average citizen." Corning read the book in the fall of his freshman year at Yale. Seven years later, Corning was elected to the State Assembly, the beginning of a forty-eight-year career in continuous elected office as the standard bearer of the Albany Democratic machine.

"I just couldn't believe that these great artifacts were going for nothing," Falk said. "I heard a lot of comments from people about the son selling off these things. It bothered me to see that nobody had taken the time to go through all these books and papers and records to see that they had a lot of historical value and they were more or less being dumped." The books were only one piece of putting Corning's ongoing education into context. "He had a remarkable lust for information," Falk said. "He saved newspaper clippings pertaining to the author or subject and stuck them in the books. He would save scholarly articles from obscure journals. He subscribed to the *Journal of Cycle Research*, which looked at the scientific basis for nature's cycles. Show me another mayor in the country who subscribed to that."

Then came the phonograph records. Falk snapped up three boxes packed with old seventy-eight r.p.m. records, the only bidder at $7.50 for hundreds of records, including thirty-three r.p.m. albums of more recent vintage. The recordings showed Erastus and Betty's middlebrow taste in music. Their home collection included several *Reader's Digest* collections, such as "Down Memory Lane" and "On Wings of Song" and "Great Music From The Movies." There were selections from Mitch Miller, Lawrence Welk, Burl Ives, Fred Waring, Eddie Davis and an album of "127 Polkas."

Closer to the mayor's heart was the collection of Roger Tory Peterson's bird calls and albums of the calls of whales and loons and a well-worn copy of the record, "What Is Heard In Duck Blinds." Falk was most interested in the vintage aluminum records covered with vinyl containing early speeches by Mayor Corning: nominating Oscar R. Ewing at the Democratic national convention after the end of the Truman era; Corning welcoming residents from Nymegen to Albany during a goodwill visit shortly after World War II; the black vaudeville singer Tom Fletcher singing "Here Comes The Groom" at the wedding reception of the mayor's younger brother, Eddie Corning, at Schuyler Meadows just after World War II.

Falk purchased for thirty dollars the mayor's fifteen bound volumes (1945-1977) of *The Conservationist*, published by the New York State Department of Environmental Conservation, for which Corning occasionally wrote essays on his outdoor experiences. Falk is enthralled by these fragments of the Corning enigma. "I've been a longtime admirer of the mayor and I'm grateful to have these things of his," Falk said. "I feel he'll always be with me now and that whenever I look at one of these things, I'll remember him." Falk bought two pairs of the mayor's snowshoes with which Corning tramped untold miles through snowy Maine woods. Falk bought kitchen utensils, including multiple sets of decorative Victorian skewers. And he bought a large box of expensive, plush monogrammed sheets and towels that belonged to Betty's mother and the mayor's mother. The whole lot for ten bucks. "I couldn't believe the children would sell everything off, right down to the bed sheets," Falk said. "It made me wonder."

"The auction clearly was symbolic for my brother," said Bettina Corning Dudley. "He wanted to rid himself of these things, these memories of his father. As to why, I won't speak for him."

Her brother, who has maintained virtually no contact with his sister, strongly disagreed with that characterization of his motivations. Erastus III said the auction was a straightforward business proposition commonly used to close out estates. The mayor's grandson, Robert Dudley, Bettina's son, believed the sterling Corning legacy in politics went to the grave with Erastus 2nd. "Rasty utterly failed to live up to the family legacy for whatever reason," Dudley said. "He had every opportunity with his family, Groton and Yale, and an era when jobs were abundant. He had the name and could have gone back to Albany and cleaned up. Instead, what I find strange, is that he went so far away and kind of dithered away his inheritance. It's an odd end to the Corning lineage. That's nature. Even successful species are eventually transformed or become extinct."

Who knows what will become now of the scattered Corning legacy – forged in the nineteenth century and dissipated as the twentieth century draws to a close – those objects of an important family sold at auction and gracing living rooms and museums and offices in Albany and far, far, beyond? It makes you wonder. But at least one piece of posthumous reunification took place following the auction. In the Fourth Ward Democratic offices on Broadway in north Albany, ward leader Joe McElroy fashioned a hat rack from a Hedrick's beer barrel. On one side rests Dan O'Connell's fedora; on the other, Erastus Corning 2nd's fedora. The hats were purchased at auction by McElroy's brother, Mike, so that Albany's two legendary bosses could ride together once more, after death, the ghosts of urban machine politics, still voting, early and often, and voting Democrat to be sure.

Selected Bibliography

Abramson, Rudy. *Spanning The Century: The Life of W. Averell Harriman.* New York: William Morrow & Co., 1992.

Allen, Oliver E. The Tiger: *The Rise and Fall of Tammany Hall.* Reading, Mass.: Addison-Wesley, 1993.

Alsop, Joseph. *FDR: A Centenary Remembrance.* Viking, 1982.

Alsop, Joseph and Adam Platt. *I've Seen The Best of It: Memoirs.* New York: W.W. Norton, 1992.

Alsop, Stewart. *Stay of Execution: A Sort of Memoir.* Philadelphia: J.B. Lippincott Company, 1973.

Ambrose, Stephen E. *Eisenhower: Soldier and President.* New York: Simon & Schuster, 1990.

Anderson, Alice Sloane. *Our Garden Heritage: Articles from the Bulletins of The Garden Club of America.* New York: Dodd, Mead & Company, 1961.

Anderson, Paul. *Janet Reno: Doing the Right Thing.* New York: John Wiley & Sons, 1994.

Barker, Albert S. *Everyday Life in the Navy.* Boston: Gorham Press, 1928.

Beatty, Jack. *The Rascal King: The Life and Times of James Michael Curley, 1874-1958.* Reading, Mass.: Addison-Wesley, 1992.

Bennett, Allison P. *The People's Choice: A History of Albany County in Art and Architecture.* Albany: The Albany County Historical Association, 1980.

Bigelow, John. *Retrospections of an Active Life.* New York: 1913.

Bissell, Richard M. Jr. *Memoirs of a Cold Warrior: From Yalta to the Bay of Pigs.* New Haven: Yale University Press, 1996.

Bleecker, Samuel E. *The Politics of Architecture: A Perspective on Nelson A. Rockefeller.* New York: Rutledge Press, 1981.

Bonney, Catharina V.R., ed. *A Legacy of Historical Gleanings, vol. II.* Albany: J. Munsell, 1875.

Bradley, Bill. *Time Present, Time Past.* New York: Alfred A. Knopf, 1996.

Bristol, Litynski and P.C Wojcik. *The Pine Bush Intermunicipal Technical Report Study.* Albany: City of Albany, Guilderland and Colonie, 1980.

Callow, Alexander B. Jr. *The Tweed Ring.* New York: Oxford University Press, 1966.

Caro, Robert A. *The Power Broker: Robert Moses And The Fall Of New York.* New York: Alfred A. Knopf, 1974.

Cobb, Gary and Albert H. Fenton. *The History of Pierce Pond.* Farmington, Maine: Knowlton & McLeary, 1992.

Connable, Alfred and Edward Silberfarb,. *Tigers of Tammany: Nine Men Who Ran New York.* New York: Holt, Rinehart and Winston, 1967.

Corry, John. *Golden Clan: The Murrays, the McDonnells, and the Irish American Aristocracy.* Boston: Houghton Mifflin Company, 1977.

Coyne, Jim. *Questions That Bother Him So!* Albany: Kokomo Publishing, 1992.

Cuomo, Mario M. and Harold Holzer, eds. *Lincoln on Democracy.* New York: Cornelia & Michael Bessie/HarperCollins, 1990.

Cutter, William Richard. *Genealogical and Family History of Central New York.* New York: Lewis Historical Publishing Company, 1912.

DeMille, George. *Pioneer Cathedral: A Brief History of the Cathedral of All Saints.* Albany: All Saints, 1967.

Desmond, James. *Nelson Rockefeller: A Political Biography.* New York: Macmillan, 1964.

Donaldson, Alfred L. *A History of the Adirondacks, Vols. I & II.* Harrison, N.Y.: Harbor Hill Books, 1977.

Dupuy, Trevor N. *Hitler's Last Gamble: The Battle of the Bulge, December 1944-January 1945.* New York: HarperCollins, 1994.

Elstner Publishing. *The Industries of Albany, Cohoes and Vicinity: A Resume of Her Past History and Progress.* Albany: Elstner Publishing Co., 1889.

Finnegan, Thomas. *Saving Union Station, Albany, New York: An Inside Look at Historic Preservation.* Albany: Washington Park Press, 1988.

Fitch, Charles Elliott. *Encyclopedia of Biography of New York.* New York: The American Historical Society, 1923.

Fort Orange Club. *Historical Sketch of the Fort Orange Club of Albany, N.Y.* Albany: Fort Orange Club Press, 1977.

Fort Orange Publishing. *Prominent People of the Capital District.* Albany: Fort Orange Recording Bureau Inc., 1923.

Freedman, Samuel. *The Inheritance: How Three Families And America Moved From Roosevelt To Reagan And Beyond.* New York: Simon & Schuster, 1996.

Freidel, Frank. *Franklin D. Roosevelt: A Rendezvous With Destiny.* Boston: Little, Brown and Company, 1990.

Gervasi, Frank. *The Real Rockefeller.* New York: Atheneum, 1974.

Groton School Trustees. *Views From The Circle: Seventy-five years of Groton School.* Groton, Mass: Groton School, 1960.

Gunther, Gerald. *Learned Hand: The Man and the Judge.* New York: Alfred A. Knopf, 1994.

Hamlin, Huybertie Pruyn. *An Albany Girlhood.* Ed. Alice P. Kenney. Albany: Washington Park Press, 1990.

Hershkowitz, Leo. *Tweed's New York: Another Look.* Garden City, N.Y. Anchor Press/Doubleday, 1977.

Hinman, Royal R. *A Catalogue of the Names of the Early Puritan Settlers of the Colony of Connecticut.* Hartford: Case, Tiffany and Company, 1852.

Hislop, Codman. *Albany: Dutch, English, and American.* Albany: The Argus Press, 1936.

Hotaling, Edward. *They're Off! Horse Racing at Saratoga.* Syracuse: Syracuse University Press, 1995.

Howell, George R. and Jonathan Tenney, eds. *Bi-Centennial History of Albany: History of the County of Albany, N.Y., from 1609 to 1886.* New York: W.W. Munsell & Co., 1886.

Johnson, Eugene J. *Style Follows Function: Architecture of Marcus T. Reynolds.* Albany: Washington Park Press and Mount Ida Press, 1993.

Josephson, Matthew. *The Robber Barons.* New York: Harcourt Brace, 1934.

Kennedy, William. *O Albany! Improbable City of Political Wizards, Fearless Ethnics, Spectacular Aristocrats, Splendid Nobodies, and Underrated Scoundrels.* Albany and New York Washington Park Press/Viking, 1983.

Kennedy, William. *Riding the Yellow Trolley Car.* New York: Viking, 1993.

Kenney, Alice P. *The Transformation of the Albany Patricians, 1778-1860.* New York: New York History, 1987.

Kent, Frank R. *The Great Game of Politics.* Garden City, N.Y.: Doubleday, 1928.

Kinnear, David M. *A Loyal and Well Beloved Son of Albany: William Stormont Hackett.* Albany: Argus Company, 1926.

Kramer, Michael and Sam Roberts. *I Never Wanted to be Vice-President of Anything! An Investigative Biography of Nelson Rockefeller.* New York: Basic Books, 1976.

Lewis, R.W.B. *The Jameses: A Family Narrative.* New York: Farrar, Straus and Giroux, 1991.

Lizzi, Dominick C. *Governor Martin H. Glynn: Forgotten Hero.* Valatie, N.Y.: Valatie Press, 1994.

Mallon, Thomas. *Henry and Clara.* New York: Ticknor & Fields, 1994.

Mallon, Thomas. *Rockets and Rodeos and other American Spectacles.* New York: Ticknor & Fields, 1993.

Maraniss, David. *First In His Class: A Biography of Bill Clinton.* New York: Simon & Schuster, 1995.

McElvaine, Robert S. *Mario Cuomo: A Biography.* New York: Charles Scribner's Sons, 1988.

McEneny, John J. *Albany: Capital City On The Hudson.* Albany: Windsor Publications, 1981.

Mele, Andre. *Polluting for Pleasure.* New York: W.W. Norton & Company, 1993.

Merry, Robert W. *Taking On The World: Joseph and Stewart Alsop – Guardians of the American Century.* New York: Viking, 1996.

Moscow, Warren. *Politics in the Empire State.* New York: Knopf, 1948.

Moscow, Warren. *Last of the Big-time Bosses: The Life and Times of Carmine De Sapio and the Rise and Fall of Tammany Hall.* New York: Stein and Day, 1971.

Munsell, Joel, ed. *Collections of the History of Albany, From Its Discovery to the Present Time, Vol. I.* Albany: J. Munsell, 1865.

Neu, Irene D. *Erastus Corning, Merchant and Financier, 1794-1872.* Ithaca: Cornell University Press, 1960.

Newhouse, Victoria. *Wallace K. Harrison, Architect.* New York: Rizzoli, 1989.

O'Connor, Edwin. *The Last Hurrah.* New York: Atlantic Monthly Press, 1956.

O'Connor, Richard. *The First Hurrah: A Biography of Alfred E. Smith.* New York: G.P. Putnam's Sons, 1970.

O'Neill, Thomas P. Jr. with William Nowak. *Man of the House: The Life and Political Memoirs of Speaker Tip O'Neill.* New York: Random House, 1987.

O'Neill, Tip with Gary Humel. *All Politics Is Local and Other Rules of the Game.* New York: Times Books, 1994.

Oppel, Frank, ed. *New York: Tales of the Empire State.* Secaucus, N.J.: Castle, 1988.

Paolantonio, S.A. *Frank Rizzo: The Last Big Man in Big City America.* Philadelphia: Camino Books, 1993.

Parker, Amasa J., ed. *Landmarks of Albany County, N.Y.* Syracuse, N.Y.: D. Mason & Company, 1897.

Persico, Joseph E., *The Imperial Rockefeller: A Biography of Nelson A. Rockefeller.* New York: Simon & Schuster, 1982.

Pringle, Henry F. *Alfred E. Smith: A Critical Study.* New York: Macy-Masius, 1927.

Rensselaer Polytechnic Institute School of Architecture. *The Pine Bush: A Special Study of Natural Resources Of A Unique Area.* Troy: RPI, 1974.

Reynolds, Cuyler. *Hudson-Mohawk Genealogical and Family Memoirs.* New York: Lewis Historical Publishing Company, 1911.

Reynolds, Cuyler. *Albany Chronicles, a History of the City Arranged Chronologically.* Albany: J.B. Lyon Co., 1906.

Ringwald, Donald C. *Hudson River Day Line.* New York: Fordham University Press, 1990.

Riordon, William L. *Plunkitt of Tammany Hall.* New York: E.P. Dutton, 1963.

Rittner, Don. *Pine Bush: Albany's Last Frontier.* Albany: Pine Bush Historic Preservation Project, 1976.

Roberts, Anne F. and Judith A. Van Dyk, eds. *Experiencing Albany: Perspectives on a City's Grand Past.* Albany: The Nelson A. Rockefeller Institute of Government, 1986.

Robinson, Frank S. *Albany's O'Connell Machine: An American Political Relic.* Albany: The Washington Park Spirit, 1973.

Rooney, Andy. *My War.* New York: Times Books, 1995.

Roseberry, C.R. *Flashback: A Fresh Look At Albany's Past.* Ed. Susanne Dumbleton. Albany: Washington Park Press, 1986.

Rowley, William Esmond. *Albany: A Tale of Two Cities 1820-1880.* Ph.D. Thesis, Cambridge: Harvard University, 1967.

Salzmann, Kenneth. *Albany Scrapbook.* Albany: Aurania Book Co., 1985.

Savell, Isabelle K. *The Executive Mansion in Albany: A Century of New York History.* Albany: New York State Office of General Services, 1982.

Schenck, Martin. *Up Came Hill: The Story of the Light Division and its Leaders.* Harrisburg, Penn: The Stackpole Company, 1958.

Schuyler, Montgomery. *American Architecture and Other Writings.* Cambridge: Belknap Press of Harvard University Press, 1961.

Shaver, Peter D. (editor). *The National Register of Historic Places in New York State.* New York: Rizzoli, 1993.

Sheaffer, Louis. *O'Neill: Son and Artist.* Boston: Little, Brown and Company, 1973.

Skaaren, Lorna. *Albany International: The First One Hundred Years.* Albany: Albany International Corp., 1995.

Solomon, Noal. *When Leaders Were Bosses: An Inside Look at Political Machines & Politics.* Hicksville, N.Y.: Exposition Press, 1975.

Stevens, Frank Walker. *The Beginning of the New York Central Railroad, A History.* New York: G.P. Putnam's Sons, 1926.

Still, Bard, ed. *Mirror for Gotham: New York as Seen by Contemporaries from Dutch Days to the Present.* New York: Fordham University Press, 1994.

Stolberg, Mary M. *Fighting Organized Crime: Politics, Justice and the Legacy of Thomas E. Dewey.* Chicago: Northeastern University Press, 1995.

Tomlan, Mary Raddant, ed. *A Neat Plain Modern Stile: Philip Hooker and His Contemporaries 1796-1836.* Clinton, N.Y.: Hamilton College, 1993.

Van Deusen, Glyndon G. *Thurlow Weed, Wizard of the Lobby.* Boston: 1947.

Ward, Geoffrey C. *A First Class Temperament: The Emergence of Franklin Roosevelt.* New York: Harper & Row, 1989.

Ward, Geoffrey C. *Before The Trumpet: Young Franklin Roosevelt 1882-1905.* New York: Harper & Row, 1985.

Wills, Garry. *Certain Trumpets: The Call of Leaders.* New York: Simon & Schuster, 1994.

Wilson, Derek. *The Astors: 1763-1992.* New York: St. Martin's Press, 1993.

Worth, Gorham A. *Random Recollections of Albany, From 1800 to 1808.* Albany: J. Munsell, 1866.

Sources and Interviews

Library and Archival Sources
Albany Academy Archives
Albany County Hall of Records
Albany Institute of History and Art,
    McKinney Library
Albany Public Library, Pruyn Room
    (Special Collections)
Groton School Archives
New York State Library
New York State Archives
New York State Legislative Library
Yale University Archives
Corning Family Private Collections

Newspapers and Periodicals
Albany Times Union
Knickerbocker News
Schenectady Gazette
The Evangelist
Washington Park Spirit
New York Times
Ellsworth (Maine) American
New York State Legislative Index
Atlantic Monthly
Fortune
New York magazine
Progressive Architecture
Time

Selected Personal Interviews
Reszin Adams, Center Square activist and
    environmentalist (3/24/96).
Angelo Amore, Corning's tailor
    (2/20/95).
Shirley Armstrong, *Times Union* reporter
    (3/19/96).
David S. Ball, Bishop of Albany Episcopal
    diocese (7/19/94).
Joe Barbagallo Sr., World War II buddy
    (11/7/94).
Joe Barbagallo Jr., Albany firefighter
    (11/7/94).
Lawrence Barry, World War II buddy
    interviewed in 1990 by John Curley
    (4/10/96).

Martha Becker, Corning family friend
    (3/21/95).
Dr. Richard Beebe, friend and physician
    to mayor (1/23/95).
Jean Beebe, Corning family friend
    (2/16/94).
Robert Bennett, butler and
    superintendent governors' Executive
    Mansion (12/8/94).
Francis Bergan, state Court of Appeals
    judge (1/18/93).
Sarah Birn, co-chair of McGovern
    campaign with Corning (6/1/95).
Ann Bissell, widow of Richard Bissell,
    Groton Class of '28 (1/28/95).
Bruce Bouchard, founder Capital
    Repertory Company (2/24/95).
Nebraska Brace, alderman (10/20/95).
David Bray, superintendent Albany
    schools (11/28/94).
Paul Bray, founder Albany Roundtable
    (3/11/94).
Alfred Bremm, police officer and
    O'Connell bodyguard (2/13/93).
Douglas Brown, Groton School archivist
    (9/22/94).
Thomas Brown, county legislator and
    state Assemblyman (10/25/93).
Dan Button, *Times Union* editor and
    Republican Congressman (11/23/93).
John Byron, South Mall construction
    director (10/21/95).
Vincent Bytner, mayoral candidate
    (10/29/95).
Alice Carey, widow of World War II
    buddy Jake Carey (10/23/94).
Daniel Catlin, Corning roommate Yale
    Class of '32 (2/12/94).
Dr. F. Sargent Cheever, classmate Groton
    Class of '28 (1/30/94).
Thomas Clingan, Albany county clerk
    and archivist (10/14/96).
Peter Clough, founder Capital Repertory
    Company (2/24/95).
Gary Cobb, Maine fishing guide
    (2/13/94).

Nancy Connell, *Times Union* reporter (3/17/96).

Edward Conway, state Supreme Court judge (3/14/94).

Amy Corning, mayor's granddaughter (11/19/95).

Elizabeth Corning, mayor's wife (5/24/93).

Erastus Corning III, mayor's son (12/16/93).

Mario Cuomo, governor of New York (5/10/96).

Matilda Cuomo, wife of Gov. Mario Cuomo (5/18/94).

Harry D'Agostino, Colonie GOP chairman (2/26/95).

Ed Dague, TV news reporter, anchor and managing editor (3/6/96).

Robert Danzig, *Times Union* publisher and head of Hearst newspaper group (3/20/96).

Carol DeMare, *Times Union* reporter (1/25/96).

Bob Denney, mayor's duck hunting buddy at Alcove Reservoir (10/16/92).

Charles Devens, classmate Groton Class of '28 (3/31/94)

Thelma Dooley, mayor's secretary (2/27/95).

Mary Arthur Doolittle, Corning family friend (3/21/95).

Frank Duci, mayor of Schenectady (2/24/96).

Bettina Corning Dudley, mayor's daughter (12/3/94).

Christopher Dudley, mayor's grandson (11/10/95).

George Dudley, architect on South Mall (6/8/94).

Robert Dudley, mayor's grandson (11/12/95).

Robert Falk, historian and Corning auction buyer (3/10/95).

Milan Fiske, orchid expert (3/27/94).

Gerald Fitzgerald, bank president (3/27/94).

Alexander Forbes, classmate Groton Class of '28 (11/19/94).

Ruben Gersowitz, ward leader (8/11/93).

Austin Goodyear, Maine lumber supply owner (5/10/94).

Mary Anne Grassie, Dan O'Connell's grand-niece (11/11/95).

Flora Gray, Maine caretaker (2/13/94).

Harold Greenstein, alderman (9/17/94).

George Grober, mayor's office assistant (3/27/93).

Albert Hartheimer, mayoral candidate (7/16/95).

Mark Heller, law firm partner of Howard Nolan and Nolan's campaign manager (10/20/95).

Albert Hessberg II, lawyer and attorney Albany Associates (2/26/94).

Harriet Rawle Hemenway, cousin of Corning (9/15/94).

William Hennessy, state transportation commissioner (10/20/95).

Jacob Herzog, city court judge and county treasurer (5/10/94).

Grace Holmes, daughter of Corning nanny's friend (10/27/95).

John Holt-Harris Jr., recorder court judge (4/10/96).

Dorothy Hoysradt, widow of John Hoysradt, Corning's drama teacher at Groton (12/29/94).

Donald Huntley, Adirondack deer hunter (3/27/94).

George Infante, Albany County sheriff (10/29/95).

Karen Johnson, mayor of Schenectady (5/12/94).

Betty Lou Johnston, Maine caretakers (1/30/94).

Ray Joyce Jr., city treasurer (1/16/95).

Howard Kahn, Corning's accountant (5/3/94).

Bill Keefe, mayor's executive assistant (4/12/93).

Ron Kermani, *Times Union* reporter (3/26/96).

Ray Kinley Jr., election commissioner (3/29/94).

Maggie Kirwin, organizer of anti-Springboks rallies (3/19/96).

Bela Kollarits Jr., Corning Hill caretaker's son (10/26/94).

Olga Kollarits, Corning Hill caretaker (10/26/94).

Harold Koreman, Court of Claims judge (4/21/94).

Duane LaFleche, *Knickerbocker News* editor (4/18/94).

Edith Lasker, widow of World War II buddy Howard Lasker (3/27/94).

James Lenden, Fort Orange Club member and mayor's lunch companion (3/28/95).

Joanne Lenden, gardening friend of Betty Corning (3/28/95).

Harvey Lifset, state Assemblyman (3/2/95).

George Louis, World War II buddy (12/8/94).

Joe Mahoney, *Times Union* reporter (1/12/94).

Pat Mahoney, engineer on city projects, including ANSWERS (6/7/94).

Harry Maikels, commissioner public works and county legislator (1/2/94).

Dan Malmed, Albany merchant and mayor's friend (6/8/93).

Clifford Manchester, Maine caretaker (2/13/94).

Vincent McArdle Jr., corporation counsel (4/26/94).

John McElroy, mayor's cousin and Yale classmate (3/27/94).

John McEneny, Corning aide and state Assemblyman (12/6/94).

Donald McKay, CEO Tougher Industries (10/20/95).

Alexander McKenzie, mayor's classmate at Albany Academy (10/10/94).

John McLean, Noonan cousin and mayor's hunting partner (11/16/95).

John McLoughlin, *Times Union* reporter and TV reporter (3/18/96).

E.J. McMahon Jr., *Times Union* and *Knickerbocker News* reporter (3/26/96).

John McNulty Jr., Green Island political boss (10/22/95).

Frank Mele, Catskills trout stream conservationist (4/12/94).

Chris Mercogliano, Mansion neighborhood activist and Free School teacher (3/9/96).

Robert Meringolo, Corning auction agent (12/30/93).

Alan Miller, *Times Union* reporter (3/19/96).

Donald Miller, state OGS engineer (2/4/96).

John "Dusty" Miller, mayor's driver (8/10/94).

Roberta Miller, mayor's secretary (2/27/95).

Gerald Mineau, Albany Associates account broker (1/5/95).

William Murphy, campaign manager for Congressman Sam Stratton (11/13/95).

Howard Nolan, mayoral candidate and state senator (6/13/94).

Peter Noonan Jr., Polly Noonan's son and hunting partner and insurance associate of mayor (11/7/95).

Polly Noonan, Corning's political advisor and confidante (9/7/95).

Daniel O'Connell, Dan O'Connell's grand-nephew (11/6/95).

Lewis Oliver, Save The Pine Bush attorney (2/28/96).

Richard Patrick, city planner (8/2/93).

Joseph Persico, Rockefeller biographer (9/20/95).

Joe Picchi, *Times Union* reporter (3/6/96).

John Polk Jr., World War II buddy (10/22/95).

Thomas Pollard, Maine guide (1/30/94).

Thomas Prime, World War II buddy (10/26/94).

John Quine, Maine camp owner and mayor of Meriden, Conn. (3/27/94).

Michael Quirk, World War II buddy (11/21/94).

Janet Reno, U.S. Attorney General and longtime friend of mayor's daughter (7/11/97).

Norman Rice, emeritus director of Albany Institute of History and Art and Corning family friend (2/15/94).

Don Rittner, Albany archaeologist and Pine Bush historian (3/6/93).

Francis Rivett, *Times Union* reporter and editor (11/7/93).

Frank Robinson, author of book on the machine (11/6/93).

Robert Roche, Corning family attorney (11/5/95).

Rev. Joseph Romano, Catholic priest and union organizer city fire department (5/31/94).

Harry Rosenfeld, *Times Union* editor (3/7/96).

William Rowley, *Knickerbocker News* reporter and SUNYA journalism professor (11/5/95).

Lewis Rubenstein, state historic preservationist (5/10/96).

Harold Rubin, president Center Square Neighborhood Association (11/6/95).

Douglas Rutnik, Corning political adviser (6/15/94).

Polly Rutnik, Polly Noonan's daughter and lawyer (2/9/93).

Martin Schenck, county court judge (11/21/93).

Rev. Charles Sheerin, Groton teacher and Episcopal Minister (10/30/95).

Mike Sheridan, committeeman and head of city youth bureau (6/6/94).

Edwin Shultes III, mayor's classmate at Albany Academy (10/12/94).

Nathan Singer, World War II buddy (11/21/94).

Wharton Sinkler III, Corning cousin (10/5/96).

Lorna Skaaren, Albany International corporate historian (3/27/95).

Raymond Skuse, state Assemblyman (7/21/95).

Herb Starr, radio and TV reporter (3/13/96).

Ivan Steen, SUNYA history professor (12/15/92).

Anita Inglehart Swatkovsky, granddaughter of Parker Corning (7/10/95).

John Tabner, county Republican committee attorney (10/23/95).

Jon Teaford, political scientist (5/12/95).

Michael Tepedino, city court judge (9/17/95).

Charlie Torche, lawyer and lobbyist (9/16/93).

James Tortorici, World War II buddy (10/22/94).

Carl Touhey, GOP mayoral candidate (9/9/93).

John Treffiletti, grocer and friend of O'Connell and Corning (12/3/95).

Leon Van Dyke, organizer of the black activist group The Brothers (4/11/96).

Frank Verenini, World War II buddy (12/6/94).

Paul Vitello, *Knickerbocker News* reporter (3/13/96).

Leonard Weiss, state Supreme Court judge and Democratic Party chairman (3/17/96).

Thomas M. Whalen III, mayor of Albany (3/23/94).

Anneke Wheeler, widow of Erastus "Tip" Corning Jr. (10/22/95).

Malcolm Wilson, governor of New York (9/9/93).

John Wolcott, Pine Bush activist (3/13/96).

Catherine Wojtowicz, widow of World War II buddy Stanley Wojtowicz (3/27/94).

Stanley Zimmer, World War II buddy (11/10/94).

Index

About the Author

Paul Grondahl is the author of four books, including the acclaimed political biography *I Rose like a Rocket: The Political Education of Theodore Roosevelt* (Free Press, 2004). He has been a staff writer at the *Albany Times Union* since 1984, where his work has received local, state, and national recognition, including the Scripps Howard Foundation National Journalism Award for Web reporting, a first prize in feature writing from the American Association of Sunday and Feature Editors, and over a dozen New York State Associated Press writing awards. He has also written for numerous other publications, including the *New York Times Book Review*, *Newsday*, and the *Houston Chronicle*.

Grondahl holds a bachelor's degree in English literature from the University of Puget Sound in Tacoma, Washington, and a master's degree in English literature from the University at Albany, where he was named a distinguished alumnus in arts and letters in 2005. He lives in Guilderland, New York. For more information visit www.paulgrondahl.com.